THE SOURCES OF

CATHOLIC DOGMA

Denzinger

THE SOURCES OF
CATHOLIC DOGMA

Translated by ROY J. DEFERRARI

from the Thirtieth Edition of

Henry Denzinger's *Enchiridion Symbolorum*

B. HERDER BOOK CO.

15 & 17 South Broadway, St. Louis 2, Mo.

AND *33 Queen Square, London, W.C.*

This translation was made from the thirtieth edition of *Enchiridion Symbolorum*, by Henry Denzinger, revised by Karl Rahner, S.J., published in 1954 by Herder & Co., Freiburg.

NIHIL OBSTAT

Dominic Hughes, O.P.
Censor Deputatus

IMPRIMATUR

✠ Patrick A. O'Boyle
Archbishop of Washington

April 25, 1955

Library of Congress Catalog Card Number: 57-5963

Translator's Preface

WE present herewith an English version of Henry Denzinger's *Enchiridion Symbolorum, definitionum et declarationum de rebus fidei et morum,* a handbook of articles of faith and morals. It is to be noted that Clement Bannwart, S.J., is responsible for the tenth edition, John Baptist Umberg, S.J., for the 18th through the 20th, and Charles Rahner, S.J., for the 28th, 29th, and 30th editions.

Every effort has been made to present an accurate as well as a readable translation. We have followed the basic principles usually accepted in this age for producing scientific translations: close adherence to the original in all matters pertaining to style, insofar as accuracy and smooth English permit. It is our belief that such adherence to the original will make not only for greater accuracy but for crispness and vitality in the translation.

It is our hope that this work will increase among English-speaking people both the knowledge of our faith and the appreciation of its continuity from the days of our Lord to our own times. Perhaps it is not too much to hope that it will also bring out more sharply the role played by the Fathers of the Church in the establishment and formulation of the basic dogmas of the faith.

Certainly we do not wish that this English version replace the original Latin and Greek, but we feel that there is great need of this translation in the institutions of higher learning in English speaking countries, where unfortunately a working knowledge of Greek no longer exists, and a practical knowledge of Latin is fast disappearing, but where, most fortunately, a desire for a systematic knowledge of theology is increasing daily. In fact, it may be said that an intense desire for a knowledge of theology is characteristic not only of the students of our institutions of higher education but in general of persons of cultivated taste in our age.

I wish to thank the Very Reverend Joseph C. Fenton, professor of dogmatic theology at The Catholic University of America for first suggesting this task to me. I wish also to acknowledge assistance given me by the Reverend Dominic Hughes, O.P., especially in the translation of the Systematic Index; also the practical help of the following in the early part of our work: Sister Mary Dorothea, S.S.N.D., of Mount Mary College, Milwaukee, Wisconsin; Sister Mary Gratia, S.S.N.D., of the College of Notre Dame of Maryland, Baltimore, Maryland; Sister M. Kathleen, O.S.B., of Donnelly College, Kansas City, Kansas; Sister M. La Salette, R.S.M., of St. Vincent's Academy, Savannah, Georgia; and Sister Marie Carolyn, O.P., of The Catholic University of America.

Roy J. Deferrari

Catholic University of America
Washington, D.C.

General Index

(Chronological)

CREEDS

DOCUMENTS OF THE ROMAN PONTIFFS
AND OF THE COUNCILS

St. Clement I, 90(?)–99(?)

HONORIUS III, 1216–1227

GREGORY IX, 1227–1241

INNOCENT IV, 1243–1254
COUNCIL OF LYONS I, 1245
(Ecumenical XIII)

ALEXANDER IV, 1254–1261

GREGORY X, 1271–1276
COUNCIL OF LYONS II, 1274
(Ecumenical XIV)

BONIFACE VIII, 1294–1303

Paul III, 1534–1549
Council of Trent, 1545–1563
(Ecumenical XIX)

Julius III, 1550–1555
Council of Trent (Continued)

Pius IV, 1559–1565

Council of Trent (Conclusion)

THE VATICAN COUNCIL, 1869–1870
(Ecumenical XX)

Leo XIII, 1878–1903

Pius X, 1903–1914

Benedict XV, 1914–1922

Pius XI, 1922–1939

Pius XII, 1939—

APPENDIX

Index of Signs

used for citing frequent sources . . .

CICFrdbg = *Corpus Iuris Canonici,* editio Lipsiensis IIa: Aemilius Friedberg, 2 vol. Lipsiae, 1879–1881.

CICRcht = *Corpus Iuris Canonici . . . ad exemplar Romanum denuo edidit Aemilius Ludovicus Richter* (2 partes). Lipsiae, 1836–1839.

CL = *Acta et Decreta sacrorum Conciliorum recentium . . .* Collectio Lacensis, auctoribus presbyteris S.J. e domo B.M.V. . . . ad Lacum. Friburgi, 1870 (tomus I) ff.

CSEL = *Corpus Scriptorum Ecclesiasticorum Latinorum . . .* Academiae litterarum caesareae Vindobonensis. Vindobonae, 1866 (tomus I) ff.

CspANQ = CASPARI, C.P. *Alte und neue Quellen zur Geschichte des Taufsymbols und der Glaubensregel.* Christiania, 1879.

CspQ = CASPARI, C.P., *Ungedruckte . . . Quellen zur Geschichte des Taufsymbols und der Glaubensregel.* tomi II, III. Christiania, 1869, 1875.

Cst = COUSTANT, PETRUS, O.S.B., *Epistolae Romanorum Pontificum a S. Clemente I usque ad Innocentium III.* Tomus I (unicus), Parisiis, 1721.

CTr = *Concilium Tridentinum, Diariorum, Actorum, Epistularum, Tractatuum* Nova Collectio. Edidit Societas Goerresiana promovendis inter Germanos Catholicos Litterarum Studiis. Friburgi Brisgoviae, 1901 (tomus I) ff.

DCh = DENIFLE, HENRICUS, O.P., *Chartularium Universitatis Parisiensis.* Parisiis, 1889 (tomus I) ff.

DuPl = DU PLESSIS D'ARGENTRÉ, CAROLI, *Collectio Iudiciorum de novis erroribus, qui ab initio XII saeculi . . . usque ad a. 1713 in Ecclesia proscripti sunt et notati,* 3 vol. geminata: Lutetiae Parisiorum, 1755 ff.

EB = *Enchiridion Biblicum,* Documenta ecclesiastica S. Scripturam spectantia, auctoritate Pontificiae Commissionis de Re Biblica edita. Romae, 1927.

H = HAHN (Aug. und) G.L., *Bibliothek der Symbole und Glaubensregeln der alten Kirche.* 3. Aufl. Mit einem Anhang von A. Harnack, Breslau, 1897.

Hfl = HEFELE, CARL JOSEPH v. (Hergenröther-Knöpfler), *Conciliengeschichte.* 9 Bände. Freiburg, 1873 (Band I) ff.

Hrd = HARDUINI, P. IOHANNIS S.J., *Conciliorum Collectio regia maxima,* (Labbei et Cossartii) sive: *Acta Conciliorum et Epistolae Decretales ac Constitutiones Summorum Pontificum.* Parisiis, 1715 (tomus I) ff.

Hrt = HURTER, H., S.J., *Nomenclator litterarius Theologiae catholicae*. Ed. 3. Oeniponte, 1903.

Jf = JAFFÉ, PHILIPPUS, *Regesta Pontificum Romanorum a condita Ecclesia* ad a.p. Chr. n. 1198, Ed. altera (Wattenbach). 2 tomi. Lipsiae, 1885, 1888.

K = KATTENBUSCH, FERDINAND, *Das apostolische Symbol*. 2 Bände. Leipzig, 1894, 1900.

KAnt = KÜNSTLE, KARL, *Antipriscilliana*. Freiburg, 1905.

KBdS = KÜNSTLE, KARL, *Eine Bibliothek der Symbole und theologischer Traktate zur Bekämpfung des Priscillianismus* . . . [Ehrhard-Kirsch, Forschungen I, 4]. Mainz, 1900.

Kch = KIRCH, C., *Enchiridion fontium historiae ecclesiasticae antiquae*. Ed. 4. Friburgi, 1923.

L = LIETZMANN, H., *Symbole der alten Kirche*. [Kleine Texte für Vorlesungen und Übungen 17, 18]. 2. Aufl. Bonn, 1914.

MBR = *Magnum Bullarium Romanum a beato Leone Magno usque ad Benedictum XIV*, Laertii Cherubini, ed. novissima cum Continuatione, Luxemburgi [potius; Genevae, cf. Scherer, *Handbuch des Kirchenrechts* I, Graz, 1886, 293 n. 11], 1727 (1742) (tomus I) ff.

MGh = *Monumenta Germaniae historica,* edidit Societas aperiendis fontibus rerum Germanicarum medii aevi.—Legum Sectio III: Concilia. Hannoverae, 1904.—*Epistolae selectae* I. Berolini, 1916.

ML, MG = MIGNE, *Patrologiae Cursus completus. Series prima Latina*. Parisiis, 1844 (tomus I) ff. *Series Graeca*. Parisiis, 1857 (tomus I) ff.

Msi = MANSI, IOHANN. DOMINICI, *Sacrorum Conciliorum nova et amplissima collectio*. Tomus I. Florentiae, 1759 ff. (postea Parisiis, Lipsiae).

MThCc = MIGNE, J.P., *Theologiae Cursus completus*. [Parisiis] (tomus I) ff.

Pth = POTTHAST, AUG., *Regesta Romanorum Poontificum inde ab a.p. Chr.* 1198 [v. Jf] ad a. 1304, 2 vol. Berolini, 1874, 1875.

R = ROUËT DE JOURNEL, M. J., *Enchiridion Patristicum*. Ed. 7. Friburgi, 1929.

Rcht = RICHTER, AEMIL. LUDOV., *Canones et Decreta Concilii Tridentini ex editione Romana anni 1834*. repetiti . . . Lipsiae, 1853.

RskMm   = Roskovány, Aug. de, *De Matrimoniis mixtis*. Typis Lycei episcopalis [Agriensis?] 1842 (tomus II) [cf. eiusdem auctoris: *Matrimonium in Ecclesia catholica*. Pestinis, 1870 ff.].

RskRP   = Roskovány, Aug. de, *Romanus Pontifex tamquam Primas Ecclesiae et Princeps Civilis e monumentis omnium saeculorum demonstratus*. Nistriae et Comaromii, 1867 (tomus I) ff.

Th   = Thiel, Andreas, *Epistolae Romanorum Pontificum . . . a S. Hilario usque ad Pelagium II* [cf. Cst]. Tomus I (unicus). Brunsbergae, 1868.

Viva   = Viva, Domin., S.J., *Damnatarum Thesium theologica Trutina*. Patavii, 1756 (tomus I, p. 1, ed. 15), et Beneventi, 1753 (tomus II, p. 4, ed. 5).

Z   = Zahn, Theodor, *Geschichte des neutestamentlichen Kanons*. 2 Bände. Erlangen, 1888.

CREEDS

THE APOSTOLIC CREED [1]

Most Ancient Forms of the Apostolic Creed

THE creed which is called Apostolic is composed essentially of (1) a Trini- **1**
tarian part, three articles professing faith in three divine persons; (2) **a**
Christological part which was added to the first section.

There are extant, however, certain formulae composed in the manner of
creeds, but lacking the Christological part. These formulae seem to be more
ancient than the Apostolic Creed. An achristological formula of this kind—
which seems to be the most ancient of all—exists in a work infected with
Gnosticism written between the years 150 and 180, *Testamentum in Galilaea
D.N.I. Christi* (or in an almost identical work *Gespräche Jesu mit seinen
Jüngern nach der Auferstehung*) where the short Creed (reads):

"[I believe] in the Father almighty,—and in Jesus Christ, our Savior;
—and in the Holy Spirit, the Paraclete, in the holy Church, and in the
remission of sins."

Another achristological formula, perhaps already used in the liturgy of Egypt
probably in the third century, is shown by a papyrus discovered in *Dér-Balyzeh,*
written in the seventh or eighth century (cf. *Dict. d'Archéol. chrét. et de Lit.*
s. v. Canon, II, 2, 1882 ff.):

---

[1] Of the Catholic authors, cf. S. Baeumer O.S.B., *Das Apostolische Glaubensbekenntnis. Seine Geschichte und sein Inhalt* (Mainz: 1893); Cl. Blume S.J., *Das Apostolische Glaubensbekenntnis* (Freiburg:1893); W. M. Peitz S.J., *Das Glaubensbekenntnis der Apostel* [Stimmen der Zcit 94 (1918), 553 ff.]; A. Nussbaumer O. Cap.,
Das Ursymbolum nach der Epideixis des hl. Irenäus und dem Dialog Justins (Paderborn: 1921); B. Capelle O.S.B., *Le Symbole romain au second siècle* [Revue Bénédictine 39 (1927), 33 ff.]; idem, *Les origines du Symbole romain* [Rech. de Théol.
anc. et médiév. 2 (1930), 5 ff.].—Items which are marked by an asterisk (*) are considered at least as the more probable.

"I believe in God almighty;—and in his only-begotten Son, our Lord Jesus Christ;—and in the Holy Spirit and in the resurrection of the body <in> the holy Catholic Church."

The More Ancient Western Form of the Apostolic Creed

[Called Roman (R)]

Sources

A. [The following] show at least elements of some Creed or a rule of faith or questions in common use at baptism:

St. Justin Martyr, martyred 167.—Apology I and II; Dial. c. Tryph. [MG 6, 328 pp.]—A twofold form, western and eastern can be conjectured with some probability; therefore, a comparison will be made below [n. 8].

St. Irenaeus, died 202, bishop of Lyons.—Adv. haer. 1, 10, 1; 3, 4, 1 and 2; 16, 5 (which are the chief places) [MG 7, 549 A 855 B 924 B]. He shows (1, 10, 1) almost all the elements of the Roman creed as a faith which the Church received from the apostles and their disciples (1, 10, 1).— Εἰς ἐπίδειξιν τοῦ ἀποστολικοῦ κηρύγματος c. 3 and 6. [Karapat Ter-Mekerttschian und Erwand Ter-Minassiantz, *Des hl. Irenäus Schrift zum Erweise der apostolischen Verkündigung* (Texte und Untersuchungen, Harnack-Schmidt XXXI, 1) Leipzig: 1907].

St. Hippolytus, died 235, Roman presbyter.—*Paradosis*—He shows the baptismal creed by means of questions from "You believe in Jesus Christ . . ." [H. Elfers, *Die Kirchenordnung Hippolyts von Rom,* 1938, 321. E. Hauler, Didasc. apost. fragm., Veron. 1900, 110 f., L 10 f. R.-H. Connolly, The so-called Egyptian Church Order and derived documents, 1916].

Tertullian, died after 225 (probably in 240), perhaps a presbyter in Carthage.—*De praescr. haer. 13, De virg. vel. 1; De carne Chr. 20; Adv. Prax. 2*[ML2, 26B 88 B 785B 856B]. He says that the church at Carthage received the rule of faith from the church at Rome (*De praescr. haer. 36*) and that it was common to the apostolic churches; (l.c. 21) the form of the creed was somewhat fixed.

Origen, died 254, presbyter at Alexandria.—*De princip. 1, praef. 4 et 5* [MG 11, 117 A]. He has a rule of faith similar to the creed.

Canones Hippolyti, of uncertain date (Some 200–235, others about 500). [Achelis, *Die ältesten Quellen des oriental Kirchenrects* I 38 (Texte und Untersuchungen, Gebhardt-Harnack VI) Leipzig: 1891].—They contain questions.

Text

[According to the Psalter of Rufinus (The Roman form)]

2 1. I believe in God, the Father almighty;

2. and in Christ Jesus, His only-begotten Son, our Lord,

3. who was born of the Holy Spirit and the Virgin Mary,

4a. was crucified by Pontius Pilate, and was buried;
  b.
5. the third day He arose again from the dead;
6a. He ascended into heaven,
  b. sits at the right hand of the Father,
7. whence He is coming to judge the living and the dead;
8. and in the Holy Spirit,
9a. the holy [Church,]
  b.
10a.
  b. the forgiveness of sins,
11. the resurrection of the body. Amen.

[According to the Psalter of Aethelstane]

1. I believe in God the Father almighty
2. and in Christ Jesus, His only begotten Son, our Lord
3. born of the Holy Spirit and Mary the virgin
4a. was crucified by Pontius Pilate and was buried
  b.
5. the third day He arose again from the dead
6a. He ascended into heaven
  b. sits at the right hand of the Father
7. whence He is coming to judge the living and the dead
8. and in the Holy Spirit
9a. the holy [Church]
  b.
10a.
  b. the forgiveness of sins
11. the resurrection of the body. Amen.
12.

B. [*The following*] *show a fixed form of the Creed.*

Psalter of Aethelstane (in Greek), in the third part, written in the **4** ninth century (at the beginning perhaps) [H. sect. 18; L. 10; CspQ. III 5].— The Creed is of uncertain date, very old,* was in liturgical use.

Codex Laudianus, (E. Actium, lat.) [H. sect. 20; CspQ. III 162].—The Creed is of uncertain date, written in the seventh century.*

Codex Swainson (Latin) [Swainson, *The Nicene and Apostles' Creeds,* London: 1875, 161; H. sect. 23]—The Creed is of uncertain date, written in the eighth century.

Marcellus Ancyranus, fourth century, bishop of Angora in Galatia of Asia Minor—*Epist. ad Iulium Papam* written in the year 337* (In Epiphanius, Haer. 72) [MG 42, 385 D; H. sect. 17].

Priscillian, died 385,* lived at Avila in Spain.—*Lib. ad Damasum tract. II* [ed. Schepss (CSEL XVIII [1889] 34). Cf. also KAnt. 20 ff.; H. sect. 53; L 13].

PHOEBADIUS, died after 392, bishop of Agen in Aquitania secunda [Guyenna]. —*De fide orthodoxa contra Arianos* at the end [H. sect. 59; ML 20, 49 B. "Libellus fidei"]; the book is genuine* (some ascribe it to Gregorius Baeticus, died after 392, bishop of Illiberi [Elivira-Granada].

RUFINUS, died 410, presbyter of Aquileia—*Expositio in Symbolum* (otherwise *Commentarius in Symbolum apostolorum*) [H. sect. 19; ML 21, 335 B]. —The form of the creed of both the Church at Rome and of the Church at Aquileia is gathered from this.

NICETAS OF ROMATIANA,* wrote 380*-420,* Romatiana [Remesiana] in Dacia.*—*Explanatio Symboli habita ad competentes* [H. sect. 40; ML 52, 865 D].

ST. AUGUSTINE, died 430, bishop of Hippo.—Chief sources: *De Fide et Symbolo; serm. 212-214 in traditione Symboli; serm. 215 in redditione Symboli* [ML 40, 181; 38, 1058, 1072; H sect. 47; L 13. Serm. 215 is genuine*; many believe with Caspari that the creed of Hippo is given in Serm. 215, and that the Creed of Milan is handed down in the rest].

ST. PETER CHRYSOLOGUS, died before 458, bishop of Ravenna.—*Serm. 57-62* [H sect. 35; L. 12; ML 52, 357 A].

ST. MAXIMUS, middle of the fifth century, bishop of Turin,— *Hom. 83 de expositione Symboli* [H. sect. 34; L. 13; ML 57, 433 A].

ST. FULGENTIUS OF RUSPE, died 533 (Ruspe in Africa) *Liber 10. contra Fabianum Arianum* [H. sect. 49; L 14; ML 65, 822].

ST. MARTIN, died 580, bishop of Braga [Braga in Spain, now Portugal].— *De correctione rusticorum* [H. sect. 54; ed. Caspari, Christiania 1883.—Cf. K I 153].

TRACTATUS SYMBOLI in a Missal and Sacramentarium for the use of a certain Florentine church furnishes a Florentine* Creed of the seventh* century; manuscript is of the twelfth century. [H. sect. 39; Csp ANQ 290].

ST. ILDEFONSE,* died 669, bishop of Toledo.—*Liber de cognitione baptismi* c. 35 [H. sect. 55; L 13 f.; ML 96, 127 B].

ETHERIUS, Eighth century bishop of Osmo and Beatus (Biaco), eighth century, presbyter of Astorga in Spain.—*Etherii episcopi Uxamensis et Beati presbyteri adv. Elpiandum archiep. Toletanum libri duo,* written in the year 785 [H. sect. 56 f.; L 13 f.; ML 96, 906 D].

LITURGIA MOZARABICA: Seventh century Liber Ordinum [ed. Férotin, p. 185; H. sect. 58; L 14; ML 85, 395 A].

The More Recent Western Form of the Apostolic Creed

[The received western text called (T)]

Sources

FAUSTUS OF REI, died after 485, in Riez in France. *Duae homiliae de Symbolo; Tractatus de Symbolo** [H. sect. 61, L 14; CspQ. II 200].

5 ST. CAESARIUS OF ARLES, died 543, Primate of Gaul [Arles].—Sermo 10

[G. Morin, S. Caesarii Arel. Sermones I, 1, Maretioli 1937, p. 51 ff.; ML 39, 2149]. The elements of the Creed are possessed, an exact formula cannot be worked out; seems to be the same as the two following:

SACRAMENTARIUM GALLICANUM [Mabillon, Museum Italicum I, Paris 1687, 312, H. sect. 66; L 15], 7/8th century, composed in Gaul,* (others, Missale Vesontiense [Besançon], Missale Bobbiense [Bobbio]); contains two formulae and a Creed in the manner of questions—(The first form is regarded).

MISSALE GALLICANUM VETUS, of the beginning of the eighth century [Mabillon, *De liturgia Gallicana III,* Paris: 1685, 339. H. sect. 67; L 15].

ST. PIRMINIUS, born in Gallia merid.*; died 753, bishop of the Meldi (?), afterwards abbot of the monastery of Reichenau [Reichenau in Germany]. Words of the Abbot Pirminius on the individual canonical books scarapsus; written between 718 and 724.* [G. Jecker, *Die Heimat des hl. Pirmin,* Münster: 1927, 34 ff.; the creed itself in the customary form n. 10 and 28 a, in the form of questions n. 12. H. sect. 92; ML 89, 1034 C].

CODEX AUGIENSIS CXCV, perhaps of the eighth century [CspQ III 512].—Creed written by a certain Irish monk(?).

ORDO VEL BREVIS EXPLANATIO DE CATECHIZANDIS RUDIBUS, c. a. 850 ad 950* [H sect. 71; CspANQ 282].

ORDO ROMANUS, ancient of the year 950 [H. sect. 25; Hittorp, De divinis catholicae ecclesiae officiis, Cologne 1568].—Shows the usual form.

Text

[According to "the Roman Order"]

1a. I believe in God the Father almighty   6
  b. creator of heaven and earth
2. and in Jesus Christ, His only son, our Lord
3. who was conceived of the Holy Spirit, born of the Virgin Mary
4a. suffered under Pontius Pilate, crucified, died, and was buried
  b. descended into hell
5. on the third day He arose from the dead
6a. He ascended to heaven
  b. sits at the right hand of God the Father Almighty
7. thence He shall come to judge the living and the dead
8. I believe in the Holy Spirit
9a. the holy Catholic Church
  b. the communion of saints
10. the remission of sins
11. the resurrection of the body
12. and life everlasting.

The Eastern Form of the Apostolic Creed

Sources

8   St. Justin Martyr. See above [n. 1]

Coptic Apostolic Constitutions (*Constitutiones Apostolicae Copticae*) or the Constitutions of the Egyptian Church in Funk, Didasc. et Const. Apost. II (1905) 97 ff., show the Apostolic Tradition (Paradosis) of Hippolytus (on which see above n. 2–3) in the Orient also changed as a creed. Therefore, it seems to be a witness also for the eastern form of the Apostolic Creed.

Text

[of Saint Cyril of Jerusalem] [1]

9   1a. We believe in one God the Father Almighty

  b. The creator of heaven and earth

  c. and of all things visible and invisible

  2a. and in one Lord Jesus Christ the only begotten Son of God

  b. who was begotten of the Father

  c. true God

  d. before all ages

  e. by whom all things were made

  3a. (who for our salvation)

  b. was made flesh (of the Holy Spirit and Mary the virgin) and was made man

  4a. was crucified (under Pontius Pilate) and was buried

  b.

  5a. arose on the third day

  b. (according to the Scriptures)

  6a. and ascended into heaven

  b. and sits at the right hand of the Father

  7a. and comes in glory to judge the living and the dead

  b. of whose kingdom there will be no end

  8a. and in one Holy Spirit the Paraclete

  b.

  c.

  d.

  e. who spoke among the prophets

---

[1] What is included within curved brackets (—) probably should be added to the form of St. Cyril; what is included within square brackets [—] should be omitted [Cf. K I 237 f.].

9 [1]. and one holy [Catholic] church
10a. and in one baptism of repentance
  b. in the dismissal of sins
11. and in the resurrection of the flesh
12. and in life everlasting

EUSEBIUS, died about 340, bishop of Caesarea, *Ep. ad suam dioec.* [Socrates, 12
Hist. eccl. I, 8, 38; MG 67, 69; H. sect. 123; L 18]. Eusebius offered his creed
to the Nicene council in 325, which used it to establish its own form.

ST. CYRIL, bishop of Jerusalem—*Catecheses 6–18,* held before 350 (351)
[H sect. 124; L. 19; MG 33, 535 ff.]. He gives out a Creed used before 325;
its text is construed otherwise by some [Macarius of Jerusalem, predecessor
of St. Cyril, seems to have had the same creed, at least according to the
headings].

ST. EPIPHANIUS, died in 403, bishop of Salamis in Cyprus.—*Ancoratus,*
written about the year 374; contains at the end two formulae, of which the
shorter (ἡ ἁγία πίστις τῆς καθολικῆς ἐκκλησίας) is here considered; [cf.
the longer, n. 13 f.]; the Creed is believed to be older than the Ancoratus
[H. sect. 125; L 19 f.; ed. K. Holl. 1915, 148; MG 43, 232 C].

CONSTITUTIONES APOSTOLORUM VII 41, of the beginning* of the fifth century
[otherwise, of middle of fourth century; it contains certainly more ancient
materials (MG 1, 1041 C. Funk, *Didascalia et Constitutiones Apostolorum* 1,
Paderborn: 1905, 445)]. The Creed, as far as many parts are concerned, belongs to Lucian Martyr* (died 312); it shows a Syro-Palestinian* form.

THE CREED OF EPIPHANIUS [2]

Longer Form

(Exposition of Nicene Creed proposed to certain catechumens
in the Orient)

We believe in one God, the father almighty, the creator of all things in- 13
visible and visible; and in one lord Jesus Christ, the son of God, the only
begotten born of God the father, that is of the substance of the Father, God
of God, light of light, true God of true God, begotten not made, consubstantial to the father, by whom all things were made, both those in
heaven and those on earth, both visible and invisible, who for us men
and for our salvation came down and became man, that is was completely
born of holy Mary ever-virgin by the Holy Spirit, was made man, that is,
assumed perfect human nature, soul and body and mind, and all whatever
is man except sin, not from the seed of man nor by means of man, but

---

[1] In the Catecheses, articles 9 and 10a and b are arranged in the reverse order; in
the creed itself, probably in the right order.
[2] MG, 43, 234 f.; coll. H. sect. 126.

having fashioned unto himself a body into one holy unity; not as he lived in the prophets and talked and worked in them, but became man completely ("for the word was made flesh," he did not submit to an alteration, nor did he change his own divine nature into human nature); he combined both the divine nature and the human into the only holy perfection of himself; (for there is one Lord Jesus Christ, and not two; the same God, the same Lord, the same King); but the same suffered in the flesh and arose again and ascended into heaven with the very body and sits in glory at the right hand of the Father, in that very body he is coming in glory to judge the living and the dead; of whose kingdom there shall be no end:—and we believe in the Holy Spirit who spoke in the law, and taught by the prophets, and descended to the Jordan, spoke by the Apostles, and lives in the saints; thus we believe in him: that he is the Holy Spirit, the Spirit of God, the perfect Spirit, the Spirit Paraclete, uncreated, proceeding from the Father and receiving of the Son, in whom we believe.

14   We believe in one catholic and apostolic Church, and in one baptism of repentance, and in the resurrection of the dead, and the just judgment of souls and bodies, and in the kingdom of heaven, and in life eternal.

But those who say that there was a time when the Son or the Holy Spirit was not, that he was made from nothing or is of another substance or essence, alleging that the Son of God or the Holy Spirit was changed or altered, these the catholic and apostolic Church, your mother and our mother, anathematizes. We also anathematize those who do not confess the resurrection of the dead, and besides all the heresies which are not consistent with this true faith.

THE FORMULA CALLED THE "FAITH OF DAMASUS" [1]

[Of uncertain author and time; from Gaul about 500 (?)]

15   We believe in one God the Father almighty and in our one Lord Jesus Christ the Son of God and in (one) Holy Spirit God. Not three Gods, but Father and Son and Holy Spirit one God do we worship and confess: not one God in such a way as to be solitary, nor the same in such wise that he himself is Father to himself and he himself is Son to himself; but the Father is he who begot, and the Son is he who is begotten; the Holy Spirit in truth is neither begotten nor unbegotten, neither created nor made, but proceeding from the Father and the Son, coeternal and coequal and the cooperator with the Father and the Son, because it is written: *"By the*

---

[1] KAnt 47 ff.; KBdS 10 et 43 ff.; H sect. 200; cf. Cst, Appendix 101 B f.

word of the Lord the heavens were established" (that is, by the Son of God), *"and all the power of them by the spirit of his mouth"* [Ps. 32:6], and elsewhere: *"Send forth thy spirit and they shall be created and thou shalt renew the face of the earth"* [Ps. 103:30]. And therefore we confess one God in the name of the Father and of the Son and of the Holy Spirit, because god is the name of power, not of peculiarity. The proper name for the Father is Father, and the proper name for the Son is Son, and the proper name for the Holy Spirit is Holy Spirit. And in this Trinity we believe in one God, because what is of one nature and of one substance and of one power with the Father is from one Father. The Father begot the Son, not by will, nor by necessity, but by nature.

The Son in the fullness of time came down from the Father to save us **16** and to fulfill the Scriptures, though he never ceased to be with the Father, and was conceived by the Holy Spirit and born of the Virgin Mary; he took a body, soul, and sense, that is, he assumed perfect human nature; nor did he lose, what he was, but he began to be, what he was not; in such a way, however, that he is perfect in his own nature and true in our nature.

For he who was God, was born a man, and he who was born a man, operates as God; and he who operates as God, dies as a man; and he who dies as a man, arises as God. He having conquered the power of death with that body, with which he was born, and suffered, and had died, arose on the third day, ascended to the Father, and sits at his right hand in glory, which he always has had and always has. We believe that cleansed in his death and in his blood we are to be raised up by him on the last day in this body with which we now live; and we have hope that we shall obtain from him either life eternal, the reward of good merit or the penalty of eternal punishment for sins. Read these words, keep them, subject your soul to this faith. From Christ the Lord you will receive both life and reward.

THE FORMULA "THE MERCIFUL TRINITY"[1]

[Of uncertain author and time; from Gaul about 500(?)]

The merciful Trinity is one divine Godhead. Consequently the Father **17** and the Son and the Holy Spirit are one source, one substance, one virtue, and one power. We say that God the Father and God the Son and God the Holy Spirit are not three gods, but we very piously confess

---

[1] Gregorianum 14 (1933) 487 f. [I. A. Aldama]. KAnt 65 ff. (cf. KBdS 12 and 147 f.).

one God. For although we name three persons, we publicly declare with the catholic and apostolic voice that they are one substance. Therefore the Father and the Son and the Holy Spirit, *these three are one* [cf. I John 5:7]. Three, neither confused, nor separated, but both distinctly joined, and, though joined, distinct; united in substance, but differentiated in name, joined in nature, distinct in person, equal in divinity, entirely similar in majesty, united in trinity, sharers in splendor. They are one in such a way, that we do not doubt that they are also three; and they are three in such a way that we acknowledge that they cannot be disjoined from one another. Therefore there is no doubt, that an insult to one is an affront to all, because the praise of one pertains to the glory of all.

18   'For this is the principal point of our faith according to the Gospel and the apostolic doctrine, that our Lord Jesus Christ and the Son of God are not separated from the Father either in the acknowledgement of honor, or in the power of virtue, or in the divine nature of substance, or by an interval of time.'[1] And therefore if anyone says that the Son of God, who just as he is truly God, so also is true man except in sin alone, did not possess something belonging to human nature or did not possess something belonging to the Godhead, he should be judged wicked and hostile to the Catholic and apostolic Church.

THE CREED OF THE COUNCIL OF TOLEDO OF THE YEAR 400 [AND 447][2]

[Formula, "A little book like a Creed"]

The rule of the Catholic faith against all heresies [(Here) begin the rules of the Catholic faith against all heresies, and especially indeed against the Priscillianists, which the bishops of Tarraco, Carthage, Lusitania, and Baetica have composed and with a command of Pope Leo of the City transmitted to Balconius, bishop of Gallicia. . . .].

---

[1] S. Hilarius, *De synodis* 61 [ML 10, 522].

[2] I. A. de Aldama, *El simbolo Toledano* I. [Analecta Gregoriana VII.] 1934, pag. 29 ff. KAnt 43 ff. KBdS 8 f. and 31 ff.; H 209 ff.; ap. Msi III 1003 A; Hrd I 993 A; cf. Hfl II 306 ff. According to de Aldama there exist two forms of this antipriscillianist creed, the one shorter, which is due to the council of Toledo of the year 400, the other longer, worked out with great care by Pastor, the Palencian bishop, and approved in the council of Toledo of the year 447. These changes (not very light ones) which are due to the council of the year 447, are shown in the text enclosed in brackets. A similar refutation of errors is found in "Statutis ecclesiae antiquis" [falsely held for acts of the fourth Council of Carthage; cf. note ad n. 150] in the form of questions which ought to be proposed to bishops about to be ordained [ML 56, 879 A f.].

We believe in one true God, Father, and Son and Holy Spirit, maker 19 of the visible and the invisible, by whom were created all things in heaven and on earth. This God alone and this Trinity alone is of divine name [divine substance]. The Father is not [himself] the Son, but has the Son, who is not the Father. The Son is not the Father, but the Son is of God by nature [is of the Father's nature]. The Spirit is also the Paraclete, who is himself neither the Father, nor the Son, but proceeds from the Father [proceeding from the Father and the Son]. Therefore the Father is unbegotten, the Son is begotten, the Paraclete is not begotten, but proceeding from the Father [and the Son]. The Father is he whose words were heard from the heavens: *This is my beloved Son, in whom I am well pleased, hear ye him.* [Matt. 17:5; II Peter 1:17. Cf. Matt. 3:17]. The Son is he who says: *I came forth from the Father, and am come into the world* [cf. John 16:28]. The Paraclete himself [the Spirit] is he, concerning whom the Son says: *Unless I go to the Father, the Paraclete will not come to you* [John 16:17]. This Trinity, though distinct in persons, is one substance [united], virtue, power, majesty [in virtue and in power and in majesty] indivisible, not different. [We believe] there is no divine nature except that [this], either of angel or of spirit or of any virtue, which is believed to be God.

Therefore this Son of God, God, born of the Father entirely before every 20 beginning, has sanctified in the womb [the womb] of the Blessed Mary Virgin, and from her has assumed true man, human nature having been begotten without the [virile] seed of man; [of not more or not less than two natures, namely, of God and of flesh, meeting completely in one person], that is, [our] Lord Jesus Christ. Not [And not] an imaginary body or one constituted of form alone [*in place of this:* or that it belong to some phantasm in him]; but a firm [and true] one. And this man hungered and thirsted and grieved and wept and felt all the pains of a body [*in place of this:* suffered all the injuries of a body]. Finally he was crucified [by the Jews], died and was buried, [and] on the third day he arose again; afterwards he conversed with [his] disciples; the fortieth day [after the resurrection] he ascended to the heavens [heaven]. This son of man is called [named] also the Son of God; but the Son of God, God, is not (likewise) called the Son of man [calls the Son of man (thus)].

We believe that there [will] assuredly [be] a resurrection of the human flesh [for the body]. However, the soul of man is not a divine substance, or a part of God, but a creature [we say] which did not fall by the divine will [created].

1. If therefore [however] anyone says and [or] believes, that this world 21 and all its furnishings were not made by God almighty, let him be anathema.

22   2. If anyone says and [or] believes, that God the Father is the same person as the Son or the Paraclete, let him be anathema.

23   3. If anyone says and [or] believes that God the Son [of God] is the same person as the Father or the Paraclete, let him be anathema.

24   4. If anyone says and [or] believes that the Paraclete the Spirit is either the Father or the Son, let him be anathema.

25   5. If anyone say and [or] believes that the man Jesus Christ was not assumed by the Son of God [*in place of this:* that a body only without a soul was assumed by the Son of God], let him be anathema.

26   6. If anyone says and [or] believes, that the Son of God, as God, suffered [*in place of this:* that Christ cannot be born], let him be anathema.

27   7. If anyone says and [or] believes that the man Jesus Christ was a man incapable of suffering [*in place of this:* the divine nature of Christ was changeable or capable of suffering], let him be anathema.

28   8. If anyone says and [or] believes, that there is one God of the old Law, another of the Gospels, let him be anathema.

29   9. If anyone says and [or] believes, that the world was made by another God than [and not] by him, concerning whom it is written: *In the beginning God created heaven and earth* [cf. Gen. 1, 1], let him be anathema.

30   10. If anyone says and [or] believes that the human bodies will not rise again [do not rise] after death, let him be anathema.

31   11. If anyone says and [or] believes that the human soul is a part of God or is God's substance, let him be anathema.

32   12. If anyone either believes that any scriptures, except those which the Catholic Church has received, ought to be held in authority or venerates them [If anyone says or believes other scriptures, besides those which the Catholic Church receives, ought to be held in authority or ought to be venerated], let him be anathema.

33   [13. If anyone says or believes that there is in Christ one nature of the Godhead of humanity, let him be anathema.]

34   [14. If anyone says or believes that there is anything that can extend itself beyond the divine Trinity, let him be anathema.]

35   [15. If anyone holds that astrology and the interpretation of stars (sic) ought to be believed, let him be anathema.]

36   [16. If anyone says or believes, that the marriages of men, which are considered licit according to divine law, are accursed, let him be anathema.]

37   [17. If anyone says or believes that the flesh of birds or of animals, which has been given for food, not only ought to be abstained from for the chastising of the body, but ought to be abhorred, let him be anathema.]

38   [18. If anyone follows the sect of Priscillian in these errors or publicly

professes it, so that he makes a change in the saving act of baptism contrary to the chair of Holy Peter, let him be anathema.]

THE CREED "QUICUMQUE"

[Which is called "Athanasian"] [1]

Whoever wishes to be saved, needs above all to hold the Catholic faith; **39** unless each one preserves this whole and inviolate, he will without a doubt perish in eternity.—But the Catholic faith is this, that we venerate one God in the Trinity, and the Trinity in oneness; neither confounding the persons, nor dividing the substance; for there is one person of the Father, another of the Son, (and) another of the Holy Spirit; but the divine nature of the Father and of the Son and of the Holy Spirit is one, their glory is equal, their majesty is coeternal. Of such a nature as the Father is, so is the Son, so (also) is the Holy Spirit; the Father is uncreated, the Son is uncreated, (and) the Holy Spirit is uncreated; the Father is immense, the Son is immense, (and) the Holy Spirit is immense; the Father is eternal, the Son is eternal, (and) the Holy Spirit is eternal: and nevertheless there are not three eternals, but one eternal; just as there are not three uncreated beings, nor three infinite beings, but one uncreated, and one infinite; similarly the Father is omnipotent, the Son is omnipotent, (and) the Holy Spirit is omnipotent: and yet there are not three omnipotents, but one omnipotent; thus the Father is God, the Son is God, (and) the Holy Spirit is God; and nevertheless there are not three gods, but there is one God; so the Father is Lord, the Son is Lord, (and) the Holy Spirit is Lord: and yet there are not three lords, but there is one Lord; because just as we are

---

[1] KAnt 232 f.; H 174 ff.; ML 88, 565 A f.; Msi II 1354 B f. (*Brevier. Rom.*: Dom. ad Prim.)—It is certain that this profession of faith is not the work of Athanasius. The Latin text seems to be the first; but there are also Greek versions. In certain ancient codices this creed is attributed to "ANASTASIUS" (II), because "The Faith of ANASTASIUS" and "The Creed of ANASTASIUS" are inscribed on it. Künstle ("Antipriscillians" p. 204 ff.) attempted to prove the anti-Priscillian and Spanish origin of this Creed. But Henry Brewer rejects the arguments by which he establishes his opinion, and contends that the author of the ("Athanasian") creed is St. Ambrose the Milanese bishop [*Das sog. Athanasianische Glaubensbekenntnis ein Werk des hl. Ambrosius*, Paderb.; 1909]. So also P. Scheepens (*Rev. d'hist eccl.* 32 [1936] 548 ff.). Cf. what G. Morin in *Journal of Theol. Stud.* 12 (1911) 161 ff. 337 ff., and A. E. Burn, ib. 27 (1926) 19, have written about the same matter. J. Stiglmayr thinks this creed ought to be assigned to Fulgentius Ruspensis: *Zeitschr. f. kath. Theol.* 49 (1926) 341 ff.—Actually this "creed" afterwards received such great authority in both the western and the eastern Church, that it was accepted in liturgical use and ought to be considered as a true definition of the faith.—The words which are enclosed in brackets [. .] indicate the liturgical text; those in parentheses (. .) are lacking in the same.

compelled by Christian truth to confess singly each one person as God and [and also] Lord, so we are forbidden by the Catholic religion to say there are three gods or lords. The Father was not made nor created nor begotten by anyone. The Son is from the Father alone, not made nor created, but begotten. The Holy Spirit is from the Father and the Son, not made nor created nor begotten, but proceeding. There is therefore one Father, not three Fathers; one Son, not three Sons; one Holy Spirit, not three Holy Spirits; and in this Trinity there is nothing first or later, nothing greater or less, but all three persons are coeternal and coequal with one another, so that in every respect, as has already been said above, both unity in Trinity, and Trinity in unity must be venerated. Therefore let him who wishes to be saved, think thus concerning the Trinity.

40   But it is necessary for eternal salvation that he faithfully believe also the incarnation of our Lord Jesus Christ. Accordingly it is the right faith, that we believe and confess, that our Lord Jesus Christ, the Son of God is God and man. He is God begotten of the substance of the Father before time, and he is man born of the substance of his mother in time: perfect God, perfect man, consisting of a rational soul and a human body, equal to the Father according to his Godhead, less than the Father according to humanity. Although he is God and man, yet he is not two, but he is one Christ; one, however, not by the conversion of the Divinity into a human body, but by the assumption of humanity in the Godhead; one absolutely not by confusion of substance, but by unity of person. For just as the rational soul and body are one man, so God and man are one Christ. He suffered for our salvation, descended into hell, on the third day arose again from the dead, ascended to heaven, sits at the right hand of God the Father almighty; thence he shall come to judge the living and the dead; at his coming all men have to arise again with their bodies and will render an account of their own deeds: and those who have done good, will go into life everlasting, but those who have done evil, into eternal fire.—This is the Catholic faith; unless every one believes this faithfully and firmly, he cannot be saved.

DOCUMENTS OF
THE ROMAN PONTIFFS
AND OF THE COUNCILS

ST. PETER THE APOSTLE (?)–67 (?)

under whose name two canonical epistles are extant.

St. Linus 67 (?)–79 (?)   St. (Ana)Cletus 79 (?)–90 (?)

ST. CLEMENT I 90 (?)–99 (?)
The Primacy of the Roman Pontiff [1]

[From the letter "Διὰ τὰς αἰφνιδίους" to the Corinthians]

(1) BECAUSE of the sudden calamities that have followed one another **41** in turn and because of the adverse circumstances which have befallen us, we think, brethren, that we have returned too late to those matters which are being inquired into among you, beloved, and to the impious and detestable sedition . . . which a few rash and presumptuous men have aroused to such a degree of insolence that your honorable and illustrious name . . . is very much reviled. . . . In order to remind you of your duty, we write. . . . (57) You, therefore, who have laid the foundations of this insurrection, be subject in obedience to the priests and receive correction unto repentance. . . . (59) But if some will not submit to them, let them learn what He [Christ] has spoken through us, that they will involve themselves in great sin and danger; we, however, shall be innocent of this transgression. . . . (63) Indeed you will give joy and gladness to us, if having become obedient to what we have written through the Holy Spirit, you will cut out the unlawful application of your zeal according to the exhortation which we have made in this epistle concerning peace and union.

---

[1] Funk, *Patres apost.* I 60 ff.; ed. K. Bihlmeyer I (1924) 35 ff.; Jf 9; Cst 9 ff.; MG 1, 205 A ff.; Msi I 171 A ff.

42   **Concerning the Hierarchy and the Status of the Laity** [1]

[From the same epistle to the Corinthians]

(40) (For) they do not go astray who follow the commands of the Lord. Inasmuch as peculiar gifts have been bestowed upon the chief priest, a special place has been assigned to the priests, and particular duties are incumbent upon the Levites. The layman is bound by the precepts pertaining to the laity.

(41) Let each of us, brethren, "in his own order" [I Cor. 15:23] with a good conscience not transgressing the prescribed rule of his own office give thanks to God honorably.

(42) The Apostles were made preachers of the Gospel to us by the Lord Jesus Christ; Jesus Christ was sent by God. . . . Accordingly, when they had proclaimed the word through country districts and cities and had tested the first converts of these by the spirit, they appointed bishops and deacons of those who were to believe.

St. Evaristus (99) (?)–107 (?)	St. Pius I 140 (?)–154 (?)
St. Alexander I 107 (?)–116 (?)	St. Anicetus 154 (?)–165 (?)
St. Sixtus I 116 (?)–125 (?)	St. Soter 165 (?)–174 (?)
St. Telesphorus 125 (?)–136 (?)	St. Eleutherius 174 (?)–189 (?)
St. Hyginus 136 (?)–140 (?)	St. Victor 189 (?)–198 (?) [2]

ST. ZEPHYRINUS 198 (?)–217
resp. ST. CALLISTUS I 217–222

The Incarnate Word [3]

[From St. Hippolytus's *Philosophy* IX 11, about the year 230]

42a   "[Callistus], however, influenced ZEPHYRINUS himself to speak to the people openly: I know one God Christ Jesus, and besides him no other begotten and passible; then indeed [CALLISTUS] said: The Fa-

---

[1] Funk, op. cit., 110 f.; ed. Bihlmeyer 47 f.; Cet 28 E.

[2] At the time of VICTOR the primacy of the Roman Pontiff was acknowledged by all. For, when in the controversy concerning the celebration of Easter, Victor wished to excommunicate the churches of Asia, they indeed accused him of too great severity (as Irenaeus), but no bishop called into question either his right or his authority. Cf. Eusebius, *Historia eccl.* 5, 24 [MG 20, 439 ff.; Schwartz-Mommsen, Euseb. II 1, 491 ff.].

[3] *Refutatio omnium haeresium*, ed. P. Wendland 1916, 246; MG 16 c, 3380. Concerning this matter see Zeitschr. f. kath. Theol. 41 (1917) 595 ff.; 52 (1928) 225 ff. (Konr. Preysing); 48 (1924) 314 ff. (H. Dieckmann).

ther did not die, but the Son: in such a way as this he kept up the perpetual dispute among the people.

When we had learned his [CALLISTUS'S] purposes, we did not yield, refuting and resisting for the sake of truth: driven to madness, especially because all agreed to his pretext—not we, however—he invoked two gods, voluntarily discharging the virus which lay hidden in his internal organs."

The Absolving of Sins [1]

[Fragment from Tertullian's "De pudicitia" c. 1]

"I also hear that an edict is published and is indeed final. Evidently the **43** Supreme Pontiff, because he is the bishop of bishops, declares: I forgive the sins of adultery and fornication to those who have performed the penance." [2]

St. Urbanus 222–230	St. Anterus 235–236
St. Pontianus 230–235	St. Fabianus 235–250

ST. CORNELIUS I 251–253
The Monarchical Constitution of the Church [3]

[From epistle (6) "Quantam solicitudinem" to Cyprian, bishop
of Carthage, 252]

"We know that CORNELIUS, bishop of the most holy Catholic **44** Church, was chosen by God almighty and by Christ our Lord; we confess our error; we have suffered imposture; we have been deceived by treachery and captious loquacity; for although we seemed to have held, as it were, a certain communication with a schismatical and heretical man, nevertheless our heart has always been in the Church; for we are not ignorant that there is one God and that there is one Lord Christ, whom we have confessed, that there is one Holy Spirit and that there ought to be one bishop in the Catholic Church."

*Concerning the written proof for teaching the Holy Spirit,
see Kirch n. 256 R n. 547; concerning the Trinity,
see R n. 546.*

---

[1] CSEL XX 1, 220; Jf 79; ML 2, 981 A.

[2] These words are ascribed by some to St. Zephyrinus, by others to St. Callistus, by others to St. Agrippinus, Bishop of Carthage.

[3] Jf 111; Cst 137 B; ML 3, 721 A f.; Msi I 831 C. This profession of faith by the schismatics Maximus, Urban, Sidonius, and others was offered to CORNELIUS and accepted by him.

The Ecclesiastical Hierarchy [1]

[From the epistle " "Ἵνα δὲ γνῷς" to Fabius, bishop of
Antioch, in the year 251]

45   Therefore did not that famous defender of the Gospel [Novatian]
know that there ought to be one bishop in the Catholic Church [of the city
of Rome]? It did not lie hidden from him (for how could it be concealed?) that in this there were forty-six priests, seven deacons, seven
subdeacons, forty-two acolytes, and fifty-two exorcists and lectors together
with porters and more than a thousand five hundred widows and [needy]
eunuchs.

Sᴛ. Lᴜᴄɪᴜs I 253–254

ST. STEPHAN I 254–257

The Baptism of Heretics [2]

[Fragment of a letter to Cyprian, from his letter (74) to Pompey]

46   (1) . . . "If therefore any come to you from any heresy whatsoever,
let nothing be renewed except what has been transmitted, so that the hand
is placed upon them for repentance, since the heretics among themselves
properly do not baptize those coming to them, but only give them communion."

[Fragment from a letter of Stephan from a letter (75) of
Firmilianus to Cyprian]

47   (18) "But," he [STEPHAN] says, "the name of Christ conduces greatly
to faith and to the sanctification of baptism, so that whoever has been
baptized anywhere in the name of Christ, at once obtains the grace of
Christ." [3]

Sᴛ. Xʏsᴛᴜs (Sɪxᴛᴜs) II 258

---

[1] Cst 149 B f.; Jf 106 c. Add.; ML 3, 741 A f. and MG 20, 622; Msi I 821 A f.

[2] CSEL III 2, 799 and 822 (Cypr. Opp., ed. Hartel); Jf 125; ML 3, 1128 B f. and
1169 C f.

[3] In the same epistle (75) Firmilianus attests to these statements:
(8) . . . "STEPHAN and those who agree with him contend that the remission
of sins and a second birth can result in the baptism of heretics. . . . (9) They do
not think that inquiry ought to be made as to who it was that baptized, because he
who was baptized could have gotten the grace by invoking the Trinity of names of
the Father and the Son and the Holy Ghost" [CSEL III 2, 815; ML 3, 1161 B f.].
And a little later Firmilianus says with indignation:
(17) . . . "STEPHAN, who brags so about the place of his bishopric, and asserts

ST. DIONYSIUS 259–268

The Trinity and the Incarnation [1]

[Fragment from epistle (2) against the Tritheists and
Sabellians, about the year 260]

(1) Now assuredly it is just to preach against those who destroy the **48**
one power which is the most sacred teaching of the Church of God, dividing and rending it into some three powers and distinct substances and
three deities. For I have heard that some who preach and explain the
divine word among you are teachers of this belief; yet they, so to speak,
are diametrically opposed to the opinion of Sabellius.

For the latter blasphemes when he says that the Son himself is the
Father and the reverse: the former indeed in a certain measure proclaim
three gods, when they divide the sacred unity into three different substances altogether distinct from one another. For it is necessary that the
divine Word be united to the God of all, and that the Holy Spirit abide in
God and dwell in Him: and thus the divine Trinity is reduced to and gathered into one, as it were, into a certain head, that is into the omnipotent
God of all. For foolish Marcion's doctrine which divides and separates
the monarchy into three principles is surely diabolical; moreover, it is not of
the true disciples of Christ or of those to whom the teaching of the Savior is
pleasing. For these know well that the Trinity is indeed proclaimed in
divine Scripture, moreover, that three gods are taught neither in the Old
nor in the New Testament.

(2) But none the less they should be blamed who think that the Son is **49**
a work, and that the Lord was made just as one of those things which
were actually created; since divine statements bear witness that He was
begotten, as is proper and fitting, not created or made.

It is therefore not a trifling, but a very great irreverence to say that the
Lord was made in some way. For if the Son was made, there was a time
when He did not exist; and yet He always was, if He undoubtedly is, as
He himself declares, in the Father [John 14:10 f.]. Moreover, and if Christ
is the word, the wisdom, and the power (for the divine Scriptures teach
that Christ is [John 1:14; I Cor. 1:24], as you yourselves know), surely
these are the powers of God. Wherefore, if the Son was made, there was a

---

that he holds the succession of PETER on which the foundations of the Church
have been laid . . . is not fired with any zeal against the heretics, granting to them
no scant power of grace, but the greatest, so that he says and declares positively
that they through the sacrament of baptism wash away the uncleanness of the old
man and forgive the old deadly sins and make sons of God by heavenly regeneration
and retrieve for eternal life by the sanctification of the divine bath." [CSEL III 2,
821; ML 3, 1169 A].

[1] Cst 273 ff.; Jf 136; MG 25, 462 C ff.; Msi I 1011 A ff.

time when these powers did not exist; and so there was a time when God was without them; which is very absurd.

50 But why should I treat further about these matters with you, man full of the Spirit, and especially who understand what absurdities follow from that opinion which asserts that the Son was made? It seems to me that the leaders of this belief did not consider these at all, and thus have completely strayed from the truth, when they explain differently from what the divine and prophetic Scripture wishes, the passage: "The Lord created man in the beginning of his ways" [Prov. 8:22: LXX]. Certainly there is not, as you know, only one meaning of the word "created." For in this passage "created" is the same as "he set him over works made by Him," made, I say, by the Son Himself.

But here "created" ought not to be understood exactly as "made." For "to make" and "to create" differ from each other. "Is not he thy father that hast possessed thee, and made thee, and created thee?" [Dt. 32, 6:LXX] said Moses in the great canticle of Deuteronomy. And so who can rightly refute them: O rash and inconsiderate men, was he then a made thing "the first born of every creature" [Col. 1:15], "begotten from the womb before the daystar" [Ps. 109:3:LXX] of whom as Wisdom says, "before all the hills he brought me forth"? [Prov. 8:25:LXX]. Finally anybody may read in many passages of the divine statements that the Son was "begotten," but nowhere "made." By reason of this they who dare to call His divine and inexplicable begetting a making, are clearly proved to speak falsely about the Lord's generation.

51 (3) Neither therefore ought the admirable and divine unity be separated into three godheads, nor ought the dignity and supreme magnitude of the Lord be lessened by the designation of making; but we must believe in God the Father Almighty, and in Christ Jesus his Son, and in the Holy Spirit, that the Word, moreover, is united to the God of all.

For He said: "I and the Father are one" [John 10:30], and: "I am in the Father, and the Father in me" [John 14:10]. Thus it is evident that the divine Trinity and the holy proclamation of the monarchy will be preserved intact.

| St. Felix I 269–274 | St. Caius 283–296 |
| St. Eutychianus 275–283 | St. Marcellinus 296–304 |

COUNCIL OF ILLIBERI [1] BETWEEN 300/306 [2]

The Indissolubility of Matrimony

52a Can. 9. Likewise let the faithful woman, who has left an adulterous husband and attracts another faithful one, be forbidden to marry; if she

---

[1] Elvira in Spain.

[2] Msi II 10 C f.; Hrd I 251 ff.; coll. Hfl I 166 and 168. See other canons of this Council in Kch n. 330 ff.

should marry, let her not receive communion unless he whom she has left has previously departed this world; unless by chance the exigency of illness should compel the giving.

The Celibacy of the Clergy

Can. 27. A bishop, or any priest at all, may have with him only a sister **52b** or a virgin daughter dedicated to God; it is decided that he by no means have a stranger.

Can. 33. It is decided that marriage be altogether prohibited to bishops, **52c** priests, and deacons, or to all clerics placed in the ministry, and that they keep away from their wives and not beget children; whoever does this, shall be deprived of the honor of the clerical office.

Baptism and Confirmation

Can. 38. If people are traveling by sea in a foreign place or if there is no **52d** church in the neighborhood, a person of the faith who keeps his baptism sound and is not twice married, can baptize a catechumen placed in the exigency of sickness, on condition that, if he survives, he bring him to a bishop, in order that it may be made perfect by the imposition of the hand.

Can. 77. If any deacon ruling the people without a bishop or priest **52e** baptizes some, the bishop will have to confirm these by a blessing; but if they should depart the world beforehand, in the faith in which anyone of them has believed, that one can be justified.

St. Marcellus 308–309   St. Eusebius 309 (or 310)

St. Militiades 311–314

ST. SYLVESTER I 314–335

COUNCIL OF ARELAS[1] I 314

Plenary (against the Donatists)

The Baptism of Heretics[2]

Can. 8. Concerning the Africans, because they use their own law so as **53** to rebaptize, it has been decided that, if anyone from a heretical sect come to the Church, he should be asked his creed, and if it is perceived that he has been baptized in the Father and the Son and the Holy Spirit, only the hand should be imposed upon him, in order that he may receive the Holy Spirit. But if upon being questioned he does not answer this Trinity, let him be baptized.

Can. 15. That deacons may not offer, see Kch 373.   **53***

---

[1] Arles in Gaul.

[2] Msi II 472 A; Hrd I 265 A; Hfl I 209.

COUNCIL OF NICEA I 325

Ecumenical I (against the Arians).

The Nicene Creed [1]

54   [Version of Hilary of Poictiers]

We believe in one God the Father almighty, creator of all things visible and invisible. And in our one Lord Jesus Christ the Son of God, the only-begotten born of the Father, that is of the substance of the Father, God of God, light of light, true God of true God, born, not made, of one substance with the Father (which they call in Greek "homousion"), by whom all things were made, which are in heaven and on earth, who for our salvation came down, and became incarnate and was made man, and suffered, and arose again on the third day, and ascended into heaven, and will come to judge the living and the dead. And in the Holy Spirit.

But those who say: "There was [a time] when he was not," and, "Before he was born, he was not," and "Because he was made from non-existing matter, he is either of another substance or essence," and those who call "God the Son of God changeable and mutable," these the Catholic Church anathematizes.[2]

The Baptism of Heretics and the Viaticum of the Dying [3]

55   [Version of Dionysius Exig.[4]]

Can. 8. Concerning those who call themselves Cathari [Novatians] that is, clean, if at any time they come to the Catholic Church, it has been decided by the holy and great Council, that, provided they receive the imposition of hands, they remain among the clergy. However, because they are accepting and following the doctrines of the Catholic and Apostolic Church, it is fitting that they acknowledge this in writing before all; that is, both that they communicate with the twice married and with those who have lapsed during a persecution.

56   Can. 19. Concerning the Paulianists who take refuge with the Catholic Church, a decree has been published that they should be fully baptized.

---

[1] Orientalia christiana periodica (Roma) 2 (1936) 342 f. (J. Ortiz de Urbina). H 160 ff.; coll. Hfl I 314; ML 10, 536 A; Msi II 666 C f. (cf. V 688): Hrd I 946 E 311 (1244); cf. KBdS 146; Bar(Th) ad 325 n. 73 ff. (4, 127b ff.); C. H. Turner, *Eccl. occid. monumenta iuris antiquissima.* T. I, fasc. I, pars 2 (1904) 106 ff.

[2] The Latin text of this condemnation is taken from ACOec I 3 P. 1, p. 121.

[3] Hrd I 326 D f. 331 C 330 B (cf. 431 E 437 A 434 E f.); coll. Hfl I 407, 417, 427; Msi II 671 B (cf. 896) 675 B 673 D f. (cf. 900).

[4] C. H. Turner, *Eccl. occid. mon. iuris antiq.* T. I, fasc. I, p. 2, 262 ff.

If, however, any of these in time past have been in the clerical order, if indeed they have appeared spotless and above reproach, after being baptized, let them be ordained by the bishop of the Catholic Church. . . .

Can. 13. Concerning these, who approach death, even now the ancient **57** and regular law will be kept; so that, if anyone is departing from the body, he be not deprived of the last and necessary viaticum. But if after being despaired of, and receiving communion, and being made a sharer of the oblation, he again regains his health, let him be among those who receive only the communion of prayer. Generally, however, to everyone without exception placed at death and requesting that the grace of communion be given him, the bishop probably ought to give from the oblation.

Synodal letter to the Egyptians concerning the error of Arius   **57***
and the ordinations made by Melitius see Kch n 410 f.

St. Marcus 336

ST. JULIUS I 337–352
The Primacy of the Roman Pontiff [1]

[From the epistle " 'Ανέγνων τὰ γράμματα" to the Antiochenes, in the year 341]

For if, indeed as you assert, some sin has risen among them, a judicial **57a** investigation ought to have been made according to the ecclesiastical canon, and not in this manner. Everyone should have written to us, in order that thus what was just might be decided by all; for the bishops were the ones who suffered, and it was not the ordinary churches that were harassed, but which the apostles themselves governed in person. Yet why has nothing been written to us, especially regarding the Alexandrian church? Or do you not know that it is the custom to write to us first, and that here what is just is decided? Certainly if any suspicion of this nature did fall upon the bishop of that city, the fact should have been written to this church.

COUNCIL OF SERDICA 343–344
The Primacy of the Roman Pontiff [2]

[Authentic text] [Can. 3] (Isid.   [Greek version] 3. Hosius the **57b**
4). Caius the bishop said: That also,   bishop said: It is necessary to de-

---

[1] Cst 385 B; ML 8, 906 A.
[2] C. H. Turner, *Eccl. occid. monumenta iuris antiquissima.* T. I, fasc. 2, para. 3,

that a bishop may not cross from one province into another province, in which there are bishops, unless perchance on the invitation of his brothers, lest we seem to have shut the door of charity.—That too should be provided; if perchance in any province some bishop has a dispute with a brother bishop, let no one of these summon the bishops from another province.—But if any bishop has been judged in some case, and he thinks he has a good case, so that a new trial may be given, if it seems good to you, let us honor the memory of the most holy Apostle, PETER: either let those who have examined the case or the bishops who reside in the next province write to the Roman bishop; and if he should judge that the judicial investigation ought to be repeated, let it be repeated, and let him appoint judges. But if he should determine that the case is such, that what has been finished should not be reopened, his decree shall be confirmed. Is this agreeable to all? The synod replied: It is agreeable.

clare this in order that no bishop may keep crossing from his own province into a different province in which there are bishops, unless perchance he should be invited by his brothers, so that we may not seem to close the doors of charity. And this too, one must provide for, that, if in any province one of the bishops should have trouble with his brother and fellow-bishop, neither of these two call to his aid as judges the bishops of another province. Yet on the other hand, if one of the bishops should think that he is being condemned in some trouble, and thinks that he has not an unsound, but a good case, in order that a new trial may be held, if it seems good to your charity, let us honor the memory of Peter the apostle, and let these judges write to Julius the bishop of Rome so that through the bishops who border on the province, if it should be necessary, the trial be reopened, and he himself should furnish the judges. But if it cannot be proven that this matter is of such a nature as to need a new trial, let not the decisions made once be set aside, but let them be confirmed.

(Isid. 5). Gaudentius the bishop said: To this very holy opinion which you have offered, if it is agreeable, we ought to add: when any bishop has been deposed by the

4. Gaudentius the bishop said: If it is decided, we ought to add to this decision which you have offered full of pure charity: that, if a bishop has been deposed by the judgment

---

492 ff. Concerning the name "Serdica" (in place of "Sardica") *ibid.*, p. 533. Hrd I 637 E f. Cf. Hfl I 560 ff.; Kch n. 500 ff. C. H. Turner (*The Journal of Theological Studies* 3 [1902] 370–397) has vindicated the genuineness of the canons of Serdica impugned by J. Friedrich (1901).

judgment of those bishops who abide in the neighboring places, and when he has proclaimed that he must plead his case in the city of Rome, another bishop may not be ordained for his place in the same office after the appeal of him who seems to have been deposed, unless his case has been decided by the judgment of the bishop of Rome.

[Can. 3b] (Isid. 6.) Osius the bishop said: However it has been agreed, that, if a bishop has been accused, and the assembled bishops of the same province have judged and deprived him of his office, and he appears to have appealed, and has taken refuge with the most blessed bishop of the Roman church and has desired to be heard, and he has thought it just that an examination be made anew, let him deign to write to these bishops who are in the adjoining and neighboring province so that they themselves may diligently make all inquiries and decide according to their pledge of truth. But if anyone asks that his case be heard again and by his plea moves the Roman bishop to send a presbyter from his own side, what he [the presbyter] wishes or what he determines will be in the power of the bishop; and if he decrees those ought to be sent who in person may judge with the bishops and who have the authority [of him] by whom they have been appointed, it [this decree] will be within his decision. But if he believes that the bishops suffice to put an end to the affair, he will do that which he de-

of these bishops who are in the neighborhood, and he alleges that the business of defense will again fall upon himself, another may not be ordained to his office unless previously the bishop of Rome has come to a decision concerning him and has published his judgment.

5. Hosius the bishop said: It has **57d** been agreed that, if a bishop has been accused, and the assembled bishops of the same region have deposed him from his rank, and in as much as he has appealed and taken refuge with the most blessed bishop of the Roman church, and he has wished to hear him, if he thinks it is just to renew the examination of his difficulty, let him deign to write to these bishops who live in the neighboring province so that they themselves may examine carefully and with exactness each matter and declare their vote on the problem according to their pledge of truth. But if anyone should ask that his case be heard again, and by his prayer seems to move the bishop of Rome to dispatch elders from his side; what he decides is good is in the power of the bishop himself, and if he determines that it is necessary to send those who will judge with the bishops and who have the absolute authority of him by whom they were sent, this also must be granted. But if he should consider it sufficient by reason of the examination of the difficulty and the sentence of

cides in accordance with his own very wise deliberation.

the bishop, he will do what he thinks is good according to his very wise deliberation. The bishops gave an answer. What was said was agreeable.

[From the epistle "Quod semper" by which the synod transmitted its acts to St. Julius] [1]

57e   For this will seem to be best and most fitting indeed, if the priests from each and every province refer to the head, that is, to the chair of PETER the apostle.

ST. LIBERIUS 352–366

Concerning the Baptism of Heretics, see St. SIRICIUS [n. 88]

ST. DAMASUS I 366–384

COUNCIL OF ROME, 382 [2]

The Trinity and the Incarnation [3]

[Tome of DAMASUS [4]]

58   [After this Council, which was assembled in the city of Rome by the Catholic bishops,[5] they made additions concerning the Holy Spirit]. And because afterwards this error became so fixed that they even dared to say with sacrilegious words that the Holy Spirit was made by the Son:

59   (1) We anathematize those who proclaim quite freely that he is not of one power and substance with the Father and the Son.

60   (2) We anathematize those also who follow the error of Sabellius, saying that the same one is Father as well as Son.

---

[1] CSEL 65, 127; Cst 395 ff.; Msi III 40 ff.; Hrd I 653 f. Concerning the genuineness of this passage, cf. "Scholastik" I (1926), 260 (A. Feder).

[2] P. Galtier, *Rech. de science rel.* 26 (1936) 385 ff., shows that the "Tomus Damasi" is due to this council.

[3] C. H. Turner, *Eccl. occid. monumenta iuris antiquissima.* T. I, fasc. II, pars 1 (1913) 284 ff. "Tomus Damasi contains (after the Nicene Creed) the following canons: Cst 511 A ff. (cf. 518); coll. H. 272 ff.; If 235 c. Add.; ML 13, 358 B f. and 56, 686 B ff.; Msi III 481 D ff. (cf. 486 C. ff.); Hrd. I 802 B f.

[4] The canons of this tome have been taken, as it seems, from the Council of Constantine I, and are praised as law by Celestine I [ML 53, 290 A] and Vigilius [ML 69, 176 B; Jf 937].

[5] Namely, the bishops gathered at Rome [cf. ML 56, 687 note a].

(3) We anathematize Arius and Eunomius who with equal impiety, **61**
though in different terms, declare that the Son and Holy Spirit are
creatures.

(4) We anathematize the Macedonians who, springing from the root **62**
of Arius, have changed not the perfidy, but the name.

(5) We anathematize Photinus who, renewing the heresy of Ebion, **63**
confesses that the Lord Jesus Christ was of Mary only.

(6) We anathematize those who say (there are) two Sons, one eternal, **64**
and the other after the assumption of flesh from the Virgin.

(7) We anathematize those who say that instead of the rational and in- **65**
tellectual soul of man, the Word of God dwelt in a human body, although the Son Himself and Word of God was not in His own body instead of a rational and intellectual soul, but assumed our soul without sin
(that is the rational and intellectual soul) and saved it.

(8) We anathematize those who contend that the Word, the Son of **66**
God, has extension or collection (of members) and is separate from the
Father, is unsubstantial, and will have an end.

(9) Those also who have moved from churches to churches, we hold as **67**
not belonging to our communion until they return to those cities in which
they were first established. But if one is ordained in the place of one who
is living, while another is moving, let him who has left his own city be
without the dignity of the priestly office until his successor rests in the
Lord.

(10) If anyone does not say that the Father does always exist, the Son **68**
does always exist, and the Holy Spirit does always exist, he is a heretic.

(11) If anyone does not say that the Son was begotten of the Father, **69**
that is, of the divine substance of Him Himself, he is a heretic.

(12) If anyone does not say that the Son of God is true God just as [His] **70**
Father is true God [and] He is all-powerful and omniscient and equal to
the Father, he is a heretic.

(13) If anyone says that because He was established in the flesh when **71**
He was on earth, He was not in heaven with the Father, he is a heretic.

(14) If anyone says, that in the passion of the cross God felt pain, and **72**
not the body with the soul which the Son of God Christ had assumed—the
form of a servant, which He had taken upon himself [cf. Phil. 2:7], as says
the Scripture—, he does not think rightly.

(15) If anyone does not say that He sits at the right hand of the Father, **73**
in the flesh, in which He will come to judge the living and the dead, he is
a heretic.

(16) If anyone does not say that the Holy Spirit, just as the Son, is truly **74**
and properly of the Father, of divine substance, and is not true God, he is
a heretic.

(17) If anyone does not say that the Holy Spirit can do all things and **75**

knows all things and is everywhere just as the Son and the Father, he is a heretic.

76   (18) If anyone says that the Holy Spirit is a creature, or was made by the Son, he is a heretic.

77   (19) If anyone does not say that the Father made all things through the Son and His Holy Spirit, that is, the visible and the invisible; he is a heretic.

78   (20) If anyone does not say that there is one divinity of Father, and Son, and Holy Spirit, one sovereignty, one majesty, one power, one glory, one dominion, one kingdom, and one will and truth, he is a heretic.

79   (21) If anyone does not say there are three true persons of Father, and of Son, and of Holy Spirit, equal, immortal, containing all things visible and invisible, ruling all things, judging all things, vivifying all things, creating all things, saving all things, he is a heretic.

80   (22) If anyone does not say that the Holy Spirit ought to be adored by every creature just as the Son and Father, he is a heretic.

81   (23) If anyone thinks well of the Father and the Son, but does not rightly esteem the Holy Spirit, he is a heretic, because all heretics who think erroneously about the Son [of God] and the [Holy] Spirit are found in the perfidy of the Jews and the pagans.

82   (24) But if anyone divides,[1] saying that God [Christ's] Father, and God His Son, and God the Holy Spirit are gods, and does not thus say God on account of the one divinity and power which we believe and know (to be) the Father's, and the Son's, and the Holy Spirit's, but taking away the Son or the Holy Spirit, thus believes that the Father alone is called God, or in this manner believes God one, he is a heretic in every respect, nay rather a Jew, because the name of gods was attached and given both to angels and to all the saints from God, but of the Father, and of the Son, and of the Holy Spirit because of their one and equal divinity, not the name of gods, but of God is declared and revealed to us, in order that we may believe, because we are baptized only in the Father, and the Son, and the Holy Spirit and not in the names of archangels or angels, as heretics, or Jews, or even demented pagans.

This then is the salvation of Christians, that believing in the Trinity, that is, in the Father, and in the Son, and in the Holy Spirit, [and] baptized in this, we believe without doubt that there is only one true divinity and power, majesty and substance of the same.

---

[1] "Partiatur" (not "putat") should be read according to P. Galtier [l.c. 566 ff.].

The Holy Spirit [1]

["Decree of DAMASUS" from the acts of the Roman Synod,
in the year 382]

It has been said: We must first treat of the sevenfold Spirit, which re- 83
poses in Christ, the Spirit of wisdom: *Christ, the power of God and the
wisdom of God* [I Cor. 1:24]. The Spirit of understanding: *I will give
thee understanding, and I will instruct thee in this way, in which thou
shalt go* [Ps. 31:8]. The Spirit of counsel: *And his name shall be called
angel of great counsel* [Is. 9:6: LXX]. The Spirit of power (as above):
The power of God and the wisdom of God [I Cor. 1:24]. The Spirit of
knowledge: *on account of the excellence of the knowledge of Christ Jesus
the apostle* [Eph. 3:19]. The Spirit of truth: *I am the way and the life and
the truth* [John 14:6]. The Spirit of fear [of God]: *The fear of the Lord is
the beginning of wisdom* [Ps. 110:10] . . . [*there follows an explanation
of the various names of Christ:* Lord, Word, Flesh, Shepherd, etc.] . . .
For the Holy Spirit is not only the Spirit of the Father or not only the Spirit
of the Son, but the Spirit of the Father and of the Son. For it is written:
If anyone love the world, the Spirit of the Father is not in him [I John 2:15;
Rom. 8:9]. Likewise it is written: *Now if any man have not the Spirit of
Christ, he is none of his* [Rom. 8:9]. When the Father and the Son are
mentioned in this way, the Holy Spirit is understood, of whom the Son
himself says in the Gospel, that the Holy Spirit *proceedeth from the Father*
[John 15:26], and *he shall receive of mine and shall announce it to you*
[John 16:14.]

The Canon of Sacred Scripture [2]

[From the same decree and the acts of the same Roman Synod]

Likewise it has been said: Now indeed we must treat of the divine 84
Scriptures, what the universal Catholic Church accepts and what she
ought to shun.

---

[1] C. H. Turner, Latin lists of the canonical books: *The Journal of Theological
Studies* 1 (1900) 556 ff. ML 19, 787 B ff.: Jf 251 c. Add. 700; cf. ML 59, 157 A ff.;
Hrd I 775 D ff.: Z II 259 ff.—This and what follows concerning the canon of the
Scripture are the first part of a very celebrated document "De libris recipiendis
vel non recipiendis," which is called "Decretum GELASII" [see n. 162 ff.]. Andr.
Thiel. [Epp. Rom. PP. 44 ff.] especially contends that this, conceived and edited by
DAMASUS, was in truth repeated by GELASIUS; and Turner [1 c. 554] holds
(this) as certain, Ed. Schwartz (*Zeitschr. f. neutest. Wissenschaft* 29 [1930] 161 ff.)
as probable, who says that the words referred to in n. 83 "Spiritus enim Sanctus . . .
Nominato itaque Patre et Filio intelligitur Spiritus" were interpolated from St. Augustine's tract, on John 9, n. 7 in opposition to Dobschüts, *Das Decretum Gelasianum*
(Leipzig: 1912), p. 4 245 f.

[2] Turner 1. c.; ML 19 700 B ff. (cf. 59, 157 A ff.); Msi VIII 145 C ff.

The order of the Old Testament begins here: Genesis one book, Exodus one book, Leviticus one book, Numbers one book, Deuteronomy one book, Josue Nave one book, Judges one book, Ruth one book, Kings four books, Paralipomenon two books, Psalms one book, Solomon three books, Proverbs one book, Ecclesiastes one book, Canticle of Canticles one book, likewise Wisdom one book, Ecclesiasticus one book.

Likewise the order of the Prophets. Isaias one book, Jeremias one book, with Ginoth, that is, with his lamentations, Ezechiel one book, Daniel one book, Osee one book, Micheas one book, Joel one book, Abdias one book, Jonas one book, Nahum one book, Habacuc one book, Sophonias one book, Aggeus one book, Zacharias one book, Malachias one book.

Likewise the order of the histories. Job one book, Tobias one book, Esdras two books, Esther one book, Judith one book, Machabees two books.

Likewise the order of the writings of the New and eternal Testament, which the holy and Catholic Church supports. Of the Gospels, according to Matthew one book, according to Mark one book, according to Luke one book, according to John one book.

The Epistles of Paul [the apostle] in number fourteen. To the Romans one, to the Corinthians two, to the Ephesians one, to the Thessalonians two, to the Galatians one, to the Philippians one, to the Colossians one, to Timothy two, to Titus one, to Philemon one, to the Hebrews one.

Likewise the Apocalypse of John, one book. And the Acts of the Apostles one book.

Likewise the canonical epistles in number seven. Of Peter the Apostle two epistles, of James the Apostle one epistle, of John the Apostle one epistle, of another John, the presbyter, two epistles, of Jude the Zealot, the Apostle one epistle, see n. 162 ff.[1]

The canon of the New Testament ends here.

COUNCIL OF CONSTANTINOPLE I 381

Ecumenical II (against the Macedonians, etc.)

Condemnation of the Heretics [2]

85   The faith of the three hundred and eighteen Fathers who assembled at Nicea in Bithynia is not

Can. 1. [Version of Dionysius Exig.] The faith of three hundred and eighteen Fathers, who con-

---

[1] Certain ones even attribute to DAMASUS that part of the "Decree of Gelasius" which treats of the Primacy and the Patriarchal Sees [see n. 163]: cf. Zahn et Thiel 11 cc. and C. H. Turner, *Eccl. occid. monumenta iuris antiquisissima* T. I, fasc. 1, pars 2, p. 155 ff. and fasc. 2, pars 1, p. xiv.

[2] Msi III gr. 557 E., lat. 566 D. coll. Hfl II 14; Hrd I 809 A.

to be disregarded; but it remains authoritative, and all heresy is to be anathematized: and especially that of the Eunomians or of the Anomians, and that of the Arians, or that of the Eudoxians, and that of the Macedonians, that is to say of those opposing the Spirit, and that of the Sabellians, of the Marcellians and that of the Photinians and that of the Apollinarians.

vened at Nicea in Bithynia, ought not to be violated; but remains firm and stable. Every heresy ought to be anathematized, and especially those of the Eunomians or Anomians, and of the Arians or Eudoxians, and of the Macedonians or those who oppose the Holy Spirit, and of the Sabellians, and of the Marcellians, and of the Photinians, and of the Apollinarians.

The "Nicene-Constantinopolitan" [1] Creed

We believe in one God, Father omnipotent, maker of heaven and earth, and of all things visible and invisible. And in one Lord Jesus Christ, the only begotten Son of God, born of the Father before all ages, light of light, true God of true God, begotten not made, consubstantial with the Father, by whom all things were made, who for us men and for our salvation came down and was made flesh by the Holy Spirit and of the Virgin Mary, and became man, and was crucified for us by Pontius Pilate, suffered, and was buried and arose again the third day, according to the Scripture, and ascended into heaven, and sits at the right hand of the Father, and is coming again with glory to judge the living and the dead;

[Version of Dionysius Exiguus] 86
We believe [I believe] in one God the Father almighty, maker of heaven and earth, and of all things visible and invisible. And in one Lord Jesus Christ, the Son of God, born of the Father [the only begotten Son of God. And born of the Father] before all ages. [God of God, light of light] true God of true God. Born [Begotten], not made, consubstantial with the Father, by whom all things were made. Who for us men and our salvation [and for our salvation] came down from heaven. And was incarnate by the Holy Spirit of the Virgin Mary, and was made human [was made man]. And he was crucified [He was crucified also] for us under Pontius Pilate, [suffered]—and was buried. And on the third day he rose again,

---

[1] ACOec II 1 P. 2, 80; Msi III 565 A; H 165 f.; Missale Romanum; Hrd I 813 B; ML 48, 772 A; Bar(Th)ad 381 n. 29 (5, 461b). Cf. *Rev. d'hist. eccl.* 32 (1936) 809 ff. (J. Lebon). See the text slightly changed of Theodorus Mops. in A. Rücker, *Ritus baptismi et Missae* . . . , Monasterii 1933, 42 f. This creed, after the Synods of EPHEUS and CHALCEDON, passed into the liturgical use of the Oriental Church, and this same thing took place in the West about the end of the eighth century through St. Paulinus of Aquileia against the Adoptians. Those words which are enclosed in brackets show the liturgical text almost as it was prepared by St. Paulinus, *Rech. de théol. anc. et méd.* 1 [1929] 7 ff. (B. Capelle).

[according to the Scriptures. And] ascended into heaven, sits at the right hand of the Father, [and] will come again with glory to judge the living and the dead;

of whose kingdom there shall be no end. And in the Holy Spirit, the Lord, the giver of life, who proceeds from the Father, who together with the Father and Son is worshipped and glorified, who spoke through the prophets. In one holy, Catholic, and Apostolic Church. We confess one baptism for the remission of sins. We look for the resurrection of the dead, and the life of eternity to come. Amen.	of whose kingdom there shall not be an end. And in the Holy Spirit, the Lord and giver of life, proceeding from the Father, [who proceeds from the Father and the Son,[1] who] to be adored with the Father and the Son [is adored together with] and to be glorified together with (them) [and is glorified together with], who spoke through the holy Prophets [by the Prophets]. And in one holy Catholic and apostolic Church. We confess [I confess] one baptism for the remission of sins. We expect [And I expect] the resurrection of the dead, and the life of a future age [to come]. Amen.

ST. SIRICIUS 384–398

The Primacy of the Roman Pontiff [2]

[From the epistle (1) "Directa ad decessorem" to Himerius, Bishop of Terracina, Feb. 10, 385]

87 . . . To your inquiry we do not deny a legal reply, because we, upon whom greater zeal for the Christian religion is incumbent than upon

---

[1] The addition "and the Son" was first made in Spain. From here this custom passed over into Gaul, then into Germany, as is clear from the Gallican liturgy of Moneius at the beginning of the fifth century, from the Synod of the Forum Julii 791, of Frankfurt 794, of Aquisgranum (Aachen), 809, which asked Leo III that it be reaccepted by the Roman Church. This, however, Leo refused, not because he rejected the dogma, but because he feared to add anything to the traditional form [cf. n. 125, 148, 159]. Afterwards, indeed, when St. Henry obtained from Benedict VIII his request that the creed be sung among the ceremonies of the Masses, the addition was accepted. This finally was admitted simultaneously by the Latins and the Greeks in the ecumenical Synods of Lyons II [n. 460] and of Florence [n. 691].

[2] Cst 624; Jf 255 c. Add.; ML 13, 1132 C; Msi III 655 D; Hrd I 847 C.

the whole body, out of consideration for our office do not have the liberty to dissimulate, nor to remain silent. We carry the weight of all who are burdened; nay rather the blessed apostle PETER bears these in us, who, as we trust, protects us in all matters of his administration, and guards his heirs.

The Baptism of Heretics [1]

[From the same letter to Himerius]

(1, 1) And so on the first page of your letter you have indicated that **88** very many baptized by the impious Arians are hastening to the Catholic faith and that certain of our brothers wish to baptize these same ones again. This is not allowed since the Apostle forbids it to be done [cf. Eph. 4:5; Heb. 6:4 ff. (?)] and the canons oppose it, and after the cessation of the Council of Ariminum general decrees [2] sent to the provinces by my predecessor LIBERIUS of venerable memory prohibit it. These together with the Novatians and other heretics we join to the company of the Catholics through the sole invocation of the sevenfold Spirit by the imposition of a bishop's hands, just as it was determined in the Synod, which, too, the whole East and West observe. It is proper that you also do not deviate from this course henceforth, if you do not wish to be separated from our company by synodal decision.[3]

Christian Marriage [4]

[From the same epistle to Himerius]

(4, 5) But you have inquired concerning the marriage veil, whether one **88a** can receive in matrimony a girl betrothed to another. Let this not be done. We prohibit it in every way, because, if that blessing which the priest gives to the bride is violated by any transgression, it is like a kind of sacrilege among the faithful.

---

[1] Cst 624 C f.

[2] These decrees do not seem to be extant now.

[3] After this that very famous controversy concerning rebaptism finally reached an end [see n. 46 f. 53, 55]. The Council of Carthage I under Gratus in the year 348 or 349, can. 1 [Msi III 145 B] forbade rebaptism; that of Laodicea between 341 and 381, can. 7 and 8, decided that the Cataphrygians ought to be rebaptized, but the Novatians and the Quartodecimans ought only to be anointed with chrism (see Kch. n. 521 f.); that of Arles II of the year 443 (452 ?) can. 16 gave orders to baptize the Photinians or the Paulianists (see Kch. n. 878). There even exists concerning this matter the canon (7) [Msi III 563 B] of the Synod of CONSTANTINOPLE I of the year 381, which however seems to have arisen in the Council of Constantinople of the year 382.

[4] Cst 628 C, ML 13, 1136 f.; Msi III 657 A; Hrd I 848 B.

88* (5, 6) *The relapses into passions to be forgiven finally before death,* see Kch. n. 657.

The Celibacy of the Clergy [1]

[From the same epistle to Himerius]

89 (7, 8 ff.) Let us come now to the most sacred orders of the clergy, which we find so abused and so disorderly throughout your provinces to the injury of venerable religion, that we ought to say in the words of Jeremias: *Who will water to my head, or a fountain of tears to my eyes? and I will weep for this people day and night* (Jer. 9:1). . . . For we have learned that very many priests and levites of Christ, after long periods of their consecration, have begotten offspring from their wives as well as by shameful intercourse, and that they defend their crime by this excuse, that in the Old Testament it is read that the faculty of procreating was given to the priests and the ministers.

Whoever that follower of sensual desires is let him tell me now: . . . Why does [the Lord] forewarn those to whom the holies of holies were to be entrusted saying: Be ye holy, because I your Lord God am holy [Lev. 20:7; I Pet. 1:16]? Why also were the priests ordered to dwell in the temple at a distance from their homes in the year of their turn? Evidently for this reason that they might not be able to practise carnal intercourse with their wives, so that shining with purity of conscience they might offer an acceptable gift to God. . . .

Therefore also the Lord Jesus, when He had enlightened us by His coming, testifies in the Gospel, that *he came to fulfill the Law, not to destroy it* [Matt. 5:17]. And so He has wished the beauty of the Church, whose spouse He is, to radiate with the splendor of chastity, so that on the day of judgment, when He will have come again, He may be able to find her *without spot or wrinkle* [Eph. 5:27] as He instituted her through His Apostle. All priests and levites are bound by the indissoluble law of these sanctions, so that from the day of our ordination, we give up both our hearts and our bodies to continence and chastity, provided only that through all things we may please our God in these sacrifices which we daily offer. *"But those who are in the flesh,"* as the vessel of election says, *"cannot please God"* [Rom. 8:8].

But those, who contend with an excuse for the forbidden privilege, so as to assert that this has been granted to them by the Old Law, should know that by the authority of the Apostolic See they have been cast out of every ecclesiastical office, which they have used unworthily, nor can they

---

[1] Cst 629 D ff. It must be noted that in this document celibacy was not instituted, but is supposed to have existed for a long time.

ever touch the sacred mysteries, of which they themselves have deprived themselves, so long as they give heed to impure desires. And because existing examples warn us to be on our guard for the future should any bishop, priest, or deacon be found such, which henceforth we do not want, let him now understand that every approach to indulgence is barred through us, because it is necessary that the wounds which are not susceptible to the healing of warm lotions be cut out with a knife.

The Ordinations of Monks [1]

[From the same epistle to Himerius]

(13) We both desire and will that monks also, whom however the austerity of their manners and the holy disposition of their lives and faith commend, be added to the offices of the clergy . . . [cf. n. 1580].   **90**

The Virginity of the Blessed Virgin Mary [2]

[From epistle (9) "Accepi litteras vestras" to Anysius,
Bishop of Thessalonica, 392]

(3) Surely, we cannot deny that regarding the sons of Mary the state-   **91** ment is justly censured, and your holiness has rightly abhorred it, that from the same virginal womb, from which according to the flesh Christ was born, another offspring was brought forth. For neither would the Lord Jesus have chosen to be born of a virgin, if he had judged she would be so incontinent, that with the seed of human copulation she would pollute that generative chamber of the Lord's body, that palace of the eternal King. For he who imputes this, imputes nothing other than the falsehood of the Jews, who say that he could not have been born of a virgin. For, if they accept this authority from the priests, that Mary seems to have brought forth many children, they strive to sweep away the truth of faith with greater zeal.

COUNCIL OF CARTHAGE (III) 397

The Canon of the Sacred Scripture [3]

Can. 36 (or otherwise 47). [It has been decided] that nothing except   **92** the Canonical Scriptures should be read in the church under the name of the Divine Scriptures. But the Canonical Scriptures are: Genesis, Exo-

---

[1] Cst 635.

[2] Cst 681 B f.: Jf 261; ML 13, 1177 B; Msi III 675 A; Hrd I 859 C f.—There is a discussion of the error of Bonosius.

[3] ML 56, 428 A f. (cf. 871); Msi III 924 A; Hrd I 968 A; c. Hfl II 68; Z II 251; EB n. 11 ff.—Cf. Z II 251 f.

dus, Leviticus, Numbers, Deuteronomy, Josue, Judges, Ruth, four books
of Kings, Paralipomenon two books, Job, the Psalter of David, five books
of Solomon, twelve books of the Prophets, Isaias, Jeremias, Daniel,
Ezechiel, Tobias, Judith, Esther, two books of Esdras, two books of the
Machabees. Moreover, of the New Testament: Four books of the Gospels,
the Acts of the Apostles one book, thirteen epistles of Paul the Apostle, one
of the same to the Hebrews, two of Peter, three [1] of John, one of James,
one of Jude, the Apocalypse of John. Thus [it has been decided] that the
Church beyond the sea may be consulted regarding the confirmation of
that canon; also that it be permitted to read the sufferings of the martyrs,
when their anniversary days are celebrated.

ST. ANASTASIUS I 398–401

The Orthodoxy of the Pope LIBERIUS [2]

[From the epistle "Dat mihi plurimum" to Venerius,
Bishop of Milan, about the year 400]

93   That which is done for the love of Christ gives me very much joy;
Italy, as victor with that zeal and aroused ardor for the godhead, retained
that faith whole which was handed down from the Apostles and placed in
the whole world by our ancestors. For at this time when Constantius of
holy memory held the world as victor, the heretical African faction was
not able by any deception to introduce its baseness because, as we believe,
our God provided that that holy and untarnished faith be not contaminated
through any vicious blasphemy of slanderous men—that faith which had
been discussed and defended at the meeting of the synod in Nicea by the
holy men and bishops now placed in the resting-place of the saints.

For this faith those who were then esteemed as holy bishops gladly endured exile, that is Dionysius, thus a servant of God, prepared by divine
instruction, or those following his example of holy recollection, LIBERIUS
bishop of the Roman Church, Eusebius also of Vercelli, Hilary of the
Gauls, to say nothing of many, on whose decision the choice could rest to
be fastened to the cross rather than blaspheme God Christ, which the Arian
heresy compelled, or call the Son of God, God Christ, a creature of the
Lord. [3]

93*   *Council of Toledo the year 400, The Minister of Unction
and Anointing* (can. 20) *see Kch n. 712.*

---

[1] Cf. Decr. DAMASI [n. 84].

[2] *Revue d'hist. et litt. relig.* (Paris) 4 (1899) 5–8 (J. van den Gheyn). Pitra,
Analecta novissima Spicilegii Solesmensis (1885) I 463 f. (cf. 20 ff.); Jf 281 c. Add.
(cf. Cst p. XIII).

[3] There follows the condemnation of the errors of Origen.

ST. INNOCENT I 401–417 [1]

The Baptism of Heretics [2]

[From epistle (2) "Etsi tibi" to Vitricius, Bishop of
Rouen, Feb. 15, 404]

(8) That those who come from the Novatians or the Montanists should **94**
be received by the imposition of the hand only, because although they
were baptized by heretics, nevertheless they were baptized in the name
of Christ.

Reconciliation in the Moment of Death [3]

[From the epistle "Consulenti tibi" to Exuperius, Bishop
of Toulouse, Feb. 20, 405]

(2) . . . It has been asked, what must be observed with regard to **95**
those who after baptism have surrendered on every occasion to the pleasures of incontinence, and at the very end of their lives ask for penance
and at the same time the reconciliation of communion. Concerning them
the former rule was harder, the latter more favorable, because mercy
intervened. For the previous custom held that penance should be granted,
but that communion should be denied. For since in those times there were
frequent persecutions, so that the ease with which communion was
granted might not recall men become careless of reconciliation from
their lapse, communion was justly denied, penance allowed, lest the
whole be entirely refused; and the system of the time made remission more
difficult. But after our Lord restored peace to his churches, when terror
had now been removed, it was decided that communion be given to the
departing, and on account of the mercy of God as a viaticum to those
about to set forth, and that we may not seem to follow the harshness and
the rigor of the Novatian heretic who refused mercy. Therefore with
penance a last communion will be given, so that such men in their ex-
tremities may be freed from eternal ruin with the permission of our
Savior [see n. 1538].

Reconciliation outside of the danger of death; see Kch. n. 727.   **95***

---

[1] The authorities of Innocent I and Zosimus on original sin and grace are in the
letter of Celestine [n. 130 ff.], of Zosimus also n. 1090.

[2] Cst 752 A; Jf 286 c. Add.; ML 20, 475 B; Msi III 1034 D.

[3] Cst 792 B f.; Jf 293 c. Add.; ML 20, 498 B f.; Msi III 1039 C f.

The Canon of the Holy Scripture and the Apocryphal Books [1]

[From the same epistle to Exuperius]

96   (7) A brief addition shows what books really are received in the canon. These are the desiderata of which you wished to be informed verbally: of Moses five books, that is, of Genesis, of Exodus, of Leviticus, of Numbers, of Deuteronomy, and Josue, of Judges one book, of Kings four books, and also Ruth, of the Prophets sixteen books, of Solomon five books, the Psalms. Likewise of the histories, Job one book, of Tobias one book, Esther one, Judith one, of the Machabees two, of Esdras two, Paralipomenon two books. Likewise of the New Testament: of the Gospels four books, of Paul the Apostle fourteen epistles, of John three [cf. n. 84, 92] epistles of Peter two, an epistle of Jude, an epistle of James, the Acts of the Apostles, the Apocalypse of John.

Others, however, which were written by a certain Leucius under the name of Matthias or of James the Less, or under the name of Peter and John (or which were written by Nexocharis and Leonidas the philosophers under the name of Andrew), or under the name of Thomas, and if there are any others, you know that they ought not only to be repudiated, but also condemned.

The Baptism of the Paulianists [2]

[From the epistle (17) "Magna me gratulatio" to Rufus
and other bishops of Macedonia, Dec. 13, 414]

97   *From the canon of Nicea* [n. 56] *indeed the Paulianists coming to the Church ought to be baptized, but not the Novatians* [see n. 55]: (5) . . . What therefore is distinct in the two heresies themselves, clear reason declares, because the Paulianists do not at all baptize in the name of the Father, and of the Son, and of the Holy Spirit, and the Novatians do baptize in the same tremendous and venerable names, and among them the question has not ever been raised concerning the unity of the divine power, that is of the Father, and of the Son, and of the Holy Spirit.

The Minister of Confirmation [3]

[From the epistle (25) "Si instituta ecclesiastica" to
Decentius the Bishop of Gubbio, March 19, 416]

98   (3) But in regard to the signing of little children, it is evident that it may not be done by any other than a bishop. For the presbyters, although

---

[1] Cst 795 B f.; ML 20, 501 A f.; Msi III 1040 E f.; EB n. 16.
[2] Cst 836 BC; Jf 303; ML 20, 533 B; Msi III 1061 E.
[3] Cst 858 A f.; Jf 311 c. Add.; ML 20, 554 B f.; Msi III 1029 B.

they are second priests, nevertheless do not possess the crown of the pontificate. That this power of a bishop, however, is due to the bishops alone, so that they either sign or give the Paraclete the Spirit, not only ecclesiastical custom indicates, but also that reading in the Acts of the Apostles which declares that Peter and John were directed to give the Holy Spirit to those already baptized [cf. Acts 8:14–17]. For to presbyters it is permitted to anoint the baptized with chrism whenever they baptize, whether without a bishop or in the presence of a bishop, but (with chrism) that has been consecrated by a bishop; nevertheless (it is) not (allowed) to sign the forehead with the same oil; that is due to the bishops alone when they bestow the Spirit, the Paraclete. Indeed, I cannot say the words lest I seem to go further than to reply to the inquiry.

The Minister of Extreme Unction [1]

[From the same letter to Decentius]

(8) Truly since your love has wished to take counsel regarding this **99** just as concerning other (matters), my son Celestine, the deacon, has also added in his letter that what was written in the epistle of the blessed Apostle James has been proposed by your love: *If anyone among you is sick, let him call the priests, and let them pray over him, anointing him with oil in the name of the Lord: and the prayer of faith shall save the sufferer, and the Lord shall raise him up, and if he has committed sin, he shall pardon him* [Jas. 5:14 f.]. There is no doubt that this anointing ought to be interpreted or understood of the sick faithful, who can be anointed with the holy oil of chrism, which prepared by a bishop, is permitted not only to priests, but also to all as Christians for anointing in their own necessity or in the necessity of their (people). Moreover, we see that addition to be superfluous; that what is undoubtedly permitted the presbyters is questioned regarding bishops. For, on this account it was said to priests, because the bishops being hindered by other business cannot go to all the sick. But if a bishop, to whom it belongs to prepare the chrism, is able (to do it) or thinks someone is worthy to be visited by him, he can both bless and anoint with the chrism without delay. For, that cannot be administered to penitents, because it is a kind of sacrament. For, how is it supposed that one species (of sacrament) can be granted to those to whom the rest of the sacraments are denied?

---

[1] Cst 862 B ff.; ML 20, 559 B f.; Msi III 1030 E.

The Primacy and the Infallibility of the Roman Pontiff [1]

[From the epistle (29) "In requirendis" to the African
bishops, Jan. 27, 417]

100   (1) In seeking the things of God . . . preserving the examples of ancient tradition . . . you have strengthened the vigor of your religion . . . with true reason, for you have confirmed that reference must be made to our judgment, realizing what is due the Apostolic See, since all of us placed in this position desire to follow the Apostle, from whom the episcopate itself and all the authority of this name have emerged. Following him we know how to condemn evils just as (well as how) to approve praiseworthy things. Take this as an example, guarding with your sacerdotal office the practices of the fathers you resolve that (they) must not be trampled upon, because they made their decisions not by human, but by divine judgment, so that they thought that nothing whatever, although it concerned separated and remote provinces, should be concluded, unless it first came to the attention of this See, so that what was a just proclamation might be confirmed by the total authority of this See, and from this source (just as all waters proceed from their natal fountain and through diverse regions of the whole world remain pure liquids of an uncorrupted source), the other churches might assume what [they ought] to teach, whom they ought to wash, those whom the water worthy of clean bodies would shun as though defiled with filth incapable of being cleansed.

100*   *For another rescript of Innocent I concerning the same matter, see Kch n. 720–726.*

ST. ZOSIMUS 417-418

COUNCIL OF MILEUM II 416, APPROVED BY INNOCENT AND COUNCIL OF CARTHAGE (XVI) 418, APPROVED BY ZOSIMUS

(against the Pelagians) [2]

Original Sin and Grace [3]

101   Can. 1. All the bishops established in the sacred synod of the Car-

---

[1] Cst 888 C f.; Jf 321; ML 20, 582 C f.; Msi III 1071 D.

[2] It is not well established that the following canons were determined even in the council of Mileum. Cf. Cst 888 ff.; Msi III 1071; Jf 321; ML 20, 582 B [see n. 100]. Fr. Maassen, *Geschichte der Quellen und der Literatur des canonischen Rechts* I (1870) 167; Hfl II 113 ff.—Can. 1 (n. 101), 2 (n. 102), 6 (n. 106), 7 (n. 107) and 8 (n. 108) are referred to by Brachiarius (7 century) in his work "De ecclesiasticis dogmatibus" cap. 33–37 [ML 83, 1235 f.; *App. ad opera S. Isidori Hispal.*].

[3] Hrd I 926 E ff. coll. H 213 ff.; cf. Hrd I 1217 D ff.; ML 56, 486 B ff.; Msi III 811 A ff. (IV 326 C ff.).

thaginian Church have decided that whoever says that Adam, the first man, was made mortal, so that, whether he sinned or whether he did not sin, he would die in body, that is he would go out of the body not because of the merit of sin but by reason of the necessity of nature,[1] let him be anathema.

Can. 2. Likewise it has been decided that whoever says that infants 102 fresh from their mothers' wombs ought not to be baptized, or says that they are indeed baptized unto the remission of sins, but that they draw nothing of the original sin from Adam, which is expiated in the bath of regeneration, whence it follows that in regard to them the form of baptism "unto the remission of sins" is understood as not true, but as false, let him be anathema. Since what the Apostle says: *"Through one man sin entered into the world (and through sin death), and so passed into all men, in whom all have sinned"* [cf. Rom. 5:12], must not to be understood otherwise than as the Catholic Church spread everywhere has always understood it. For on account of this rule of faith even infants, who in themselves thus far have not been able to commit any sin, are therefore truly baptized unto the remission of sins, so that that which they have contracted from generation may be cleansed in them by regeneration.[2]

Can. 3. Likewise it has been decided that whoever says that the grace 103 of God, by which man is justified through Jesus Christ, our Lord, has power only for the remission of sins which have already been committed, and not also for help, that they be not committed, let him be anathema.

Can. 4. In like manner, whoever says that the same grace of God through 104 Jesus Christ, our Lord, helps us not to sin only for this reason, that through it the understanding of the commands is revealed and opened to us, that we may know what we ought to strive after, what we ought to avoid, but that through this [the power] is not also given to us to love and to be able to do that which we know ought to be done, let him be anathema. For since the Apostle says: *"Knowledge puffs up, but charity edifies"* [I Cor. 8:1], it is very impious for us to believe that for that which puffs up, we have the grace of Christ, and for that which edifies we have not, although each is a gift of God, both to know what we ought to do and to love in order that we may do it, so that while charity edifies, knowledge may not

---

[1] Cf. St. Augustine, *De pecc. mer. et rem.* 1, 1, 2 [ML 44, 109].

[2] *There is added here in a certain codex another authentic canon:*

Can. 3. It has been decided likewise that if anyone says that for this reason the Lord said: *"In my Father's house there are many mansions"* [John 14:2]: that it might be understood that in the kingdom of heaven there will be some middle place or some place anywhere where the blessed infants live who departed from this life without baptism, without which they cannot enter into the kingdom of heaven, which is life eternal, let him be anathema. For when the Lord says: "Unless a man be born again of water and the Holy Ghost, he shall not enter into the kingdom of God" [John 3:5], what Catholic will doubt that he will be a partner of the devil who has not deserved to be a coheir of Christ? For he who lacks the right part will without doubt run into the left [Hrd 1 927 B note].

be able to puff us up. Moreover, just as it is written of God: *"Who teaches man knowledge"* [Ps. 93:10], so also it is written: *"Charity is from God"* [I John 4:7].

105   Can. 5. It has likewise been decided that whoever says that the grace of justification is given to us for this reason: that what we are ordered to do through free will, we may be able to accomplish more easily through grace, just as if, even if grace were not given, we could nevertheless fulfill the divine commands without it, though not indeed easily, let him be anathema. For concerning the fruits of His commands the Lord spoke not when He said: *"Without me you can accomplish with greater difficulty,"* but when He said: *"Without me you can do nothing"* [John 15:5].

106   Can. 6. It has likewise been decided that what St. John the Apostle says: *If we say, that we have not sin, we deceive ourselves, and the truth is not in us* [I John 1:8], whoever thinks that this ought to be interpreted thus: that he asserts that this ought to be said on account of humility, namely, that we have sin, and not because it is truly so, let him be anathema. For the Apostle continues and adds: *If however we confess our sins, he is faithful and just, who remits our sins and cleanses us from all iniquity* [I John 1:9], wherein it is quite clear, that this is said not only humbly but truly. For the Apostle could have said: *If we say: we have not sin, we extol ourselves, and humility is not in us.* But when he says: *We deceive ourselves, and the truth is not in us,* he shows clearly that he who said he had not sin, spoke not the truth but a falsehood.

107   Can. 7. It has likewise been decided that whoever says that for this reason the saints say in the Lord's prayer: *"Forgive us our debts"* [Matt. 6:12], that they say this not for themselves, because that petition is not now necessary for them, but for others who are sinners among their people, and that on this account each one of the saints does not say: *Forgive me my debts,* but, *Forgive us our debts;* so that the just man is understood to seek this for others rather than for himself, let him be anathema. For the Apostle James was holy and just, when he said: *"For in many things we all offend"* [Jas. 3:2]. For why was "all" (*omnes*) added, unless that this meaning was proper and in the Psalm where one reads: *Enter not into judgment with thy servant, because no (ne omnes) living person shall be justified in thy sight* [Ps. 142:2]. And in the prayer of wisest Solomon: *There is not a man who has not sinned* [III Kings 8:46]. And in the book of holy Job: *In the hand of every (omnis) man he signs, so that every (omnis) man may know his infirmity* [Job 37:7]. Hence also holy and just Daniel, when he spoke in the plural in his prayer: *"We have sinned, we have done evil"* [Dan. 9:5, 15], and the rest which he there truly and humbly confesses, lest it should be thought, as certain ones do think, that he said this not about his own sins, but rather about the sins of his people, declared afterwards: *"When . . . I prayed and confessed* *my sins and the sins of my people"* [Dan. 9:20] to the Lord my God; he did not wish to say "our sins," but he said the sins of his people and his own sins, since as a prophet he foresaw there would be those who would thus misunderstand.

Can. 8. It has likewise been decided that whoever wishes that the   108
words themselves of the Lord's prayer, where we say: *"Forgive us our debts"* [Matt. 6:12] be said by the saints so as to be spoken humbly, not truthfully, let him be anathema. For who would tolerate one praying and lying, not to men, but to the Lord himself, who says with his lips that he wishes to be forgiven, and in his heart holds that he does not have debts to be forgiven?

The Primacy and the Infallibility of the Roman Pontiff [1]

[From the epistle (12) "Quamvis Pátrum traditio" to
the African bishops, March 21, 418]

Although the tradition of the Fathers has attributed such great authority   109
to the Apostolic See that no one would dare to disagree wholly with its judgment, and it has always preserved this [judgment] by canons and rules, and current ecclesiastical discipline up to this time by its laws pays the reverence which is due to the name of PETER, from whom it has itself descended . . . ; since therefore PETER the head is of such great authority and he has confirmed the subsequent endeavors of all our ancestors, so that the Roman Church is fortified . . . by human as well as by divine laws, and it does not escape you that we rule its place and also hold power of the name itself, nevertheless you know, dearest brethren, and as priests you ought to know, although we have such great authority that no one can dare to retract from our decision, yet we have done nothing which we have not voluntarily referred to your notice by letters . . . not because we did not know what ought to be done, or would do anything which by going against the advantage of the Church, would be displeasing. . . .

Original Sin [2]

[From the epistle "Tract(at)oria ad Orientales ecclesias,
Aegypti diocesim, Constantinopolim, Thessalonicam,
Hierosolymam," sent after March, 418]

The Lord [is] faithful in his words [Ps. 144:13] and His baptism holds   109a
the same plenitude in deed and words, that is in work, confession, and

---

[1] Cst 974 B f.; Jf 342; ML 20, 676 A f.; Msi IV 366 D f.; Bar(Th) to 418 n. 4 (7, 107a).

[2] Cst 994 E ff.; Jf 343; ML 20, 693 B.—From this same epistle "Tract(at)oria" these points, which have been cited, have been drawn n. 134 f.

true remission of sins in every sex, age, and condition of the human race. For no one except him who is the servant of sin is made free, nor can he be said to be redeemed unless he has previously truly been a captive through sin, as it is written: *"If the Son liberates you, you will be truly free* [John 8:36]. For through Him we are reborn spiritually, through Him we are crucified to the world. By His death that bond of death introduced into all of us by Adam and transmitted to every soul, that bond contracted by propagation is broken, in which no one of our children is held not guilty until he is freed through baptism.

ST. BONIFACE I 418–422
The Primacy and Infallibility of the Roman Pontiff [1]
[From the epistle (13) "Retro maioribus tuis" to
Rufus, Bishop of Thessaly, March 11, 422]

110   (2) . . . To the Synod [of Corinth] . . . we have directed such writings that all the brethren may know . . . that there must be no withdrawal from our judgment. For it has never been allowed that that be discussed again which has once been decided by the Apostolic See.

ST. CELESTINE I 422–432
Reconciliation in the Moment of Death [2]
[From the epistle (4) "Cuperemus quidem" to the
bishops of the provinces of Vienne and Narbo,
July 26, 428]

111   (2) We acknowledge that penance is being denied the dying and no assent is given to the ardent wishes of those who at the time of their death desire to come to the assistance of their souls with this remedy. We are horrified, I confess, that anyone is found of such great impiety, that he despairs of the love of God, as if He were not able at any time whatever to hasten to the aid of the one who runs to Him for help and to free from his burden a man endangered by the weight of sins, from which he longs to be liberated. For what else is this, I ask, than to add death to the dying and to kill his soul with one's own cruelty, that it may not be able to be

   [1] C. Silva-Tarouca S.J. *Epistularum Rom. Pontificum . . . collectio Thessalonicensis*, Romae: 1937, 33 [Textus et documenta, Ser. theol. 23]. Cst 1035 C; Jf 363; ML 20, 776 A; Msi VIII 754 E f.
   [2] Cst 1067 C f.; Jf 369; ML 50, 431 B; Msi IV 465 B.

absolved? Since God, most ready to succor, inviting to repentance, thus promised: *In whatever day,* He says, *the sinner shall be converted, his sins shall not be imputed to him* [cf. Ezech. 33:16]. . . . Since therefore the Lord is the examiner of the heart, penance must not be denied at any time to one who asks for (it). . . .

COUNCIL OF EPHESUS 431

Ecumenical III (against the Nestorians)

The Incarnation [1]

[From the epistle II of St. Cyril of Alexandria to Nestorius, read and approved in action I]

For we do not say that the nature of the Word was changed and made **111a** flesh, nor yet that it was changed into the whole man (composed) of soul and body but rather (we say) that the Word uniting with Himself according to person is a body animated by a rational soul, marvelously and incomprehensibly was made man, and was the Son of man, not according to the will alone or by the assumption of a person alone, and that the different natures were brought together in a real union, but that out of both in one Christ and Son, not because the distinction of natures was destroyed by the union, but rather because the divine nature and the human nature formed one Lord and Christ and Son for us, through a marvelous and mystical concurrence in unity. . . . For in the first place no common man was born of the holy Virgin; then the Word thus descended upon him; but being united from the womb itself he is said to have endured a generation in the flesh in order to appropriate the producing of His own body. Thus [the holy Fathers] did not hesitate to speak of the holy Virgin as the Mother of God.

The Primacy of the Roman Pontiff [2]

[From the speech of Philip the Roman legate in action III]

No one doubts, but rather it has been known to all generations, that the **112** holy and most blessed Peter, chief and head of the Apostles, the pillar of the faith, the foundation stone of the Catholic church, received the keys of the kingdom from our Lord Jesus Christ the Savior and Redeemer of the human race, and that the power of binding and loosing sins was

---

[1] ACOec T. 1, vol. 1, part 1, p. 25 f.; cf. *ibid.*, part 2, p. 13; vol. II, p. 38; vol. III, p. 21; vol. V, part 1, p. 50; Msi IV 1138; Hrd I 1273; II 115; Hfl II 160, 185.

[2] Msi IV 1295 B f.; Hrd I 1477 B; Hfl II 200 f.; ACOec I, I, 3, 106.

given to him, who up to this moment and always lives in his successors, and judges [see n. 1824].

The Anathemas of the Chapter of Cyril [1] (against Nestorius) [2]

113   Can. 1. If anyone does not confess that God is truly Emmanuel, and that on this account the Holy Virgin is the Mother of God (for according to the flesh she gave birth to the Word of God become flesh by birth), let him be anathema.

114   Can. 2. If anyone does not confess that the Word of God the Father was united to a body by hypostasis and that one is Christ with his own body, the same one evidently both God and man, let him be anathema.

115   Can. 3. If anyone in the one Christ divides the subsistences after the union, connecting them by a junction only according to worth, that is to say absolute sway or power, and not rather by a joining according to physical union, let him be anathema.

116   Can. 4. If anyone portions out to two persons, that is to say subsistences, the words in the Gospels and the apostolic writings, whether said about Christ by the saints, or by Him concerning Himself, and attributes some as if to a man specially understood beside the Word of God, others as befitting God alone, to the Word of God the Father, let him be anathema.

117   Can. 5. If anyone ventures to say that Christ is a man inspired by God, and not rather that He is truly God, as a son by nature, as the Word was made flesh and has shared similarly with us in blood and flesh, let him be anathema.

118   Can. 6. If anyone ventures to say that God or the Lord is the Word of Christ from God the Father and does not rather confess the same as at once both God and man, since the Word was made flesh according to the Scriptures, let him be anathema.

119   Can. 7. If anyone says that Jesus as man was assisted by the Word of God, and that the glory of the Only-begotten was applied as to another existing beside Him, let him be anathema.

120   Can. 8. If anyone ventures to say that the assumed man must be worshipped and glorified along with God the Word, and bears the same title

---

[1] Nestorius was condemned by the council of EPHESUS, as it were *"in globo"* and was deposed on the twenty-second of June, 431 [Msi IV 1211 C]. Those anathematized, who were added to the epistle which St. Cyril and the synod of Alexandria in the year 430 had given to Nestorius, the Council V [of CONSTANTINOPLE II] brought back and highly extolled (this) as part of "the achievements which were effected at Ephesus" [Msi IX 327 C f.]. P. Galtier, *Rech. de science rel.* 23 (1933) 45 ff., shows that the Council of Ephesus approved the letter of St. Cyril placed as n. 111a, but not this one. The Anathematized of Nestorius against Cyril, see Kch n. 796 ff.

[2] ACOec T. I, vol. I, pars I, p. 4 ff.; ML 48, 840 A ff.; Msi IV 1081 D ff. (gr.) H 312 ff.; Hrd I 1291 E ff.; cf. Hfl II 170 ff.; Bar(Th) to 439 n. 50 ff. (7, 323 ff.).

with Him, as the one in the other, for the "σύν" always being added will force (one) to understand this, and does not rather honor Emmanuel with one worship and apply one glory to Him, according as the Word was made flesh, let him be anathema.

Can. 9. If anyone says that the one Lord Jesus Christ was glorified by   121
the Spirit, as it were using through Him a power belonging to another, and that He received from Him the power to work against unclean spirits, and to perform miracles for men, and does not say rather that the Spirit through which He worked the miracles was His own; let him be anathema.

Can. 10. The Divine Scripture says that Christ was made a high priest   122
and apostle of our confession [Heb. 3:1] and in the odor of fragrance offered himself to God and the Father for us [Eph. 5:2]. Therefore, if anyone says that the Word of God Himself was not made our High-priest and Apostle, when He was made flesh [John 1:14] and man in our likeness, but that as it were another besides Himself specifically a man (born) of a woman, or if anyone says that He offered the oblation for Himself and not rather for us alone, for He who knew not sin would not have needed oblations, let him be anathema.

Can. 11. If anyone does not confess that the flesh of the Lord is life-   123
giving and belongs personally to the Word of God, the Father, but that it is of someone else besides Him, but joined to Him according to worthiness, as having only the divine indwelling, and not rather as we said, is life-giving, since He was made the Word's own, and has power to give life to all things, let him be anathema.

Can. 12. If anyone does not confess that the Word of God suffered in   124
the flesh, and tasted death in the flesh, and was made the firstborn from the dead [Col. 1:18] according to which as God He is both the life and the life-giver, let him be anathema.

Faith and the Tradition to be Guarded [1]

. . . The holy synod decided that no one is allowed to declare or at   125
any rate to compose or devise a faith other than that defined by the holy fathers who with the Holy Spirit came together at Nicea. . . .

. . . If any should be discovered, whether bishops or priests, or lay persons, who believe or teach those things in the exposition conveyed by Charisius the priest concerning the Incarnation [2] of the Only-begotten Son of God, or at any rate the abominable and distorted dogmas of Nestorius . . . , let them be subject to the decision of this holy and ecumenical synod. . . .

---

[1] ACOec I, I, 7, p. 105 f.; Msi IV 1362 D ff.; Hrd I 1526 D; cf. Hfl II 207.
[2] Msi IV 1345 ff.

Condemnation of the Pelagians [1]

126 Can. 1. Whether a metropolitan of the province after revolting against the holy and ecumenical synod . . . , heeded or will heed the (opinions) of Celestius, this person is in no wise able to accomplish anything against the bishops of the province, since thereafter he is debarred by the synod from all ecclesiastical communion and is rendered inefficacious. . . .

127 Can. 4. But if some of the clergy should rebel, and dare to hold the opinions of Nestorius or Celestius either in private or in public, it has been judged by the holy synod that they too are deposed.

The Authority of St. Augustine [2]

[From Ep. (21) "Apostolici Verba Praecepti" to the bishops of the Gauls, May 15 (?), 431]

128 Chapter 2. We have always held Augustine a man of holy memory because of his life and also of his services in our communion, nor has even report ever sullied him with unfavorable suspicion. We recall him as having once been a man of such great knowledge that even by my predecessors in the past he was always accounted among the best teachers.[3]

The Catalog or the Authoritative Statements of the Past Bishops of the Holy See [4] Concerning the Grace of God

129 Because some, who glory in the name of Catholic, linger in the condemned view of heretics whether through perverseness or through ig-

---

[1] ACOec I, I, 3 p. 27 f.; Msi IV 1471 C ff.; Hrd I 1621 D; cf. Hfl II 205 ff.

[2] Cst 1187 C ff.; Jf 381 c. Add.; ML 50, 530 A; Msi IV 455 E ff.; Hrd I 1254 B ff.

[3] In the same way the authority of St. Augustine is commended by Boniface II in his epistle to the Fathers of Orange, and he was reckoned among the Fathers, who had written correctly about grace. Note, however, what is said by St. Celestine, c. 173 of this epistle, the words of St. HORMISDAS to the Defendant [see n. 173a], proposition 30 condemned by ALEXANDER VIII [see n. 1320], and the admonition of PIUS XI, encyclical "Ad salutem," 22 Apr., 1930, lest "the authority of Augustine speaking be preferred even to the supreme authority of the Church teaching" [AAS 22 (1930) 204], finally the words of Augustine himself *De dono perseverantiae*, chapter 21: "I would not wish anyone so to esteem my (writings) that he would follow me except in those matters in which he has clearly seen I do not err: for on this account I am now composing books in which I have undertaken to examine my works, so that I may show that I myself have not conformed to myself in all things" [ML 45, 1027 f.].

[4] They seem to have been collected at Rome by St. Prosper of Aquitaine (according to M. Cappuyns, *Revue Bénédictine* 41 [1929] 156 ff.) shortly after CELESTINE I, between 435 and 442, and, about the year 500 to have been recognized universally as the genuine doctrine of the Apostolic See: cf. *Epist. Petri Diaconi* (year 520), c. 8, n. 7 [ML 45, 1775], and Brachiarius (7th century) *De ecclesiasticis dogmatibus,*

norance, and presume to oppose the very pious disputers, and, although they do not hesitate to anathematize Pelagius and also Caelestius, nevertheless contradict our teachers, as if they overstepped the necessary limit, and profess to follow and approve only those [doctrines] which the most sacred See of the Blessed Apostle PETER has sanctioned and taught against the enemies of the grace of God through the office of its leaders, it has become necessary to inquire diligently as to what the rulers of the Roman Church judged concerning the heresy which had arisen in their times, and in opposition to the most harmful [heretics] what the defenders of free will decreed should be thought with regard to the grace of God. Thus, too, we have added certain opinions of the African Councils, which the apostolic high-priests have assuredly made their own when they approved [them]. In order therefore that [those] who doubt in any [matter] may be the more fully instructed, we are making public the definitions of the Holy Fathers in a brief catalogue, in which, if anyone is not a little contentious, he will recognize that the organic union of all reasonings depends upon this concise [catalogue] of supporting authorities, and no reason for contradiction remains to him, if he believes and speaks with the Catholics.

Chapter 1. In the transgression of Adam all men lost their "natural   130 power" [1] and innocence, and no one can rise from the depth of that ruin through free will, unless the grace of a merciful God raise him up, [according as] Pope INNOCENT of blessed memory proclaimed and said in his letter [2] to the Council of Carthage: [3] "For he, having once braved every consequence of free choice, while he used his goods too unadvisedly, fell and was overwhelmed in the depth of his transgression, and found no [way] by which he was able to rise from it; and beguiled forever by his own liberty he would have lain prostrate by the weight of this ruin, if the coming of Christ had not afterwards lifted him up by virtue of His grace, who through the purification of a new regeneration washed away in the bath of His baptism every past sin."

Chapter 2. For no one is good of himself, unless He gives [him] a   131 participation of Himself, who alone is good.

In the same writings the opinion of the same pontiff bears witness to this, stating: [4] "Shall we after this judge anything to be right in the minds of those who think they owe to themselves the fact that they are

---

c. 22–32 [ML 83, 1232–1234], Gennadius Massil., *De eccl. dogmatibus*, c. 30 [ML 58 987 D].

[1] St. Aug., *D. Nat. et grat.* XL, 47 [ML 44, 270].
[2] Ep. 29 "In requirendis" n. 6 [ML 20, 586 B].
[3] Of the year 416.
[4] Ep. 29 "In requirendis" n. 3 [ML 20, 584 B].

good, and do not consider Him, whose grace they obtain daily; who feel
sure that they are able to secure [it] alone without Him?"

132   Chapter 3. No one even after having been restored by the grace of
baptism is capable of overcoming the snares of the devil and subduing the
concupiscenses of the flesh, unless he has received through the daily help
of God the perseverance of the good way of life. The doctrine of the same
high-priest confirms this in the same letter, declaring [1]: "For although He
had redeemed man from his past sins, nevertheless knowing that he would
be able to sin again, He saved many things for reparation to Himself,
offering him daily remedies by which He might be able to correct him
even after those (sins), and, if we do not struggle relying upon these
[remedies] and trusting in them, we shall by no means be able to conquer
human mistakes. For it is necessary that, as we are victorious with His
aid, we shall again be defeated if He does not help us."

133   Chapter 4. The same teacher in the epistle to the council of Mileum [2]
proclaims that no one uses his free will well, except through Christ, asserting: [3] "Note finally, O perverse doctrine of most distorted minds, that
liberty itself so deceived the first man, that, while he used his bridle too
indulgently, he fell into transgression by presumption. Nor would he
have been able to be rescued from this, had not the coming of Christ the
Lord reestablished for him the state of pristine liberty by the providence
of regeneration."

134   Chapter 5. That all the zeal and all the works and merits of the saints
ought to be referred to the glory and praise of God; because no one pleases
Him with anything except with that which He Himself has given. To
this view the regular authority of the Pope ZOSIMUS of blessed memory
directs us, when, writing to the bishops of the whole world, he says: [4]
"We, however, by the inspiration of God (for all good things must be
assigned to their author, whence they derive their origin) have referred
all things to the conscience of our brothers and co-bishops." However, the African bishops honored with such great praise this discourse
radiating with the light of sincerest truth, that they wrote thus to the
same man: "That statement indeed, which you made in the letter, that
you caused to be sent to all the provinces, saying: 'We nevertheless by the
inspiration of God, etc.,' we have accepted the words thus: that you, as
it were moving swiftly with the drawn sword of truth have cut off those
who extol the freedom of the human will in opposition to the help of God.
For you have done nothing with free will except refer all things to the
conscience of our lowliness. And yet you have faithfully and wisely seen

---

[1] *Ibid.*, n. 6 [ML 20, 586 C ff.].

[2] Of the year 416.

[3] Ep. 30 "Inter ceteras," n. 3 [ML 20, 591 A].

[4] Ep. *tract(at)oria* a. 418.

that it was done by the inspiration of God, and you have spoken truly and confidently. Therefore assuredly, because *the good will is provided beforehand by the Lord* [Prov. 8:35: LXX], and that the good may accomplish something, He Himself touches the hearts of His sons with paternal inspirations. *For all that are moved by the Spirit of God, they are the Sons of God* [Rom. 8:14]; so that we do not think that our free will is lacking; and we do not doubt that in each and every good movement of the human will, His help is more powerful."

Chapter 6. That God thus operates in the hearts of men and in the **135** free will itself, so that a holy thought, a pious plan, and every motion of good will is from God, because we can do anything good through Him, *without whom we can do nothing* [John 15:5]. For to this profession the same teacher ZOSIMUS trained us, who, when he spoke [1] to the bishops of the whole world concerning the assistance of divine grace, said: "What time therefore occurs in which we do not need His help? Accordingly in all acts, situations, thoughts, and movements He ought to be implored as helper and protector. Indeed, it is arrogant for human nature to take anything to itself since the Apostle declares: *Our struggle is not against flesh and blood, but against princes and powers of this atmosphere, against the spirits of wickedness in high places* [Eph. 6:12]. And thus He Himself said again: *Unhappy* man (that) *I* (am), *who will free me from the body of this death? The grace of God through Jesus Christ our Lord* [Rom. 7:24]. And again: *By the grace of God I am what I am, and His grace in me has not been void; but I have labored more than all those; yet not I, but the grace with me* [I Cor. 15:10]."

Chapter 7. Furthermore that which was determined in the decrees of **136** the synod of Carthage,[2] we have embraced as the Apostolic See's own, namely, what was defined in the third chapter: "That whoever says that the grace of God, by which we are justified through Jesus Christ our Lord, has power only for the remission of sins which have already been committed, and not also for help, that they may not be committed, let him be anathema." [see n. 103].

And again in the fourth chapter: "That whoever says that the grace **137** of God through Jesus Christ on this account alone helps us not to sin, that through it an understanding of the commands is revealed and opened to us, so that we know what we ought to strive after and what we ought to shun, but that through it [the power] is not also given to us to love and to be able to do that which we know ought to be done, let him be anathema. For since the Apostle says: *Knowledge puffs up, but charity edifies* [I Cor. 8:1]; it is very impious, for us to believe, that for that which puffs up, we have the grace of Christ, and for that which edifies, we have not,

---

[1] Ep. *tract(at)oria* a. 418.

[2] In the year 418 [see n. 101 ff.].

although each is a gift of God, both to know what we ought to do, and to love in order that we may do it, so that since charity edifies, knowledge may not be able to puff up. Moreover just as it is written of God: *Who teaches man knowledge* [Ps. 93:10], so also it is written: *Charity is from God* [I John 4:7];" [see n. 104].

138   Likewise in the fifth chapter: "That whoever says, that for this reason the grace of justification is given to us, that what we are ordered to do through free will we may be able to accomplish more easily through grace, just as if, even were grace not given, we could nevertheless fulfill the divine commands without it, though not indeed easily, let him be anathema. For of the fruits of his commands the Lord did not speak when He said: *Without me you can accomplish (them) with more difficulty,* but when He said: *Without me you can do nothing* [John 15:5]" [See n. 105].

139   Chapter 8.[1] But besides these hallowed ordinances of the most blessed and Apostolic See, in accordance with which the most pious Fathers, after casting aside the pride of pernicious novelty, have taught us to refer to Christ's grace both the beginnings of good will, and the advances in commendable devotions and the perseverance in these unto the end, let us be mindful also of the sacraments of priestly public prayer, which handed down by the Apostles are uniformly celebrated in the whole world and in every Catholic Church, in order that the law of supplication may support the law of believing.

For when the leaders of the holy nations perform the office of ambassador entrusted to them, they plead the cause of the human race before divine Clemency, and while the whole Church laments with them, they ask and pray that the faith may be granted to infidels; that idolaters may be delivered from the errors of their impiety; that the veil of their hearts may be removed and the light of truth be visible to the Jews; that heretics may come to their senses through a comprehension of the Catholic faith; that schismatics may receive the spirit of renewed charity; that the remedy of repentance may be bestowed upon the lapsed; that finally after the catechumens have been led to the sacraments of regeneration, the royal court of heavenly mercy may be opened to them. Moreover, the effect of these prayers shows that these are not sought from the Lord perfunctorily and uselessly, since indeed God deigns to attract from every kind of error very many whom, *torn from the power of darkness, He transfers into the kingdom of the Son of his love* [Col. 1:13], and *from vessels of wrath* He makes *vessels of mercy* [Rom. 9:22 f.]. This is felt to be so completely a divine work that the action of the graces and the acknowledgement of praise on account of the illumination or correction

---

[1] This chapter 8 agrees fully in the matter with St. Prosper's *De vocatione omnium gentium* 1, 12 [ML 51, 664 C f.]. Cf. prayers in the Mass of the Presanctified.

of such [persons] should always be referred to God who effects these
things.

That also, which the holy Church uniformly does in the whole world 140
with regard to those to be baptized, we do not observe with indifferent
respect. Since whether children or youths come to the sacrament of regeneration, they do not approach the fountain of life, before the unclean
spirit is driven away from them by the exorcisms and the breathings upon
them of the priests; so that then it is truly manifest how *the prince of
this world is sent forth* [John 12:31], and how *the strong* [man] *is first
bound* [Matt. 12:29], and thereafter *his vessels are plundered* [Mark
3:27], having been transferred to the possession of the victor, who *leads
captivity captive* [Eph. 4:8] and *gives gifts to man* [Ps. 67:19].

Therefore, in accordance with the ecclesiastical rules and documents 141
taken on divine authority, we are so strengthened by our Lord's aid that
we confess openly that God [is] the author of all good dispositions of
mind, and also of works, and of all zeal, and of all virtues by which from
the beginning of faith we tend towards God; and we do not doubt that all
the merits of man are preceded by His grace, through whom it is brought
to pass, that we begin both *to will* and *to do* [Phil. 2:13] anything good.
Assuredly free choice is not taken away by this aid and gift of God, but it
is set at liberty, that light may come from darkness, right from wrong,
health from sickness, and prudence from imprudence. For, so great is the
goodness of God towards all men that He wishes the merits, which are His
own gifts, to be ours, and in consideration of those which He has conferred, He intends to give eternal rewards.[1] For He acts in us that we
may both will and do what He wishes, nor does He allow those gifts to
be idle in us which He has given to be used and not to be neglected,
that we also may be cooperators with the grace of God. And if we
see that there is any listlessness in us as a result of our relaxation,
let us carefully have recourse to Him, *who heals all our weaknesses
and redeems our life from destruction* [Ps. 102:3 f.], and *to whom
we daily say: Lead us not into temptation, but deliver us from evil*
[Matt. 6:13].

Chapter 10. But although we do not dare to esteem lightly the deeper 142
and more difficult parts of the questions which they have treated[2] in
more detail who have resisted the heretics, yet we do not consider it
necessary to add what their writings, according to the aforementioned
regulation of the Apostolic See, have taught us, because we believe that
it is quite enough to confess the grace of God, from whose work and
honor nothing should be entirely taken away, so that we do not deem

---

[1] Cf. St. Augustine, Ep. 194 to Sixtus 5, 19 [ML 33, 880].

[2] Viva, Theses damn. ab ALEXANDRO VIII n. XXX reads: ". . . Augustine and
others investigated, who . . ."

that to be at all Catholic which appears to be contrary to the views presented above.

Sᴛ. Sɪxᴛᴜs III 432–440

"Creed of the union" of the year 433, by which peace was restored between St. Cyril of Alexandria and the Antiochenes [St. Cyril, Ep. 39: MG 77, 176 D f. 7; see R n. 2060; approved by St. Sixtus III, App. n. 5002 ff.]

ST. LEO I, THE GREAT 440–461

The Incarnation [1] (against Eutyches) [2]

[From the dogmatic epistle (28) "Lectis dilectionis tuae" to Flavian, Patriarch of Constantinople, June 13, 449]

(2) . . . *see R n. 2182.*

143   (3) The uniqueness of each nature being preserved and combined in one person, humility was assumed by majesty, weakness by strength, mortality by eternity, and for the sake of paying the debt of our creation, an inviolable nature was joined to a passible nature; so that, because it was adapted to our relief, *one* and the same *mediator of God and men, the man Jesus Christ* [I Tim. 2:5] both could die by reason of the one, and could not die on account of the other. Accordingly, in the whole and perfect nature of true man, true God was born, complete in His own, complete in ours. . . .

144   (4) Consequently, the Son of God entered into these lowly conditions of the world, after descending from His celestial throne, and though He did not withdraw from the glory of the Father, He was generated in a new order and in a new nativity. In a new order, because invisible in His own, He was made visible in ours; incomprehensible [in His own], He wished to be comprehended; permanent before times, He began to be in time; the Lord of the universe assumed the form of a slave, concealing the immensity of His majesty; the impassible God did not disdain to be a passible man and the immortal [did not disdain] to be subject to the laws of death. Moreover, He was generated in a new nativity, because inviolate virginity [that] did not know concupiscence furnished the material of His body. From the mother of the Lord, nature, not guilt, was assumed; and in the Lord Jesus Christ born from the womb of the Virgin, because His birth was miraculous, nature was not for that

---

[1] The Fathers of Council IV of CHALCEDON received this epistle, crying, "PETER has spoken through LEO" [Hrd II 305 E].

[2] Cf. Silva-Tarouca, S.J., *S. Leonis M. Tomus ad Flavianum*, episc. Cstpl., Romae, 1932, 24 ff. ML 54, 763 A ff.; Jf 423; Hfl II 356 Nota; Msi V 1371 D ff.; Hrd II 291 E ff.; BR(T) App. (I) 29a f.

reason different from ours. For He who is true God, is likewise true man, and there is no falsehood in this unity, as long as there are alternately the lowliness of man and the exaltedness of the Divinity. For, just as God is not changed by His compassion, so man is not destroyed by His dignity. For each nature does what is proper to it with the mutual participation of the other; the Word clearly effecting what belongs to the Word, and the flesh performing what belongs to the flesh. One of these gleams with miracles; the other sinks under injuries. And just as the Word does not withdraw from the equality of the paternal glory, so His body does not abandon the nature of our race [For more see R n. 2183 f. 2188].

> *Matrimony as a sacrament* [*Eph. 5:32*] *see R n. 2189;*   **144***
> *The creation of the soul and original sin, see*
> *R n. 2181.*

Secret Confession [1]

[From epistle "Magna indign." to all the bishops through
Campania, etc., March 6, 459]

(2) I also decree that that presumption against the apostolic regula-   **145**
tion, which I recently learned is being committed by some through unlawful usurpation, be banished by all means.

With regard to penance, what is demanded of the faithful, is clearly not that an acknowledgement of the nature of individual sins written in a little book be read publicly, since it suffices that the states of consciences be made known to the priests alone in secret confession. For although the fullness of faith seems to be laudable, which on account of the fear of God is not afraid to blush before men, nevertheless since the sins of all are not such that those who ask for penance do not dread to publish them, so objectionable a custom should be abolished. . . . For that confession is sufficient, which is first offered to God, then also to a priest, who serves as an intercessor for the transgressions of the penitents. For then, indeed, more will be able to be incited to penance, if the conscience of the one confessing is not exposed to the ears of the people.

The Sacrament of Penance [2]

[From epistle (108) "Solicitudinis quidem tuae" to
Theodore, Bishop of Forum Julii, June 11, 452]

(2) The manifold mercy of God came to the assistance of fallen men   **146**
in such a way that the hope of eternal life might be recovered not only

---

[1] ML 54, 1210 C f.; Jf 545; Msi VI 410 C f.; BT(T) 80 a.
[2] ML 54, 1011 B ff.; Jf 485; Msi VI 209 A f.; BR(T) App. I 102b ff.

by the grace of baptism, but also by the remedy of penance, that those
who have violated the gifts of regeneration, condemning themselves by
their own judgment, might attain to the remission of their sins; the help
of divine goodness having been so ordered that the indulgence of God
cannot be obtained except by the supplications of the priests. For *"the
Mediator of God and of men, the man Christ Jesus* [I Tim. 2:5] has
entrusted this power to the leaders of the Church, that they might both
grant the action of penance to those confessing, and admit the same
[persons] cleansed by salutary satisfaction to the communion of the sacraments through the gate of reconciliation. . . .

147   (5) It is necessary that each and every Christian hold a trial of his
own conscience, lest from day to day he defer being converted to God,
and choose the difficulties of that time when neither the confession of
the penitent nor the reconciliation of the priest can take place. But, as
I have said, the need even of such should be served, so that neither the
action of penance nor the grace of communion may be denied them, even
if the function of speech has been lost, and they ask it through the signs
of a sound sense. But if they are so oppressed by some violent illness,
that what they asked a little while before, they are not able to signify
in the presence of the priest, the testimonies of the faithful standing
about ought to be advantageous to them, that they may gain simultaneously the benefit of both penance and reconciliation, the regulation
of the canons of the Fathers, however, being observed regarding the persons of those who have sinned against God by deserting the faith.

COUNCIL OF CHALCEDON 451
Ecumenical IV (against the Monophysites)

Definition of the Two Natures of Christ [1]

148   Therefore, following the holy
fathers, we all teach that with one
accord we confess one and the
same Son, our Lord Jesus Christ,
the same perfect in human nature,
truly God and the same with a rational soul and a body truly man,
consubstantial with the Father according to divinity, and consubstantial with us according to hu-

[Version of Rusticus] Therefore,
following the holy Fathers, we all
teach that with one accord we confess one and the same Son, our
Lord Jesus Christ, the same perfect
in Godhead and the same perfect
in human nature, true God and
true man, the same with a rational
soul and a body, consubstantial
with the Father according to di-

---

[1] ACOec T. II, vol. I, pars 2, p. [325] 129 f.; Msi VII 115 B f.; coll. Hfl II
471 f.; Hrd II 455 B f.; cf. Bar(Th) to 451 n. 32 ff. (8, 104 ff.).

man nature, like unto us in all things except sin, [cf. Heb. 4:15]; indeed born of the Father before the ages according to divine nature, but in the last days the same born of the virgin Mary, Mother of God according to human nature; for us and for our deliverance, one and the same Christ only begotten Son, our Lord, acknowledged in two natures,[1] without mingling, without change, indivisibly, undividedly, the distinction of the natures nowhere removed on account of the union but rather the peculiarity of each nature being kept, and uniting in one person and substance, not divided or separated into two persons, but one and the same Son only begotten God Word, Lord Jesus Christ, just as from the beginning the prophets taught about Him and the Lord Jesus Himself taught us, and the creed of our fathers has handed down to us.

Therefore, since these have been arranged by us with all possible care and diligence, the holy and ecumenical synod has declared that no one is allowed to profess or in any case to write up or to compose or to devise or to teach others a different faith.

vine nature, consubstantial with us according to the human nature, *like unto us in all things except sin* [cf. Heb. 4:15]: indeed born of the Father before the ages according to divinity, but in the latest days the same born of the virgin Mary, Mother of God according to the humanity; for us and for our salvation, one and the same Christ, only begotten Son, our Lord, acknowledged in two natures without mingling, without change, indivisibly, undividedly, the distinction of the natures removed on account of the union, but rather the uniqueness of each nature being kept and uniting in one person and one substance, not divided or separated into two persons, but one and the same Son only begotten God Word, Lord Jesus Christ, just as from the beginning the prophets taught about Him and the Lord Jesus Christ Himself taught us, and as the creed of the Fathers has handed down to us [see n. 54 86].

Therefore, since these having been arranged by us with all possible care and diligence, the sacred and universal Synod has declared that no one is allowed to profess or to write up or to compose or to devise or to teach others a different faith.

---

[1] The reading should be so, but not ἐκ δύο φύσεων (out of two natures), which the Greek text, as reported by some Collections of the Councils, has, and which Petavius, 1.3. de Inc., c. 6, n. 11 and Hfl II 470 note 1 show very well.

The Primacy of the Roman Pontiff [1]

[From the epistles of the Synod "Repletum est gaudio"
to Leo the Pope, at the beginning of November,
451]

149   For if where two or three are gathered together in His name, there He says He is in the midst of them, how great an intimacy did He show with regard to the five hundred and twenty consecrated men, who preferred to both native land and to labor the knowledge of confession for Him. Over these you ruled as a head over the members, among those holding office, displaying your good will.

[The more ancient version.] For if *where two or three are gathered together in his name, there he says he is in the midst of them* [cf. Matt. 18:20], how great an intimacy will He show in regard to the five hundred and twenty priests, who have preferred to both native land and to labor the knowledge of confession for Him. Over these you ruled as a head over the members, among those holding office, displaying your good will.

149*   *The words of St. LEO himself regarding the primacy of the Roman Pontiff, see Kch n. 891–901*

The Ordination of the Clergy [2]

[From "Ancient Statutes of the Church," or
"Ancient Statutes of the East"]

150   Can. 2 (90). When a bishop is ordained, let two bishops place (expose) and hold the book of the Gospels above his head, and while one pours forth the benediction upon him, let all the remaining bishops, who are present, touch his head with their hands.

151   Can. 3 (91). When a priest is ordained, while the bishop is blessing

---

[1] ML 54, 952 B (Greek text) 959 C (Latin text); cf. Hrd II 655 f.; Msi VI 147 ff. 155; Hfl II 545 ff.

[2] ML 56, 887 C f. (*Ball. Append. Opp. Leon. I*); Msi III 951 A f. (Hrd I 979).— These canons were once falsely ascribed to a certain Council of CARTHAGE IV (398), which is now considered as certainly never to have been held. They seem to have arisen after the beginning of the Pelagian and Monophysite heresies, but before the end of the sixth century. In fact they are cited as "Instituta seniorum" in the acts which are said to be of some Council of Arles but which was not held. Their author or composer is now thought to be Caesarius, Bishop of Arles (502–542). —Cf. the prayer, used on Feria VI in Holy Week, in which the same series of orders is placed in such a way, however, that the psalmists or cantors are called "confessor": "Let us pray for all Bishops, Priests, Deacons, Subdeacons, Acolytes, Exorcists, Lectors, Porters, Confessors, Virgins, Widows."

[him] and holding his hands over his head, let all the priests also, who are present, hold their hands close to the hands of the bishop above his head.

Can. 4 (92). When a deacon is ordained, let the bishop alone, who 152 blesses him, place his hands above his head, because he is consecrated not for the priesthood, but for the ministry.

Can. 5 (93). When a subdeacon is ordained, because he does not re- 153 ceive the imposition of hands, let him receive the empty paten from the hand of the bishop, and the empty chalice. But from the hand of the archdeacon let him receive the cruet with the water and the maniple, and the towel.

Can. 6 (94). When an acolyte is ordained, let him indeed be taught 154 by the bishop how he ought to conduct himself in his office; let him receive from the archdeacon the candlestick with the wax tapers, so that he may know that he is about to be given the right to kindle the lights of the church. Let him also receive the empty cruet for carrying the wine at the Eucharist of the blood of Christ.

Can. 7 (95). When the exorcist is ordained, let him receive from the 155 hand of the bishop the little book in which the exorcisms are written, while the bishop says to him: *Receive and commit to memory, and have the power of imposing the hand upon one possessed of the devil, whether [he be] baptized or a catechumen.*

Can. 8 (96). When a lector is ordained, let the bishop speak a word 156 concerning him to the people, pointing out his faith, his life, and his ability. After this, while the people look on, let him hand him the book, from which he is about to read, saying to him: *Receive and be the reporter of the word of God; if you fulfill the office faithfully and usefully, you will have a part with those who have administered the word of God.*

Can. 9 (97). When a porter is ordained, after he has been instructed 157 by the archdeacon as to how he ought to live in the house of God, at the suggestion of the archdeacon let the bishop hand him the keys of the church from the altar, saying: *So act as if you were about to give God the reason for these things which are opened with those keys.*

Can. 10 (98). The psalmist, that is the cantor, can receive his office 158 of singing without the knowledge of the bishop, by the sole order of the presbyter, the presbyter saying to him: *See that what you sing with your heart, and what you believe with your heart, you confirm with your deeds.*

[*There follow the regulations for consecrating virgins, widows: can. 101 on matrimony, see Kch n. 952*]

St. Hilarius 461–468

ST. SIMPLICIUS 468-483

The Necessity of Guarding the Faith Which Has Been Handed Down [1]

[From the epistle "Quantum presbyterorum" to Acacius,
Bishop of Constantinople, January 9, 476]

159   (2) Because, according to the extant doctrine of our predecessors of sacred memory, against which it is wrong to argue, whoever seems to understand rightly, does not desire to be taught by new assertions, but all [matters] in which either he who has been deceived by heretics can be instructed, or he who is about to be planted in the vineyard of the Lord can be trained, are clear and perfect; after imploring trust in your most merciful leader, have the request for calling a synod refused. . . . (3) I urge (therefore), dearest brother, that by every means resistance be offered to the efforts of the perverse to call a synod, which has not always been enjoined in other cases, unless something new arose in distorted minds or something ambiguous in a pronouncement so that, if there were any obscurity, the authority of sacerdotal deliberation might illumine those who were treating the ambiguous pronouncement in common, just as first the impiety of Arius and then that of Nestorius, lastly that of Dioscorus and also of Eutyches caused this to be done. And —may the mercy of Christ our God (and) Savior avert this—it must be made known, abominable [as it is], that [the purpose is] to restore [to their former positions] in opposition to the opinions of the priests of the Lord of the whole world and of the principal rulers of both [*scil.,* worlds] those who have been condemned. . . .

The Unchangeableness of Christian Doctrine [2]

[From the epistle "Cuperem quidem" to Basiliscus
Augustus January 10, 476]

160   Those genuine and clear [truths] which flow from the very pure fountains of the Scriptures cannot be disturbed by any arguments of misty subtlety. For this same norm of apostolic doctrine endures in the successors of him upon whom the Lord imposed the care of the whole sheepfold [John 21:15 ff.], whom [He promised] He would not fail even to the end of the world [Matt. 28:20], against whom He promised that the gates of hell would never prevail, by whose judgment He testified that what was bound on earth could not be loosed in heaven [Matt.

---

[1] Th 178 f.; Jf 572; ML 58, 41 B f.; Msi VII 977 D f.; BR(T) App. I 207 b f.
[2] Th 182; Jf 573; ML 58, 40 A; Msi VII 975 A; BR(T) App. I 210 b f.

16:18 ff.]. (6) . . . *Let whoever,* as the Apostle proclaimed, *attempts to disseminate something other, than what we have received, be anathema* [Gal. 1:8 f.]. Let no approach to your ears be thrown open to the pernicious plans of undermining, let no pledge of revising any of the old definitions be granted, because, as it must be repeated very often, what has deserved to be cut away with the sharp edge of the evangelical pruning-hook by apostolic hands with the approval of the universal Church, cannot acquire the strength for a rebirth nor is it able to return to the fruitful shoot of the master's vine, because it is evident that it has been destined to eternal fire. Thus, finally, the machinations of all heresies laid down by decrees of the Church are never allowed to renew the struggles of their crushed attack.

COUNCIL OF ARLES 475 (?)

[From the letter of submission of Lucidus, the priest] [1]

Grace and Predestination

Your public reproof is public salvation, and your opinion is medicine. 160a From this I also draw the highest remedy, that by blaming past errors I excuse [them], and by healing confession I wash myself. Just so in consequence of the recent statutes of the Council about to be published, I condemn with you that view which states that the work of human obedience does not have to be united with divine grace; which says that after the fall of the first man the free choice of the will was totally destroyed; which states that Christ our Lord and Savior did not incur death for the salvation of all; which states that the foreknowledge of God violently impels man to death, or that they who perish, perish by the will of God; which affirms that whoever sins after baptism which has been legitimately received dies in Adam; which states that some have been condemned to death, others have been predestined to life; which states that from Adam even to Christ none of the nations has been saved unto the coming of Christ through the first grace of God, that is, by the law of nature, and that they lost free will in the first parent; which states that the patriarchs and prophets or every one of the highest saints, even before the times of the redemption, entered into paradise. All these I condemn as impious and replete with sacrileges.

But I declare that the grace of God is such that I always unite the striving and efforts of man with grace, and I proclaim that the liberty of the human will was not destroyed but enfeebled and weakened, and that he who is saved, was tried; and he who perished, could have been saved.

---

[1] ML 53, 683 ff.; Hfl sect. 212; Msi VII 1010 f.; Hrd II 809 f.

160b Also that Christ, God and Redeemer, as far as it pertained to the riches of His goodness, offered the price of death for all, and because He, who is the Savior of all, especially of the faithful, does not wish anyone to perish, *rich unto all who call upon him* [Rom. 10:12]. . . . Now by the authority of the sacred witnesses, which are found in great profusion through the extent of the Divine Scriptures, in accordance with the doctrine of our elders made clear by reason, I freely confess that Christ came also for the lost, because they perished although He did not will [it]. For it is not right that the riches of His boundless goodness and His divine benefits be confined to those only who seem to have been saved. For if we say that Christ extended assistance only to those who have been redeemed, we shall seem to absolve the unredeemed, who, it is established, had to be punished for having despised redemption. I declare further that by reason and through the regular succession of the centuries some have been saved by the law of grace, others by the law of Moses, others by the law of nature, which God has written in the hearts of all, in the expectation of the coming of Christ; nevertheless from the beginning of the world, they were not set free from the original slavery except by the intercession of the sacred blood. I acknowledge, too, that the eternal fires and the infernal flames have been prepared in advance for capital deeds, because divine judgment, which they deservedly incur, who have not believed these [truths] with their whole heart, justly follows those who persist in human sins. Pray for me, holy lords and apostolic fathers.

I, Lucius the priest, have signed this my letter with my own hand, and I affirm the things which are asserted in it, and I condemn what has been condemned.

Felix II (III) 483–492

ST. GELASIUS I 492–496

Errors Once Condemned, not to be Discussed Again [1]

[From the epistle "Licet inter varias" to Honorius,
Bishop of Dalmatia, July 28, 493 (?)]

161 (1) . . . [For] it has been reported to us, that in the regions of the Dalmatians certain men had disseminated the recurring tares of the Pelagian pest, and that their blasphemy prevails there to such a degree that they are deceiving all the simple by the insinuation of their deadly

---

[1] Th 321 f.; Jf 625 c. Add.; ML 59, 31 A; Msi VIII 20 E f.; BR(T) App. I
277 b f.

madness. . . . [But] since the Lord is superior, the pure truth of Catholic faith drawn from the concordant opinions of all the Fathers remains present. . . . (2) . . . What pray permits us to abrogate what has been condemned by the venerable Fathers, and to reconsider the impious dogmas that have been demolished by them? Why is it, therefore, that we take such great precautions lest any dangerous heresy, once driven out, strive anew to come [up] for examination, if we argue that what has been known, discussed, and refuted of old by our elders ought to be restored? Are we not ourselves offering, which God forbid, to all the enemies of the truth an example of rising again against ourselves, which the Church will never permit? Where is it that it is written: *Do not go beyond the limits of your fathers* [Prov. 22:28], and: *Ask your fathers and they will tell you, and your elders will declare unto you* [Deut. 32:7]? Why, accordingly, do we aim beyond the definitions of our elders, or why do they not suffice for us? If in our ignorance we desire to learn something, how every single thing to be avoided has been prescribed by the orthodox fathers and elders, or everything to be adapted to Catholic truth has been decreed, why are they not approved by these? Or are we wiser than they, or shall we be able to stand constant with firm stability, if we should undermine those [dogmas] which have been established by them? . . . .

The Authority and the Priesthood, and the Primacy of **161***
the Roman Pontiff. See *Kch n. 959*

The Canon of Sacred Scripture [1]

[From the epistle 42, or decretal "de recipiendis et non
recipiendis libris," in the year 495]

An enumeration of the canonical books similar to that, which we have 162
placed under DAMASUS [n. 84] *is accustomed in certain codices
to be set before the special Decree of GELASIUS. Nevertheless among
others it is no longer read in this place.* Of John the Apostle one
epistle, of the other John the priest two epistles, but, of the Apostle John
three epistles [cf. n. 84, 92, 96].

---

[1] ML 59, 157 A; Jf 700 c. Add.; cf. Th 44 ff.; Z II 261 ff.; EB n. 19 f.—the first part of this most celebrated "Decree of Gelasius" which Thiel, Turner, Ed. Schwartz and others attributed to Damasus, see n. 83 f. Turner and Ed. Schwartz think that even this part ought to be ascribed to DAMASUS (see n. 83 n.). Afterwards the same decree with a few additions necessary by reason of the time seems to have been repeated by HORMISDAS [n. 173 ff.] (Th 49).

Then follows:

The Primacy of the Roman Pontiff and the Patriarchal Sees [1]

[From the same epistle or "Decretal," in the year 495]

163 (1) After (all these) prophetic and evangelical and apostolic writings (which we have set forth above), on which the Catholic Church by the grace of God is founded, we have thought this (fact) also ought to be published, namely that, although the universal Catholic Church spread throughout the world has the one marriage of Christ, nevertheless the holy Roman Church has not been preferred to the other churches by reason of synodical decrees, but she has held the primacy by the evangelical voice of the Lord and Savior saying: *Thou art Peter, and upon this rock I will build my Church, and the gates of hell shall not prevail against it, and I will give unto thee the keys of the kingdom of heaven, and whatsoever thou shalt bind upon earth, it shall be bound also in heaven, and whatsoever thou shalt loose upon earth, it shall be loosed also in heaven* [Matt. 16:18 f.]. There is added also the association of the most blessed Paul the Apostle, the vessel of election, who not at a different time, as the heretics say, but at the one time, on one and the same day, while contending for the prize together with Peter was crowned with a glorious death under Caesar Nero in the City of Rome; and equally have they consecrated the above-mentioned Church of Rome to Christ the Lord and have raised it above all other cities in the whole world by their presence and their venerable triumph.

Accordingly the see of PETER the Apostle of the Church of Rome is first, *having neither spot, nor wrinkle, nor anything of this kind* [Eph. 5:27]. But the second see at Alexandria was consecrated in the name of blessed PETER by Mark his disciple and evangelist . . . but the third in honor is considered the see of the most blessed Apostle PETER at Antioch. . . .

The Authority of the Councils and the Fathers [2]

[From the same epistle or "Decretal"]

164 (2) And although *no one can lay a foundation other than that, which has been laid, which is Christ Jesus* [cf. I Cor. 3:11], nevertheless for the purpose of instruction the holy, that is, the Roman Church, does not

---

[1] C. H. Turner: *The Journal of Theological Studies* I (1900) 560. Th 454 ff.; ML 59, 159 B f.; Msi VIII 147 B ff.; BR (T) I 122 f.—There are those who even wish this part of the "Decree of Gelasius" to be attributed to DAMASUS, as for example, Turner and Schwartz: see n. 83 ff.; cf. Bar(Th) to 382 n. 19 (5, 492 b).

[2] Th 456 ff.; ML 59, 159 ff.

forbid these writings also, that is: the Sacred Synod of NICEA . . .
EPHESUS . . . [and] CHALCEDON . . . to be received after those
of the Old or New Testament, which we regularly accept.

(3) Likewise the works of blessed Caecilius Cyprian . . . [*and in the*   **165**
same way the works of Gregory Nazianzen, Basil, Athanasius, John
(Chrysostom), Theophilus, Cyril of Alexandria, Hilary, Ambrose, Augustine, Jerome, (and) Prosper *may be admitted*]. Also the epistle of
blessed LEO the Pope to Flavian [dogmatic, see n. 143 f.] . . . ; if
anyone argues concerning the text of this one even in regard to one iota,
and does not receive it in all respects reverently, let him be anathema.

Likewise it decrees that the works and treatises of all the orthodox
Fathers who in no [way] have deviated from the society of the holy
Roman Church . . . ought to be read.

Likewise, too, the decretal epistles, which the most blessed Popes . . .
have written, ought to be received with reverence.

Likewise the deeds of the holy martyrs . . . [which] with remarkable
caution are not read in the holy Roman Church . . . because the names
of those who wrote (them) are entirely unknown . . . lest an occasion
of light mockery arise. We, however, with the aforementioned Church
venerate with every devotion both all the martyrs and the glorious combats of those who are known to God rather than to men.

Likewise we acknowledge with all honor the lives of the Fathers, of
Paul, of Anthony, of Hilary, and of all the hermits, which however the
most blessed Jerome has described.

[Finally many other writings are enumerated and praised, with addition however:]

But . . . let the judgment of blessed Paul the Apostle lead the way:
"*Prove . . . all things, hold that which is good*" [I Thess. 5:21].

Other things which have been written or published by heretics or
schismatics, the Catholic and apostolic Roman Church in nowise receives. We believe that a few of these . . . ought to be appended.

The Apocrypha "which are not accepted" [1]

[From the same epistle or "Decretal"]

(4) [*After the long series of apocrypha has been presented, the Decree*   **166**
of Gelasius is thus concluded:] These and [writings] similar to these,
which . . . all the heresiarchs and their disciples, or the schismatics
have taught or written . . . , we confess have not only been rejected,
but also banished from the whole Roman Catholic and apostolic Church

---

[1] Th 469 ff.—Here is as it were the first "Index of forbidden books."

and with their authors and the followers of their authors have been condemned forever under the indissoluble bond of anathema.

The Remission of Sins [1]

[From the Tome of GELASIUS, "Ne forte," concerning the bond of the anathema, about the year 495]

167 (5) The Lord said that *to those sinning against the Holy Spirit, it should not be forgiven either here or in the future world* [Matt. 12:32]. But how many do we know that sin against the Holy Spirit, such as various heretics . . . who return to the Catholic faith, and here have received the pardon of their blasphemy, and have enjoyed the hope of gaining indulgence in the future? And not on this account is the judgment of the Lord not true, or will it be thought to be in any way weakened, since with respect to such men, if they continue to be thus, the judgment remains never to be relaxed at all; moreover, never because of such effects is it not imposed. Just as consequently is also that of the blessed John the Apostle: *There is a sin unto death: I do not say that prayer should be offered for this: and there is a sin not unto death: I do say that prayer should be offered for this* [I John 5:16, 17]. It is a sin unto death for those persisting in the same sin; it is not a sin unto death for those withdrawing from the same sin. For there is no sin for whose remission the Church does not pray, or which she cannot forgive those who desist from that same sin, or from which she cannot loose those who repent, since the power has been divinely given to her, to whom it was said: *Whatsoever you shall forgive upon earth* . . . [cf. John 20:23]; *"whatsoever you shall loose upon earth, shall be loosed also in heaven"* [Matt. 18:18]. In *whatsoever* all are [included], howsoever great they may be, and of whatsoever kind they may be, although the judgment of them nevertheless remains true, by which he is denounced [as] never to be loosed who continues in the course of them, but not after he withdraws from this same [course].

The Two Natures of Christ [2]

[From the Tome of GELASIUS, "Necessarium," on the two natures in Christ, (492–) 496]

168 (3) Although, I say, in accordance with this confession this must piously be believed regarding the conception of our Lord, although it can in no wise be explained, the *Eutychians* assert that there is one na-

---

[1] Th 562; Jf 701; ML 59, 105 A; Msi VIII 90 C f.
[2] Th 532 f.; Jf 670.

ture, that is, the divine; and *Nestorius* none the less mentions a single [nature], namely, the human; if we must maintain two against the Eutychians, because they draw out one, it follows that we should without doubt proclaim also in opposition to Nestorius who declares one, that not one, but rather two existed as a unity from His beginning, properly adding the human, contrary to Eutyches, who attempts to defend one, that is, the divine only, in order to show that the two, upon which that remarkable mystery rests, endure there; in opposition to *Nestorius* indeed, who similarly says one, namely, the human, we nevertheless substitute the divine, so that in like manner we hold that two against his *one* with a true division have existed in the plenitude of this mystery from the primordial effects of His union, and we refute both who chatter in a different way of *single* [natures], not each of them in regard to one only, but both in respect to the abiding possession of two natures: to wit, the human and divine, united from His beginning without any confusion or defect.

(4) For although one and the same person is the Lord Jesus Christ, and the whole God man and the whole man God, and whatever there is of humanity, the God man makes his own, and whatever there is of God, the man God possesses, nevertheless, granted that this remains a mystery and cannot be explained in any degree, thus the whole man continues to be what God is, [as?] the whole God continues to be whatever man is. . . .[1]

ST. ANASTASIUS II 496–498

The Ordinations of Schismatics [2]

[From the epistle (1) "Exordium Pontificatus mei" to
Anastasius Augustus, 496]

(7) According to the most sacred custom of the Catholic Church, let **169** the heart of your serenity acknowledge that no share in the injury from the name of Acacius should attach to any of these whom Acacius *the schismatic bishop* has baptized, or to any whom he has ordained priests or levites according to the canons, lest perchance the grace of the sacrament seem less powerful when conferred by an unjust [person]. . . . For if the rays of that visible sun are not stained by contact with any pollution when they pass over the foulest places, much less is the virtue

---

[1] See the whole tractate in Thiel, who then adds many "Testimonia veterum de duab. nat. in Christo" p. 541 ff.

[2] Th 620 f.; Jf 744 c. Add; Msi VIII 190 E f.; CIC Decr. I, 19, 8; Frdbg I 63; Rcht I 56.

of him who made that visible [sun] fettered by any unworthiness in the minister.

(8) Therefore, then, this person has only injured himself by wickedly administering the good. For the inviolable sacrament, which was given through him, held the perfection of its virtue for others.

The Origin of Souls and Original Sin [1]

[From the epistle "Bonum atque iucundum" to the
bishops of Gaul, August 23, 498]

170 (1) . . . *Certain heretics in Gaul think* that by a rational assertion they are persuaded of this, that just as the parents transmit bodies to the human race from material dregs, so also they bestow the vital principle of the living souls. . . . How (therefore) do they, contrary to God's will, with a very carnal mind think that the soul made to the image of God is diffused and insinuated by the mixture of human beings, when that very action by Him, who did this in the beginning, has not ceased even today, just as He Himself said: *My Father works up to this time, and I work* [cf. John 5:17]? Although likewise they ought to know what is written: *"He who lives unto eternity, created all things at the same time"* [Ecclus. 18:1]. If, then, previously according to the Scripture He placed order and reason by single species in every individual creature (potentially), which cannot be denied, and causally in the work pertaining to the creation of all things at the same time, after the consummation of which He rested on the seventh day, but now operates visibly in the work pertaining to the passage of time even up to the present,[2] let the sound doctrines then rest, namely, that He, who calls those, *which are not, just as those that are* [cf. Rom. 4:17], imparts souls.

(4) By the reasoning of which they think perhaps that they speak piously and well, in declaring that the souls are justly handed down by parents, since they are entangled with sins, they ought to be separated from them by this wise sundering, because nothing else can be transmitted by them than what has been brought to pass by their own evil presumption, that is, guilt and the punishment of sin, which their offspring have followed through the vine-branch [3] and clearly show so that men are born vicious and distorted. In this alone at any rate God is clearly seen to have no communion, (and) lest any fall into this necessary destruction, He has prevented it by an inborn terror of death and

---

[1] Th 634 ff.; Jf 751 c. Add; BR(T) App. I 342 b ff. There is doubt about the authenticity of this letter.

[2] St. Aug., *De Gen. ad litt.* VI, 4, 5 [ML 34, 341].

[3] It is evident that the substitution of this word here is different from that in which the "Traducianists" employed it.

has given warning of it. Therefore, through the vine-branch what is transmitted by the parents evidently appears, and what God has operated from the beginning even to the end, and what He is operating is shown.

St. Symmachus 498–514

ST. HORMISDAS 514–523

The Infallibility of the Roman Pontiff [1]

["Libellus professionis fidei" added to the epistle
"Inter ea quae" to the bishops of Spain, April 2, 517]

[Our] first safety is to guard the rule of the right faith and to deviate **171** in no wise from the ordinances of the Fathers; because we cannot pass over the statement of our Lord Jesus Christ who said: *"Thou art Peter and upon this rock I will build my church"* . . . [Matt. 16:18]. These [words] which were spoken, are proved by the effects of the deeds, because in the Apostolic See the Catholic religion has always been preserved without stain. Desiring not to be separated from this hope and faith and following the ordinances of the Fathers, we anathematize all heresies, especially the heretic Nestorius, who at one time was bishop of the city of Constantinople, condemned in the Council of EPHESUS by the blessed CELESTINE, Pope of the City of Rome,[2] and by the venerable man Cyril, high priest of the City of Alexandria. Similiarly anathematizing both Eutyches and Dioscorus of Alexandria condemned in the holy Synod of CHALCEDON [see n. 148] which we follow and embrace, which following the sacred Council of NICEA proclaimed the apostolic faith, we detest both Timothy the parricide, surnamed the Cat, and likewise his disciple and follower in all things, Peter of Alexandria. We condemn, too, and anathematize Acacius, formerly bishop of Constantinople, who was condemned by the Apostolic See, their con-

---

[1] Th 795 f.; Jf 788; W. Haacke, *Die Glaubensformel des Papstes Hormisdas in Acacianischen Schisma* [Rome 1939] p. 10 ff. This rule of faith, after it was proposed to the bishops who had been sharers of the Acacian schism, was subscribed to by all the bishops of the Orient, by the emperor Justinian, and by the Constantinopolitan patriarchs Epiphanius, John, Menna, and finally in the eighth ecumenical Synod (Constantinople IV), act. 1, by the Greek and Latin Fathers [cf. n. 1833 and Bar(Th) to 869 n. 19 (15, 153 a f.)]. That "Libellus" in almost the same words occurs in various epistles of that age. The formula placed above is that which HORMISDAS proposed to the bishops of Spain for receiving the oriental clerics into the communion of the Church. It almost agrees with that which John the Patriarch of Constantinople sent signed to HORMISDAS [CSEL 35, 608 ff.; cf. *ibid.*, 338, 340, 520, 800].

[2] Epistolae 22 ff. [ML 50, 537 ff.].

federate and follower, or those who remained in the society of their communion, because Acacius justly merited a sentence in condemnation like theirs in whose communion he mingled. No less do we condemn Peter of Antioch with his followers, and the followers of all mentioned above.

172　　Moreover, we accept and approve all the letters of blessed LEO the Pope, which he wrote regarding the Christian religion, just as we said before, following the Apostolic See in all things, and extolling all its ordinances. And, therefore, I hope that I may merit to be in the one communion with you, which the Apostolic See proclaims, in which there is the whole and the true and the perfect solidity of the Christian religion, promising that in the future the names of those separated from the communion of the Catholic Church, that is, those not agreeing with the Apostolic See, shall not be read during the sacred mysteries. But if I shall attempt in any way to deviate from my profession, I confess that I am a confederate in my opinion with those whom I have condemned. However, I have with my own hand signed this profession of mine, and to you, HORMISDAS, the holy and venerable Pope of the City of Rome, I have directed it.

The Canon, Primacy, Councils, Apocrypha [1]

[From epistle 125 or "Decretal . . . on divine
scriptures" in the year 520]

173　　*Besides those which are contained in the Decretal of Gelasius,* [n. 162] here, after the Synod of Ephesus "Constantinopolitana (I)" was also inserted: *then was added:* But even if any councils thus far have been instituted by the holy Fathers, we have decreed that after the authority of those four they must be both kept and received.

The Authority of St. Augustine

[From the epistle "Sicut rationi" to Possessor, August 13, 520] [2]

173a　　5. Yet what the Roman, that is the Catholic, Church follows and preserves concerning free will and the grace of God can be abundantly recognized both in the various books of the blessed Augustine, and especially [in those] to Hilary and Prosper, but the prominent chapters are contained in the ecclesiastical archives and if these are lacking there and you believe them necessary, we establish [them], although he who

---

[1] Th 932; Jf 862; ML 69, 166. This "Decretum HORMISDAE" he contends is a repetition and adaptation of the "Decretum Damaso—Gelasiani" (n. 162 ff.) Th. 51.

[2] ACOec T. IV, vol. II 46; CSEL 35, 700; ML 63, 493 A; Jf 850; Msi VIII 500 A.

diligently considers the words of the apostle, should know clearly what he ought to follow.

S<small>T</small>. J<small>OHN</small> I 523–526

ST. FELIX III 526–530

COUNCIL OF ORANGE II 529 [1]

Confirmed by Boniface II (against the Semipelagians)

Original Sin, Grace, Predestination [2]

To us, according to the admonition and authority of the Apostolic See, **173b** it has seemed just and reasonable that we should set forth to be observed by all, and that we should sign with our own hands, a few chapters transmitted [3] to us by the Apostolic See, which were collected by the ancient fathers from the volumes of the Sacred Scripture especially in this cause, to teach those who think otherwise than they ought. . . .

[I. Original sin] Can. 1. If anyone says that by the offense of Adam's **174** transgression not the whole man, that is according to body and soul, was changed for the worse [St. Augustine],[4] but believes that while the liberty of the soul endures without harm, the body only is exposed to corruption, he is deceived by the error of Pelagius and resists the Scripture which says: *"The soul, that has sinned, shall die"* [Ezech. 18:20]; and: *"Do you not know that to whom you show yourselves servants to obey, you are the servants of him whom you obey?"* [Rom. 6:16]; and: *Anyone is adjudged the slave of him by whom he is overcome* [II Pet. 2:19].

Can. 2. If anyone asserts that Adam's transgression injured him alone **175** and not his descendants, or declares that certainly death of the body only, which is the punishment of sin, but not sin also, which is the death of the soul, passed through one man into the whole human race, he will do an injustice to God, contradicting the Apostle who says: *Through one man sin entered in the world, and through sin death, and thus death*

---

[1] Orange in Gaul. This Council approved by Boniface II [see n. 200 a f.] obtained such authority in the Church that it is worthily held as an infallible rule. Cf. P. Lejay, "Le rôle théologique de S. Césaire d'Arles" [*Rev. d'hist. et litt. rel.* 10 (1905) 217 ff.].

[2] MGh Legum sectio III, Concilia T. I (Fr. Massen, 1903) 46 ff.; Msi VIII 712 B ff.; coll. Hfl II 726 ff. and H 221 ff. The canons 1–8, 13, 19, 21 and n. 199 by Brachiarius (s. 7) are referred to. *De Ecclesiasticis Dogmatibus* c. 38–49 [ML 83, 1236–1239]. On the origin of the canons, cf. *Rech. de Théol. anc. et méd.* 6 (1934) 120 ff. [M. Cappuyns].

[3] They seem to be n. 174–181; cf. Msi VIII 722 f.

[4] *De nupt. et concup.* 2, 34, 57 [ML 44, 471].

passed into all men, in whom all have sinned [Rom. 5:12; cf. St. Augustine].[1]

176   [II Grace] Can. 3. If anyone says that the grace of God can be bestowed by human invocation, but that the grace itself does not bring it to pass that it be invoked by us, he contradicts Isaias the Prophet, or the Apostle who says the same thing: *"I was found by those who were not seeking me: I appeared openly to those, who did not ask me"* [Rom. 10:20; cf. Isa. 65:1].

177   Can. 4. If anyone contends that in order that we may be cleansed from sin, God waits for our good will, but does not acknowledge that even the wish to be purged is produced in us through the infusion and operation of the Holy Spirit, he opposes the Holy Spirit Himself, who says through Solomon: *"Good will is prepared by the Lord"* [Prov. 8:35: LXX], and the Apostle who beneficially says: *"It is God, who works in us both to will and to accomplish according to his good will"* [Phil. 2:13].

178   Can. 5. If anyone says, that just as the increase [of faith] so also the beginning of faith and the very desire of credulity, by which we believe in Him who justifies the impious, and (by which) we arrive at the regeneration of holy baptism (is) not through the gift of grace, that is, through the inspiration of the Holy Spirit reforming our will from infidelity to faith, from impiety to piety, but is naturally in us, he is proved (to be) antagonistic to the doctrine of the Apostles, since blessed Paul says: *We trust, that he who begins a good work in us, will perfect it unto the day of Christ Jesus* [Phil. 1:6]; and the following: *It was given to you for Christ not only that you may believe in Him, but also, that you may suffer for Him* [Phil. 1:29]; and: *By grace you are made safe through faith, and this not of yourselves; for it is the gift of God* [Eph. 2:8]. For those who say that faith, by which we believe in God, is natural, declare that all those who are alien to the Church of Christ are in a measure faithful [cf. St. Augustine].[2]

179   Can. 6. If anyone asserts that without the grace of God mercy is divinely given to us when we believe, will, desire, try, labor, pray, watch, study, seek, ask, urge, but does not confess that through the infusion and the inspiration of the Holy Spirit in us, it is brought about that we believe, wish, or are able to do all these things as we ought, and does not join either to human humility or obedience the help of grace, nor agree that it is the gift of His grace that we are obedient and humble, opposes the Apostle who says: *What have you, that you have not received?* [I Cor. 4:7]; and: *By the grace of God I am that, which I am* [I Cor. 15:10; cf. St. Augustine and St. Prosper of Aquitaine].[3]

---

[1] Against two epistles of the Pelagians 4, 4–7 [ML 44, 611–614].

[2] *De praedest. Sanct.* [ML 44, 959–992].

[3] *De dono persev.* 23, 64; *Contra collat.* 2, 6 [ML 45, 1032 resp. 1804].

Can. 7. If anyone affirms that without the illumination and the in-   180
spiration of the Holy Spirit,—who gives to all sweetness in consenting
to and believing in the truth,—through the strength of nature he can
think anything good which pertains to the salvation of eternal life, as he
should, or choose, or consent to salvation, that is to the evangelical
proclamation, he is deceived by the heretical spirit, not understanding
the voice of God speaking in the Gospel: *"Without me you can do
nothing"* [John 15:5]; and that of the Apostle: *Not that we are fit to
think everything by ourselves as of ourselves, but our sufficiency is from
God* [II Cor. 3:5; cf. St. Augustine].[1]

Can. 8. If anyone maintains that some by mercy, but others by free   181
will, which it is evident has been vitiated in all who have been born of
the transgression of the first man, are able to come to the grace of
baptism, he is proved to be inconsistent with the true faith. For he asserts
that the free will of all was not weakened by the sin of the first man, or
assuredly was injured in such a way, that nevertheless certain ones have
the power without revelation of God to be able by themselves to seek the
mystery of eternal salvation. How contrary this is, the Lord Himself
proves, who testifies that not some, but no one can come to Him, except *whom the Father draws* [John 6:44], and just as he says to PETER:
*"Blessed art thou, Simon Bar-Jona, because flesh and blood hath not
revealed it to you, but my Father, who is in heaven"* [Matt. 16:17]; and
the Apostle: *No one can say Lord Jesus except in the Holy Spirit* [I Cor.
12:3; cf. St. Prosper].[2]

Can. 9. *"The assistance of God.* It is a divine gift, both when we think   182
rightly and when we restrain our feet from falsity and injustice; for as
often as we do good, God operates in us and with us, that we may work"
[St. Prosper].[3]

Can. 10. *The assistance of God.* The assistance of God ought to be   183
implored always even by those who have been reborn and have been
healed, that they may arrive at a good end, or may be able to continue
in good work [cf. St. Prosper].[4]

Can. 11. *"The obligation of vows.* No one would rightly vow anything   184
to God, unless he accepts from Him what he vows" [St. Prosper] [5] as it
is written: *And what we have received from your hand, we give to you*
[I Par. 29:14].

Can. 12. *"God loves such as us.* God loves us, such as we shall be by   185
His gift, not such as we are by our own merit" [St. Prosper].[6]

---

[1] *De gratia Christi* 25, 26–26, 27 [ML 44, 373 f.].

[2] *Contra collat.* 5, 13; 19, 55 (Sixth definition) [ML 45, 1806 f.; 1829].

[3] Thoughts taken from Augustine, *Sent.* 22 [ML 45, 1861].

[4] *Contra collat.* 11, 31–36 [ML 45, 1815 ff.].

[5] Thoughts taken from Augustine, *Sent.* 54 [ML 45, 1864]; from St. Augustine's
"City of God" 17, 4, 7 [ML 41, 530].

[6] Thoughts taken from St. Augustine, *Sent.* 56 [ML 45, 1864].

186   Can. 13. The restoration of free will. Freedom of will weakened in the first man cannot be repaired except through the grace of baptism; "once it has been lost, it cannot be restored except by Him by whom it could be given. Thus Truth itself says: *If the Son liberates you, then you will be truly free*" [John 8:36; St. Prosper].[1]

187   Can. 14. "No wretched person is freed from misery, however small, unless he is first reached by the mercy of God" [St. Prosper],[2] just as the Psalmist says: *Let thy mercy, Lord, speedily anticipate us* [Ps. 78:8]; and also: *"My God, His mercy will prevent me"* [Ps. 58:11].

188   Can. 15. "From that which God fashioned, Adam was changed by his own iniquity, but for the worse. From that which injustice has effected, the faithful (man) is changed by the grace of God, but for the better. Therefore, the former change was (the result) of the first transgression, the latter according to the Psalmist *is the change of the right hand of the Most High* [Ps. 76:11]" [St. Prosper].[3]

189   Can. 16. "Let no one glory in that which he seems to possess, as if he did not receive (it), or think that he has received (it) for this reason, because the sign appeared from without, either that it might be read, or sounded that it might be heard. For thus says the Apostle: *If justice* (is) *through the law, then Christ died for nothing* [Gal. 2:21]: *ascending on high he led captivity captive, he gave gifts to men* [Eph. 4:8; cf. Ps. 67:19]. Whoever has, has from Him, but whoever denies that he has from Him, either does not truly possess, or that, *which he possesses, is taken away from him* [Matt. 25:29]" [St. Prosper].[4]

190   Can. 17. "Worldly desire creates the fortitude of the Gentiles, but the *charity* of God, which *is diffused in our hearts,* not by free will, which is from us, but *by the Holy Spirit, which is given to us* [Rom. 5:5] produces the fortitude of the Christians" [St. Prosper].[5]

191   Can. 18. *"That grace is preceded by no merits.* A reward is due to good works, if they are performed; but grace, which is not due, precedes, that they may be done" [St. Prosper].[6]

192   Can. 19. *"That no one is saved except by God's mercy.* Even if human nature remained in that integrity in which it was formed, it would in no way save itself without the help of its Creator; therefore, since without the grace of God it cannot guard the health which it received, how

---

[1] Thoughts taken from St. Augustine, *Sent.* 152; from Augustine's "City of God" 14, 11, 1 [ML 45, 1871 f.; resp. 41, 418].

[2] *Ibid., Sent.* 211 [ML 45, 1876].

[3] *Ibid., Sent.* 225; from St. Aug., *Enarr. in ps.,* serm. 1, 2 [ML 45, 1878;—36, 841].

[4] *Ibid., Sent.* 259; from St. Aug., *De spiritu et litt.* 29, 50 [ML 45, 1880;—44 231].

[5] *Ibid., Sent.* 295; from St. Aug., *Opus imperf. c. Iulian.* 1, 83 [ML 45, 1884;—45, 1104].

[6] *Ibid., Sent.* 297; from St. Aug., *Opus imperf. c. Iulian.* 1, 133 [ML 45, 1885;—45, 1133].

without the grace of God will it be able to recover what it has lost?"
[St. Prosper].[1]

Can. 20. "*That without God man can do no good.* God does many good   **193**
things in man, which man does not do; indeed man can do no good that
God does not expect that man do" [St. Prosper].[2]

Can. 21. "*Nature and grace.* Just as the Apostle most truly says to those,   **194**
who, wishing to be justified in the law, have fallen even from grace:
If justice is from the law, then Christ died in vain [Gal. 2:21]; so it is
most truly said to those who think that grace, which the faith of Christ
commends and obtains, is nature: If justice is through nature, *then
Christ* died in vain. For the law was already here, and it did not justify;
nature, too, was already present, and it did not justify. Therefore, Christ
did not die in vain, that the law also might be fulfilled through Him,
who said: *I came not to destroy the law, but to fulfill (it)* [Matt. 5:17],
and in order that nature ruined by Adam, might be repaired by Him,
who said: He came *to seek and to save that which had been lost* [Luke
19:10]" [St. Prosper].[3]

Can. 22. "*Those things which are peculiar to men.* No one has any-   **195**
thing of his own except lying and sin. But if man has any truth and
justice, it is from that fountain for which we ought to thirst in this
desert, that bedewed by some drops of water from it, we may not falter
on the way" [St. Prosper].[4]

Can. 23. "*The good will of God and of man.* Men do their own will,   **196**
not God's, when they do what displeases God; but when they do what
they wish, in order to serve the divine will, even though willingly they
do what they do, nevertheless, it is the will of Him by whom what they
will is both prepared and ordered" [St. Prosper].[5]

Can. 24. "*The branches of the vine.* Thus there are *branches in the*   **197**
vine, not that they may bestow anything upon the vine, but that they may
receive from it the means by which they may live; so truly the vine is
in the branches, that it may furnish vital nourishment to these, not take
it from them. And by this it is an advantage to the disciples, not to
Christ, that each have Christ abiding in him, and that each abide in
Christ. For if the branch is cut off, another can sprout forth from the

---

[1] *Ibid., Sent.* 308; from St. Aug., *Ep.* 186, 11, 37 [ML 45, 1186;—33, 830].

[2] Thoughts taken from St. Augustine, *Sent.,* 312; from St. Aug., *Contra duas epist.
Pelag.* 2, 8, 21 [ML 45, 1886;—44, 586].

[3] *Ibid., Sent.* 315; from St. Augustine's *De gratia el libero arbitr.* 13, 25 [ML 45,
1887; —44, 896].

[4] *Ibid., Sent.* 323; from St. Augustine's *In Joann.* tract. 5, 1 [ML 45, 1887;—35,
1414].

[5] *Ibid., Sent.* 338; from St. Augustine's *In Joann.* tract. 19, 19 [ML 45, 1189;—
35, 1555].

living root; but that which has been cut off, cannot live without the root [John 15:5 ff.]" [St. Prosper].[1]

198   Can. 25. *"The love with which we love God.* Truly to love God is a gift of God. He Himself has granted that He be loved, who though not loved loves. Although we were displeasing we were loved, so that there might be produced in us [something] by which we might please. For the *Spirit* whom we love together with the Father and the Son *pours forth the charity* [of the Father and the Son] *in our hearts* [Rom. 5:5]" [St. Prosper].[2]

199   And thus according to the statements of the Holy Scriptures written above, or the explanations of the ancient Fathers, God being propitious, we ought to proclaim and to believe that through the sin of the first man free will was so changed and so weakened that afterwards no one could either love God as he ought, or believe in God, or perform what is good on account of God, unless the grace of divine mercy reached him first. Therefore, we believe that in the [case of] the just Abel, and Noe, and Abraham, and Isaac, and Jacob, and all the multitude of the ancient saints that illustrious faith which the Apostle Paul proclaims in their praise [Heb. 11], was conferred not by the good of nature, which had been given before in [the case of] Adam, but through the grace of God. Even after the coming of the Lord we know and likewise believe that this grace was not held in the free will of all who desired to be baptized, but was bestowed by the bounty of Christ, according to what has already been said often, and Paul the Apostle declares: *It has been given to you for Christ, not only, that you may believe in him, but also that you may suffer for him* [Phil. 1:29]; and this: *God, who has begun a good work in you, will perfect it even to the day of our Lord* [Phil. 1:6]; and this: *By grace you are made safe through faith, and this not of yourselves: for it is the gift of God* [Eph. 2:8]; and that which the Apostle says about himself: *I have obtained mercy, that I may be faithful* [I Cor. 7:25; I Tim. 1:13]; he did not say: "because I was," but: *"that I may be."* And that: *What have you, that you have not received?* [I Cor. 4:7]. And that: *Every good gift, and every perfect gift is from above, coming down from the Father of lights* [Jas. 1:17]. And that: *No one has anything, except it has been given him from above* [John 3:27]. Innumerable are the testimonies of the Sacred Scriptures which can be brought forward to prove grace, but they are passed over out of a desire for brevity; also because, in truth, more [proofs] will not profit those for whom a few do not suffice.

---

[1] *Ibid., Sent.,* 366; from St. Augustine's, *In Joann.* tract. 81, 1 [ML 45, 1893;— 35, 1841].

[2] *Ibid., Sent.* 370; from St. Augustine's, *In Joann.* tract. 102, 5 [ML 45, 1894;— 35, 1898].

[III. Predestination] According to the Catholic faith we believe this **200** also, that after grace has been received through baptism, all the baptized with the help and cooperation of Christ can and ought to fulfill what pertains to the salvation of the soul, if they will labor faithfully. We not only do not believe that some have been truly predestined to evil by divine power, but also with every execration we pronounce anathema upon those, if there are [any such], who wish to believe so great an evil. This, too, we profess and believe unto salvation, that in every good work we do not begin, and afterwards are helped by the mercy of God, but He Himself, with no preceding good services [on our part], previously inspires us with faith and love of Him, so that we may both faithfully seek the sacraments of baptism, and after baptism with His help be able to perform those [acts] which are pleasing to Him. So very clearly we should believe that the faith—so admirable—both of that famous thief, whom the Lord restored to his native land of paradise [Luke 23:43], and of Cornelius the centurion, to whom the angel of the Lord was sent [Acts 10:3], and of Zacheus, who deserved to receive the Lord Himself [Luke 19:6], was not from nature, but a gift of God's bounty.

BONIFACE II 530–532

Confirmation of the Council of Orange II [1]

[From the letter "Per filium nostrum" to Caesarius of Arles, January 25, 531].

1 . . . To your petition, which you have composed with laudable **200a** solicitude for the Faith, we have not delayed to give a Catholic reply. For you point out that some bishops of the Gauls, although they now agree that other goods are born of God's grace, think that faith, by which we believe in Christ, is only of nature, not of grace; and that (faith) has remained in the free will of man from Adam—which it is a sin to say— and is not even now conferred on individuals by the bounty of God's mercy; asking that, for the sake of ending the ambiguity, we confirm by the authority of the Apostolic See your confession, in which in the opposite way you explain that right faith in Christ and the beginning of all good will, according to Catholic truth, is inspired in the minds of individuals by the preceding grace of God.

2. And therefore, since many Fathers, and above all Bishop Augustine **200b** of blessed memory, but also our former high priests of the Apostolic See are proved to have discussed this with such detailed reasoning that there

---

[1] ML 65, 31 ff. (45, 1790 f.); Jf 881; Msi VIII 735 ff.; Bar(Th) to 529 n. 1 ff. (9, 375 ff.); Hfl II 737.

should be no further doubt in anyone that faith itself also comes to us from grace, we have thought that we should desist from a complex response, especially since according to these statements from the Apostle which you have arranged, in which he says: *I have obtained mercy, that I may be faithful* [I Cor. 7:25], and elsewhere: *It has been given to you, for Christ, not only that you may believe in Him, but also that you may suffer for Him* [Phil. 1:29], it clearly appears that the faith by which we believe in Christ, just as all blessings, comes to each man from the gift of supernal grace, not from the power of human nature. And this, too, we rejoice that your Fraternity, after holding a meeting with certain priests of the Gauls, understood according to the Catholic faith, namely in these matters in which with one accord, as you have indicated, they explained that the faith, by which we believe in Christ, is conferred by the preceding grace of God; adding also that there is no good at all according to God, that anyone can will, or begin, or accomplish without the grace of God, since our Savior Himself says: *Without Me you can do nothing"* [John 15:5]. For it is certain and Catholic that in all blessings of which the chief is faith, though we do not will it, the mercy of God precedes us, that we may be steadfast in faith, just as David the prophet says: *"My God, his mercy will prevent me"* [Ps. 58:11]; and again: *My mercy is with him* [Ps. 88:25]; and elsewhere: *His mercy follows me* [Ps. 22:6]. And similarly blessed Paul says: *Or did anyone first give to him, and will he be rewarded by him? Since from him, and through him, and in him are all things* [Rom. 11:35 f.]. So we marvel very much that those, who believe the contrary, are oppressed by the remains of an ancient error even to the point that they do not believe that we come to Christ by the favor of God, but by that of nature, and say that the good of that very nature, which is known to have been perverted by Adam's sin, is the author of our faith rather than Christ; and do not perceive that they contradict the statement of the master who said: *No one comes to me, except it be given to him by my Father* [John 6:44]; but they also oppose blessed Paul likewise, who exclaims to the Hebrews: *Let us run in the contest proposed to us, looking upon the author and finisher of faith, Jesus Christ* [Heb. 2:1 f.]. Since this is so, we cannot discover what they impute to the human will without the grace of God for belief in Christ, since Christ is the author and consummator of faith.

3. Therefore, we salute [you] with proper affection, and approve your confession written above in agreement with the Catholic rules of the Fathers.

JOHN II 533–535
"One of the Trinity Suffered," and the Blessed Virgin Mary, Mother of God [1]

[From epistle (3) "Olim quidem" to the senators of Constantinople, March, 534]

[Since] Justinian the Emperor, our son, as you have learned from the 201 tenor of his epistle, has signified that arguments have arisen with regard to these three questions, whether one of the Trinity can be called Christ and our God, that is, one holy person of the three persons of the Holy Trinity; whether the God Christ incapable of suffering because of deity endured [suffering in] the flesh; whether properly and truly <the Mother of God and the Mother of God's Word become incarnate from her> the Mother of our Lord God Christ ought to be called Mary ever Virgin. In these matters we have recognized the Catholic faith of the Emperor, and we show that this is clearly so from the examples of the prophets, and of the Apostles, or of the Fathers. For in these examples we clearly point out that one of the Holy Trinity is Christ, that is, one of the three persons of the Holy Trinity is a holy person or substance, which the Greeks call ὑπόστασις, [various witnesses are brought forward, as Gen. 3:22; I Cor. 8:6; the Nicene Creed; Proclus' letter to the Westerners, etc.]; but let us confirm by these examples that God truly endured in the flesh [Deut. 28:66; John 14:6; Matt. 3:8; Acts 3:15: 20, 28; I Cor. 2:8; Cyrilli anath. 12; LEO ad Flavium etc.].

We rightly teach that the glorious Holy ever Virgin Mary is acknowl- 202 edged by Catholic men [to be] both properly and truly the one who bore God, and the Mother of God's Word, become incarnate from her. For He Himself deigned from earliest times properly and truly to become incarnate and likewise to be born of the holy and glorious Virgin Mother. Therefore, because the Son of God was properly and truly made flesh from her and born of her, we confess that she was properly and truly

---

[1] ACOec Tom. IV, Vol. II, p. 206 ff.; Msi VIII 803 E ff.; Jf 885; Hrd II 1150 C ff.; ML 66, 20 C ff.; BR(T) App. I 496 a ff.—Certain monks at Scythian Constantinople announced the proposition: One of the Trinity suffered. For this reason it happened that they came under suspicion of the Monophysite heresy, and they set out to HORMISDAS, the Pope, to defend their own Roman orthodoxy. He did not give judgment in this matter, but in epistle 70 to Possessor [ML 63, 490 ff.] he showed that he bore the impudence of the Scythians with difficulty. But when other monks, namely the Acoemetae of Constantinople, attacked the same proposition out of a feeling of perversity, JOHN II approved the letter of Justinian the emperor, in which he accused them of the Nestorian heresy [ML 66, 17 f.], and in another letter directed to the Constantinopolitan senators he decreed as above regarding this matter.

the Mother of God made incarnate and born from her, and <properly indeed>, lest it be believed that the Lord Jesus received the name of God through honor or grace, as the foolish Nestorius thinks; but truly for this reason, lest it be believed that He took flesh in a phantasm or some other manner, not true flesh from the virgin, just as the impious Eutyches has asserted.

St. Agapetus I 535–536   St. Silverius 536–(537)–540

VIGILIUS (537) 540–555

Canons against Origen [1]

[From the Book against Origen of the Emperor Justinian, 543]

203   Can. 1. If anyone says or holds that the souls of men pre-existed, as if they were formerly minds and holy powers, but having received a surfeit of beholding the Divinity, and having turned towards the worse, and on this account having shuddered (apopsycheisas) at the love of God, in consequence being called souls (psychae) and being sent down into bodies for the sake of punishment, let him be anathema.

204   Can. 2. If anyone says and holds that the soul of the Lord pre-existed, and was united to God the Word before His incarnation and birth from the Virgin, let him be anathema.

205   Can. 3. If anyone says or holds that the body of our Lord Jesus Christ was first formed in the womb of the holy Virgin, and that after this God, the Word, and the soul, since it had pre-existed, were united to it, let him be anathema.

206   Can. 4. If anyone says or holds that the Word of God was made like all the heavenly orders, having become a Cherubim for the Cherubim, a Seraphim for the Seraphim, and evidently having been made like all the powers above, let him be anathema.

207   Can. 5. If anyone says or maintains that in resurrection the bodies of men are raised up from sleep spherical, and does not agree that we are raised up from sleep upright, let him be anathema.

208   Can. 6. If anyone says that the sky, and the sun, and the moon and

---

[1] Msi IX 533 A f.; Hrd III 279 C.—These canons, which the native synod under Menna the Patriarch edited in the year 543, the Supreme Pontiff VIGILIUS seems to have confirmed by his signature, as Cassiodorus testifies, *De inst. div. litt.* c. 2 [MG 70, 1111]: "It appears that he [evidently Origen] . . . has nevertheless in the present time been condemned anew by VIGILIUS the Pope, a most blessed man." [Cf. Fr. Diekamp, *Die originistischen Streitigkeiten* in 6. Jahrhundert und das 5. allg. Konzil. Münster: 1899, 46 ff.].

the stars, and the waters above the heavens are certain living and material [1] powers, let him be anathema.

Can. 7. If anyone says or holds that the Lord Christ in the future age 209 will be crucified in behalf of the demons, just as (He was) for the sake of men, let him be anathema.

Can. 8. If anyone says or holds that the power of God is limited, and 210 that He has accomplished as much as He has comprehended, let him be anathema.

Can. 9. If anyone says or holds that the punishment of the demons and 211 of impious men is temporary, and that it will have an end at some time, that is to say, there will be a complete restoration of the demons or of impious men, let him be anathema.

COUNCIL OF CONSTANTINOPLE II 553

Ecumenical V (concerning the three Chapters)

Ecclesiastical Tradition [2]

We confess that (we) hold and declare the faith given from the begin- 212 ning by the great God and our Savior Jesus Christ to the Holy Apostles, and preached by them in the whole world; which the sacred Fathers both confessed and explained, and handed down to the holy churches, and especially [those Fathers] who assembled in the four sacred Synods, whom we follow and accept through all things and in all things . . . judging as at odds with piety all things, indeed, which are not in accord with what has been defined as right faith by the same four holy Councils, we condemn and anathematize them.

Anathemas Concerning the Three Chapters [3]

[In part identical with "Homologia" of the Emperor, in the year 551]

Can. 1. If anyone does not confess that (there is) one nature or sub- 213 stance of the Father and of the Son and of the Holy Spirit, and one power and one might, and that the Trinity is consubstantial, one Godhead being worshipped in three subsistences, or persons, let such a one be anathema. For there is one God and Father, from whom are all things, and one Lord Jesus Christ, through whom are all things, and one Holy Spirit, in whom are all things.

---

[1] We should read: λογικάς, resp. "endowed with reason."

[2] Msi IX 201B; Hrd III 70 D f.; cf. Bar(TH) to 553 n. 20 ff. (10, 87 ff.).

[3] Msi IX 375 D ff.; coll. Hfl. II 892 ff.; Hrd III 193 D ff.

214   Can. 2. If anyone does not confess that there are two generations of the Word of God, the one from the Father before the ages, without time and incorporeally, the other in the last days, when the same came down from heaven, and was incarnate of the holy and glorious Mother of God and ever Virgin Mary, and was born of her, let such a one be anathema.

215   Can. 3. If anyone says that one [person] is the Word of God who performed miracles, and another the Christ who suffered, or says that God the Word was with Christ when He was born of a woman, or was with Him as one in another, but not that the same [person] is our Lord Jesus Christ, the Word of God, incarnate and made man, and that both the miracles and the sufferings which He voluntarily endured in the flesh were of the same person, let such a one be anathema.

216   Can. 4. If anyone says that the union of the Word of God with man was made according to grace, or according to operation, or according to dignity, or according to equality of honor, or according to authority or relation, or temperament, or power, or according to good will—as if man was pleasing to God the Word because it seemed well to Him regarding Himself, as [mad] Theodore declares; or according to homonymy, by which the Nestorians who call God the Word Jesus and Christ, and name the man separately Christ and the Son, and, though plainly speaking of two persons, pretend to speak of one person and one Christ according to name only, and honor, and dignity, and worship, but does not confess that the union of the Word of God to a body animated with a rational and intellectual soul, took place according to composition or according to subsistence, as the Holy Fathers have taught, and on this account one subsistence of Him, who is the Lord Jesus Christ, one of the Holy Trinity, let such a one be anathema. For, since the union is thought of in many ways, some following the impiety of Appollinaris and Eutyches, consenting to the disappearance of those who have come together, worship the union according to confusion; others thinking like Theodore and Nestorius, rejoicing in the division, introduce the accidental union. But the Holy Church of God, rejecting the impiety of each heresy, confesses the union of God's Word to the body according to composition, that is according to subsistence. For the union through composition in the mystery about Christ not only preserves unconfused what have come together but besides does not admit a division.

217   Can. 5. If anyone accepts the one subsistence of our Lord Jesus Christ as admitting the significance of many subsistences, and on this account attempts to introduce in the mystery about Christ two subsistences or two persons, and of the two persons introduced by him, he speaks of one person according to dignity, and honor, and adoration, just as mad Theodore and Nestorius have written, and he falsely accuses the sacred synod of Chalcedon of using the expression "of one subsistence" ac-

cording to this impious conception, but does not confess that the word of God was united to a body according to subsistence, and on this account one subsistence of Him, that is one person, and that thus, too, the holy Council of Chalcedon confessed one subsistence of our Lord Jesus Christ, let such a one be anathema. For, the Holy Trinity did not receive the addition of a person or of a subsistence when one of the Holy Trinity, God the Word, became incarnate.

Can. 6. If anyone says that the holy glorious ever-virgin Mary is **218** falsely but not truly the Mother of God; or (is the Mother of God) according to relation, as if a mere man were born, but as if the Word of God became incarnate [and of her] from her, but the birth of the man according to them being referred to the Word of God as being with the man when he was born, and falsely accuses the holy synod of Chalcedon of proclaiming the Virgin Mother of God according to this impious conception which was invented by Theodore; or, if anyone calls her the mother of the man or the mother of the Christ, as if the Christ were not God, but does not confess that she is exactly and truly the Mother of God, because God the Word, born of the Father before the ages, was made flesh from her in the last days, and that thus the holy Synod of Chalcedon confessed her (to be), let such a one be anathema.

Can. 7. If anyone speaking on two natures does not admit that our **219** Lord Jesus Christ is acknowledged as in the Divinity, in order that through this he may signify the distinction of the natures from which without confusion the marvelous union was born, and that the nature of the Word was not changed into that of the flesh, nor was the nature of the flesh changed into that of the Word (for each remains exactly as it is by nature, and the union has been made according to subsistence) but with a view to division by part; if he receives such an expression as this with regard to the mystery of Christ, or, acknowledging the number of the natures in the same one Lord our Jesus the Word of God made flesh, but does not accept the difference of these [natures] of which He is composed by reason alone, which is not destroyed by the union (for one is from both, and through one both), but uses number in such a way, as if each nature had its own subsistence separately, let such a one be anathema.

Can. 8. If anyone who agrees that a union has been born of the two **220** natures of divinity and humanity, or who says that one nature of the Word of God has been made flesh, does not accept these (expressions) as the holy Fathers have taught, namely, that of the nature of God and of that of man, the union having taken place according to subsistence, one Christ was produced; but from such words attempts to introduce one nature or substance of Godhead and humanity of Christ, let such be anathema. For, while asserting that the only-begotten Word is united according to subsistence, we do not say that any confusion of the natures with each other has been produced; but rather we believe that while each remains exactly as it is, the Word has been united to the flesh. Therefore, there is one Christ, God and man, the same [person being] consubstantial with the Father according to the Divinity, and the same consubstantial with us according to the humanity, for the Church of God equally detests and anathematizes those who divide or cut part by part, and those who confuse the mystery of the divine dispensation of Christ.

221 Can. 9. If anyone says that Christ is adored in two natures and as a result of this two (forms of) adoration are introduced, a special one for God the Word, and a special one for the man; or, if anyone with a view to the destruction of the humanity, or to the confusing of Divinity and the humanity, talking of one nature or substance of those who have come together, thus adores Christ but does not adore with one worship God the Word incarnate with His own flesh, just as the Church of God has accepted from the beginning, let such a one be anathema.

222 Can. 10. If anyone does not confess that Jesus Christ, our Lord, who was crucified in the flesh is true God, and Lord of glory, and one of the Holy Trinity, let such a one be anathema.

223 Can. 11. If anyone does not anathematize Arius, Eunomius, Macedonius, Apollinarius, Nestorius, Eutyches, and Origen, in company with their sinful works, and all other heretics, who have been condemned by the Holy Catholic and Apostolic Church and by the four holy synods above-mentioned, and those of the above-mentioned heretics who have thought or think likewise, and have remained in their impiety until the end, let such a one be anathema.

224 Can. 12. If anyone defends the impious Theodore of Mopsuestia, who said that one was God the Word, and another the Christ, who was troubled by the sufferings of the soul and the longings of the flesh, and who gradually separated Himself from worse things, and was improved by the progress of His works, and rendered blameless by this life, so as to be baptized as mere man in the name of the Father, and of the Son, and of the Holy Spirit, and on account of the baptism received the grace of the Holy Spirit, and was deemed worthy of adoption as a son, and according to the likeness of the royal image is worshipped in the person of God the Word, and after the resurrection became unchangeable in thoughts and absolutely unerring, and again the same impious Theodore having said that the union of God the Word with the Christ was such as the Apostle (spoke of) with reference to man and woman: *"They shall be two in one flesh"* [Eph. 5:31]; and in addition to his other innumerable blasphemies, dared to say that after the resurrection, the Lord when He breathed on His disciples and said: *"Receive ye the holy ghost"* [Isa. 20:22], did not give them the Holy Spirit, but breathed only

figuratively. But this one, too, said that the confession of Thomas on touching the hands and the side of the Lord, after the resurrection, *"My Lord and my God"* [Isa. 20:28], was not said by Thomas concerning Christ, but that Thomas, astounded by the marvel of the resurrection, praised God for raising Christ from the dead;

and what is worse, even in the interpretation of the Acts of the 225 Apostles made by him, the same Theodore comparing Christ to Plato and Manichaeus, and Epicurus, and Marcion, says that, just as each of those after inventing his own doctrine caused his disciples to be called Platonists, and Manichaeans, and Epicureans, and Marcionites, and Christ invented His own way of life and His own doctrines [caused His disciples] to be called Christians from Him; if, then, anyone defends the aforementioned most impious Theodore and his impious writings, in which he sets forth the aforesaid and other innumerable blasphemies against the great God and our Savior Jesus Christ, but does not anathematize him and his impious writings, and all those who accept or even justify him, or say that he preached in an orthodox manner, and those who wrote in his defense or in defense of his wicked writings, and those who think the same things, or have thought them up to this time and acquiesced in such heresy until their deaths, let such a one be anathema.

Can. 13. If anyone defends the impious writings of Theodoritus, which 226 are against the true faith and the first holy synod (held) in Ephesus, and (against) Cyril in the number of the saints, and his twelve chapters [see note 113 ff.], and defends all that he has written on behalf of the impious Theodore and Nestorius, and on behalf of others who think the same as the above-mentioned Theodore and Nestorius, and accepts them and their godlessness; and because of them calls the teachers of the Church impious, who believe in the union of the Word of God according to subsistence; and if he does not anathematize the said impious writings, and those who have thought or think similarly with these, and all those who have written against the true faith, or against Cyril among the saints and his twelve chapters, and have died in such impiety, let such a one be anathema.

Can. 14. If anyone defends the epistle which Ibas is said to have 227 written to Maris the Persian, which denied that God the Word became incarnate of the holy Mother of God and ever virgin Mary, was made man, but which said that a mere man was born of her, whom he calls a temple, so that God the Word is one, and the man another; and which slandered as a heretic Cyril in the number of the saints for having proclaimed the right faith of the Christians; and as one who wrote in a manner like that of the wicked Apollinaris, and blamed the first holy synod (held) in Ephesus, because it condemned Nestorius without an inquiry; and the same impious letter stigmatizes the twelve chapters of Cyril [see n. 113 ff.] in the number of the saints as wicked and opposed to the true faith, and justifies Theodore and Nestorius and their impious doctrines and writings; if anyone then defends the said letter, and does not anathematize it, and those who defend it, and say that it is true, or part of it is, and those who have written and are writing in its defense, or in defense of the wicked (ideas) included in it, and dare to justify it or the impiety included in it in the name of the holy Fathers, or of the holy synod (held) in Chalcedon, and have persisted in these (actions) until death, let such a one be anathema.

228   When then these things have been so confessed, which we have received from Holy Scripture, and from the teaching of the Holy Fathers, and from what was defined with regard to one and the same faith by the aforesaid four holy synods, and from that condemnation formulated by us against the heretics and their impiety, and besides, that against those who have defended or are defending the aforementioned three chapters, and who have persisted or do persist in their own error; if anyone should attempt to transmit [doctrines] opposed to those piously molded by us, or to teach or to write [them] if indeed he be a bishop, or belongs to the clergy, such a one, because he acts in a manner foreign to the sacred and ecclesiastical constitutions, shall be stripped of the office of bishop or cleric, but if he be a monk or a layman, he shall be anathematized.

PELAGIUS I 556-561
The Last Things [1]
[From *Fide PELAGII* in the letter "Humani generis"
to Childebert I, April, 557]

For I confess that all men from Adam, even to the consummation of   228a
the world, having been born and having died with Adam himself and his
wife, who were not born of other parents, but were created, the one from
the earth, the other [*al.: altera*], however, from the rib of the man [cf.
Gen. 2:7, 22], will then rise again and *stand before the judgment seat of
Christ, that every one may receive the proper things of the body, according as he has done, whether it be good or bad* [Rom. 14:10; II Cor. 5:10];
and indeed by the very bountiful grace of God he will present the just, as
vessels of mercy prepared beforehand for glory [Rom. 9:23], with the
rewards of eternal life; namely, they will live without end in the society
of the angels without any fear now of their own fall; the wicked, however, remaining by choice of their own with *vessels of wrath fit for
destruction* [Rom. 9:22], who either did not know the way of the Lord,
or knowing it left it when seized by various transgressions, He will give
over by a very just judgment to the punishment of eternal and inex-
tinguishable fire, that they may burn without end. This, then, is my
faith and hope, which is in me by the gift of the mercy of God, in
defense of which blessed PETER taught [cf. I Pet. 3:15] that we ought
to be especially ready to answer everyone who asks us for an accounting.

The Form of Baptism [2]
[From the epistle "Admonemus ut" to Gaudentius,
Bishop of Volterra, about the year 560]

There are many who assert that they are baptized in the name of   229
Christ alone with only one immersion. But the evangelical precept
which the very God, our Lord and Savior Jesus Christ, handed down
warns us to give each one holy baptism in the name of the Trinity and
with a triple immersion also, since our Lord Jesus Christ said to his
disciples: *Go, baptize all nations in the name of the Father and of the
Son and of the Holy Ghost* [Matt. 28:19].

If, in fact, those of the heretics, who are said to remain in places near

---

[1] MGh Epistles III (1892) 79; Jf 946; ML 69, 410 BC.
[2] CIC Decr. III, 4, 82 and 30; Frdbg I 1389 and 1370; Rcht I 1212 and 1196;
Jf 980.

your love, confess perchance that they have been baptized only in the name of the Lord, without any uncertainty of doubt you will baptize them in the name of the Holy Trinity, if they come to the Catholic faith. But if . . . by a clear confession it becomes evident that they have been baptized in the name of the Trinity, you will hasten to unite them to the Catholic faith, employing only the grace of reconciliation, in order that nothing other than what the evangelical authority orders may seem to be accomplished.

The Primacy of the Roman Pontiff [1]

[From epistle (26) "Adeone te" to a certain bishop
(John ?), about the year 560]

230 Has the truth of your Catholic mother so failed you, who have been placed in the highest office of the priesthood, that you have not at once recognized yourself as a schismatic, when you withdrew from the apostolic sees? Being appointed to preach the Gospel to the people, had you not even read that the Church was founded by Christ our Lord upon the chief of the Apostles, so that *the gates of hell* might not be able *to prevail against it* [cf. Matt. 16:18]? If you had read this, where did you believe the Church to be outside of him in whom alone are clearly all the apostolic sees? To whom in like measure as to him, who had received *the keys,* has the power *of binding and of loosing* been granted [cf. Matt. 16:19]? But for this reason he gave first to him alone, what he was about to give also to (in) all, so that, according to the opinion of blessed Cyprian the martyr who explains this very thing, the Church might be shown to be one. Why, therefore, did you, already dearest in Christ, wander away from your portion, or what hope did you have for your salvation?

(JOHN III 561–574)

COUNCIL OF BRAGA [2] II 561

Anathemas against Heretics, especially the Priscillianists [3]

231 1. If anyone does not confess that the Father, and the Son, and the Holy Spirit (are) three persons of one substance, and virtue, and power,

---

[1] From Coll. Brit. Löwenfeld, *Epistolae Pontificum Romanorum ineditae,* Lipsiae: 1885, n. 28, p. 15 f.; Jf 998 c. Add.

[2] Braga, then in Spain but now in Portugal.

[3] Msi IX 774 C ff.; coll. KAnt 36 ff. and H 230 ff.; Hrd III 348 B ff.; Hfl III 15 ff.—Concerning the rules of the faith of the church of Spain and their connection with this council, see KAnt 25 ff. and 36 ff.—Almost with the same words and

just as the Catholic and apostolic Church teaches, but says there is only one and a solitary person, so that He Himself is the Father who is the Son, and also He Himself is the Paraclete, the Spirit, just as Sabellius and Priscillian have asserted, let him be anathema.

2. If anyone introduces some other names of the Godhead in addition to the Holy Trinity, because, as he says, there is in the Godhead himself a Trinity of the Trinity, just as the Gnostics and Priscillians have stated, let him be anathema. **232**

3. If anyone says that the Son of God our Lord did not exist before He was born of the Virgin, just as Paul of Samosata and Photinus and Priscillian have said, let him be anathema. **233**

4. If anyone does not truly honor the birthday of Christ according to the flesh, but pretends that he honors (it), fasting on the very day and on the Lord's Day, because, like Cerdon, Marcion, Manichaeus, and Priscillian, he does not believe that Christ was born in the nature of man, let him be anathema. **234**

5. If anyone believes, as Manichaeus and Priscillian have said, that human souls or angels have arisen from the substance of God, let him be anathema. **235**

6. If anyone says that human souls first sinned in the heavenly habitation and in view of this were hurled down into human bodies on earth, as Priscillian has affirmed, let him be anathema. **236**

7. If anyone says that the devil was not first a good angel made by God, and that his nature was not a work of God, but says that he came forth from darkness, and does not have any author of himself, but is himself the origin and substance of evil, as Manichaeus and Priscillian have said, let him be anathema. **237**

8. If anyone believes that the devil made some creatures in the world and by his own authority the devil himself causes thunder and lightning, and storms and spells of dryness, just as Priscillian has asserted, let him be anathema. **238**

9. If anyone believes that human souls [*al.* souls and human bodies] are bound by a fatal sign [*al.* by fatal stars], just as the pagans and Priscillian have affirmed, let him be anathema. **239**

10. If anyone believes that the twelve signs or stars, which the astrologers are accustomed to observe, have been scattered through single members of the soul or body, and say that they have been attributed to the names of the Patriarchs, just as Priscillian has asserted, let him be anathema. **240**

11. If anyone condemns human marriage and has a horror of the **241**

---

order the errors rejected by this council stand condemned in a letter of LEO the Great to Turibius, Bishop of Asturia [Astorga in Spain] Jf 412; ML 54, 680 ff.; Msi V 1290 ff. (cf. n. 21 ff.).

procreation of living bodies, as Manichaeus and Priscillian have said, let him be anathema.

242   12. If anyone says that the formation of the human body is a creation of the devil, and says that conceptions in the wombs of mothers are formed by the works of demons, and for this reason does not believe in the resurrection of the body, just as Manichaeus and Priscillian have said, let him be anathema.

243   13. If anyone says that the creation of all flesh is not the work of God, but belongs to the wicked angels, just as Priscillian has said, let him be anathema.

244   14. If anyone considers the foods of the flesh unclean, which God has given for the use of men; and, not for the affliction of his body, but as if he thought it unclean, so abstains from these that he does not taste vegetables cooked with meats, just as Manichaeus and Priscillian have said, let him be anathema.

[15 and 16 consider only ecclesiastical discipline].

245   17. If anyone reads the Scriptures, which Priscillian has distorted according to his own error, or Dictinius's treatises, which Dictinius himself wrote before he was converted; or whatsoever writings of the heretics under the name of the Patriarchs, of the Prophets, or of the Apostles they have devised in agreement with their own error, and follows or defends their impious creations, let him be anathema.

BENEDICT I 575–579

PELAGIUS II 579–590

The Unity of the Church [1]

[From epistle (1) "Quod ad dilectionem" to the schismatic bishops of Istria, about 585]

246   (For) you know that the Lord proclaims in the Gospel: *Simon, Simon, behold Satan has desired to have you, that he might sift you as wheat: but I have asked the Father for thee, that thy faith fail not; and thou being once converted, confirm thy brethren* [Luke 22:31 f.].

Consider, most dear ones, that the Truth could not have lied, nor will the faith of PETER be able to be shaken or changed forever. For although the devil desired to sift all the disciples, the Lord testifies that He Himself asked for PETER alone and wished the others to be confirmed by him; and to him also, in consideration of a greater love which

---

[1] ACOec Tom. I, vol. IV, pars 2, 105 ff.; Msi IX 892 A f.; Jf 1054; ML 72, 707 B ff.; Hrd III 414 E ff.

he showed the Lord before the rest, was committed the care *of feeding the sheep* [cf. John 21:15 ff.]; and to him also He handed over *the keys of the kingdom of heaven,* and upon him He promised *to build his Church,* and He testified that *the gates of hell would* not prevail against it [cf. Matt. 16:16 ff.]. But, because the enemy of the human race even until the end of the world does not abstain from sowing cockle [Matt. 13:25] over the good seed in the Church of the Lord, and therefore, lest perchance anyone with malignant zeal should by the instigation of the devil presume to make some alterations in and to draw conclusions regarding the integrity of the faith; and (lest) by reason of this your minds perhaps may seem to be disturbed, we have judged it necessary through our present epistle to exhort with tears that you should return to the heart of your mother the Church, and to send you satisfaction with regard to the integrity of faith. . . .

[*The faith of the Synods of* NICEA, CONSTANTINOPLE I, EPHESUS I, *and especially of* CHALCEDON, *and likewise of the dogmatic epistle of* LEO *to Flavian having been confirmed, he proceeds thus:*]

If anyone, however, either suggests or believes or presumes to teach contrary to this faith, let him know that he is condemned and also anathematized according to the opinion of the same Fathers. . . . Consider (therefore) the fact that whoever has not been in the peace and unity of the Church, cannot have the Lord [Gal. 3:7]. . . .

The Necessity of Union with the Church [1]

[From epistle (2) "Dilectionis vestrae" to the schismatic
bishops of Istria, about 585]

. . . Do not (therefore) because of a love of ostentation, which is al-   247
ways next to pride, remain in the vice of obstinacy; since in the day of judgment no one can excuse himself. . . .

For although it is evident from the word of the Lord Himself in the Sacred Gospel [cf. Matt. 16:18] where the Church is established, let us hear nevertheless what the blessed Augustine, mindful of the opinion of the same Lord, has explained. For he says that the Church of God is established among those who are known to preside over the apostolic sees, through the succession of those in charge, and whoever separates himself from the communion or authority of these sees, is shown to be in schism. And following additional remarks (he says): "If you are put outside, for the name of Christ you will also die. Suffer for Christ among

---

[1] ACOec IV, II, 108 ff.; Msi IX 897 D ff.; Jf 1055; ML 72, 712 D ff.; Hrd III 419 B ff.

the members of Christ; clinging to the body, fight for the head." But the blessed Cyprian . . . among other things, says the following: "The beginning starts from unity, and the primacy is given to PETER, so that the Church and the chair of Christ may be shown (to be) one: and they are all shepherds, but the flock, which is fed by the Apostles in unanimous agreement, is shown to be one." [1] And after a few (remarks he adds): "Does he who does not hold this unity of the Church believe that he has the faith? Does he who deserts and resists the chair of PETER, on which the Church was founded, have confidence that he is in the Church?" Likewise after other remarks (he asserts): "They cannot arrive at the reward of peace, because they disrupt the peace of the Lord by the fury of discord. . . . Those who were not willing to be at agreement in the Church of God, cannot remain with God; although given over to flames and fires, they burn, or thrown to wild beasts, they lay down their lives, there will not be [for them] that crown of faith, but the punishment of faithlessness, not a glorious result (of religious virtue), but the ruin of despair. Such a one can be slain, he cannot be crowned. . . . For the crime of schism is worse than that which they [commit] who have offered sacrifice, who, nevertheless, having been disposed to penance for their sins prayed to God with the fullest satisfaction. In this case the Church is sought and solicited; in the other the Church is opposed. So in this case he who has fallen, has injured only himself; in the other, who attempts to cause a schism deceives many by dragging (them) with himself. In this case there is the loss of one soul; in the other there is danger to many. Certainly the one knows that he has sinned and laments and bewails (it); the other puffed up with pride in his sin and pluming himself on the sins themselves, separates sons from their mother, seduces the sheep from the shepherds, disturbs the sacraments of God, and, whereas the former having stumbled sinned once, the latter sins daily. Lastly although the lapsed, if afterwards he acquired martyrdom, is able to secure the promises of the kingdom; if the other is slain outside of the Church, he cannot attain to the rewards of the Church." [2]

---

[1] *De unit.* 4 [ML 4,500; but, cf. CSEL 3, 1, 212 f.].
[2] *De unit.* 11, 14, 19, [ML 4, 511, 514; CSEL 3, 1, 213, 223, 227].

ST. GREGORY I, THE GREAT 590–604

The Knowledge of Christ (against the Agnoetae) [1]

[From the epistle "Sicut aqua frigida" to Eulogius,
Patriarch of Alexandria, August, 600]

(But) concerning that which has been written: *That neither the Son,*   248
nor the angels know the day and the hour [cf. Mark 13:32], indeed,
your holiness has perceived rightly, that since it most certainly should
be referred not to the same son according to that which is the head, but
according to his body which we are . . . , He [Augustine] also says
. . . that this can be understood of the same son, because omnipotent
God sometimes speaks in a human way, as he said to Abraham: *Now I*
know that thou fearest God [Gen. 22:12], not because God then knew
that He was feared, but because at that time He caused Abraham to
know that he feared God. For, just as we say a day is happy not because
the day itself is happy, but because it makes us happy, so the omnipotent
Son says He does not know the day which He causes not to be known,
not because He himself is ignorant of it, but because He does not permit
it to be known at all. Thus also the Father alone is said to know, because
the Son (being) consubstantial with Him, on account of His nature,
by which He is above the angels, has knowledge of that, of which the
angels are unaware. Thus, also, this can be the more precisely understood
because the Only-begotten having been incarnate, and made perfect man
for us, in His human nature indeed did know the day and the hour of
judgment, but nevertheless He did not know this from His human nature. Therefore, that which in (nature) itself He knew, He did not
know from that very (nature), because God-made-man knew the day
and hour of the judgment through the power of His Godhead. . . .
Thus, the knowledge which He did not have on account of the nature of
His humanity—by reason of which, like the angels, He was a creature—
this He denied that He, like the angels, who are creatures, had. Therefore (as) God and man He knows the day and the hour of judgment; but
on this account, because God is man. But the fact is certainly manifest
that whoever is not a Nestorian, can in no wise be an Agnoeta. For
with what purpose can he, who confesses that the Wisdom itself of God
is incarnate say that there is anything which the Wisdom of God does
not know? It is written: *In the beginning was the Word, and the*
Word was with God, and the Word was God. . . . *All things were*
made by him [John 1:13]. If *all,* without doubt also the day of judg-

[1] ML 77, 1097 A f.; Jf 1790.

ment and the hour. Who, therefore, is so foolish as to presume to assert that the Word of the Father made that which He does not know? It is written also: *Jesus knowing, that the Father gave him all things into his hands* [John 13:3]. If all things, surely both the day of judgment and the hour. Who, therefore, is so stupid as to say that the Son has received in His hands that of which He is unaware?

Baptism and the Orders of Heretics [1]

[From the epistle "Quia charitati" to the bishops of
Spain, about June 22, 601]

249   From the ancient institution of the Fathers we have learned that those who are baptized in the name of the Trinity, although amid heresy, whenever they return to the holy Church, may be recalled to the bosom of their mother the Church either with the anointing of chrism, or the imposition of hands, or with a profession of faith alone . . . , because the holy baptism, which they received among the heretics, at that time restores the power of cleansing in them when they have been united to the holy faith and the heart of the universal Church. But these heretics who are not baptized in the name of the Trinity . . . , whenever they come to the holy Church, are baptized, because whatever those placed in error received not in the name of the Trinity—was not baptism. Nor can that baptism itself, which, as has been said, had not been given in the name of the Trinity, be called repeated.

Therefore . . . without any hesitation your holiness may receive in your assembly all whoever return from the perverse error of Nestorius, their own orders preserved for them so that, while . . . through gentleness you make no opposition or difficulty in regard to their own orders, you may snatch them from the mouth of the ancient enemy.

The Time of the Hypostatic Union [2]

[From the same epistle to the bishops of Spain]

250   (But) the flesh was not first conceived in the womb of the Virgin and afterwards the divinity came into the flesh; but, as soon as the Word came into the womb, directly, the power of His own nature being preserved, the Word was made flesh. . . . Nor was He conceived first and afterwards anointed; but that He was conceived of the Holy Spirit from the flesh of the Virgin, was anointed by the Holy Spirit, this was.

---

[1] ML 77, 1205 A ff.; Jf 1844; CIC Decr. III, 4, 44 and 84; Frbg I 1380, 1390.
[2] ML 77, 1207 D f.

Sabianus 604–606   St. Boniface IV 608–615
Boniface III 607   St. Deusdedit 615–618
          Boniface V 619–625

HONORIUS I 625-638

Two Wills and Operations in Christ [1]

[From the epistle (1) "Scripta fraternitatis vestrae"
to Sergius, Patriarch of Constantinople in the year 634]

. . . With God as a leader we shall arrive at the measure of the right 251
faith which the apostles of the truth have extended by means of the
slender rope of the Sacred Scriptures. Confessing that the Lord *Jesus
Christ, the mediator of God and of men* [I Tim. 2:5], has performed
divine (works) through the medium of the humanity naturally [gr.
hypostatically] united to the Word of God, and that the same one performed human works, because flesh had been assumed ineffably and
particularly by the full divinity [gr. in—] distinctly, unconfusedly, and
unchangeably . . . so that truly it may be recognized that by a wonderful design [passible flesh] is united [to the Godhead] while the differences of both natures marvelously remain. . . . Hence, we confess one
will of our Lord Jesus Christ also, because surely our nature, not our
guilt was assumed by the Godhead, that certainly, which was created
before sin, not that which was vitiated after the transgression. For
Christ . . . was conceived of the Holy Spirit without sin, and was also
born of the holy and immaculate Virgin mother of God without sin,
experiencing no contagion of our vitiated nature. . . . For there was no
other law in His members, or a will different from or contrary to the
Savior, because He was born above the law of the human nature. . . .
There are extensive works of sacred literature pointing out very clearly
that the Lord Jesus Christ, the Son and the Word of God, *by whom all
things were made* [John 1:3], is Himself the one operator of divinity
and of humanity. But whether on account of the works of divinity and
of humanity, one or two operations ought to be said or understood to be

---

[1] Msi XI 538 D f. and 579 D ff.; Jf 2018 and 2024 c. Add.; Hrd III 1319 B ff.
and 1351 E ff.; ML 80, 471 B ff. and 475 A. This text is the Latin version of the
Greek version. More from this and the following epistle in Kch 1057 ff.

derived, such (questions) should not concern us, leaving them to the grammarians, who are accustomed to sell to children words acquired by derivation. For in sacred literature we have perceived that the Lord Jesus Christ and His Holy Spirit operated not one operation or two, but we have learned that (He) operated in many ways.

[From the epistle (2) "Scripta dilectissimi filii" to the same Sergius]

252   ... So far as pertains to ecclesiastical doctrine, what we ought to hold or to preach on account of the simplicity of men and the inextricable ambiguities of questions (which) must be removed . . . , is to define not one or two operations in the mediator of God and of men, but both natures united in one Christ by a natural union, when we should confess those operating with the participation of the other and the operators, both the divine, indeed, performing what is of God, and the human performing what is of the flesh; teaching [that they operate] neither separately, nor confusedly, nor interchangeably, the nature of God changed into man, and the human changed into God; but confessing the complete differences of the natures. . . . Therefore, doing away with . . . the scandal of the new invention, we, when we are explaining, should not preach one or two operations; but instead of one operation, which some affirm, we should confess one operator, Christ the Lord, in both natures; and instead of two operations—when the expression of two operations has been done away with—rather of the two natures themselves, that is of divinity and of the flesh assumed, in one person, the Only-begotten of God the Father unconfusedly, inseparably, and unchangeably performing their proper (works) with us.

[*More from this epistle see Kch. n. 1065–1069*]

Severinus 640

JOHN IV 640–642

The Meaning of the Words of HONORIUS about the Two Wills [1]

[From the epistle "Dominus qui dixit" to Constantius the Emperor, 641]

253   ... *One* and He alone is without sin, *the mediator of God and of men,* the man Christ Jesus [cf. I Tim. 2:5] who was conceived and born *free among* the dead [Ps. 87:6]. Thus in the dispensation of His sacred

---

[1] Msi X 684 A ff.; Jf 2042; Hrd III 611 D ff.; ML 80, 604 B ff.

flesh, He never had two contrary wills, nor did the will of His flesh resist the will of His mind. . . . Therefore, knowing that there was no sin at all in Him when He was born and lived, we fittingly say and truthfully confess one will in the humanity of His sacred dispensation; and we do not preach two contrary wills, of mind and of flesh, as in a pure man, in the manner certain heretics are known to rave. In accord with this method, then, our predecessor (already mentioned) [HONORIUS] is known to have written to the (aforenamed) Sergius the Patriarch who was asking questions, that in our Savior two contrary wills did not exist internally, that is, in His members, since He derived no blemish from the transgression of the first man. . . . This usually happens, that, naturally where there is a wound, there medicinal aid offers itself. For the blessed Apostle is known to have done this often, preparing himself according to the custom of his hearers; and sometimes indeed when teaching about the supreme nature, he is completely silent about the human nature, but sometimes when treating of the human dispensation, he does not touch on the mystery of His divinity. . . . So, my aforementioned predecessor said concerning the mystery of the incarnation of Christ, that there were not in Him, as in us sinners, contrary wills of mind and flesh; and certain ones converting this to their own meaning, suspected that He taught one will of His divinity and humanity which is altogether contrary to the truth. . . .

THEODORUS I 642–649

ST. MARTIN I 649–653 (655)

THE LATERAN COUNCIL 649

(Against the Monothelites)

The Trinity, the Incarnation, etc.[1]

Can. 1. If anyone does not confess properly and truly in accord with **254** the holy Fathers that the Father, and the Son, and the Holy Spirit [are a] Trinity in unity, and a unity in Trinity, that is, one God in three subsistences, consubstantial and of equal glory, one and the same Godhead, nature, substance, virtue, power, kingdom, authority, will, operation of the three, uncreated, without beginning, incomprehensible, im-

---

[1] Hrd III 922 A ff.; Msi X 1151 A ff.; coll. Hfl III 223 ff. and H 238 ff.; cf. Bar(Th) about 649, n. 2 ff. (11, 388 ff.), Can.: n. 22 f. (11, 392 ff.). These canons are recognized by AGATHO with all the western synods in a letter given to the emperors on the occasion of the ecumenical Synod VI CONSTANTINOPLE III): see below n. 288. Cf. Zeitschr. f. Kirchengesch. 51 (1932) 75 ff. [E. Caspar].

mutable, creator and protector of all things, let him be condemned [see n. 78–82, 213].

255   Can. 2. If anyone does not properly and truly confess in accordance with the Holy Fathers that God the Word himself, one of the holy and consubstantial and venerable Trinity, descended from heaven, and was incarnate of the Holy Spirit and Mary ever Virgin, and was made man, was crucified in the flesh, voluntarily suffered for us and was buried, and arose again on the third day, and ascended into heaven, and sits at the right hand of the Father, and will come again with paternal glory, with his flesh assumed by Him and intellectually animated, to judge the living and the dead, let him be condemned [see n. 2, 6, 65, 215].

256   Can. 3. If anyone does not properly and truly confess in accord with the holy Fathers, that the holy Mother of God and ever Virgin and immaculate Mary in the earliest of the ages conceived of the Holy Spirit without seed, namely, God the Word Himself specifically and truly, who was born of God the Father before all ages, and that she incorruptibly bore [Him?], her virginity remaining indestructible even after His birth, let him be condemned [see n. 218].

257   Can. 4. If anyone does not properly and truly confess according to the holy Fathers, two nativities of our one Lord and God Jesus Christ, as before the ages from God and the Father incorporally and eternally, and as from the holy ever Virgin, Mother of God Mary, corporally in the earliest of the ages, and also one and the same Lord of us and God, Jesus Christ, consubstantial with man and His Mother according to the human nature, and the same one passible in the flesh, and impassible in the Godhead, circumscribed in the body, uncircumscribed in Godhead, the same one uncreated and created, terrestial and celestial, visible and intelligible, comprehensible and incomprehensible, that all mankind which fell under sin, might be restored through the same complete man and God, let him be condemned [see n. 214].

258   Can. 5. If anyone does not properly and truly confess according to the holy Fathers one incarnate nature of God the Word, in this way, that our substance is called incarnate perfectly in Christ God and without diminution, [see n. 220] provided substance is signified without sin, let him be condemned.

259   Can. 6. If anyone does not properly and truly confess according to the holy Fathers, that from two and in two natures substantially united unconfusedly and undividedly there is one and the same Lord and God, Jesus Christ, let him be condemned [see n. 148].

260   Can. 7. If anyone does not properly and truly confess according to the holy Fathers, the substantial difference of the natures preserved in Him, unconfusedly and undividedly, let him be condemned [see n. 148].

261   Can. 8. If anyone does not properly and truly confess according to the

holy Fathers the substantial union of the natures recognized in Him undividedly and unconfusedly, let him be condemned [see n. 148].

Can. 9. If anyone does not properly and truly confess according to the holy Fathers, the natural properties of His Godhead and of His humanity preserved without diminution and without injury in Him, let him be condemned. **262**

Can. 10. If anyone does not properly and truly confess according to the holy Fathers two wills of one and the same Christ our God, united uninterruptedly, divine and human, and on this account that through each of His natures the same one of His own free will is the operator [Editors add: operator] of our salvation, let him be condemned. **263**

Can. 11. If anyone does not properly and truly confess according to the holy Fathers two operations of one and the same Christ our God uninterruptedly united, divine and human, from this that through each of His natures He naturally is the same operator of our salvation, let him be condemned. **264**

Can. 12. If anyone according to the wicked heretics confesses one will and one operation of Christ our God, to the destruction of the confession of the holy Fathers and to the denial of the same dispensation of our Savior, let him be condemned. **265**

Can. 13. If anyone according to the wicked heretics, contrary to the doctrine of the Fathers, confesses both one will and one operation, although two wills and two operations, divine and human, have been substantially preserved in union in Christ God, and have been piously preached by our holy Fathers, let him be condemned. **266**

Can. 14. If anyone according to the wicked heretics, together with one will and one operation, which is impiously confessed by the heretics, denies and rejects both two wills and in like manner two operations, that is, divine and human, which are preserved in unity in the very Christ God, and are proclaimed in regard to Him in an orthodox manner by the holy Fathers, let him be condemned. **267**

Can. 15. If anyone according to the wicked heretics unwisely accepts the divine—human operation, which the Greeks call θεανδρικήν, as one operation, but does not confess that it is twofold according to the holy Fathers, that is, divine and human, or that the new application itself of the word "divine—human" which has been used is descriptive of one, but not demonstrative of the marvelous and glorious union of both, let him be condemned. **268**

Can. 16. If anyone according to the wicked heretics in the destruction of the two wills and the two operations, that is, divine and human, preserved essentially in unity in Christ God, and piously preached by the holy Fathers, foolishly connects discords and differences with the mystery of His dispensation, and so attributes the evangelical and **269** apostolic words about the same Savior not to one and the same person and essentially to the same Lord Himself and God, our Jesus Christ, according to blessed Cyril, so that he is shown to be by nature God and likewise man, let him be condemned.

270   Can. 17. If anyone in word and mind does not properly and truly confess according to the holy Fathers all even to the last portion that has been handed down and preached in the holy, Catholic, and apostolic Church of God, and likewise by the holy Fathers and the five venerable universal Councils, let him be condemned.

271   Can. 18. If anyone according to the holy Fathers, harmoniously with us and likewise with the Faith, does not with mind and lips reject and anathematize all the most abominable heretics together with their impious writings even to one least portion, whom the holy Catholic and apostolic Church of God, that is, the holy and universal five Synods and likewise all the approved Fathers of the Church in harmony, rejects and anathematizes, we mean Sabellius, Arius, Eunomius, Macedonius, Apollinaris, Polemon, Eutyches, Dioscurus, Timothy Aelurus, Severus, Theodosius, Colluthus, Themistius, Paul of Samosata, Diodorus, Theodore, Nestorius, Theodulus the Persian, Origen, Didymus, Evagrius, and briefly all the remaining heretics, who have been condemned and cast out by the Catholic Church; whose teachings are the fruit of diabolical operation, and those, who unto the end have obstinately suggested (ideas) similar to these, or do suggest (them), or are believed to suggest (them), with whom (they are) justly (associated), inasmuch as (they are) like them and (are) possessed of a similar error, according to which they are known to teach and by their own error determine their lives, we mean, Theodore formerly Bishop of Pharan, Cyrus of Alexandria, Sergius of Constantinople, or his successors, Pyrrhus and Paul, persisting in their treachery, and all their impious writings; and those, who have unto the end obstinately suggested, or are suggesting, or are believed to suggest (ideas) similar to those, that is, one will and one operation of the divinity and humanity of Christ, and besides these the very impious Ecthesis, which was composed at the persuasion of the same Sergius by Heraclius, formerly emperor in opposition to the orthodox faith, defining that one will of Christ God, and one operation from the composite are to be venerated; but also everything, which has been impiously written or done by them in defense of it, and those who accept it, or any thing that has been written or done in defense of it; and together with those again the wicked Typus, who on the persuasion of the aforementioned Paul was prepared recently by the most serene Emperor Constantine [read: Constantius], the emperor against the Catholic Church, inasmuch as he promulgates equally the denial and by silence the binding together of two natural wills and operations, divine and

human, which are piously preached by the holy Fathers in the very Christ, true God and our Savior, together with one will and operation, which is impiously venerated in Him by the heretics, and inasmuch as he unjustly defines that together with the holy Fathers the wicked heretics also are freed from all reprehension and condemnation, unto the trimming down of the definitions or of the rule of the Catholic Church.

If anyone therefore, as has been said, does not in agreement with us **272** reject and anathematize all these most impious teachings of their heresy, and those matters which have been impiously written by anyone in defense of them or in definition of them, and the specifically designated heretics, we mean Theodore, Cyrus and Sergius, Pyrrhus and Paul, seeing that they are the rebels against the Catholic Church; or if anyone holds as condemned and entirely deposed some one of these who were in writing, or without writing, in any manner or place or time whatsoever rashly deposed or condemned by them (heretics) or by persons like them, inasmuch as the one condemned does not believe at all like them but with us confesses the doctrine of the holy Fathers—but, on the contrary (anyone) does not consider everybody who has been of this class—that is, whether bishop or priest or deacon or a member of any other ecclesiastical rank, or monk or layman—pious and orthodox and a defender of the Catholic Church, and also more firmly settled in the order to which he has been called by the Lord, but believes such (to be) impious and their judgments in defense of this detestable, or their opinions vain and invalid and weak, nay more wicked and execrable or worthy of condemnation, let such a person be condemned.

Can. 19. If anyone who indubitably has professed and also under- **273** stands those (teachings) which the wicked heretics suggest, through vain impudence says that these are teachings of piety, which the investigators and ministers of the Word have handed down from the beginning, that is to say, the five holy and universal Synods, certainly calumniating the holy Fathers themselves and the five holy Synods mentioned, in the deception of the simple, or in the acceptance of their own impious treachery, let such a person be condemned.

Can. 20. If anyone according to the wicked heretics in any manner **274** whatsoever, by any word whatsoever, or at any time or place whatsoever illicitly *removing the bounds* which the holy *Fathers* of the Catholic Church *have* rather firmly *established* [Prov. 22:28], that is, the five holy and universal Synods, in order rashly to seek for novelties and expositions of another faith; or books, or letters, or writings, or subscriptions, or false testimonies, or synods, or records of deeds, or vain ordinations unknown to ecclesiastical rule; or unsuitable and irrational tenures of place; and briefly, if it is customary for the most impious heretics to do anything else, (if anyone) through diabolical operation crookedly and cunningly acts contrary to the pious preachings of the orthodox (teachers) of the Catholic Church, that is to say, its paternal and synodal proclamations, to the destruction of the most sincere confession unto the Lord our God, and persists without repentance unto the end impiously doing these things, let such a person be condemned forever, *and let all the people say: so be it, so be it* [Ps. 105:48].

ST. EUGENIUS I 654 (655)–657   ST. VITALIANUS 657–672

(ADEODATUS 672–676)

COUNCIL OF TOLEDO XI 675 [1]

Creed of Faith (especially concerning the Trinity and the Incarnation) [2]

["Exposition of faith" against the Priscillianists]

275   [The Trinity] We confess and believe the holy and ineffable Trinity, the Father, and the Son, and the Holy Spirit, one God naturally, to be of one substance, one nature, and also of one majesty and power. And we profess that the Father, indeed, is not begotten, not created but unbegotten. For He from whom both the Son received His nativity and the Holy Spirit His procession takes His origin from no one. Therefore, He is the source and origin of all Godhead; also is the Father Himself of His own essence, He who ineffably begot the Son [Another version: Father, essence indeed ineffable, Son of His own substance] from an ineffable substance; nor did He, however, beget other than what He Himself is: God God, light light, from Him, therefore, is *all paternity* **276** *in heaven and on earth* [Eph. 3:15].—We confess also that the Son was born, but not made, from the substance of the Father without beginning before all ages, because neither the Father without the Son, nor the Son without the Father ever at any time existed. And yet not as the Son from the Father, so the Father from the Son, because the Father did not receive generation from the Son, but the Son from the

---

[1] KAnt 73 ff. [cf. n. 15 ff.] thinks that this creed was composed by a certain unknown theologian of the fifth century and was received by this Council. It is not certain that this same creed was approved by INNOCENT III: cf. *Zeitschr. f. kath. Theologie* 48 (1924) 322 ff. (H. Lennerz, S.J.).

[2] Msi XI 132 E ff.; coll. J. Madoz, S.J., *Le symbole du XIe concile de Tolède*, 1938, 16 ff.; H. 242 ff. and KAnt 74 ff.; Hrd III 1020 A ff.; ML 12, 959 A ff.; cf. Hfl III 114 ff.; Bar(Th) ad 675 n. 1 ff. (11, 588 ff.).—See in Madox *op. cit.* 31 ff., 206 ff. the citations of the Fathers, etc., occurring in this document.

Father. The Son, therefore, is God from the Father; the Father, however, is God, but not from the Son; Father indeed of the Son, not God
from the Son. He, however, is Son of the Father and God from the
Father. However, the Son is equal in all things to God the Father, because at no time did He either begin or cease to be born. We believe that
He is of one substance with the Father, and because of this we say
that He is ὁμοούσιος to the Father, that is, of the same substance with
the Father, for ὅμος in Greek means one, οὐσία means substance, and
the two joined together mean "one substance." For, neither from nothing, nor from any other substance, but from the womb of the Father,
that is, from His substance, we must believe that the Son was begotten
or born. Therefore, the Father is eternal, and the Son is eternal. But if
He always was Father, He always had a Son to whom He was Father;
and by reason of this we confess that the Son was born of the Father
without beginning. Neither do we call the same Son of God a part of a
divided nature because of the fact that He is begotten of the Father; but
we assert that the perfect Father begot the perfect Son without diminution or division, because it is a characteristic of Divinity alone not to
have an unequal Son. Also, this Son is Son of God by nature, not by
adoption,[1] whom we must believe God the Father begot neither by will
nor by necessity; for, neither does any necessity happen [*al. capit,* 'take
hold'] in God, nor does will precede wisdom.—We believe also that the **277**
Holy Spirit, who is the third person in the Trinity, is God, one and
equal with God the Father and the Son, of one substance, also of one
nature; that He is the Spirit of both, not, however, begotten nor created
but proceeding from both. We believe also that this Holy Spirit is
neither unbegotten nor begotten, lest if we say unbegotten, we should
affirm two Fathers, or if begotten, we should be proven to declare two
Sons; He is said to be the Spirit, however, not only of the Father but
at the same time of the Father and the Son. For, neither does He proceed from the Father into the Son, nor does He proceed from the Son
to sanctify the creature, but He is shown to have proceeded at the same
time from both, because He is acknowledged to be the love or holiness
of both. Therefore, we believe that this Holy Spirit was sent by both,
as the Son was sent by the Father; but He is not considered less than
the Father and the Son, as the Son, on account of the body He assumed,
testifies that He Himself is less than the Father and the Holy Spirit.

This is the account of the Holy Trinity that has been handed down. **278**
We must call and believe it to be not triple but triune. Neither can we
rightly say that in one God is the Trinity, but that one God is the

---

[1] This proclaimed against the Bonosians who declared the Son of God to be according to divine nature a son by adoption only, although the later Adoptionists said
this with reference to human nature.

Trinity. In the relative names of persons, however, the Father refers to the Son, the Son to the Father, and the Holy Spirit to both, in that while relatively three persons are asserted, we yet believe they are one nature or substance. Neither as three persons, so do we predicate three substances, but one substance, however three persons. For, as He is Father, not to Himself, but to the Son; and as He is Son not to Himself but to the Father, similarly also the Holy Spirit refers in a relative sense not to Himself, but to the Father and to the Son, in that He is proclaimed the Spirit of the Father and the Son.—Likewise when we say "God," no relationship is expressed, as the Father to the Son, or the Son

279 to the Father, or the Holy Ghost to the Father and the Son, but God applies especially to Himself. For, if we are asked concerning the individual persons, we must confess that each is God. Therefore, we say that the Father is God, the Son is God, and the Holy Spirit is God each singly; yet there are not three Gods, but there is one God. Likewise also we say that the Father is omnipotent, the Son is omnipotent, and the Holy Spirit is omnipotent, each singly; not, however, three omnipotent Gods, but one omnipotent God, as also we predicate one light and one principle. We confess and believe, therefore, that singly each person is wholly God and that all three persons are one God; they have one indivisible and equal Godhead, majesty or power, neither is it lessened in the single person, nor increased in the three persons, because it does not have anything less when each person of God is spoken of singly,

280 nor more when all three persons are called one God.—Therefore, this Holy Trinity, which is the one and true God, neither excludes number nor is it contained in number.—For in the relation of persons number appears, but in the substance of divinity, what might be enumerated is not understood. Therefore, in this alone they imply number, that they are related to each other; and in this, that they are to themselves, they lack number. For natural unity is so suitable to this Holy Trinity that there cannot be a plurality in the three persons. For this reason, then, we believe that saying in Sacred Scripture: "Great is our Lord and great is his power; and of his Wisdom there is no number" [Ps. 146:5]. Neither because we have said that these three persons are one God, are we able to say that the same one is the Father who is the Son, or that He is the Son who is the Father, or that He who is the Holy Spirit is either the Father or the Son. For He is not the Father who is the Son, nor is He the Son who is the Father, nor is the Holy Spirit He who is either the Father or the Son, even though the Father is the same as the Son, the Son the same as the Father, the Father and the Son the same as the Holy Spirit; that is, in nature one God. For, when we say that the same one is not the Father as the Son, we refer to the distinction of persons. When, however, we say that the Father is the same

as the Son, the Son the same as the Father, the Holy Spirit the same as the Father and the Son, it is plain that the reference is to the nature or substance by which He is God, because in substance they are one; for we are distinguishing persons, we are not dividing the Deity.—We ac- **281** knowledge, therefore, the Trinity in a distinction of persons; we profess unity on account of the nature or substance. Therefore, the three are one, that is, in nature, not in person. We must not, however, consider these three persons separable, since we believe that no one before the other, no one after the other, no one without the other ever existed or did anything. For, they are found inseparable both in that which they are, and in that which they do, because between the generating Father and the generated Son and the proceeding Holy Spirit we believe that there was no interval of time in which either the begetter at any time preceded the begotten, or the begotten was lacking to the begetter, or the proceeding Holy Spirit appeared after the Father or the Son. There- fore, for this reason we proclaim and believe that this Trinity is insep- arable and unconfused. These three, therefore, are called persons, as our ancestors define, that they may be recognized, not that they may be separated. For, if we give attention to that which Holy Scripture says of Wisdom: "She is the brightness of eternal light" [Wisd. 7:26], as we see the splendor inhering inseparably in light, so we confess that the Son cannot be separated from the Father. Therefore, just as we do not confuse these three persons of one and inseparable nature, so do we in nowise declare them separable. Since, indeed, the Trinity itself has so deigned to show this clearly to us that even in these names by which it wished the persons to be recognized singly, it does not permit one to be understood without the other; for neither is the Father recognized with- out the Son, nor is the Son found without the Father. Indeed, the very relation of personal designation forbids the persons to be separated, whom, even when it does not name them together, it implies together. Moreover, no one can hear anyone of those names without being con- strained to think also of another. Since, then, these three are one and the one three, there is yet remaining to each person His own property. For the Father has eternity without nativity, the Son eternity with nativity, and the Holy Spirit procession without nativity with eternity.

[The Incarnation] Of these three persons we believe that for the **282** liberation of the human race only the person of the Son became true man without sin from the holy and immaculate Virgin Mary, from whom He is begotten in a new manner and by a new birth; in a new manner, because invisible in divinity, He became visible in flesh; by a new birth, however, is He begotten, because inviolate virginity without the experience of sexual intercourse supplied the material of human flesh made fruitful by the Holy Spirit. This Virgin birth is neither grasped by reason nor illustrated by example, because if grasped by reason, it is not miraculous; if illustrated by example, it will not be unique.[1] Yet we must not believe that the Holy Spirit is Father of the Son, because of the fact that Mary conceived by the overshadowing of the same Holy Spirit, lest we seem to assert that there are two Fathers of the Son,

283 which is certainly impious to say.—In this marvelous conception, with Wisdom building a house for herself, *the Word was made flesh and dwelt among us* [John 1:14]. The Word itself, however, was not so converted and changed that He who willed to become man ceased to be God; but the *Word was made flesh* in such a way that not only are the Word of God and the flesh of man present, but also the soul of a rational man, and this whole is called God on account of God, and man on account of man. In this Son of God we believe there are two natures, one of divinity, the other of humanity, which the one person of Christ so united in Himself that the divinity can never be separated from the humanity, nor the humanity from the divinity. Christ, therefore, is perfect God and perfect man in the unity of one person; but it does not follow, because we have asserted two natures in the Son, that there are two persons in Him, lest—which God forbid—a quaternity be predicated of the Trinity. For God the Word has not received the person of man, but the nature, and to the eternal person of divinity He has united the

284 temporal substance of flesh.—Likewise we believe that the Father, the Son, and the Holy Spirit are of one substance, but we do not say that the Virgin Mary gave birth to the unity of the Trinity, but only to the Son, who alone assumed our nature in the unity of His person. Also, we must believe that the entire Trinity accomplished the Incarnation of the Son of God, because the works of the Trinity are inseparable. However, only the Son *took the form of a servant* [cf. Phil. 2:7] in the singleness of His person, not in the unity of His divine nature; in what is proper to the Son, not in what is common to the Trinity; and this form was adapted to Him for unity of person so that the Son of God and the Son of man is one Christ, that is, Christ in these two natures exists in three substances; of the Word, which must refer to the essence of God alone, of the body, and of the soul, which pertain to true man.

285 He has, therefore, in Himself the twofold substance of His divinity and our humanity. We understand, however, that by the fact that He proceeded from God the Father without beginning, He was born only, for He was neither made nor predestined; by the fact, however, that He was born of the Virgin Mary, we must believe that He was born, made, and predestined. Yet both births in Him are marvelous, because He was both begotten by the Father without a mother before all ages and in the end of the ages He was born of a mother without a father; He who,

---

[1] Cf. St. Augustine, Ep. 137, 2, 8 [ML 33, 519].

however, according as He is God created Mary, according as He is man was created from Mary; He is both father and son of His mother Mary. Likewise by the fact that He is God, He is equal to the Father; by the fact that He is man, He is less than the Father. Likewise we must believe that He is both greater and less than Himself; for in the form of God even the Son Himself is greater than Himself on account of the humanity He assumed, than which the divinity is greater; in the form, however, of a servant He is less than Himself, that is, in His humanity, which is recognized as less than His divinity. For, as by reason of the body which He assumed He is believed to be not only less than the Father but also less than Himself, so according to His divinity He is coequal with the Father, and both He and the Father are greater than man, which the person of the Son alone assumed. Likewise to the question whether the Son could so be equal to and less than the Holy Spirit, as we believe that He is now equal to, now less than the Father, we reply: According to the form of God He is equal to the Father and to the Holy Spirit, according to the form of a servant, He is less than both the Father and the Holy Spirit; because neither the Holy Spirit nor the Father, but only the person of the Son assumed a body, by which He is believed to be less than those two persons. Likewise we believe that this Son, inseparable from God the Father and the Holy Spirit, is distinguished from them by His person, and distinguished from other men by the nature He assumed [another version, from the manhood assumed]. Likewise with reference to man it is His person that is preeminent; but with reference to the Father and the Holy Spirit it is the divine nature or substance. Yet we must believe that the Son was sent not only by the Father but also by the Holy Spirit; because He himself said through the prophet *And now the Lord has sent me and His Holy Spirit* [Isa. 48:16]. We believe also that He was sent by Himself, because we acknowledge that not only the will but also the works of the whole Trinity are inseparable. For, He who before all ages was called the only begotten, in time became the first born; the only begotten on account of the substance of the Godhead, the first born on account of the nature of the body which He assumed.

[The Redemption] In this form of assumed human nature we be- 286 lieve according to the truth of the Gospels that He was conceived without sin, born without sin, and died without sin, who alone *for us became sin* [II Cor. 5:21], that is, a sacrifice for our sin. And yet He endured His passion without detriment to His divinity, for our sins, and condemned to death and to the cross, He accepted the true death of the body; also on the third day, restored by His own power, He arose from the grave.

In this example, therefore, of our Head we confess is accomplished 287 [another version: with true faith] the true resurrection of the body of all the dead. Neither do we believe that we shall rise in an ethereal or any other body (as some madly say) but in that in which we live and exist and move. When this example of His holy resurrection was finished, our same Lord and Savior returned by ascending to His paternal home, which in His divinity He had never left. There sitting at the right hand of the Father, He awaits the end of time to be the judge of all the living and the dead. Thence with the holy angels and men He will come to judge, and to render to everyone the due of his own reward, according *as each one* living in the body *has done good or evil* [II Cor. 5:10]. We believe that the holy Catholic Church, purchased by the price of His blood, will reign with Him for eternity. Established in her bosom we believe in and confess one baptism for the remission of all sins. In this faith we both truly believe in the resurrection of the dead and we await the joys of the future life. We must pray and beg for this only, that when, the judgment finished and over, the Son *will hand over the kingdom to God the Father* [I Cor. 15:24], that He may render us participators of His kingdom, so that through this faith in which we cling to Him, we may reign with Him without end.—This exposition is the pledge of our confession through which the teaching of all heretics is destroyed, through which the hearts of the faithful are cleansed, through which also we ascend gloriously to God for all eternity. Amen.

Donus 676–678

ST. AGATHO 678–681

ROMAN COUNCIL 680

The Hypostatic Union [1]

[From the dogmatic epistle of Agatho and the Roman
Synod "Omnium bonorum spes" to the Emperors [2]]

288   We acknowledge (indeed) that one and the same our Lord Jesus Christ, the only begotten Son of God, from two and in two substances subsists, unconfusedly without change, indivisibly, inseparably [see n. 148], never the difference of natures destroyed on account of the union,

---

[1] Msi XI 290 E f.; Jf 2110; Hrd III 1119 D f.; ML 87, 1221 B; cf. Hfl III 252 f.

[2] The Fathers of Synod VI (Constplt. III) accepted this letter, asserting that Peter spoke through Agatho. "The highest chief of the Apostles struggled with us; for we had his imitator and the successor to the See as a supporter and illustrator of the divine sacrament through a letter. That ancient city of Rome offered you [Constantinus] a confession written by God" [Hrd III 1422 E f.].

but rather the property of each nature preserved and concurring in one person and in one subsistence; not shared or divided in a duality of persons, nor fused into one composite nature; but we acknowledge, even after the subsistential union, one and the same only begotten Son, the Word God, our Lord Jesus Christ [see n. 148], neither each in a different way, nor the one and the other, but the very same in two natures, that is, in the Godhead and in the humanity, because neither has the Word been changed into the nature of the flesh, nor has the flesh been transformed into the nature of the Word; for each remains what by nature it was; indeed in contemplation alone do we discern a difference of the united natures in that from which unfusedly, inseparably, and incommutably it was composed; for one from both and each through one, because at the same time there are present both the dignity of the Godhead and the humility of the flesh, each nature, even after the union, preserving without defect its own property, "and each form doing with the mutual participation of the other what it holds as its own (work); the Word doing what is of the Word, and the flesh accomplishing what is of the flesh; the one of which shines forth in miracles, the other submits to injuries." [1] Thus, it follows that as we truly confess that He has two natures or substances, that is, the Godhead and the humanity, unfusedly, indivisibly, incommutably, so also He has both two natural wills and two natural operations, since the rule of piety instructs us that perfect God and perfect man is one and the same Lord Jesus Christ [see n. 254–274], because it is shown that the apostolic and evangelical tradition and the teaching of the holy Fathers, whom the holy, apostolic, and Catholic Church and the venerable Synods accept, have taught us this.

COUNCIL OF CONSTANTINOPLE III
680–681

Ecumenical VI (against the Monothelites)

Definition of the Two Wills of Christ [2]

This present holy and universal Synod faithfully receiving and will-   **289** ingly accepting such a suggestion which was made by the most holy and most blessed Agatho, Pope of ancient Rome, to Constantine, our very good and most faithful ruler, which (decree) by name has excommunicated those who have taught or have preached, as has been said

---

[1] Letter of Pope Leo dogmat. ad Flavianum [see n. 144].

[2] Msi XI 635 C ff.; Hrd III 1397 E ff.; cf. Hfl III 283 ff.; Bar(Th) ad 680 n. 41 ff. (12, 11 ff.).—See Letter of Leo II. Msi XI 725 ff.

above, that there is one will and one operation in the dispensation of the Incarnation of our Lord Jesus Christ, our true God [see n. 288], likewise has accepted another Synodal decree, which was sent by the Sacred Council which, under the same most holy Pope, is made up of one hundred and twenty-five bishops [1] pleasing to God, in accordance with a tranquillity established by God, in so far as they are in agreement with the holy Council of Chalcedon, and the [see n. 148] letter of this most holy and most blessed Pope Leo of ancient Rome which was directed to holy Flavian [see n. 143], and which (letter) the Synod has called a monument of this kind of orthodox faith.

290   Besides, both in Synodical letters which were written by blessed Cyril against the impious Nestorius and to the oriental bishops, following also the five holy ecumenical councils and the holy and trusted Fathers, and defining harmoniously with them it confesses that our Lord Jesus Christ, our true God, one of the holy and consubstantial Trinity and giving forth the origin of life, perfect in Godhead and the same perfect in humanity, truly God and truly man, Himself of a rational soul and body; it confesses the same consubstantial with the Father according to Godhead, and consubstantial with us according to humanity, *through all things like to us except in sin* [Heb. 4:15], before ages, indeed, begotten of the Father according to Godhead, in the last days, however, the same for us and for our salvation of the Holy Spirit and of the Virgin Mary properly and truly the mother of God according to humanity, one and the same Christ, the only begotten Lord God in two natures recognized unfusedly, unchangeably, inseparably, indivisibly, never the difference of these natures destroyed on account of union, but rather the property of each nature saved and in one person and in one substance concurring, not into two persons portioned or divided but one and the same only begotten Son of God the Word, our Lord Jesus Christ, just as formerly the prophets taught us about Him, and our Lord Jesus Christ Himself has taught us, and the creed of the holy Fathers has handed down to us [Conc. Chal., see n. 148].

291   And so we proclaim two natural wills in Him, and two natural operations indivisibly, inconvertibly, inseparably, unfusedly according to the doctrine of the holy Father, and two natural wills not contrary, God forbid, according as impious heretics have asserted, but the human will following and not resisting or hesitating, but rather even submitting to His divine and omnipotent will. For, it is necessary that the will of the flesh act, but that it be subject to the divine will according to the most wise Athanasius.[2] For, as His flesh is called and is the flesh of the Word

---

[1] Msi XI 185 ff.

[2] Tractate on the following: "Nunc anima mea turbata est" [John 12:27]. This tractate is now not extant; cf. MG 26, 124.

of God, so also the natural will of His flesh is called and is the proper will of the Word of God as He Himself says: "Because I came down from heaven, not to do my own will but the will of my Father who sent me" [cf. John 6:38], calling the will of the flesh His own. For the body became His own. For as His most holy and immaculate animated flesh deified has not been destroyed but in its own status and plan remained, so also His human will deified has not been destroyed, but on the contrary it has been saved according to the theologian Gregory who says: [1] "For to wish of that one an entire deification, which is understood in the Savior, is not contrary to God."

But we glorify two natural operations indivisibly, inconvertibly, unfusedly, inseparably in our Lord Jesus Christ Himself, our true God, that is, the divine operation and the human operation, according to Leo the divine preacher who very clearly asserts: "For each form does what is proper to itself with the mutual participation of the other, that is, the Word doing what is of the Word and the flesh accomplishing what is of the flesh" [see n. 144]. For at no time shall we grant one natural operation to God and to the creature, so that neither what was created, we raise into divine essence, nor what is especially of divine nature, we cast down to a place begetting creatures. For of one and the same we recognize the miracles and the sufferings according to the one and the other of these natures from which He is and in which He has to be as the admirable Cyril says. Therefore we, maintaining completely an unconfused and undivided (opinion), in a brief statement set forth all: that we, believing that He is one of the Holy Trinity, our Lord Jesus Christ our true God, and after the incarnation assert that His two natures radiate in His one substance, in which His miracles and His sufferings through all His ordained life, not through phantasy but truly He has shown, on account of the natural difference which is recognized in the same single substance, while with the mutual participation of the other, each nature indivisibly and without confusion willed and performed its own works; according to this plan we confess two natural wills and operations concurring mutually in Him for the salvation of the human race. **293**

These things, therefore, having been determined by us with all caution and diligence, we declare that no one is permitted to introduce, or to describe, or to compare, or to study, or otherwise to teach another faith. But whoever presumes to compare or to introduce or to teach or to pass on another creed to those wishing to turn from the belief of the Gentiles or of the Jews or from any heresy whatsoever to the acknowledgement of truth, or who (presumes) to introduce a novel doctrine or an invention of discourse to the subversion of those things which now have been determined by us, (we declare) these, whether they are bishops or clerics,

---

[1] St. Gregory Nazianzenus, Or. 30, 12 [MG 36, 117].

to be excommunicated, bishops indeed from the bishopric, but priests from the priesthood; but if they are monks or laymen, to be anathematized.

Sᴛ. Lᴇᴏ II 682–683 [1]   Jᴏʜɴ V 685–686

Sᴛ. Bᴇɴᴇᴅɪᴄᴛ II 684–685   Cᴏɴᴏɴ 686–687

(ST. SERGIUS I 687–701)

COUNCIL OF TOLEDO XV 685

Protestation concerning the Trinity and the Incarnation [2]

[From "Liber responsionis" or the "Apologia" of Julian, Archbishop of Toledo]

294   . . . We have found that in that book of response to our faith, which we had sent to the Roman Church through Peter the regent, it had seemed to the Pope already mentioned (Benedict) that we had carelessly written that first chapter where we said according to divine essence: "Will begot will, as also wisdom, wisdom," because that man in a hurried reading thought that we had used these very names according to a relative sense, or according to a comparison of the human mind; and so in his reply he commanded us to give warning saying: "In the natural order we recognize that the word takes its origin from the mind, just as reason and will, and they cannot be changed, so that it may be said that, as the word and the will proceed from the mind, so also the mind from the word or the will, and from this comparison it seemed to the Roman Pontiff that the will cannot be said to be from the will." We, however, not according to this comparison of the human mind, nor according to a relative sense, but according to essence have said: Will from will, as also wisdom from wisdom. For this being is to God as willing: this willing as understanding. But this we cannot say concerning man. For it is one thing for man not to will that which is, and another thing to will even without understanding. In God, however, it is not so, be-

---

[1] Letters in which (is treated) the Anathema against Honorius, see Kch 1085 ff.

[2] Msi XII 10 E ff.; Hrd III 1761 B ff.; cf. Hfl III 325 f.; Bar (Th) ad 688 n. 1 ff. (12, 96 ff.).—The Spanish fathers of the Council of Toledo XIV had accepted a certain work of St. Julian, in which these propositions occurred: Will begot will, just as also wisdom, wisdom; and that there are three substances in Christ. Benedict II indicated by an announcement that he had difficulty accepting these. But when St. Julian explained his meaning, in this meaning Sergius I acknowledged that they were orthodox. Thus in the Synod of Toledo XV and XVI, the Spanish fathers explained their minds again.

cause so perfect is His nature, that this being is to Him as willing, as understanding. . . .

Passing also to a re-examination of the second chapter in which the 295 same Pope thought that we had uncautiously said that three substances are professed in Christ, the Son of God, as we will not be ashamed to defend the things that are true, so perchance others will be ashamed to be ignorant of the things that are true. For who does not know that every man consists of two substances, namely of the soul and of the body? . . . Therefore when the divine nature has been joined to the human nature, they can be called both three personal and two personal substances. . . .

COUNCIL OF TOLEDO XVI 693

Profession of Faith concerning the Trinity [1]

Let the designation of this "holy will"—although through a compara- 296 tive similitude of the Trinity, where it is called memory, intelligence, and will—refer to the person of the Holy Spirit; according to this, how-ever, what applies to itself, is predicated substantially. For the will is the Father, the will is the Son, the will is the Holy Spirit; and many other similar things, according to substance, which those who live as protectors of the Catholic faith do not for any reason hesitate to say. And just as it is Catholic to say: God from God, light from light, life from life, so it is a proved assertion of true faith to say the will from the will; just as wisdom from wisdom, essence from essence, and as God the Father begot God the Son, so the Will, the Father, begot the Son, the Will. Thus, although according to essence the Father is will, the Son is will and the Holy Spirit is will, we must not however believe that there is unity according to a relative sense, since one is the Father who refers to the Son, another the Son, who refers to the Father, another the Holy Spirit who, because He proceeds from the Father and the Son, refers to the Father and the Son; not the same but one in one way, one in another, because to whom there is one being in the nature of deity, to these there is a special property in the distinction of persons.

John VI 701–705	Sisinnius 708
John VII 705–707	Constantine I 708–715

---

[1] J. Madoz, *El símbolo del Concilio XVI de Toledo* (Madrid: 1946) 27; Msi XII 67 B; Hrd III 1792 B; cf. Hfl III 350; Bar(Th) ad 693 n. 1 ff. (12, 135 f.).

ST. GREGORY II 715–731
The Form and Minister of Baptism [1]

[From the epistle "Desiderabilem mihi" to St. Boniface, Nov. 22, 726]

296a   You have said that some without the profession of the Creed were baptized by adulterous and unworthy priests. In these cases may your love hold to the ancient custom of the Church: that, whoever has been baptized in the name of the Father and of the Son and of the Holy Spirit, may in no case be rebaptized; for not in the name of the one baptizing, but in the name of the Trinity has one received the gift of this grace. And let that which the Apostle says be observed: *One God, one faith, one baptism* [Eph. 4:5]. But we recommend that to such you teach more zealously the spiritual doctrine.

ST. GREGORY III 731–741
Baptism and Confirmation [2]

[From the epistle "Doctoris omnium" to St. Boniface, Oct. 29, 739]

296b   However, because they were baptized in the name of the Trinity, it is necessary that those indeed who were baptized through a diversity and a variation of the relationship of languages, be strengthened through the hands of imposition [another version: imposition] and of the holy chrism.

ST. ZACHARY 741–752
The Form and Minister of Baptism [3]

[From the epistle "Virgilius et Sedonius" to St. Boniface, July 1, 746 (?)]

297   For they have reported that there was a priest in that province, who was so completely ignorant of the Latin language that when he was baptizing, because of his ignorance of the Latin speech, breaking up the

---

[1] MGh Epp. III 1, n. 26; Jf 2174; Hrd III 1859 D; ML 89, 525 CD.
[2] MGh Epp. III 1, n. 45; Msi XII 285 D; Jf 2251; ML 89, 584 C.
[3] MGh Epp. III 1, n. 68 and 80; Msi XII 339 D f.; Jf 2276 2286 c. Add.; Hrd III 1888 1910 C; ML 89, 929 C 943 D f.

language, said: "Baptizo te in nomine Patria et Filia et Spiritus Sancti." And on account of this your honored brotherhood has considered re-baptizing. But . . . if that one who baptized, not introducing an error or a heresy, but through mere ignorance of the Roman speech by break-ing up the language, baptizing he said, as we mentioned above, we do not agree that they should be baptized a second time.

[From the epistle (10 resp. 11) "Sacris liminibus" to
St. Boniface, May 1, 748 (?)]

In that (synod of the Angles) it is distinctly recognized that such a   297a
decree and judgment is very firmly commanded and diligently demon-strated, so that whoever had been washed without the invocation of the Trinity, he has not been perfected, unless he shall have been baptized in the name of the Father, and of the Son, and of the Holy Spirit.

(STEPHEN II 752)   ST. PAUL I 757–767
ST. STEPHEN III 752–757 [1]   STEPHEN IV 768–772

HADRIAN I 772–795

The Primacy of the Roman Pontiff [2]

[From the epistle "Pastoralibus Curis" to the Patriarch
Tarasius in the year 785]

. . . Let that false assembly, which without the Apostolic See . . . was   298
held contrary to the traditions of the venerable fathers against the divine images, be declared anathema in the presence of our delegates, and let the word of our Lord Jesus Christ be fulfilled, that "the gates of hell shall not prevail against her" (Matt. 16:18); and again: "Thou art Peter . . ." (Matt. 16:18–19), whose throne holding the first place in all

---

[1] The replies of Stephen III given in the year 754 are extant [ML 89, 1024 ff.], in one of which imperfect divorce is permitted, "if the weakness of an evil spirit or the stain of leprosy occurs"; and in the third of these it is decreed: "If anyone in a foreign land should take a slave woman in marriage, and afterwards on return-ing to his own country should take a free-born woman, and it should again happen that he return to the very country in which he had been before, and that slave woman, whom he previously had, had associated with another man, this person in such circumstances can take another woman, but not while that free-born woman is living whom he had in his own country." The Council of Verberia, 756 can., 5–12 [ML 96 1507 f.] and of Compiegne, 756, can. 11, 13, 16 [ML 96, 1514] undoubtedly made certain erroneous decisions on the indissolubility of marriage.

[2] Msi XII 1081D; Jf 2449 c. Add.; Hrd IV 102 B; cf. Hfl III 448 ff.—This Greek version (from which the Latin version has been made) was read at the Council of Nicea II.

the world shines forth and holds its place as the head of the whole Church of God.

The Errors of the Adoptionists [1]

[From the epistle "Institutio universalis" to the bishops of Spain, in the year 785]

299   . . . And then from your country a plaintive chapter came to us that certain bishops living there, namely Eliphandus and Ascaricus with others agreeing with them, do not blush to confess the Son of God adopted, although no heretical leader, however great, has dared to utter such blasphemy, except that perfidious Nestorius who has declared that the Son of God is pure man. . . .

Predestination and the Various Abuses of the Spaniards [2]

[From the same epistle to the bishops of Spain]

300   As for that, however, which some of these say, that predestination to life or to death is in the power of God and not in ours; they say: "Why do we try to live, because it is in the power of God?"; again others say: "Why do we ask God, that we may not be overcome by temptation, since it is in our power, as in the freedom of will?" For truly they are able to render or to accept no plan, being ignorant . . . [of the words] of blessed Fulgentius [3] [against a certain Pelagius]: "Therefore, God in the eternity of His changelessness has prepared works of mercy and justice . . . but for men who are to be justified He has prepared merits; He has prepared rewards for those who are to be glorified; but for the wicked He has not prepared evil wills or evil works, but He has prepared for them just and eternal punishments. This is the eternal predestination of the future works of God, which as we have always acknowledged to be taught to us by apostolic doctrine, so also faithfully we proclaim. . . ."

301   Dearly beloved ones, in regard to those diverse chapters, which we have heard from those parts, namely, that many saying that they are Catholics, living a life common with the Jews and nonbaptized pagans, as in food so in drink or in diverse errors, say that they are not being harmed; and that which has been practised, for although it is not permitted for any-

---

[1] MGh Epp. III 637; Jf 2479; Msi XII 815 D f.; ML 98, 376 A; cf. Hfl III 661.

[2] MGh Epp. III 642 f.; Jf 2479; ML 98, 383 B ff.; Msi XII 811 et 813.—This text occurs also the same, as far as the words go, in another letter. "Audientes orthodoxam," in which Egilas is praised. ML 98, 336 ff.; Jf 2445 show this; but Msi has the first part of this text in one letter, the latter part only in another.

[3] Letter to Eugypius which is not now extant; but cf. in the same meaning the work of St. Fulgentius *De veritate praedestinationis* 3, 6, 9 f. [ML 65, 656 f.].

one to marry an infidel, they bless their daughters with one, and so they are entrusted to a pagan people; and that without examination these aforesaid priests are ordained in order that they may preside; and also another great deadly error has grown strong, that although the husband is living, these false priests choose women for themselves in marriage; and at the same time we have heard from these parts about the liberty of the will, and many other things which are too numerous to mention. . . .

COUNCIL OF NICEA II 787

Ecumenical VII (against the Iconoclasts)

Definition of the Sacred Images and Tradition [1]

ACTION VII

(I. Definition) . . . We, continuing in the regal path, and following 302 the divinely inspired teaching of our Holy Fathers, and the tradition of the Catholic Church, for we know that this is of the Holy Spirit who certainly dwells in it, define in all certitude and diligence that as the figure of the honored and life-giving Cross, so the venerable and holy images, the ones from tinted materials and from marble as those from other material, must be suitably placed in the holy churches of God, both on sacred vessels and vestments, and on the walls and on the altars, at home and on the streets, namely such images of our Lord Jesus Christ, God and Savior, and of our undefiled lady, or holy Mother of God, and of the honorable angels, and, at the same time, of all the saints and of holy men. For, how much more frequently through the imaginal formation they are seen, so much more quickly are those who contemplate these, raised to the memory and desire of the originals of these, to kiss and to render honorable adoration to them, not however, to grant true *latria* according to our faith, which is proper to divine nature alone; but just as to the figure of the revered and life-giving Cross and to the holy gospels, and to the other sacred monuments, let an oblation of incense and lights be made to give honor to these as was the pious custom with the ancients. "For the honor of the image passes to the original"; [2] and he who shows reverence to the image, shows reverence to the substance of Him depicted in it.

(II. Proof) For thus the doctrine of our Holy Fathers, that is, the 303 tradition of the Catholic Church which has received the Gospel from and even to the end of the world is strengthened. Thus we follow Paul, who

---

[1] Msi XIII 378 C ff.; Hrd IV 455 A f.; cf. Hfl III 472 ff.; Bar(Th) ad 787 n. 1 ff. (13, 195 ff.).
[2] Cf. St. Basil, *De Spiritu Sancto* 18, 45 [MG 32, 149C].

spoke in Christ [II Cor. 2:17], and all the divine apostolic group and the paternal sanctity *keeping the traditions* [II Thess. 2:14] which we have received. Thus prophetically we sing the triumphal hymns for the Church: *Rejoice exceedingly, O daughter of Sion, sing forth, O daughter of Jerusalem: be joyful and be happy with all your heart. The Lord has taken from you the injustices of those adverse to you: He has redeemed you from the power of your enemies. The Lord is king in your midst: You will not see more evils* [Wisd. 3:14 f.: LXX] *and peace to you unto time eternal.*

304   (III. Declaration) Those, therefore, who dare to think or to teach otherwise or to spurn according to wretched heretics the ecclesiastical traditions and to invent anything novel, or to reject anything from these things which have been consecrated by the Church: either the Gospel or the figure of the Cross, or the imaginal picture, or the sacred relics of the martyr; or to invent perversely and cunningly for the overthrow of anyone of the legitimate traditions of the Catholic Church; or even, as it were, to use the sacred vessels or the venerable monasteries as common things; if indeed they are bishops or clerics, we order (them) to be deposed; monks, however, or laymen, to be excommunicated.

The Sacred Elections [1]

ACTION VIII

305   Can. 3. Let every election of a bishop or of a presbyter or of a deacon made by the leaders remain invalid according to the canon (Apostolic Canon 30), which says: If any bishop, using secular powers, obtains a church by means of these, let him be deposed and let all be segregated who join with him. For, it is necessary that he who is going to enter upon the office of bishop, be elected by bishops, as it has been defined by the Holy Fathers who met at Nicea, in the canon (Canon 4) which says: Indeed it is especially fitting that a bishop be ordained by all the bishops who are in the province. If, however, this is difficult either because of pressing necessity or because of the length of the journey, nevertheless, in any case with three meeting together for this very thing, and the absent ones in agreement and joining by letter, then the consecration may be held. The authority, however, over what is done in each province is granted to the metropolitan bishop.

---

[1] Msi XIII 419 D ff.; Hrd IV 487 c f.; cf. Hfl III 476; cf. CIC Decr. 63, 7: Frdbg I 237; Rcht I 203.

Images, the Humanity of Christ, Tradition [1]

ACTION VIII

We admit that images should be venerated. Those of us who are not so **306** minded we subject to anathema. . . .

If anyone does not confess that Christ, our Lord, has been described **307** according to His humanity . . . let him be anathema.

If anyone rejects all ecclesiastical tradition either written or not written **308** . . . let him be anathema.

The Errors of the Adoptionists [2]

[From the epistle of Hadrian "Si tamen licet" to the bishops of Gaul and of Spain, 793]

On that occasion selections of perfidious words from a disordered pen **309** were read; among other things which must be rejected, was the matter arranged with false arguments giving rise, however, to perfidy concerning the adoption of Jesus Christ, the Son of God according to the flesh. This the Catholic Church has never believed, has never taught, has never given assent to those believing wickedly. . . .

. . . O, you impious, and you who are ungrateful for so many benefits, **310** do you not fear to whisper with a poisonous mouth that He, our liberator, is an adopted Son, as it were, a mere man subject to human misfortune, and what is a disgrace to say, that He is a servant. . . . Why are you not afraid, O, querulous detractors, O, men odious to God, to call Him servant, who has freed you from the servitude of the devil? . . . For, although in the imperfect representation of the prophet He was called *servant* [cf. Job 1:8 ff.] because of the condition of servile form which He assumed from the Virgin . . . we understand that this was said both historically of holy Job and allegorically of Christ. . . .

---

[1] Msi XIII 415 AC; Hrd IV 483 CE.

[2] MGh of the laws section III, II 1, 123, 126; Jf 2482; Msi XIII 865 D 869 **A**; Hrd IV 866 B 869 B; cf. Hfl III 685 f.

COUNCIL OF FRANKFURT 794 [1]

Christ, the Natural, not the Adopted Son of God [2]

[From the synodical epistle of the bishops of France
to the Spaniards]

311   . . . For in the beginning of your little book we have found written
what you have laid down: "We confess and we believe that God, the
Son of God before all ages without beginning, was begotten from the
Father, co-eternal and consubstantial, not by adoption but by birth." Likewise after a few words in the same place we read: "We confess and we
believe that He *was made from a woman, made under the law* [cf. Gal.
4:4], that not by birth is He the Son of God but by adoption; not by nature
but by grace." Behold the serpent hiding among the fruit bearing trees of
Paradise, that he may deceive every unwary one. . . .

312   That also which you added in the following [cf. n. 295] we have not
found expressed in the profession of the Nicene Creed, that in Christ
there are two natures and three substances [cf. n. 295] and "man deified
and God made human." What is the nature of man, but soul and body?
or what is the difference between nature and substance, that it is necessary
for us to say three substances, and not rather simply, as the Holy Fathers
have said, that they confess our Lord Jesus Christ true God and true man
in one person? Certainly the person of the Son remained in the Holy
Trinity, to which person human nature was joined so that it was one
person, God and man, not man deified and God made human, but God
man and man God, on account of the unity of the person one Son of God,
and the same Son of man, perfect God, perfect man . . . Ecclesiastical
custom is wont to name two substances in Christ, namely of God and
of man. . . .

313   If, therefore, He is true God, who was born of the Virgin, how then
can He be adopted or a servant? For by no means do you dare to confess
God a servant or one adopted; and if the prophet called Him servant,
it is not, however, from the condition of servitude, but from the obedience

---

1 Frankfurt in Germany.

2 MGh Of the laws, section III, II, 1, 144, 150, 152, 165; Msi XIII 884 E 890 B
909 C; Hrd IV 883 D ff. 904 C; cf. Hfl III 678 ff.; Bar(Th) ad 794 n. 1 ff. (13, 274
a ff.).—The heresy of the Adoptionists, which arose in Spain, was already rejected
in the year 792 at the Synod of Ratisbon with King Carol presiding; then at this
Synod of Frankfurt, called together by the same King and held in the month of
June of the year 794 in the presence of legates of the Apostolic See, it was condemned
again. Cf. *Rev. des sciences rel.* 16 (1936) 281 ff. [E. Amann].

of humility, by which He was *made obedient* to the Father *even unto death* [Phil. 2, 8].

[From "Capitulari"]

(1) . . . In the beginning of the chapters there arose the question   **314** concerning the impious and abominable heresy of Elephandus, Bishop of the see of Toledo, and of Felix of Orgellitana, and of their followers, who, thinking wrongly, asserted adoption in the Son of God; the most Holy Fathers, who previously rejected all these, have unanimously protested against this and they have determined that this heresy must be thoroughly eradicated from the Holy Church.

ST. LEO III 795–816

COUNCIL OF FRIULI [1] 796

Christ, the Natural, not the Adopted [2] Son of God

[From the Symbol of Faith]

Neither was the human and temporal nativity absent from the divine   **314a** and eternal nativity, but in one person of Christ Jesus true Son of God and true Son of man. Not one Son of man and another of God . . . not the supposed Son of God, but true; not adopted, but His own, because never was He alien from the Father because of the human nature which He assumed. And so in each nature we confess that He is the true and not the adopted Son of God, because unconfusedly and inseparably, man having been assumed, one and the same is the Son of God and the Son of man. By nature Son to the mother according to humanity, however, true Son to the Father in both natures.[3]

Stephan V 816–817	Valentine 827
St. Paschal I 817–824	Gregory IV 828–844
Eugenius II 824–827	Sergius II 844–847

---

[1] Friaul.

[2] Msi XIII 844; ML 99, 294.

[3] Leo XIII accepted the profession of faith offered by Nicephorus, Patriarch of Constantinople, in the year 811, according to which God "also preserved the virgin who supernaturally and ineffably had given birth; after the bringing forth, her virginity according to nature in no part being changed or destroyed." [MG 100, 186 B].

ST. LEO IV 847–855

COUNCIL OF TICINUS [1] 850

The Sacrament of Extreme Unction [2]

315   (8) That saving sacrament also which James the Apostle commends saying: *If anyone is sick . . . it will be remitted him* [Jas. 5:14], must be made known to the people by skilful teaching; a truly great mystery and one exceedingly to be sought, through which, if the faithful ask, and their sins are forgiven, it may even follow that health of body is restored. . . . This, however, must be known, that, if he who is sick has not been freed from public penance, he cannot receive the remedy of this mystery, unless first by the prescribed reconciliation he has merited the communion of the body and blood of Christ. He to whom the other sacraments have been restricted, is by no means permitted to use this one.

COUNCIL OF QUIERSY [3] 853

(Against Gottschalk and the Predestinarians)

Redemption and Grace [4]

316   Chap. 1. Omnipotent God created man noble without sin with a free will, and he whom He wished to remain in the sanctity of justice, He placed in Paradise. Man using his free will badly sinned and fell, and became the "mass of perdition" of the entire human race. The just and good God, however, chose from this same mass of perdition according to His foreknowledge those whom through grace He predestined to life [Rom. 8:29 ff.; Eph. 1:11], and He predestined for these eternal life; the others, whom by the judgment of justice he left in the mass of perdition,[5] however, He knew would perish, but He did not predestine that they would perish, because He is just; however, He predestined eternal punishment for them. And on account of this we speak of only one predestination of God, which pertains either to the gift of grace or to the retribution of justice.

317   Chap. 2. The freedom of will which we lost in the first man, we have received back through Christ our Lord; and we have free will for good, preceded and aided by grace, and we have free will for evil, abandoned by

---

[1] Pavia.

[2] Msi XIV 932 E f.; Hrd V 27 A; cf. Hfl IV 77.

[3] Quiersy in Gaul.

[4] Msi XIV 920 D ff.; Hrd V 18 C ff.; Hfl IV 187; ML 125, 49 (129) ff.

[5] Cf. St. Augustine, Ep. 190, 3, 9 [ML 33, 859]; *de dono persev.* 14, 35 [ML 45, 1014].

grace. Moreover, because freed by grace and by grace healed from corruption, we have free will.

Chap. 3. Omnipotent God wishes *all men* without exception *to be* 318 *saved* [I Tim. 2:4] although not all will be saved. However, that certain ones are saved, is the gift of the one who saves; that certain ones perish, however, is the deserved punishment of those who perish.

Chap. 4. Christ Jesus our Lord, as no man who is or has been or ever 319 will be whose nature will not have been assumed in Him, so there is, has been, or will be no man, for whom He has not suffered; although not all will be saved by the mystery of His passion. But because all are not redeemed by the mystery of His passion, He does not regard the greatness and the fullness of the price, but He regards the part of the unfaithful ones and those not believing in faith those things *which He has worked through love* [Gal. 5:6], because the drink of human safety, which has been prepared by our infirmity and by divine strength, has indeed in itself that it may be beneficial to all; but if it is not drunk, it does not heal.

COUNCIL OF VALENCE [1] III 855

(Against John Scotus)

Predestination [2]

Can. 1. We have faithfully and obediently heard that Doctor of the 320 Gentiles warning in faith and in truth: "O Timothy, guard that which has been entrusted to you, avoiding the profane novelties of words, and oppositions under the false name of knowledge, which some promising concerning faith have destroyed" [II Tim. 6:20 f.]; and again: "Shun

---

[1] Valence in Gaul.

[2] Msi XV 3 A ff.; Hrd V 88 E ff.; Hfl IV 193 ff.; cf. ML 125, 49 ff.; Bar(Th) ad 855 n. 1 ff. (14, 422 a ff.). These canons were taken up by the Synod of Tulle I at Saponariae in the year 859 and repeated. It is not to be denied that they were directed against the chapters of Quiersy. But when the entire difference came out of this, namely that the Fathers of both councils thought that two or one predestination should be mentioned with a different sense, and that the Valentinians thought that Hincmar, the president of the meeting at Quiersy, favored the errors of John Scotus, as soon as the mistake was detected, at the Synod of Langres 859 the same bishops who had been present at that of Valence removed from canon 4 of Valence the note attached to the chapters of Quiersy, which we have included in the text within square brackets [ ], and both parties in the Council of Tulle II meeting at Tusiacum in the year 860 entered an agreement and accepted a synodal letter written by Hincmar and some chapters of Quiersy and Valence. On the relation of this council to the Council of Quiersy [n. 316 ff.], cf. *Book on maintaining the truth of Scripture without change* [ML 121, 1083 ff.], composed by St. Remigius, Bishop of Lyons, who himself is the author of the canons of the Council of Valence. Cf. "Gregorianum" 3 (1922) 78.

profane and useless talk; for they contribute much toward ungodliness, and their speech spreadest like an ulcer" [II Tim. 2:16 f.]; and again: "Avoid foolish and unlearned questions, knowing that they beget strifes; but the servant of the Lord must not quarrel" [II Tim. 2:23 f.] and again: "Nothing through contention, nothing through vain glory" [Phil. 2:3]: desiring to be zealous for peace and charity, in so far as God has given, attending the pious counsel of this same apostle: "Solicitous to preserve the unity of the spirit in the bond of peace" [Eph. 4:3], let us with all zeal avoid novel doctrines and presumptuous talkativeness, whence rather the smoke of contention and of scandal between brothers can be stirred up, than any increase of the fear of God arise. Without hesitation, however, to the doctors piously and correctly discussing the word of truth, and to those very clear expositors of Sacred Scripture, namely, Cyprian, Hilary, Ambrose, Jerome, Augustine, and others living tranquilly in Catholic piety, we reverently and obediently submit our hearing and our understanding, and to the best of our ability we embrace the things which they have written for our salvation. For concerning the foreknowledge of God, and predestination, and other questions in which the minds of the brethren are proved not a little scandalized, we believe that we must firmly hold that only which we are happy to have drawn from the maternal womb of the Church.

321   Can. 2. We faithfully hold that "God foreknows and has foreknown eternally both the good deeds which good men will do, and the evil which evil men will do," because we have that word of Scripture which says: "Eternal God, who are the witness of all things hidden, who knew all things before they are" [Dan. 13:42]; and it seems right to hold "that the good certainly have known that through His grace they would be good, and that through the same grace they would receive eternal rewards; that the wicked have known that through their own malice they would do evil deeds, and that through His justice they would be condemned by eternal punishment"; [1] so that according to the Psalmist: "Because power belongs to God and mercy to the Lord, so that He will render to each man according to his works" [Ps. 61:12 f.], and as apostolic doctrine holds: "To them indeed, who according to patience in good works, seek glory and honor and incorruption, eternal life; but to them that are contentious, and who obey not the truth, but give credit to iniquity, wrath and indignation, tribulation and anguish upon every soul of man doing evil" [Rom. 2:7 ff.]. In the same sense, this same one says elsewhere: "In the revelation of the Lord Jesus from heaven with the angels of His power, in a flame of fire, giving vengeance to them who do not know God, and who do not obey the gospel of our Lord Jesus Christ, who shall suffer eternal punishment in destruction . . . when He shall come to be glorified

---

[1] Florus the Deacon, *Sermon on Predestination* [ML 119, 97 A–B].

in His Saints, and to be made wonderful in all them who have believed [II Thess. 1:7 ff.]. Certainly neither (do we believe) that the foreknowledge of God has placed a necessity on any wicked man, so that he cannot be different, but what that one would be from his own will, as God, who knew all things before they are, He foreknew from His omnipotent and immutable Majesty. "Neither do we believe that anyone is condemned by a previous judgment on the part of God but by reason of his own iniquity." [1] "Nor (do we believe) that the wicked thus perish because they were not able to be good; but because they were unwilling to be good, they have remained by their own vice in the mass of damnation either by reason of original sin or even by actual sin." [2]

Can. 3. But also it has seemed right concerning predestination and **322** truly it is right according to the apostolic authority which says: "Or has not the potter power over the clay, from the same lump, to make one vessel unto honor, but another unto dishonor?" [Rom. 9:21] where also he immediately adds: "What if God willing to show His wrath and to make known His power, endured with much patience vessels of wrath fitted or prepared for destruction, so that He might show the riches of His grace on the vessels of mercy, which He has prepared unto glory" [Rom. 9:22 f.]: faithfully we confess the predestination of the elect to life, and the predestination of the impious to death; in the election, moreover, of those who are to be saved, the mercy of God precedes the merited good. In the condemnation, however, of those who are to be lost, the evil which they have deserved precedes the just judgment of God. In predestination, however, (we believe) that God has determined only those things which He Himself either in His gratuitous mercy or in His just judgment would do [3] according to Scripture which says: "Who has done the things which are to be done" [Isa. 45:11, LXX]; in regard to evil men, however, we believe that God foreknew their malice, because it is from them, but that He did not predestine it, because it is not from Him. (We believe) that God, who sees all things, foreknew and predestined that their evil deserved the punishment which followed, because He is just, in whom, as Saint Augustine [4] says, there is concerning all things everywhere so fixed a decree as a certain predestination. To this indeed he applies the saying of Wisdom: "Judgments are prepared for scorners, and striking hammers for the bodies of fools" [Prov. 19:29]. Concerning this unchangeableness of the foreknowledge of the predestination of God, through which in Him future things have already taken place, even in Ecclesiastes the saying is well understood: "I know that all the works which God has made

[1] Florus the Deacon, *Sermon on Predestination* [ML 119, 99 B].
[2] Florus the Deacon, *ibid.* [ML 119, 100 A].
[3] Florus the Deacon, *ibid.* [ML 119, 99 D].
[4] Cf. *On Predestination* 17, 34 [ML 44, 986].

continue forever. We cannot add anything, nor take away those things which God has made that He may be feared" [Eccles. 3:14]. "But we do not only not believe the saying that some have been predestined to evil by divine power," namely as if they could not be different, "but even if there are those who wish to believe such malice, with all detestation," as the Synod of Orange, "we say anathema to them" [see n. 200].

323   Can. 4. Likewise concerning the redemption of the blood of Christ, because of the great error which has arisen from this cause, so that some, as their writings indicate, declare that it has been shed even for those impious ones who from the beginning of the world even up to the passion of our Lord, have died in their wickedness and have been punished by eternal damnation, contrary to that prophet: "O death, I will be Thy death, O hell, I will be thy bite" [Osee 13:14]; it seems right that we should simply and faithfully hold and teach according to the evangelical and apostolic truth, because we hold this price to have been paid for those concerning whom our Lord Himself says: "As Moses lifted up the serpent in the desert, so it is necessary that the Son of man be lifted up, that all, who believe in Him, may not perish, but may have eternal life. For God so loved the world that He gave His only begotten Son: that all, who believe in Him, may not perish but may have eternal life" [John 3:14 ff.], and the Apostle: "Christ," he said, "once has been offered to exhaust the sins of many" [Heb. 9:28]. Furthermore, although they are becoming widely spread, we completely remove from the pious hearing of the faithful the chapters (four, which by the council of our brothers have been unwisely accepted, because of the uselessness or even the harmfulness, and the error contrary to truth, and other reasons) absurdly concluded with nineteen syllogisms, and not outstanding in learning, in which the machination of the devil rather than any tenet of faith is found, and that such and similar things may be avoided through all (chapters), we by the authority of the Holy Spirit forbid (them); we believe also that those who introduce these novel doctrines must be punished lest they become too harmful.

324   Can. 5. Likewise we believe that we must hold most firmly that all the multitude of the faithful, regenerated "from the water and the Holy Spirit" [John 3:5], and through this truly incorporated in the Church, and according to the apostolic doctrine *baptized in the death of Christ* [Rom. 6:3], in His blood has been absolved from its sins; that neither for these could there have been true regeneration unless there were true redemption; since in the sacraments of the Church there is nothing false, nothing theatrical, but certainly everything true, dependent upon truth itself and sincerity. Moreover, from this very multitude of the faithful and the redeemed some are preserved in eternal salvation, because through

the grace of God they remain faithfully in their redemption, bearing in their hearts the voice of their God Himself: "Who . . . perseveres even unto the end, he will be saved" [Matt. 10:22; 24:13]; that others, because they were unwilling to remain in the safety of faith, which in the beginning they received, and because they choose by wrong teaching or by a wrong life to make void rather than to preserve the grace of redemption, came in no way to the fullness of salvation and to the reception of eternal beatitude. In both certainly we have the doctrine of the holy Doctor: "We who are baptized in Christ Jesus, are baptized in His death" [Rom. 6:3], and: "All you who are baptized in Christ have put on Christ" [Gal. 3:27], and again: "Let us approach with a true heart in fullness of faith, having our hearts sprinkled from an evil conscience, and our bodies washed with clean water let us hold unwavering the confession of our hope" [Heb. 10:22], and again: "For to us sinning willfully after the accepted knowledge of the truth, there is now left no sacrifice for sins" [Heb. 10:26], and again: "He who making void the law of Moses, dies without mercy with two or three witnesses. How much more do you think he deserves worse punishments, who has crushed under foot the son of God, and has considered the blood of the testament unclean, by which he was sanctified, and has offered insult to the Spirit of grace?" [Heb. 10:28].

Can. 6. Likewise concerning grace, through which thos: who believe **325** are saved, and without which never has a rational creature lived happily, and concerning free will weakened through sin in our first parents, but reintegrated and healed through the grace of our Lord Jesus for His faithful, we most constant and in complete faith confess the same, which the most Holy Fathers by the authority of the Sacred Scriptures have left for us to hold, which the Synod of Africa and the Synod of Orange [n. 174 ff.] have professed, which the most blessed Pontiffs of the Apostolic See in the Catholic faith have held; but also concerning nature and grace, we presume in no manner to change to another way. We thoroughly refute, however, *the foolish questions,* and the utterly *old wives' tales,* the porridge of the Scoti bearing nausea to the purity of faith, which in these most dangerous and grave times, to the summit of cur labors even up to the dividing of charity wretchedly and tearfully have arisen, lest Christian minds henceforth *be corrupted and cut off* even from the purity of faith, *which is in Christ* [II Cor. 11:3] *Jesus,* and we warn by the love of our Lord Christ that brotherly charity, by being on its guard, protects the hearing from such things. Let the brotherhood recall that it is hard pressed by the very grave evils of the world, by the excessive harvest of iniquity, and that it is most cruelly suffocated by the chaff of light men. Let it have zeal to conquer these things; let it labor to correct these things; and let it not burden the assembly with the inanities of those who grieve and weep piously, but rather in certain and true faith, let that be embraced which has been sufficiently determined by the Holy Fathers concerning these and similar things.

BENEDICT III 855–858

ST. NICHOLAS I 858–867

ROMAN COUNCIL 860 AND 863

Primacy, the Passion of Christ, Baptism [1]

326   Chap. 5. If anyone condemns dogmas, mandates, interdicts, sanctions or decrees, promulgated by the one presiding in the Apostolic See, for the Catholic faith, for the correction of the faithful, for the emendation of criminals, either by an interdict of threatening or of future ills, let him be anathema.[2]

327   Chap. 7. Truly indeed we must believe and in every way profess that our Lord Jesus Christ, God and Son of God, suffered the passion of the Cross only according to the flesh; in the Godhead however, he remained impassible, as the apostolic authority teaches and the doctrine of the Holy Fathers most clearly shows.

328   Chap. 8. Let these however be anathema, who say that our Redeemer Jesus Christ and Son of God sustained the passion of the Cross according to His Godhead, since it is impious and detestable to Catholic minds.

329   Chap. 9. For all those who say that these who believing in the most holy font of baptism are reborn in the Father, in the Son, and in the Holy Spirit, are not equally cleansed from original sin, let it be anathema.

The Immunity and Independence of the Church [3]

[From epistle (8) "Proposueramus quidem" to Michael
the Emperor, 865]

330   . . . Neither by Augustus, nor by all the clergy, nor by religious, nor by the people will the judge be judged [4]. . . . "The first seat will not be judged by anyone" [5] [see n. 352 ff.].

---

[1] Msi XV 652 E 658 f.; Jf 2692; Hrd V 574 E; cf. Hfl IV 260, 272 ff.

[2] This chapter is due to the council of the year 863, the following to the council of the year 861.

[3] Msi XV 196 D ff.; cf. Jf 2796 c. Add; Hrd V 154 C ff.; ML 119, 938 D ff.; cf. Hfl IV 334 f.

[4] These are alleged to be the words of St. Sylvester.

[5] From the acts of the apocryphal synod of Sinuessa (between Rome and Capua), 303 [cf. Hfl I 143 ff.].

. . . Where have you ever read that your former rulers were present **331** in synodal meetings, unless perchance in those in which (matters) concerning faith were discussed, which is universal, which is common to all, which pertains not only to the clergy but even to the laity and certainly to all Christians? . . . The greater the complaint which is brought to the judgment of a more powerful authority, so much the higher authority must be sought, until gradually it comes to this See, whose cause either from itself, as the merits of the matters demand, is changed for the better or is left without question to the will of God alone.

Furthermore if you have not heard us, it remains for you to be with us **332** of necessity, such as our Lord Jesus Christ has commanded those to be considered, who disdained to hear the Church of God, especially since the privileges of the Roman Church, built on Blessed Peter by the word of Christ, deposited in the Church herself, observed in ancient times and celebrated by the sacred universal Synods, and venerated jointly by the entire Church, can by no means be diminished, by no means infringed upon, by no means changed; for the foundation which God has established, no human effort has the power to destroy and what God has determined, remains firm and strong. . . . Thus the privileges granted to this holy Church by Christ, not given by the Synod, but now only celebrated and venerated. . . .

Since, according to the canons, where there is a greater authority, the **333** judgment of the inferiors must be brought to it to be annulled, or to be substantiated, certainly it is evident that the judgment of the Apostolic See, of whose authority there is none greater, is to be refused by no one. If indeed they wish the canon to be appealed to any part of the world; from it, however, no one may be permitted [1] to appeal. . . . We do not deny that the opinion of this See can be changed for the better, when either something shall have been stealthily snatched from it, or by the very consideration of age or time, or by a dispensation of grave necessity, it shall have decided to regulate something. We beseech you, however, never question the judgment of the Church of God; that indeed bears no prejudgment on your power, since it begs eternal divinity for its own stability, and it beseeches in constant prayer for your well being and eternal salvation. Do not usurp the things that belong to it; do not wish to snatch away that which has been intrusted to it alone, knowing that without doubt every administrator of mundane affairs ought to be removed from sacred affairs, just as it is proper that no one from the group of clergy and those militant for God be implicated in any secular affairs. Finally, we are completely without knowledge of how those to whom it has been intrusted only to be in charge of human affairs presume to judge concerning those through whom divine affairs are ministered. These

---

[1] St. Gelasius I, letter 26 to the bishops of Dardania, n. 5 [Th 399].

things existed before the coming of Christ, so that some figuratively lived
at one and the same time as kings and priests; this, sacred history shows
how holy Melchisedech was, and this the devil imitated in his members,
since he always hastens to assume for himself in a tyrannical spirit the
things which are becoming to the divine culture, so that these pagan
emperors were also called supreme pontiffs. But when it came to the same
true king and pontiff, neither has He, the emperor, voluntarily taken to
himself the rights of the pontiff, nor as pontiff has He usurped the name
of the emperor. Since the same "mediator of God and man, the man
Christ Jesus" [I Tim. 2:5] by His own acts and distinct dignities, has
so decreed the duties of each power, wishing His own to be lifted up by
His salutary humility, not to be submerged again by human pride, so that
Christian rulers for eternal life may need pontiffs, and that pontiffs may
use imperial laws only for the course of temporal affairs; because spiritual
action differs from carnal efforts.

The Form of Matrimony [1]

[From the responses of Nicholas to the decrees of
the Bulgars, Nov., 866]

334   Chap. 3 . . . According to the laws, let the consent alone of those
suffice concerning whose union there is question; and if by chance this
consent alone be lacking in the marriage, all other things, even when
solemnized with intercourse itself, are in vain.

The Form and Minister of Baptism [2]

[From the responses to the decrees of the Bulgars, Nov., 866]

334a   Chap. 15. You ask whether those persons who received baptism from
that man [who imagines himself a priest] are Christians or ought to be
baptized again. If they have been baptized in the name of the highest and
indivisible Trinity, they certainly are Christians; and it is not proper that
they be baptized again, by whatever Christian they have been baptized.
. . . An evil person by ministering blessings brings an accumulation of
harm not upon others but upon himself, and by this it is certain that no
portion of injury touched those whom that Greek baptized, because: "He
it is that baptizeth" [John 1:33], that is Christ, and again: "God . . .
giveth the increase" [I Cor. 3:7] is heard; and not man.

335   Chap. 104. You assert that in your fatherland many have been baptized

---

[1] Msi XV 403 B; Jf 2812 (c. Add); Hrd V 355 A; ML 119, 980 C; cf. Hfl IX 347.
[2] Msi XV 408 f. 432 C; Jf 2812 (c. Add); Hrd V 360, 383 E; ML 119, 986 f. and
1014 D; Hfl IV 348 ff.

by a certain Jew, you do not know whether Christian or pagan, and you consult us as to what should be done about them. If indeed they have been baptized in the name of the Holy Trinity or only in the name of Christ, as we read in the Acts of the Apostles [cf. Acts 2:38; 19:5], (surely it is one and the same, as Saint Ambrose [1] sets forth) it is established that they should not be baptized again.

HADRIAN II 867–872
COUNCIL OF CONSTANTINOPLE IV
869–870

Ecumenical VIII (against Photius)

Canons against Photius [2]

In actio I the rule of faith of Hormisdas is read and subscribed [see n. 171 f.]

(Text of Anastasius:) Canon 1— We, wishing to advance without offense through the just and regal way of divine justice, ought to retain the definitions and opinions of the Holy Fathers who live according to God as lamps always burning and illuminating our steps. Therefore, judging and believing these as favorable words according to the great and very wise Dionysius,[3] likewise regarding these with the divine David we most readily sing: "The Command of the

We, wishing to advance without offense through the just and royal way of divine justice, ought to control the definitions of the Holy Fathers as lamps always burning. Therefore, we confess to keep and guard the rules which have been handed down in the Catholic and Apostolic Church by the holy and noted Apostles and by the universal and local orthodox synods or by any Father, teacher of the Church, speaking the word of God. For the great Apostle Paul expressly

336

---

[1] *De Spiritu Sancto* 1, 3, 42 [ML 16, 714].

[2] Msi XVI 160 A ff. (lat.) 397 D ff. (gr.); ML 129, 150 B ff.; Hrd V 899 A ff.; cf. Hfl IV 417 ff.; Bar(Th) ad 869 n. 11 ff. (15, 151 a ff.).—The authentic acts of this council are not extant. A double form of these canons is preserved, one in Greek the shorter and exhibiting fewer canons, the other from a version of Anastasius, a librarian, who accuses the Greeks of falsifying, and affirms that they transferred something from the authentic acts preserved in the archives of the Roman church. Yet it is remarkable that those acts which favor the Roman pontiff are present in the Greek, and that those which [favor] the Constantinopolitan high priest are lacking.

[3] Pseudo-Dionysius Areop., *De eccl. hier.* 1, 4 [MG 3, 375].

Lord is a light illumining our eyes" [Ps. 18:9], and, "Thy light [law] is a lamp to my feet and a light to my ways" [Ps. 118:105], and with the writer of Proverbs we say: "Thy command is a light and Thy law is a light" [Prov. 6:23]; and with a loud voice with Isaias we cry to the Lord God: "Thy precepts are a light upon the earth" [Isa. 26:9: LXX]. For to the light truly have been assimilated the exhortations and dissuasions of the divine canons, according as that which is better is discerned from that which is worse, and the expedient and profitable from that which is recognized as not expedient but even harmful. Therefore we profess to keep and guard the rules, which have been handed down for the holy, Catholic and Apostolic Church by the holy, noted apostles as well as by the universal and also the local Councils of the orthodox or even by any Father or teacher of the Church speaking the word of God; guiding by these both our own life and morals and also the whole group of priests, but also all those who are known by the name Christian, resolving to submit canonically to these punishments and condemnations and on the other hand, to the receptions and justifications which through these have been brought forth and defined; Paul, the great apostle, openly gave warning *to hold* indeed the traditions which we have received *either through the word or through the epistle* [II Thess. 2:14] of the Saints who have previously been distinguished.

exhorted us *to hold the traditions* which we have received either through word or epistles of the Saints who have been distinguished before.

337   Can. 3. We decree that the sacred image of our Lord Jesus Christ, the Liberator and Savior of all, be adored in equal honor with the book of the holy Gospels. For, as through the eloquence of the syllables which are in the book, we should all attain salvation, so through the imaginal energies of colors both all the wise and the unwise from that which is manifest enjoy usefulness; for the things which are the sermon in syllables, these things also the writing which is in colors, teaches and commands; and it is fitting, that according to the suitableness of reason and very

We adore the sacred image of our Lord Jesus Christ in like honor with the book of the Holy Gospels. For as through the syllables carried in it, we all attain salvation, so through the imaginal energies of the colors both all the wise and the unwise from that which is manifest enjoy usefulness; for the things which are the sermon in syllables, those things also the writing which is in colors teaches and commands. If, therefore, anyone does not adore the image of Christ the Savior, let him not see His form in the second coming. And we likewise honor and adore the image of His undefiled ancient tradition on account of honor, because they refer to the very principal things, it follows likewise that the images will be honored and adored equally as the sacred book of the holy Gospels and the figure of the precious Cross. Mother and the images of the holy angels, just as Divine Scripture characterizes them in words. And let those who do not hold thus be anathema.

If, therefore anyone does not adore the image of Christ the Savior, let him not see His form when *He will come* in paternal glory *to be glorified and to glorify His saints* [II Thess. 1:10]; but let him be separated from His communion and glory; likewise, however, also the image of Mary, His undefiled Mother, and Mother of God; moreover, we also represent the images of the holy Angels, just as Divine Scripture shows them in words; and also of the Apostles most worthy of praise, of the Prophets, of the Martyrs and of holy men; at the same time also of all the saints we both honor and venerate. And whoever does not hold thus, let him be anathema from the Father, and the Son, and the Holy Spirit.

Can. 11. Although the Old and the New Testaments teach that man has one rational and intellectual soul, and all the Fathers speaking the word of God and all the teachers of the Church declare the same opinion, certain persons giving attention to the inventors of evil, have reached such a degree of impiety that they impudently declare that man has two souls, and by certain irrational attempts "through wisdom which has been made foolish" [I Cor. 1:20], they try to strengthen their own heresy. Hastening to root out as the very worst cockle this wicked opinion

Although the Old and New **338** Testaments teach that man has one rational and intellectual soul, and all the Fathers and teachers of the Church teach the same opinion, there are some who think that he has two souls, and by certain irrational attempts they strengthen their own heresy. Therefore, this holy and ecumenical synod loudly anathematizes the originators of such impiety and those who agree with them; and if anyone shall dare to speak contrary to the rest, let him be anathema.

currently germinating, and furthermore carrying "the firebrand in the hand of Truth" [Matt. 3:12; 3:17], and wishing to transmit with the unquenchable fire all the chaff and "to show forth the cleansed threshing floor of Christ" [Matt. 3:12; Luke 3:17] this holy and universal Synod with a loud voice declares anathema all inventors and perpetrators of such impiety and those believing things similar to these, and it defines and promulgates that no one have or keep in any way the statutes of the authors of this impiety. If, however, anyone should presume to act contrary to this holy and great Synod, let him be anathema, and let him be separated from the faith and worship of Christians.

339   Can. 12. In accord with the apostolic and synodical canons forbidding promotions and consecrations of bishops made by the power and precept of princes, we define and offer the opinion also that, if any bishop through the craftiness or tyranny of princes should accept a consecration of such dignity, let him by all means be deposed, since he wished or agreed to possess the house of God not from the will of God both by ecclesiastical rite and decree, but from a desire of carnal sense, from men and through men.

340   From Can. 17. . . . Moreover, we cast aside from our ears as something poisonous what is said by certain ignorant men, namely, that it is not possible to hold a synod without the presence of the civil ruler, since never did the sacred canons order secular leaders to meet in councils, but only bishops. Thus neither do we find that they were present in the synods, ecumenical councils excepted; for neither is it right that secular rulers be spectators of things which sometimes happen to the priests of God.

(12) There came to our ears the statement that a synod cannot be held without the presence of the civil ruler. But nowhere do the sacred canons order secular leaders to come together in synods, but only bishops. Thus we do not find that their presence was effected except for ecumenical synods. For it is not right that secular rulers be spectators of the things that happen to the priests of God.

341   Can. 21. We, believing that the word of the Lord which Christ spoke to His Apostles and disciples: "Who receives you, receives Me" [Matt. 10:40]: "and who spurns you, spurns me" [Luke 10:16], was said to all, even to those who after them according to them have been made Supreme Pontiffs and chiefs of the pastors, declare that absolutely no one of the powerful of this world may try to dishonor or move from his throne anyone of those who are in command of the patriarchial sees, but that they judge them worthy of all reverence and honor; especially indeed the most holy Pope of senior Rome; next the Patriarch of Constantinople; then certainly of Alexandria and of Antioch and of Jerusalem; but that no one compose or prepare any writings and words against the most holy Pope of older Rome under the pretext, as it were, of some evil crimes, a thing which both Photius did recently, and Dioscorus long ago.

Whoever, moreover, shall use such boasting and boldness that,

(13) If anyone should employ such daring as, like Photius and

following Photius or Dioscorus, in writings or without writings he may arouse certain injuries against the See of Peter, the chief of the Apostles, let him receive the equal and same condemnation as those. But if anyone enjoying some secular power or being influential should try to depose the above mentioned Pope of the Apostolic Chair or any of the other Patriarchs, let him be anathema. But if the universal Synod shall have met, and there will have arisen even concerning the holy church of the Romans any doubt or controversy whatever, it is necessary with veneration and with fitting reverence to investigate and to accept a solution concerning the proposed question, either to offer to have offered but not boldly to declare an opinion contrary to the Supreme Pontiffs of senior Rome.

Dioscorus, in writings or without writings, to rouse certain inquiries against the See of Peter, the chief of the Apostles, let him receive the same condemnation as those; but if, when the ecumenical synod has met, any doubt arises even about the church of the Romans, it is possible to make an investigation reverently and with fitting respect concerning the question at hand, and to accept the solution either to be assisted or to assist, but not boldly to deliver (an opinion) contrary to the Supreme Pontiffs of senior Rome.

JOHN VIII 872-882	JOHN X 914-928
MARINUS I 882-884	LEO VI 928
ST. HADRIAN III 884-885	STEPHAN VIII 929-931
STEPHAN VI 885-891	JOHN XI 931-935
FORMOSUS 891-896	LEO VII 936-939
BONIFACE VI, 896	STEPHAN IX 939-942
STEPHAN VII 896-897	MARINUS II 942-946
ROMANUS 897	AGAPETUS II 946-955
THEODORE II 897	JOHN XII 955-963
JOHN IX 898-900	LEO VIII 963-964
BENEDICT IV 900-903	BENEDICT V 964 (†966)
LEO V 903	JOHN XIII 965-972
SERGIUS III 904-911	BENEDICT VI 973-974
ANASTASIUS III 911-913	BENEDICT VII 974-983
LANDO 913-914	JOHN XIV 983-984

JOHN XV 985–996

ROMAN COUNCIL 993

(For the Canonization of St. Udalrich)

The Worship of the Saints [1]

342 . . . By common agreement we have decreed that we should venerate the memory of that one, namely, St. Udalrich the bishop, with all pious affection and most faithful devotion, since we so venerated and worship the relics of the martyrs and confessors that Him whose martyrs and confessors they are, we may adore; we honor the servants that honor may redound to the Lord, who said: "Who receives you, receives me" [Matt. 10:40]; and thus we who do not have the pledge of our justice, by their prayers and merits may be helped jointly before the most clement God, because the salutary divine precepts both of the holy Canons and of the venerable Fathers effaciously taught that by the attentive study of all the churches, and by the effort of apostolic guidance, the documents accomplish a degree of usefulness and an integrity of strength; just as the memory of the already mentioned venerable Bishop Udalrich dedicated to divine worship exists and is always advantageous in most devoutly giving praise to God.

Gregory V 996–999	John XIX 1024–1032
Sylvester II 999–1003	Benedict IX 1032–1044
John XVII 1003	Sylvester III 1045
John XVIII 1004–1009	Gregory VI 1045–1046
Sergius IV 1009–1012	Clement II 1046–1047
Benedict VIII 1012–1024	Damasus II 1048

ST. LEO IX 1049–1054

Symbol of faith [2]

[From the epistle "Congratulamur vehementer" to Peter, Bishop of Antioch, April 13, 1053]

343 For I firmly believe that the Holy Trinity, the Father and the Son and the Holy Spirit, is one omnipotent God, and in the Trinity the whole

---

[1] Msi XIX 170 E f.; cf. Jf 2945; Hrd VI, I 727 f.; Hfl IV 642; Bar(Th) ad 983 n. 1 ff. (16, 313).

[2] Msi XIX 662 B ff.; cf. Jf 4297 c. Add.; ML 143, 771 C ff.; Hrd VI I 923 C ff.—

Godhead is co-essential and consubstantial, co-eternal and co-omnipotent, and of one will, power, and majesty; the creator of all creation, from whom all things, through whom all things, in whom all things [Rom. 11:36] which are in heaven or on earth, visible or invisible. Likewise I believe that each person in the Holy Trinity is the one true God, complete and perfect.

I believe also that the Son of God the Father, the Word of God, was 344 born eternally before all time from the Father, consubstantial, co-omnipotent, and co-equal to the Father through all things in divinity; born of the Holy Spirit from the ever virgin Mary in time, with a rational soul, having two nativities, the one from the Father, eternal, the other from the Mother, in time; having two wills and operations, true God and true man, individual in each nature and perfect, not having suffered a fusion and division, not adopted or phantastical, the one and only God, the Son of God in two natures, but in the singleness of one person, incapable of suffering and immortal in divinity; but in humanity for us and for our salvation suffered in the true passion of the body and was buried, and arose from the dead on the third day in the true resurrection of the body; because of which we must declare with the disciples that He ate from no need of food but only from will and power; on the fortieth day after His resurrection with the flesh in which He arose, and with His soul He ascended into heaven and sits at the right hand of the Father, whence on the tenth day He sent the Holy Spirit, and thence, as He ascended, He will come to judge the living and the dead, and will render to each one according to his works.

I believe also that the Holy Spirit, complete and perfect and true God, 345 proceeding from the Father and the Son, co-equal, co-essential, co-omnipotent and co-eternal with the Father and the Son in all respects, has spoken through the prophets.

That this holy and individual Trinity is not three Gods, but in three 346 persons and in one nature or essence [is] one God omnipotent, external, invisible and incommutable, so I believe and confess, so that I may truly proclaim that the Father is not begotten, the Son is the only begotten one, and the Holy Spirit is neither begotten nor unbegotten, but proceeds from the Father and the Son.

(Variant Readings:) I believe that the one true Church is holy, Catholic 347 and apostolic, in which is given one baptism and the true remission of all sins. I also believe in a true resurrection of this body, which now I bear, and in eternal life.

The articles of this creed almost agree with the questions which were customarily proposed according to the "Ancient statutes of the Church" [cf. n. 150 not.] to those to be consecrated bishops.—See the canon in ML 56, 879 B ff. [cf. also the Creed of Palaeologus n. 461 ff.].

348 I believe also that there is one author of the New and Old Testament, of the law both of the Prophets and of the Apostles, namely the omnipotent God and Lord. (I believe) that God predestined only the good things, but that He foreknew the good and the evil. I believe and profess that the grace of God precedes and follows man, yet in such a manner that I do not deny free will to the rational creature. I also believe and declare that the soul is not a part of God but was created from nothing and was without baptism subject to original sin.

349 Furthermore, I declare anathema every heresy raising itself against the holy Catholic Church, and likewise him whosoever has honored or believes that any writings beyond those which the Catholic Church accepts ought to be held in authority or has venerated them. I accept entirely the four Councils and I venerate them as the four Gospels, because through four parts of the world the universal Church, upon these as on square stone, has been founded [1]. . . . Equally I accept and venerate the three remaining Councils. . . . Whatever the above mentioned seven holy and universal Councils believe and praise I also believe and praise, and whomever they declare anathema, I declare anathema.

The Primacy of the Roman Pontiff [2]

[From the epistle "In terra pax hominibus" to Michael
Cerularius and to Leo of Achrida, September 2, 1053]

350 Chap. 5 . . . You are said to have condemned publicly in a strange presumption and incredible boldness the Apostolic and Latin Church, neither heard nor refuted, for the reason chiefly that it dared to celebrate the commemoration of the passion of the Lord from the Azymes. Behold your incautious reprehension, behold your evil boasting, when "you put your mouth into heaven. When your tongue passing on to the earth" [Ps. 72:9], by human arguments and conjectures attempts to uproot and overturn the ancient faith. . . .

351 Chap. 7 . . . The holy Church built upon a rock, that is Christ, and upon *Peter* or Cephas, the son of John who first was called Simon, because by the gates of Hell, that is, by the disputations of heretics which lead the vain to destruction, it would never be overcome; thus Truth itself promises, through whom are true, whatsoever things are true: "The gates of hell will not prevail against it" [Matt. 16:18]. The same Son declares that He obtained the effect of this promise from the Father by prayers, by saying to Peter: "Simon, behold Satan etc." [Luke 23:31]. Therefore, will

---

[1] Cf. St. Gregory the Great, Letter 1, 1 ep. 25 [ML 77, 478].

[2] Msi XIX 638 B ff.; cf. Jf 4302; ML 143, 747 C ff.; Hrd VI, I 929 E ff.; cf. Hfl IV 768 ff.—It is not established that this letter was really transmitted (cf. A. Michel, *Humbert and Kerullarios I* [1925], p. 55).

there be anyone so foolish as to dare to regard His prayer as in anyway vain whose being willing is being able? By the See of the chief of the Apostles, namely by the Roman Church, through the same Peter, as well as through his successors, have not the comments of all the heretics been disapproved, rejected, and overcome, and the hearts of the brethren in the faith of Peter which so far neither has failed, nor up to the end will fail, been strengthened?

Chap. 11. By passing a preceding judgment on the great See, concern- 352 ing which it is not permitted any man to pass judgment, you have received anathema from all the Fathers of all the venerable Councils. . . .

Chap. 32 . . . As the hinge while remaining immovable opens and 353 closes the door, so Peter and his successors have free judgment over all the Church, since no one should remove their status because "the highest See is judged by no one." [see n. 330 ff.]

Victor II 1055–1057   Stephen IX 1057–1058
Benedict X, 1058–1059

NICHOLAS II 1059–1061

ROMAN COUNCIL 1060

The Ordinations by Simoniacs [1]

Lord Pope Nicholas presiding at the Synod in the Basilica of Constantine 354 said: "We judge that in preserving dignity no mercy is to be shown toward the simoniacs; but according to the sanctions of the canons and the decrees of the Holy Fathers we condemn them entirely and by apostolic authority we decree that they are to be deposed. Concerning those, however, who have been ordained by the simoniacs, not through money but gratis, because the question from long standing has been drawn out still longer, we absolve from every manner [another version: knot or impediment] of doubt; so that with regard to this chapter let us permit no one later to doubt. . . . Thus, moreover, by the authority of the holy Apostles Peter and Paul we entirely forbid that at any time any of our successors from this our permission take or fix a rule for himself or another, because the authority of the ancient Fathers has not promulgated this by order or grant, but too great a necessity of the time has forced us to permit it. . . ."

Alexander II 1061–1073

---

[1] Msi XIX 899 B; cf. Jf post 4398; Hrd VI, I 1163 D; Hfl IV 825 and CIC Decr. II, 1, 1, 100: Frdbg I 401; Bar(Th) ad 1059 n. 34 (17, 150b).

ST. GREGORY VII 1073–1085

ROMAN COUNCIL VI 1079

(Against Berengarius)

The Most Holy Eucharist [1]

(Oath taken by Berengarius)

355   I, Berengarius, in my heart believe and with my lips confess that through the mystery of the sacred prayer and the words of our Redeemer the bread and wine which are placed on the altar are substantially changed into the true and proper and living flesh and blood of Jesus Christ, our Lord, and that after consecration it is the true body of Christ which was born of the Virgin and which, offered for the salvation of the world, was suspended on the Cross, and which sitteth at the right hand of the Father, and the true blood of Christ, which was poured out from His side not only through the sign and power of the sacrament, but in its property of nature and in truth of substance, as here briefly in a few words is contained and I have read and you understand. Thus I believe, nor will I teach contrary to this belief. So help me God and these holy Gospels of God.

VICTOR III 1087

URBAN II 1088–1099

COUNCIL OF BENEVENTO 1091

The Sacramental Nature of the Diaconate [2]

356   Can. 1. Let no one be chosen in order of succession into the episcopacy except one who has been found living religiously in sacred orders. More-

---

[1] Msi XX 524 D; cf. Jf post 5102; ML 148, 811; Hrd VI I 1585 B; cf. Hfl V 129; Bar(Th) ad 1079 n. 3 (17, 453 b f.).—Berengarius was condemned by St. Leo IX in the Council of Rome 1050 [Msi XIX 759 ff.] and of Vercelli 1050 [Msi XIX 773 ff.]; by Victor II in the Synod of Florence 1055 [Msi XIX 837 f.]; by Nicholas II in the Synod of Rome 1059 [Msi XIX 900 A]; by St. Gregory VII in two councils of Rome 1078 [Msi XX 516 C] and 1079. In this extremity he was compelled to subscribe to this formula, after he had frequently either deluded the judges or returned to his vomit.

[2] Msi XX 738 E; Jf post 5444; cf. CIC Decr. I, 60, 4; Frdbg I 227; Rcht I 195.—According to a decision of Innocent III even a subdeacon can be elected to the episcopacy (Benedict XIV, *De syn. dioec.* VIII, 9, 9 f.).

over we call sacred orders the diaconate and the priesthood. Since we read that the early Church had only these, only concerning these do we have the precept of the Apostle.

PASCHAL II 1099–1118

LATERAN COUNCIL 1102

(Against Henry IV)

The Obedience Owed the Church [1]

[Formula prescribed for all the cities of the Eastern Church]

I declare anathema every heresy and especially that one which disturbs **357** the position of the present Church, which teaches and declares that excommunication is to be despised and that the restrictions of the Church are to be cast aside. Moreover, I promise obedience to Paschal, the supreme Pontiff of the Apostolic See, and to his successors under the testimony of Christ and the Church, affirming what the holy and universal Church affirms and condemning what she condemns.

COUNCIL OF GUASTALLA [2] 1106

The Ordinations by Heretics and Simoniacs [3]

For many years now the broad extent of the Teutonic kingdom has **358** been separated from the unity of the Apostolic See. In this schism indeed

---

[1] Msi XX 1147 C; Hrd VI, II 1863 A; Bar(Th) ad 1102 n. 2 (18, 130 b); cf. Hfl V 266 ff.

[2] Guastalla of Lombardy.

[3] Msi XX 1209 f.; Jf post 6094; Hrd VI, II 1183 (primo) A; Bar(Th) ad 1106 n. 29 (18, 171 a). Because of this a serious controversy had arisen in the tenth century as to whether ordinations by heretics and simoniacs were valid or not, because certain of the more ancient authorities seemed to have decided that they are invalid. Cf. the Council of Rome, 964 [Msi XVIII 474], Urban II ep. to Lanzo etc., 1091 [Msi XX 705 f.]. But presently Clement II in a synod of Rome 1047 [Msi XIX 627 f.], when inflicting punishments on those ordained simoniacally, ignored the validity of the ordinations. Leo IX confirmed this decree in a Roman synod 1049, and declared that the ordinations by heretics were valid through a snare [Hrd VI, II 991]. But Nicholas II in a Roman Synod 1059, permitted those who thus far had been ordained gratis by simoniacs to remain in their office [see n. 354]. Urban II in Placentina 1094, made the same decision regarding those who unknowingly had been ordained by simoniacs, and regarding those ordained by schismatics whom, however, manner of life and knowledge commended [Msi XX 805; cf. 809]. Paschal II decided similarly. But the entire question was only slowly lulled to sleep: see Hfl V op. 380 f., 440, 442, 514, 712, 718, 725. On reordinations which are said to

so great a danger has arisen that—and we say this with sorrow—only a few priests or Catholic clergy are found in such a broad extent of territory. Therefore, with so many sons living in this condition, the necessity of Christian peace demands that regarding this (group) the maternal womb of the Church be open. Therefore instructed by the examples and writings of our Fathers, who in different times received into their ranks the Novatians, the Donatists, and other heretics, we are receiving in the episcopal office the bishops of the above-mentioned region who have been ordained in schism, unless they are proven usurpers, simoniacs, or criminals. We decree the same concerning the clergy of any rank whom way of life together with knowledge commends.

Gᴇʟᴀsɪᴜs II 1118–1119

CALLISTUS II 1119–1124
LATERAN COUNCIL I 1123

Ecumênical IX (concerning investitures)

Simony, Celibacy, Investiture, Incest [1]

359   Can. 1. "Following the examples of the Holy Fathers" and renewing the duty of our office "we forbid in every way by the authority of the Apostolic See that anyone by means of money be ordained or promoted in the Church of God. But if anyone shall have acquired ordination or promotion in the Church in this way, let him be entirely deprived of his office." [2]

---

have been made by Alexander III, Lucius III, Urban III, and others, see L. Saltet, *Les réordinations,* Paris 1907.

[1] Msi XXI 282 A ff.; Hrd VI, II 1111 C ff.; cf. Hfl V 379 ff.; Bar(Th) ad 1122 n. 1 ff. (18, 343 a ff.).

[2] From the Council of Tolosa 1119, held by Callistus II, can. 1 [Msi XXI 226]. The following are against the heresy of simony, which was called a heresy because the simoniacs not only sinned against the law but contended that the payment of money for holy orders is licit; and so they attacked the law of good morals, or they said that what they themselves on the other hand opposed were not prohibited by it (simony). Against this curse the Pontiffs and Councils fought with the following decrees: Chalcedon 451, can. 2 [Msi VII 393 B]; Clement II in Roman Synod 1047 [Msi XIX 627 f.]; Leo IX in Roman Synod I 1049 [Msi XIX 721 C], Remen. 1049 c. 2 [Msi XIX 741 E], Mogunt 1049 [Msi XIX 749 c]; Nicholas II in Roman Synod 1059 c. 9 [Msi XIX 909 A]; Alexander II in Roman Synod 1063 c. 1 f. [Msi XIX 1023 f.]; Gregory VII in Roman Synod 1073 [Msi XX 173 E]; 1074, c. 6–10 [Msi XX 408 ff.]; 1078 [Msi XX 503 D]; 1078, c. 4 [Msi XX 509 E]; Urban II in Melfit. 1089, c. 1 [Msi XX 721 f.]; Placentina 1095, c 1–7 [Msi XX 805 f.]; Claromontan. 1095 [Msi XX 916 D]; Roman. 1099 c 1–7 [Msi XX 961 f.]; Callistus II in Tolosa 1119, c. 1 [Msi XXI 225 C]; Remen c. 1 [Msi XXI 235 B]; ecumenical

Can. 3. We absolutely forbid priests, deacons, or subdeacons the in- 360
timacy of concubines and of wives, and cohabitation with other women,
except those with whom for reasons of necessity alone the Nicene Synod
permits them to live, that is, a mother, sister, paternal or maternal aunt,
or others of this kind concerning whom no suspicion may justly arise
[see n. 52 b f.].[1]

Can. 4. "Besides according to the sanction of the most blessed Pope 361
Stephen we have decided that laymen, although they are religious, nevertheless have no faculty for determining anything concerning ecclesiastical
possessions; but according to the Canons of the Apostles let the bishop
have the care of all ecclesiastical business, and let him dispense these things
as in the sight of God. If, therefore, any civil ruler or other layman ap-
propriates to himself either a donation of property or of ecclesiastical
possessions, let him be judged sacrilegious."[2]

Can. 5. "We forbid that the marriages of blood relatives take place 362
since both divine and secular laws forbid these. For divine laws not only
cast out but also call wicked those who do this, and those who are born

---

synods, Lat. 1 hoc can. 1; Lat. II 1139, can. 1 and 2 [see n. 364]; Lat. III 1179,
can. 7 and 15 [see n. 400]; Lat. IV 1215, can. 63 [Msi XXII 1051]. By these
decrees simoniac ordinations and promotions of any kind and purchases of things
of the altar are prohibited.

[1] The following are against the heresy of the Nicolaites, that is, of incontinent
clergy, who were regarded as heretics in so far as they not only infringed upon the
church law of celibacy and practiced concubinage, but also dishonored the law as
impossible for them to keep, and harmful to morals. The following decrees also
pertain to this: Leo IX in Mainz 1049 [Msi XIX 749 C]; Gregory VII in Roman
Synod 1073 [Msi XX 173 E]; 1074, c. 11–21 [Msi XX 413 ff. 434]; 1078, c. 11
[Msi XX 510 E]; Urban II in Melfi 1089, c. 2 12 [Msi XX 723 f.]; Claromontana
1095, c. 1 [Msi XX 906 A]; Callistus II in Remensi 1119, c. 5 [Msi XXI 236 B];
Lat. I oec., hoc can. 3; Lat. II 1139, can. 6 7 8, which declares the marriages of
older clergy and regulars invalid [Msi XXI 527 f.]; Lateran III, 1179 c. 11 [Msi
XXII 224 f.].

[2] From Pseudo-Isidore [Hinschius, *Decretales Pseudo-Isidorianae*, Lipsiae 1863 p.
186]. With this and the following can. 10 the very lengthy struggle on investitures
was finished, which pertains to this in so far as it is also concerned with the principle, whether or not the power of the *magisterium* and of the ecclesiastical ministry
flows from the civil magistrate by his own right. The following, moreover, pertains
to this: Nicholas II in Roman Synod 1059, c. 6 [Msi XIX 909 A] and in Synod
of Tours 1060, c. 4 [Msi XIX 927 C]; St. Gregory VII in Roman Synod 1075
[Hfl V 41, 46 f.; Msi XX 434 f.], 1078 c. 2 [Msi XX 509 C; cf. 517 f.]; 1080,
c. 1 f. [Msi XX 531 f.] etc.; Victor III [Msi XX 637, 639 ff.]; Urban II in the
Synod of Melfi 1089 c. 5 [Msi XX 723 B], in Claromontana c. 15 [Msi XX 817 D],
in Barensis 1098; [Msi XX 1061 E], Roman Synod 1099 c. 17 [Msi XX 964 B];
Paschal II in Roman Synod 1110, c. 4 [Msi XXI 7]; 1116 [Msi XXI 147 D]; in
Synod of Guastalla 1106 [Msi XX 1210 E]. Trecan. 1107 [Msi XX 1223 B], in
Synod of Benevento 1108 [Msi XX 1231 B]; in Council of Vienne 1112, c. 1 [Msi
XXI 74 D]; Callistus II in Remen. 1119, c. 2 [Msi XXI 235 D]; Lat. II 1139, c.
25 [Msi XXI 532 D].

from these (marriages); but secular laws call such disreputable, and they cast them off from inheritance. We, therefore, following our Fathers point them out in disgrace, and we declare that they are disreputable." [1]

363   Can. 10. Let no one unless canonically elected extend his hand for consecration to the episcopacy. But if he should presume to do so, let both the one consecrated and the one consecrating be deposed without hope of restoration.

Honorius II 1124–1130

INNOCENT II 1130–1143
LATERAN COUNCIL II 1139

Ecumenical X (against pseudo-pontiffs)

Simony, Usury, False Penitence, the Sacraments [2]

364   Can. 2. If anyone with the intervention of the accursed ardor of avarice has acquired through money an allowance from the state, or a priory, or a deanery, or honor, or some ecclesiastical promotion, or any ecclesiastical sacrament, namely chrism or holy oil, the consecrations of altars or of churches, let him be deprived of the honor evilly acquired. And let the buyer and the seller and the mediator be struck with the mark of disgrace. And not for food nor under the pretense of any custom before or after may anything be demanded from anyone, nor may he himself presume to give, since he is a simoniac. But freely and without any diminution let him enjoy the dignity and favor acquired for himself. [3]

---

[1] From Pseudo-Isidore [Hinschius, *Pseudo-Isidoran Decretals* p. 140]. These are against the heresy of the incestuous. Those were so called who contended that unions of relatives were not illicit and counted the grades of consanguinity according to the norm of civil law. Against these the following defended canonical law and doctrine: Leo IX in Roman Synod I, 1049 [Msi XIX 722 D] and Remen. 1049, c. 11 [Msi XIX 742 C]; Nicholas II in Roman Synod, 1059, c. 11 [Msi XIX 898 e]; Alexander II in Roman Synod, 1063, c. 9 [Msi XIX 1026 A]; but especially indeed in Rom., 1065, in which he publishes a decretal, *quae causa 35, q. 5, c. 2 habetur;* Urban II in syn. Troian., 1089 [Msi XX 721 C]; Lat. oec. II, 1139, c. 17 [Msi XXI 530 E]: "We forbid absolutely the formation of unions of blood-relatives; for incest of this kind, which has almost come into general practice under the stimulus of the enemy of the human race, the institutions of the Holy Fathers and the Holy Church of God despise." But Lat. IV reduced the prohibited grades to the number of four, c. 50 [Msi XXII 1035 E].

[2] Msi XXI 526 C ff.; Hrd VI, II 1028 B ff.; cf. Hfl V 440 ff.; Bar(Th) ad 1139 n. 4 f. (18, 566 a ff.).

[3] The following have decreed that nothing be exacted for holy oil, chrism, visitation and anointing of the sick, funeral obsequies, burial, baptism, the eucharist,

Can. 13. Moreover the detestable and shameful and, I say, insatiable **365** rapacity of money lenders, forbidden both by divine and human laws throughout the Scripture in the Old and in the New Testament, we condemn, and we separate them from all ecclesiastical consolation, commanding that no archbishop, no bishop, no abbot of any rank, nor anyone in an order and in the clergy presume to receive moneylenders except with the greatest caution. But during their whole life let them be considered disreputable and, unless they repent, let them be deprived of Christian burial.[1]

Can. 22. "Certainly because among other things there is one thing **366** which especially disturbs the Holy Church, namely, false repentance, we warn our confreres and priests lest by false repentance the souls of the laity are allowed to be deceived and to be drawn into hell. It is clear, moreover, that repentance is false when, although many things have been disregarded, repentance is practiced concerning one thing only; or when it is practiced concerning one thing, in such a way that he is not separated from another. Therefore, it is written: "He who shall observe the whole law yet offends in one thing, has become guilty of all," [Jas. 2: 10], with respect to eternal life. For just as if he had been involved in all sins, so if he should remain in only one, he will not enter the gate of eternal life. Also that repentance becomes false if when repenting one does not withdraw from either court or business duty, a thing which for no reason can be done without sin, or if hatred is kept in the heart, or if satisfaction be not made to one who has been offended, or if the offended one does not forgive the one offending, or if anyone take up arms against justice."[2]

---

the blessing of bridal couples, and other sacraments and blessings: Leo IX in syn. Remen. 1049, c. 2 and 5 [Msi XIX 741 f.]; Urban II in Placentin. 1095, c. 2 and 13 [Msi XX 805 f.]; Callistius II in Tolosana 1119, c. 9 [Msi XXI 227 E], and Remensi 1119, c. 4 [Msi XXI 236 A]; Lateran II 1139, c. 2 and 24 [Msi XXI 526 A 532 D]; Lateran. III 1179, De Simonia c. 10 [Msi XXII 249 D]; Lateran IV 1215, c. 66 [Msi XXII 1054 D]. This is to be understood of those who in the manner of a sale exact something for the sacred thing itself, or as a provision to avoid the risk of simony.

[1] Cf. Leo IX in syn. Remen. 1049, c. 7 [Msi XIX 742 B]; Lat. III 1179, c. 25 [Msi XXII 231 B]; Gregory X in Lugd. II oec. [CIC VI, 5, 5, 1 and 2; Frdbg II 1081 f.]. Many seem to have held this sanction of the Council as a positive prohibition only. Hence Alexander III [CIC Decr. V, 19, 4: Frdbg II 812 f.] declares that dispensation cannot be given in the case of receiving money for usury, and not even that the poor, who are held in captivity by the Saracens, can be liberated by the same money, just as Sacred Scripture prohibits lying to save the life of another. *Ibid.* c. 5 rejects the exception of some, (declaring) that only those usuries are to be restored which were accepted after the decree of Lateran II. Finally c. 9 decrees that heirs themselves, sons, or outsiders, be held for restitution. By many decrees Innocent III also (under the same title) urges the observance of these decrees.

[2] The following had already issued decrees on false penance: Gregory VII in Syn. Rom. V 1078, can. 5, and Rom. VII 1080, can. 5 [Msi XX 510 A 533 B], and

367　　Can. 23. "Those, moreover, who pretending a kind of piety condemn the sacrament of the Body and Blood of the Lord, the baptism of children, the sacred ministry and other ecclesiastical orders, and the bonds of legitimate marriages, we drive as heretics from the Church of God, and we both condemn and we command them to be restrained by exterior powers. We bind their defenders also by the chain of this same condemnation." [1]

COUNCIL OF SENS [2] 1140 or 1141

The Errors of Peter Abelard [3]

368　　1. That the Father is complete power, the Son a certain power, the Holy Spirit no power.

369　　2. That the Holy Spirit is not of the substance [another version: [4] power] of the Father or of the Son.

370　　3. That the Holy Spirit is the soul of the world.

371　　4. That Christ did not assume flesh to free us from the yoke of the devil.

372　　5. That neither God and man, nor this Person which is Christ, is the third Person in the Trinity.

373　　6. That free will is sufficient in itself for any good.

374　　7. That God is only able to do or to omit those things, either in that manner only or at that time in which He does (them), and in no other.

375　　8. That God neither ought nor is He able to prevent evil.

376　　9. That we have not contracted sin from Adam, but only punishment.

377　　10. That they have not sinned who being ignorant have crucified Christ, and that whatever is done through ignorance must not be considered as sin.

Urban II in Synod of Melfi 1089, can. 16 [Msi XX 724 C]; from this last canon, Lateranensis has been taken word for word.

[1] This canon is against Peter de Bruis and the Neomanichaeans, from whom have arisen the Albigenses, and has been taken word for word from the Council of Toulouse of the year 1119, held in the presence of Callistus II [Msi XXI 234 A].

[2] In Gaul.

[3] Msi XXI 568 C: Gotti, *Veritas rel. Christ.* II 352 b ff.; Hrd VI, II 1224 E; Hfl V 476; cf. Bar(Th) ad 1140 n. 7 f. (18, 583 a ff.); Paul Ruf and Mart. Grabmann, *Ein neuaufgefundenes Bruchstück der Apologia Abaelarda* (Sitzungsberichte der Bayr. Akad. d. Wiss. Philos.—hist. Abtlg. 1930, Heft 5], München 1930; in this fragment (p. 10 f.) all errors here noted in n. 368–386 are examined in the same order—Peter Abelard (Baiolardus), born 1079 in the town of Pallet, made a monk of St. Denis, taught in Paris. His errors were already condemned in 1121 in the Council of Sens, collected by St. Bernard, and set forth and rejected in the Council of Sens. He died April 21, 1142.

[4] Cf. *Rev. Apologétique* 52 (1931) 397.

11. That the spirit of the fear of the Lord was not in Christ.   378

12. That the power of binding and loosing was given to the Apostles 379 only, not to their successors.

13. That through work man becomes neither better nor worse.   380

14. That to the Father, who is not from another, properly or es- 381 pecially belongs power,[1] not also wisdom and kindness.

15. That even chaste fear is excluded from future life.   382

16. That the devil sends forth evil suggestion through the operation [2] 383 of stones and herbs.

17. That the coming at the end of the world can be attributed to the 384 Father.

18. That the soul of Christ did not descend to hell by itself but only 385 by power.

19. That neither action nor will, neither concupiscence nor delight, 386 when [3] it moves it [the soul] is a sin, nor ought we to wish to extinguish (it).[4]

[From the letter of Innocent II "Testante Apostolo" to Henry the Bishop of Sens, July 16, 1140 [5]]

And so we who though unworthily are observed to reside in the chair 387 of St. Peter, to whom it has been said by the Lord: "And thou being once converted, convert thy brethren" (Luke 22:33), after having taken counsel with our brethren the principal bishops, have condemned by the authority of the sacred canons the chapters sent to us by your discretion and all the teachings of this Peter (Abelard) with their author, and we have imposed upon him as a heretic perpetual silence. We declare also that all the followers and defenders of his error must be separated from the companionship of the faithful and must be bound by the chain of excommunication.

Baptism of Desire (an unbaptized priest) [6]

[From the letter "Apostolicam Sedem" to the Bishop   388 of Cremona, of uncertain time]

To your inquiry we respond thus: We assert without hesitation (on the authority of the holy Fathers Augustine and Ambrose) that the

---

[1] In the Ruf-Grabmann fragment: omnipotentia, *full power.*

[2] *Ibid.: appositionem.*

[3] *Ibid.: quae* [i.e., which arouse it].

[4] *Ibid.: exstingui* [i.e., that it be extinguished].

[5] Msi XXI 565 B; Jf 8148; ML 179, 517 A.

[6] ML 179, 624 Df; Jf 8272; CIC Decr. Greg. III, 43, 2: Frdbg II 648; Rcht II 623. This document is ascribed to Innocent III in CIC.

priest whom you indicated (in your letter) had died without the water of baptism, because he persevered in the faith of holy mother the Church and in the confession of the name of Christ, was freed from original sin and attained the joy of the heavenly fatherland. Read (brother) in the eighth book of Augustine's "City of God"[1] where among other things it is written, "Baptism is ministered invisibly to one whom not contempt of religion but death excludes." Read again the book also of the blessed Ambrose concerning the death of Valentinian[2] where he says the same thing. Therefore, to questions concerning the dead, you should hold the opinions of the learned Fathers, and in your church you should join in prayers and you should have sacrifices offered to God for the priest mentioned.

CELESTINE II 1143–1144   LUCIUS II 1144–1145

EUGENIUS III 1145–1153

COUNCIL OF RHEIMS[3] 1148

Confession of Faith in the Trinity[4]

389   1. We believe and confess that God is the simple nature of divinity, and that it cannot be denied in any Catholic sense that God is divinity, and divinity is God. Moreover, if it is said that God is wise by wisdom, great by magnitude, eternal by eternity, one by oneness, God by divinity, and other such things, we believe that He is wise only by that wisdom which is God Himself; that He is great only by that magnitude which is God Himself; that He is eternal only by that eternity which is God Himself; that He is one only by the oneness which is God Himself; that He is God only by that divinity which He is Himself; that is, that He is wise, great, eternal, one God of Himself.

390   2. When we speak of three persons: Father, Son, and Holy Spirit, we confess that they are one God, one divine substance. And contrariwise,

---

[1] Cf. *De civ. Dei* 13, 7 [ML 41, 381]. De facto the Pontiff seems to have regard for St. Augustine's *De baptismo* IV 22, 29 [ML 43, 173].

[2] Cap. 51 [ML 16, 1374].

[3] In Gaul.

[4] Msi XXI 712 Ef (725); coll. Hfl V 524; Hrd VI, II 1299 Df (1309). ML 185, 617 Bf; Bar(Th) ad 1148 n. 9 (19, 18 bf).—In the case of Gilbert Porretanus, on the testimony of Otto of Freising, "the Roman Pontiff defined that no reasoning should make a division between nature and person in theology, and that God should be called divine essence not only according to the sense of the ablative but also according to the sense of the nominative. This creed was set forth in council.—In the same council Eon of Stella and Henry were condemned.

when we speak of one God, one divine substance, we confess that the one God himself, the one divine substance are three persons.

3. We believe (and we confess) that only God the Father and Son and Holy Spirit are eternal, and not by any means other things, whether they be called relations or peculiarities or singularities or onenesses, and that other such things belong to God, which are from eternity, which are not God. **391**

4. We believe (and confess) that divinity itself, whether you call it divine substance or nature, is incarnate only in the Son. **392**

Anastasius IV 1153–1154   Hadrian IV 1154–1159

ALEXANDER III 1159–1181

Erroneous Proposition concerning the Humanity of Christ [1]

[Condemned in the letter "Cum Christus" to Willelmus, Archbishop of Rheims, February 18, 1177]

Since Christ perfect God is perfect man, it is strange with what temerity anyone dares to say that "Christ is not anything else but man." [2] Moreover lest so great an abuse of God be able to spring up in the Church . . . by our authority you should place under anathema, lest anyone dare to say this concerning the other . . . because just as He is true God, so He is true man existing from a rational soul and human flesh. **393**

The Illicit Contract of a Sale [3]

[From the letter "In civitate tua" to the Archbishop of Geneva, of uncertain time]

In your city you say that it often happens that when certain ones are purchasing pepper or cinnamon or other wares which at that time are not the value of more than five pounds, they also promise to those from whom they receive these wares that they will pay six pounds at a stated time. However, although a contract of this kind according to such a form cannot be considered under the name of usury, yet nevertheless the sellers incur sin, unless there is a doubt that the wares would be of **394**

---

[1] CIC *Decr. Greg.* V, 7, 7: Frdbg II 779; Rcht II 751; Jf 12785; Msi XXI 1081 C f.; cf. DuPl I, I 116 b; DCh I n. 9.

[2] This sentence was Abelard's; cf. *Opera sancti Bonaventurae* ed. Quaracchi tom. 3, p. 156 f., Schol.

[3] CIC *Decr. Greg.* V, 19, 6: Frdbg II 813; Rcht II 784; Jf 13965.

more or less value at the time of payment. And so your citizens would look well to their own interests, if they would cease from such a contract, since the thoughts of men cannot be hidden from Almighty God.

The Bond of Matrimony [1]

[From the letter "Ex publico instrumento" to the
Bishop of Brescia, of uncertain time]

395   Since the aforesaid woman, although she has been espoused by the aforesaid man, yet up to this time, as she asserts, has not been known by him, in instructing your brotherhood through Apostolic writings we order that if the aforesaid man has not known the said woman carnally and this same woman, as it is reported to us on your part, wishes to enter religion, after she has been made sufficiently mindful that she ought either to enter religion or return to her husband within two months, you at the termination of her objection and appeal absolve her from the sentence (of excommunication); that if she enters religion, each restore to the other what each is known to have received from the other, and the man himself, when she takes the habit of religion, have the liberty of passing over to other vows. Certainly what the Lord says in the Gospel: "It is not permitted to man unless on account of fornication to put away his wife" [Matt. 5:32; 19:9], must be understood according to the interpretation of the sacred words concerning those whose marriage has been consummated by sexual intercourse, without which marriage cannot be consummated, and so, if the aforesaid woman has not been known by her husband, it is permissible (for her) to enter religion.

[From fragments of a letter to the Archbishop of
Salerno, of uncertain time]

396   After legitimate consent in the present case it is permitted to the one, even with the other objecting, to choose a monastery, as some saints have been called from marriage, as long as sexual intercourse has not taken place between them. And to the one remaining, if, after being advised, he is unwilling to observe continency, he is permitted to pass over to second vows; because, since they have not been made one flesh, it is quite possible for the one to pass over to God, and the other to remain in the world.[2]

---

[1] CIC *Decr. Greg.* III, 32, 7: Frdbg II 581; Rcht II 559; Jf 13787;—III. 32, 2: Frdbg II 579; Rcht II 558; Jf 14091;—IV, 4, 3: Frdbg II 681, Rcht, II 656.

[2] The same holy Pontiff in a letter to the Bishop of Poitiers (of uncertain date) [CIC *Decr. Greg.* IV, 13, 2] decided that a valid marriage, not consummated [or, as it is called in CIC l.c., "a betrothal of the future"] is dissolved by a subsequent affinity. Innocent III, however, in a letter to the prefect of Magdeburg in the year 1200 [CIC *Decr. Greg.* IV, 13, 6] clearly denies the dissolubility of such a marriage, valid but not consummated.

If between the man and the woman legitimate consent . . . occurs in **397** the present, so indeed that one expressly receives another by mutual consent with the accustomed words, . . . whether an oath is introduced or not, it is not permissible for the woman to marry another. And if she should marry, even if carnal intercourse has taken place, she should be separated from him, and forced by ecclesiastical order to return to the first, although some think otherwise and also judgment has been rendered in another way by certain of our predecessors.

The Form of Baptism [1]

[From fragments of the letter to (Pontius, the Bishop
of Clermont?), of uncertain time]

Certainly if anyone immerses a child in water three times in the name **398** of the Father and of the Son and of the Holy Spirit, Amen, and he does not say: "I baptize you in the name of the Father and of the Son and of the Holy Ghost, Amen," the child is not baptized.

Let those concerning whom there is a doubt, whether or not they have **399** been baptized, be baptized after these words have first been uttered: "If you are baptized I do not baptize you; if you are not yet baptized, I baptize you, etc."

LATERAN COUNCIL III 1179

Ecumenical XI (against the Albigenses)

Simony [2]

Chap. 10. Let monks not be received in the monastery at a price. . . . **400** If anyone, however, on being solicited gives anything for his reception, let him not advance to sacred orders. Let him, however, who accepts (a price) be punished by the taking away of his office.[3]

Heresies that Must be Avoided [4]

Chap. 27. As Blessed Leo [5] says: "Although ecclesiastical discipline, **401** content with sacerdotal judgment, does not employ bloody punishments, it is nevertheless helped by the constitutions of Catholic rulers, so that

---

[1] CIC *Decr. Greg.* III, 42, 1 and 2: Frdbg II 644; Rcht II 619; Jf 14200.
[2] Msi XXII 224 B; Jf post 13331; Hrd VI, II 1678 C; cf. Hfl V 713 ff.; Bar(Th) ad 1179 n. 1 ff. (19, 472 a ff.).
[3] Thus also Urban II in the Synod of Melfi 1089, c. 7 [Msi XX 723 C].
[4] Msi XXII 231 E f.; Hrd VI, II 1683 D f.
[5] Letter to Turibius, Proem. [MS 54, 680 A].

men often seek a salutary remedy, when they fear that corporal punishment is coming upon them." For this reason, since in Gascony, in Albegesium, and in parts of Tolosa and in other places, the cursed perversity of the heretics whom some call Cathari, others Patareni, others Publicani, others by different names, has so increased that now they exercise their wickedness not as some in secret, but manifest their error publicly and win over the simple and weak to their opinion, we resolve to cast them, their defenders, and receivers under anathema, and we forbid under anathema that anyone presume to hold or to help these in their homes or on their land or to do business with them.[1]

LUCIUS III 1181–1185
COUNCIL OF VERONA 1184
The Sacraments (against the Albigenses) [2]
[From the decree "Ad abolendum" against the heretics]

402　　All who, regarding the sacrament of the Body and Blood of our Lord Jesus Christ, or regarding baptism or the confession of sins, matrimony or the other ecclesiastical sacraments, do not fear to think or to teach otherwise than the most holy Roman Church teaches and observes; and in general, whomsoever the same Roman Church or individual bishops through their dioceses with the advice of the clergy or the clergy themselves, if the episcopal see is vacant, with the advice if it is necessary of neighboring bishops, shall judge as heretics, we bind with a like bond of perpetual anathema.

URBAN III 1185–1187
Usury [3]
[From the epistle "Consuluit nos" to a certain priest of Brescia]

403　　Your loyalty asks us whether or not in the judgment of souls he ought to be judged as a usurer who, not otherwise ready to deliver by loan,

---

[1] Furthermore the council proclaims a holy war against the Brebantiones, Navarri, Baschi, and others, who were laying everything to waste, and were sparing neither age nor sex.

[2] CIC *Decr. Greg.* V, 7, 9: Frdbg II 780; Rcht II 752; Jf 15109; Msi XXII 477 B; Hrd VI, II 1878 E; cf. Hfl V 724 ff.

[3] CIC *Decr. Greg.* V, 19, 10: Frdbg II 814; Rcht II 785; Jf 15726.

loans his money on this proposition that without any agreement he nevertheless receive more by lot; and whether he is involved in that same state of guilt who, as it is commonly said, does not otherwise grant a similar oath, until, although without payment, he receives some gain from him; whether or not that negotiator ought to be condemned with a like punishment, who offers his wares at a price far greater, if an extension of the already extended time be asked for making the payment, than if the price should be paid to him at once. But since what one must hold in these cases is clearly learned from the Gospel of Luke in which is said: "Give mutually, hoping nothing thereby" [cf. Luke 6:35], men of this kind must be judged to act wrongly on account of the intention of gain which they have, since every usury and superabundance are prohibited by law, and they must be effectively induced in the judgment of souls to restore those things which have been thus received.

GREGORY VIII 1187   CLEMENT III 1187–1191
CELESTINE III 1191–1198

INNOCENT III 1198–1216

The Form of the Sacrament of Matrimony [1]

[From the letter, "Cum apud sedem" to Humbert,
Archbishop of Arles, July 15, 1198]

You have asked us whether the dumb and the deaf can be united to **404** each other in marriage. To this question we respond to your brotherhood thus: Since the edict of prohibition concerning the contracting of marriage is that whoever is not prohibited, is consequently permitted, and only the consent of those concerning whose marriages we are speaking is sufficient for marriage, it seems that, if such a one wishes to contract (a marriage), it cannot and it ought not to be denied him, since what he cannot declare by words he can declare by signs.

[From the letter to the Bishop of Mutina, in the year 1200] [2]

Besides in the contracting of marriages we wish you to observe this: when, as in the present case legitimate agreement exists between legitimate persons, which is sufficient in such cases according to canonical sanctions, and if this alone is lacking, other things are made void, even

---

[1] CIC *Decr. Greg.* IV, 1, 23 (cf. 25: Frdbg II 669 f.; Rcht II 645; Pth 329; ML 214, 304 C.—In these decrees of Innocent III, in order that similar materials might be presented together, the chronological order has not been strictly observed.

[2] CIC *Decr. Greg.* IV, 4, 5; Frdbg II 682; Rcht II 657; Pth 1238.

if sexual intercourse itself has taken place, if persons legitimately married afterwards actually contract (marriage) with others, what before had been done according to law cannot be annulled.

On the Bond of Marriage and the
Pauline Privilege [1]

[From the letter "Quanto te magis" to Hugo, Bishop of Ferrara, May 1, 1199]

405   Your brotherhood has announced that with one of the spouses passing over to heresy the one who is left desires to rush into second vows and to procreate children, and you have thought that we ought to be consulted through your letter as to whether this can be done under the law. We, therefore, responding to your inquiry regarding the common advice of our brothers make a distinction, although indeed our predecessor seems to have thought otherwise, whether of two unbelievers one is converted to the Catholic Faith, or of two believers one lapses into heresy or falls into the error of paganism. For if one of the unbelieving spouses is converted to the Catholic faith, while the other either is by no means willing to live with him or at least not without blaspheming the divine name or so as to drag him into mortal sin, the one who is left, if he wishes, will pass over to second vows. And in this case we understand what the Apostle says: "If the unbeliever depart, let him depart: for the brother or sister is not subject to servitude in (cases) of this kind" [I Cor. 7:15]. And likewise (we understand) the canon in which it is said that "insult to the Creator dissolves the law of marriage for him who is left." [2]

406   But if one of the believing spouses either slip into heresy or lapse into the error of paganism, we do not believe that in this case he who is left, as long as the other is living, can enter into a second marriage; although in this case a greater insult to the Creator is evident. Although indeed true matrimony exists between unbelievers, yet it is not ratified; between believers, however, a true and ratified marriage exists, because the sacrament of faith, which once was admitted, is never lost, but makes the sacrament of marriage ratified so that it itself lasts between married persons as long as the sacrament of faith endures.

---

[1] CIC *Decr. Greg.* IV, 19, 7: Frdbg II 722 f.; Rcht II 696 f.; Pth 684; ML **214**, 588 D f.

[2] Cf. *Decr. Grat.* II, causa 28, q. 2, c. **2**.

Marriages of Pagans and the Pauline Privilege [1]

[From the letter "Gaudemus in Domino" to the Bishop
of Tiberias, in the beginning of 1201]

You have asked to be shown through Apostolic writings whether **407**
pagans receiving wives in the second, third, or further degree ought, thus
united, to remain after their conversion with the wives united to them or
ought to be separated from them. Regarding this we reply to your brotherhood thus, that, since the sacrament of marriage exists between believing
and unbelieving spouses as the Apostle points out when he says: "If any
brother has an unbelieving wife, and she consents to live with him, let
him not put her away" [I Cor. 7:12], and since in the aforesaid degree
matrimony is lawfully contracted with respect to them by pagans who are
not restricted by canonical constitutions, ("For what is it to me?" according to the same Apostle, "to judge concerning those which are
outside?" [I Cor. 5:12]); in favor especially of the Christian religion
and faith, from receiving which many fearing to be deserted by their
wives can easily be restrained, such believers, having been joined in
marriage, can freely and licitly remain united, since through the sacrament of baptism marriages are not dissolved but sins are forgiven.

But since pagans divide their conjugal affection among many women **408**
at the same time, it is rightly doubted whether after conversion all or
which one of all they can retain. But this (practice) seems to be in
disagreement with and inimical to the Christian Faith, since in the beginning one rib was changed into one woman, and Divine Scripture testifies
that "on account of this, man shall leave father and mother and shall
cling to his wife and they shall be two in one flesh" [Eph. 5:31; Gen.
2:24; cf. Matt. 19:5]; it does not say "three or more" but *two;* nor did
it say "he will cling to wives" but *to a wife.* Never is it permitted to
anyone to have several wives at one time except to whom it was granted
by divine revelation. This custom existed at one time, sometimes was
even regarded as lawful, by which, as Jacob from a lie, the Israelites
from theft, and Samson from homicide, so also the Patriarchs and other
just men, who we read had many wives at the same time, were excused
from adultery. Certainly this opinion is proved true also by the witness
of Truth, which testifies in the Gospel: "Whosoever puts away his wife
(except) on account of fornication, and marries another commits adultery," [Matt. 19:9; cf. Mark 10:11]. If, therefore, when the wife has been
dismissed, another cannot be married according to law, all the more she
herself cannot be retained; through this it clearly appears that regarding

---

[1] CIC *Decr. Greg.* IV, 19, 8: Frdbg II 723 f.; Rcht II 697 f.; Pth 1325; ML 216,
1269 C ff.

marriage plurality in either sex—since they are not judged unequally—
must be condemned. Moreover, he who according to his rite puts away
a lawful wife, since Truth in the Gospel has condemned such a repudiation, never while she lives, even after being converted to the faith of
Christ, can he have another wife, unless after his conversion she refuses
to live with him, or even if she should consent, yet not without insult to
the Creator, or so as to lead him into mortal sin. In this case to the one
seeking restitution, although it be established regarding unjust spoliation,
restitution would be denied, because according to the Apostle: "A brother
or sister is not subject to servitude in (cases) of this kind" [I Cor. 7, 12].
But if her conversion should follow his conversion to faith, before, on
account of the above mentioned causes, he would marry a legitimate
wife, he would be compelled to take her back again. Although, too,
according to the Evangelical truth, "he who marries one put aside is
guilty of adultery" [Matt. 19:9], yet the one doing the dismissing will
not be able to upbraid the one dismissed with fornication because he
married her after the repudiation, unless she shall otherwise have committed fornication.

The Dissolubility of Valid Marriage by Religious Profession [1]

[From the letter "Ex parte tua" to Andrew, the
Archbishop of Lyons, Jan. 12, 1206]

409   Unwilling to depart suddenly on this point from the footsteps of our
predecessors who, on being consulted, responded that before marriage
has been consummated by sexual intercourse, it is permitted for one of
the parties, even without consulting the remaining one, to pass over to
religion, so that the one left can henceforth legitimately marry another;
we advise you that this must be observed.

The Effect of Baptism (and the Character) [2]

410   (For) they assert that baptism is conferred uselessly on children. . . .
We respond that baptism has taken the place of circumcision. . . .
Therefore as "the soul of the circumcised did not perish from the people"
[Gen. 17:4], so "he who has been reborn from water and the Holy
Spirit will obtain entrance to the kingdom of heaven" [John 3:5]. . . .
Although original sin was remitted by the mystery of circumcision, and
the danger of damnation was avoided, nevertheless there was no ar-
riving at the kingdom of heaven, which up to the death of Christ was
barred to all. But through the sacrament of baptism the guilt of one

---

[1] CIC *Decr. Greg.* III, 32, 14: Frdbg II 584; Rcht II 562; Pth 2651; ML 215, 774 A.
[2] CIC *Decr. Greg.* III, 42, 3: Frdbg II 644 f.; Rcht II 619 f.; Pth 1479.

made red by the blood of Christ is remitted, and to the kingdom of heaven one also arrives, whose gate the blood of Christ has mercifully opened for His faithful. For God forbid that all children of whom daily so great a multitude die, would perish, but that also for these the merciful God who wishes no one to perish has procured some remedy unto salvation. . . . As to what opponents say, (namely), that faith or love or other virtues are not infused in children, inasmuch as they do not consent, is absolutely not granted by most. . . , some asserting that by the power of baptism guilt indeed is remitted to little ones but grace is not conferred; and some indeed saying both that sin is forgiven and that virtues are infused in them as they hold virtues as a possession not as a function, until they arrive at adult age. . . . We say that a distinction must be made, that sin is twofold: namely, original and actual: original, which is contracted without consent; and actual which is committed with consent. Original, therefore, which is committed without consent, is remitted without consent through the power of the sacrament; but actual, which is contracted with consent, is not mitigated in the slightest without consent. . . . The punishment of original sin is deprivation of the vision of God, but the punishment of actual sin is the torments of everlasting hell. . . .

This is contrary to the Christian religion, that anyone always unwilling **411** and interiorly objecting be compelled to receive and to observe Christianity. On this account some absurdly do not distinguish between unwilling and unwilling, and forced and forced, because he who is violently forced by terrors and punishments, and, lest he incur harm, receives the sacrament of baptism, such a one also as he who under pretense approaches baptism, receives the impressed sign of Christianity, and he himself, just as he willed conditionally although not absolutely, must be forced to the observance of Christian Faith. . . . But he who never consents, but inwardly contradicts, receives neither the matter nor the sign of the sacrament, because to contradict expressly is more than not to agree. . . . The sleeping, moreover, and the weak-minded, if before they incurred weak-mindedness, or before they went to sleep persisted in contradiction, because in these the idea of contradiction is understood to endure, although they have been so immersed, they do not receive the sign of the sacrament; not so, however, if they had first lived as catechumens and had the intention of being baptized; therefore, the Church has been accustomed to baptize such in a time of necessity. Thus, then the sacramental operation impresses the sign, when it does not meet the resisting obstacle of a contrary will.

The Matter of Baptism [1]

[From the letter "Non ut apponeres" to Thorias
Archbishop of Nidaros] [2]

412   You have asked whether children ought to be regarded as Christians
whom, when in danger of death, on account of the scarcity of water and
the absence of a priest, the simplicity of some has anointed on the head
and the breast, and between the shoulders with a sprinkling of saliva for
baptism. We answer that since in baptism two things always, that is,
"the word and the element," [3] are required by necessity, according to
which Truth says concerning the word: "Going into the world etc."
[Luke 16:15; cf. Matt. 28:19], and the same concerning the element
says: "Unless anyone etc." [John 3:5] you ought not to doubt that those
do not have true baptism in which not only both of the above mentioned
(requirements) but one of them is missing.

The Minister of Baptism and the Baptism of Spirit [4]

[From the letter "Debitum pastoralis officii" to Berthold,
the Bishop of Metz, August 28, 1206]

413   You have, to be sure, intimated that a certain Jew, when at the point of
death, since he lived only among Jews, immersed himself in water while
saying: "I baptize myself in the name of the Father, and of the Son, and
of the Holy Spirit, Amen."

We respond that, since there should be a distinction between the one
baptizing and the one baptized, as is clearly gathered from the words of
the Lord, when he says to the Apostles: "Go baptize all nations in the
name etc." [cf. Matt. 28:19], the Jew mentioned must be baptized again
by another, that it may be shown that he who is baptized is one person,
and he who baptizes another. . . . If, however, such a one had died
immediately, he would have rushed to his heavenly home without delay
because of the faith of the sacrament, although not because of the sacrament of faith.

---

[1] CIC *Decr. Greg.* III, 42, 5: Frdbg II 674; Rcht II 622; Pth 2696; ML 215, 813 A.
[2] Drontheim in Norvegia.
[3] St. Augustine, In Io. tract. 80, 3 [ML 35, 1840].
[4] CIC *Decr. Greg.* III, 42, 4: Frdbg II 646 f.; Rcht II 621 f.; Pth 2875; ML 215,
986 A.

The Form of the Eucharistic Sacrament and its Elements [1]

[From the letter "Cum Marthae circa" to a certain
John, Archbishop of Lyons, Nov. 29, 1202]

You have asked (indeed) who has added to the form of the words which   **414**
Christ Himself expressed when He changed the bread and wine into the
body and blood, that in the Canon of the Mass which the general Church
uses, which none of the Evangelists is read to have expressed. . . . In the
Canon of the Mass that expression, *"mysterium fidei,"* is found inter-
posed among His words. . . . Surely we find many such things omitted
from the words as well as from the deeds of the Lord by the Evangelists,
which the Apostles are read to have supplied by word or to have expressed by deed. . . . From the expression, moreover, concerning which
your brotherhood raised the question, namely "mysterium fidei," certain
people have thought to draw a protection against error, saying that in the
sacrament of the altar the truth of the body and blood of Christ does not
exist, but only the image and species and figure, inasmuch as Scripture
sometimes mentions that what is received at the altar is sacrament and
mystery and example. But such run into a snare of error, by reason of the
fact that they neither properly understand the authority of Scripture, nor
do they reverently receive the sacraments of God, equally "ignorant of the
Scriptures and the power of God" [Matt. 22:29]. . . . Yet "mysterium
fidei" is mentioned, since something is believed there other than what is
perceived; and something is perceived other than is believed. For the
species of bread and wine is perceived there, and the truth of the body
and blood of Christ is believed and the power of unity and of love. . . .

We must, however, distinguish accurately between three things which   **415**
are different in this sacrament, namely, the visible form, the truth of the
body, and the spiritual power. The form is of the bread and wine; the
truth, of the flesh and blood; the power, of unity and of charity. The
first is the "sacrament and not reality." The second is "the sacrament
and reality." The third is "the reality and not the sacrament." But the
first is the sacrament of a twofold reality. The second, however, is a
sacrament of one and the reality (is) of the other. But the third is the
reality of a twofold sacrament. Therefore, we believe that the form of
words, as is found in the Canon, the Apostles received from Christ,
and their successors from them. . . .

---

[1] CIC *Decr. Greg.* III 41, 6: Frdbg II 637 f.; Rcht II 612 f.; Pth 1179; ML 214,
1119 A f.; Bar(Th) ad 1202 n. 14 ff. (20, 114 a f.).

Water Mixed with Wine in the Sacrifice of the Mass [1]

[From the same letter to John, Nov. 29, 1202]

416   You have asked (also) whether the water with the wine is changed into the blood. Regarding this, however, opinions among the scholastics vary. For it seems to some that, since from the side of Christ two special sacraments flowed—of the redemption in the blood and of regeneration in the water—into those two the wine and water, which are mixed in the chalice, are changed by divine power. . . . But others hold that the water with the wine is transubstantiated into the blood; when mixed with the wine, it passes over into the wine. . . . Besides it can be said that water does not pass over into blood but remains surrounded by the accidents of the original wine. . . . This, however, is wrong to think, which some have presumed to say, namely, that water is changed into phlegm. . . . But among the opinions mentioned that is judged the more probable which asserts that the water with the wine is changed into blood.

[From the letter "In quadam nostra" to Hugo, Bishop of Ferrara, March 5, 1209]

417   You say that you have read in a certain decretal letter of ours that it is wrong to think what certain ones have presumed to say, namely, that the water of the Eucharist is changed into phlegm, for they say falsely that from the side of Christ not water but a watery liquid came forth. Moreover, although you recall that great and authentic men have thought this, whose opinions in speech and in writings up to this time you have followed, from whose (opinions), however, we differ, you are compelled to agree with our opinion. . . . For if it had not been water but phlegm which flowed from the side of the Savior, he *who saw* and *gave testimony* to the truth [cf. John 19:35] certainly would not have said water but phlegm. . . . It remains, therefore, that of whatever nature that water was, whether natural, or miraculous, or created anew by divine power, or resolved in some measure of component parts, without doubt it was true water.

---

[1] CIC *Decr. Greg.* III 41, 6: Frdbg II 638 f.; Rcht II 614 f.; ML 214, 1121 C ff.; Bar(Th) ad 1202 n. 17 ff.—Another letter: *Decr. Greg.* III, 41, 8; Frdbg II 640 f.; Rcht II 615 f.; ML 216, 16 B f.

The Feigned Celebration of Mass [1]

[From the letter "De homine qui" to the rectors of the
Roman brotherhood, September 22, 1208]

(For) you have asked us what we think about the careless priest who, **418**
when he knows that he is in mortal sin, hesitates because of the consciousness of his guilt to celebrate the solemnity of the Mass, which he
however, cannot omit on account of necessity . . . and, when the other
details have been accomplished, pretends to celebrate Mass; and after
suppressing the words by which the body of Christ is effected, he merely
takes up the bread and wine. . . . Since, therefore, false remedies must
be cast aside, which are more serious than true dangers, it is proper
that he who regards himself unworthy on account of the consciousness
of his own crime ought reverently to abstain from a sacrament of this
kind, and so he sins seriously if he brings himself irreverently to it; yet
without a doubt he seems to offend more gravely who so fraudently
presumes to feign (the sacrifice of the Mass); since the one by avoiding
sin, as long as he acts, falls into the hands of the merciful God alone;
but the other by committing sin, as long as he lives, places himself under
obligation not only to God whom he does not fear to mock, but also to
the people whom he deceives.

The Minister of Confirmation [2]

[From the letter "Cum venisset" to Basil, Archbishop
of Tirnova, Feb. 25, 1204]

The imposition of the hands is designated by the anointing of the **419**
forehead which by another name is called confirmation, because through
it the Holy Spirit is given for an increase (of grace) and strength. Therefore, although a simple priest or presbyter is able to give other anointings,
this one, only the highest priest, that is the bishop, ought to confer, because we read concerning the Apostles alone, whose successors the
bishops are, that through the imposition of the hands they gave the Holy
Spirit [cf. Acts 8:14 ff.].

---

[1] CIC *Decr. Greg.* III 41, 7: Frdbg II 640; Rcht II 615; Pth 3503; ML 215, 1463 C f.
[2] CIC *Decr. Greg.* I 15, 1 *sect.* 7; Frdbg II 133; Rcht II 128; Pth 2138; ML 215,
285 C.

Profession of Faith Prescribed for Durand of Osca and His Waldensian Companions [1]

[From the letter "Eius exemplo" to the Archbishop of Terraco, Dec. 18, 1208]

420   By the heart we believe, by faith we understand, by the mouth we confess, and by simple words we affirm that the Father and the Son and the Holy Spirit are three Persons, one God, and entire Trinity, co-essential and consubstantial and co-eternal and omnipotent, and each single Person in the Trinity complete God as is contained in "Credo in Deum," [see n. 2] in "Credo in unum Deum" [see n. 86], and in "Quicumque vult" [see n. 39].

421   By the heart we believe and by the mouth we confess that the Father also and the Son and the Holy Spirit, one God, concerning whom we are speaking, is the creator, the maker, the ruler, and the dispenser of all things corporal and spiritual, visible and invisible. We believe that God is the one and same author of the Old and the New Testament, who existing in the Trinity, as it is said, created all things from nothing; and that John the Baptist, sent by Him, was holy and just, and in the womb of his mother was filled with the Holy Spirit.

422   By the heart we believe and by the mouth we confess that the Incarnation of the Divinity took place neither in the Father, nor in the Holy Spirit, but in the Son only; so that He who was in the Divinity the Son of God the Father, true God from the Father, was in the humanity the son of man, true man from a mother, having true flesh from the womb of his mother and a human rational soul; at the same time of each nature, that is God and man, one Person, one Son, one Christ, one God with the Father and the Holy Spirit, the author and ruler of all, born from the Virgin Mary in a true birth of the flesh; He ate and drank, He slept and, tired out from a journey, He rested, He suffered in the true passion of His flesh; He died in the true death of His body, and He arose again in the true resurrection of His flesh and in the true restoration of His soul to the body in which, after He ate and drank, He ascended into heaven, sits at the right hand of the Father, and in the same will come to judge the living and the dead.

423   By the heart we believe and by the mouth we confess the one Church,

---

[1] ML 215, 1510 C ff.; Pth 3571.—This formula occurs again in letter "Cum inaestimabile pretium universis Archiepiscopis et Episc., ad quos litterae istae pervenerint" sent on the 12th of May, 1210 [ML 216, 274 D], and, slightly changed, in another letter "Cum inaestimabile pretium," likewise regarding the matter of Waldensian converts, on June 14, 1210 [ML 216, 289 C ff.]. In this letter the conversion of Bernard the First and of others is announced, and it is prescribed that heretics be received back into the bosom of the Church by a similar profession.

not of heretics but the Holy Roman, Catholic, and Apostolic (Church) outside which we believe that no one is saved.

The sacraments also which are celebrated in it with the inestimable **424** and invisible power of the Holy Spirit cooperating, although they may be administered by a priest who is a sinner, as long as the Church accepts him, in no way do we reprove nor from ecclesiastical offices or blessings celebrated by him do we withdraw; but we receive with a kind mind as from the most just, because the wickedness of a bishop or priest does no harm to the baptism of an infant, nor to consecrating the Eucharist, nor to the other ecclesiastical duties celebrated for subjects. We approve, therefore, the baptism of infants, who, if they died after baptism, before they commit sins, we confess and believe are saved; and in baptism all sins, that original sin which was contracted as well as those which voluntarily have been committed, we believe are forgiven. We decree that confirmation performed by a bishop, that is, by the imposition of hands, is holy and must be received reverently. Firmly and without doubt with a pure heart we believe and simply in faithful words we affirm that the sacrifice, that is, the bread and wine [Other texts: in the sacrifice of the Eucharist those things which before consecration were bread and wine] after the consecration is the true body and blood of our Lord Jesus Christ, in which we believe nothing more by a good nor less by a bad priest is accomplished because it is accomplished not in the merits of the one who consecrates but in the word of the Creator and in the power of the Holy Spirit. Therefore, we firmly believe and we confess that however honest, religious, holy, and prudent anyone may be, he cannot nor ought he to consecrate the Eucharist nor to perform the sacrifice of the altar unless he be a priest, regularly ordained by a visible and perceptible bishop. And to this office three things are necessary, as we believe: namely, a certain person, that is a priest as we said above, properly established by a bishop for that office; and those solemn words which have been expressed by the holy Fathers in the canon; and the faithful intention of the one who offers himself; and so we firmly believe and declare that whosoever without the preceding episcopal ordination, as we said above, believes and contends that he can offer the sacrifice of the Eucharist is a heretic and is a participant and companion of the perdition of Core and his followers, and he must be segregated from the entire holy Roman Church. To sinners truly penitent, we believe that forgiveness is granted by God, and with them we communicate most gladly. We venerate the anointing of the sick with the consecrated oil. According to the Apostle [cf. I Cor. 7] we do not deny that carnal unions should be formed, but ordinarily we forbid absolutely the breaking of the contracts. Man also with his wife we believe and confess are saved, and we do not even condemn second or later marriages.

Variations

425 We do not at all censure the receiving of the flesh. Nor do we condemn an oath; on the contrary, we believe with a pure heart that with truth and judgment and justice it is permissible to swear. [In the year 1210, the following sentence was added:] Concerning secular power we declare that without mortal sin it is possible to exercise a judgment of blood as long as one proceeds to bring punishment not in hatred but in judgment, not incautiously but advisedly.

426 We believe that preaching is exceedingly necessary and praiseworthy, yet that it must be exercised by the authority or license of the Supreme Pontiff or by the permission of prelates. But in all places where manifest heretics remain and renounce and blaspheme God and the faith of the holy Roman Church, we believe that, by disputing and exhorting in all ways according to God, we should confound them, and even unto death oppose them openly with the word of God as adversaries of Christ and the Church. But ecclesiastical orders and everything which in the holy Roman Church is read or sung as holy, we humbly praise and faithfully venerate.

427 We believe that the devil was made evil not through creation but through will. We sincerely believe and with our mouth we confess the resurrection of this flesh which we bear and not of another. We firmly believe and affirm also that judgment by Jesus Christ will be individually for those who have lived in this flesh, and that they will receive either punishment or rewards. We believe that alms, sacrifice, and other benefits can be of help to the dead. We believe and confess that those who remain in the world and possess their own wealth, by practicing alms, and other benefits from their possessions, and by keeping the commands of the Lord are saved. We believe that tithes and first fruits and oblations should be paid to the clergy according to the Lord's command.

LATERAN COUNCIL IV 1215

Ecumenical XII (against the Albigensians, Joachim, Waldensians etc.

The Trinity, Sacraments, Canonical Mission, etc.[1]

Chap. 1. The Catholic Faith

[Definition directed against the Albigensians and other heretics]

428 Firmly we believe and we confess simply that the true God is one alone, eternal, immense, and unchangeable, incomprehensible, omni-

---

[1] Msi XXII 982 ff.; Hrd VII 15 ff.; cf. Hfl V 878 ff.; Pth post 5006; Bar(Th) ad 1215 n. 1 ff. (20, 339 a ff.), [CIC *Decr. Greg.* I, i, 1: Frdbg II 5 f.; Rcht II 5 f.]..

potent and ineffable, *Father and Son and Holy Spirit:* indeed three Persons but one essence, substance, or nature entirely simple. The Father from no one, the Son from the Father only, and the Holy Spirit equally from both; without beginning, always, and without end; the Father generating, the Son being born, and the Holy Spirit proceeding; consubstantial and coequal and omnipotent and coeternal; one beginning of all, creator of all visible and invisible things, of the spiritual and of the corporal; who by His own omnipotent power at once from the beginning of time created each creature from nothing, spiritual, and corporal, namely, angelic and mundane, and finally the human, constituted as it were, alike of the spirit and the body. For the devil and other demons were created by God good in nature, but they themselves through themselves have become wicked. But man sinned at the suggestion of the devil. This Holy Trinity according to common essence undivided, and according to personal properties distinct, granted the doctrine of salvation to the human race, first through Moses and the holy prophets and his other servants according to the most methodical disposition of the time.

And finally the only begotten Son of God, Jesus Christ, incarnate by 429 the whole Trinity in common, conceived of Mary ever Virgin with the Holy Spirit cooperating, made true man, formed of a rational soul and human flesh, one Person in two natures, clearly pointed out the way of life. And although He according to divinity is immortal and impassible, the very same according to humanity was made passible and mortal, who, for the salvation of the human race, having suffered on the wood of the Cross and died, descended into hell, arose from the dead and ascended into heaven. But He descended in soul, and He arose in the flesh, and He ascended equally in both, to come at the end of time, to judge the living and the dead, and to render to each according to his works, to the wicked as well as to the elect, all of whom will rise with their bodies which they now bear, that they may receive according to their works, whether these works have been good or evil, the latter everlasting punishment with the devil, and the former everlasting glory with Christ.

One indeed is the universal Church of the faithful, outside which no 430 one at all is saved,[1] in which the priest himself is the sacrifice, Jesus Christ, whose body and blood are truly contained in the sacrament of the altar under the species of bread and wine; the bread (changed) into His body by the divine power of transubstantiation, and the wine into the blood, so that to accomplish the mystery of unity we ourselves receive from His (nature) what He Himself received from ours. And surely no

---

[1] St. Cyprian "There is no salvation outside the Church," Ep. 73, To Iubaianus, n. 21 [ML 3, 1123 B].

one can accomplish this sacrament except a priest who has been rightly ordained according to the keys of the Church which Jesus Christ Himself conceded to the Apostles and to their successors. But the sacrament of baptism (which at the invocation of God and the indivisible Trinity, namely, of the Father and of the Son and of the Holy Spirit, is solemnized in water) rightly conferred by anyone in the form of the Church is useful unto salvation for little ones and for adults. And if, after the reception of baptism, anyone shall have lapsed into sin, through true penance he can always be restored. Moreover, not only virgins and the continent but also married persons pleasing to God through right faith and good work merit to arrive at a blessed eternity.

Chap. 2. The Error of Abbot Joachim [1]

431　　We condemn, therefore, and we disapprove of the treatise or tract which Abbot Joachim published against Master Peter Lombard on the unity or essence of the Trinity, calling him heretical and senseless because in his *Sentences* he said: "Since it is a most excellent reality—the Father, and the Son, and the Holy Spirit, and it is not generating, nor generated, nor proceeding." [2] Thus he (Joachim) declares that Peter Lombard implies not so much a Trinity as a quaternity in God, namely the three Persons and that common essence as a fourth, openly protesting that there is no matter which is the Father and the Son and the Holy Spirit; neither is there essence, nor substance, nor nature, although he concedes that the Father, and the Son, and the Holy Spirit are one essence, one substance, and one nature. But he says that unity of this kind is not true and proper, but is something collective and similar, as many men are called one people, and many faithful, one Church, according to the following: "Of the multitude believing there was one heart and one mind" [Acts 4:32]; and, "He who clings to God is one spirit with him" [I Cor. 6:17]; likewise, "He who . . . plants and he who waters are one" [I Cor. 3:8]; and, "we are all one body in Christ" [Rom. 12:5]; again in the Book of Kings [Ruth]: "My people and your people are one" [Ruth 1:16]. Moreover, to add to this opinion of his he brings the following most powerful expression, that Christ spoke in the Gospel about the faithful: "I will, Father, that they are one in us as we are one, so that they may be perfected in unity" [John 17:22 f.]. For not, (as he says), are the faithful of Christ one, that is, a certain one matter which is common to all, but in this way are they one, that is, one Church because of the unity of the Catholic faith; and finally one kingdom, because of the union of indissoluble love, as in the canonical letter of John the Apostle we read: "For there are three that give testimony in heaven, the

---

[1] Msi XXII 982 ff.
[2] Cf. *Sent.* I, 1, dist. 5.

Father, and the Son, and the Holy Spirit, and these three are one" [I John 5:7], and immediately is added: "And there are three who give testimony on earth, the Spirit, the water, and the blood, and these three are one" [I John 5:8], as is found in certain texts.

We, however, with the approval of the sacred Council, believe and confess with Peter Lombard that there exists a most excellent reality, incomprehensible indeed and ineffable, which truly is the Father, and the Son, and the Holy Spirit, at the same time three Persons, and anyone of the same individually; and so in God there is Trinity only, not a quaternity; because any one of the three Persons is that reality, namely, substance, essence or divine nature, which alone is the beginning of all things, beyond which nothing else can be found, and that reality is not generating, nor generated, nor proceeding, but it is the Father who generates, the Son who is generated, and the Holy Spirit who proceeds, so that distinctions are in Persons and unity in nature. Therefore, although "one is the Father, another the Son, and another the Holy Spirit, yet they are not different"[1] but what is the Father is the Son and the Holy Spirit entirely the same, so that according to the true and Catholic Faith they are believed to be consubstantial. For the Father from eternity by generating the Son gave His substance to Him according to which He Himself testifies: "That which the Father has given to me is greater than all things" [John 10:29]. But it cannot be said that He (the Father) has given a part of His substance to Him (the Son), and retained a part for Himself, since the substance of the Father is indivisible, namely, simple. But neither can it be said that the Father has transferred His substance to the Son in generating, as if He had given that to the Son which he did not retain for Himself; otherwise the substance would have ceased to exist. It is clear, therefore, that the Son in being born without any diminution received the substance of the Father, and thus the Father and the Son have the same substance, and so this same reality is the Father and the Son and also the Holy Spirit proceeding from both. But when Truth prays to the Father for His faithful saying: "I will that they may be one in us, as we also are one" [John 17:22]: this word "one" indeed is accepted for the faithful in such a way that a union of charity in grace is understood, for the divine Persons in such a way that a unity of identity in nature is considered, as elsewhere Truth says: "Be . . . perfect, as also your heavenly Father is perfect" [Matt. 5:48], as if He said more clearly, "Be perfect" in the perfection of grace "as your heavenly Father is perfect" in the perfection of grace, that is, each in his own manner, because between the Creator and the creature so great a likeness cannot be noted without the necessity of noting a greater dissimilarity between them. If anyone, therefore, shall

432

---

[1] St. Gregory Nazianzenus, Ep. 1 ad Cledon [MG 37, 179].

presume to defend or approve the opinion or doctrine of the above mentioned Joachim, let him be refuted as a heretic by all.

433   Yet on this account we do not wish to detract from the monastery in Florence (whose founder is Joachim himself), since both the institution there is regular and the observance salutary, especially since Joachim himself has ordered all his writings to be assigned to us, to be approved or even corrected by the judgment of the Apostolic See, dictating a letter which he signed with his own hand in which he firmly confesses that he holds that Faith which the Roman Church, which (the Lord disposing) is the mother and master of all the faithful, holds. We reprove also and we condemn that very perverse dogma of the impious Almaricus, whose mind the father of lies has so blinded that his doctrine must be considered not so heretical as insane.

Chap. 3. The Heretics [Waldensian] [1]
[The necessity of a canonical mission]

434   Because some indeed "under the pretext of piety, denying his power" (according to what the Apostle says) [II Tim. 3:5], assume to themselves the authority of preaching, when the same Apostle says: "How . . . shall they preach, unless they are sent?" [Rom. 10:15], let all who, being prohibited or not sent, without having received authority from the Apostolic See, or from the Catholic bishop of the place, shall presume publicly or privately to usurp the duty of preaching [2] be marked by the bond of excommunication; and unless they recover their senses, the sooner the better, let them be punished with another fitting penalty.

Chap. 4. The Pride of the Greeks Against the Latins [3]

435   Although we wish to cherish and honor the Greeks who in our days are returning to the obedience of the Apostolic See, by sustaining their customs and rites in as far as we are able with the Lord, yet we do not wish nor are we able to defer to them in these things which engender danger to souls and which detract from ecclesiastical honor. For when the church of the Greeks with certain accomplices and their protectors withdrew itself from the obedience of the Apostolic See, the Greeks began to detest the Latins so much that among other things which they impiously committed to their dishonor, if at any time Latin priests celebrated Mass on their altars, they themselves were unwilling to sacrifice on these (altars), before they washed them, as if defiled on account of this (sacrifice by the Latin priests); these same Greeks presumed with

---

[1] Msi XXII 990 A. CIC *Decret. Greg.* V, 7, 13: Frdbg II 788; Rcht II 759.
[2] From the Council of Verona 1184, under Lucius III [Msi XXII 477 A].
[3] Msi XXII 990.

indiscreet boldness to rebaptize those baptized by the Latins, and up to
this time, as we have learned, certain ones do not fear to do this. Therefore, wishing to remove such scandal from the Church, on the recommendation of the Sacred Council, we strictly command that they do not
presume such things in the future, conforming themselves as obedient
sons to the holy Roman Church, their mother, so that there may be "one
flock and one shepherd" [John 10:16]. If anyone, however, shall presume
any such thing, struck by the sword of excommunication, let him be
deposed from every office and ecclesiastical favor.

Chap. 5. The Dignity of the Patriarchs [1]

Renewing the ancient privilege of the patriarchal sees, with the ap- **436**
proval of the sacred universal synod, we sanction that after the Roman
Church, which by the ordering of the Lord before all others holds the
first place of ordinary power as the mother and teacher of all the faithful
of Christ, the (Church of) Constantinople holds the first, Alexandria
the second, Antioch the third, and Jerusalem the fourth place.

Chap. 21. The Obligation of Making Confession and of its not being Revealed by the Priest, and the Obligation of Receiving the Sacrament at least in Paschal Time. [2]

Let everyone of the faithful of both sexes, after he has arrived at the **437**
years of discretion, alone faithfully confess all his sins at least once a year
to his own priest, and let him strive to fulfill with all his power the
penance enjoined upon him, receiving reverently the sacrament of the
Eucharist at least in Paschal time, unless by chance on the advice of his
own priest for some reasonable cause it shall be decided that he must
abstain from the precept temporarily; otherwise both while living let him
be barred from entrance to the church, and when dying let him be
deprived of Christian burial. Therefore, let this salutary law be published frequently in the churches, lest anyone assume a pretext of
excuse in the blindness of ignorance. Moreover if anyone from a just
cause shall wish to confess his sins to another priest, let him first ask
and obtain permission from his own priest, since otherwise that one
(the other priest) cannot absolve or bind him. Let the priest, however,
be discreet and cautious, so that skilled by practise "he may pour wine
and oil" [Luke 10:34] on the wounds of the wounded, diligently inquiring into both the circumstances of the sinner and the sin, by which
prudently he may understand what kind of advice he ought to give to
him, and, using various experiments to save the sick, what kind of a
remedy he ought to apply.

---

[1] Msi XXII 990.

[2] *Ibid.* 1007 E. ff. CIC *Decr. Greg.* V, 38, 12: Frdbg II 887; Rcht II 862.

438   Moreover, let him constantly take care, lest by word or sign or any other way whatsoever he may at any time betray the sinner; but if he should need more prudent counsel, he should seek it cautiously without any mention of the person, since he who shall presume to reveal a sin entrusted to him in confession, we decree not only must be deposed from priestly office but must also be thrust into a strict monastery to do perpetual penance.

Chap. 41. The Continuation of Good Faith in Every Precept [1]

439   Since "everything . . . which is not from faith is a sin" [Rom. 14:23], by synodal judgment we define that no precept either canonical or civil without good faith has any value, since that which cannot be observed without mortal sin must in general be rejected by every constitution and custom. Therefore, it is necessary that he who lay down a rule at no time be conscious of anything wrong.

Chap. 62. The Relics of the Saints [2]

440   Since, because certain ones expose the relics of saints for sale and exhibit them at random, the Christian religion has often suffered detraction; so that it may not suffer detraction in the future, we have ordered by the present decree that from now on ancient relics may by no means be exhibited or exposed for sale outside a case. Moreover let no one presume that newly found relics be venerated publicly, unless first they have been approved by the authority of the Roman Pontiff. . . .

HONORIUS III 1216–1227

The Matter of the Eucharist [3]

[From the letter "Perniciosus valde" to Olaus, Archbishop
of Upsala Dec. 13, 1220]

441   An exceedingly pernicious abuse, as we have heard, has arisen in your area, namely, that in the sacrifice water is being used in greater measure than wine; when according to the reasonable custom of the general Church more of wine than of water should be used. And so to your brotherhood through the apostolic writings we order that in the future

---

[1] Msi XXII 1027 A, CIC *Decr. Greg.* II, 26, 20: Frdbg II 393; Rcht II 379.

[2] Msi XXII 1049 f.; the full title of this chapter is: Let the relics of saints not be shown outside a receptacle; let no new relics be held in veneration without the Roman Church.

[3] CIC *Decr. Greg.* III 41, 13: Frdbg II 643; Rcht 618; Pth 6441.

you do not do this, and that you do not allow it to be done in your province.

GREGORY IX 1227–1241

The Necessity of Preserving Theological Terminology and Tradition [1]

[From the letter "Ab Aegyptiis" to the theologians of Paris, July 7, 1228]

"Touched inwardly with sorrow of heart" [Gen. 6:6], "we are filled **442** with the bitterness of wormwood" [cf. Lam. 3:15], because as it has been brought to our attention, certain ones among you, distended like a skin by the spirit of vanity, are working with profane novelty to pass beyond the boundaries which thy fathers have set [cf. Prov. 22:28], the understanding of the heavenly page limited by the fixed boundaries of expositions in the studies of the Holy Fathers by inclining toward the philosophical doctrine of natural things, which it is not only rash but even profane to transgress; (they are doing this) for a show of knowledge, not for any profit to their hearers; so that they seem to be not taught of God or speakers of God, but rather revealed as God. For, although they ought to explain theology according to the approved traditions of the saints and not with carnal weapons, "yet with (weapons) powerful for God to destroy every height exalting itself against the knowledge of God and to lead back into captivity every understanding unto the obedience of Christ" [cf. II Cor. 10:4 f.], they themselves "led away by various and strange doctrines" [cf. Heb. 13:9] reduce the "head to the tail" [cf. Deut. 28:13, 44] and they force the queen to be servant to the handmaid, that is, by earthly documents attributing the heavenly, which is of grace, to nature. Indeed relying on the knowledge of natural things more than they ought, returning "to the weak and needy elements" of the world, which they served while they were "little" and "serving them again" [Gal. 4:9] as foolish in Christ they feed on "milk and not solid food" [Heb. 5:12 f.], and they seem by no means to have established "the heart in grace" [cf. Heb. 13:9]; and so despoiled of their rewards "plundered and wounded by their natural possessions [2] they do not reduce to memory that (saying) of the Apostle which we believe they have already frequently read: "Avoiding the profane novelties of words, and the oppositions of knowledge falsely so called, which some seeking have

---

[1] DCh I 59.—Bar(Th) ad 1228 n. 20 (20, 555 b f.); Pth 8231; cf. DuPl. I, I 137 b.

[2] Peter Lombard, *Sent.* 1. 2. dist. 25 c. 7; cf. Luke 10: 30, according to St. Ambrose, *In Luc.* 1. 7, n. 73 [ML 15, 17, 18 B], St. Aug., *Quaest. evang.* 1, 2, n. 19 [ML 35, 134 D], St. Bede, *In Luc.* lib. 3, c. 10 [ML 92, 468 D].

erred concerning the faith" [cf. I Tim. 6:20 f.]. "O foolish and slow of heart in all things" which the protectors of divine grace, namely "the prophets" the evangelists and the apostles "have spoken" [cf. Luke 24:25], since nature in itself cannot (work) anything for salvation unless it is helped by grace [see n. 105, 138]. Let presumers of this kind speak, who embracing the doctrine of natural things offer the leaves and not the fruit of words to their hearers, whose minds as if fed with husks remain empty and vacant; and their soul cannot be "delighted in fatness" [Isa. 55:2], because thirsty and dry it cannot drink "from the waters of Siloe running with silence" [cf. Isa. 8:6] but rather from those which are drawn from the philosophical torrents, of which it is said: "The more they are drunk, the more the waters are thirsted for, because they do not bring satiety, but rather anxiety and labor. And while by extorted, nay rather distorted, expositions they turn the sacred words divinely inspired to the sense of the doctrine of philosophers who are ignorant of God, "do they not place the ark of the covenant by Dagon" [I Kings 5:2], and set up the image of Antiochus to be adored in the temple of the Lord? And while they try to add to faith by natural reason more than they ought, do they not render it in a certain way useless and empty since "faith does not have merit for one to whom human reason furnishes proof?" [1] Finally, nature believes what is understood, but faith by its freely given power comprehends what is believed by the intelligence, and bold and daring it penetrates where natural intellect is not able to reach. Will such followers of the things of nature, in whose eyes grace seems to be proscribed, say that "the Word which was in the beginning with God, was made flesh, and dwelt in us" [John 1] is of grace or of nature? As for the rest, God forbid that a "most beautiful woman" [Cant. 5:9], with "eyes painted with stiblic" [IV Kings 9:30] by presumers, be adorned with false colors, and that she who "girded with clothes" [Ps. 44:10] and "adorned with jewels" [Isa. 61:10] proceeds splendid as a queen, be clothed with stitched semi-girdles of philosophers, sordid apparel. God forbid that "cows ill favored" and consumed with leanness, which "give no mark of being full would devour the beautiful" [Gen. 41:18 ff.] and consume the fat.

443   Therefore, lest a rash and perverse dogma of this kind "as a canker spreads" [II Tim. 2:17], and infects many and makes it necessary that "Rachel bewail her lost sons" [Jer. 31:15], we order and strictly command by the authority of those present that, entirely forsaking the poison mentioned above, without the leaven of worldly knowledge, that you teach theological purity, not "adulterating the word of God" [II Cor. 2:17] by the creations of philosophers, lest around the altar of God you seem to wish to plant a grove contrary to the teaching of the Lord, and

---

[1] St. Gregory the Great, *In evang.* hom. l. 2, hom. 26, n. 1 [ML 76, 1197].

by a commingling of honey to cause the sacrifice of doctrine to ferment which is to be presented "with the unleavened bread of sincerity and truth" [I Cor. 5:8]. But content with the terminology established by the Fathers, you should feed the minds of your listeners with the fruit of heavenly words, so that after the leaves of the words have been removed, "they may draw from the fountains of the Savior" [Isa. 12:3]; the clear and limpid waters which tend principally to this, that they may build up faith or fashion morals, and refreshed by these they may be delighted with internal richness.[1]

Condemnation of Various Heretics [2]

[From the form of anathema published Aug. 20, 1229 (?)]

"We excommunicate and anathematize . . . all heretics": the Cathari, **444** the Patareni, the Pauperes of Lyons, the Passagini, the Josephini, the Arnoldistae, the Speronistae, and others, "by whatever names they may be known; having different faces indeed, but "tails coupled to each other" [Judg. 15:4], because from vanity they come together at the same point." [3]

The Matter and Form of Ordination [4]

[From the letter to Olaus, Bishop of Lyons, Dec. 9, 1232]

When a priest and deacon are ordained, they receive the imposition **445** of a hand by corporal touch, by the rite introduced by the Apostles; and if this shall be omitted, it must not be partially repeated, but at an established time for conferring orders of this kind, what through error was omitted must be carefully supplied. Moreover, the suspension of hands over the head must be made, when the prayer of ordination is uttered over the head.

The Invalidity of Marriage Subject to Conditions [5]

[From fragments of the Decrees n. 104, about the years 1227–1234]

If conditions contrary to the nature of marriage are inserted, for **446** example, if one says to the other: "I contract marriage with you, if you

---

[1] Cf. Greg. IX and John XXII in Bar(Th) ad 1231 n. 48 (21, 46a), and ad 1317 n. 15 (24, 49 b f.).

[2] CIC *Decr. Greg.* V, 7, 15: Frdbg II 789; Rcht II 760; Pth 9675 (cf. 8445); cf. Bar(Th) ad 1229 n. 37 ff. (21, 11 a ff.).

[3] From the Fourth Lateran Council, 1215, chapter 3, on heretics [Msi XXII 986].

[4] CIC *Decr. Greg.* I, 16, 3: Frdbg II 135; Rcht II 1305; Pth 9056.

[5] CIC *Decr. Greg.* IV, 5, 7: Frdbg II 684; Rcht II 650 f.; Pth 9664; Msi XXIII 141 **A.**

avoid the generation of children," or "until I find another more worthy by reason of reputation or riches," or, "if you surrender yourself to adultery for money," the marriage contract, however favorable it may be, is lacking in effect; although some conditions appended in matrimony, if they are disgraceful or impossible, because of its esteem, are to be considered as not added.

The Matter of Baptism [1]

[From the letter "Cum, sicut ex" to Sigurd, Archbishop of Nidaros,[2] July 8, 1241]

447   Since as we have learned from your report, it sometimes happens because of the scarcity of water, that infants of your lands are baptized in beer, we reply to you in the tenor of those present that, since according to evangelical doctrine it is necessary "to be reborn from water and the Holy Spirit" [John 3:5] they are not to be considered rightly baptized who are baptized in beer.

Usury [3]

[From a letter to brother R. in fragments of Decree n. 69, of uncertain date]

448   He who loans a sum of money to one sailing or going to market, since he has assumed upon himself a risk, is [not] to be considered a usurer who will receive something beyond his lot. He also who gives ten solidi, so that at another time just as many measures of grain, wine, and oil may be payed back to him, and although these are worth more at the present time, it is probably doubtful whether at the time of payment they will be worth more or less, for this reason should not be considered a usurer. By reason of this doubt he also is excused, who sells clothing, grain, wine, oil, or other wares so that at a set time he receives for them more than they are worth at that time, if, however, he had not intended so to sell them at the time of the contract.

CELESTINE IV 1241

---

1 Bar(Th) ad 1241 n. 42 (21, 241 b); Pth 11048.
2 Drontheim in Norwegia.
3 CIC *Decr. Greg.* V, 19, 19: Frdbg II 816; Rcht II 787; Pth 9678; Msi XXIII 131 E f.

INNOCENT IV 1243–1254
COUNCIL OF LYONS I 1245

Ecumenical XIII (against Frederick II)

He did not send out dogmatic decrees.

The Rites of the Greeks [1]

[From the letter "Sub Catholicae" to the Bishop of
Tusculum, of the Legation of the Apostolic
See among the Greeks, March 6, 1254]

1. And so concerning these matters our deliberation has resulted **449**
thus, that Greeks of the same kingdom in the anointings, which are
made with respect to baptism, should hold to and observe the custom of
the Roman Church.—2. But the rite or custom which they are said to
have, of anointing completely the bodies of those to be baptized may be
tolerated, if it cannot be given up or be removed without scandal, since,
whether or not it be done, it makes no great difference with regard to
the efficacy or effect of baptism.—3. Also it makes no difference whether
they baptize in cold or in hot water, since they are said to affirm that
baptism has equal power and effect in each.

4. Moreover, let bishops alone mark the baptized on the forehead with **450**
chrism, because this anointing is not to be given except by bishops, since
the apostles alone, whose places the bishops take, are read to have imparted the Holy Spirit by the imposition of the hand, which confirmation, or the anointing of the forehead represents.—5. Also all bishops
individually in their own churches on the day of the Lord's Supper can,
according to the form of the Church, prepare chrism from balsam and
olive oil. For the gift of the Holy Spirit is given in the anointing with
chrism. And particularly the dove, which signifies the Spirit Himself,
is read to have brought the olive branch to the ark. But if the Greeks
should wish rather to preserve their own ancient rite in this, namely,
that the patriarch together with the archbishops and bishops, his suffragans and the archbishops with their suffragans, prepare chrism at the
same time, let them be tolerated in such a custom of theirs.

6. Moreover no one may merely be anointed with some unction by **451**
priests or confessors for satisfaction of penance.—7. But upon the sick
according to the word of James the Apostle [Jas. 5:4] let extreme unction be conferred.

---

[1] MBR I (Luxemburg 1742) 100 f.; Msi 23, 574; Pth 15 265; *Les régistres d'Innocent
IV*, by Elie Berger, III (1897) n. 7338.

452   8. Furthermore in the application of water, whether cold or hot or tepid, in the sacrifice of the altar, let the Greeks follow their own custom if they wish, as long as they believe and declare that, when the form of the canon has been preserved, it is accomplished equally by each (kind of water).—9. But let them not preserve the Eucharist consecrated on the day of the Lord's Supper for a year on the pretext of the sick, that with it they may obviously communicate themselves. It may be permitted them, however, in behalf of the sick themselves, to consecrate the body of Christ and to preserve it for fifteen days, but not for a longer period of time, lest through its long preservation, perchance by a change in the species, it be rendered less suitable to receive, although the truth and its efficacy always remain entirely the same, and never by any length of time or the mutability of time do they grow weak.—10. But in the celebration of solemn and other Masses, and concerning the hour of celebrating these, as long as in the preparation and in the consecration they observe the form of words expressed and handed down by the Lord, and (as long as) in celebrating they do not pass the ninth hour, let them be permitted to follow their own custom.

453   18. Moreover concerning fornication which an unmarried man commits with an unmarried woman, there must not be any doubt at all that it is a mortal sin, since the Apostle declares that "fornicators as adulterers are cast out from the kingdom of God" [I Cor. 6:9].

454   19. In addition to this we wish and we expressly command that the Greek bishops in the future confer the seven orders according to the custom of the Roman Church, since they are said to have neglected or to have hitherto omitted three of the minor ones with respect to those to be ordained. But let those who already have been so ordained by them, because of their exceedingly great number, be kept in the orders thus received.

455   20. Because according to the Apostle "a woman if her husband is dead is freed from the law of her husband" so "that she has the free power of marrying whom she will in the Lord" [cf. Rom. 7:2; I Cor. 7:39], let the Greeks in no measure reprehend second or third or even later marriages; nor should they condemn but rather approve them between persons who otherwise can licitly be united to one another in marriage. Priests, however, should not by any means bless those who marry a second time.

456   23. Finally, since Truth in the Gospel asserts that "if anyone shall utter blasphemy against the Holy Spirit, neither in this life nor in the future will it be forgiven him" [cf. Matt. 12:32], by this it is granted that certain sins of the present be understood which, however, are forgiven in the future life, and since the Apostle says that "fire will test the work of each one, of what kind it is," and " if any man's work burn,

he shall suffer loss, but he himself shall be saved, yet so as by fire"
[I Cor. 3:13, 15], and since these same Greeks truly and undoubtedly
are said to believe and to affirm that the souls of those who after a
penance has been received yet not performed, or who, without mortal
sin yet die with venial and slight sin, can be cleansed after death and
can be helped by the suffrages of the Church, we, since they say a place
of purgation of this kind has not been indicated to them with a certain
and proper name by their teachers, we indeed, calling it purgatory according to the traditions and authority of the Holy Fathers, wish that
in the future it be called by that name in their area. For in that transitory
fire certainly sins, though not criminal or capital, which before have not
been remitted through penance but were small and minor sins, are
cleansed, and these weigh heavily even after death, if they have been
forgiven in this life.

24. Moreover, if anyone without repentance dies in mortal sin, with-   **457**
out a doubt he is tortured forever by the flames of eternal hell.—25. But
the souls of children after the cleansing of baptism, and of adults also
who depart in charity and who are bound neither by sin nor unto any
satisfaction for sin itself, at once pass quickly to their eternal fatherland.

ALEXANDER IV 1254-1261

Errors of William of St. Amour (concerning Mendicants) [1]

[From Constit. "Romanus Pontifex," October 5, 1256]

They have published, I say, and they have rushed forth into wicked   **458**
falsehoods out of an excessive passion of soul, rashly composing an exceedingly pernicious and detestable treatise. After this treatise was carefully read, and opportunely and rigidly examined, and a complete report
concerning it was made to us by these, because in it (there are) some
perverse and wicked things:

against the power and authority of the Roman Pontiff and of his
bishops;

some against those who overcome the world with its riches by voluntary indigence, and for the sake of God beg in very strict poverty;

others even against those who, ardently zealous for the salvation of

---

[1] MBR 1, 112 a f.; BR(T) 3, 644 a ff.; cf. Bar(Th) ad 1256 n. 22 f. (21, 508 b f.).
Gotti, *Verit. relig. christ.* II 375; Pth 16565; cf. DuPl I, I 168 ff.; DCh I 331 ff.—This
condemnation has been repeated many times, e.g., in Const. "Veri solis radiis," Oct. 17,
1256; "Non sine multa cordis amaritudine," Oct. 19, 1256, and "Quidam Scripturae
sacrae," Oct. 19, 1256.

souls and caring for sacred interests, bring about much spiritual progress in the Church of God and make much fruit there;

459   moreover, certain statements against the salutary state of the poor or religious mendicants, as are the beloved sons, the Brother Preachers and Minor, who in the vigor of spirit after abandoning the world with its riches, aspire to their heavenly fatherland alone with all effort;

and because also we find many other disagreements, certainly worthy of confutation and lasting confusion clearly contained;

and because, too, this same treatise was a festering center of great scandal and matter of much disturbance, and induced a loss of souls, since it distracted the faithful from ordinary devotion and the customary giving of alms and from conversion and entrance into religion,

We by the advice of our Brethren, by Apostolic authority have thought that this same book which begins thus: "Behold seeing they will cry from abroad," and which according to its title is called "a brief tract concerning the dangers of most recent times" as something wicked, criminal, and detestable, and the rules and documents handed down in it as wicked, false, and impious, must be rejected, and must be condemned forever, and we rigidly command that whoever has that treatise will take care to burn it and entirely destroy it immediately in whole and in any of its parts within eight days from the time at which he shall know of such a rejection and condemnation of ours.

URBAN IV 1261–1264   CLEMENT IV 1265–1268

GREGORY X 1271–1276
COUNCIL OF LYONS II 1274

Ecumenical XIV (concerning the union of the Greeks)

Declaration Concerning the Procession of the Holy Spirit [1]

[The Most Exalted Trinity and the Catholic Faith]

460   In faithful and devout profession we declare that the Holy Spirit proceeds eternally from the Father and the Son, not as from two beginnings, but from one beginning, not from two breathings but from one breathing. The most holy Roman Church, the mother and teacher of all the faithful, has up to this time professed, preached, and taught this; this she firmly holds, preaches, declares, and teaches; the unchangeable and true opinion of the orthodox Fathers and Doctors, Latin as well

---

[1] Msi XXIV 81 B; Pth 20 950; Hrd VII 705; cf. Hfl VI 132 ff.; Baɪ(Th) ad 1274 n. 1 ff. (22, 321 ff.).

as Greek, holds this. But because some through ignorance of the irresistible aforesaid truth have slipped into various errors, we in our desire to close the way to errors of this kind, with the approval of the sacred Council, condemn and reject (those) who presume to deny that the Holy Spirit proceeds eternally from the Father and the Son; as well as (those) who with rash boldness presume to declare that the Holy Spirit proceeds from the Father and the Son as from two beginnings, and not as from one.

Profession of Faith of Michael Palaeologus [1]

We believe that the Holy Trinity, the Father, and the Son, and the   461 Holy Spirit, is one God omnipotent and entire Deity in the Trinity, coessential and consubstantial, coeternal and co-omnipotent, of one will, power, and majesty, the creator of all creatures, from whom are all things, in whom are all things, through whom all things which are in the heavens and on the earth, visible, invisible, corporal, and spiritual. We believe that each individual Person in the Trinity is one true God, complete and perfect.

We believe that the same Son of God, the Word of God, is eternally   462 born from the Father, consubstantial, co-omnipotent, and equal through all things to the Father in divinity, temporally born from the Holy Spirit and Mary ever Virgin with a rational soul; having two births, one eternal birth from the Father, the other temporal from the mother; true God and true man, proper and perfect in each nature, not adopted nor phantastic, but the one and only Son of God, in two and from two natures, that is divine and human, in the singleness of one person impassible and immortal in divinity, but in humanity for us and for our salvation having suffered in the true passion of the flesh, died, and was buried, descended to hell, and on the third day arose again from the dead in the true resurrection of the flesh, on the fortieth day after the resurrection with the flesh in which He arose and with His soul ascended into heaven and sits at the right hand of God the Father, whence

---

[1] Msi XXIV 70 A f.; Hrd VII 694 C ff.; Hfl VI 139 nota; cf. Bar(Th) ad 1274 n. 19 (22, 329a).—This profession of faith was proposed in the year 1267 by Clement IV to Michael Palaeologus [Bar(Th) ad ann. 1267, n. 72–81], and by him offered at the Council of Lyons to Gregory X, and was also proposed again by Urban VI on Aug. 1, 1385, to the orthodox Greeks returning to the Church. Up to the words: "Haec est vera fides" it is the same profession which with a few changes in words is even now put forth by questions and responses at the consecrations of bishops according to "the ancient statutes of the Church" (which once were falsely considered as "the decrees of the Fourth Council of Carthage"; cf. n. 150 ff.; n. 353 ff.; ML 56, 879 B f.).—Cf. the profession of faith of John Veccus [Bar(Th) in the year 1277, n. 34–39] and the letter of Gregory X, October 24, 1272 [Msi XX 47].

He will come to judge the living and the dead, and will return to each one according to his works whether they were good or evil.

463   We believe also that the Holy Spirit is complete and perfect and true God, proceeding from the Father and the Son, coequal and consubstantial, co-omnipotent, and coeternal through all things with the Father and the Son. We believe that this holy Trinity is not three Gods but one God, omnipotent, eternal, invisible, and unchangeable.

Variant Readings

464   We believe that the true Church is holy, Catholic, apostolic, and one, in which is given one holy baptism and true remission of all sins. We believe also in the true resurrection of this flesh, which now we bear, and in eternal life. We believe also that the one author of the New and the Old Testament, of the Law, and of the Prophets and the Apostles is the omnipotent God and Lord. This is the true Catholic Faith, and this in the above mentioned articles the most holy Roman Church holds and teaches. But because of diverse errors introduced by some through ignorance and by others from evil, it (the Church) says and teaches that those who after baptism slip into sin must not be rebaptized, but by true penance attain forgiveness of their sins. Because if they die truly repentant in charity before they have made satisfaction by worthy fruits of penance for (sins) committed and omitted, their souls are cleansed after death by purgatorical or purifying punishments, as Brother John [1] has explained to us. And to relieve punishments of this kind, the offerings of the living faithful are of advantage to these, namely, the sacrifices of Masses, prayers, alms, and other duties of piety, which have customarily been performed by the faithful for the other faithful according to the regulations of the Church. However, the souls of those who after having received holy baptism have incurred no stain of sin whatever, also those souls who, after contracting the stain of sin, either while remaining in their bodies or being divested of them, have been cleansed, as we have said above, are received immediately into heaven. The souls of those who die in mortal sin or with original sin only, however, immediately descend to hell, yet to be punished with different punishments. The same most holy Roman Church firmly believes and firmly declares that nevertheless on the day of judgment "all" men will be brought together with their bodies "before the tribunal of Christ" "to render an account" of their own deeds [Rom. 14:10].

465   The same holy Roman Church also holds and teaches that the ecclesiastical sacraments are seven: namely, one is baptism, concerning which we have spoken above; another is the sacrament of confirmation which

---

[1] Brother John Parastron, O.F.M.

the bishops confer through the imposition of hands when anointing the reborn; another is penance; another the Eucharist; another the sacrament of orders; another is matrimony; another extreme unction, which according to the doctrine of St. James is given to the sick. The same Roman Church prepares the sacrament of the Eucharist from unleavened bread, holding and teaching that in the same sacrament the bread is changed into the body, and the wine into the blood of Jesus Christ. But concerning matrimony it holds that neither one man is permitted to have many wives nor one woman many husbands at the same time. But she (the Church) says that second and [1] third marriages successively are permissible for one freed from a legitimate marriage through the death of the other party, if another canonical impediment for some reason is not an obstacle.

Also this same holy Roman Church holds the highest and complete **466** primacy and spiritual power over the universal Catholic Church which she truly and humbly recognizes herself to have received with fullness of power from the Lord Himself in Blessed Peter, the chief or head of the Apostles whose successor is the Roman Pontiff. And just as to defend the truth of Faith she is held before all other things, so if any questions shall arise regarding faith they ought to be defined by her judgment. And to her anyone burdened with affairs pertaining to the ecclesiastical world can appeal; and in all cases looking forward to an ecclesiastical examination, recourse can be had to her judgment, and all churches are subject to her; their prelates give obedience and reverence to her. In her, moreover, such a plentitude of power rests that she receives the other churches to a share of her solicitude, of which many patriarchal churches the same Roman Church has honored in a special way by different privileges—its own prerogative always being observed and preserved both in general Councils and in other places.

INNOCENT V 1276	MARTIN IV 1281–1285
HADRIAN V 1276	HONORIUS IV 1285–1287
JOHN XXI 1276–1277	NICHOLAS IV 1288–1292
NICHOLAS III 1277–1280	ST. CELESTINE V 1294–(†1295)

---

[1] Thus in the formula subscribed by Palaeologus; Clement IV had written so: *tertias et deinceps nuptias* (third and fourth marriages).

BONIFACE VIII 1294-1303

Indulgences [1]

[From the Jubilee Bull "Antiquorum habet" Feb. 22, 1300]

467   A faithful report of the ancients holds that to those approaching the honorable Basilica of the Prince of the Apostles are granted great remissions of sins and indulgences. We . . . confirm and by apostolic authority approve all such remissions and indulgences, holding them all and individually valid and pleasing. . . .

The Unity and Power of the Church [2]

[From the Bull "Unam Sanctam" November 18, 1302]

468   With Faith urging us we are forced to believe and to hold the one, holy, Catholic Church and that, apostolic, and we firmly believe and simply confess this (Church) outside which there is no salvation nor remission of sin, the Spouse in the Canticle proclaiming: "One is my dove, my perfect one. One she is of her mother, the chosen of her that bore her" [Cant. 6:8]; which represents the one mystical body whose head is Christ, of Christ indeed, as God. And in this, "one Lord, one faith, one baptism" [Eph. 4:5]. Certainly Noe had one ark at the time of the flood, prefiguring one Church which perfect on one cubit had one ruler and guide, namely Noe, outside which we read all living things on the earth were destroyed. Moreover this we venerate and this alone, the Lord in the prophet saying: "Deliver, O God, my soul from the sword; my only one from the hand of the dog" [Ps. 21:21]. For in behalf of the soul, that is, in behalf of himself, the head itself and the body he prayed at the same time, which body he called the "Only one" namely, the Church, because of the unity of the spouse, the faith, the

---

[1] CIC Extr. comm. V, 9, 1: Frdbg II 1303; Rcht II 1218; Pth 24917; BR(T) 4, 156 b; MBR 1, 179 a; Bar(Th) ad 1300 n. 4 (23, 263 b f.).

[2] CIC Extr. comm. I, 8, 1; Frdbg II 1245; Rcht II 1159 f.; Bar(TH) ad 1302 n. 13 (23, 303 f.; cf. Hfl VI 346 ff.—Philip IV, King of France, made ill use of this bull when he said that it was defined by it that the Pope had direct power over kings; but Boniface by no means intended this; in a consistory held on this matter he expressly declared that the statement was falsely applied to him, "that we had ordered the king to recognize his kingdom as from us. For forty years we have been experienced in the law, and we know that there are two powers ordained by God. Therefore, who should or can believe that such foolishness, such folly is or has been in our head? We say that we wish to usurp the jurisdiction of a king in nothing; and this did our brother Portuensis say. It cannot be denied that a king or any other person among the faithful is subject to us by reason of sin." Cf. Du Puy, *Histoire du différend*, etc., 77.

sacraments, and the charity of the Church. This is that "seamless tunic" of the Lord [John 19:23], which was not cut, but came forth by chance. Therefore, of the one and only Church (there is) one body, one head, not two heads as a monster, namely, Christ and Peter, the Vicar of Christ and the successor of Peter, the Lord Himself saying to Peter: "Feed my sheep" [John 21:17]. He said "My," and generally, not individually these or those, through which it is understood that He entrusted all to him. If, therefore, the Greeks or others say that they were not entrusted to Peter and his successors, of necessity let them confess that they are not of the sheep of Christ, since the Lord says in John, "to be one flock and one Shepherd" [John 10:16].

And we are taught by evangelical words that in this power of his are **469** two swords, namely spiritual and temporal. . . . Therefore, each is in the power of the Church, that is, a spiritual and a material sword. But the latter, indeed, must be exercised for the Church, the former by the Church. The former (by the hand) of the priest, the latter by the hand of kings and soldiers, but at the will and sufferance of the priest. For it is necessary that a sword be under a sword and that temporal authority be subject to spiritual power. . . . It is necessary that we confess the more clearly that spiritual power precedes any earthly power both in dignity and nobility, as spiritual matters themselves excel the temporal. . . . For, as truth testifies, spiritual power has to establish earthly power, and to judge if it was not good. . . . Therefore, if earthly power deviates, it will be judged by spiritual power; but if a lesser spiritual deviates, by its superior; but if the supreme (spiritual power deviates), it can be judged by God alone, not by man, as the Apostle testifies: "The spiritual man judges all things, but he himself is judged by no one" [I Cor. 2:15]. But this authority, although it is given to man and is exercised by man, is not human, but rather divine, and has been given by the divine Word to Peter himself and to his successors in him, whom the Lord acknowledged an established rock, when he said to Peter himself: "Whatsoever you shall bind" etc. [Matt. 16:19]. Therefore, "whosoever resists this power so ordained by God, resists the order of God" [cf. Rom. 13:2], unless as a Manichaean he imagines that there are two beginnings, which we judge false and heretical, because, as Moses testifies, not "in the beginnings" but "in the beginning God created the heaven and earth" [cf. Gen. 1:1]. Furthermore, we declare, say, define, and proclaim to every human creature that they by necessity for salvation are entirely subject to the Roman Pontiff.

BENEDICT XI 1303-1304
The Repeated Confession of Sins [1]
[From the order "Inter cunctas sollicitudines" Feb. 17, 1304]

470   . . . Although . . . it is not necessary to confess the same sins a second time, nevertheless, because of the shame which is a large part of repentance, we consider it of benefit to repeat the confession of the same sins, we strongly enjoin the Brothers [Preachers and Minors] carefully to advise those confessing, and in their sermons exhort that they confess to their own priests at least once in a year, declaring that without doubt this pertains to the advancement of souls.

CLEMENT V 1305-1314

COUNCIL OF VIENNE 1311-1312
Ecumenical XV (abolition of the Templars)

The Errors of the Beghards and the Beguines (the State of Perfection) [2]

471   1. That man in the present life can acquire so great and such a degree of perfection that he will be rendered inwardly sinless, and that he will not be able to advance farther in grace; for, as they say, if anyone could always advance, he could become more perfect than Christ.

472   2. That it is not necessary for man to fast or to pray, after he has attained a degree of such perfection; because then his sensuality is so perfectly subject to the spirit and to reason that man can freely grant to the body whatever it pleases.

473   3. That those who are in the aforementioned degree of perfection and in that spirit of liberty are not subject to human obedience, nor are they bound to any precepts of the Church, because (as they assert) "where the spirit of the Lord is, there is liberty [II Cor. 3:17].

474   4. That man can so attain final beatitude according to every degree of perfection in the present life, as he will obtain it in the blessed life.

---

[1] CIC Extr. comm. V, 7, 1; Frdbg II 1298 f.; Rcht II 1213; Pth 25 370; cf. Bar(Th) ad 1304 n. 21 (23, 355 b). The constitution "Inter cunctas" was again abrogated after seven years at the Council of Vienne (1311).

[2] CIC Clem. V, 3, 3; Frdbg II 1183; Rcht II 1100; Msi XXV 410 A; Hrd VII 1358 E f.; Gotti, *Verit. reliq. christ.* II 382; cf. Hfl VI 544; Bar (Th) ad 1312 n. 17 f. (28, 514 a ff.).

5. That any intellectual nature in its own self is naturally blessed, 475
and that the soul does not need the light of glory raising it to see God
and to enjoy Him beatifically.

6. That it is characteristic of the imperfect man to exercise himself 476
in acts of virtue, and the perfect soul gives off virtues by itself.

7. That a woman's kiss, since nature does not incline to this, is a 477
mortal sin; but the carnal act, since nature inclines to this, is not a sin,
especially when the one exercising it is tempted.

8. That in the elevation of the body of Jesus Christ they ought not to 478
arise nor to show reverence to it, declaring that it would be characteristic
of the imperfection in them, if from the purity and depth of their con-
templations they should descend to such a degree as to think about
other things regarding the minister [other text, mystery] or the sacrament of the Eucharist or the passion of the humanity of Christ.

A judgment: We with the approval of the Sacred Council condemn
and disapprove completely that sect together with its past errors, restraining more strictly lest anyone in the future hold, approve, or defend
them.

Usury [1]

[From the edict "Ex gravi ad nos"]

If anyone shall fall into that error, so that he obstinately presumes to 479
declare that it is not a sin to exercise usury, we decree that he must be
punished as a heretic.

The Errors of Peter John Olivi (The Wounds of Christ, the Union of the Soul and Body, and Baptism [2])

[From the edict "De Summa Trinitate et fide catholica"]

(The incarnation). Clinging firmly to the "foundation" of the Cath- 480
olic faith "against which," as the Apostle testifies "no one is able to
place anything different" [cf. I Cor. 3:11], we openly acknowledge with
holy mother Church that the only begotten Son of God in all these
things in which God the Father is, existing eternally together with the

---

[1] CIC Clem. V, 5: Frdbg II 1184; Rcht II 1101; Msi XXV 411 D; Hrd VII 1360 A;
cf. Hfl VI 546; Bar(Th) ad 1312 n. 21 (23, 523 b).

[2] CIC Clem. I, 1: Frdbg II 1133 f.; Rcht II, 1057 f.; Msi XXV 410 E f.; Hrd VII
1359 C f.; cf. Hfl VI 536 f.; Bar(Th) ad 1312 n. 19 f. (23, 522 a ff.).—Peter of John
Olivi, O.Fr.M., born 1248 in Sérignan in Gaul. For his errors on the soul see Quaracchi
edition (B. Jansen, S.J.) 1922–1926, tom. II p. 104 ff., 136 ff., 302 ff. He died with a
most beautiful profession of faith published March 14, 1298 (or 1297) [Hrt II[3] 404
ff.]. Cf. *Theol. Quartalschrift* (Tübingen) 113 (1932) 142 ff. [I. Koch].

Father, parts of our nature as well as unity, from which He Himself existing as true God in Himself became true man, namely, a human body capable of suffering and an intellective or rational soul, forming the body by Himself and essentially, assumed it temporarily in the Virginal womb unto the unity of its substance and person. And that the same Word of God in this assumed nature, for working out the salvation of all, wished not only to be fastened to the Cross and to die on it, but also, after His Spirit had been given up, permitted His side to be pierced with a lance, that in the streams of water and blood which flowed from it there might be formed the one and only immaculate virgin, holy Mother Church, the Spouse of Christ, just as from the side of the first man asleep Eve was formed into a marriage with him, that so truth should respond to a certain figure of the first and ancient Adam "who," according to the Apostle, "is formed for the future" [cf. Rom. 5:14], in our new Adam, that, is, Christ. That is, I say, the truth, made strong by the testimony of that very great eagle which the prophet Ezechiel saw flying around the other evangelical animals, namely of St. John, the Apostle and Evangelist, who narrating in his Gospel the condition and order of this sacrament said: "But after they were come to Jesus, when they saw that He was already dead, they did not break His legs. But one of the soldiers with a spear opened His side, and immediately there came out blood and water. And he that saw it has given testimony and his testimony is true. And he knows that he speaks the truth, that you [also] may believe" [John 19:33-35]. We, therefore, turning our attention to such remarkable testimony and to the common opinion of apostolic reflection of the Holy Fathers and the Doctors in accord with which alone it is proper to declare these things, with the approval of the sacred council we declare that the above mentioned Apostle and Evangelist John had kept the right order of the deed accomplished in the aforesaid, when he said that Christ "already dead, one of the soldiers opened His side with a lance."

481   [The soul as a form of the body]. Furthermore, with the approval of the above mentioned sacred council we reprove as erroneous and inimical to the Catholic faith every doctrine or position rashly asserting or turning to doubt that the substance of the rational or intellective soul truly and in itself is not a form of the human body, defining, so that the truth of sincere faith may be known to all, and the approach to all errors may be cut off, lest they steal in upon us, that whoever shall obstinately presume in turn to assert, define, or hold that the rational or intellective soul is not the form of the human body in itself and essentially must be regarded as a heretic.

482   Besides, one baptism which regenerates all who are baptized in Christ must be faithfully confessed by all just as "one God and one faith"

[Eph. 4:5], which celebrated in water in the name of the Father and of the Son and of the Holy Spirit we believe to be commonly the perfect remedy for salvation for adults as for children.

But because certain theological doctors are found to have contrary **483** opinions as to how great the effect of baptism (is) in the case of children, certain of these saying that through the power of baptism indeed sin is remitted to children, but grace is not conferred, others asserting on the contrary that sin is remitted for them in baptism and virtues and forming grace are infused as a habit [see n. 410], although not for them at the time as a function, we, however, considering the general efficacy of the death of Christ, which through baptism is applied equally to all the baptized, with the approval of the sacred council, consider the second opinion to be preferred, which says that forming grace and virtue are conferred on children as on adults, as more probable, more consonant and more in agreement with the words of the saints and the modern doctors of theology.

JOHN XXII 1316–1334

The Errors of the Fraticelli (the Church and the Sacraments) [1]

[Condemned in the law "Gloriosam Ecclesiam," January 23, 1318]

As a report worthy of faith holds, the sons of the above mentioned **484** rashness and impiety have been driven to this weakness of mind, that they think impiously in opposition to the most renowned and salutary truth of the Christian faith; they contemn the sacraments of the Church which should be venerated, and in an attack of blind fury they who should be crushed by it, press against the glorious primacy of the Roman Church, saying that it ought to be overthrown by all nations.

(1) Thus, the first error which breaks forth from their dark work- **485** shop invents two churches, the one carnal, packed with riches, overflowing with riches [others, luxuries], stained with crimes which they declare the Roman prefect and other inferior prelates dominate; the other spiritual, cleansed by frugality, beautiful in virtue, bound by poverty, in which they only and their companions are held, and which they, because of the merit of their spiritual life, if any faith should be applied to lies, rule.

(2) The second error, by which the conscience of the above mentioned **486** insolent is stained, cries out that the venerable priests of the Church and

---

[1] Gotti, *Verit. relig. christ.* II 379; cf. CIC Extr. IOH. XXII, 7; Frdbg II 1213 f.; Rcht II 1128 f. Cf. *Theol. Quartalschrift* (Tübingen) 113 (1932): 145 ff. [I. Koch].

other ministers of jurisdiction and order [1] are so devoid of authority that they cannot pass sentences, nor perform the sacraments nor instruct nor teach the subject people, imagining that these have been deprived of all ecclesiastical power, whom they see are free of their own heresy; because only in themselves (as they themselves vainly think), just as the sanctity of a spiritual life, so authority remains; and in this matter they are following the error of the Donatists. . . .

487 (3) The third error of these men conspires with the error of the Waldensians, since both declare that an oath was to be taken in no case, propounding that who happen to be bound by the sacredness of an oath are defiled by the contagion of mortal sin and are bound by punishment.

488 (4) The fourth blasphemy of such wicked men, breaking forth from the poisoned fount of the Waldensian teachings pretends that priests rightly and even legitimately ordained according to the form of the Church, yet weighed down by any sins cannot consecrate or confer the ecclesiastical sacraments. . . .

489 (5) The fifth error so blinds the minds of these that they declare that the Gospel of Christ has been fulfilled in them alone at this time, because up to now (as they foolishly think) it has been concealed or indeed entirely extinct. . . .

490 There are many other things which these very presumptuous men are said to babble against the venerable sacrament of matrimony; many things which they foolishly believe concerning the course of time and the end of time; many things which they propagate with lamentable vanity concerning the coming of the Antichrist which they declare even now to be close at hand. All these things, because we recognize them as partly heretical, partly senseless, partly fabulous, we decree must be condemned together with their authors rather than pursued or refuted with a pen. . . .

The Errors of John of Pouilly ("Confession and the Church") [2]

[Examined and condemned in the edict "Vas electionis," July 21, 1321]

491 (1). That they who have confessed to brothers having the general permission of hearing confessions are bound to confess again those same sins which have been confessed, to their own priest.

---

[1] The clause of the bulls does not have "et ordinis," *Dipl. et privil. SS. Rom. Pontificum,* Taurensis editio, T. IV., Aug. Taur. 1859, page 264.

[2] DCh. II 243 f. and DuPl I, I 301; CIC *Extr. comm.* V, 3, 2; Frdbg II 291; Rcht II 1207; Gotti l.c. II 377a; Bar(Th) ad 1321 n. 37 (24, 161a.—John of Pouilly wrote the work "Quodlibeta" which embraces almost all theology; he himself retracted his own errors. He died after the year 1321 [Hrt II³ 488 f.]. Cf. *Theol. Quartalschrift* (Tübingen) 113 (1932) 141 f., 147 ff. [I. Koch].

(2). That under the existing law "everyone of each sex" published in 　492
the General Council [Later. IV. see n. 437] the Roman Pontiff cannot
bring it about that parishioners be not bound to confess all their sins　‐
once a year to their own priest, who, it says, is the parish curate; indeed
neither could God do this, because, as it says, this involves contradiction.

(3). That the Pope cannot give the general power of hearing confes-　493
sions, indeed neither can God, without the one who has confessed to one
having general power being bound to confess these same sins again to
his own priest, who, it says, as we have already indicated, is the parish
curate. . . .

All the above mentioned articles and each one of them we, by apostolic
authority, condemn and reprove as false and erroneous and deviating
from sound authority . . . , declaring that the true and Catholic doctrine is contrary to them.

Hell and Limbo(?) [1]

[From the letter "Nequaquam sine dolore" to the Armenians,
Nov. 21, 1321]

It (The Roman Church) teaches . . . that the souls . . . of those 　493a
who die in mortal sin, or with only original sin descend immediately
into hell; however, to be punished with different penalties and in different places.

The Poverty of Christ [2]

[From the edict "Cum inter nonnullos," Nov. 13, 1323]

Since among some learned men it often happens that doubt is again 　494
raised as to whether it should be branded as heretical to affirm persistently that our Redeemer and Lord Jesus Christ and His apostles did not
possess anything either in particular or even in common, even though
there are different and adverse opinions on that question, we, in a desire
to put an end to this controversy, declare on the advice of our brethren
by this perpetual edict that a persistent assertion of this kind shall henceforth be branded as erroneous and heretical, since it expressly contradicts Sacred Scripture, which in many passages asserts that they did
have some possessions; and since with regard to the aforementioned it

---

[1] Bar(Th) approximately the year 1321, n. II. Cf. *Zeitschr. f. kath. Theologie* 52
(1928): 79 ff. (A. Straub); *Estudios eclesiásticos* 5 (1926): 438 ff. (F. Segarra).

[2] DuPl I, I 295b f.; CIC Extr. IOH XXII 14, 4: Frdbg II 1229 f.; Rcht II 1143
f.; Bar(Th) about 1323 n. 61 (24, 332b).—As to how this definition of John
XXII does not contradict the constitution of Nicholas III, "Exiit qui seminat," see in
Natalis Alexander, *Hist. eccl.* of the 12th and 14th centuries, diss. 11, art. 1.

openly submits that Sacred Scripture itself, by which surely the articles of orthodox faith are approved, contains a ferment of falsehood and consequently, in so far as in it lies, completely voicing the faith of Scripture it renders the Catholic faith, by destroying its approval, doubtful and uncertain. Moreover, in the future to affirm persistently that the right to use these same possessions which Sacred Scripture testifies that they had was by no means appropriate to our aforesaid Redeemer and His apostles, and that they did not have the right to sell or to donate them or to acquire others by means of them, which, nevertheless, Sacred Scripture testifies that they did according to the aforesaid or submits expressly that they could have done, since such an assertion evidently includes use and deeds on their part, in the aforesaid, it is not just; since surely it is wicked, contrary to Sacred Scripture, and inimical to Catholic doctrine about the use, actions, or deeds on the part of our Redeemer, the Son of God, we declare on the advice of our brethren that the persistent assertion shall henceforth be worthily branded as erroneous and heretical.

Errors of Marsilius of Padua and John of Jandun

(The Constitution of the Church) [1]

[Examined and condemned in the edict "Licet iuxta doctrinam" Oct. 23, 1327]

495   (1) That what we read about Christ in the Gospel of St. Matthew, that He Himself paid tribute to Caesar, when He ordered the stater which had been taken from the mouth of the fish [cf. Matt. 17:26] to be given to those who sought a drachma, He did this not with condescension out of liberality or piety, but forced by necessity.

[*Thence according to the Bull they concluded*]:

That all temporal affairs of the Church are subject to the emperor and he can accept these things as his own.

496   (2) That blessed Peter the Apostle had no more authority than the other Apostles had nor was he the head of the other apostles. Likewise that God did not send forth any head of the Church, nor did He make anyone His vicar.

497   (3) That it pertains to the emperor to correct, to appoint, to depose, and to punish the pope.

498   (4) That all priests, whether the pope or archbishop or a simple

---

[1] *Dict. de Théol. Cath.* 10 I col. 167–172. DuPl I, I 304a f.; cf. 397b; cf. Gotti, *Verit. reliq. christ.* II 385 ff.—Marsilius of Padua, born in the year 1280 (?), was rector of the University of Paris in 1312. He died, unreconciled to the Church, before April 10, 1343. John of Jandun together with Marsilius was excommunicated by name in 1327 [Hrt II³ 529 note].

priest, are by the institution of Christ equal in authority and jurisdiction.

(5) That the whole Church joined together can punish no man by 499 forced punishment, unless the emperor permits this.

We declare by sentence the above mentioned articles . . . to be *con-* 500 *trary to Sacred Scripture* and *enemies of the Catholic faith, heretics,* or *heretical and erroneous,* and also that the above mentioned Marsilius and John, will be heretics—rather they will be manifest and notorious archheretics.

Errors of Eckart (The Son of God, etc.) [1]

[Examined and condemned in the edict "In agro dominico,"
Mar. 27, 1329]

(1) And when asked why God did not create the world first, he 501 answered that God was not able to create the world first,[2] because He cannot make things before He is; therefore, as soon as God was, He immediately created the world.

(2) Likewise it can be granted that the world existed from eternity. 502

(3) Likewise at the same time and once, when God was, when He 503 begot the Son coeternal with Himself, through all things coequal God, He also created the world.

(4) Likewise in every work, even evil, evil I say, as of punishment 504 and of sin, the glory of God is manifested and reflects equally.

(5) Likewise he who blames anyone, in the blame itself by the sin 505 of blaming praises God, and the more he blames and the more gravely he sins, the more he praises God.

(6) Likewise anyone by blaspheming God Himself, praises God. 506

(7) Also he seeking anything here or there seeks evil and badly be- 507 cause he seeks the denial of good and the denial of God, and he prays God to be denied to him.

(8) In those men who do not seek after wealth, or honors, or utility, 508 or interior devotion, or sanctity or reward, or the kingdom of heaven, but renounce all these things even that which is theirs, God is honored.

(9) Recently I have considered whether I would wish to receive or to 509 wish for anything from God; I wish to deliberate exceedingly well about this, because when I was receiving from God, then I was under Him

---

[1] Denifle, *Archiv. f. litt.* and K.G. II (1886) 638 ff.; DuPl I, I 312a ff.; Gotti, *Verit. relig. christ.* II 348 f.—Eckart, O. P., was born about the middle of the 13th century at Hockheim, Germany, and taught in Paris and Strassburg. He withdrew his errors, which had been reported to the Pope, before sentence was passed. After his death (†1327) the errors were condemned [Hrt II³ 615 ff.; D Ch II 148]. Cf. *Theol., Quartalschrift* (Tübingen) 113 (1932) 150 ff. [I. Koch].

[2] *Should be corrected:* prius, (previously).

or below Him, as a servant or slave, and He [was] as a master in giving, and thus we ought not to be in eternal life.

510   (10) We are transformed entirely in God, and we are changed into
Him; in a similar manner as in the sacrament the bread is changed into
the body of Christ; so I am changed into Him because He Himself
makes me to be one with Him, not like (to Him); through the living
God it is true that there is no distinction there.

511   (11) Whatever God the Father gave to His only begotten Son in human nature, all this He has given to me; here I except nothing, neither
union, nor sanctity, but He has given all to me as to Himself.

512   (12) Whatever Sacred Scripture says about Christ, all this also is
verified with respect to every good and divine man.

513   (13) Whatever is proper to divine nature, all this is proper to the
just and divine man; because of this that man operates whatever God
operates, and together with God he created heaven and earth, and he is
the generator of the eternal Word, and God without such a man does
not know how to do anything.

514   (14) A good man ought so to conform his will to the divine will that
he himself wishes whatever God wishes; because God wishes me to have
sinned in some way, I would not wish that I had not committed sins,
and this is true repentance.

515   (15) If man had committed a thousand mortal sins, if such a man
were rightly disposed, he ought not to wish that he had not committed
them.

516   (16) God properly does not prescribe an exterior act.

517   (17) An exterior act is not properly good or divine, neither does God
properly operate it or produce it.

518   (18) We bring forth the fruit not of exterior actions which do not
make us good, but of interior actions which the Father abiding in us
does and operates.

519   (19) God loves souls, not works outside.

520   (20) A good man is the only begotten Son of God.

521   (21) A noble man is that only begotten Son of God whom the Father
has begotten from eternity.

522   (22) The Father begot me His son and the same Son. Whatever God
does, this is one; because of this He Himself begot me His Son without any distinction.

523   (23) God is one in all ways and according to every reason, so that
in Himself He cannot find any multitude in intellect or outside intellect;
for he who sees two, or sees a distinction, does not see God, for God is
one beyond the above number, neither is He counted one [read: num-
ber] with anyone. It follows, therefore, that no distinction can exist or
be understood in God Himself.

(24) Every distinction is foreign to God, either in nature or in person; **524**
it is proved that nature itself is one and this oneness, and any person is
one and the oneness which is nature.

(25) When it is said: "Simon, do you love me more than these?" **525**
[I John 21:15 f.], the sense is: That is, more than those and indeed well
but not perfectly. For in the *first* and *the second* and *more* and *less* there
is both a degree and a rank; in *oneness,* however, there is no degree nor
rank. Therefore, he who loves God more than his neighbor, (loves) indeed well but not yet perfectly.

(26) All creatures are one pure nothing; I do not say that they are **526**
something ordinary or anything, but that they are one pure nothing.

In addition there is an objection against the above said Eckart, because he preached two other articles under these words:

(1) Something is in the soul which is uncreated and incapable of **527**
creation; if the entire soul were such, it would be uncreated and incapable of creation, and this is the intellect.

(2) That God is not good nor better nor best; so I speak badly when- **528**
ever I call God good, as if I should call white black.

. . . We condemn and expressly disapprove the first fifteen articles **529**
and also the two last ones as "heretical," but the eleven others already
mentioned as "evil-sounding, rash, and suspected of heresy," and no less
any books or works of this Eckart containing the above mentioned
articles or any one of them.

BENEDICT XII 1334–1342

The Beatific Vision of God and the Last Days [1]

[From the edict "Benedictus Deus," Jan. 29, 1336]

By this edict which will prevail forever, with apostolic authority we **530**
declare: that according to the common arrangement of God, souls of
all the saints who departed from this world before the passion of our
Lord Jesus Christ; also of the holy apostles, the martyrs, the confessors,
virgins, and the other faithful who died after the holy baptism of Christ
had been received by them, in whom nothing was to be purged, when
they departed, nor will there be when they shall depart also in the
future; or if then there was or there will be anything to be purged in
these when after their death they have been purged; and the souls of
children departing before the use of free will, reborn and baptized in

---

[1] DuPl I, I 321b f.; cf. Msi XXV 986 D; BR(T) 4, 346b; MBR 1, 217b; Bar(Th)
ad 1336 n. 3 (25, 50b f.).

that same baptism of Christ, when all have been baptized, immediately after their death and that aforesaid purgation in those who were in need of a purgation of this kind, even before the resumption of their bodies and the general judgment after the ascension of our Savior, our Lord Jesus Christ, into heaven, have been, are, and will be in heaven, in the kingdom of heaven and in celestial paradise with Christ, united in the company of the holy angels, and after the passion and death of our Lord Jesus Christ have seen and see the divine essence by intuitive vision, and even face to face, with no mediating creature, serving in the capacity of an object seen, but divine essence immediately revealing itself plainly, clearly, and openly, to them, and seeing thus they enjoy the same divine essence, and also that from such vision and enjoyment their souls, which now have departed, are truly blessed and they have eternal life and rest; and also [the souls] of those who afterwards will depart, will see that same divine essence, and will enjoy it before the general judgment; and that such vision of the divine essence and its enjoyment makes void the acts of faith and hope in them, inasmuch as faith and hope are proper theological virtues; and that after there has begun or will be such intuitive and face-to-face vision and enjoyment in these, the same vision and enjoyment without any interruption [intermission] or departure of the aforesaid vision and enjoyment exist continuously and will continue even up to the last judgment and from then even unto eternity.

531   Moreover, we declare that according to the common arrangement of God, the souls of those who depart in actual mortal sin immediately after their death descend to hell where they are tortured by infernal punishments, and that nevertheless on the day of judgment all men with their bodies will make themselves ready to render an account of their own deeds before the tribunal of Christ, "so that everyone may receive the proper things of the body according as he has done whether it be good or evil" [II Cor. 5:10].

Errors of the Armenians [1]

[From the book "Iam dudum" sent to the Armenians
in the year 1341]

532   (4) Also that the Armenians say and hold that the personal sin of our first parents themselves was so serious that all of their children propagated from their seed up to the passion of Christ have been deservedly condemned for the aforesaid personal sin, and they have been

---

[1] Bar(Th) ad 1341 n. 49 ff. (25, 250 a ff.); cf. Msi XXV 1188 B ff.; where the same articles together with the responses of the Council of the Armenians are repeated.

thrust into hell after death, not because they themselves have contracted •some original sin from Adam, since they say that children have no original sin at all, neither before the passion of Christ nor after, but that the aforementioned condemnation before the passion of Christ followed them by reason of the gravity of the personal sin which Adam and Eve committed by transgressing the divine precept which had been given to them; but after the passion of our Lord, by which the sin of our first parents was erased, the children who are born from the sons of Adam are not subject to this condemnation, nor are they to be thrust into hell by reason of the aforesaid sin, because Christ erased entirely the sin of our first parents in His passion.

(5) Also that a certain teacher of the Armenians called Mechitriz, **533** which is interpreted the paraclete, has again introduced and taught that the human soul of the son is propagated from the soul of his father, as the body from his body; and also one angel from another, because since a human soul is rational and an angel is of intellectual nature, they are in a way spiritual lights, and from themselves they propagate other spiritual lights.

(6) Also the Armenians say that the souls of children who are born **534** from Christian parents after the passion of Christ, if they die before they are baptized, go to a terrestial Paradise in which Adam was before sin; but the souls of children who are born after the passion of Christ from non-Christian parents and who die without baptism go to the place where the souls of their parents are.

(17) Also that the Armenians commonly believe and hold that in **535** another world there is no purgation of souls, because, as they say, if a Christian confesses his sins, all his sins and the punishments of his sins are forgiven him. They do not even pray for the dead, that their sins may be forgiven them in another world, but in general they pray for all the dead, as for blessed Mary, the apostles. . . .

(18) Also that the Armenians believe and hold that Christ descended **536** from heaven and became incarnate for the salvation of men, not on account of the fact that the sons propagated from Adam and Eve after their sin contracted from them original sin, from which through the incarnation and death of Christ they will be saved, since they say that no such sin exists in the sons of Adam; but they say that Christ for the salvation of man became incarnate and suffered, because through His passion the sons of Adam who preceded the aforesaid passion have been freed from hell in which they were, not because of original sin which was in them, but because of the gravity of the personal sin of our first parents. They also believe that Christ for the salvation of children who were born after His passion became incarnate and suffered, because by His passion He entirely destroyed hell. . . .

537   (19) In such a degree they (the Armenians) say that (the aforesaid)
concupiscence of the flesh is a sin and evil, that even Christian parents •
when they lie together in marriage commit a sin . . . , because they
say that the marriage act and even matrimony itself is a sin. . . .

538   (40) Some indeed say that bishops and priests of the Armenians do
nothing toward the remission of sins either principally or ministerially,
but God alone remits sins; neither bishops nor priests are employed to
perform the aforesaid remission of sins, except that they have received
the power of speaking from God, and so when they absolve they say:
"May God forgive you your sins" or, "I forgive you your sins on earth
and God forgives you in heaven."

539   (42) Also the Armenians hold and say that the passion of Christ
alone, without any other gift of God, even grace, suffices for the remission of sins; they do not say that sanctifying grace is required for the
granting of remission of sins, nor that in the sacraments of the new law
sanctifying grace is given.

540   (48) Also the Armenians say and hold that, if the Armenians commit any crime whatsoever once, certain ones excepted, their church can
absolve them, as far as the fault and the punishment of the aforesaid
sins are concerned; but, if afterwards anyone should commit the aforesaid sins again, he could not be absolved by their church.

541   (49) Also they say that if any one . . . takes a third [wife] or a
fourth, one after another, he cannot be absolved by their church, because
they say that such a marriage is fornication. . . .

542   (58) Also the Armenians hold and say that for what is true baptism,
these three things are required: namely water, chrism . . . and the
Eucharist, so that if anyone should baptize another in water while saying: "I baptize you in the name of the Father and of the Son and of the
Holy Spirit, Amen" and afterwards he should not be anointed with the
(aforesaid) chrism, he would not be baptized. . . .

543   (64) Also the Catholicon of lesser Armenia says that the sacrament of confirmation is of no value, and if it has any value he himself has given permission to his priests that they confer the same sacrament.

544   (67) Also that the Armenians do not say that, after the aforesaid
words of the consecration of bread and wine are said, the transubstantiation of bread and wine into the true body and blood of Christ, which
was born of the Virgin Mary, suffered, and arose again, is accomplished;
but they hold that this sacrament is an example or likeness or figure
of the true body and blood of the Lord . . . on account of which they
do not call the sacrament of the Altar the body and blood of the Lord,
but a victim or sacrifice or communion. . . .

545   (68) Also the Armenians say and hold that if an ordained priest or

bishop commits fornication, even in secret, he loses the power of consecrating and of administering all the sacraments.

(70) Also the Armenians do not say nor hold that the sacrament of **546** the Eucharist worthily received operates in him who receives remission of sin, or the relaxation of punishments due to sin, or that through it the grace of God or its increase is granted; but . . . the body of Christ enters into his body and is changed into him as other foods are changed in the one who has been fed. . . .

(92) Also that among the Armenians there are only three orders, **547** namely the offices of acolyte, deacon, and priest, which orders the bishops confer after money has been promised or received. And in the same manner the aforesaid orders of the priesthood and diaconate are confirmed, that is, through the imposition of the hands, by saying certain words, with this change only, that in the ordination of the deacon the order of diaconate is expressed, and in the ordination of the priest the order of the priesthood. For no bishop among them can ordain another bishop except the Catholicon alone. . . .

(95) Also that the Catholicon of lesser Armenia gave power to a cer- **548** tain priest that he might be able to ordain to the diaconate those of his subjects whom he wished.

(109) Also that among the Armenians no one is punished for any **549** error whatsoever which he may hold. . . . [117 numbers are extant].

CLEMENT VI 1342-1352

The Satisfaction of Christ, the Treasure of the Church,   **550**
Indulgences [1]

[From the Bull of Jubilee, "Unigenitus Dei Filius," Jan. 25, 1343]

The only begotten Son of God . . . "made unto us from God, wisdom, justice, sanctification and redemption" [I Cor. 3], "neither by the blood of goats or of calves, but by His own blood entered once into the holies having obtained eternal redemption" [Heb. 9:12]. "For not with corruptible things as gold or silver, but with the precious blood of His very (Son) as of a lamb unspotted and unstained He has redeemed us" [cf. I Pet. 1:18–19], who innocent, immolated on the altar of the Cross is known to have poured out not a little drop of blood, which however on account of union with the Word would have been sufficient for the redemption of the whole human race, but copiously as a kind of flowing stream, so that "from the soles of His feet even to the top of His Head no soundness was found in Him" [Isa. 1:6]. Therefore, how great **a**

---

[1] CIC Extr. comm. V, 9, 2: Frdbg II 1304 f.; Rcht II 1218 f.

treasure did the good Father acquire from this for the Church militant, so that the mercy of so great an effusion was not rendered useless, vain or superfluous, wishing to lay up treasures for His sons, so that thus the Church is an infinite treasure to men, so that they who use it, become the friends of God [Wisd. 7:14].

551   Indeed this treasure . . . through blessed Peter, the keeper of the keys of heaven and his successors, his vicars on earth, He has committed to be dispensed for the good of the faithful, both from proper and reasonable causes, now for the whole, now for partial remission of temporal punishment due to sins, in general as in particular (according as they know to be expedient with God), to be applied mercifully to those who truly repentant have confessed.

552   Indeed, to the mass of this treasure the merits of the Blessed Mother of God and of all the elect from the first just even to the last, are known to give their help; concerning the consumption or the diminution of this there should be no fear at any time, because of the infinite merits of Christ (as was mentioned before) as well as for the reason that the more are brought to justification by its application, the greater is the increase of the merits themselves.

Errors (philosophical) of Nicholas of Autrecourt [1]

[Condemned and publicly recalled by him in the year 1347]

553   1 . . . That through natural appearances no certainty, as it were, be had regarding things; yet that measure can be had in a short time, if men turn their intellect to things and not to the intellect of Aristotle and his commentator.

554   2 . . . That clearly from the above mentioned evidence from one matter another matter cannot be inferred or concluded, or from the nonexistence of one, the nonexistence of another.

555   3 . . . That the propositions: "God is" and "God is not" signify entirely the same thing, although in a different way.

556   9 . . . That the certainty of evidence does not have degrees.

557   10 . . . That we do not have from our soul the certainty of evidence concerning another material substance.

---

[1] DCh II 580 f.; DuPl I, I 355 a f.—William called "of the four crowned saints," presbyter, cardinal in the year 1346 on the day before the nineteenth of May, as the legate of Clement VI, decreed that the books of Nicholas of Autrecourt be burned, as "containing many false, dangerous, presumptuous, suspected together with erroneous and heretical" statements, and the propositions from which these, which we have placed above, have been taken he ordered to be recalled as "erroneous, false, doubtful, presumptuous, and suspected," and this Nicholas did in the year 1347. This genuine text is drawn from DCh II 576 ff. n. 1124.

11 . . . That with the certainty of faith excepted there was not an- **558** other certainty except the certainty of the first principle, or that which can be resolved into the first principle.

14 . . . That we do not know clearly that other things can be from **559** God because of some effect—that some cause works efficiently which is not God—that some efficient cause is or can be natural.

15 . . . That we do not know clearly whether any effect is or can be **560** produced naturally.

17 . . . That we do not know clearly that in any production the sub- **561** ject concurs.

21 . . . That in any demonstrated matter whatever no one knows **562** clearly that in truth it surpasses all others in nobility.

22 . . . That in any demonstrated matter no one knows clearly that **563** this thing is not God, if by God we understand the most noble substance.

25 . . . That one does not know clearly that in truth it can be reason- **564** ably conceded, "if any matter has been produced, God has been produced."

26 . . . That it cannot be shown clearly that in truth any matter at **565** all is eternal.

30 . . . That these consequences are not clear: "An act of understand- **566** ing exists; therefore intelligence exists. An act of willing exists, therefore will exists."

31 . . . That it cannot be shown clearly that in truth all things which **567** are apparent are true.

32 . . . That God and the creature are not something. **568**

40 . . . That whatever exists in the universe is better that, than not **569** that.

53 . . . That this is the first principle and not another: "If something **570** is, it is something."

The Primacy of the Roman Pontiff [1]

[From the letter "Super quibusdam" to the Consolator, the Catholicon of the Armenians, Sept. 20, 1351]

3 . . . We ask: In the first place, whether you and the Church of the **570a** Armenians which is obedient to you, believe that all those who in baptism have received the same Catholic faith, and afterwards have withdrawn and will withdraw in the future from the communion of this same Roman Church, which one alone is Catholic, are schismatic and heretical, if they remain obstinately separated from the faith of this Roman Church.

In the second place, we ask whether you and the Armenians obedient to **570b**

---

[1] Bar(Th) about 1351 n. 3 and 15 (25, 503 a and 508 a).

you believe that no man of the wayfarers outside the faith of this Church, and outside the obedience of the Pope of Rome, can finally be saved.

570c But in the second chapter . . . we ask:

First, whether you have believed, believe, or are prepared to believe with the Church of the Armenians which is obedient to you, that blessed Peter received complete power of jurisdiction over all faithful Christians from our Lord Jesus Christ; and that every power of jurisdiction, which in certain lands and provinces and in different parts of the world especially and particularly Jude Thaddeus and the other Apostles had, was completely subject to the authority and power which blessed Peter received from our Lord Jesus Christ Himself, over whomsoever are believers in Christ in all parts of the world, and that no apostle or any other one whosoever received that very complete power over all Christians except Peter alone.

570d In the second place, whether you have believed, have held, or are prepared to believe and to hold with the Armenians subject to you that all the Roman Pontiffs, who succeeding blessed Peter have entered canonically and will enter canonically, have succeeded blessed Peter the Roman Pontiff and will succeed in the same plentitude in the jurisdiction of power over the complete and universal body of the militant church which blessed Peter himself received from our Lord Jesus Christ.

570e In the third place, if you and the Armenians subject to you have believed and do believe that the Roman Pontiffs who have been and we who now are the Roman Pontiff and, those who in future will be successively as legitimate vicars of Christ and full of power in the highest degree, have received immediately from Christ Himself over the complete and universal body of the church militant, every jurisdiction of power which Christ as fitting head had in human life.

570f In the fourth place, if you have believed and now believe that all the Roman Pontiffs who have been and we who are, and others who will be in the future from the plentitude of past power and authority have been able, are able, and will be able directly by our own power and theirs both to judge all those subject to our jurisdiction and theirs, and to establish and delegate ecclesiastical judges to judge whomsoever we wish.

570g In the fifth place, if you have believed and now believe that to such an extent has been, is, and will be both pre-eminent authority together with juridical power of the Roman Pontiffs who have been, of us who are, and of those who in future will be, has been, is, and will be so extensive, that by no one have they been, can we be, or will they in the future be able to be judged; but they have been, we are, and they will be reserved for judgment by God alone; and that from our sentences and judgments it has not been possible nor will it be possible for an appeal to be made to any judges.

In the sixth place, if you have believed and still believe that the plentitude 570h
of the power of the Roman Pontiff extends so far that it is possible to
transfer patriarchs, the Catholicon, the archbishops, bishops, abbots, and
whatsoever other prelates from the offices in which they have been established to other offices of greater or lesser jurisdiction, or, as their sins
demand, to demote, to depose, excommunicate, or to surrender them
to Satan.

In the seventh place, if you have believed and still believe that the 570i
Pontifical authority cannot or ought not to be subject to any imperial
or regal or other secular power, in so far as pertains to a judicial institution, to correction or to deposition.

In the eighth place, if you have believed and now believe that the Roman 570k
Pontiff alone is able to establish sacred general canons, to grant plenary
indulgences to those who visit the thresholds of the Apostles, Peter and
Paul, or to those who go to the Holy Land, or to any of the faithful who
are truly and fully repentant and have confessed.

In the ninth place, if you have believed and do believe that all who have 570l
raised themselves against the faith of the Roman Church and have
died in final impenitence have been damned and have descended to the
eternal punishments of hell.

In the tenth place, if you have believed and still believe that the Roman 570m
Pontiff regarding the administration of the sacraments of the Church,
can tolerate and even permit different rites of the Church of Christ, in
order that they may be saved, provided that those matters are always
preserved which belong to the integrity and necessity of the sacraments.

In the eleventh place, if you have believed and now believe that the 570o
Armenians, who are obedient to the Roman Pontiff in different parts of
the world and who observe studiously and with devotion the forms and
rites of the Roman Church in the administration of the sacraments and in
ecclesiastical duties, fasts, and other ceremonies do well, and by doing this
merit eternal life.

In the twelfth place, if you have believed and now believe that no one 570p
can be transferred from episcopal offices to the archiepiscopal, patriarchal,
or to the Catholicon by his own authority, nor even by the authority of
any secular leader whomsoever, whether he be king or emperor, or any one
also distinguished by any such power or earthly office.

In the thirteenth place if you have believed, and still believe that the 570q
Roman Pontiff alone, when doubts arise regarding the Catholic faith,
through authentic decision can impose the limit to which all must inviolably adhere, and that whatever by the authority of the keys handed
to him by Christ, he determines to be true is true and Catholic, and what
he determines to be false and heretical, must be so regarded.

In the fourteenth place, if you have believed and now believe that the

New and Old Testaments in all their books, which the authority of the Roman Church has given to us, contain undoubted truth in all things.

Purgatory [1]

[From the same letter to Consolator]

570s   We ask if you have believed and now believe that there is a purgatory to which depart the souls of those dying in grace who have not yet made complete satisfaction for their sins. Also, if you have believed and now believe that they will be tortured by fire for a time and that as soon as they are cleansed, even before the day of judgment, they may come to the true and eternal beatitude which consists in the vision of God face to face and in love.

The Matter and Minister of Confirmation [2]

[From the same letter to Consolator]

571   (12) You have given responses which influence us to ask the following from you: first, concerning the consecration of chrism, whether you believe that the chrism can rightly and deservedly be consecrated by no priest who is not a bishop.

572   Second, whether you believe that the sacrament of confirmation cannot ordinarily be administered by any other than by the bishop by virtue of his office.

573   Third, whether you believe that by the Roman Pontiff alone, having a plentitude of power, the administration of the sacrament of confirmation can be granted to priests who are not bishops.

574   Fourth, whether you believe that those confirmed by any priests whatsoever, who are not bishops and who have not received from the Roman Pontiff any commission or concession regarding this, must be anointed again by a bishop or bishops.

The Errors of the Armenians

[From the same letter to Consolator]

574a   (15) After all the above mentioned, we are forced to wonder strongly that in a certain letter, which begins, "To the honorable Fathers in Christ," you retract fourteen chapters from the first fifty-three chapters. First, that

---

[1] Bar(Th) about the year 131, n. 8. Cf. *Zeitschr. f. kath. Theologie* 52 (1928) 82 ff. (A. Straub); *Estudios eclesiásticos* 6 (1927); 96 ff., 7 (1928); 376 ff., 542 ff. (F. Segarra).

[2] Bar(Th) ad 1351 n. 12 resp. 15 (25, 506b ff.).

the Holy Spirit proceeds from the Father and the Son. Third, that children contract original sin from their first parents. Sixth, that souls separated from their bodies, when entirely cleansed, clearly see God. Ninth, that the souls of those departing in mortal sin descend into hell. Twelfth, that baptism destroys original and actual sins. Thirteenth, that Christ did not destroy a lower hell by descending into hell. Fifteenth, that the angels were created good by God. Thirtieth, that the pouring out of the blood of animals works no remission of sins. Thirty-second, those who eat of fish and oil on the days of fasts, shall not judge. Thirty-ninth, that having been baptized in the Catholic Church, if they become unfaithful and afterwards are converted, they must not be baptized again. Fortieth, that children can be baptized before the eighth day and that baptism cannot be by any liquid other than pure water. Forty-second, that the body of Christ after the words of consecration is the same in number as the body born from the Virgin and immolated on the Cross. Forty-fifth, that no one even a saint can consecrate the body of Christ, unless he is a priest. Forty-sixth, that it is necessary for salvation to confess all mortal sins perfectly and distinctly to one's own priest or with his permission (to another priest).

Innocent VI 1352–1362

URBAN V 1362–1370

Errors of Dionysius Foullechat (Perfection and Poverty) [1]

[Condemned in the order "Ex supremae clementiae dono," Dec. 23, 1368]

(1) This blessed, indeed most blessed and sweetest law, namely, the **575** law of love, takes away all propriety and power,—*false, erroneous, heretical.*

(2) The actual renunciation of sincere will and temporal powers shows **576** and produces the most perfect state of dominion or authority—*false, erroneous, heretical.*

(3) That Christ did not renounce such possession and right in temporal **577** things is not held according to the New Law, but rather the opposite—*false, erroneous, heretical.*

---

[1] DuPl I, I 382 b ff. 384 b ff.; cf. D Ch III 187 ff.; Bar(Th) ad 1368 n. 16 (26, 158 a f.).—Dennis Foullechet (Soulechet), O. Fr. M., a Gaul, a Doctor of Paris, put forth these errors for the first time in the year 1363; he publicly retracted them [Hrt II³ 626] afterwards on two occasions (1364 and 1369).

GREGORY XI 1370–1378

Errors of Peter of Bonageta and of John of Lato

(The Most Holy Eucharist) [1]

[Examined and condemned by the Inquisitors according
to the mandate of the Pontiff]

578 (1) That if a consecrated host fall or is cast into a sewer, into mud, or some disgraceful place, that, while the species remain, the body of Christ ceases to be under them and the substance of bread returns.

579 2. That if the consecrated host is gnawed by a mouse or is consumed by an animal, that, while the so-called species remains, the body of Christ ceases to be under them and the substance of bread returns.

580 3. That if the consecrated host is consumed by a just man or by a sinner, that while the species is being crushed by the teeth, Christ is snatched up to heaven and He is not cast into the stomach of man.

URBAN VI 1378–1389   INNOCENT VII 1404–1406
BONIFACE IX 1389–1404   GREGORY XII 1406–1415

MARTIN V 1417–1431

COUNCIL OF CONSTANCE
1414–1418

Ecumenical XVI (against Wycliffe, Hus, etc.)

SESSION VIII (May 4, 1415)

Errors of John Wycliffe [2]

[Condemned in Council and by the Bulls "Inter Cunctas"
and "In eminentis" Feb. 22, 1418]

581 1. In the sacrament of the altar the material substance of bread and likewise the material substance of wine remain.

---

[1] DuPl I, I 390 b f.—Each from the Order of Brothers Minor.

[2] Msi XXVII 1207 E ff. (cf. 632 1215 ff.); coll. Rcht II, 131 f.; Hrd VIII, 909 E ff. (cf. 299 918 ff.); BRT 4, 669 b ff.; MBR 1, 290 b ff.; cf. DuPl I, II 49 a ff.; where the censures of the theologians are added to the individual theses; cf. Hfl VII 116 ff.; Bar(Th) to 1415 n. 35 (27, 404 a f.).

2. In the same sacrament the accidents of the bread do not remain with-   582
out a subject.

3. In the same sacrament Christ is not identically and really with His   583
own bodily presence.

4. If a bishop or priest is living in mortal sin, he does not ordain, nor   584
consecrate, nor perform, nor baptize.

5. It is not established in the Gospel that Christ arranged the Mass.   585

6. God ought to obey the devil.   586

7. If man is duly contrite, every exterior confession on his part is   587
superfluous and useless.

8. If the pope is foreknown and evil, and consequently a member of   588
the devil, he does not have power over the faithful given to him by anyone,
unless perchance by Caesar.

9. After Urban VI no one should be received as pope, unless he live   589
according to the customs of the Greeks under their laws.

10. It is contrary to Sacred Scripture that ecclesiastical men have   590
possessions.

11. No prelate should excommunicate anyone, unless first he knows   591
that he has been excommunicated by God; and he who so excommunicates becomes, as a result of this, a heretic or excommunicated.

12. A prelate excommunicating a cleric who has appealed to the king,   592
or to a council of the kingdom, by that very act is a traitor of the king
and the kingdom.

13. Those who cease to preach or to hear the word of God because of   593
the excommunication of men, are themselves excommunicated, and in the
judgment of God they will be considered traitors of Christ.

14. It is permissible for any deacon or priest to preach the word of God   594
without the authority of the Apostolic See or a Catholic bishop.

15. No one is a civil master, no one a prelate, no one a bishop, as long   595
as he is in mortal sin.

16. Temporal rulers can at their will take away temporal goods from   596
the Church, when those who have possessions habitually offend, that
is, offend by habit, not only by an act.

17. People can at their will correct masters who offend.   597

18. The tithes are pure alms and parishioners can take these away at   598
will because of the sins of their prelates.

19. Special prayers applied to one person by prelates or religious are not   599
of more benefit to that person than general (prayers), all other things
being equal.

20. One bringing alms to the Brothers is excommunicated by that very   600
thing.

21. If anyone enters any private religious community of any kind, of   601

those having possessions or of the mendicants, he is rendered unfit and unsuited for the observance of the laws of God.

602   22. Saints, instituting private religious communities, have sinned by instituting them.

603   23. Religious living in private religious communities are not of the Christian religion.

604   24. Brothers are bound to acquire their food by the labor of hands and not by begging.

605   25. All are simoniacs who oblige themselves to pray for others who assist them in temporal matters.

606   26. The prayer for the foreknown is of avail to no one.

607   27. All things happen from absolute necessity.

608   28. The confirmation of youths, ordination of clerics, and consecration of places are reserved to the pope and bishops on account of their desire for temporal gain and honor.

609   29. Universities, studies, colleges, graduations, and offices of instruction in the same have been introduced by a vain paganism; they are of as much value to the Church as the devil.

610   30. The excommunication of the pope or of any prelate whatsoever is not to be feared, because it is the censure of the Antichrist.

611   31. Those who found cloisters sin and those who enter (them) are diabolical men.

612   32. To enrich the clergy is contrary to the rule of Christ.

613   33. Sylvester, the Pope, and Constantine, the Emperor, erred in enriching the Church.

614   34. All of the order of mendicants are heretics, and those who give alms to them are excommunicated.

615   35. Those entering religion or any order, by that very fact are unsuited to observe divine precepts, and consequently to enter the kingdcm of heaven, unless they apostatize from these.

616   36. The pope with all his clergy who have possessions are heretics, because they have possessions; and all in agreement with these, namely all secular masters and other laity.

617   37. The Roman Church is a synagogue of Satan, and the pope is not the next and immediate vicar of Christ and His apostles.

618   38. The decretal letters are apocryphal and they seduce from the faith of Christ, and the clergy who study them are foolish.

619   39. The emperor and secular masters have been seduced by the devil to enrich the Church with temporal goods.

620   40. The election of the pope by cardinals was introduced by the devil.

621   41. It is not necessary for salvation to believe that the Roman Church is supreme among other churches.

622   42. It is foolish to believe in the indulgences of the pope and bishops.

43. Oaths are illicit which are made to corroborate human contracts and 623
civil commerce.

44. Augustine, Benedict, and Bernard have been damned, unless they 624
repented about this, that they had possessions and instituted and entered
religious communities; and thus from the pope to the last religious, all
are heretics.

45. All religious communities without distinction have been introduced 625
by the devil.

*See the theological censures of these 45 articles to be proposed to the Wyclif-
fites and Hussites, n.* 11 (661 below).

Session XIII (June 15, 1415)

Definition of Communion under One Species [1]

Since in some parts of the world certain ones have rashly presumed 626
to assert that Christian people should receive the sacrament of the Eucharist
under both species of bread and wine, and since they give communion to
the laity indiscriminately, not only under the species of bread, but also
under the species of wine, after dinner or otherwise when not fasting,
and since they pertinaciously assert that communion should be enjoyed
contrary to the praiseworthy custom of the Church reasonably approved
which they try damnably to disprove as a sacrilege, it is for this reason
that this present Council . . . declares, decides, and defines, that, although
Christ instituted that venerable sacrament after supper and administered
it to His disciples under both species of bread and wine; yet, notwithstanding this, the laudable authority of the sacred canons and the approved
custom of the Church have maintained and still maintain that a sacrament of this kind should not be consecrated after supper, nor be received
by the faithful who are not fasting, except in case of sickness or of another
necessity granted or admitted by law or Church; and although such a
sacrament was received by the faithful under both species in the early
Church, yet since then it is received by those who consecrate under both
species and by the laity only under the species of bread [another reading:
And similarly, although this sacrament was received by the faithful in the
early Church under both species, nevertheless this custom has been reasonably introduced to avoid certain dangers and scandals, namely, that
it be received by those who consecrate it under both species, and by the
laity only under the species of bread], since it must be believed most
firmly and not at all doubted that the whole body of Christ and the blood
are truly contained under the species of bread as well as under the species
of wine. Therefore, to say that to observe this custom or law is a sacrilege

---

[1] Msi XXVII 727 C, Hrd VIII 381 B; cf. Hfl VII 173 f.; Bar(Th) about 1415, **n.**
25 (27, 399b f.).

or illicit must be considered erroneous, and those pertinaciously asserting the opposite of the above mentioned must be avoided as heretics and should be severely punished, either by the local diocesan officials or by the inquisitors of heretical depravity.

SESSION XV (July 6, 1415)

Errors of John Hus [1]

[Condemned in the Council and by the above mentioned
Bulls in 1418]

627 1. One and only is the holy universal Church which is the aggregate of the predestined.

628 2. Paul never was a member of the devil, although he did certain acts similar to the acts of those who malign the Church.

629 3. The foreknown are not parts of the Church, since no part of it finally will fall away from it, because the charity of predestination which binds it will not fall away.

630 4. Two natures, divinity and humanity, are one Christ.[2]

631 5. The foreknown, although at one time he is in grace according to the present justice, yet is never a part of the holy Church; and the predestined always remains a member of the Church, although at times he may fall away from additional grace, but not from the grace of predestination.

632 6. Assuming the Church as the convocation of the predestined, whether they were in grace or not according to the present justice, in that way the Church is an article of faith.

633 7. Peter is not nor ever was the head of the Holy Catholic Church.

634 8. Priests living criminally in any manner whatsoever, defile the power of the priesthood, and as unfaithful sons they think unfaithfully regarding the seven sacraments of the Church, the keys, the duties, the censures, customs, ceremonies, and sacred affairs of the Church, its veneration of relics, indulgences, and orders.

635 9. The papal dignity has sprung up from Caesar, and the perfection and institution of the pope have emanated from the power of Caesar.

636 10. No one without revelation would have asserted reasonably regarding himself or anyone else that he was the head of a particular church, nor is the Roman Pontiff the head of a particular Roman Church.

637 11. It is not necessary to believe that the one whosoever is the Roman

---

[1] Msi XXVII 1209 C ff. (754 A ff., 794 B ff.); coll. Rcht II, 133 f.; Hrd VIII 911 D ff. (410 C ff., 457 C ff.); BR(T) 4, 671 a ff.; MBR 1, 291 a ff.; Bar(Th) ad 1415 n. 41 (27, 409 a ff.); cf. Hfl VII 193 ff.—Cf. n. 659 ff.

[2] Cf. Hfl VII 201.

Pontiff, is the head of any particular holy church, unless God has pre-destined him.

12. No one takes the place of Christ or of Peter unless he follows 638 him in character, since no other succession is more important, and not otherwise does he receive from God the procuratorial power, because for that office of vicar are required both conformity in character and the authority of Him who institutes it.

13. The pope is not the true and manifest successor of Peter, the first 639 of the apostles, if he lives in a manner contrary to Peter; and if he be avaricious, then he is the vicar of Judas Iscariot. And with like evidence the cardinals are not the true and manifest successors of the college of the other apostles of Christ, unless they live in the manner of the apostles, keeping the commandments and counsels of our Lord Jesus Christ.

14. Doctors holding that anyone to be emended by ecclesiastical cen- 640 sure, if he is unwilling to be corrected, must be handed over to secular judgment, certainly are following in this the priests, scribes, and pharisees, who, saying that "it is not permissible for us to kill anyone" (John 18:31), handed over to secular judgment Christ Himself, who did not wish to be obedient to them in all things, and such are homicides worse than Pilate.

15. Ecclesiastical obedience is obedience according to the invention of 641 the priest of the Church, without the expressed authority of Scripture.

16. The immediate division of human works is: that they are either 642 virtuous or vicious, because, if a man is vicious and does anything, then he acts viciously; and if he is virtuous and does anything, then he acts virtuously; because as vice, which is called a crime or mortal sin, renders the acts of man universally vicious, so virtue vivifies all the acts of the virtuous man.

17. Priests of Christ, living according to His law and having a knowl- 643 edge of Scripture and a desire to instruct the people, ought to preach without the impediment of a pretended excommunication. But if the pope or some other prelate orders a priest so disposed not to preach, the subject is not obliged to obey.

18. Anyone who approaches the priesthood receives the duty of a 644 preacher by command, and that command he must execute, without the impediment of a pretended excommunication.

19. By ecclesiastical censures of excommunication, suspension, and in- 645 terdict, the clergy for its own exaltation supplies for itself the lay populace, it multiplies avarice, protects wickedness, and prepares the way for the Antichrist. Moreover, the sign is evident that from the Antichrist such censures proceed, which in their processes they call fulminations, by which the clergy principally proceed against those who uncover the wickedness of the Antichrist, who will make use of the clergy especially for himself.

646   20. If the pope is wicked and especially if he is foreknown, then as Judas, the Apostle, he is of the devil, a thief, and a son of perdition, and he is not the head of the holy militant Church, since he is not a member of it.

647   21. The grace of predestination is a chain by which the body of the Church and any member of it are joined insolubly to Christ the Head.

648   22. The pope or prelate, wicked and foreknown, is equivocally pastor and truly a thief and robber.

649   23. The pope should not be called "most holy" even according to his office, because otherwise the king ought also to be called "most holy" according to his office, and torturers and heralds should be called holy, indeed even the devil ought to be called holy, since he is an official of God.

650   24. If the pope lives in a manner contrary to Christ, even if he should ascend through legal and legitimate election according to the common human constitution, yet he would ascend from another place than through Christ, even though it be granted that he entered by an election made principally by God; for Judas Iscariot rightly and legitimately was elected by God, Jesus Christ, to the episcopacy, and yet he ascended from another place to the sheepfold of the sheep.

651   25. The condemnation of the forty-five articles of John Wycliffe made by the doctors is irrational and wicked and badly made; the cause alleged by them has been feigned, namely, for the reason that "no one of them is a Catholic but anyone of them is either heretical, erroneous, or scandalous."

652   26. Not for this reason, that the electors, or a greater part of them, agreed by acclamation according to the observance of men upon some person, is that person legitimately elected; nor for this reason is he the true and manifest successor or vicar of the Apostle Peter, or in the ecclesiastical office of another apostle. Therefore, whether electors have chosen well or badly, we ought to believe in the works of the one elected; for, by the very reason that anyone who operates for the advancement of the Church in a manner more fully meritorious, has from God more fully the faculty for this.

653   27. For there is not a spark of evidence that there should be one head ruling the Church in spiritual affairs, which head always lives and is preserved with the Church militant herself.

654   28. Christ through His true disciples scattered through the world would rule His Church better without such monstrous heads.

655   29. The apostles and faithful priests of the Lord strenuously in necessities ruled the Church unto salvation, before the office of the pope was introduced; thus they would be doing even to the day of judgment, were the pope utterly lacking.

30. No one is a civil master, no one is a prelate, no one is a bishop **656**
while he is in mortal sin [see n. 595].

*See the theological censures of these thirty articles among "Questions of
Wycliffe and Hus to be proposed" n. 11 (661 below).*

Questions to be Proposed to the Wycliffites and Hussites [1]

[From the Bull above mentioned "Inter Cunctas," Feb. 22, 1418]

Articles 1–4, 9–10 treat of communion with said heretics.

5. Likewise, whether he believes, holds, and declares, that every general **657**
Council, including that of CONSTANCE, represents the universal
Church.[2]

6. Likewise, whether he believes that what the sacred Council of Con- **658**
stance, which represents the Catholic Church, has approved and does
approve in favor of faith, and for the salvation of souls, must be approved
and maintained by all the faithful of Christ; and that what (the Council)
has condemned and does condemn to be contrary to faith and good morals,
this must be believed and proclaimed by the same as considered worthy
of condemnation.

7. Likewise, whether he believes that the condemnations of John Wy- **659**
cliffe, John Hus, and Jerome of Prague, made by the sacred general Council of CONSTANCE, concerning their persons, books, and documents
have been duly and justly made, and that they must be considered and
firmly declared as such by every Catholic whatsoever.

8. Likewise, whether he believes, holds, and declares, that John Wycliffe **660**
of England, John Hus of Bohemia, and Jerome of Prague have been

---

[1] Msi XXVII 1211 B ff.; Hrd VIII 914 A ff.; BR(T) 4, 673 a ff.; MBR 1, 292 b ff.

[2] It is clear that the statements made here on the authority of the Council of
Constance are to be understood according to the mind of the Apostolic See itself,
which never confirmed all its decrees. (They are to be understood) definitely according to this opinion: (the Synod of Constance) "has power immediately from Christ,
to which anyone of whatever status or dignity, even if it be papal, is bound to give
obedience in matters pertaining to faith. . . ." In the Fourth and Fifth Sessions (Msi
XXVII 585 B 590 D) Eugenius IV, Sept. 4, 1439, expressly rejected the statute as
impious and scandalous, and on July 22, 1446 he wrote the following to his delegates
living in Germany: "As they [*our predecessors*] were accustomed to accept, embrace,
and venerate the general Councils lawfully established and canonically celebrated
in their own times, so we with every reverence and devotion accept and venerate the
general councils of Constance and Basil from the beginning even to the translation
made by us, yet without prejudice to the right, dignity, and pre-eminence of the
holy Apostolic See, and to the power conceded to it by Christ and residing canonically
in the same in the person of Saint Peter" [Bar(Th) about 1446 n. 3 (28, 461 a)]; cf.
Hergenröther-Kirsch, *Handb. der allgem. Kirchengesch.* 6. Aufl. III (1925): 153 f.

heretics and are to be considered and classed as heretics, and that their books and doctrines have been and are perverse; and because of these books and these doctrines and their obstinacy, they have been condemned as heretics by the sacred Council of CONSTANCE.

661   11. Likewise, let the especially learned person be asked, whether he believes that the decision of the sacred Council of CONSTANCE passed concerning the forty-five articles of John Wycliffe and the thirty of John Hus described above, would be true and Catholic: namely, that the above mentioned forty-five articles of John Wycliffe and the thirty of John Hus are not Catholic, but some of them are notedly heretical, some erroneous, others audacious and seditious, others offensive to the ears of the pious.

662   12. Likewise, whether he believes and maintains that in no case one may take an oath.

663   13. Likewise, whether he believes that by the order of a judge an oath must be uttered regarding truth, or anything else suitable for a cause be allowed, even if it must be done for the purification of infamy.

664   14. Likewise whether he believes, that perjury knowingly committed, for whatever cause or occasion, for the conservation of one's own bodily life or that of another, even in favor of faith, is a mortal sin.

665   15. Likewise, whether he believes that anyone deliberately despising the rite of the Church, the ceremonies of exorcism and catechism, of consecrated baptismal water, sins mortally.

666   16. Likewise, whether he believes, that after the consecration by the priest in the sacrament of the altar under the semblance of bread and wine, it is not material bread and material wine, but the same Christ through all, who suffered on the Cross and sitteth at the right (hand) of the Father.

667   17. Likewise, whether he believes and maintains that after the consecration by the priest, under the sole species of bread only, and aside from the species of wine, it is the true body of Christ and the blood and the soul and the divinity and the whole Christ, and the same body absolutely and under each one of these species separately.

668   18. Likewise, whether he believes that the custom of giving communion to lay persons under the species of bread only, which is observed by the universal Church, and approved by the sacred Council of CONSTANCE, must be preserved, so that it be not allowed to condemn this or to change it at pleasure without the authority of the Church, and that those who obstinately pronounce the opposite of the aforesaid should be arrested and punished as heretics or as suspected of heresy.

669   19. Likewise, whether he believes that a Christian who rejects the reception of the sacraments of confirmation, or extreme unction, or the solemnization of marriage sins mortally.

670   20. Likewise, whether he believes that a Christian in addition to contrition of heart is obligated out of necessity for salvation to confess to

a priest only (the priest having the proper faculties), and not to a layman or laymen however good and devout.

21. Likewise, whether he believes, that the priest in cases permitted 671 to him can absolve from sins a sinner who has confessed and become contrite, and enjoin a penance upon him.

22. Likewise, whether he believes that a bad priest, employing the 672 proper matter and form and having the intention of doing what the Church does, truly consecrates, truly absolves, truly baptizes, truly confers the other sacraments.

23. Likewise, whether he believes that blessed Peter was the vicar 673 of Christ, possessing the power of binding and loosing on earth.

24. Likewise, whether he believes that the pope canonically elected, 674 who lived for a time, after having expressed his own name, is the successor of the blessed Peter, having supreme authority in the Church of God.

25. Likewise, whether he believes that the authority of jurisdiction of 675 the pope, archbishop, and bishop in loosing and binding is greater than the authority of the simple priest, even if he has the care of souls.

26. Likewise, whether he believes that the pope, for a pious and just 676 reason, especially to those who visit holy places and to those who extend their helping hands can grant indulgences for the remission of sins to all Christians truly contrite and having confessed.

27. And whether he believes that from such a concession they who 677 visit these very churches and they who lend helping hands can gain indulgences of this kind.

28. Likewise, whether he believes that individual bishops can grant in- 678 dulgences of this kind to their subjects according to the limitation of the sacred canons.

29. Likewise, whether he believes or maintains that it is lawful that 679 the relics and images of the saints be venerated by the faithful of Christ.

30. Likewise, whether he believes that objects of religious veneration 680 approved by the Church were duly and reasonably introduced by the holy Fathers.

31. Likewise, whether he believes that a pope or another prelate, the 681 proper titles of the pope for the time having been expressed, or whether their vicars can excommunicate their ecclesiastical or secular subject for disobedience or contumacy, so that such a one should be considered as excommunicated.

32. Likewise, whether he believes that with the growing disobedience 682 or contumacy of the excommunicated, the prelates or their vicars in spiritual matters have the power of oppressing and of oppressing him again, of imposing interdict and of invoking the secular arm; and that these censures must be obeyed by his inferiors.

683   33. Likewise, whether he believes that the pope and other prelates and their vicars in spiritual matters have the power of excommunicating priests and disobedient and contumacious lay men and of suspending them from office, benefaction, entrance to a church, and the administration of the sacraments of the Church.

684   34. Likewise, whether he believes that it is permissible for ecclesiastical personages to hold possessions and temporal goods of this world without sin.

685   35. Likewise, whether he believes that it is not permissible for the laity to take away these temporal goods by their own power; that on the contrary, if they do take them away, seize, and lay hold on these ecclesiastical goods, they are to be punished as sacrilegious persons, even if the ecclesiastical personages possessing goods of this kind were living bad lives.

686   36. Likewise, whether he believes that a seizure and an attack of this kind thoughtlessly or violently committed or wrought against any priest whatsoever, even though living an evil life, leads to sacrilege.

687   37. Likewise, whether he believes that it is permissible for the laity of both sexes, namely men and women, freely to preach the word of God.

688   38. Likewise, whether he believes that it be freely permitted to individual priests to preach the word of God, wheresoever, and whenever, and to whomsoever it may be pleasing, even though they are not sent.

689   39. Likewise, whether he believes that all mortal sins, particularly manifest, should be publicly corrected and eradicated.

Condemnation of the Proposition Concerning Tyrannicide [1]

690   The holy Synod, July 6, 1415 declares and defines this opinion: "Any tyrant can lawfully and meritoriously be killed and ought so to be killed by any vassal or subject of his, even by secret plots, and subtle flattery and adulation, regardless of any oath of fealty or any pact made with him, without waiting for an opinion or command of any judge whatsoever" . . . is erroneous in faith and morals, and it (the Synod) condemns and rejects it as heretical, scandalous, and as offering a way to frauds, deceptions, lies, treasons, and false oaths. In addition it declares, decrees, and defines that those who persistently sow this most pernicious doctrine are heretics. . . .

---

[1] Msi XXVII 765 E f.; Hrd VIII 424 C; Hfl VII 175 ff. This condemnation was not approved as a definition by the Holy Pontiff (cf. V. Cathrein, *Moral-philosophie* II 5 pg. 596), but was renewed by Paul V, letter "Cura Dominici gregis," January 24, 1615.

EUGENIUS IV 1431–1447

COUNCIL OF FLORENCE 1438–1445

Ecumenical XVII (Union with the Greeks, Armenians, Jacobites)

Decree for the Greeks [1]

[From the Bull "Laetentur coeli," July 6, 1439]

[The procession of the Holy Spirit] In the name of the Holy Trinity, **691** of the Father, and of the Son, and of the Holy Spirit, with the approbation of this holy general Council of Florence we define that this truth of faith be believed and accepted by all Christians, and that all likewise profess that the Holy Spirit is eternally from the Father and the Son and has His essence and His subsistent being both from the Father and the Son, and proceeds from both eternally as from one principle and one spiration; we declare that what the holy Doctors and Fathers say, namely, that the Holy Spirit proceeds from the Father through the Son, tends to this meaning, that by this it is signified that the Son also is the cause, according to the Greeks, and according to the Latins, the principle of the subsistence of the Holy Spirit, as is the Father also. And that all things, which are the Father's, the Father Himself has given in begetting His only begotten Son; without being Father, the Son Himself possesses this from the Father, that the Holy Spirit proceeds from the Son from whom He was moreover eternally begotten. We define in addition that the explanation of the words "Filioque" for the sake of declaring the truth and also because of imminent necessity has been lawfully and reasonably added to the Creed.

We have likewise defined that the body of Christ is truly effected in **692** unleavened or leavened wheaten bread; and that priests ought to effect the body of our Lord in either one of these, and each one namely according to the custom of his Church, whether that of the West or of the East.

[*De novissimis*] [2] It has likewise defined, that, if those truly penitent **693** have departed in the love of God, before they have made satisfaction by worthy fruits of penance for sins of commission and omission, the souls of these are cleansed after death by purgatorial punishments; and so that they may be released from punishments of this kind, the suffrages of the living faithful are of advantage to them, namely, the sacrifices of Masses,

---

[1] Msi XXXI 1030 D f. (1696 D f.); Hrd IX 422 B f. (986 B f.); BR(T) 5, 41 a f.; MBR 1, 335 b f.; Hfl VII 737 (746) ff.; cf. Bar(Th) about 1439 n. 1 ff.; n. 8 (28, 282 b f.); cf. M Th Cc 5, 452 ff.

[2] On the origin of this definition, cf. "Gregorianum" 18 (1937) 337 ff. [G. Hofmann, S.J.].

prayers, and almsgiving, and other works of piety, which are customarily performed by the faithful for other faithful according to the institutions of the Church. And that the souls of those, who after the reception of baptism have incurred no stain of sin at all, and also those, who after the contraction of the stain of sin whether in their bodies, or when released from the same bodies, as we have said before, are purged, are immediately received into heaven, and see clearly the one and triune God Himself, just as He is, yet according to the diversity of merits, one more perfectly than another. Moreover, the souls of those who depart in actual mortal sin or in original sin only, descend immediately into hell but to undergo punishments of different kinds [see n. 464].

694   We likewise define that the holy Apostolic See, and the Roman Pontiff, hold the primacy throughout the entire world; and that the Roman Pontiff himself is the successor of blessed Peter, the chief of the Apostles, and the true vicar of Christ, and that he is the head of the entire Church, and the father and teacher of all Christians; and that full power was given to him in blessed Peter by our Lord Jesus Christ, to feed, rule, and govern the universal Church; just as is contained in the acts of the ecumenical Councils and in the sacred canons.

Decree for the Armenians [1]

[From the Bull "Exultate Deo," Nov. 22, 1439]

695   In the fifth place we have reduced under this very brief formula the truth of the sacraments of the Church for the sake of an easier instruction of the Armenians, the present as well as the future. There are seven sacraments of the new Law: namely, baptism, confirmation, Eucharist, penance, extreme unction, orders, and matrimony, which differ a great deal from the sacraments of the Old Law. For those of the Old Law did not effect grace, but only pronounced that it should be given through the passion of Christ; these sacraments of ours contain grace, and confer it upon those who receive them worthily. Of these the five first ones are ordained for

---

[1] Msi XXXI 1054 B ff.; Hrd IX 473 D ff.; BR(T) 5, 48 a ff.; M B R 1. 355 b ff.; cf. Hfl VII 788 ff.; Bar(Th) ad 1439 n. 12 ff.; n. 15 (28, 289 a ff.).—This decree contains the Nicean Constantinopolitan creed, the decree regarding the acceptance of the Chalcedonian Synod and the letter of Leo the Great, an instruction on the sacraments, which we include, the Athanasian creed, the decree of the union of the Greeks, and the decree on celebrating feasts. On this decree, cf. *Bulletin de litt. ecclés.* (Toulouse) 1919: 81 ff., 195 ff. (J. de Guibert). The decree at the end distinguishes between chapters (*capitula*), declarations (*declarationes*), definitions (*diffinitiones*), traditions (*traditiones*), precepts (*praecepta*), statutes (*statuta*), and doctrine (*doctrinam*) which are contained in it.—This instruction is taken almost word for word from St. Thomas' work "On the Articles of Faith and the Sacraments of the Church" (*De articulis fidei et Ecclesiae sacramentis*).

the spiritual perfection of each and every one in himself, the last two for the government and increase of the entire Church. For, through baptism we are spiritually reborn; through confirmation we increase in grace, and are made strong in faith; reborn, however, we are strengthened and nourished by the divine sustenance of the Eucharist. But if through sin we incur the disease of the soul, through penance we are spiritually healed; spiritually and corporally, according as is expedient to the soul, through extreme unction; through orders the Church is truly governed and spiritually propagated; through matrimony corporally increased. All these sacraments are dispensed in three ways, namely, by things as the matter, by words as the form, and by the person of the minister conferring the sacrament with the intention of doing as the Church does; if any of these is lacking the sacrament is not fulfilled. Among these sacraments there are three, baptism, confirmation, and orders, which imprint an indelible sign on the soul, that is, a certain character distinctive from the others. Hence they should not be repeated in the same person. The remaining four do not imprint a sign and admit of repetition.

Holy baptism, which is the gateway to the spiritual life, holds the first place among all the sacraments; through it we are made members of Christ and of the body of the Church. And since death entered into the universe through the first man, "unless we are born of water and the Spirit, we cannot," as the Truth says, "enter into the kingdom of heaven" (cf. John 3:5). The matter of this sacrament is real and natural water; it makes no difference whether cold or warm. The form is: *I baptize thee in the name of the Father and of the Son and of the Holy Ghost.* Yet we do not deny that through these words: *Such a* (this) *servant of Christ is baptized in the name of the Father and of the Holy Ghost* [1] or: *Such a one is baptized by my hands in the name of the Father and of the Son and of the Holy Ghost,* a true baptism is administered since the principal causes, from which baptism has its power is the Holy Trinity; the instrumental cause, however, is the minister, who bestows the sacrament externally; if the act which is performed through the minister himself, is expressed with the invocation of the Holy Trinity, the sacrament is effected. The minister of this sacrament is a priest, who is competent by office to baptize. In case of necessity, however, not only a priest or a deacon, but even a layman or a woman, yes even a pagan and a heretic can baptize, so long as he preserves the form of the Church and has the intention of doing as the Church does. The effect of this sacrament is the remission of every sin, original and actual, also of every punishment which is due to the sin itself. Therefore, no satisfaction must be enjoined for past sins upon those who immediately attain to the kingdom of heaven and the vision of God.

696

---

[1] Many Greeks so baptize.

697   The second sacrament is confirmation; its matter is the chrism prepared from the oil, which signifies the excellence of conscience, and from
the balsam, which signifies the fragrance of a good reputation, and is
blessed by a bishop. The form is: *I sign thee with the sign of the cross,
and I confirm thee with the chrism of salvation, in the name of the Father
and of the Son and of the Holy Ghost.* The ordinary minister is a bishop.
And although a simple priest has the power in regard to other anointings,
only a bishop can confer this sacrament, because according to the apostles,
whose place the bishops hold, we read that through the imposition of
hands they conferred the Holy Spirit, just as the lesson of the Acts of the
Apostles reveals: "Now, when the apostles, who were in Jerusalem, had
heard that the Samaria had received the word of God, they sent unto them
Peter and John. Who, when they were come, prayed for them that they
might receive the Holy Ghost. For He was not as yet come upon any of
them: but they were only baptized in the name of the Lord Jesus. Then
they laid their hands upon them; and they received the Holy Ghost" [Acts
8:14 ff.]. But in the Church confirmation is given in place of this imposition of hands. Nevertheless we read that at one time, by dispensation
of the Apostolic See for a reasonable and urgent cause, a simple priest
administered this sacrament of confirmation after the chrism had been
prepared by the bishop. The effect of this sacrament, because in it the Holy
Spirit is given for strength, was thus given to the Apostles on the day of
Pentecost, so that the Christian might boldly confess the name of Christ.
The one to be confirmed, therefore, must be anointed on the forehead,
which is the seat of reverence, so that he may not be ashamed to confess
the name of Christ and especially His Cross, which is indeed a "stumbling-
block to the Jews and unto the Gentiles foolishness" [cf. I Cor. 1:23]
according to the Apostle; for which reason one is signed with the sign of
the Cross.

698   The third is the sacrament of the Eucharist; its matter is wheat bread
and wine of grape, with which before consecration a very slight amount
of water should be mixed. Now it is mixed with water because according
to the testimonies of the holy Fathers and Doctors of the Church in a
disputation made public long ago, it is the opinion that the Lord Himself
instituted this sacrament in wine mixed with water; and, moreover, this
befits the representation of the Lord's passion. For blessed Alexander,[1]
the fifth Pope after blessed Peter, says: "In the offerings of the sacraments
which are offered to the Lord within the solemnities of Masses, let only
bread and wine mixed with water be offered as a sacrifice. For either wine
alone or water alone must not be offered in the chalice of the Lord, but
both mixed, because it is read that both, that is, blood and water, flowed

---

[1] From Pseudo-Isidore (P. Hinschius, *Decretales Pseudo-Isidorianae*, Lipsiae: 1863,
p. 99).

from the side of Christ." Then also, because it is fitting to signify the effect of this sacrament, which is the union of the Christian people with Christ. For water signifies the people, according to the passage in the Apocalypse: "the many waters . . . are many people" [cf. Apoc. 17:15]. And Julius,[1] the second Pope after blessed Sylvester, says: "The chalice of the Lord according to the precept of the canons, mixed with wine and water, ought to be offered, because we see that in water the people are understood, but in wine the blood of Christ is shown. Therefore, when wine and water are mixed in the chalice the people are made one with Christ, and the multitude of the faithful is joined and connected with Him in whom it believes." Since, therefore, the holy Roman Church taught by the most blessed Apostles Peter and Paul, as well as all the rest of the churches of the Latins and the Greeks, in which the lights of all sanctity and doctrine have shown, have so preserved this from the beginning of the nascent church and are now preserving it, it seems very unfitting that any other region differ from this universal and reasonable observance. We order, therefore, that the Armenians themselves also conform with all the Christian world, and that their priests mix a little water with the wine in the offering of the chalice, as has been said. The words of the Savior, by which He instituted this sacrament, are the form of this sacrament; for the priest speaking in the person of Christ effects this sacrament. For by the power of the very words the substance of the bread is changed into the body of Christ, and the substance of the wine into the blood; yet in such a way that Christ is contained entire under the species of bread, and entire under the species of wine. Under any part also of the consecrated host and consecrated wine, although a separation has taken place, Christ is entire. The effect of this sacrament which He operates in the soul of him who takes it worthily is the union of man with Christ. And since through grace man is incorporated with Christ and is united with His members, it follows that through this sacrament grace is increased among those who receive it worthily; and every effect that material food and drink accomplish as they carry on corporal life, by sustaining, increasing, restoring, and delighting, this the sacrament does as it carries on spiritual life, in which, as Pope Urban says, we renew the happy memory of our Savior, are withdrawn from evil, are greatly strengthened in good, and proceed to an increase of the virtues and the graces.

The fourth sacrament is penance, the matter of which is, as it were, **699** the acts of the penitent, which are divided into three parts. The first of these is contrition of heart, to which pertains grief for a sin committed together with a resolution not to sin in the future. The second is oral confession, to which pertains that the sinner confess integrally to his

---

[1] Julius I (ML 8, 970 BG).

priest all sins of which he has recollection. The third is satisfaction for sins according to the decision of the priest, which is accomplished chiefly by prayer, fasting, and alms. The words of absolution which the priest utters when he says: *Ego te absolvo,* etc., are the form of this sacrament, and the minister of this sacrament is the priest who has either ordinary authority for absolving or has it by the commission of a superior. The effect of this sacrament is absolution from sins.

700   The fifth sacrament is extreme unction, whose matter is the olive oil blessed by the bishop. This sacrament should be given only to the sick of whose death there is fear; and he should be anointed in the following places: on the eyes because of sight, on the ears because of hearing, on the nostrils because of smell, on the mouth because of taste and speech, on the hands because of touch, on the feet because of gait, on the loins because of the delight that flourishes there. The form of this sacrament is the following: *Per istam sanctam unctionem et suam piissimam misericordiam indulgeat tibi Dominus, quidquid per visum,* etc. (Through this holy anointing and his most kind mercy may the Lord forgive you whatever through it, etc.). And similarly on the other members. The minister of this sacrament is the priest. Now the effect is the healing of the mind and, moreover, in so far as it is expedient, of the body itself also. On this sacrament blessed James, the Apostle says: "Is any man sick among you? Let him bring in the priests of the church, and let them pray over him, anointing him with oil in the name of the Lord. And the prayer of faith shall save the sick man; and the Lord shall raise him up: and if he be in sins, they shall be forgiven him" [Jas. 5:14, 15].

701   The sixth sacrament is that of order, the matter of which is that through whose transmission the order is conferred:[1] just as the priesthood is transmitted through the offering of the chalice with wine and of the paten

---

[1] On the sense and force of this part see what is set forth by G. M. Card. van Rossum, *De essentia sacramenti Ordinis,* Friburgi, Brisq., ed. 2 (1931): 174 ff. On the same subject Benedict XIV [*De Synodo* l. 8, c. 10, n. 8 ff. (ed. Mechl. II, 223 ff.)] had already acted, but it is not clear from his words to what opinion he decrees that adherence should be given [see *ibid.* n. 11]. It is established that for nine centuries earlier the imposition of hands alone prevailed in the Church, not only Western but also Eastern, and that this is the only matter even to the present day among some Easterners, as, for example, the Greeks. Clement VIII in Instr. "Presbyteri Graeci," August 31, 1595 [MBR 3, 53 a sect. 7], ordered that a Greek bishop be always present in Rome to confer orders on Greek students in this rite, and Urban VIII in a brief "Universalis Ecclesiae," Nov. 23, 1624 [MBR 4, 172 a ff.] confirmed this. Benedict XIV in the Bull "Etsi pastoralis," May 26, 1742, issued for Italo-Greeks, said: "Let Greek bishops in conferring orders preserve their own Greek rite as described in the Euchologium," and in Const. "Demandatum coelitus," Dec. 24, 1743, he forbade that any innovation be made in the rites of the Greeks [cf. BB (M) 1, 342 ff.; 2, 148 ff.; MBR 16, 99 a ff.; 166 b ff.]. Finally Leo XIII in the Bull "Orientalium dignitas Ecclesiarum," Nov. 30, 1894, confirmed this Constitution of Benedict XIV [cf. ASS 27 (1894/95) 257; AL V 303 ff.].

with bread; the diaconate, however, by the giving of the book of the Gospels; but the subdiaconate by the giving of the empty chalice with the empty paten superimposed; and similarly with regard to the others by allotment of things pertaining to their ministry. The form of such priesthood is: *Accipe potestatem offerendi sacrificium in ecclesia pro vivis et mortuis, in nomine Patris et Filii et Spiritus Sancti.* And thus with regard to the forms of the other orders, as is contained extensively in the Roman Pontifical. The ordinary minister of this sacrament is the bishop. The effect is increase of grace, so that the one ordained be a worthy minister.

The seventh is the sacrament of matrimony, which is the sign of the **702** joining of Christ and the Church according to the Apostle who says: "This is a great sacrament; but I speak in Christ and in the church" [Eph. 5:32]. The efficient cause of matrimony is regularly mutual consent expressed by words in person. Moreover, there is allotted a threefold good on the part of matrimony. First, the progeny is to be accepted and brought up for the worship of God. Second, there is faith which one of the spouses ought to keep for the other. Third, there is the indivisibility of marriage, because it signifies the indivisible union of Christ and the Church. Although, moreover, there may be a separation of the marriage couch by reason of fornication, nevertheless, it is not permitted to contract another marriage, since the bond of a marriage legitimately contracted is perpetual.

A Decree in Behalf of the Jacobites [1]

[From the Bull "Cantata Domino," February 4, Florentine style, 1441, modern, 1442]

The sacrosanct Roman Church, founded by the voice of our Lord and **703** Savior, firmly believes, professes, and preaches one true God omnipotent, unchangeable, and eternal, Father, Son, and Holy Ghost; one in essence, three in persons; Father unborn, Son born of the Father, Holy Spirit proceeding from Father and Son; that the Father is not Son or Holy Spirit, that Son is not Father or Holy Spirit; that Holy Spirit is not Father or Son; but Father alone is Father, Son alone is Son, Holy Spirit alone is Holy Spirit. The Father alone begot the Son of His own substance; the Son alone was begotten of the Father alone; the Holy Spirit alone proceeds at the same time from the Father and Son. These three persons are one God, and not three gods, because the three have one substance, one essence, one nature, one divinity, one immensity, one eternity, where no opposition of relationship interferes.[2]

---

[1] Msi XXXI 1735 D ff.; Hrd IX 1023 A ff.; BT (T) 5, 59 b ff.; MBR 1, 344 b ff.; cf. Hfl VII 794 ff.; cf. Bar(Th) ad 1441 n. 1 ff. (28, 354 a ff.).

[2] On the Council of Florence, John, the theologian of the Latins, testified: "Indeed, according to the Doctors, Greek as well as Latin, it is the only relation which

704   "Because of this unity the Father is entire in the Son, entire in the Holy Spirit; the Son is entire in the Father, entire in the Holy Spirit, the Holy Spirit is entire in the Father, entire in the Son. No one either excels another in eternity, or exceeds in magnitude, or is superior in power. For the fact that the Son is of the Father is eternal and without beginning; and that the Holy Spirit proceeds from the Father and the Son is eternal and without beginning." [1] Whatever the Father is or has, He does not have from another, but from Himself; and He is the principle without principle. Whatever the Son is or has, He has from the Father, and is the principle from a principle. Whatever the Holy Spirit is or has, He has simultaneously from the Father and the Son. But the Father and the Son are not two principles of the Holy Spirit, but one principle, just as the Father and the Son and the Holy Spirit are not three principles of the creature, but one principle.

705   Whoever, therefore, have adverse and contrary opinions the Church disapproves and anathematizes and declares to be foreign to the Christian body which is the Church. Hence it condemns Sabellius who confuses the persons and completely takes away their real distinction. It condemns the Arians, the Eunomians, the Macedonians who say that only the Father is the true God, but put the Son and the Holy Spirit in the order of creatures. It condemns also any others whatsoever who place grades or inequality in the Trinity.

706   Most strongly it believes, professes, and declares that the one true God, Father and Son and Holy Spirit, is the creator of all things visible and invisible, who, when He wished, out of His goodness created all creatures, spiritual as well as corporal; good indeed, since they were made by the highest good, but changeable, since they were made from nothing, and it asserts that nature is not evil, since all nature, in so far as it is nature, is good. It professes one and the same God as the author of the Old and New Testament, that is, of the Law and the Prophets and the Gospel, since the saints of both Testaments have spoken with the inspiration of the same Holy Spirit, whose books, which are contained under the following titles it accepts and venerates. [The books of the canon follow, cf. n. 784; EB n. 32].

707   Besides it anathematizes the madness of the Manichaeans, who have established two first principles, one of the visible, and another of the

---

multiplies the persons in the divine processions, which is called the relation of origin, to which only two pertain: the one from whom, and the one who from another." [Hrd IX 203]. Similarly, the very learned Cardinal Bessarion, Archbishop of Nicea, theologian of the Greeks in the same Council declared: "No one is ignorant of the fact that the personal names of the Trinity are relative" (Hrd IX 339). Cf. St. Anselm, *De proc. Spiritus* S. c. 2 [ML 158, 288].

[1] Cf. St. Fulgentius, *De fide,* ad Petrum c. 1, n. 4 [MI 65, 674].

invisible; and they have said that there is one God of the New Testament, another God of the Old Testament.

It believes, professes, and proclaims that one person of the Trinity, true **708** God, Son of God born from the Father, consubstantial and coeternal with the Father, in the plenitude of time which the inscrutable depth of divine counsel has disposed for the salvation of the human race, assumed true and complete human nature from the immaculate womb of the Virgin Mary, and joined with itself in the unity of person, with such unity that whatever is of God there, is not separated from man, and whatever is of man, is not divided from the Godhead; He is one and the same undivided, both natures, God and man, remaining in their own peculiar properties, God and man, Son of God and Son of man, equal to the Father according to divinity, less than the Father according to humanity, immortal and eternal from the nature of divinity, passible and temporal from the condition of assumed humanity.

It firmly believes, professes, and proclaims that the Son of God in **709** the assumed humanity was truly born of the Virgin, truly suffered, truly died and was buried, truly rose again from the dead, ascended into heaven, and sits at the right hand of the Father, and will come at the end of time to judge the living and the dead.

It, moreover, anathematizes, execrates, and condemns every heresy that **710** suggests contrary things. And first it condemns Ebion, Cerinthus, Marcion, Paul of Samosata, Photinus, and all similar blasphemers, who, being unable to accept the personal union of humanity with the Word, denied that our Lord Jesus Christ was true God, proclaiming Him pure man, who was called divine man by reason of a greater participation in divine grace, which He had received by merit of a more holy life. It anathematizes also Manichaeus with his followers, who, thinking vainly that the Son of God had assumed not a true but an ephemeral body, entirely do away with the truth of the humanity in Christ. And also Valentinus who asserts that the Son of God took nothing from the Virgin Mary, but assumed a heavenly body and passed through the womb of the Virgin just as water flows and runs through an aqueduct. Arius also, who asserted that the body assumed from the Virgin lacked a soul, and would have the Godhead in place of the soul. Also Apollinaris, who, understanding that there was no true humanity if in Christ the soul is denied as giving the body form, posited only a sensitive soul, but held that the Godhead of the Word took the place of a rational soul. It also anathematizes Theodore of Mopsuestia and Nestorius who assert that humanity was united with the Son of God through grace, and hence there are two persons in Christ, just as they confess that there are two natures, since they were unable to understand that the union of humanity with the Word was hypostatic, and so refused to accept the subsistence of God. For according to this blasphemy, the Word was not made flesh, but the Word through grace lived in the flesh; that is, He was made not the Son of God, but rather the Son of God lived in man. It anathematizes also, execrates, and condemns Eutyches the archimandrite; since he believed according to the blasphemy of Nestorius that the truth of the Incarnation is excluded, and therefore it is fitting that humanity was so united to the Word of God that the person of the Godhead and of humanity were one and the same, and also, he could not grasp the unity of person as long as a plurality of natures existed, just as he established that there was one person of the Godhead and humanity in Christ, so he asserted that there was one nature, meaning that before the union there was a duality of natures, but in the assumption they passed over into one nature, with the greatest blasphemy and impiety granting either that humanity was turned into Godhead, or Godhead into humanity. It also anathematizes, execrates, and condemns Macarius of Antioch and all who hold similar views; although he had a correct understanding of the duality of natures and the unity of person, yet he erred greatly concerning the operations of Christ when he said that in Christ there was one operation and one will on the part of both natures. All these, together with their heresies, the Holy Roman Church anathematizes, affirming that there are two wills and two operations in Christ.

711 It firmly believes, professes, and teaches that no one conceived of man and woman was ever freed of the domination of the Devil, except through the merit of the mediator between God and men, our Lord Jesus Christ; He who was conceived without sin, was born and died, through His death alone laid low the enemy of the human race by destroying our sins, and opened the entrance to the kingdom of heaven, which the first man by his own sin had lost with all succession; and that He would come sometime, all the sacred rites of the Old Testament, sacrifices, sacraments, and ceremonies disclosed.

712 It firmly believes, professes, and teaches that the matter pertaining to the law of the Old Testament, of the Mosiac law, which are divided into ceremonies, sacred rites, sacrifices, and sacraments, because they were established to signify something in the future, although they were suited to the divine worship at that time, after our Lord's coming had been signified by them, ceased, and the sacraments of the New Testament began; and that whoever, even after the passion, placed hope in these matters of the law and submitted himself to them as necessary for salvation, as if faith in Christ could not save without them, sinned mortally. Yet it does not deny that after the passion of Christ up to the promulgation of the Gospel they could have been observed until they were believed to be in no way necessary for salvation; but after the promulgation of the Gospel it asserts that they cannot be observed without the loss of eternal salvation. All, therefore, who after that time observe circumcision and the Sabbath and the other requirements of the law, it declares alien to the Christian faith and not in the least fit to participate in eternal salvation, unless someday they recover from these errors. Therefore, it commands all who glory in the name of Christian, at whatever time, before or after baptism, to cease entirely from circumcision, since, whether or not one places hope in it, it cannot be observed at all without the loss of eternal salvation. Regarding children, indeed, because of danger of death, which can often take place, when no help can be brought to them by another remedy than through the sacrament of baptism, through which they are snatched from the domination of the Devil and adopted among the sons of God, it advises that holy baptism ought not to be deferred for forty or eighty days, or any time according to the observance of certain people, but it should be conferred as soon as it can be done conveniently, but so that, when danger of death is imminent, they be baptized in the form of the Church, early without delay, even by a layman or woman, if a priest should be lacking, just as is contained more fully in the decree of the Armenians [n. 696].

It believes firmly, professes, and proclaims that "every creature of God **713** is good, and nothing is to be rejected that is received with thanksgiving" [I Tim. 4:4], since, according to the word of the Lord [Matt. 15:11], "not that which goeth into the mouth defileth a man"; and it asserts that the indifference of clean and unclean foods of the Mosiac law pertains to the ceremonials which, with the rise of the Gospel passed out of existence and ceased to be efficacious. And it says also that the prohibition of the apostles "from things sacrificed to idols, and from blood and from things strangled [Acts 15:29] befitted that time in which one Church arose from the Jews and the Gentiles, who before lived according to different ceremonies and customs, so that even the Gentiles observed some things in common with the Jews, and occasion was furnished for coming together into one worship of God and one faith, and ground for dissension was removed; since to the Jews, by reason of an ancient custom, blood and things strangled seemed abominable, and they could think that the Gentiles would return to idolatry because of the eating of things sacrificed. But when the Christian religion is so propagated that no carnal Jew appears in it, but all passing over to the Church, join in the same rites and ceremonies of the Gospel, believing "all things clean to the clean" [Tit. 1:15], with the ending of the cause for this apostolic prohibition, the effect also ended. Thus it declares that the nature of no food, which society admits, is to be condemned, and no distinction is to be made by anyone at all, whether man or woman, between animals, and by whatever kind of death they meet their end; although for the health of body, for the exercise of virtue, for regular and ecclesiastical discipline many things not denied should be given up, since, according to the Apostle, "all things are lawful, but all things are not expedient" [I Cor. 6:12; 10:22].

714   It firmly believes, professes, and proclaims that those not living within the Catholic Church, not only pagans, but also Jews and heretics and schismatics cannot become participants in eternal life, but will depart "into everlasting fire which was prepared for the devil and his angels" [Matt. 25:41], unless before the end of life the same have been added to the flock; and that the unity of the ecclesiastical body is so strong that only to those remaining in it are the sacraments of the Church of benefit for salvation, and do fastings, almsgiving, and other functions of piety and exercises of Christian service produce eternal reward, and that no one, whatever almsgiving he has practiced, even if he has shed blood for the name of Christ, can be saved, unless he has remained in the bosom and unity of the Catholic Church.[1]

(The decrees for Greeks and Armenians of the ecumenical Synod accepted by the Roman Church follow.)

715   But since in the above written decree of the Armenians the form of the words, which in the consecration of the body and blood of the Lord the holy Roman Church confirmed by the teaching and authority of the Apostles had always been accustomed to use, was not set forth, we have thought that it ought to be inserted here. In the consecration of the body the Church uses this form of the words: "For this is my body"; but in the consecration of the blood, it uses the following form of the words: "For this is the chalice of my blood, the new and eternal testament, the mystery of faith, which will be poured forth for you and many for the remission of sins." But it makes no difference at all whether the wheaten bread in which the sacrament is effected was cooked on that day or before; for, provided that the substance of bread remains, there can be no doubt but that after the aforesaid words of the consecration of the body have been uttered with the intention of effecting, it will be changed immediately into the substance of the true body of Christ.

The decrees for the Syrians, Chaldeans, Meronites contain nothing new

NICHOLAS V 1447–1455

---

[1] Cf. St. Fulgentius, *De fide,* ad Petrum c. 37 ff., n. 78 ff. [ML 65, 703 f.].

CALLISTUS III 1455–1458

Usury and Contract for Rent [1]

[From the Constitution "Regimini universalis," May 6, 1455]

A petition recently addressed to us proposed the following matter: For **716** a very long time, and with nothing in memory running to the contrary, in various parts of Germany, for the common advantage of society, there has been implanted among the inhabitants of those parts and maintained up to this time through constant observance, a certain custom. By this custom, these inhabitants—or, at least, those among them, who in the light of their condition and indemnities, seemed likely to profit from the arrangement—encumber their goods, their houses, their fields, their farms, their possessions, and inheritances, selling the revenues or annual rents in marks, florins, or groats (according as this or that coin is current in those particular regions), and for each mark, florin, or groat in question, from those who have bought those coins, whether as revenues or as rents, have been in the habit of receiving a certain price appropriately fixed as to size according to the character of the particular circumstances, in conformity with the agreements made in respect of the relevant properties between themselves and the buyers. As guarantee for the payment of the aforesaid revenues and rents they mortgage those of the aforesaid houses, lands, fields, farms, possessions, and inheritances that have been expressly named [2] in the relevant contracts. In the favor of the sellers it is added to the contract that in proportion as they have, in whole or in part, returned to the said buyers the money thus received, they are entirely quit and free of the obligation to pay the revenues and rents corresponding to the sum returned. But the buyers, on the other hand, even though the said goods, houses, lands, fields, possessions, and inheritances might by the passage of time be reduced to utter destruction and desolation, would not be empowered to recover even in respect of the price paid.

Now, by some a certain doubt and hesitation is entertained as to whether contracts of this kind are to be considered licit. Consequently, certain debtors, pretending these contracts would be usurious, seek to find thereby an occasion for the nonpayment of revenues and rents owed by them in this way. . . . We, therefore, . . . in order to remove every doubt springing from these hesitations, by our Apostolic authority, do declare by

---

[1] CIC Extr. comm. III 5, 2; Frdbg II 1271 f.; Rcht II 1186.—This constitution is a confirmation of a Bull of Martin V on the material that is chapter 1 there: Frdbg II 1269 ff.

[2] It seems necessary to read: "quae . . . expressa."

these present letters that the aforesaid contracts are licit and in agreement with law, and that the said sellers, yielding all opposition, are effectively bound to the payment of the rents and revenues in conformity with the terms of the said contracts. [The reader is referred to the discussion of this text given by L. Choupin in A.Vacant-E Mangenot, *Dict. de théol. cath.* 2 (Paris, 1905) 1351–1362 (art. 'Calliste III,' sec. ii). The Translator.]

PIUS II 1458–1464

Appeal to the General Council [1]

[From the Bull "Exsecrabilis," [2] Jan. 18; in the ancient Roman opinion 1459; that of today 1460]

717   The execrable and hitherto unheard of abuse has grown up in our day, that certain persons, imbued with the spirit of rebellion, and not from a desire to secure a better judgment, but to escape the punishment of some offense which they have committed, presume to appeal to a future council from the Roman Pontiff, the vicar of Jesus Christ, to whom in the person of the blessed PETER was said: "Feed my sheep" [John 21:17], and, "Whatever thou shalt bind on earth, shall be bound in heaven" [Matt. 16:19]. . . . Wishing therefore to expel this pestiferous poison far from the Church of Christ and to care for the salvation of the flock entrusted to us, and to remove every cause of offense from the fold of our Savior . . . we condemn all such appeals and disprove them as erroneous and detestable.

Errors of Zanini de Solcia [3]

[Condemned in the letter "Cum sicut," Nov. 14, 1459]

717a   (1) That the world should be naturally destroyed and ended by the heat of the sun consuming the humidity of the land and the air in such a way that the elements are set on fire.

717b   (2) That all Christians are to be saved.

717c   (3) That God created another world than this one, and that in its time many other men and women existed and that consequently Adam was not the first man.

717d   (4) Likewise, that Jesus Christ suffered and died not for the redemp-

---

[1] BR(T) 5, 149 b; MBR 1, 369 b f.

[2] This Bull was confirmed by the Highest Pontiffs, Sixtus IV and Julius II; then the prohibition of appeal from the Highest Pontiff to the general Council was accepted in the Bull "Coenae" (art. 2).

[3] DuPl I, II 254 a; Bar(Th) ad 1459, n. 31 (29, 192 b).

tion because of His love of the human race, but by the law of the stars.

(5) Likewise, that Jesus Christ, Moses, and Mohammed ruled the 717e world by the pleasure of their wills.

(6) And that the same Lord our Jesus is illegitimate, and that He 717f exists in the consecrated hosts not with respect to His humanity but with respect to His divinity only.

(7) That wantonness outside of matrimony is not a sin, unless by 717g the prohibition of positive laws, and that these have not disposed of the matter well, and are checked by ecclesiastical prohibition only from following the opinion of Epicurus as true.

(8) Moreover that the taking away of another's property is not a 717h mortal sin, even though against the will of the master.

(9) Finally that the Christian law through the succession of another 717i law is about to have an end, just as the law of Moses has been terminated by the law of Christ.

Zaninus, Canon of Pergamum, is said to have presumed to affirm these propositions "in a sacrilegious attempt against the dogmas of the holy Fathers and later to assert them rashly with polluted lips," *but afterwards to have freely renounced* "these aforesaid errors."

The Blood of Christ [1]

[From the Bull "Ineffabilis summi providentia Patris," Aug. 1, 1464]

. . . By apostolic authority by the tenor of these presents we state and 718 ordain that none of the aforesaid Brethren (Minors and Preachers) hereafter be allowed to dispute, to preach, to make a statement either publicly or privately, concerning the above mentioned doubt, or to persuade others, that it may be heretical or a sin to hold or to believe that the most sacred blood itself (as is set before us) in the three days of the passion of the same Lord Jesus Christ from the divinity Himself was or was not divided or separated in some way, until beyond a question of a doubt of this kind what must be held has been defined by us and the Apostolic See.

PAUL II 1464–1471

---

[1] BR(T) 5, 181 a f.; MBR 1, 380 b.

SIXTUS IV 1471-1484

Errors of Peter de Rivo (concerning the Truth of Future Contingencies) [1]

[Condemned in the Bull "Ad Christi vicarii," Jan. 3, 1474]

719 (1) When Elizabeth spoke to the Blessed Virgin Mary saying: "Blessed art thou that hast believed because those things shall be accomplished that were spoken to thee by the Lord" [Luke 1:45], she seemed to intimate that those propositions, namely: "Thou shalt bring forth a son and thou shalt call his name Jesus: He shall be great, etc." [Luke 1:31], do not yet contain truth.

720 (2) Likewise, when Christ after His resurrection said: "All things must needs be fulfilled which are written in the law of Moses and in the prophets and in the psalms concerning me" [Luke 24:44] seems to have implied that such propositions were devoid of truth.

721 (3) Likewise, when the Apostle said: "For the law, having a shadow of the good things to come, not the very image of things [Heb. 10:1], he seems to imply that the propositions of the Old Law which concerned the future, did not yet contain the prescribed truth.

722 (4) Likewise, that it does not suffice for the truth of the proposition concerning the future, that the thing will be, but there is required that it will be without impediment.

723 (5) Likewise, it is necessary to say one of two things, either that in the articles of faith concerning the future actual truth is not present, or that what is signified in them through divine power could not have been hindered.

They were condemned as "scandalous and deviating from the path of Catholic faith"; *they were revoked by the written word of Peter himself.*

Indulgence for the Dead

[From the Bull in favor of the Church of St. Peter of Xancto, Aug. 3, 1476] [2]

723a In order that the salvation of souls may be procured rather at that time when they need the prayers of others more, and when they can be

---

[1] DuPl I, II 279 b ff.—Peter de Rivo of Alost, taught at Louvain from the year 1460 [Hrt II³ 1034].

[2] Archives historiques de la Saintonge et de l'Aunis, T.X Saintes 1882, p. 56 ff.; N. Paulus in: *Historisches Jahrbuch* XXI (1900), p. 649 f., note 4.

of benefit to themselves less, by Apostolic authority from the treasure of the Church wishing to come to the aid of the souls who departed from the life united with Christ through charity, and who, while they lived, merited that they be favored by such indulgence; desiring this with paternal affection, in so far as with God's help we can, confident in the mercy of God and in the plenitude of His power, we both concede and grant that, if any parents, friends, or other faithful of Christ, moved in behalf of these souls who are exposed to purgatorial fire for the expiation of punishments due them according to divine justice, during the aforementioned ten year period give a certain sum of money for the repair of the church of Xancto, or a value according to an arrangement with the dean or overseer of said church, or our collector by visiting said church or send it during said ten year period through messengers delegated by the same, we grant as a suffrage a plenary remission to assist and intercede for the souls in purgatory, in whose behalf they paid the said sum of money or the value, as mentioned above, for the remission of punishments.

Errors of Peter de Osma (the Sacrament of Penance) [1]

[Condemned in the Bull "Licet ea," August 9, 1479]

(1) That the confession of sins in species will be found really in a 724 statute of the universal Church, not in divine law;

(2) that mortal sins with respect to blame and punishment of the 725 other world are abolished without confession, by contrition of heart only;

(3) moreover, bad thoughts are forgiven by displeasure only;   726

(4) that it is not demanded of necessity that confession be secret; [2]   727

(5) that those who confess should not be absolved, if penance has not 728 been done;

(6) that the Roman Pontiff cannot remit the punishment of purga- 729 tory; [3]

---

[1] MBR 1, 416 f.; DuPl I, II 298 b ff.; Gotti, *Verit. rel. christ.* II 410 b; cf. Aguirre, *Coll. Conc. Hisp.* III 687 a; BR(T) 5, 265 a.—Peter Martinez, called "of Osma" from his native city, taught at Salamanca. His errors (among which also is "The Church of the city of Rome can err" [n. 730 in former editions]), rejected by a gathering of theologians at Alcala and afterwards condemned by the Archbishop of Toledo (which condemnation Sixtus IX confirmed by this Bull), he retracted publicly before the publication of the Bull. Cf. Rom. Quartalschr. 43 (1935) 205 ff. [Fr. Stegmüller].

[2] The Archbishop of Toledo by authority of the Holy Pontiff had proscribed the opinion of Peter of Osma in this sense, that "confession ought to be secret, that is about secret sins, not manifest sins." Cf. Rom. Quartalschr. l.c. 244.

[3] Cf. *Zeitschr. f. kath. Theol.* 33 (1909) 599–608, where Nic. Paulus proves that Peter of Osma denied that the Highest Pontiff could so concede indulgences to the

731   (7) and cannot dispense with respect to what the universal Church has established;

732   (8) also that the sacrament of penance, as far as concerns the accumulation of grace, is of nature, but not of the institution of the New or Old Testament.

733   *On these propositions we read in the Bull,* Sect. 6:

. . . We declare each and all the above mentioned propositions to be false, contrary to the holy Catholic faith, erroneous, and scandalous, and entirely at variance with the truth of the Gospels, also contrary to the decrees of the holy Fathers and other apostolic constitutions and to contain manifest heresy.

The Immaculate Conception of the B.V.M.[1]

[From the Constitution "Cum praeexcelsa," Feb. 28, 1476]

734   While in an examination of devout deliberation we are thoroughly investigating the distinguished marks of merit, by which the Queen of Heaven, the glorious Virgin Mother of God, is preferred to all in the heavenly courts; just as among the stars the morning star foretells the dawn, we consider it just, even a duty, that all the faithful of Christ for the miraculous conception of this immaculate Virgin, give praise and thanks to Almighty God (whose providence beholding from all eternity the humility of this same Virgin, to reconcile with its author human nature exposed to eternal death because of the fall of the first man, by the preparation of the Holy Spirit constituted her the habitation of His Only-begotten Son, from whom He took on the flesh of our mortality for the redemption of His people, and the Virgin remained immaculate even after childbirth), and therefore that they say Masses and other divine offices instituted in the Church of God, and that they attend them to ask by indulgences and by the remission of sins to become more worthy of divine grace by the merits of and by the intercession of this same Virgin.

[From the Constitution "Grave nimis," Sept. 4, 1483]

735   Although the Holy Roman Church solemnly celebrates the public feast of the conception of the immaculate Mary ever Virgin, and has ordained a special and proper office for this feast, some preachers of different orders, as we have heard, in their sermons to the people in public throughout different cities and lands have not been ashamed to affirm

---

living, and accordingly that by the power of the keys, the penalties of purgatory themselves are certainly wiped out.

[1] CIC Extr. comm. III 12, 1 and 2: Frdbg II 1285 f.; Rcht II 1201 f.

up to this time, and daily cease not to affirm, that all those who hold or assert that the same glorious and immaculate mother of God was conceived without the stain of original sin, sin mortally, or that they are heretical, who celebrate the office of this same immaculate conception, and that those who listen to the sermons of those who affirm that she was conceived without this sin, sin grievously. . . .

We reprove and condemn assertions of this kind as false and erroneous and far removed from the truth, and also by apostolic authority and the tenor of these present [letters] we condemn and disapprove on this point published books which contain it . . . [but these also we reprehend] who have dared to assert that those holding the contrary opinion, namely, that the glorious Virgin Mary was conceived with original sin are guilty of the crime of heresy and of mortal sin, since up to this time there has been no decision made by the Roman Church and the Apostolic See.

INNOCENT VIII 1484–1492   PIUS III 1503
ALEXANDER VI 1492–1503   JULIUS 1503–1513

LEO X 1513–1521

LATERAN COUNCIL V 1512–1517

Ecumenical XVIII (The Reform of the Church)

The Human Soul (against the Neo-Aristotelians) [1]

[From the Bull "Apostolici Regiminis" (Session VIII), Dec. 19, 1513]

Since in our days (and we painfully bring this up) the sower of cockle, **738** ancient enemy of the human race, has dared to disseminate and advance in the field of the Lord a number of pernicious errors, always rejected by the faithful, especially concerning the nature of the rational soul, namely, that it is mortal, or one in all men, and some rashly philosophizing affirmed that this is true at least according to philosophy, in our desire to offer suitable remedies against a plague of this kind, with the approval of this holy Council, we condemn and reject all who assert that the intellectual soul is mortal, or is one in all men, and those who cast doubt on these truths, since it [the soul] is not only truly in itself and essentially the form of the human body, as was defined in the canon of Pope

---

[1] Msi XXXII 842 A; Hrd IX 1719 C f.; BR(T) 5, 601 b f.; MBR 1, 542 a f.; Bar(Th) ad 1513 n. 92 (31, 40 a f.); cf. Hfl VIII 585 f.

CLEMENT V our predecessor of happy memory published in the (general) Council of VIENNE [n. 481] but it is also multiple according to the multitude of bodies into which it is infused, multiplied, and to be multiplied, . . . And since truth never contradicts truth, we declare [see n. 1797] every assertion contrary to the truth of illumined faith to be altogether false; and, that it may not be permitted to dogmatize otherwise, we strictly forbid it, and we decree that all who adhere to errors of this kind are to be shunned and to be punished as detestable and abominable infidels who disseminate most damnable heresies and who weaken the Catholic faith.

"Mountains of Piety" and Usury [1]

[From the Bull "Inter multiplices," April 28
(Session X, May 4), 1515]

739   With the approval of the holy Council, we declare and define that the aforesaid "Mountains of piety" established by the civil authorities and thus far approved and confirmed by the authority of the Apostolic See, in which a moderate rate of interest is received exclusively for the expenses of the officials and for other things pertaining to their keeping, as is set forth, for an indemnity of these as far as this matter is concerned, beyond the capital without a profit for these same Mountains, neither offer any species of evil, nor furnish an incentive to sin, nor in any way are condemned, nay rather that such a loan is worthwhile and is to be praised and approved, and least of all to be considered usury. . . . Moreover, we declare that all religious and ecclesiastics as well as secular persons, who henceforth shall dare to preach or dispute in word or in writing against the form of the present declaration and sanction, incur the penalty of excommunication of a sentence [automatically] imposed [*latae sententiae*], a privilege of any nature whatsoever notwithstanding.

The Relation Between the Pope and the Councils [2]

[From the Bull "Pastor Aeternus" (Session XI) Dec. 19, 1516]

740   Nor should this move us, that the sanction [pragmatic] itself, and the things contained in it were proclaimed in the Council of Basle . . . , since all these acts were made after the translation of that same Council of Basle from the place of the assembly at Basle, and therefore could have

---

[1] Msi XXXII 906 D f.; Hrd IX 1747 C; BR(T) 5, 622 b ff.; MBR 1, 554 a ff.; Bar(Th) ad 1515 n. 3 (31, 90 b f.); cf. Hfl VIII 645.

[2] Msi XXXII 967 C; Hrd IX 1228 D; BR(T) 5, 661 a f.; MBR 1, 570 b f.; Bar(Th) ad 1516 n. 25 (31, 121 a); cf. Hfl VIII 710 ff.

no weight, since it is clearly established that the Roman Pontiff alone, possessing as it were authority over all Councils, has full right and power of proclaiming Councils, or transferring and dissolving them, not only according to the testimony of Sacred Scripture, from the words of the holy Fathers and even of other Roman Pontiffs, of our predecessors, and from the decrees of the holy canons, but also from the particular acknowledgment of these same Councils.

Indulgences [1]

[From the Bull "Cum postquam" to the Legate Cajetan de Vio, Nov. 9, 1518]

And lest in the future anyone should allege ignorance of the doctrine **740a** of the Roman Church concerning such indulgences and their efficacy, or excuse himself under pretext of such ignorance, or aid himself by pretended protestations, but that these same persons may be convicted as guilty of notorious lying and be justly condemned, we have decided that you should be informed by these presents that the Roman Church, which the other churches are bound to follow as their mother, has decreed that the Roman Pontiff, the successor of PETER the key bearer, and the Vicar of Jesus Christ on earth, by the power of the keys, to which it belongs to open the kingdom of heaven, by removing the obstacles in the faithful of Christ (namely the fault and punishment due to actual sins, the fault by means of the sacrament of penance, but the temporal punishment due for actual sins according to divine justice by means of the indulgence of the Church), for the same reasonable causes can concede indulgences from the superabundant merits of Christ and the saints to these same faithful of Christ, who belong to Christ by the charity that joins the members, whether they be in this life or in purgatory; and by granting an indulgence by apostolic authority to the living as well as to the dead, has been accustomed to dispense from the treasury of the merits of Jesus Christ and the saints, and by means of absolution to confer that same indugence or to transfer it by means of suffrage. And for that reason that all, the living as well as the dead, who have truly gained such indulgences, are freed from such temporal punishment due for their actual sins according to divine justice, as is equivalent to the indulgence granted and acquired. And thus by apostolic authority in accordance with the tenor of these letters we decree that it should be held by all and be preached under punishment of excommunication, of a sentence [automatically] imposed [*latae sententiae*]. . . .

---

[1] Iod. le Plat, a very full collection II of records pertaining to the history of the Council of Trent (Lovanii 1782) 23 f.; cf. Caietanus de Vio, In 3 P., f. 48, a 5 (1903, 469) et *Zeitschr. f. kath. Theologie* 37 (1913): 394 ff. (N. Paulus.)

Leo X sent this Bull to the Swiss in the year 1519 with a letter dated April 30, 1519, in which he concluded as follows concerning the doctrine of the Bull:

740b You will be solicitous about a thorough consideration and preservation of the power of the Roman Pontiff in the granting of such indulgences according to the true definition of the Roman Church, which we have commanded should be observed and preached by all . . . according to these letters which we are ordering to be delivered to you . . . You will firmly abide by the true decision of the Holy Roman Church and to this Holy See, which does not permit errors.

Errors of Martin Luther [1]

[Condemned in the Bull "Exsurge Domine," June 15, 1520]

741 1. It is an heretical opinion, but a common one, that the sacraments of the New Law give pardoning grace to those who do not set up an obstacle.

742 2. To deny that in a child after baptism sin remains is to treat with contempt both Paul and Christ.

743 3. The inflammable sources [*fomes*] of sin, even if there be no actual sin, delays a soul departing from the body from entrance into heaven.

744 4. To one on the point of death imperfect charity necessarily brings with it great fear, which in itself alone is enough to produce the punishment of purgatory, and impedes entrance into the kingdom.

745 5. That there are three parts to penance: contrition, confession, and satisfaction, has no foundation in Sacred Scripture nor in the ancient sacred Christian doctors.

746 6. Contrition, which is acquired through discussion, collection, and detestation of sins, by which one reflects upon his years in the bitterness of his soul, by pondering over the gravity of sins, their number, their baseness, the loss of eternal beatitude, and the acquisition of eternal damnation, this contrition makes him a hypocrite, indeed more a sinner.

747 7. It is a most truthful proverb and the doctrine concerning the contritions given thus far is the more remarkable: "Not to do so in the future is the highest penance; the best penance, a new life."

748 8. By no means may you presume to confess venial sins, nor even all mortal sins, because it is impossible that you know all mortal sins. Hence in the primitive Church only manifest mortal sins were confessed.

749 9. As long as we wish to confess all sins without exception, we are

---

[1] BR(T) 5, 750 a ff.; MBR 1, 610 b ff.; Msi XXII 1051 C ff.; Hrd IX 1893 A ff.; CIC Rcht, II 134 ff. (Primo); cf. Bar(Th) ad 1520 n. 53 (31, 272 b ff.).

doing nothing else than to wish to leave nothing to God's mercy for pardon.

10. Sins are not forgiven to anyone, unless when the priest forgives   750 them he believes they are forgiven; on the contrary the sin would remain unless he believed it was forgiven; for indeed the remission of sin and the granting of grace does not suffice, but it is necessary also to believe that there has been forgiveness.

11. By no means can you have reassurance of being absolved because of   751 your contrition, but because of the word of Christ: "Whatsoever you shall loose, etc." [Matt. 16:19]. Hence, I say, trust confidently, if you have obtained the absolution of the priest, and firmly believe yourself to have been absolved, and you will truly be absolved, whatever there may be of contrition.

12. If through an impossibility he who confessed was not contrite, or   752 the priest did not absolve seriously, but in a jocose manner, if nevertheless he believes that he has been absolved, he is most truly absolved.

13. In the sacrament of penance and the remission of sin the pope or   753 the bishop does no more than the lowest priest; indeed, where there is no priest, any Christian, even if a woman or child, may equally do as much.

14. No one ought to answer a priest that he is contrite, nor should the   754 priest inquire.

15. Great is the error of those who approach the sacrament of the   755 Eucharist relying on this, that they have confessed, that they are not conscious of any mortal sin, that they have sent their prayers on ahead and made preparations; all these eat and drink judgment to themselves. But if they believe and trust that they will attain grace, then this faith alone makes them pure and worthy.

16. It seems to have been decided that the Church in common Council   756 established that the laity should communicate under both species; the Bohemians who communicate under both species are not heretics, but schismatics.

17. The treasures of the Church, from which the pope grants indul-   757 gences, are not the merits of Christ and of the saints.

18. Indulgences are pious frauds of the faithful, and remissions of   758 good works; and they are among the number of those things which are allowed, and not of the number of those which are advantageous.

19. Indulgences are of no avail to those who truly gain them, for the   759 remission of the penalty due to actual sin in the sight of divine justice.

20. They are seduced who believe that indulgences are salutary and   760 useful for the fruit of the spirit.

21. Indulgences are necessary only for public crimes, and are properly   761 conceded only to the harsh and impatient.

762   22. For six kinds of men indulgences are neither necessary nor useful; namely, for the dead and those about to die, the infirm, those legitimately hindered, and those who have not committed crimes, and those who have committed crimes, but not public ones, and those who devote themselves to better things.

763   23. Excommunications are only external penalties and they do not deprive man of the common spiritual prayers of the Church.

764   24. Christians must be taught to cherish excommunications rather than to fear them.

765   25. The Roman Pontiff, the successor of PETER, is not the vicar of Christ over all the churches of the entire world, instituted by Christ Himself in blessed PETER.

766   26. The word of Christ to PETER: "*Whatsoever you shall loose on earth, etc.*" (Matt. 16) is extended merely to those things bound by Peter himself.

767   27. It is certain that it is not in the power of the Church or the pope to decide upon the articles of faith, and much less concerning the laws for morals or for good works.

768   28. If the pope with a great part of the Church thought so and so, he would not err; still it is not a sin or heresy to think the contrary, especially in a matter not necessary for salvation, until one alternative is condemned and another approved by a general Council.

769   29. A way has been made for us for weakening the authority of Councils, and for freely contradicting their actions, and judging their decrees, and boldly confessing whatever seems true, whether it has been approved, or disapproved by any Council whatsoever.

770   30. Some articles of John Hus, condemned in the Council of CONSTANCE, are most Christian, wholly true and evangelical; these the universal Church could not condemn.

771   31. In every good work the just man sins.

772   32. A good work done very well is a venial sin.

773   33. That heretics be burned is against the will of the Spirit.

774   34. To go to war against the Turks is to resist God who punishes our iniquities through them.

775   35. No one is certain that he is not always sinning mortally; because of the most hidden vice of pride.

776   36. Free will after sin is a matter of title only; and as long as one does what is in him, one sins mortally.

777   37. Purgatory cannot be proved from Sacred Scripture, which is in the canon.

778   38. The souls in purgatory are not sure of their salvation, at least not all; nor is it proved by any arguments or by the Scriptures that they are beyond the state of meriting or of increasing in charity.

39. The souls in purgatory sin without intermission, as long as they **779** seek rest and abhor punishments.

40. The souls freed from purgatory by the suffrages of the living are **780** less happy than if they had made satisfactions by themselves.

41. Ecclesiastical prelates and secular princes would not act badly if **781** they destroyed all of the money-bags of beggary.

Censure of the Holy Pontiff: "All and each of the above mentioned articles or errors, so to speak, as set before you, we condemn, disapprove, and entirely reject as respectively heretical, or scandalous, or false, or offensive to pious ears, or seductive of simple minds, and in opposition to Catholic truth.

HADRIAN VI 1522-1523   CLEMENT VII 1523-1534

PAUL III 1534-1549

COUNCIL OF TRENT 1545-1563

Ecumenical XIX (Contra Novatores 16 cent.)

SESSION III (Feb. 4, 1546)

The Creed of the Catholic Faith is Accepted [1]

This sacred and holy ecumenical and general Synod of Trent, lawfully **782** assembled in the Holy Spirit, with the three legates of the Apostolic See presiding over it, in consideration of the magnitude of the matters to be transacted, especially those which are comprised under these two heads, the extirpation of heresies and the reform of morals, because of which chiefly the Synod was convoked . . . , has proposed that the creed of faith, which the Holy Roman Church utilizes, inasmuch as it is that principle, wherein all who profess the faith of Christ necessarily agree, and is the firm and sole foundation, against which the "gates of Hell shall never prevail" [Matt. 16:18], be expressed in the very same words in which it is read in all the churches. This creed is as follows:

[The Nicean-Constantinopolitan Creed follows, see n. 86.]

---

[1] C Tr IV 579 f.; Rcht 10; Msi XXXIII 19 B; Hrd X 19 E f.; Bar(Th) ad 1546 n. 15 f. (33, 124 ff.).

SESSION IV (April 8, 1546)

The Sacred Books and the Traditions of the Apostles
are Accepted [1]

783   The sacred and holy ecumenical and general Synod of Trent, lawfully
assembled in the Holy Spirit, with the same three Legates of the Apostolic
See presiding over it, keeping this constantly in view, that with the
abolishing of errors, the purity itself of the Gospel is preserved in the
Church, which promised before through the Prophets in the Holy Scriptures our Lord Jesus Christ the Son of God first promulgated with His
own mouth, and then commanded "to be preached" by His apostles "to
every creature" as the source of every saving truth and of instruction in
morals [Matt. 28:19 ff., Mark 16:15], and [the Synod] clearly perceiving
that this truth and instruction are contained in the written books and in
the unwritten traditions, which have been received by the apostles from
the mouth of Christ Himself, or from the apostles themselves, at the dictation of the Holy Spirit, have come down even to us, transmitted as
it were from hand to hand, [the Synod] following the examples of the
orthodox Fathers, receives and holds in veneration with an equal affection
of piety and reverence all the books both of the Old and of the New Testament, since one God is the author or both, and also the traditions themselves, those that appertain both to faith and to morals, as having been
dictated either by Christ's own word of mouth, or by the Holy Spirit,
and preserved in the Catholic Church by a continuous succession. And so
that no doubt may arise in anyone's mind as to which are the books that
are accepted by this Synod, it has decreed that a list of the Sacred books
be added to this decree.

784   They are written here below:

Books of the Old Testament: The five books of Moses, namely, Genesis,
Exodus, Leviticus, Numbers, Deuteronomy; Josue, Judges, Ruth, four
books of Kings, two of Paralipomenon, the first book of Esdras, and the
second which is called Nehemias, Tobias, Judith, Esther, Job, the Psalter
of David consisting of 150 psalms, the Proverbs, Ecclesiastes, the Canticle
of Canticles, Wisdom, Ecclesiasticus, Isaias, Jeremias with Baruch, Ezechiel, Daniel, the twelve minor Prophets, that is Osee, Joel, Amos, Abdias,
Jonas, Michaeas, Nahum, Habacuc, Sophonias, Aggaeus, Zacharias, Malachias; two books of the Machabees, the first and the second.

Books of the New Testament: the four Gospels, according to Matthew,
Mark, Luke, and John; the Acts of the Apostles, written by Luke the

---

[1] CTr V 91; Rcht 11 f.; Msi XXXIII 22 A; Hrd X 22 C f.; Bar(Th) ad 1546 n.
48 ff. (33, 136 b ff.); FB n. 42 ff.

Evangelist, fourteen epistles of Paul the Apostle, to the Romans, to the Corinthians two, to the Galatians, to the Ephesians, to the Philippians, to the Colossians, two to the Thessalonians, two to Timothy, to Titus, to Philemon, to the Hebrews; two of Peter the Apostle, three of John the Apostle, one of the Apostle James, one of the Apostle Jude, and the Apocalypse of John the Apostle. If anyone, however, should not accept the said books as sacred and canonical, entire with all their parts, as they were wont to be read in the Catholic Church, and as they are contained in the old Latin Vulgate edition, and if both knowingly and deliberately he should condemn the aforesaid traditions let him be anathema. Let all, therefore, understand in what order and in what manner the said Synod, after having laid the foundation of the confession of Faith, will proceed, and what testimonies and authorities it will mainly use in confirming dogmas, and in restoring morals in the Church.

The Vulgate Edition of the Bible is Accepted and the Method is Prescribed for the Interpretation of (Sacred) Scripture, etc.[1]

785 Moreover, the same sacred and holy Synod taking into consideration that no small benefit can accrue to the Church of God, if it be made known which one of all the Latin editions of the sacred books which are in circulation is to be considered authentic, has decided and declares that the said old Vulgate edition, which has been approved by the Church itself through long usage for so many centuries in public lectures, disputations, sermons, and expositions, be considered authentic, and that no one under any pretext whatsoever dare or presume to reject it.

786 Furthermore, in order to curb impudent clever persons, the synod decrees that no one who relies on his own judgment in matters of faith and morals, which pertain to the building up of Christian doctrine, and that no one who distorts the Sacred Scripture according to his own opinions, shall dare to interpret the said Sacred Scripture contrary to that sense which is held by holy mother Church, whose duty it is to judge regarding the true sense and interpretation of holy Scriptures, or even contrary to the unanimous consent of the Fathers, even though interpretations of this kind were never intended to be brought to light. Let those who shall oppose this be reported by their ordinaries and be punished with the penalties prescribed by law. . . . [Then laws are listed concerning the printing and approbation of books, for which among other matters the decree is:] that henceforth the Sacred Scripture, especially the aforesaid old and Vulgate edition, be printed as correctly as

---

[1] CTr V 91 f.; Rcht 12; Msi XXXIII 22 E f.; Hrd X 23 B f.; Bar(TL) ad 1546 n. 48 ff. (33, 136 b ff.); EB n. 46 ff.

possible, and that no one be allowed either to print or cause to be printed any books whatever concerning sacred matters without the name of the author, nor to sell them in the future or even to keep them, unless they have been first examined and approved by the ordinary. . . .

Session v (June 17, 1546)

Decree On Original Sin [1]

787   That our Catholic faith, "without which it is impossible to please God" [Heb. 11:16] may after the purging of errors continue in its own perfect and spotless purity, and that the Christian people may not be "carried about with every wind of doctrine" [Eph. 4:14], since that old serpent, the perpetual enemy of the human race, among the very many evils with which the Church of God in these our times is troubled, has stirred up not only new, but even old dissensions concerning original sin and its remedy, the sacred ecumenical and general Synod of Trent lawfully assembled in the Holy Spirit with the same three legates of the Apostolic See presiding over it, wishing now to proceed to the recalling of the erring and to the confirming of the wavering, and following the testimonies of the Holy Scriptures and of the holy Fathers and of the most approved Councils, as well as the judgment and the unanimity of the Church itself, has established, confesses, and declares the following concerning original sin:

788   1. If anyone does not confess that the first man Adam, when he had transgressed the commandment of God in Paradise, immediately lost his holiness and the justice in which he had been established, and that he incurred through the offense of that prevarication the wrath and indignation of God and hence the death with which God had previously threatened him, and with death captivity under his power, who thenceforth "had the empire of death" [Heb. 2:14], that is of the devil, and that through that offense of prevarication the entire Adam was transformed in body and soul for the worse [see n. 174], let him be anathema.

789   2. If anyone asserts that the transgression of Adam has harmed him alone and not his posterity, and that the sanctity and justice, received from God, which he lost, he has lost for himself alone and not for us also; or that he having been defiled by the sin of disobedience has transfused only death "and the punishments of the body into the whole human race, but not sin also, which is the death of the soul," let him be anathema, since he contradicts the Apostle who says: "By one man sin entered into

---

[1] CTr V 238 ff.; Rcht 13 ff.; Msi XXXIII 27 A ff.; Hrd X 27 C ff.; Bar(Th) ad 1546 n. 65 f. (33, 146 a ff.).

the world, and by sin death, and so death passed upon all men, in whom all have sinned" [Rom. 5:12; see n. 175].

3. If anyone asserts that this sin of Adam, which is one in origin and **790** transmitted to all is in each one as his own by propagation, not by imitation, is taken away either by the forces of human nature, or by any remedy other than the merit of the one mediator, our Lord Jesus Christ [see n. 711], who has reconciled us to God in his own blood, "made unto us justice, sanctification, and redemption" [I Cor. 1:30]; or if he denies that that merit of Jesus Christ is applied to adults as well as to infants by the sacrament of baptism, rightly administered in the form of the Church: let him be anathema. "For there is no other name under heaven given to men, whereby we must be saved . . ." [Acts 4:12]. Whence that word: "Behold the lamb of God, behold Him who taketh away the sins of the world" [John 1:29]. And that other: "As many of you as have been baptized, have put on Christ" [Gal. 3:27].

4. "If anyone denies that infants newly born from their mothers' **791** wombs are to be baptized," even though they be born of baptized parents, "or says they are baptized indeed for the remission of sins, but that they derive nothing of original sin from Adam, which must be expiated by the laver of regeneration" for the attainment of life everlasting, whence it follows, that in them the form of baptism for the remission of sins is understood to be not true, but false: let him be anathema. For what the Apostle has said: "By one man sin entered into the world, and by sin death, and so death passed upon all men, in whom all have sinned" [Rom. 5:12], is not to be understood otherwise than as the Catholic Church spread everywhere has always understood it. For by reason of this rule of faith from a tradition of the apostles even infants, who could not as yet commit any sins of themselves, are for this reason truly baptized for the remission of sins, so that in them there may be washed away by regeneration, what they have contracted by generation, [see n. 102]. "For unless a man be born again of water and the Holy Ghost, he cannot enter into the kingdom of God" [John 3:5].

5. If anyone denies that by the grace of our Lord Jesus Christ, which is **792** conferred in baptism, the guilt of original sin is remitted, or even asserts that the whole of that which has the true and proper nature of sin is not taken away, but says that it is only touched in person or is not imputed, let him be anathema. For in those who are born again, God hates nothing, because "there is no condemnation, to those who are truly buried together with Christ by baptism unto death" [Rom. 6:4], who do not "walk according to the flesh" [Rom. 8:1], but putting off "the old man" and putting on the "new, who is created according to God" [Eph. 4:22 ff.; Col. 3:9 ff.], are made innocent, immaculate, pure, guiltless and beloved sons of God, "heirs indeed of God, but co-heirs with Christ" [Rom.

8:17], so that there is nothing whatever to retard their entrance into heaven. But this holy Synod confesses and perceives that there remains in the baptized concupiscence of an inclination, although this is left to be wrestled with, it cannot harm those who do not consent, but manfully resist by the grace of Jesus Christ. Nay, indeed, "he who shall have striven lawfully, shall be crowned" [II Tim. 2:5]. This concupiscence, which at times the Apostle calls *sin* [Rom. 6:12 ff.] the holy Synod declares that the Catholic Church has never understood to be called sin, as truly and properly sin in those born again, but because it is from sin and inclines to sin. But if anyone is of the contrary opinion, let him be anathema.

6. This holy Synod declares nevertheless that it is not its intention to include in this decree, where original sin is treated of, the blessed and immaculate Virgin Mary mother of God, but that the constitutions of Pope SIXTUS IV of happy memory are to be observed, under the penalties contained in these constitutions, which it renews [see n. 734 ff.:].

Session vi (Jan. 13, 1547)

Decree On Justification [1]

Introduction

792a   Since at this time not without the loss of many souls and grave detriment to the unity of the Church there is disseminated a certain erroneous doctrine concerning justification, the holy ecumenical and general synod of Trent lawfully assembled in the Holy Spirit, the Most Reverends John Maria, Bishop of Praeneste, de Monte, and Marcellus, priest of the Holy Cross in Jerusalem, cardinals of the Holy Roman Church and apostolic legates *a latere,* presiding therein in the name of our Most Holy Father and Lord in Christ, Paul, the third Pope by the providence of God, for the praise and glory of Almighty God, for the tranquillity of the Church and the salvation of souls, purpose to expound to all the faithful of Christ the true and salutary doctrine of justification, which the "son of justice" [Mal. 4:2], Christ Jesus, "the author and finisher of our faith" [Heb. 12:2] taught, the apostles transmitted and the Catholic Church, under the instigation of the Holy Spirit, has always retained, strictly forbidding that anyone henceforth may presume to believe, preach or teach, otherwise than is defined and declared by this present decree.

Chap. 1. On the Inability of Nature and of the Law to Justify Man

793   The holy Synod decrees first that for a correct and sound understanding of the doctrine of justification it is necessary that each one recognize and

---

[1] CTr V 791 ff.; Rcht 23 ff.; Msi XXXIII 33 A ff.; Hrd X 33 C ff.; Bar(Th) ad 1547 n. 6 ff. (33, 192 b ff.).

confess that, whereas all men had lost their innocence in the prevarication of Adam [Rom. 5:12; I Cor. 15:22: see n. 130], "having become unclean" [Isa. 64:6], and (as the Apostle says), "by nature children of wrath" [Eph. 2:3], as it (the Synod) has set forth in the decree on original sin, to that extent were they the servants of sin [Rom. 5:20], and under the power of the devil and of death, that not only the gentiles by the force of nature [can. 1], but not even the Jews by the very letter of the law of Moses were able to be liberated or to rise therefrom, although free will was not extinguished in them [can. 5], however weakened and debased in its powers [see n. 81].

Chap. 2. On the Dispensation and Mystery of the Advent of Christ

Whereby it came to pass that the heavenly Father, "the Father of **794** mercies and the God of all comfort" [II Cor. 1:3], when that "blessed fullness of time" was come [Eph. 1:10; Gal. 4:4] sent to men Christ Jesus [can. 1], his Son, who had been announced and promised [cf. Gen. 49:10, 18], both before the Law and at the time of the Law to many holy Fathers, that He might both redeem the Jews, who were under the Law, and the "gentiles, who did not follow after justice, might attain to justice" [Rom. 9:30], and that all men "might receive the adoption of sons" [Gal. 4:5]. "Him God has proposed as a propitiator through faith in his blood, for our sins" [Rom. 3:25], and not for our sins only, but also for those of the whole world [I John 2:2].

Chap. 3. Who are Justified Through Christ

But although Christ died for all [II Cor. 5:15], yet not all receive **795** the benefit of His death, but those only to whom the merit of His passion is communicated. For, as indeed men would not be born unjust, if they were not born through propagation of the seed of Adam, since by that propagation they contract through him, in conception, injustice as their own, so unless they were born again in Christ, they never would be justified [can. 2 and 10], since in that new birth through the merit of His passion, the grace, whereby they are made just, is bestowed upon them. For this benefit the Apostle exhorts us always to "give thanks to the Father who has made us worthy to be partakers of the lot of the saints in light" [Col. 1:12], "and has delivered us from the power of darkness, and has translated us into the kingdom of the Son of his love, in whom we have redemption and remission of sins [Col. 1:13 ff.].

Chap. 4. A Description of the Justification of the Sinner, and Its Mode in the State of Grace is Recommended

In these words a description of the justification of a sinner is given **796** as being a translation from that state in which man is born a child of the first Adam to the state of grace and of the "adoption of the sons" [Rom. 8:15] of God through the second Adam, Jesus Christ, our Savior; and this translation after the promulgation of the Gospel cannot be effected except through the laver of regeneration [can. 5 *de bapt.*], or a desire for it, as it is written: "Unless a man be born again of water and the Holy Spirit, he cannot enter into the kingdom of God" [John 3:5].

Chap. 5. *On the Necessity of Preparation for Justification of Adults, and Whence it Proceeds*

797   It [the Synod] furthermore declares that in adults the beginning of that justification must be derived from the predisposing grace [can. 3] of God through Jesus Christ, that is, from his vocation, whereby without any existing merits on their part they are called, so that they who by sin were turned away from God, through His stimulating and assisting grace are disposed to convert themselves to their own justification, by freely assenting to and cooperating with the same grace [can. 4 and 5], in such wise that, while God touches the heart of man through the illumination of the Holy Spirit, man himself receiving that inspiration does nothing at all inasmuch as he can indeed reject it, nor on the other hand can he [can. 3] of his own free will without the grace of God move himself to justice before Him. Hence, when it is said in the Sacred Writings: "Turn ye to me, and I will turn to you" [Zach. 1:3], we are reminded of our liberty; when we reply: "Convert us, O Lord, to thee, and we shall be converted" [Lam. 5:21], we confess that we are anticipated by the grace of God.

Chap. 6. *The Manner of Preparation*

798   Now they are disposed to that justice [can. 7 and 9] when, aroused and assisted by divine grace, receiving faith "by hearing" [Rom. 10:17], they are freely moved toward God, believing that to be true which has been divinely revealed and promised [can. 12 and 14], and this especially, that the sinner is justified by God through his grace, "through the redemption which is in Christ Jesus" [Rom. 3:24], and when knowing that they are sinners, turning themselves away from the fear of divine justice, by which they are profitably aroused [can. 8], to a consideration of the mercy of God, they are raised to hope, trusting that God will be merciful to them for the sake of Christ, and they begin to love him as the source of all justice and are therefore moved against sins by a certain hatred and detestation [can. 9], that is, by that repentance, which must be performed before baptism [Acts 2:38]; and finally when they resolve to receive baptism, to begin a new life and to keep the commandments of God. Concerning this disposition it is written: "He that cometh to God must believe, that he is and is a rewarder to them that seek him"

[Heb. 11:6], and, "Be of good faith, son, thy sins are forgiven thee" [Matt. 9:2; Mark 2:5], and, "The fear of the Lord driveth out sin" [Eccles. 1: 27], and, "Do penance, and be baptized every one of you in the name of Jesus Christ for the remission of your sins, and you shall receive the Holy Spirit" [Acts 2:38], and, "Going therefore teach all nations, baptizing them in the name of the Father and of the Son and of the Holy Spirit, teaching them to observe all things whatsoever I have commanded you" [Matt. 28:19], and finally, "Prepare your hearts unto the Lord" [I Kings 7:3].

Chap. 7. In What the Justification of the Sinner Consists, and What are its Causes

Justification itself follows this disposition or preparation, which is not **799** merely remission of sins [can. 11], but also the sanctification and renewal of the interior man through the voluntary reception of the grace and gifts, whereby an unjust man becomes a just man, and from being an enemy becomes a friend, that he may be "an heir according to hope of life everlasting" [Tit. 3:7]. The causes of this justification are: the final cause indeed is the glory of God and of Christ and life eternal; the efficient cause is truly a merciful God who gratuitously "washes and sanctifies" [I Cor. 6:11], "signing and anointing with the Holy Spirit of promise, who is the pledge of our inheritance" [Eph. 1:13 f.]; but the meritorious cause is His most beloved only-begotten Son, our Lord Jesus Christ, "who when we were enemies" [cf. Rom. 5:10], "for the exceeding charity wherewith he loved us" [Eph. 2:4], merited justification for us [can. 10] by His most holy passion on the wood of the Cross, and made satisfaction for us to God the Father; the instrumental cause is the sacrament of baptism, which is the "sacrament of faith," [1] without which no one is ever justified. Finally the unique formal cause is the "justice of God, not that by which He Himself is just, but by which He makes us just" [2] [can. 10 and 11], that, namely, by which, when we are endowed with it by him, we are renewed in the spirit of our mind, and not only are we reputed, but we are truly called and are just, receiving justice within us, each one according to his own measure, which the "Holy Spirit distributes to everyone as he wills" [I Cor. 12:11], and according to each one's own disposition and cooperation.

For although no one can be just but he to whom the merits of the **800** passion of our Lord Jesus Christ are communicated, yet this does take place in this justification of the ungodly when by the merit of that same most holy passion "the charity of God is poured forth by the Holy Spirit

---

[1] St. Ambrose, *De Spiritu Sancto*, I, 3, 42 [ML 16, 714]. St. Aug. Letter 98, to Boniface 9 ff. [ML 33, 364]. Innoc. III [see n. 406, 413].

[2] Cf. St. Augustine, *De Trin.*, 14, 12, 15 [ML 42, 1048].

in the hearts" [Rom. 5:5] of those who are justified, and inheres in them [can. 11]. Hence man through Jesus Christ, into whom he is ingrafted, receives in the said justification together with the remission of sins all these [gifts] infused at the same time: faith, hope, and charity. For faith, unless hope and charity be added to it, neither unites one perfectly with Christ, nor makes him a living member of his body. For this reason it is most truly said that "faith without works is dead" [Jas. 2:17 ff.], and is of no profit [can. 19], and "in Christ Jesus neither circumcision availeth anything, nor uncircumcision, but faith, which worketh by charity" [Gal. 5:6; 6:15]. This faith, in accordance with apostolic tradition, catechumens beg of the Church before the sacrament of baptism, when they ask for "faith which bestows life eternal," [1] which without hope and charity faith cannot bestow. Thence also they hear immediately the word of Christ: "If thou wilt enter into life, keep the commandments" [Matt. 19:17; can. 18–20]. Therefore, when receiving true and Christian justice, they are commanded immediately on being reborn, to preserve it pure and spotless as the "first robe" [Luke 15:22] given to them through Christ Jesus in place of that which Adam by his disobedience lost for himself and for us, so that they may bear it before the tribunal of our Lord Jesus Christ and have life eternal.[2]

Chap. 8. How One is to Understand the Gratuitous Justification of a Sinner by Faith

801   But when the Apostle says that man is justified "by faith" [can. 9] and "freely" [Rom. 3:22, 24], these words must be understood in that sense in which the uninterrupted consent of the Catholic Church has held and expressed, namely, that we are therefore said to be justified by faith, because "faith is the beginning of human salvation," [3] the foundation and root of all justification, "without which it is impossible to please God" [Heb. 11:6] and to come to the fellowship of His sons; and are, therefore, said to be justified gratuitously, because none of those things which precede justification, whether faith, or works merit the grace itself of justification; for, "if it is a grace, it is not now by reason of works; otherwise (as the same Apostle says) grace is no more grace" [Rom. 11:6].

Chap. 9. Against the Vain Confidence of Heretics

802   Although it is necessary to believe that sins are neither forgiven, nor ever have been forgiven, except gratuitously by divine mercy for Christ's sake, yet it must not be said that sins are forgiven or have been forgiven

---

[1] *Rit. Rom., Ordo Baptismi* note 1 f.

[2] *Ibid.*, n. 24.

[3] St. Fulgentius, *De fide*, to Peter, note 1 [ML 65, 671].

to anyone who boasts of his confidence and certainty of the forgiveness of his sins and rests on that alone, since among heretics and schismatics this vain confidence, remote from all piety [can. 12], may exist, indeed in our own troubled times does exist, and is preached against the Catholic Church with vigorous opposition. But neither is this to be asserted, that they who are truly justified without any doubt whatever should decide for themselves that they are justified, and that no one is absolved from sins and is justified, except him who believes with certainty that he is absolved and justified, and that by this faith alone are absolution and justification effected [can. 14], as if he who does not believe this is doubtful of the promises of God and of the efficacy of the death and resurrection of Christ. For, just as no pious person should doubt the mercy of God, the merit of Christ, and the virtue and efficacy of the sacraments, so every one, when he considers himself and his own weakness and indisposition, may entertain fear and apprehension as to his own grace [can. 13], since no one can know with the certainty of faith, which cannot be subject to error, that he has obtained the grace of God.

Chap. 10. Concerning the Increase of Justification Received

Having, therefore, been thus justified and having been made the **803** "friends of God" and "his domestics" [John 15:15; Eph. 2:19], "advancing from virtue to virtue" [Ps. 83:8], "they are renewed" (as the Apostle says) "from day to day" [II Cor. 4:16], that is, by mortifying the members of their flesh [Col. 3:5], and by "presenting them as instruments of justice" [Rom. 6:13, 19], unto sanctification through the observance of the commandments of God and of the Church; in this justice received through the grace of Christ "faith cooperating with good works" [Jas. 2:22], they increase and are further justified [can. 24 and 32], as it is written: "He that is just, let him be justified still" [Apoc. 22:11], and again: "Be not afraid to be justified even to death" [Eccles. 18:22], and again: "You see, that by works a man is justified and not by faith only" [Jas. 2:24]. And this increase of justice Holy Church begs for, when she prays: "Give unto us, O Lord, an increase of faith, hope and charity" [13th Sun. after Pent.].

Chap. 11. The Observance of the Commandments, and the Necessity and Possibility thereof

But no one, however much justified, should consider himself exempt **804** from the observance of the commandments [can. 20]; no one should make use of that rash statement forbidden under an anathema by the Fathers, that the commandments of God are *impossible* to observe for a man who is justified [can. 18 and 22: cf. n. 200]. "For God does not command impossibilities, but by commanding admonishes you both to do what you can do, and to pray for what you cannot do, and assists you that you may be able"; [1] "whose commandments are not heavy" [I John 5:3], "whose yoke is sweet and whose burden is light" [Matt. 11:30]. For they who are the sons of God, love Christ: "but they who love him, (as He Himself testifies) keep his words" [John 14:23], which indeed with the divine help they can do. For although in this mortal life men however holy and just fall at times into at least light and daily sins, which are also called venial [can. 23], they do not for that reason cease to be just. For that word of the just, "Forgive us our trespasses" [Matt. 6:12; cf. n. 107], is both humble and true. Thus it follows that the just ought to feel themselves more bound to walk in the way of justice, in that having been now "freed from sin and made servants of God" [Rom. 6:22], "living soberly and justly and piously" [Tit. 2:12], they can proceed onwards through Christ Jesus, through whom they "have access unto this grace" [Rom. 5:2]. For God "does not forsake those who have once been justified by His grace, unless He be first forsaken by them." [2] And so no one should flatter himself because of faith alone [can. 9, 19, 20], thinking that by faith alone he is made an heir and will obtain the inheritance, even though he suffer not with Christ "that he may be also glorified" [Rom. 8:17]. For even Christ Himself (as the Apostle says), "whereas he was the Son of God, he learned obedience by the things which he suffered and being made perfect he was made to all who obey him the cause of eternal salvation" [Heb. 5:8 ff.] For this reason the Apostle himself admonishes those justified saying: "Know you not, that they who run in the race, all run indeed, but one receiveth the prize? So run, that you may obtain. I therefore so run, not as at an uncertainty, I so fight, not as one beating the air, but I chastise my body and bring it under subjection, lest perhaps when I have preached to others, I myself should become a castaway" [I Cor. 9:24 ff.]. So also the chief of the Apostles, Peter: "Labor the more, that by good works you may make sure your calling and election; for doing these things, you shall not sin at any time" [II Pet. 1:10]. Thence it is clear that they are opposed to the teaching of orthodox religion who say that the just man sins at least venially in every good work [can. 25], or (what is more intolerable) that he merits eternal punishments; and that they also who declare that the just sin in all works, if in those works, in order to stimulate their own sloth and to encourage themselves to run in the race, with this (in view), that above all God may be glorified, they have in view also the eternal reward [can. 26, 31], since it is written: "I have inclined my heart to do thy justifications on account of the reward" [Ps. 118:112], and of Moses the Apostle says, that he "looked to the reward" [Heb. 11:26].

---

[1] Cf. St. Augustine, *De nat. et gratia*, c. 43, n. 50 [ML 44, 271].
[2] Cf. St. Augustine, *Op. cit.*, c. 26, n. 29 [ML 44, 261].

Chap. 12. Rash Presumption of Predestination is to be Avoided

No one moreover, so long as he lives in this mortal state, ought so far   805
to presume concerning the secret mystery of divine predestination, as to
decide for certain that he is assuredly in the number of the predestined
[can. 15], as if it were true that he who is justified either cannot sin any
more [can. 23], or if he shall have sinned, that he ought to promise himself an assured reformation. For except by special revelation, it cannot be
known whom God has chosen for Himself [can. 16].

Chap. 13. The Gift of Perseverance

So also as regards the gift of perseverance [can. 16] of which it is   806
written: He that "shall persevere to the end, he shall be saved" [Matt.
10:22; 24:13] (which gift cannot be obtained from anyone except from
Him, "who is able to make him, who stands, stand" [Rom. 14:4], that he
may stand perseveringly, and to raise him, who falls), let no one promise
himself anything as certain with absolute certitude, although all ought
to place and repose a very firm hope in God's help. For God, unless men
be wanting in His grace, as He has begun a good work, so will He perfect
it, "working to will and to accomplish" [Phil. 2:13; can. 22].[1] Nevertheless, let those "who think themselves to stand, take heed lest they fall"
[I Cor. 10:12], and "with fear and trembling work out their salvation"
[Phil. 2:12] in labors, in watchings, in almsdeeds, in prayers and oblations, in fastings and chastity [cf. II Cor. 6:3 ff.]. For they ought to fear,
knowing that they are born again "unto the hope of glory" [cf. I Rom.
Pet. 1:3], and not as yet unto glory in the combat that yet remains with
the flesh, with the world, with the devil, in which they cannot be victors,
unless with God's grace they obey the Apostle saying: "We are debtors,
not to the flesh, to live according to the flesh. For if you live according to
the flesh, you shall die. But if by the spirit you mortify the deeds of the
flesh, you shall live" [Rom. 8:12 ff.].

Chap. 14. The Fallen and Their Restoration

Those who by sin have fallen away from the received grace of justifica-   807
tion, will again be able to be justified [can. 29] when, roused by God
through the sacrament of penance, they by the merit of Christ shall have
attended to the recovery of the grace lost. For this manner of justification
is the reparation of one fallen, which the holy Fathers [2] have aptly called

---

[1] Cf. *Orat. Eccl.*: "We beseech thee, O Lord, by your inspiration anticipate our actions
and by your help attend them, that our every prayer and operation may always begin
from thee and begun be ended through thee."

[2] Cf. Tertullian, *De poenit.*, 4 7 9 12 [ML 1, 1233 ff.]; St. Jerome, *Ad Demetriadem*
ep. 130, 9 [ML 22, 1115]; *In Isaiam* 2, 3, 56 [ML 24, 65 D]; St. Pacian, Ep. 1, 5
[ML 13, 1056 A]; *De lapsu virg. consecr.* 8, 38 [ML 16, 379 A].

a second plank after the shipwreck of lost grace. For on behalf of those who after baptism fall into sin, Christ Jesus instituted the sacrament of penance, when He said: "Receive ye the Holy Ghost; whose sins you shall forgive, they are forgiven them, and whose sins you shall retain, they are retained" [I John 20:22, 23]. Hence it must be taught that the repentance of a Christian after his fall is very different from that at his baptism, and that it includes not only a cessation from sins, and a detestation of them, or "a contrite and humble heart" [Ps. 50:19], but also the sacramental confession of the same, at least in desire and to be made in its season, and sacerdotal absolution, as well as satisfaction by fasting, almsgiving, prayers, and other devout exercises of the spiritual life, not indeed for the eternal punishment, which is remitted together with the guilt either by the sacrament or the desire of the sacrament, but for the temporal punishment [can. 30], which (as the Sacred Writings teach) is not always wholly remitted, as is done in baptism, to those who ungrateful to the grace of God which they have received, "have grieved the Holy Spirit" [cf. Eph. 4:30], and have not feared to "violate the temple of God" [I Cor. 3:17]. Of this repentance it is written: "Be mindful, whence thou art fallen, do penance, and do the first works" [Apoc. 2:5], and again: "The sorrow which is according to God, worketh penance steadfast unto salvation" [II Cor. 7:10], and again: "Do penance" [Matt. 3:2; 4:17], and, "Bring forth fruits worthy of penance" [Matt. 3:8].

Chap. 15. By Every Mortal Sin Grace is Lost, but not Faith

808   Against the crafty genius of certain men also, who "by pleasing speeches and good words seduce the hearts of the innocent" [Rom. 16:18], it must be maintained that the grace of justification, although received, is lost not only by infidelity [can. 27], whereby even faith itself is lost, but also by any other mortal sin, although faith be not lost [can. 28], thereby defending the doctrine of the divine law which excludes from the kingdom of God not only the unbelievers, but also the faithful who are "fornicators, adulterers, effeminate, liers with mankind, thieves, covetous, drunkards, railers, extortioners" [I Cor. 6:9 ff.], and all others who commit deadly sins, from which with the assistance of divine grace they can refrain and for which they are separated from the grace of God [can. 27].

Chap. 16. The Fruit of Justification, that is, the Merit of Good Works, and the Reasonableness of that Merit

809   To men, therefore, who have been justified in this respect, whether they have preserved uninterruptedly the grace received, or have recovered it when lost, the words of the Apostle are to be submitted: "Abound in every good work, knowing that your labor is not in vain in the Lord" [I Cor. 15:58]; "for God is not unjust, that he should forget your work

and the love, which you have shown in his name" [Heb. 6:10], and: "Do not lose your confidence, which has a great reward" [Heb. 10:35]. And therefore to those who work well "unto the end" [Matt. 10:22], and who trust in God, life eternal is to be proposed, both as a grace mercifully promised to the sons of God through Christ Jesus, "and as a recompense" [1] which is according to the promise of God Himself to be faithfully given to their good works and merits [can. 26 and 32]. For this is that "crown of justice which after his fight and course" the Apostle declared "was laid up for him, to be rendered to him by the just judge and not only to him, but also to all that love his coming" [II Tim. 4:7 ff.]. For since Christ Jesus Himself as the "head into the members" [Eph. 4:15], and "as the vine into the branches" [John 15:5] continually infuses His virtue into the said justified, a virtue which always precedes their good works, and which accompanies and follows them, and without which they could in no wise be pleasing and meritorious before God [can. 2], we must believe that to those justified nothing more is wanting from being considered [can. 32] as having satisfied the divine law by those works which have been done in God according to the state of this life, and as having truly merited eternal life to be obtained in its own time (if they shall have departed this life in grace [Apoc. 14:13]), since Christ our Lord says: "If anyone shall drink of the water, that I will give him, he shall not thirst forever, but it shall become in him a fountain of water springing up unto life everlasting" [John 4:14]. Thus neither is "our own justice established as our own" from ourselves, nor is the justice of God [Rom. 10:3] "ignored" or repudiated; for that justice which is called ours, because we are justified [can. 10 and 11] through its inherence in us, that same is (the justice) of God, because it is infused into us by God through the merit of Christ.

Nor indeed is this to be omitted, that although in the sacred Writings **810** so much is ascribed to good works, that even "he that shall give a drink of cold water to one of his least ones" Christ promises "shall not lose his reward" [Matt. 10:42], and the Apostle testifies "that that which is at present momentary and light of our tribulation, worketh for us above measure exceedingly an eternal weight of glory" [II Cor. 4:17]; nevertheless far be it that a Christian should either trust or "glory" in himself and not "in the Lord" [cf. I Cor. 1:31; II Cor. 10:17], whose goodness towards all men is so great that He wishes the things which are His gifts [see n. 141] to be their own merits [can. 32]. And whereas "in many things we all offend" [Jas. 3:2; can. 23], each one should have before his eyes the severity and judgment as well as mercy and goodness; neither ought anyone to judge himself, even though he be "not conscious to himself of anything," since the whole life of men must be judged and examined not

---

[1] Cf. St. Augustine, *De gr. et lib. arb.* c. 8, n. 20 [ML 44, 893].

by the judgment of men, but of God, who "will bring to light the hidden things of darkness, and will make manifest the counsels of the hearts, and then shall every man have praise from God" [I Cor. 4:4 ff.], "who," as it is written, "will render to every man according to his works" [Rom. 2:6].

After this Catholic doctrine of justification [can. 33]—which, unless he faithfully and firmly accepts it, no one can be justified—it seemed good to the holy Synod to add these canons, so that all may know, not only what they must hold and follow, but also what they ought to shun and avoid.

Canons On Justification [1]

811   Can. 1. If anyone shall say that man can be justified before God by his own works which are done either by his own natural powers, or through the teaching of the Law, and without divine grace through Christ Jesus: let him be anathema [cf. n. 793 ff.].

812   Can. 2. If anyone shall say that divine grace through Christ Jesus is given for this only, that man may more easily be able to live justly and merit eternal life, as if by free will without grace he were able to do both, though with difficulty and hardship: let him be anathema [cf. n. 795, 809].

813   Can. 3. If anyone shall say that without the anticipatory inspiration of the Holy Spirit and without His assistance man can believe, hope, and love or be repentant, as he ought, so that the grace of justification may be conferred upon him: let him be anathema [cf. n. 797].

814   Can. 4. If anyone shall say that man's free will moved and aroused by God does not cooperate by assenting to God who rouses and calls, whereby it disposes and prepares itself to obtain the grace of justification, and that it cannot dissent, if it wishes, but that like something inanimate it does nothing at all and is merely in a passive state: let him be anathema [cf. n. 797].

815   Can. 5. If anyone shall say that after the sin of Adam man's free will was lost and destroyed, or that it is a thing in name only, indeed a title without a reality, a fiction, moreover, brought into the Church by Satan: let him be anathema [cf. n. 793, 797].

816   Can. 6. If anyone shall say that it is not in the power of man to make his ways evil, but that God produces the evil as well as the good works, not only by permission, but also properly and of Himself, so that the betrayal of Judas is no less His own proper work than the vocation of Paul: let him be anathema.

817   Can. 7. If anyone shall say that all works that are done before justifica-

---

[1] C. Tr V 797 ff.; Tcht 30 ff.; Msi XXXIII 40 A ff.; Hrd X 40 B ff.; Bar(Th) ad 547 n. 14 ff. (33, 195 b ff.).

tion, in whatever manner they have been done, are truly sins or deserving of the hatred of God, or that the more earnestly anyone strives to dispose himself for grace, so much the more grievously does he sin: let him be anathema [cf. n. 798].

Can. 8. If anyone shall say that the fear of hell, whereby by grieving for **818** sins we flee the mercy of God or refrain from sinning, is a sin or makes sinners worse: let him be anathema [cf. n. 798].

Can. 9. If anyone shall say that by faith alone the sinner is justified, so **819** as to understand that nothing else is required to cooperate in the attainment of the grace of justification, and that it is in no way necessary that he be prepared and disposed by the action of his own will: let him be anathema [cf. n. 798, 801, 804].

Can. 10. If anyone shall say that men are justified without the justice **820** of Christ by which He merited for us, or that by that justice itself they are formally just: let him be anathema [cf. n. 798, 799].

Can. 11. If anyone shall say that men are justified either by the sole **821** imputation of the justice of Christ, or by the sole remission of sins, to the exclusion of grace and charity, which is poured forth in their hearts by the Holy Spirit and remains in them, or even that the grace by which we are justified is only the favor of God: let him be anathema [cf. n. 799 ff., 809].

Can. 12. If anyone shall say that justifying faith is nothing else than **822** confidence in the divine mercy which remits sins for Christ's sake, or that it is this confidence alone by which we are justified: let him be anathema [cf. n. 798, 802].

Can. 13. If anyone shall say that it is necessary for every man in order **823** to obtain the remission of sins to believe for certain and without any hesitation due to his own weakness and indisposition that his sins are forgiven him: let him be anathema [cf. n. 802].

Can. 14. If anyone shall say that man is absolved from his sins and **824** justified, because he believes for certain that he is absolved and justified, or that no one is truly justified but he who believes himself justified, and that by this faith alone absolution and justification are perfected: let him be anathema [cf. n. 802].

Can. 15. If anyone shall say that a man who is born again and justified **825** is bound by faith to believe that he is assuredly in the number of the predestined: let him be anathema [cf. n. 805].

Can. 16. If anyone shall say that he will for certain with an absolute **826** and infallible certainty have that great gift of perseverance up to the end, unless he shall have learned this by a special revelation: let him be anathema [cf. n. 805 ff.].

Can. 17. If anyone shall say that the grace of justification is attained **827** by those only who are predestined unto life, but that all others, who are called, are called indeed, but do not receive grace, as if they are by divine power predestined to evil: let him be anathema [cf. n. 800].

828 Can. 18. If anyone shall say that the commandments of God are even for a man who is justified and confirmed in grace impossible to observe: let him be anathema [cf. n. 804].

829 Can. 19. If anyone shall say that nothing except faith is commanded in the Gospel, that other things are indifferent, neither commanded nor prohibited, but free, or that the ten commandments in no way pertain to Christians: let him be anathema [cf. n. 800].

830 Can. 20. If anyone shall say that a man who is justified and ever so perfect is not bound to observe the commandments of God and the Church, but only to believe, as if indeed the Gospel were a mere absolute promise of eternal life, without the condition of observation of the commandments: let him be anathema [cf. n. 804].

831 Can. 21. If anyone shall say that Christ Jesus has been given by God to men as a Redeemer in whom they should trust, and not also as a legislator, whom they should obey: let him be anathema.

832 Can. 22. If anyone shall say that he who is justified can either persevere in the justice received without the special assistance of God, or that with that [assistance] he cannot: let him be anathema [cf. n. 804, 806].

833 Can. 23. If anyone shall say that a man once justified can sin no more, nor lose grace, and that therefore he who falls and sins was never truly justified; or, on the contrary, that throughout his whole life he can avoid all sins even venial sins, except by a special privilege of God, as the Church holds in regard to the Blessed Virgin: let him be anathema [cf. n. 805, 810].

834 Can. 24. If anyone shall say, that justice received is not preserved and also not increased in the sight of God through good works but that those same works are only the fruits and signs of justification received, but not a cause of its increase: let him be anathema [cf. n. 803].

835 Can. 25. If anyone shall say that in every good work the just one sins at least venially, or (what is more intolerable) mortally, and therefore deserves eternal punishments, and that it is only because God does not impute those works unto damnation that he is not damned, let him be anathema [cf. n. 804].

836 Can. 26. If anyone shall say that the just ought not to expect and hope for an eternal recompense from God and the merit of Jesus Christ for the good works which have been performed in God, if by doing well and in keeping the divine commandments they persevere even to the end: let him be anathema [cf. n. 809].

837 Can. 27. If anyone shall say that there is no mortal sin except that of infidelity, or that grace once received is not lost by any other sin however

grievous and enormous, except the sin of infidelity: let him be anathema [cf. n. 808].

Can. 28. If anyone shall say that together with the loss of grace by sin **838** faith also is always lost, or that the faith that remains is not a true faith, though it be not a living one, or that he, who has faith without charity, is not a Christian: let him be anathema [cf. n. 808].

Can. 29. If anyone shall say that he who has fallen after baptism can- **839** not by the grace of God rise again; or that he can indeed recover lost justice, but by faith alone without the sacrament of penance, contrary to what the holy Roman and universal Church, taught by Christ the Lord and His apostles, has hitherto professed, observed, and taught: let him be anathema [cf. n. 807].

Can. 30. If anyone shall say that after the reception of the grace of **840** justification, to every penitent sinner the guilt is so remitted and the penalty of eternal punishment so blotted out that no penalty of temporal punishment remains to be discharged either in this world or in the world to come in purgatory before the entrance to the kingdom of heaven can be opened: let him be anathema [cf. n. 807].

Can. 31. If anyone shall say that the one justified sins, when he performs **841** good works with a view to an eternal reward: let him be anathema [cf. n. 804].

Can. 32. If anyone shall say that the good works of the man justified **842** are in such a way the gifts of God that they are not also the good merits of him who is justified, or that the one justified by the good works, which are done by him through the grace of God and the merit of Jesus Christ (whose living member he is), does not truly merit increase of grace, eternal life, and the attainment of that eternal life (if he should die in grace), and also an increase of glory: let him be anathema [cf. n. 803 and 809].

Can. 33. If anyone shall say that because of this Catholic doctrine of **843** justification as set forth by the holy Synod in this present decree, there is in some degree a detraction from the glory of God or from the merits of Jesus Christ our Lord, and that the truth of our faith, and in fact the glory of God and of Jesus Christ are not rather rendered illustrious: let him be anathema [cf. n. 810].

Session vii (March 3, 1547)

Foreword [1]

For the completion of the salutary doctrine of justification, which was **843a** promulgated in the last session with the unanimous consent of the Fathers,

---

[1] CTr V 994 f.; Rcht 40 f.; Msi XXXIII 52 A ff.; Hrd X 51 D f.; Bar(Th) ad 1547 n. 36 f. (33, 210 b ff.).

it has seemed fitting to treat of the most holy sacraments of the Church, through which all true justice either begins, or being begun is increased, or being lost is restored. Therefore the holy, ecumenical, and general Synod of Trent lawfully assembled in the Holy Spirit with the same legates of the Apostolic See presiding therein, in order to destroy the errors, and to uproot the heresies concerning these most holy sacraments, which in this stormy period of ours have been both revived from the heresies previously condemned by our Fathers, and also have been invented anew, which are exceedingly detrimental to the purity of the Catholic Church and to the salvation of souls; this Synod in adhering to the teaching of the Holy Scriptures, to the apostolic traditions and to the unanimous opinion of other councils and of the Fathers, has thought it proper to establish and decree these present canons, intending (with the assistance of the divine Spirit) to publish later the remaining which are wanting for the completion of the work begun.

Canons on the Sacraments in General

844   Can. 1. If anyone shall say that the sacraments of the New Law were not all instituted by Jesus Christ our Lord, or that there are more or less than seven, namely baptism, confirmation, Eucharist, penance, extreme unction, order, and matrimony, or even that anyone of these seven is not truly and strictly speaking a sacrament: let him be anathema.

845   Can. 2. If anyone shall say that these same sacraments of the new Law do not differ from the sacraments of the Old Law, except that the ceremonies are different and the outward rites are different: let him be anathema.

846   Can. 3. If anyone shall say that these seven sacraments are equal to each other in such a way that one is not for any reason more worthy than the other: let him be anathema.

847   Can. 4. If anyone shall say that the sacraments of the New Law are not necessary for salvation, but are superfluous, and that, although all are not necessary for every individual, without them or without the desire of them through faith alone men obtain from God the grace of justification; let him be anathema.

848   Can. 5. If anyone shall say that these sacraments have been instituted for the nourishing of faith alone: let him be anathema.

849   Can. 6. If anyone shall say that the sacraments of the New Law do not contain the grace which they signify, or that they do not confer that grace on those who do not place an obstacle in the way, as though they were only outward signs of grace or justice, received through faith, and certain marks of the Christian profession by which the faithful among men are distinguished from the unbelievers: let him be anathema.

Can. 7. If anyone shall say that grace, as far as concerns God's part, is 850 not given through the sacraments always and to all men, even though they receive them rightly, but only sometimes and to some persons: let him be anathema.

Can. 8. If anyone shall say that by the said sacraments of the New 851 Law, grace is not conferred from the work which has been worked [*ex opere operato*], but that faith alone in the divine promise suffices to obtain grace: let him be anathema.

Can. 9. If anyone shall say that in the three sacraments, namely, bap- 852 tism, confirmation, and orders, there is not imprinted on the soul a sign, that is, a certain spiritual and indelible mark, on account of which they cannot be repeated: let him be anathema.

Can. 10. If anyone shall say that all Christians have power to administer 853 the word and all the sacraments: let him be anathema.

Can. 11. If anyone shall say that in ministers, when they effect and 854 confer the sacraments, the intention at least of doing what the Church does is not required: let him be anathema.

Can. 12. If anyone shall say that a minister who is in mortal sin, al- 855 though he observes all the essentials which pertain to the performance or conferring of the sacrament, neither performs nor confers the sacrament: let him be anathema.

Can. 13. If anyone shall say that the received and approved rites of the 856 Catholic Church accustomed to be used in the solemn administration of the sacraments may be disdained or omitted by the minister without sin and at pleasure, or may be changed by any pastor of the churches to other new ones: let him be anathema.

Canons on the Sacrament of Baptism [1]

Can. 1. If anyone shall say that the baptism of John had the same force 857 as the baptism of Christ: let him be anathema.

Can. 2. If anyone shall say that real and natural water is not necessary 858 for baptism, and on that account those words of our Lord Jesus Christ: "Unless a man be born again of water and the Holy Spirit" (John 3:5), are distorted into some sort of metaphor: let him be anathema.

Can. 3. If anyone shall say that in the Roman Church (which is the 859 mother and the teacher of all churches) there is not the true doctrine concerning the sacrament of baptism: let him be anathema.

Can. 4. If anyone shall say that the baptism, which is also given by 860 heretics in the name of the Father and of the Son and of the Holy Spirit, with the intention of doing what the Church does, is not true baptism: let him be anathema.

---

[1] CTr V 595 f.; Rcht 41 f.; Msi XXXIII 53C; Hrd X 53 C f.; Bar(Th) ad 1547 n. 38 f. (33, 211 b f.).

861   Can. 5. If anyone shall say that baptism is optional, that is, not necessary for salvation: let him be anathema [cf. n. 796].

862   Can. 6. If anyone shall say that one who is baptized cannot, even if he wishes, lose grace, however much he may sin, unless he is unwilling to believe: let him be anathema [cf. n. 808].

863   Can. 7. If anyone shall say that those who are baptized are by baptism itself made debtors to faith alone, and not to the observance of the whole law of Christ: let him be anathema [cf. n. 802].

864   Can. 8. If anyone shall say that those baptized are free from all precepts of the holy Church, which are either written or handed down, so that they are not bound to observe them, unless they of their own accord should wish to submit themselves to them: let him be anathema.

865   Can. 9. If anyone shall say that men are to be so recalled to the remembrance of the baptism which they have received, that they understand that all the vows which have been taken after baptism are void by virtue of the promise already made in baptism itself, as if by them they detracted from the faith which they professed, and from the baptism itself: let him be anathema.

866   Can. 10. If anyone shall say that all sins which are committed after baptism are either remitted or made venial by the mere remembrance and the faith of the baptism received: let him be anathema.

867   Can. 11. If anyone shall say that baptism truly and rightly administered must be repeated for him who has denied the faith of Christ among infidels, when he is converted to repentance: let him be anathema.

868   Can. 12. If anyone shall say that no one is to be baptized except at that age at which Christ was baptized, or when at the very point of death, let him be anathema.

869   Can. 13. If anyone shall say that infants, because they have not actual faith, after having received baptism are not to be numbered among the faithful, and therefore, when they have reached the years of discretion, are to be rebaptized, or that it is better that their baptism be omitted than that they, while not believing, by their own act be baptized in the faith of the Church alone: let him be anathema.

870   Can. 14. If anyone shall say that those who have been baptized in this manner as infants, when they have grown up, are to be questioned whether they wish to ratify what the sponsors promised in their name, when they were baptized, and if they should answer that they are not willing, that they must be left to their own will, and that they are not to be forced to a Christian life in the meantime by any other penalty, except that they be excluded from the reception of the Eucharist and of the other sacraments until they repent: let him be anathema.

Canons on the Sacrament of Confirmation [1]

Can. 1. If anyone shall say that the confirmation of those baptized is an 871 empty ceremony and not rather a true and proper sacrament, or that in former times it was nothing more than a kind of catechism, by which those approaching adolescence gave an account of their faith before the Church: let him be anathema.

Can. 2. If anyone shall say that they who ascribe any power to the 872 sacred chrism of confirmation offer an outrage to the Holy Spirit: let him be anathema.

Can. 3. If anyone shall say that the ordinary minister of holy confirma- 873 tion is not the bishop alone, but any simple priest: let him be anathema.

JULIUS III 1550-1555

COUNCIL OF TRENT, continued

Session xiii (Oct. 11, 1551)

Decree On the Most Holy Eucharist [2]

The sacred and holy ecumenical and general Synod of Trent, lawfully 873a assembled in the Holy Spirit with the same legates and nuncios of the Apostolic See presiding therein, although it has convened for this purpose not without the special guidance and direction of the Holy Spirit, namely to publish the true and ancient doctrine concerning faith and the sacraments, and to provide a remedy for all the heresies and other very serious troubles by which the Church of God is at present wretchedly agitated and torn into many different factions, yet from the beginning has had this especially among its desires, to uproot the "cockles" of execrable errors and schisms, which the enemy in these troubled times of our has "sown" [Matt. 13:25 ff.], in the doctrine of the faith, in the use and worship of the sacred Eucharist, which our Savior, moreover, left in His Church as a symbol of that unity and charity with which He wished all Christians to be mutually bound and united. Therefore, this same sacred and holy synod, transmitting that sound and genuine doctrine of this venerable and divine sacrament of the Eucharist, which the Catholic Church, instructed by our Lord Jesus Christ himself and by his Apostles, and taught by the "Holy Spirit who day by day brings to her all truth"

---

[1] CTr V 996; Rcht 47; Msi XXXIII 55A; Hrd X 54 E f.; Bar(Th) ad 1547 n. 40 (33, 212 a).

[2] Rcht 62 f.; Msi XXXIII 8 D f.; Hrd X79 A f.; Bar(Th) ad 51 n. 43 f. (33, 406 b f.).

[John 14:26], has always held and will preserve even to the end of time, forbids all the faithful of Christ hereafter to venture to believe, teach, or preach concerning the Most Holy Eucharist otherwise than is explained and defined in this present decree.

Chap. 1. The Real Presence of our Lord Jesus Christ in the Most Holy Sacrament of the Eucharist

874   First of all the holy Synod teaches and openly and simply professes that in the nourishing sacrament of the Holy Eucharist after the consecration of the bread and wine our Lord Jesus Christ, true God and man, is truly, really, and substantially [can. 1] contained under the species of those sensible things. For these things are not mutually contradictory, that our Savior Himself is always seated at the right hand of the Father in heaven according to the natural mode of existing, and yet that in many other places sacramentally He is present to us in His own substance by that manner of existence which, although we can scarcely express it in words, yet we can, however, by our understanding illuminated by faith, conceive to be possible to God, and which we ought most steadfastly to believe. For thus all our forefathers, as many as were in the true Church of Christ, who have discussed this most holy sacrament, have most openly professed that our Redeemer instituted this so wonderful a sacrament at the Last Supper, when after the blessing of the bread and wine He testified in clear and definite words that He gave them His own body and His own blood; and those words which are recorded [Matt. 26:26 ff.; Mark 14:22; Luke 22:19 ff.] by the holy Evangelists, and afterwards repeated by St. Paul [I Cor. 11:23 ff.], since they contain within themselves that proper and very clear meaning in which they were understood by the Fathers, it is a most disgraceful thing for some contentious and wicked men to distort into fictitious and imaginary figures of speech, by which the real nature of the flesh and blood of Christ is denied, contrary to the universal sense of the Church, which, recognizing with an ever grateful and recollecting mind this most excellent benefit of Christ, as the pillar and ground of truth [I Tim. 3:15], has detested these falsehoods, devised by impious men, as satanical.

Chap. 2. The Reason for the Institution of this Most Holy Sacrament

875   Our Savior, therefore, when about to depart from this world to the Father, instituted this sacrament in which He poured forth, as it were, the riches of His divine love for men, "making a remembrance of his wonderful works" [Ps. 110:4], and He commanded us in the consuming of it to cherish His "memory" [I Cor. 11:24], and "to show forth his death until He come" to judge the world [I Cor. 11:26]. But He wished

that this sacrament be received as the spiritual food of souls [Matt. 26:26], by which they may be nourished and strengthened [can. 5], living by the life of Him who said: "He who eateth me, the same also shall live by me" [John 6:58], and as an antidote, whereby we may be freed from daily faults and be preserved from mortal sins. He wished, furthermore, that this be a pledge of our future glory and of everlasting happiness, and thus be a symbol of that one "body" of which He Himself is the "head" [I Cor. 11:3; Eph. 5:23], and to which He wished us to be united, as members, by the closest bond of faith, hope, and charity, that we might "all speak the same thing and there might be no schisms among us" [cf. I Cor. 1:10].

Chap. 3. The Excellence of the Most Holy Eucharist Over the Other Sacraments

This, indeed, the most Holy Eucharist has in common with the other 876 sacraments, that it is a "symbol of a sacred thing and a visible [1] form of an invisible grace"; but this excellent and peculiar thing is found in it, that the other sacraments first have the power of sanctifying, when one uses them, but in the Eucharist there is the Author of sanctity Himself before it is used [can. 4]. For the apostles had not yet received the Eucharist from the hand of the Lord [Matt. 26:26; Mark 14:22] when He Himself truly said that what He was offering was His body; and this belief has always been in the Church of God, that immediately after the consecration the true body of our Lord and His true blood together with His soul and divinity exist under the species of bread and wine; but the body indeed under the species of bread, and the blood under the species of wine by the force of the words, but the body itself under both by force of that natural connection and concomitance by which the parts of Christ the Lord, "who hath now risen from the dead to die no more" [Rom. 6:9], are mutually united, the divinity also because of that admirable hypostatic union [can. 1 and 3] with His body and soul. Therefore, it is very true that as much is contained under either species as under both. For Christ whole and entire exists under the species of bread and under any part whatsoever of that species, likewise the whole (Christ) is present under the species of wine and under its parts [can. 3].

Chap. 4. Transubstantiation

But since Christ, our Redeemer, has said that that is truly His own 877 body which He offered under the species of bread [cf. Matt. 26:26 ff.; Mark 14:22 ff.; Luke 22:19 ff.; I Cor. 11:24 ff.], it has always been a matter of conviction in the Church of God, and now this holy Synod declares it again, that by the consecration of the bread and wine a con-

---

[1] CIC Decr. Grat. III, *De consecr.* II, c. Sacrificium 32: Frdbg. I 1324; Rcht. I 1156; cf. St. Aug., *Quaest. in Hept.* 3, 84 (ML 34, 712).

version takes place of the whole substance of bread into the substance of the body of Christ our Lord, and of the whole substance of the wine into the substance of His blood. This conversion is appropriately and properly called transubstantiation by the Catholic Church [can. 2].

Chap. 5. The Worship and Veneration to be Shown to this Most Holy Sacrament

878   There is, therefore, no room left for doubt that all the faithful of Christ in accordance with a custom always received in the Catholic Church offer in veneration [can. 6] the worship of *latria* which is due to the true God, to this most Holy Sacrament. For it is not less to be adored because it was instituted by Christ the Lord to be received [cf. Matt. 26:26 ff.]. For we believe that same God to be present therein, of whom the eternal Father when introducing Him into the world says: "And let all the Angels of God adore Him" [Heb. 1:6; Ps. 96:7], whom the Magi "falling down adored" [cf. Matt. 2:11], who finally, as the Scripture testifies [cf. Matt. 28:17], was adored by the apostles in Galilee. The holy Synod declares, moreover, that this custom was piously and religiously introduced into the Church of God, so that this sublime and venerable sacrament was celebrated every year on a special feast day with extraordinary veneration and solemnity, and was borne reverently and with honor in processions through the streets and public places. For it is most proper that some holy days be established when all Christians may testify, with an extraordinary and unusual expression, that their minds are grateful to and mindful of their common Lord and Redeemer for such an ineffable and truly divine a favor whereby the victory and triumph of His death is represented. And thus, indeed, ought victorious truth to celebrate a triumph over falsehood and heresy, that her adversaries, placed in view of so much splendor and amid such deep joy of the universal Church, may either vanish weakened and broken, or overcome and confounded by shame may some day recover their senses.

Chap. 6. The Reservation of the Sacrament of the Holy Eucharist and Bearing it to the Sick

879   The custom of reserving the Holy Eucharist in a holy place is so ancient that even the age of the NICENE Council recognized it. Moreover, the injunction that the sacred Eucharist be carried to the sick, and be carefully reserved for this purpose in the churches, besides being in conformity with the greatest equity and reason, is also found in many councils, and has been observed according to a very ancient custom of the Catholic Church. Therefore this holy Synod decrees that this salutary and necessary custom be by all means retained [can. 7].

Chap. 7. The Preparation that Must be Employed to Receive the Holy Eucharist Worthily

If it is not becoming for anyone to approach any of the sacred functions   880
except solemnly, certainly, the more the holiness and the divinity of this
heavenly sacrament is understood by a Christian, the more diligently
ought he to take heed lest he approach to receive it without great reverence and holiness [can. 11], especially when we read in the Apostle those
words full of terror: "He that eateth and drinketh unworthily, eateth
and drinketh judgment to himself not discerning the body of the Lord"
[I Cor. 11:29]. Therefore, the precept, "Let a man prove himself" [I Cor.
11:28], must be recalled to mind by him who wishes to communicate.
Now ecclesiastical usage declares that this examination is necessary, that
no one conscious of mortal sin, however contrite he may seem to himself,
should approach the Holy Eucharist without a previous sacramental confession. This, the holy Synod has decreed, is always to be observed by all
Christians, even by those priests on whom by their office it may be incumbent to celebrate, provided the recourses of a confessor be not lacking to them. But if in an urgent necessity a priest should celebrate without
previous confession, let him confess as soon as possible [see n. 1138 ff.].

Chap. 8. The Use of the Admirable Sacrament

As to its use our Fathers have rightly and wisely distinguished three   881
ways of receiving this Holy Sacrament. For they have taught that some
receive it sacramentally only, as sinners; others only spiritually, namely
those who eating with desire the heavenly bread set before them, by a
living faith, "which worketh by charity" [Gal. 5:6], perceive its fruit
and usefulness; while the third receive it both sacramentally and spiritually [can. 8]; and these are they who so prove and prepare themselves
previously that "clothed with the wedding garment" [Matt. 22:11 ff.],
they approach this divine table. Now as to the reception of the sacrament
it has always been the custom in the Church of God for the laity to receive
communion from the priests, but that the priests when celebrating should
communicate themselves [can. 10]; this custom proceeding from an
apostolical tradition should with reason and justice be retained.

And finally this holy Synod with paternal affection admonishes, exhorts,   882
entreats, and beseeches, "through the bowels of the mercy of our God"
[Luke 1:78], that each and all, who are classed under the Christian name,
will now finally agree and be of the same opinion in this "sign of unity,"
in this "bond of charity," [1] in this symbol of concord, and that mindful
of so great a majesty and such boundless love of our Lord Jesus Christ,
who gave His own beloved soul as the price of our salvation, and gave

---

[1] Cf. St. August., *In Io*. tract. 26, 13 [ML 35, 1612].

us His "own flesh to eat" [John 6:48 ff.], they may believe and venerate these sacred mysteries of His body and blood with that constancy and firmness of faith, with that devotion of soul, that piety and worship, as to be able to receive frequently that "supersubstantial bread" [Matt. 6:11], and that it may be to them truly the life of the soul and the perpetual health of mind, that being invigorated by the strength thereof [III Kings 19:8], after the journey of this miserable pilgrimage, they may be able to arrive in their heavenly country to eat without any veil that same bread of angels [Ps. 77:25] which they now eat under the sacred veils.

But whereas it is not enough to declare the truth, unless errors be exposed and repudiated, it has seemed good to the holy Synod to subjoin these canons, so that all, now that the Catholic doctrine has been made known, may also understand what heresies are to be avoided and guarded against.

Canons on the Most Holy Sacrament of the Eucharist [1]

883   Can. 1. If anyone denies that in the sacrament of the most holy Eucharist there are truly, really, and substantially contained the body and blood together with the soul and divinity of our Lord Jesus Christ, and therefore the whole Christ, but shall say that He is in it as by a sign or figure, or force, let him be anathema [cf. n. 874, 876].

884   Can. 2. If anyone says that in the sacred and holy sacrament of the Eucharist there remains the substance of bread and wine together with the body and blood of our Lord Jesus Christ, and denies that wonderful and singular conversion of the whole substance of the bread into the body, and of the entire substance of the wine into the blood, the species of the bread and wine only remaining, a change which the Catholic Church most fittingly calls transubstantiation: let him be anathema [cf. n. 877].

885   Can. 3. If anyone denies that the whole Christ is contained in the venerable sacrament of the Eucharist under each species and under every part of each species, when the separation has been made: let him be anathema [cf. n. 876].

886   Can. 4. If anyone says that after the completion of the consecration that the body and blood of our Lord Jesus Christ is not in the marvelous sacrament of the Eucharist, but only in use, while it is taken, not however before or after, and that in the hosts or consecrated particles, which are reserved or remain after communion, the true body of the Lord does not remain: let him be anathema [cf. n. 876].

887   Can. 5. If anyone says that the special fruit of the most Holy Eucharist

---

[1] Rcht 66 f.; Msi XXXIII 84 C f.; Hrd X 83 A f.; Bar(Th) ad 1551 n. 50 (33, 409 a f.).

is the remission of sins, or that from it no other fruits are produced: let him be anathema [cf. 875].

Can. 6: If anyone says that in the holy sacrament of the Eucharist the 888 only-begotten Son of God is not to be adored even outwardly with the worship of *latria* (the act of adoration), and therefore not to be venerated with a special festive celebration, nor to be borne about in procession according to the praiseworthy and universal rite and custom of the holy Church, or is not to be set before the people publicly to be adored, and that the adorers of it are idolators: let him be anathema [cf. n. 878].

Can. 7. If anyone says that it is not lawful that the Holy Eucharist be 889 reserved in a sacred place, but must necessarily be distributed immediately after the consecration among those present; or that it is not permitted to bring it to the sick with honor: let him be anathema [cf. n. 879].

Can. 8. If anyone says that Christ received in the Eucharist is received 890 only spiritually, and not also sacramentally and in reality: let him be anathema [cf. n. 881].

Can. 9. If anyone denies that all and each of the faithful of Christ of 891 both sexes, when they have reached the years of discretion, are bound every year to communicate at least at Easter according to the precept of holy mother Church: let him be anathema [cf. n. 437].

Can. 10. If anyone says that it is not lawful for a priest celebrating to 892 communicate himself: let him be anathema [cf. n. 881].

Can. 11. If anyone says that faith alone is sufficient preparation for 893 receiving the sacrament of the most Holy Eucharist: let him be anathema. And that so great a Sacrament may not be unworthily received, and therefore unto death and condemnation, this holy Council ordains and declares that sacramental confession must necessarily be made beforehand by those whose conscience is burdened by mortal sin, however contrite they may consider themselves. If anyone moreover teaches the contrary or preaches or obstinately asserts, or even publicly by disputation shall presume to defend the contrary, by that fact itself he is excommunicated [cf. n. 880].

SESSION XIV (Nov. 25, 1551)

Doctrine on the Sacrament of Penance [1]

The holy ecumenical and general council of Trent, lawfully assembled 893a in the Holy Spirit with the same delegate and nuncios of the Holy Apostolic See presiding, although for a necessary reason much discussion on the sacrament of penance has been introduced in the decree on justification [see n. 807, 839], because of the kindred nature of the subjects,

---

[1] Rcht 75 ff.; Msi XXXIII 91 D ff.; Hrd X 89 E ff.; Bar(Th) ad 1551 n. 56 ff. (33, 412 a ff.).

nevertheless so great is the number of errors of various kinds about this sacrament in this our age that it will be no small public advantage to have handed down a more exact and fuller definition, in which, after all errors have been displayed and refuted, Catholic truth should become clear and manifest; and this truth which this holy synod now proposes is to be preserved for all time by all Christians.

Chap. 1. The Necessity and Institution of the Sacrament of Penance

894　If in all who have been regenerated, there were this gratitude toward God, so that they would constantly safeguard the justice received in baptism by His bounty and His grace, there would have been no need to institute [can. 2] another sacrament besides baptism for the remission of sins. But "since God, rich in mercy" [Eph. 2:4] "knoweth our frame" [Ps. 102:14], He offers a remedy of life even to those who may afterwards have delivered themselves to the servitude of sin, and to the power of Satan, namely, the sacrament of penance [can. 1], by which the benefit of the death of Christ is applied to those who have fallen after baptism. Penance has indeed been necessary for all men, who at any time whatever have stained themselves with mortal sin, in order to attain grace and justice, even for those who have desired to be cleansed by the sacrament of baptism, so that their perversity being renounced and amended, they might detest so great an offense against God with a hatred of sin and a sincere sorrow of heart. Therefore, the Prophet says: "Be converted and do penance for all your iniquities; and iniquity shall not be your ruin" [Ezech. 18:30]. The Lord also said: "Except you do penance, you shall all likewise perish" [Luke 13:3]. And the prince of the apostles, Peter, recommending penance to sinners about to receive baptism said: "Do penance and be baptized every one of you" [Acts 2:38]. Moreover, neither before the coming of Christ was penance a sacrament, nor is it after His coming to anyone before baptism. But the Lord instituted the sacrament of penance then especially, when after His resurrection from the dead He breathed upon His disciples, saying: "Receive ye the Holy Spirit: whose sins you shall forgive, they are forgiven them, and whose sins you shall retain, they are retained" [John 20:22]. In this act so significant and by words so clear, the consensus of all the Fathers has always recognized that the power of forgiving and retaining sins had been communicated to the apostles and their legitimate successors for reconciling the faithful who have fallen after baptism [can. 37], and that with good reason the Catholic Church has repudiated and condemned as heretics the Novatians, at one time stubbornly denying the power of forgiveness. Therefore, this holy Council, approving and receiving this true meaning of these words of the Lord, condemns the false interpretations of those who, contrary to the institution of this sacrament, falsely distort those words to the power of preaching the word of God and of announcing the Gospel of Christ.

Chap. 2. The Difference Between the Sacrament of Penance and that of Baptism

Moreover, it is clear that this sacrament differs in many respects from 895 baptism [can. 2]. For aside from the fact that in the matter and form, by which the essence of a sacrament is effected, it differs very widely, it is certainly clear that the minister of baptism need not be a judge, since the Church exercises judgment on no one who has not first entered it through the gateway of baptism. "For what have I to do," says St. Paul, "to judge them that are without?" [I Cor. 5:12]. It is otherwise with those of the household of the faith, whom Christ the Lord by the laver of "baptism" has once made "members of his own body" [I Cor. 12:13]. For these, if they should afterwards have defiled themselves by some crime, He did not now wish to have cleansed by the repetition of baptism, since that is in no way permitted in the Catholic Church, but to be placed, as it were, as culprits before the tribunal, so that by the sentence of the priests they may be freed not only once, but as often as they, repentant for the sins committed, have had recourse to Him. Furthermore, the fruit of baptism is one thing; that of penance is another thing. For by putting on Christ by baptism [Gal. 3:27], we are made an entirely new creature in Him, obtaining a full and complete remission of all sins, to which newness and integrity, however, we can in no way arrive by the sacrament of penance without many tears and labors on our part, for divine justice demands this, so that penance has justly been called by the holy Fathers, "a laborious kind of baptism." This sacrament of penance, moreover, is necessary for the salvation of those who have fallen after baptism, as baptism itself is for those as yet not regenerated [can. 6].

Chap. 3. The Parts and Fruits of the Sacrament of Penance

Furthermore, the holy Council teaches that the form of the sacrament 896 of penance, in which its force chiefly consists, is set down in these words of the minister: "I absolve thee, etc."; to which indeed certain prayers are laudably added according to the custom of holy Church; yet in no way do they pertain to the essence of this form, nor are they necessary for the administration of the sacrament. The matter, as it were, of this sacrament, on the other hand, consists in the acts of the penitent himself, namely contrition, confession, and satisfaction [can. 4]. These, inasmuch as by the institution of God they are required in the penitent for the integrity of the sacrament for the full and perfect remission of sins, are for this reason called the parts of penance. The reality and *effectus* of this sacrament, however, so far as concerns its force and efficacy, is reconciliation with God, which at times in pious persons and in those who receive this sacrament with devotion is wont to be followed by peace of conscience and serenity with an exceedingly great consolation of spirit. The holy Council, while recording these matters regarding the parts and effect of this sacrament, condemns the opinions of those who maintain that the parts of penance are the terrors of conscience and faith [can. 4].

Chap. 4. Contrition

897   Contrition, which has the first place among the aforementioned acts of the penitent, is a sorrow of the soul and a detestation of sin committed, with a determination of not sinning in the future. This feeling of contrition is, moreover, necessary at all times to obtain the forgiveness of sins, and thus for a person who has fallen after baptism it especially prepares for the remission of sins, if it is united with trust in divine mercy and with the desire of performing the other things required to receive this sacrament correctly. The holy Synod, therefore, declares that this contrition includes not only cessation from sin and a resolution and a beginning of a new life, but also hatred of the old, according to this statement: "Cast away from you all your transgressions, by which you have transgressed, and make to yourselves a new heart and a new spirit" [Ezech. 18:31]. And certainly, he who has considered those lamentations of the saints: "To Thee only have I sinned, and have done evil before Thee" [Ps. 50:6]; "I have labored in my groanings; I shall wash my bed every night" [Ps. 6:7]; "I will recount to Thee all my years in the bitterness of my soul" [Isa. 38:15], and others of this kind, will readily understand that they emanate from a certain vehement hatred of past life and from a profound detestation of sins.

898   The Council teaches, furthermore, that though it sometimes happens that this contrition is perfect because of charity and reconciles man to God, before this sacrament is actually received, this reconciliation nevertheless must not be ascribed to the contrition itself without the desire of the sacrament which is included in it. That imperfect contrition [can. 5] which is called attrition, since it commonly arises either from the consideration of the baseness of sin or from fear of hell and its punishments, if it renounces the desire of sinning with the hope of pardon, the Synod declares, not only does not make a person a hypocrite and a greater sinner, but is even a gift of God and an impulse of the Holy Spirit, not indeed as already dwelling in the penitent, but only moving him, assisted by which the penitent prepares a way for himself unto justice. And though without the sacrament of penance it cannot *per se* lead the sinner to justification, nevertheless it does dispose him to obtain the grace of God

in the sacrament of penance. For the Ninivites, struck in a salutary way by this fear in consequence of the preaching of Jonas which was full of terror, did penance and obtained mercy from the Lord [cf. Jonas 3]. For this reason, therefore, do some falsely accuse Catholic writers, as if they taught that the sacrament of penance confers grace without any pious endeavor on the part of those who receive it, a thing which the Church of God has never taught or pronounced. Moreover, they also falsely teach that contrition is extorted and forced, and that it is not free and voluntary [can. 5].

Chap. 5. Confession

From the institution of the sacrament of penance as already explained **899** the universal Church has always understood that the complete confession of sins was also instituted by our Lord, [Jas. 5:16; I John 1:9; (Luke 17:14)], and by divine law is necessary for all who have fallen after baptism [can. 7], because our Lord Jesus Christ, when about to ascend from earth to heaven, left behind Him priests as His own vicars [Matt. 16:19; 18:18; John 20:23], as rulers and judges, to whom all the mortal sins into which the faithful of Christ may have fallen should be brought, so that they in virtue of the power of the keys may pronounce the sentence of remission or retention of sins. For it is evident that priests could not have exercised this judgment without a knowledge of the matter, nor could they indeed have observed justice in imposing penalties, if the faithful had declared their sins in general only, and not specifically and one by one. From this it is gathered that all mortal sins of which they have knowledge after a careful self-examination must be enumerated in confession by the penitents, even though they are most secret and have been committed only against the two last precepts of the decalogue [Exod. 20:17; Matt. 5:28], sins which sometimes wound the soul more grievously, and are more dangerous than those which are committed openly. For venial sins, by which we are not excluded from the grace of God and into which we fall more frequently, although they may rightly and profitably and without any presumption be declared in confession [can. 7], as the practice of pious persons indicates, may be passed over in silence without guilt and may be expiated by many other remedies. But since all mortal sins, even those of thought, make men children of wrath [Eph. 2:3] and enemies of God, it is necessary to ask pardon for all of them from God by an open and humble confession. While, therefore, the faithful of Christ strive to confess all sins which occur to their memory, they undoubtedly lay all of them before the divine mercy to be forgiven [can. 7]. While those who do otherwise and knowingly conceal certain sins, lay nothing before the divine bounty for forgiveness by the priest. "For if one who is ill is ashamed to make known his wound to the physician, the physician does not remedy what he does not know." [1] Furthermore, it is gathered that those circumstances also must be explained in confession, which alter the species of the sin, [can. 7], because without them the sins themselves are neither honestly revealed by the penitents, nor are they known to the judges, and it would not be possible for them to judge rightly the gravity of the crimes and to impose the punishment which is proper to those penitents. Hence it is unreasonable to teach that these circumstances have been conjured up by idle men, or that one circumstance only must be confessed, namely to have sinned against a brother.

900   But it is also impious to say that a confession, which is ordered to be made in this manner [can. 8] is impossible, or to call it a torture of conscience; for it is clear that in the Church nothing else is exacted of the penitents than that each one, after he has carefully examined himself and searched all the nooks and recesses of his conscience, confess those sins by which he recalls that he has mortally offended his Lord and God; moreover, the other sins which do not occur to him after diligent thought, are understood to be included in a general way in the same confession; for these sins we trustingly say with the Prophet: "From my hidden sins cleanse me, O Lord" [Ps. 18:13]. But, truly, the difficulty of such confession and the shame of disclosing the sins might appear a burdensome matter indeed, if it were not alleviated by so many and such great advantages and consolations which are most certainly bestowed by absolution upon all those who approach this sacrament worthily.

901   Moreover, as regards the manner of confessing secretly to a priest alone, although Christ has not prohibited that one confess sins publicly in expiation for his crimes and for his own humiliation, and as an example to others, as well as for the edification of the Church offended, yet this is not commanded by divine precept, nor would it be advisedly enjoined by any human law that offenses, especially secret ones, be disclosed by a public confession [can. 6]. Therefore, since secret sacramental confession, which the holy Church has used from the beginning and which she still uses, has always been recommended by the most holy and most ancient Fathers in emphatic and unanimous agreement, the empty calumny of those who do not fear to teach that this is foreign to the divine mandate and is a human invention, and that it had its origin in the Fathers assembled in the Lateran Council [can. 8] is manifestly disproved; for neither did the Church through the Lateran Council decree that the faithful of Christ should confess, a matter which she recognized was necessary and instituted by divine law, but that the precept of confession should be fulfilled at least once a year by each and all, when they

---

[1] St. Jerome, *In Eccl. comm.* 10, 11 [ML 23, 1096].

have reached the years of discretion. Hence, this salutary custom of confessing to the great benefit of souls is now observed in the whole Church during that sacred and especially acceptable time of Lent, a custom which this holy Council completely approves and sanctions as pious and worthy to be retained [can. 8; see n. 427 f.].

Chap. 6. *The Minister of this Sacrament and Absolution*

With regard to the minister of this sacrament the holy Synod declares 902 false and entirely foreign to the truth of the Gospel all doctrines which perniciously extend the ministry of the keys to any other men besides bishops and priests [can. 10], believing that those words of the Lord: "Whatsoever you shall bind upon earth, shall be bound also in heaven, and whatsoever you shall loose upon earth, shall be loosed also in heaven" [Matt. 18:18], and "Whose sins you shall forgive, they are forgiven them, and whose sins you shall retain, they are retained" [John 20:23], were indifferently and indiscriminately addressed to all the faithful of Christ contrary to the institution of this sacrament, so that anyone may have the power of remitting sins, public sins by way of rebuke, if the rebuked acquiesces, and secret ones through a voluntary confession made to anyone. It also teaches that even priests who are bound by mortal sin exercise as ministers of Christ the office of forgiving sins by virtue of the Holy Spirit conferred in ordination, and that they are of an erroneous opinion who contend that this power does not exist in bad priests. However, although the absolution of the priest is the dispensation of the benefaction of another, yet it is not a bare ministry only, either of announcing the Gospel or declaring the forgiveness of sins, but it is equivalent to a judicial act, by which sentence is pronounced by him as if by a judge [can. 9]. And, therefore, the penitent should not so flatter himself on his own faith as to think that even though he have no contrition, and that the intention of acting earnestly and absolving effectively be wanting in the priest, nevertheless he is truly and before God absolved by reason of his faith alone. For faith without penance effects no remission of sins, and he would be most negligent of his own salvation, who would know that a priest was absolving him in a jesting manner, and would not earnestly consult another who would act seriously.

Chap. 7. *The Reservation of Cases*

Therefore, since the nature and essence of a judgment require that 903 the sentence be imposed only on subjects, there has always been the conviction in the Church of God, and this Synod confirms it as most true, that this absolution which the priest pronounces upon one over whom he has no ordinary or delegated jurisdiction has no value. It seemed to be a matter of very great importance to our most holy Fathers for the discipline of the Christian people that certain more atrocious and grave crimes should be absolved not by anyone indiscriminately, but only by the highest priests. Hence the sovereign Pontiffs, by virtue of the supreme power given them in the universal Church, could rightfully reserve to their own exclusive judgment certain more serious cases of crimes. Neither should it be a matter of doubt, since all things which are from God are well ordered, that the same may lawfully be done by all bishops each in his own diocese, "to edification," however, "not to destruction" [II Cor. 13:10], by virtue of the authority over their subjects given to them above other priests inferior in rank, especially with regard to those crimes to which the censure of excommunication is attached. That this reservation of crimes has force not only in external administration, but also in the sight of God is in accord with divine authority [can. 11]. But lest anyone perish on this account, it has always been piously observed in the same Church of God that there be no reservation at the moment of death, and that all priests, therefore, may in that case absolve all penitents from any sins and censures whatsoever; and since outside this moment priests have no power in reserved cases, let them strive to persuade penitents to this one thing, that they approach their superiors and lawful judges for the benefit of absolution.

Chap. 8. The Necessity and Fruit of Satisfaction

904   Finally with regard to satisfaction, which of all the parts of penance has been recommended by our Fathers to the Christian people in all ages, and which is especially assailed in our day under the pretext of piety by those who "have an appearance of piety, but who have denied the power thereof" [II Tim. 3:51], the holy Synod declares that it is absolutely false and contrary to the word of God that the guilt is never forgiven by the Lord without the entire punishment also being remitted [can. 12, 15]. For clear and illustrious examples are found in the Sacred Writings [cf. Gen. 3:16 f.; Num. 12:14 f.; 20:11 f.; II Kings 12:13 f., etc.], besides which divine tradition refutes this error with all possible clarity. Indeed the nature of divine justice seems to demand that those who have sinned through ignorance before baptism may be received into grace in one manner, and in another those who at one time freed from the servitude of sin and the devil, and on receiving the gift of the Holy Spirit, did not fear to "violate the temple of God knowingly" [I Cor. 3:17], "and to grieve the Holy Spirit" [Eph. 4:30]. And it befits divine clemency that sins be not thus pardoned us without any satisfaction, lest, seizing the occasion [Rom. 7:8], and considering sins trivial, we, offering injury and "affront to the Holy Spirit" [Heb. 10:29], fall into graver ones, "treasuring up to ourselves wrath against the day of wrath" [Rom. 2:5; Jas. 5:3]. For, without doubt, these satisfactions greatly restrain

from sin, and as by a kind of rein act as a check, and make penitents more cautious and vigilant in the future; they also remove the remnants of sin, and destroy vicious habits acquired by living evilly through acts contrary to virtue. Neither was there ever in the Church of God any way considered more secure for warding off impending punishment by the Lord than that men perform these works of penance [Matt. 3:28; 4:17; 11:21 etc.] with true sorrow of soul. Add to this that, while we suffer by making satisfaction for our sins, we are made conformable to Christ Jesus, "who made satisfaction for our sins" [Rom. 5:10; I John 2:1 f.], from whom is all our sufficiency [II Cor. 3:5], having also a most certain pledge from Him that "if we suffer with Him, we shall also be glorified" [cf. Rom. 8:17]. Neither is this satisfaction which we discharge for our sins so much our own as it is through Jesus Christ; for we who can do nothing of ourselves, as if of ourselves, with the cooperation "of Him who" comforts us, "we can do all things." Thus man has not wherein to glory; but all "our glorying" [cf. I Cor. 31; II Cor. 10:17; Gal. 6:14] is in Christ, "in whom we live, in whom we move" [cf. Acts 17:28], in whom we make satisfaction, "bringing forth fruits worthy of penance" [Luke 3:8] which have their efficacy from Him, by Him are offered to the Father, and through Him are accepted by the Father [can. 13 f.].

The priests of the Lord ought, therefore, so far as the spirit and pru- 905 dence suggest, to enjoin salutary and suitable satisfactions, in keeping with the nature of the crimes and the ability of the penitents, lest, if they should connive at sins and deal too leniently with penitents, by the imposition of certain very light works for grave offenses, they might become participators in the crimes of others [cf. I Tim. 5:22]. Moreover, let them keep before their eyes that the satisfaction which they impose be not only for the safeguarding of a new life and a remedy against infirmity, but also for the atonement and chastisement of past sins; for the ancient Fathers both believe and teach that the keys of the priests were bestowed not only to loose, but also to bind [cf. Matt. 16:19; John 20:23; can. 15]. Nor did they therefore think that the sacrament of penance is a tribunal of wrath or of punishments; as no Catholic ever understood that from our satisfactions of this kind the nature of the merit and satisfaction of our Lord Jesus Christ is either obscured or in any way diminished; when the Innovators wish to observe this, they teach that the best penance is a new life, in order to take away all force and practice of satisfaction [can. 13].

Chap. 9. The Works of Satisfaction

It teaches furthermore that so great is the liberality of the divine 906 munificence that not only by punishments voluntarily undertaken by us in atonement for sin can we make satisfaction to God the Father through Jesus Christ, or by punishments imposed by the judgment of the priest according to the measure of our offense, but also, (and this is the greatest proof of love) by the temporal afflictions imposed by God and patiently borne by us [can. 13].

The Doctrine of the Sacrament of Extreme Unction [1]

907   It has seemed fit to the holy Synod to add to the preceding doctrine on penance the following matters concerning the sacrament of extreme unction, which was considered by the Fathers [2] the consummation not only of penance, but also of the whole Christian life which should be a perpetual penance. In the first place, therefore, as regards its institution it declares and teaches that our most clement Redeemer, who wished that a provision be made for salutary remedies at all times for His servants against all the weapons of all enemies, just as He made provision for the greatest aids in other sacraments by which Christians, as long as they live, can preserve themselves free from every very grave spiritual injury, so He fortified the end of life with, as it were, the most powerful defense, by the sacrament of extreme unction [can. 1]. For, although "our adversary seeks" and seizes throughout our entire life occasions "to devour" [I Pet. 5:8] our souls in every manner, yet there is no time when he directs more earnestly all the strength of his cunning to ruin us completely, and if possible to drive us also from faith in the divine mercy, than when he sees that the end of life is upon us.

Chap. 1. The Institution of the Sacrament of Extreme Unction

908   This sacred unction for the sick, however, was instituted by Christ our Lord as truly and properly a sacrament of the New Testament, alluded to in Mark [Mark 6:13], indeed, but recommended to the faithful and promulgated by James the Apostle and brother of the Lord [can. 1]. "Is any man," he says, "sick among you?" "Let him bring in the priests of the Church, and let them pray over him, anointing him with oil in the name of the Lord and the prayer of faith shall save the sick man, and the Lord shall raise him up; and if he be in sins, they shall be forgiven him" [Jas. 5:14, 15]. In these words, as the Church has learned from apostolic tradition transmitted from hand to hand, he teaches the matter, form, proper ministration, and effect of this salutary sacrament. For the Church has understood that the matter is the oil blessed by the bishop, since the unction very appropriately represents the grace of the Holy

---

[1] Rcht 81 ff.; Msi XXXIII 97 E ff.; Hrd X 96 A f; Bar(Th) ad 1551 n. 59 (33, 413 b).

[2] St. Thomas, *C. gent.*, 4, 73.

Spirit, with which the soul of the sick person is visibly anointed; and that these words are the form: "By this anointing, etc."

Chap. 2. The Effect of the Sacrament

Furthermore, the significance and effect of this sacrament are explained **909** in these words: "And the prayer of faith shall save the sick man, and the Lord shall raise him up, and if he be in sins they shall be forgiven him" [Jas. 5:15]. For the thing signified is the grace of the Holy Spirit, whose anointing wipes away sins, if there be any still to be expiated, and the remains of sin, and relieves, and strengthens the soul of the sick person [can. 2] by exciting in him great confidence in divine mercy, supported by which the sick person bears more lightly the miseries and pains of his illness, and resists more easily the temptations of the evil spirit who "lies in wait for his heel" [Gen. 3:150], and sometimes attains bodily health, when it is expedient for the salvation of the soul.

Chap. 3. The Minister of this Sacrament and the Time When it Should be Administered

And now, as regards the prescribing of those who can receive and **910** administer this sacrament, this, too, was clearly expressed in the words above. For it is also indicated there that the proper ministers of this sacrament are the presbyters of the Church [can. 4], under which name in that place are to be understood not the elders by age or the foremost in rank among the people, but either bishops or priests duly ordained by them with the "imposition of the hands of the priesthood" [I Tim. 4:14; can. 4]. It is also declared that this unction is to be applied to the infirm, but especially to those who are so dangerously ill that they seem to be facing the end of life, for which reason it is also called the sacrament of the dying. But if the sick should recover after the reception of this sacrament of extreme unction, they can with the aid of this sacrament be strengthened again, when they fall into another similar crisis of life. Therefore, under no condition are they to be listened to, who contrary to so open and clear a statement of the Apostle James [Jas. 5:14] teach that this unction is either a figment of the imagination or a rite received from the Fathers, having neither a command of God nor a promise of grace [can. 1]; and likewise those who assert that this has now ceased, as though it were to be referred to the grace of healing only in the primitive Church; and those who maintain that the rite and practice which the holy Roman Church observes in the administration of this sacrament are opposed to the thought of James the Apostle, and therefore ought to be changed to another; and finally, those who affirm that this extreme unction may be contemned by the faithful without sin [can. 3]. For all these things very manifestly disagree with the clear words of this great Apostle. Nor, indeed, does the Roman Church, the mother and teacher of all others, observe anything else in the administration of this unction with reference to those matters which constitute the substance of this sacrament than what the blessed James has prescribed. Nor, indeed, could there be contempt for so great a sacrament without grievous sin and offense to the Holy Spirit.

These are the things which this sacred ecumenical Synod professes and teaches concerning the sacraments of penance and extreme unction, and it sets them forth to be believed and held by all the faithful of Christ. Moreover, the following canons, it says, must be inviolately observed, and it condemns and anathematizes forever those who assert the contrary.

Canons On the Sacrament of Penance [1]

911   Can. 1. If anyone says that in the Catholic Church penance is not truly and properly a sacrament instituted by Christ our Lord to reconcile the faithful, as often as they fall into sin after baptism: let him be anathema [cf. n. 894].

912   Can. 2. If anyone, confusing the sacraments, says that baptism itself is the sacrament of penance, as though these two sacraments are not distinct, and that therefore penance is not rightly called "a second plank after shipwreck": let him be anathema [cf. n. 894].

913   Can. 3. If anyone says that those words of the Lord Savior: "Receive ye the Holy Ghost; whose sins you shall forgive, they are forgiven them; and whose sins ye shall retain, they are retained" [John 20:22 f.], are not to be understood of the power of remitting and retaining sins in the sacrament of penance, as the Catholic Church has always understood from the beginning, but, contrary to the institution of this sacrament, distorts them to an authority for preaching the Gospel: let him be anathema [cf. n. 894].

914   Can. 4. If anyone denies that for the full and perfect remission of sins there are three acts required on the part of the penitent, as it were, the matter of the sacrament of penance, namely contrition, confession, and satisfaction, which are called the three parts of penance; or says, that there are only two parts of penance, namely the terrors of a troubled conscience because of the consciousness of sin, and the faith received from the Gospel or from absolution, by which one believes that his sins have been forgiven him through Christ: let him be anathema [cf. n. 896].

915   Can. 5. If anyone says that this contrition, which is evoked by examination, recollection, and hatred of sins "whereby one recalls his years in

---

[1] Rcht 83 ff.; Msi XXXIII 99 C ff.; Hrd X 97 D ff.; Bar(Th) ad 1551 n. 59 (33, 414 a ff.).

the bitterness of his soul" [Isa. 38:15], by pondering on the gravity of one's sins, the multitude, the baseness, the loss of eternal happiness, and the incurring of eternal damnation, together with the purpose of a better life, is not a true and a beneficial sorrow, and does not prepare for grace, but makes a man a hypocrite, and a greater sinner; finally that this sorrow is forced and not free and voluntary: let him be anathema [cf. n. 898].

Can. 6. If anyone denies that sacramental confession was either in- **916** stituted by divine law or is necessary for salvation; or says that the manner of secretly confessing to a priest alone, which the Catholic Church has always observed from the beginning and still observes, is alien to the institution and the mandate of Christ, and is a human invention: let him be anathema [cf. n. 899 f.].

Can. 7. If anyone says that in the sacrament of penance it is not **917** necessary by divine law for the remission of sins to confess each and all mortal sins, of which one has remembrance after a due and diligent examination, even secret ones and those which are against the two last precepts of the decalogue, and the circumstances which alter the nature of sin; but that this confession is useful only for the instruction and consolation of the penitent, and formerly was observed only for imposing a canonical satisfaction; or says, that they who desire to confess all their sins wish to leave nothing to be pardoned by divine mercy; or, finally, that it is not lawful to confess venial sins: let him be anathema [cf. n. 899-901].

Can. 8. If anyone says that the confession of all sins as the Church **918** observes is impossible, and is a human tradition to be abolished by the pious, or that each and all of the faithful of Christ of either sex are not bound to it once a year, according to the constitution of the great Lateran Council, and for this reason the faithful of Christ must be persuaded not to confess during the Lenten season; let him be anathema [cf. n. 900 f.].

Can. 9. If anyone says that the sacramental absolution of the priest **919** is not a judicial act, but an empty service of pronouncing and declaring to the one confessing that his sins are forgiven, provided only that he believes that he has been absolved, or [1] even if the priest does not absolve seriously, but in jest; or says that the confession of the penitent is not required, so that the priest may be able to absolve him: let him be anathema [cf. n. 902].

Can. 10. If anyone says that priests who are in mortal sin do not **920** have the power of binding and loosing, or, that not only priests are the ministers of absolution, but that these words were spoken also to each

---

[1] Read "even if" [cf. *Römische Quartalschrift* 34 (1926) 75-82] or, as had been proposed by the Fathers: "even if he be not contrite or the priest. . . ."

and all of the faithful: "Whatsoever you shall bind upon earth, shall be bound also in heaven, and whatsoever you shall loose upon earth, shall be loosed in heaven" [Matt. 18:18]; and, "Whose sins you shall forgive, they are forgiven them and whose sins you shall retain, they are retained" [John 20:23], that by virtue of these words anyone can absolve sins, public sins indeed by reproof only, if the one reproved accepts correction, secret sins by voluntary confession: let him be anathema [cf. n. 902].

921   Can. 11. If anyone says that bishops do not have the right of reserving cases to themselves, except those of external administration, and that on this account the reservation of cases does not prohibit a priest from truly absolving from reserved cases: let him be anathema [cf. n. 903].

922   Can. 12. If anyone says that the whole punishment, together with the guilt, is always pardoned by God, and that the satisfaction of penitents is nothing other than faith, by which they perceive that Christ has made satisfaction for them: let him be anathema [cf. n. 904].

923   Can. 13. If anyone says that for sins, as far as temporal punishment is concerned, there is very little satisfaction made to God through the merits of Christ by the punishments inflicted by Him and patiently borne, or by those enjoined by the priest, but voluntarily undertaken, as by fasts, prayers, almsgiving, or also by other works of piety, and that therefore the best penance is only a new life: let him be anathema [cf. n. 904 ff.].

924   Can. 14. If anyone says that the satisfactions by which penitents atone for their sins through Jesus Christ are not a worship of God, but the traditions of men, obscuring the doctrine of grace, the true worship of God, and the very beneficence of the death of Christ: let him be anathema [1] [cf. n. 905].

925   Can. 15. If anyone says that the keys have been given to the Church only to loose, and not also to bind, and that therefore priests, by imposing penalties on those who confess, act contrary to the institution of Christ; and that it is fiction that, after eternal punishment has been remitted by virtue of the keys, there usually remains a temporal punishment to be discharged: let him be anathema [cf. n. 904].

Canons on Extreme Unction [2]

926   Can. 1. If anyone says that extreme unction is not truly and properly a sacrament instituted by our Lord Jesus Christ [cf. Mark 6:13], and

---

[1] Cf. can. 2 of the Council of Laodicea (about the year 364): "Regarding those who have sinned by diverse misdeeds and persevering in the prayer of confession and penance have had a perfect conversion from evil deeds, after a period of penance has been fulfilled, in accord with the nature of the offense, communion is allowed to such because of the clemency and goodness of God" [Version of Dionysius Exiguus, Hrd I 781B].

[2] Rcht 86; Msi XXXIII 102 A; Hrd X 100 B; Bar(Th) ad 1551 n. 59 (33, 415 a f.).

promulgated by blessed James the Apostle [Jas. 5:14], but is only a rite accepted by the Fathers, or a human fiction: let him be anathema [cf. n. 907 ff.].

Can. 2. If anyone says that the sacred anointing of the sick does not 927 confer grace nor remit sins, nor alleviate the sick, but that it has already ceased, as if it had at one time only been a healing grace: let him be anathema [cf. n. 909].

Can. 3. If anyone says that the rite of extreme unction and its practice, 928 which the holy Roman Church observes, is opposed to the statement of the blessed Apostle James, and that it is therefore to be changed, and can be contemned without sin by Christians: let him be anathema [cf. n. 910].

Can. 4. If anyone says that the priests of the Church, whom blessed 929 James exhorts to be brought to anoint the sick, are not the priests ordained by a bishop, but the elders by age in each community, and that for this reason a priest alone is not the proper minister of extreme unction: let him be anathema [cf. n. 910].

Marcellus II 1555   Paulus IV 1555–1559 [1]

PIUS IV 1559–1565

COUNCIL OF TRENT, conclusion

Session xxi (July 16, 1562)

The Doctrine on Communion under both Species and that of Little Children [2]

Preface

The holy, ecumenical, and general Synod of Trent, lawfully assembled 929a in the Holy Spirit with the same legates of the Apostolic See presiding, has decreed that those things which relate to communion under both species, and to that of little children are to be explained here, since in different places various monstrous errors concerning the tremendous and most holy sacrament of the Eucharist are being circulated by the wiles of the evil spirit; and for this reason in some provinces many seem to have fallen away from the faith and from obedience to the Catholic Church. Therefore, it warns all the faithful of Christ not to venture to believe, teach, or preach hereafter about those matters, otherwise than is explained or defined in these decrees.

---

[1] See n. 993.
[2] C Tr VIII 698 ff.; Rcht 109 ff.; Msi XXXIII 122 B f.; Hrd X 119 ff.; Bar(Th) ad 1562 n. 70 f. (34, 230 b ff.).

Chap. 1. That Laymen and Clerics who not Offering Mass are not Bound by Divine Law to Communion under Both Species

930   Thus, the holy Synod itself, instructed by the Holy Spirit, who is the Spirit of wisdom and understanding, the Spirit of counsel and piety, [Isa. 112], and following the judgment and custom of the Church itself, declares and teaches that laymen and clerics not officiating are bound by no divine law to receive the sacrament of the Eucharist under both species, and that without injury to the faith there can be no doubt at all that communion under either species suffices for them for salvation. For although Christ the Lord at the Last Supper instituted and delivered to the apostles this venerable sacrament under the species of bread and wine [cf. Matt. 26:26 f.; Mark 14:22; Luke 22:19; I Cor. 11:24 f.], yet, that institution and tradition do not contend that all the faithful of Christ by an enactment of the Lord are bound [can. 1, 2] to receive under both species [can. 1, 2]. But neither is it rightly inferred from that sixth discourse in John that communion under both forms was commanded by the Lord [can. 3], whatever the understanding may be according to the various interpretations of the holy Fathers and Doctors. For, He who said: "Unless you eat the flesh of the Son of Man and drink His blood, you shall not have life in you" [John 6:54], also said: "If anyone eat of this bread, he shall live forever" [John 6:52]. And He who said: "He that eateth my flesh, and drinketh my blood hath life everlasting" [John 6:55] also said: "The bread, which I shall give, is my flesh for the life of the world" [John 6:52]: and finally, He who said: "He that eateth my flesh and drinketh my blood, abideth in me and I in him" [John 6:57], said nevertheless: "He that eateth this bread, shall live forever" [John 6:58].

Chap. 2. The Power of the Church Concerning the Administration of the Sacrament of the Eucharist

931   It [the Council] declares furthermore that this power has always been in the Church, that in the administration of the sacraments, preserving their substance, she may determine or change whatever she may judge to be more expedient for the benefit of those who receive them or for the veneration of the sacraments, according to the variety of circumstances, times, and places. Moreover, the Apostle seems to have intimated this in no obscure manner, when he said: "Let a man so account of us as of the ministers of Christ and the dispensers of the mysteries of God" [I Cor. 4:1]; and that he himself used this power is quite manifest in this sacrament as well as in many other things, not only in this sacrament itself, but also in some things set down with regard to its use, he says: "The rest I will set in order when I come" [I Cor. 11:34]. Therefore holy mother Church, cognizant of her authority in the administra-

tion of the sacraments, although from the beginning of the Christian religion the use of both species was not infrequent, nevertheless, since that custom in the progress of time has been already widely changed, induced by weighty and just reasons, has approved this custom of communicating under either species, and has decreed that it be considered as a law, which may not be repudiated or be changed at will without the authority of the Church [can. 2].

Chap. 3. Christ Whole and Entire and a True Sacrament is Received under Either Species

Moreover, it declares that although our Redeemer, as has been said **932** before, at that Last Supper instituted this sacrament and gave it to the apostles under two species, yet it must be confessed that Christ whole and entire and a true sacrament is received even under either species alone, and that on that account, as far as regards its fruit, those who receive only one species are not to be deprived of any grace which is necessary for salvation [can. 3].

Chap. 4. Little Children are not Bound to Sacramental Communion

Finally, the same holy Synod teaches that little children without the **933** use of reason are not bound by any necessity to the sacramental communion of the Eucharist [can. 4.], since having been "regenerated" through "the laver" of baptism [Tit. 3:5], and having been incorporated with Christ they cannot at that age lose the grace of the children of God which has already been attained. Nor is antiquity, therefore, to be condemned, if at one time it observed this custom in some places. For, just as those most holy Fathers had good reason for an observance of that period, so certainly it is to be believed without controversy that they did this under no necessity for salvation.

Canons on Communion Under Both Species and that of Little Children [1]

Can. 1. If anyone says that each and every one of the faithful of Christ **934** ought by a precept of God, or by necessity for salvation to receive both species of the most holy Sacrament: let him be anathema [cf. n. 930].

Can. 2. If anyone says that the holy Catholic Church has not been in- **935** fluenced by just causes and reasons to give communion under the form of bread only to layman and even to clerics when not consecrating, or that she has erred in this: let him be anathema [cf. n. 931].

Can. 3. If anyone denies that Christ whole and entire, who is the **936**

---

[1] CTr VIII 699 f.; Rcht 111; Msi XXXIII 123 C; Hrd X 121 A; Bar(Th) ad 1562 n. 71 (34, 233 a).

fountain and author of all graces, is received under the one species of bread, because, as some falsely assert, He is not received according to the institution of Christ Himself under both species: let him be anathema [cf. n. 930, 932].

937   Can. 4. If anyone says that for small children, before they have attained the years of discretion, communion of the Eucharist is necessary: let him be anathema [cf. n. 933].

SESSION XXII (Sept. 17, 1562)

The Doctrine on the Most Holy Sacrifice of the Mass [1]

937a   The holy, ecumenical, and general Synod of Trent lawfully assembled in the Holy Spirit with the same legates of the Apostolic See presiding, has decreed that the faith and doctrine concerning the great mystery of the Eucharist in the holy Catholic Church, complete and perfect in every way, should be retained and, after the errors and heresies have been repudiated, should be preserved as of old in its purity; concerning this doctrine, since it is the true and the only sacrifice, the holy Council, instructed by the light of the Holy Spirit, teaches these matters which follow, and declares that they be preached to the faithful.

Chap. 1. [The Institution of the Most Holy Sacrifice of the Mass] [2]

938   Since under the former Testament (as the Apostle Paul bears witness) there was no consummation because of the weakness of the Levitical priesthood, it was necessary (God the Father of mercies ordaining it thus) that another priest according to the order of Melchisedech [Gen. 14:18; Ps. 109:4; Heb. 7:11] arise, our Lord Jesus Christ, who could perfect [Heb. 10:14] all who were to be sanctified, and lead them to perfection. He, therefore, our God and Lord, though He was about to offer Himself once to God the Father upon the altar of the Cross by the mediation of death, so that He might accomplish an eternal redemption for them [edd.: *illic,* there], nevertheless, that His sacerdotal office might not come to an end with His death [Heb. 7:24, 27] at the Last Supper, on the night He was betrayed, so that He might leave to His beloved spouse the Church a visible sacrifice [can. 1] (as the nature of man demands), whereby that bloody sacrifice once to be completed on the Cross might be represented, and the memory of it remain even to the end of the world [I Cor. 11:23 ff.] and its saving grace be applied to the remission of those

---

[1] CTr VIII 959 ff.; Rcht 124 ff.; Msi XXXIII 128 D ff.; Hrd X 126 B ff.; Bar(Th) ad 1562 n. 101 f. (34, 254 b ff.).

[2] The inscriptions of the chapters of this session are not due to the Council but to Philip Chiffletius (17th cent.) Cf. CTr VIII 959 note 1 coll. c. 701 note 1.

sins which we daily commit, declaring Himself constituted "a priest for-ever according to the order of Melchisedech" [Ps. 109:4], offered to God the Father His own body and blood under the species of bread and wine, and under the symbols of those same things gave to the apostles (whom He then constituted priests of the New Testament), so that they might partake, and He commanded them and their successors in the priesthood in these words to make offering: "Do this in commemoration of me, etc." [Luke 22:19; I Cor. 11:24], as the Catholic Church has always under-stood and taught [can. 2]. For, after He had celebrated the ancient feast of the Passover, which the multitude of the children of Israel sacrificed [Exod. 12:1 ff.] in memory of their exodus from Egypt, He instituted a new Passover, Himself to be immolated under visible signs by the Church through the priests, in memory of His own passage from this world to the Father, when by the shedding of His blood He redeemed us and "delivered us from the power of darkness and translated us into His kingdom" [Col. 1:13].

And this, indeed, is that "clean oblation" which cannot be defiled by **939** any unworthiness or malice on the part of those who offer it; which the Lord foretold through Malachias must be offered in every place as a clean oblation [Mal. 1:11] to His name, which would be great among the gentiles, and which the Apostle Paul writing to the Corinthians has clearly indicated, when he says that they who are defiled by participation of the "table of the devils" cannot become partakers of the table of the Lord [I Cor. 10:21], understanding by table in each case, the altar. It is finally that [sacrifice] which was prefigured by various types of sacrifices, in the period of nature and the Law [Gen. 4:4; 8:20; 12:8; 22; Ex: passim], inasmuch as it comprises all good things signified by them, as being the consumma-tion and perfection of them all.

Chap. 2. [*The Sacrifice is a Visible Propitiation for the Living and the Dead*]

And since in this divine sacrifice, which is celebrated in the Mass, that **940** same Christ is contained and immolated in an unbloody manner, who on the altar of the Cross "once offered Himself" in a bloody manner [Heb. 9:27], the holy Synod teaches that this is truly propitiatory [can. 3], and has this effect, that if contrite and penitent we approach God with a sincere heart and right faith, with fear and reverence, "we obtain mercy and find grace in seasonable aid" [Heb. 4:16]. For, appeased by this oblation, the Lord, granting the grace and gift of penitence, pardons crimes and even great sins. For, it is one and the same Victim, the same one now offering by the ministry of the priests as He who then offered Himself on the Cross, the manner of offering alone being different. The fruits of that oblation (bloody, that is) are received most abundantly through this unbloody one; so far is the latter from being derogatory in any way to Him [can. 4]. Therefore, it is offered rightly according to the tradition of the apostles [can. 3], not only for the sins of the faithful living, for their punishments and other necessities, but also for the dead in Christ not yet fully purged.

Chap. 3. [Masses in Honor of the Saints]

941 And though the Church has been accustomed to celebrate some Masses now and then in honor and in memory of the saints, yet she does not teach that the sacrifice is offered to them, but to God alone, who has crowned them [can. 5]. Thence the priest is not accustomed to say: "I offer sacrifice to you, Peter and Paul," [1] but giving thanks to God for their victories, he implores their patronage, so that "they themselves may deign to intercede for us in heaven, whose memory we celebrate on earth" [Missal].

Chap. 4. [The Canon of the Mass]

942 And since it is fitting that holy things be administered in a holy manner, and this sacrifice is of all things the most holy, the Catholic Church, that it might be worthily and reverently offered and received, instituted the sacred canon many centuries ago, so free from all error [can. 6], that it contains nothing in it which does not especially diffuse a certain sanctity and piety and raise up to God the minds of those who offer it. For this consists both of the words of God, and of the traditions of the apostles, and also of pious instructions of the holy Pontiffs.

Chap. 5. [The Solemn Ceremonies of the Sacrifice of the Mass]

943 And since such is the nature of man that he cannot easily without external means be raised to meditation on divine things, on that account holy mother Church has instituted certain rites, namely, that certain things be pronounced in a subdued tone [can. 9] in the Mass, and others in a louder tone; she has likewise [can. 7] made use of ceremonies such as mystical blessings, lights, incense, vestments, and many other things of this kind in accordance with apostolic teaching and tradition, whereby both the majesty of so great a sacrifice might be commended, and the minds of the faithful excited by these visible signs of religion and piety to the contemplation of the most sublime matters which lie hidden in this sacrifice.

Chap. 6. [The Mass in which the Priest Alone Communicates]

944 The holy Synod would wish indeed that at every Mass the faithful present receive communion not only by spiritual desire, but also by the sacramental reception of the Eucharist, so that a more abundant

---

[1] St. Augustine, *C. Faustum* 20, 21 [ML 42, 384].

fruit of this most holy Sacrifice may be brought forth in them; yet if that is not always done, on that account it does not condemn [can. 8], those Masses in which the priest alone communicates sacramentally, as private and illicit, but rather approves and commends them, since indeed these Masses should also be considered as truly common, partly because at these Masses the people communicate spiritually, and partly, too, because they are celebrated by a public minister of the Church not only for himself, but for all the faithful who belong to the Body of Christ.

Chap. 7. [*The Water to be Mixed with Wine to be Offered in the Chalice*]

The holy Synod then admonishes priests that it has been prescribed by **945** the Church to mix water with the wine to be offered in the chalice [can. 9], not only because the belief is that Christ the Lord did so, but also because there came from His side water together with blood [John 19:34], since by this mixture the sacrament is recalled. And since in the Apocalypse of the blessed John the peoples are called waters [Apoc. 17:1, 15], the union of the faithful people with Christ, their head, is represented.

Chap. 8. [*The Mass not to be Celebrated in the Vernacular, and its Mysteries to be Explained to the People*]

Although the Mass contains much instruction for the faithful, it has **946** nevertheless not seemed expedient to the Fathers that it be celebrated everywhere in the vernacular [can. 9]. For this reason, since the ancient rite of each church has been approved by the holy Roman Church, the mother and teacher of all churches, and has been retained everywhere, lest the sheep of Christ suffer hunger, and "little ones ask for bread and there is none to break it unto them" [cf. Lam. 4:4], the holy Synod commands pastors and everyone who has the care of souls to explain frequently during the celebration of the Masses, either themselves or through others, some of the things which are read in the Mass, and among other things to expound some mystery of this most holy Sacrifice, especially on Sundays and feast days.

Chap. 9. [*Preliminary Remarks on the Following Canons*]

Because various errors have been disseminated at this time, and many **947** things are being taught and discussions carried on by many against this ancient faith founded on the holy Gospel, on the traditions of the apostles, and on the doctrine of the holy Fathers, the holy Synod, after long and grave deliberations over these matters, has resolved by the unanimous consent of all the fathers, to condemn and to eliminate from the holy Church by means of the following canons whatever is opposed to this most pure faith and to this sacred doctrine.

Canons on the Most Holy Sacrifice of the Mass [1]

948   Can. 1. If anyone says that in the Mass a true and real sacrifice is not offered to God, or that the act of offering is nothing else than Christ being given to us to eat: let him be anathema [cf. n. 938].

949   Can. 2. If anyone says that by these words: "Do this for a commemoration of me" [Luke 22:19; I Cor. 11:24], Christ did not make the apostles priests, or did not ordain that they and other priests might offer His own body and blood: let him be anathema [cf. n. 938].

950   Can. 3. If anyone says that the sacrifice of the Mass is only one of praise and thanksgiving, or that it is a mere commemoration of the sacrifice consummated on the Cross, but not one of propitiation; or that it is of profit to him alone who receives; or that it ought not to be offered for the living and the dead, for sins, punishments, satisfactions, and other necessities: let him be anathema [cf. n. 940].

951   Can. 4. If anyone says that blasphemy is cast upon the most holy sacrifice of Christ consummated on the Cross through the sacrifice of the Mass, or that by it He is disparaged: let him be anathema [cf. n. 940].

952   Can. 5. If anyone says that it is a deception for Masses to be celebrated in honor of the saints and to obtain their intercession with God, as the Church intends: let him be anathema [cf. n. 941].

953   Can. 6. If anyone says that the canon of the Mass contains errors, and should therefore be abrogated: let him be anathema [cf. n. 942].

954   Can. 7. If anyone says that the ceremonies, vestments, and outward signs, which the Catholic Church uses in the celebration of Masses, are incentives to impiety rather than the services of piety: let him be anathema [cf. n. 943].

955   Can. 8. If anyone says that Masses in which the priest alone communicates sacramentally, are illicit and are therefore to be abrogated: let him be anathema [cf. n. 944].

956   Can. 9. If anyone says that the rite of the Roman Church, according to which a part of the canon and the words of consecration are pronounced in a low tone, is to be condemned, or that the Mass ought to be celebrated in the vernacular only, or that water should not be mixed with the wine that is to be offered in the chalice because it is contrary to the institution of Christ: let him be anathema [cf. n. 943, 945 f.].

Session xxiii (July 15, 1563)

956a   ## The Doctrine on the Sacrament of Orders

---

[1] CTr VIII 961 f.; Tcht 127; Msi XXXIII 131 C ff.; Hrd X 129 A; Bar(Th) ad 1562 n. 102 (34, 256 b f.).

Chap. 1. [*The Institution of the Priesthood of the New Law*] [1]

Sacrifice and priesthood are so united by the ordinance of God that both 957 have existed in every law. Since, therefore, in the New Testament the Catholic Church has received from the institution of the Lord the holy, visible sacrifice of the Eucharist, it must also be confessed that there is in this Church a new visible and external priesthood [can. 1], into which the old has been translated [Heb. 7:12]. Moreover, that this was instituted by that same Lord our Savior [can. 3], and that to the apostles and their successors in the priesthood was handed down the power of consecrating, of offering and administering His body and blood, and also of forgiving and retaining sins, the Sacred Scriptures show and the tradition of the Catholic Church has always taught [can. 1].

Chap. 2. [*The Seven Orders*]

Moreover, since the ministry of this holy priesthood is a divine thing, 958 it was proper that it should be exercised more worthily and with deeper veneration, that in the most well ordered arrangement of the Church, there should be different orders of ministers [Matt. 16:19; Luke 22:19; John 20:22 f.], who by virtue of their office should administer to the priesthood, so distributed that those who already had the clerical tonsure should ascend through the minor to the major orders [can. 2]. For the Sacred Scriptures make distinct mention not only of the priests, but also of the deacons [Acts 6:5; I Tim. 3:8 f.; Phil. 1:1], and teach in the most impressive words what is especially to be observed in their ordination; and from the very beginning of the Church the names of the following orders and the duties proper to each one are known to have been in use, namely those of the subdeacon, acolyte, exorcist, lector, and porter, though not of equal rank; for the subdiaconate is classed among the major orders by the Fathers and the sacred Councils, in which we also read very frequently of other inferior orders.

Chap. 3. [*The Order of the Priesthood is Truly a Sacrament*]

Since from the testimony of Scripture, apostolic tradition, and the un- 959 animous consensus of opinion of the Fathers it is evident that by sacred ordination, which is performed by words and outward signs, grace is conferred, no one can doubt that order is truly and properly one of the seven sacraments of the Church [can. 3]. For the Apostle says: "I admonish thee that thou stir up the grace of God which is in thee by the imposition of my hands. For God has not given us the spirit of fear, but of power and of love and of sobriety" [II Tim. 1:6, 7; cf. I Tim. 4:14].

---

[1] The inscriptions of the chapters of this session are due to Philip Chiffletius, cf. C Tr. IX 620 note 1.

Chap. 4. [*The Ecclesiastical Hierarchy and Ordination*]

960   But since in the sacrament of orders, as also in baptism and in confirmation, a sign is imprinted [can. 4], which can neither be effaced nor taken away, justly does the holy Synod condemn the opinion of those who assert that the priests of the New Testament have only a temporary power, and that those at one time rightly ordained can again become laymen, if they do not exercise the ministry of the word of God [can. 1]. But if anyone should affirm that all Christians without distinction are priests of the New Testament, or that they are all endowed among themselves with an equal spiritual power, he seems to do nothing else than disarrange [can. 6] the ecclesiastical hierarchy, which is "as an army set in array" [cf. Cant. 6:3], just as if, contrary to the teaching of blessed Paul, all were apostles, all prophets, all evangelists, all pastors, all doctors [cf. I Cor. 12:29; Eph. 4:11]. Accordingly, the holy Synod declares that besides the other ecclesiastical grades, the bishops who have succeeded the Apostles, belong in a special way to this hierarchial order, and have been "placed (as the same Apostle says) by the Holy Spirit to rule the Church of God" [Acts 20:29], and that they are superior to priests, and administer the sacrament of confirmation, ordain ministers of the Church, and can perform many other offices over which those of an inferior order have no power [can. 7]. The holy Synod teaches, furthermore, that in the ordination of bishops, priests, and of other orders, the consent, or call, or authority of the people, or of any secular power or magistrate is not so required for the validity of the ordination; but rather it decrees that those who are called and instituted *only* by the people, or by the civil power or magistrate and proceed to exercise these offices, and that those who by their own temerity take these offices upon themselves, are not ministers of the Church, but are to be regarded as "thieves and robbers, who have not entered by the door" [cf. John 10:1; can. 8]. These are the matters which in general it seemed well to the sacred Council to teach to the faithful of Christ regarding the sacrament of order. It has, however, resolved to condemn the contrary in definite and appropriate canons in the following manner, so that all, making use of the rule of faith, with the assistance of Christ, may be able to recognize more easily the Catholic truth in the midst of the darkness of so many errors, and may adhere to it.

Canons on the Sacrament of Order [1]

961   Can. 1. If anyone says that there is not in the New Testament a visible and external priesthood, or that there is no power of consecrating and offering the true body and blood of the Lord, and of forgiving and retain-

---

[1] CTr IX 621 f.; Rcht 174; Msi XXXIII 139 D f.; Hrd X 137 A f.; Bar(Th) ad 1563 n. 127 (34, 398 b f.).

ing sins, but only the office and bare ministry of preaching the Gospel, or that those who do not preach are not priests at all: let him be anathema [cf. n. 957, 960].

Can. 2. If anyone says that besides the priesthood there are in the **962** Catholic Church no other orders, both major and minor, by which as by certain grades, there is an advance to the priesthood: let him be anathema [cf. n. 958].

Can. 3. If anyone says that order or sacred ordination is not truly and **963** properly a sacrament instituted by Christ the Lord, or that it is some human contrivance, devised by men unskilled in ecclesiastical matters, or that it is only a certain rite for selecting ministers of the word of God and of the sacraments: let him be anathema [cf. n. 957, 959].

Can. 4. If anyone says that by sacred ordination the Holy Spirit is not **964** imparted, and that therefore the bishops say in vain: "Receive ye the Holy Spirit"; or that by it a character is not imprinted or that he who has once been a priest can again become a layman: let him be anathema [cf. n. 852].

Can. 5. If anyone says that the sacred unction which the Church uses **965** in holy ordination, is not only not required, but is to be contemned and is pernicious as also are the other ceremonies of order: let him be anathema [cf. n. 856].

Can. 6. If anyone says that in the Catholic Church a hierarchy has not **966** been instituted by divine ordinance, which consists of the bishops, priests, and ministers: let him be anathema [cf. n. 960].

Can. 7. If anyone says that the bishops are not superior to priests; or **967** that they do not have the power to confirm and to ordain, or, that the power which they have is common to them and to the priests; or that orders conferred by them without the consent or call of the people or of the secular power are invalid, or, that those who have been neither rightly ordained nor sent by ecclesiastical and canonical authority, but come from a different source, are lawful ministers of the word and of the sacraments: let him be anathema [cf. n. 960].

Can. 8. If anyone says that the bishops who are chosen by the authority **968** of the Roman Pontiff are not true and legitimate bishops, but a human invention: let him be anathema [cf. n. 960].

Session xxiv (Nov. 11, 1563)

Doctrine (Concerning the Sacrament of Matrimony) [1]

The first parent of the human race expressed the perpetual and in- **969** dissoluble bond of matrimony under the influence of the divine Spirit,

---

[1] CTr IX 966 f.; Rcht 214 f.; Msi XXXII 149 E f.; Hrd X 147 A; Bar(Th) ad 1563 n. 193 (34, 434 a ff.).

when he said: "This now is bone of my bone, and flesh of my flesh. Wherefore a man shall leave father and mother and shall cleave to his wife, and they shall be two in one flesh" [Gen. 2:23 f.; cf. Eph. 5:31].

But that by this bond two only are united and joined together, Christ the Lord taught more openly, when referring to those last words, as having been uttered by God, He said: "Therefore now they are not two, but one flesh" [Matt. 19:6], and immediately ratified the strength of this same bond, pronounced by Adam so long ago in these words: "What therefore God has joined together, let no man put asunder" [Matt. 19:6; Mark 10:9].

But the grace which was to perfect that natural love, and confirm the indissoluble union, and sanctify those united in marriage, Christ Himself, institutor and perfector of the venerable sacraments, merited for us by His passion. The Apostle Paul intimates this, when he says: "Men, love your wives as Christ loved the Church, and delivered himself up for it" [Eph. 5:25], directly adding: "This is a great Sacrament; but I speak in Christ and in the Church" [Eph. 5:32].

970   Since, therefore, matrimony in the evangelical law, by grace through Christ, excels the ancient marriages, our holy Fathers, the Councils, and the tradition of the universal Church have with good reason always taught that it is to be classed among the sacraments of the New Law; and since impious men of this age, madly raging against this teaching, have not only formed false judgments concerning this venerable sacrament, but according to their custom, introducing under the pretext of the Gospel a carnal liberty, have in writing and in word asserted many things foreign to the mind of the Catholic Church and to the general opinion approved from the time of the apostles, not without great loss of the faithful of Christ, this holy and general Synod wishing to block their temerity has decided, lest their pernicious contagion attract more, that the more prominent heresies and errors of the aforesaid schismatics are to be destroyed, decreeing anathemas against these heretics and their errors.

971   Can. 1. If anyone says that matrimony is not truly and properly one of the seven sacraments of the evangelical Law, instituted by Christ the Lord, but that it has been invented by men in the Church, and does not confer grace: let him be anathema [cf. n. 969 f.].

972   Can. 2. If anyone says that it is lawful for Christians to have several wives at the same time, and that it is not forbidden by any divine law [Matt. 19:4 f.]: let him be anathema [cf. n. 969 f.].

973   Can. 3. If anyone says that only those degrees of consanguinity and affinity which are expressed in Leviticus [18:6 f.] can be impediments to the contract of matrimony and can dissolve it when contracted, and that the Church can dispense in some of these, or establish more to impede or invalidate: let him be anathema [cf. n. 1550 f.].

Can. 4. If anyone says that the Church could not establish impediments **974** invalidating marriage [cf. Matt. 16:19], or that she has erred in establishing them: let him be anathema.

Can. 5. If anyone says that the bond of matrimony can be dissolved **975** because of heresy, or grievous cohabitation, or voluntary absence from the spouse: let him be anathema.

Can. 6. If anyone says that matrimony contracted, but not consum- **976** mated, is not dissolved by a solemn religious profession of either one of the married persons: let him be anathema.

Can. 7. If anyone says that the Church errs,[1] inasmuch as she has **977** taught and still teaches that in accordance with evangelical and apostolic doctrine [Matt. 10: I Cor. 7] the bond of matrimony cannot be dissolved because of adultery of one of the married persons, and that both, or even the innocent one, who has given no occasion for adultery, cannot during the lifetime of the other contract another marriage, and that he, who after the dismissal of the adulteress shall marry another, is guilty of adultery, and that she also, who after the dismissal of the adulterer shall marry another: let him be anathema.

Can. 8. If anyone says that the Church errs, when she decrees that for **978** many reasons a separation may take place between husband and wife with regard to bed, and with regard to cohabitation, for a determined or indetermined time: let him be anathema.

Can. 9. If anyone says that clerics constituted in sacred orders, or **979** regulars who have solemnly professed chastity, can contract marriage, and that such marriage is valid, notwithstanding the ecclesiastical law or the vow, and that the contrary is nothing else than a condemnation of marriage, and that all who feel that they have not the gift of chastity (even though they have vowed it) can contract marriage: let him be anathema. Since God does not refuse that gift to those who seek it rightly, "neither does he suffer us to be tempted above that which we are able" [I Cor. 10:13].

Can. 10. If anyone says that the married state is to be preferred to the **980** state of virginity or celibacy, and that it is not better and happier to remain in virginity or celibacy than to be united in matrimony [cf. Matt. 19:11 f.; I Cor. 7:25 f.; 28:40]: let him be anathema.

Can. 11. If anyone says that the prohibition of the solemnization of **981**

---

[1] This form of condemnation was chosen lest the Greeks be offended, who evidently followed a contrary practice, although they did not condemn the opposite practice of the Latin Church. On this canon Pius XI (*Casti Conubii*, Dec. 31, 1930; AAS 22 [1930] 574) speaks thus: "But if the Church has not erred or does not err, when she taught or is teaching these things, and thus it is quite certain that matrimony can be dissolved not even on account of adultery, it is clear that other much weaker causes which are customarily brought forward are worth much less, and furthermore are to be considered valueless."

marriages at certain times of the year is a tyrannical superstition, derived from the superstition of the heathen, or condemns the benedictions and other ceremonies which the Church makes use of in them: let him be anathema.

982   Can. 12. If anyone says that matrimonial causes do not belong to ecclesiastical judges: let him be anathema [see n. 1500 a, 1559 f.].

SESSION XXV (Dec. 3 and 4, 1563)

Decree Concerning Purgatory [1]

983   Since the Catholic Church, instructed by the Holy Spirit, in conformity with the sacred writings and the ancient tradition of the Fathers in sacred councils, and very recently in this ecumenical Synod, has taught that there is a purgatory [see n. 940, 950], and that the souls detained there are assisted by the suffrages of the faithful, and especially by the acceptable sacrifice of the altar, the holy Synod commands the bishops that they insist that the sound doctrine of purgatory, which has been transmitted by the holy Fathers and holy Councils, be believed by the faithful of Christ, be maintained, taught, and everywhere preached. Let the more difficult and subtle "questions," however, and those which do not make for "edification" [cf. I Tim. 1:4], and from which there is very often no increase in piety, be excluded from popular discourses to uneducated people. Likewise, let them not permit uncertain matters, or those that have the appearance of falsehood, to be brought out and discussed publicly. Those matters on the contrary, which tend to a certain curiosity or superstition, or that savor of filthy lucre, let them prohibit as scandals and stumbling blocks to the faithful. . . .

Invocation, Veneration and Relics of Saints, and on Sacred Images [2]

984   The holy Synod commands all bishops and others who hold the office of teaching and its administration, that in accordance with the usage of the Catholic and apostolic Church, received from primeval times of the Christian religion, and with the consensus of opinion of the holy Fathers and the decrees of sacred Councils, they above all diligently instruct the faithful on the intercession and invocation of the saints, the veneration of relics, and the legitimate use of images, teaching them that the saints, who reign together with Christ, offer up their prayers to God for men;

---

[1] CTr IX 1077; Rcht 391; Msi XXXIII 170 D f.; Hrd X 167 C; Bar(Th) ad 1563 n. 210 (34, 445 a).

[2] CTr IX 1077 ff.; Rcht 392 ff.; Msi XXXIII 171 A f.; Hrd X 167 E ff.; Bar(Th) ad 1563 n. 211 (34, 445 a ff.).

and that it is good and useful to invoke them suppliantly and, in order to obtain favors from God through His Son Jesus Christ our Lord, who alone is our Redeemer and Savior, to have recourse to their prayers, assistance, and support; and that they who deny that those saints who enjoy eternal happiness in heaven are to be invoked, think impiously, or who assert that they do not pray for men, or that our invocation of them, to intercede for each of us individually, is idolatry, or that it is opposed to the word of God, and inconsistent with the honor of the "one mediator of God and men Jesus Christ" [cf. I Tim. 2:5], or that it is foolish to pray vocally or mentally to those who reign in heaven.

That the holy bodies of the saints and also of the martyrs and of others **985** living with Christ, who were the living "members of Christ and the temple of the Holy Spirit" [cf. I Cor. 3:16; 6:19; II Cor. 6:16], which are to be awakened by Him to eternal life and to be glorified, are to be venerated by the faithful, through which many benefits are bestowed by God on men, so that those who affirm that veneration and honor are not due to the relics of the saints, or that these and other memorials are honored by the faithful without profit, and that the places dedicated to the memory of the saints for the purpose of obtaining their help are visited in vain, let these be altogether condemned, just as the Church has for a long time condemned and now condemns them again.

Moreover, that the images of Christ, of the Virgin Mother of God, and **986** of the other saints, are to be placed and retained especially in the churches, and that due honor and veneration be extended to them, not that any divinity or virtue is believed to be in them, for which they are to be venerated, or that anything is to be petitioned from them, or that trust is to be placed in images, as at one time was done by the gentiles, who placed their hope in idols [cf. Ps. 134:15 f.], but because the honor which is shown them, is referred to the prototypes which they represent, so that by means of the images, which we kiss and before which we bare the head and prostrate ourselves, we adore Christ, and venerate the saints, whose likeness they bear. This is what was sanctioned by the decrees of the councils, especially that of the second council of NICEA, against the opponents of images [see n. 302 ff.].

Indeed let the bishops diligently teach this, that by the accounts of the **987** mysteries of our redemption, portrayed in pictures or in other representations, the people are instructed and confirmed in the articles of faith which should be kept in mind and constantly pondered over; then, too, that from all sacred images great profit is derived not only because the people are reminded of the benefits and gifts, which are bestowed upon them by Christ, but also, because through the saints the miracles of God and salutary examples are set before the eyes of the faithful, so that they may give thanks to God for those things, may fashion their own lives and conduct in imitation of the saints, and be stimulated to adore and love God, and to cultivate piety. But if anyone should teach or maintain anything contrary to these decrees, let him be anathema.

988   If any abuses shall creep into these holy and salutary observances, the holy Synod earnestly desires that they be entirely abolished, so that no representations of false dogma and those offering occasion of dangerous error to uneducated persons be exhibited. And if at times it happens that the accounts and narratives of the Holy Scripture, when this is of benefit to the uneducated people, are portrayed and exhibited, let the people be instructed that not for that reason is the divinity represented, as if it can be seen with bodily eyes, or expressed in colors and figures. . . .

Decree Concerning Indulgences [1]

989   Since the power of granting indulgences was conferred by Christ on the Church, and she has made use of such power divinely given to her, [cf. Matt. 16:19; 18:18] even in the earliest times, the holy Synod teaches and commands that the use of indulgences, most salutary to a Christian people and approved by the authority of the sacred Councils, is to be retained in the Church, and it condemns those with anathema who assert that they are useless or deny that there is in the Church the power of granting them. . . .

Clandestinity Invalidating Matrimony [2]

[From Session XXIX Chap. (I) "Tametsi" on the
reformation of matrimony]

990   Although it is not to be doubted that clandestine marriages made with the free consent of the contracting parties, are valid and true marriages, so long as the Church has not declared them invalid; and consequently that they are justly to be condemned, as the holy Synod condemns those with anathema, who deny that they are true and valid, and those also who falsely affirm that marriages contracted by minors without the consent of parents are invalid, and that parents can make them sanctioned or void, nevertheless the holy Church of God for very just reasons has always detested and forbidden them. But while the holy Synod recognizes that those prohibitions by reason of man's disobedience are no longer of any use, and considers the grave sins which have their origin in such clandestine marriage, especially, indeed, the sins of those who remain in the state

---

[1] CTr IX 1105; Rcht 468; Msi XXXIII 193 E f.; Hrd X 190 C; Bar(Th) ad 1563 n. 212 (34, 447 a).

[2] CTr IX 968 f.; Rcht 216 ff.; Msi XXXIII 152 A; Hrd X 149 B f.; cf. Bar(Th) ad 1563 n. 150 f. (34, 410 a f.).

of damnation, after abandoning the first wife, with whom they made a secret contract, while they publicly contract another, and live with her in continual adultery, since the Church, which does not judge what is hidden, cannot correct this evil, unless a more efficacious remedy be applied, therefore by continuing in the footsteps of the holy Lateran Council [IV] proclaimed under INNOCENT III, it commands that in the future, before a marriage is contracted, public announcement be made three times on three consecutive feast days in the Church during the celebration of the Masses, by the proper pastor of the contracting parties between whom the marriage is to be contracted; after these publications have been made, if no legitimate impediment is put in the way, one can proceed with the celebration of the marriage in the open church, where the parish priest, after the man and woman have been questioned, and their mutual consent has been ascertained, shall either say: "I join you together in matrimony, in the name of the Father and of the Son, and of the Holy Spirit," or use other words, according to the accepted rite of each province.

But if at some time there should be a probable suspicion that a marriage **991** can be maliciously hindered, if so many publications precede it, then either one publication only may be made, or the marriage may be celebrated at once in the presence of the parish priest and of two or three witnesses; then before its consummation the publications should be made in the church, so that, if any impediments exist, they may the more easily be detected, unless the ordinary himself may judge it advisable that the publications be dispensed with, which the holy Synod leaves to his prudence and judgment.

Those who shall attempt to contract marriage otherwise than in the **992** presence of the parish priest, or of another priest with the authorization of the parish priest or the ordinary, in the presence of two or three witnesses, the holy Synod renders absolutely incapable of thus contracting marriage, and declares that contracts of this kind are invalid and nil, inasmuch as by the present decree it invalidates and annuls them.

The Trinity and the Incarnation (against the Unitarians) [1]

[From the ordinance of Paul IV, "Cum quorundam," [2] Aug. 7, 1555]

Since the depravity and iniquity of certain men have reached such a **993** point in our time that, of those who wander and deviate from the Catholic faith, very many indeed not only presume to profess different heresies but

---

[1] BR(T) 6, 500 b f.; MBR 1, 821 b.—This document, which according to chronological order should be placed after n. 929, has been placed here, so as not to break the series of decrees of the Council of Trent.

[2] This constitution was confirmed by Clement VIII by the brief "Dominici gregis," Feb. 3, 1603 [BR(T) 11 a].

also to deny the foundations of the faith itself, and by their example lead many away to the destruction of their souls, we, in accord with our pastoral office and charity, desiring, in so far as we are able with God, to call such men away from so grave and destructive an error, and with paternal severity to warn the rest, lest they fall into such impiety, all and each who have hitherto asserted, claimed or believed that Almighty God was not three in persons and of an entirely uncomposed and undivided unity of substance and one single simple essence of divinity; or that our Lord is not true God of the same substance in every way with the Father and the Holy Spirit, or that He was not conceived of the Holy Spirit according to the flesh in the womb of the most blessed and ever Virgin Mary, but from the seed of Joseph just as the rest of men; or that the same Lord and our God, Jesus Christ, did not submit to the most cruel death of the Cross to redeem us from sins and from eternal death, and to reunite us with the Father unto eternal life; or that the same most blessed Virgin Mary was not the true mother of God, and did not always persist in the integrity of virginity, namely, before bringing forth, at bringing forth, and always after bringing forth, on the part of the omnipotent God the Father, and the Son, and the Holy Spirit, with apostolic authority we demand and advise, etc.

The Profession of Faith of the Council of Trent [1]

[From the Bull of Pius IV, "Iniunctum nobis," Nov. 13, 1565]

994   I, N., with firm faith believe and profess all and everything which is contained in the creed of faith, which the holy Roman Church uses, namely: I believe [2] in one God the Father Almighty, creator of heaven and earth, of all things visible and invisible; and in one Lord Jesus Christ, the only-begotten Son of God, and born of the Father before all ages, God of God, light of light, true God of true God, begotten not made, consubstantial with the Father, by whom all things were made; who for us men and for our salvation descended from heaven, and became incarnate by the Holy Spirit of the Virgin Mary, and was made man; he was also crucified for us under Pontius Pilate, suffered and was buried; and he rose on the third day according to the Scriptures, and ascended into heaven; he sitteth at the right hand of the Father, and will come again with glory to judge the living and the dead, of whose kingdom there shall be no end; and in the Holy Spirit, the Lord and giver of life, who proceeds from the Father and the Son; who together with the Father and the Son is adored and glorified; who spoke through the prophets; and in one holy

---

[1] Rcht App. 575 ff.; Msi XXXIII 220 B f.; Hrd X 199 D ff.; BR(T) 7, 327 b ff.; MBR 2, 138 b ff.

[2] Creed Nic.—Const.; see n. 86.

Catholic and apostolic Church. I confess one baptism for the remission of sins, and I await the resurrection of the dead, and the life of the world to come. Amen.

The apostolic and ecclesiastical traditions and all other observances and 995 constitutions of that same Church I most firmly admit and embrace. I likewise accept Holy Scripture according to that sense which our holy Mother Church has held and does hold, whose [office] it is to judge of the true meaning and interpretation of the Sacred Scriptures; I shall never accept nor interpret it otherwise than in accordance with the unanimous consent of the Fathers.

I also profess that there are truly and properly seven sacraments of the 996 New Law instituted by Jesus Christ our Lord, and necessary for the salvation of mankind, although not all are necessary for each individual; these sacraments are baptism, confirmation, the Eucharist, penance, extreme unction, order, and matrimony; and [I profess] that they confer grace, and that of these baptism, confirmation, and order cannot be repeated without sacrilege. I also receive and admit the accepted and approved rites of the Catholic Church in the solemn administration of all the aforesaid sacraments. I embrace and accept each and everything that has been defined and declared by the holy Synod of Trent concerning original sin and justification.

I also profess that in the Mass there is offered to God a true, proper sac- 997 rifice of propitiation for the living and the dead, and that in the most holy sacrament of the Eucharist there is truly, really, and substantially present the body and blood together with the soul and the divinity of our Lord Jesus Christ, and that there takes place a conversion of the whole substance of bread into the body, and of the whole substance of the wine into the blood; and this conversion the Catholic Church calls transubstantiation. I also acknowledge that under one species alone the whole and entire Christ and the true sacrament are taken.

I steadfastly hold that a purgatory exists, and that the souls there de- 998 tained are aided by the prayers of the faithful; likewise that the saints reigning together with Christ should be venerated and invoked, and that they offer prayers to God for us, and that their relics should be venerated. I firmly assert that the images of Christ and of the Mother of God ever Virgin, and also of the other saints should be kept and retained, and that due honor and veneration should be paid to them; I also affirm that the power of indulgences has been left in the Church by Christ, and that the use of them is especially salutary for the Christian people.

I acknowledge the holy Catholic and apostolic Roman Church as the 999 mother and teacher of all churches; and to the Roman Pontiff, the successor of the blessed Peter, chief of the Apostles and vicar of Jesus Christ, I promise and swear true obedience.

1000　　Also all other things taught, defined, and declared by the sacred canons and ecumenical Councils, and especially by the sacred and holy Synod of Trent, (and by the ecumenical Council of the Vatican,[1] particularly concerning the primacy of the Roman Pontiff and his infallible teaching), I without hesitation accept and profess; and at the same time all things contrary thereto, and whatever heresies have been condemned, and rejected, and anathematized by the Church, I likewise condemn, reject, and anathematize. This true Catholic faith, outside of which no one can be saved, (and) which of my own accord I now profess and truly hold, I, N., do promise, vow, and swear that I will, with the help of God, most faithfully retain and profess the same to the last breath of life as pure and inviolable, and that I will take care as far as lies in my power that it be held, taught, and preached by my subjects or by those over whom by virtue of my office I have charge, so help me God, and these holy Gospels of God.

ST. PIUS V 1566–1572

Errors of Michael du Bay (BAII)[2]

[Condemned in the Bull "Ex omnibus afflictionibus," Oct. 1, 1567]

1001　　1. Neither the merits of an angel nor of the first man still in the state of integrity are called grace.

---

[1] What is included by parentheses is now to be added from Decr. S.C. Conc. (Jan. 20, 1877), [ASS 10 (1877)].

[2] DuPl III, II 110 ff.; coll. Viva 553 a; CIC Rcht II 136 ff.—Michael Baius (du Bay), born in 1513, professor on the faculty of theology at Louvain, began to propose false doctrines in 1551. When presently others, especially Ruardus Lapperus, strenuously opposed him, in the year 1560 the theses of du Bay were sent to the faculty in Paris and were condemned by it. But when du Bay and his followers stirred up great contention, Pius IV in the year 1561 imposed silence upon him. But when du Bay did not obey, Pius V in a Bull, not then published, "Ex omnibus afflictionibus," omitting the name of the writer, noted his theses with various censures. Then du Bay sent a defense of his teaching to the Pontiff, who after reading it confirmed in the year 1569 the earlier condemnation. And when du Bay, who for appearance sake had subjected himself, was unwilling to cease spreading his errors, that condemnation was repeated and the Bull of Pius V was published by Gregory XIII in the Bull "Provisionis nostrae" on Jan. 29, 1579 [BR(T) 8, 315 a ff.; Hrd X 126 ff.], and afterwards by Urban VIII in the Bull "In eminenti Eccl. milit." on the 6th of March, 1641 [BR(T) 15, 93 a ff.].—These theses either word for word, or at least according to sense have been selected from the various works of du Bay: 1–20, "On the merits of works" (*De meritis operum*); 21–24, 26, "On the first justice of man" (*De prima hominis iustitia*); 25, 27–30, "On the virtues of the impious" (*De virtutibus impiorum*); 31–34, 36–38, 42, "On charity" (*De caritate*); 37, 39–41, 66, "On free will" (*De libero arbitrio*); 42–43, "On justice" (*De iustitia*); 44, "On justification" (*De iustificatione*); 45, "On sacrifice" (*De sacrificio*);

2. Just as an evil work by its nature is deserving of eternal death, so a **1002** good work by its own nature is meritorious of eternal life.

3. Felicity would be the reward, and not grace both for the good angels **1003** and for the first man, if he had persevered in that state even to the end of his life.

4. Eternal life was promised to integral man and to the angel in view **1004** of good works, and good works in themselves from the law of nature suffice for attaining it.

5. In the promise made both to the angel and to the first man is con- **1005** tained the disposition of natural justice, whereby for good works without any other regard eternal life is promised to the just.

6. By the natural law it has been ordained for man that, if he would **1006** persevere in obedience, he would attain to that life, in which he could not die.

7. The merits of the first integral man were the gifts of the first creation, **1007** but according to the manner of speech in Sacred Scripture they are not rightly called grace; for this reason they should be called merits only, not also grace.

8. In the redeemed through the grace of Christ no good merit can be **1008** found, which may not be freely bestowed upon one who is unworthy.

9. Gifts bestowed upon integral man and to an angel, perhaps not to **1009** be condemned by reason, can be called grace; but, according to the use of Sacred Scripture, these gifts which were bestowed through Jesus Christ upon those badly meriting and unworthy of them are understood only by the name of grace; therefore, neither the merits nor the reward, which is rendered to them, should be called grace.

10. The remission of temporal punishment, which often remains after **1010** the forgiveness of sin, and the resurrection of the body must properly be ascribed only to the merits of Christ.

11. The fact that having lived piously and justly in this mortal life **1011** even to the end of life we attain eternal life, should not be imputed to the grace of God, but to the natural order instantly ordained in the beginning of creation by the just judgment of God; neither in this recompense of goods is regard paid to the merit of Christ, but only to the first institution of the human race, in which it is ordained by the natural law that by the just judgment of God eternal life is paid for obedience to His mandates.

12. The opinion of Pelagius is: A good work performed without the **1012** grace of adoption, is not meritorious of the heavenly kingdom.

46–48, 50–55, "On original sin" (*De peccato originis*); 57–58, "On prayer for the dead" (*De oratione pro defunctis*); 59–60, "On indulgences" (*De indulgentiis*); the rest have been deduced from the principles of du Bay.—The errors of du Bay are divided by some into 76 propositions; by others into 79.

1013   13. Good works, performed by the sons of adoption, do not receive a consideration of merit from the fact that they are done through the spirit of adoption which lives in the hearts of the sons of God, but only from the fact that they are conformable to law, and because through them obedience is preferred to law.

1014   14. The good works of the just do not receive on the day of the last judgment a fuller reward than they deserve to receive by the just judgment of God.

1015   15. The reason of merit does not consist in this, that he who works well should have grace and the indwelling Holy Spirit, but in this only, that he obeys the divine law.

1016   16. That is not true obedience of the law, which is done without charity.

1017   17. They are in agreement with Pelagius who say that it is necessary for reason of merit, that man through the grace of adoption be lifted up to a deified state.

1018   18. The works of the catechumens, as faith and penance performed before the remission of sins, are merits for eternal life; and they will not attain this life, unless the impediments of preceding faults are first taken away.

1019   19. The works of justice and temperance which Christ performed, have not obtained greater value from the dignity of the person operating.

1020   20. No sin is venial by its own nature, but every sin deserves eternal punishment.

1021   21. The sublimation and exaltation of human nature in participation with the divine nature has been due to the integrity of the first condition, and hence must be called natural, and not supernatural.

1022   22. They agree with Pelagius who understand the text of the Apostle to the Romans: "The nations, who do not have a law, do naturally the things, which are of the law" [Rom. 2:14], concerning nations who do not possess the grace of faith.

1023   23. Absurd is the opinion of those who say that man from the beginning, by a certain supernatural and gratuitous gift, was raised above the condition of his nature, so that by faith, hope, and charity he cherished God supernaturally.

1024   24. By vain and idle men, in keeping with the folly of philosophers, is the opinion devised which must be referred to Pelagianism, that man was so constituted from the beginning that through gifts added upon nature by the bounty of the Creator he was raised and adopted into the sonship of God.

1025   25. All works of infidels are sins, and the virtues of philosophers are vices.

1026   26. The integrity of the first creation was not the undeserved exaltation of human nature, but its natural condition.

27. Free will, without the help of God's grace, has only power for 1027
sin.

28. It is a Pelagian error to say that free will has the power to avoid 1028
any sin.

29. Not only are they "thieves" and "robbers" who deny that Christ is 1029
the way and *"the door"* of the truth and life, but also whoever teaches that
there can be ascent [cf. John 10:1] to the way of justice (that is to any
justice) otherwise than through Him,

30. or, that man can resist any temptation without the help of His 1030
grace, so that he may not be led into it and not be overcome by it.

31. Perfect and sincere charity, which is from a "pure heart and good 1031
conscience and a faith not feigned" [I Tim. 1:5], can be in catechumens
as well as in penitents without the remission of sins.

32. That charity which is the fullness of the law is not always connected 1032
with the remission of sins.

33. A catechumen lives justly and rightly and holily, and observes the 1033
commandments of God, and fulfills the law through charity, which is
only received in the laver of baptism, before the remission of sins has
been obtained.

34. That distinction of a twofold love, namely a natural one, by which 1034
God is loved as the author of nature, and of a gratuitous love, by which
God is loved as one who blesses, is vain and false and devised to ridicule
the sacred literature and most of the testimonies of the ancients.

35. Every action which a sinner, or a slave of sin performs is a sin. 1035

36. Natural love which arises from the force of nature, is defended by 1036
some doctors according to philosophy alone through the pride of human
presumption with injury to the Cross of Christ.

37. He agrees with Pelagius, who acknowledges anything as a natural 1037
good, that is, whatever he thinks has arisen from the forces of nature
alone.

38. All love of a rational creature is either vicious cupidity, by which 1038
the world is loved, which is prohibited by John; or that praiseworthy
charity by which "when poured forth" by the Holy Spirit in our heart
[Rom. 5:5], God is loved.

39. What is voluntarily done, even though it be done by necessity, is 1039
nevertheless freely done.

40. In all his actions a sinner serves his ruling passion. 1040

41. This measure of freedom, which is of necessity, is not found in the 1041
Scriptures under the name of freedom, but is merely the name for freedom
from sin.

42. Justice, by which an impious person is justified by faith, consists 1042
formally in the obedience of mandates, which is the justice of works; not
however in any grace [habitual] infused into the soul, by which man is

adopted into the sonship of God and renewed according to the interior man and made a sharer of the divine nature, so that, thus renewed through the Holy Spirit, he can in turn live well and obey the mandates of God.

1043   43. In persons who are penitent before the sacrament of absolution, and in catechumens before baptism, there is true justification, yet separated from the remission of sin.

1044   44. In most good works performed by the faithful, simply to obey the mandates of God, such as obedience to parents, paying a trust, abstaining from homicide, theft, fornication, certain men are justified, because these are obedience to the law and the true justice of the law; and yet they do not obtain for them the increments of the virtues.

1045   45. The sacrifice of the Mass is a sacrifice for no other reason than for that general one by which "every work is performed that man may be closely connected with God in holy association." [1]

1046   46. Voluntariness does not pertain to the essence and definition of sin, nor is it a question of definition, but of cause and origin, whether every sin is bound to be voluntary.

1047   47. Therefore original sin truly has the essence of sin without any relation and respect to will, from which it had its origin.

1048   48. Original sin is voluntary in the habitual will of a child and habitually dominates the child, in this, that a child does not act contrary to the freedom of the will.

1049   49. And from an habitually dominating will it comes to pass that a small child, dying without the sacrament of regeneration, when he has attained the use of reason actually holds God in hatred, blasphemes God, and resists the law of God.

1050   50. Bad desires, to which reason does not consent, and which man unwillingly suffers, are prohibited by the precept: "Thou shalt not covet" [cf. Exod. 20:17].

1051   51. Concupiscence, whether the law of the members, and its depraved desires which men experience against their will, are the true disobediences of the law.

1052   52. Every crime is of this nature, that it can corrupt its author and all posterity in the way in which the first transgression corrupted.

1053   53. As much as arises from the force of transgression, so much of merited evils do they contract from the one generating, those who are born with lesser faults as well as those who are born with greater ones.

1054   54. This definitive opinion, that God has given no impossible commands to man, is falsely attributed to Augustine, whereas it belongs to Pelagius.

1055   55. God would not have had the power from the beginning to create such a man as is born now.

1056   56. There are two things in sin, an act and guilt; when, however, the

---

[1] Cf. St. Augustine, *De civit. Dei* 10, 6 (ML 41, 283).

act has passed, nothing remains except the guilt and the obligation to pay the penalty.

57. Therefore, in the sacrament of baptism or in the absolution of the 1057 priest the guilt of the sin only is taken away, and the ministry of the priests frees from guilt alone.

58. A penitent sinner is not vivified by the ministry of a priest who 1058 absolves, but by God alone, who by suggesting and inspiring penance, vivifies and brings him back to life; however, by the ministry of the priest on the other hand, the guilt alone is taken away.

59. When by almsgiving and other works of penance we make satis- 1059 faction to God for temporal punishments, we do not offer a worthy price to God for our sins, as some erring persons affirm (for otherwise, at least in some part, we should be redeemers); but we do something, in view of which the satisfaction of Christ is applied and communicated to us.

60. Through the sufferings of the saints communicated in indulgences, 1060 our sins are not properly atoned for; but through a communion of charity their sufferings are communicated to us, that we, who were freed by the price of the blood of Christ from punishments due to sins, may be worthy.

61. That famous distinction of the doctors, that the mandates of the 1061 divine law are fulfilled in two ways: in one way, in so far as pertains to the substance of the works alone; in the other way, in so far as pertains to a definite manner, namely, according to which they can guide the doer to eternal life (that is in the meritorious manner), is fabricated and should be rejected.

62. That distinction also by which a work is called good in two ways, 1062 either because it is right and good from its object and all its circumstances (which is usually termed moral), or because it is meritorious of the eternal kingdom, in so far as it proceeds from a living member of Christ the Spirit of charity, must be rejected.

63. Moreover that distinction of a twofold justice, one which is brought 1063 to pass through the indwelling Spirit of charity, the other which arises from the inspiration of the Holy Spirit exciting the heart to penance, but not yet dwelling in the heart and diffusing charity in it, by which the justification of the divine law may be fulfilled, is similarly condemned. 1064

64. And likewise that distinction of a twofold vivification, the one, by which a sinner is vivified, when the resolution to penance and the beginning of a new life through the grace of God inspire him; the other, by which he is vivified who is truly justified and is made a living branch on the vine for Christ, is equally deceitful and in no way consonant with the Scriptures.

65. Some good, or at least not bad use of free will can be admitted only 1065 by a Pelagian error; and he who knows and teaches this, does injury to the grace of Christ.

1066   66. Violence alone repels the natural liberty of man.

1067   67. Man sins, even to damnation, in what he does by necessity.

1068   68. Purely negative infidelity in those among whom Christ has not been preached, is a sin.

1069   69. The justification of a wicked man takes place formally through obedience to the law, not, however, through the hidden communication and the inspiration of grace, which makes those justified by it fulfill the law.

1070   70. Man existing in the state of mortal sin, or under the penalty of eternal damnation can have true charity; and even perfect charity can exist along with the guilt of eternal damnation.

1071   71. Through contrition even when joined with perfect charity and with the desire to receive the sacrament, a crime is not remitted without the actual reception of the sacrament, except in case of necessity, or of martyrdom.

1072   72. All afflictions of the just are punishments for sins themselves, therefore, both Job and the martyrs suffered what they suffered on account of sins.

1073   73. No one except Christ is free from original sin; hence, the Blessed Virgin died because of sin contracted from Adam, and all of her afflictions in this life as well as those of other just persons were the punishments for actual sin, or for original sin.

1074   74. Concupiscence in the regenerated who have fallen back into mortal sin, and in those in whom it dominates, is a sin, as also are other bad habits.

1075   75. The bad impulses of concupiscence in the state of depraved man are prohibited by the precept: "Thou shalt not covet" [Exod. 20:17]; hence, a man aware of these and not consenting, transgresses the precept: "Thou shalt not covet," although the transgression is not to be classed as a sin.

1076   76. As long as there is something of carnal concupiscence in one who loves, he does not fulfill the precept: "Thou shalt love the Lord with thy whole heart" [Deut. 6:5; Matt. 22:37].

1077   77. Laborious satisfactions of those who are justified are of no avail to expiate condignly the temporal punishments remaining after the fault has been remitted.

1078   78. The immortality of the first man was not a benefit of grace, but a natural condition.

1079   79. The opinion of the doctors that the first man could have been created by God and established without natural justice, is false.

1080   These opinions have been carefully considered and examined before us; although some of them could be maintained in some way,[1] yet in the strict

---

[1] This is the very celebrated *Comma Pianum,* which heretics transferred from this place to another, so that the sense was clearly changed. On this matter consult Tornelius,

and proper sense intended by those asserting them, we condemn them respectively as heretical, erroneous, suspect, rash, scandalous, and as giving offense to pious ears.

Exchanges (i.e., Exchanging of Money, Promissory Notes) [1]

[From the ordinance "In eam pro nostro," Jan. 28, 1571]

First (then) we condemn all those exchanges which are called fictitious, **1081** (elsewhere, *dry*), and are so devised that the contracting parties at certain market places or at other localities pretend to solemnize exchanges; at which places those who receive money, actually hand over their letters of exchange, but they are not sent, or they are so sent that, when the time has passed they are brought back void, whence they had set out; or, even when no letters of this kind were handed over, the money is finally demanded with interest, where the contract had been solemnized; for between givers and receivers even from the beginning it had been so decided, or surely such was the intention, and there is no one who in the marketplaces or the above mentioned places makes payment, when such letters are received. And similar to this evil is also that, when money or deposits or by another name fictitious exchanges are handed over so that afterwards in the same place or elsewhere they are paid back with interest.

But even in the exchanges which are called real, sometimes, as it is **1082** reported to me, bankers put off the prescribed term of payment, when a profit has been received according to tacit or expressed agreement or even only a promise. All these things we declare to be usurious, and strictly prohibit their being done.

GREGORY XIII 1572–1585

Profession of Faith Prescribed for the Greeks [2]

[From the acts concerning the union of the Greco-Russian church, 1575]

I, N., in firm faith believe and profess each and every thing which is **1083** contained in the Creed of faith, which the holy Roman Church uses,

---

Tract. de gratia Christi q. 3, sec., "Momenta ex parte materiae Bullarum adversus Baium"; also Kilber, *Tract. de gratia,* disp. 4, c. 2 "De variis circa gratiam erroribus," art. 4, quaeres 2. Viva ad prop. 31, Alexandri VIII B. n. 13 [cf. n. 1321].

[1] CIC Lib. "Sept." V 13, 2; Franc. Sentis, Clementis Papae VIII Decretalis (Frib. 1870) [ed. Boehmer (1747) App. 78; ed. Freiesleben (1773) App. 79, where 1575 is read incorrectly].

[2] BR(T) 8, 133 a ff.; MBR 2, 429 a ff.

namely: I believe in one God [as in the Nicean-Constantinopolitan Creed, n. 86, 994].

1084   I also believe, and I accept and profess all the things which the holy ecumenical Synod of FLORENCE defined and declared concerning the union of the western and eastern Church, namely that the Holy Spirit is eternally from the Father and the Son; and that He has His essence and His subsistent being from the Father and from the Son together; and that He proceeds from both eternally, as from one principle and by a single procession, since what the holy Doctors and Fathers say comes to mean the same thing, that from the Father through the Son the Holy Spirit proceeds, and that the Son, according to the Greeks, is also the cause, and according to the Latins, indeed the principle of the subsistence of the Holy Spirit, as is the Father. All things, however, which are of the Father, the Father Himself has given to His only-begotten Son in generation, outside of being the Father; the very fact that the Holy Spirit proceeds from the Son, the Son himself eternally has from the Father, by whom He has also been eternally begotten. And that the explanation of these words, "Filioque," for the sake of declaring the truth, and because of imminent necessity, has lawfully and reasonably been added to the Creed. . . . The text follows from the decrees of the union of the Greeks. Council of FLORENCE.

1085   Besides, I profess and accept all the other things which the holy Roman and Apostolic Church, according to the decrees of the holy ecumenical general Synod of TRENT, proposed and prescribed should be professed and accepted, as well as the contents in the above mentioned creeds of faith, as follows:

Apostolic . . . and all the rest, as in the profession of faith of TRENT [n. 995 ff.].

Sixtus V 1585–1590   Gregory XIV 1590–1591
Urban VII 1590   Innocent IX 1591

CLEMENT VIII 1592–1605

The Faculty of Blessing Sacred Oils [1]

[From the Instruction concerning the rites of the Italo-Greeks, August 30, 1595]

1086   (3) . . . Greek priests are not to be forced to accept the holy oils, except the chrism from the Latin diocesan bishops, since oils of this kind are

---

[1] BR(T) 10, 212 a; cf. Constit. Benedicti XIV "Etsi pastoralis," May 26, 1742 [BB (M) 1, 353; MBR 16, 96 b]; where it is stated that Greek priests cannot validly confirm

produced and blessed by them in the furnishing of the oils and the pre-sensation of the sacraments according to the ancient rite. . . . Let them be forced to accept chrism, however, which, even according to their rite, cannot be blessed except by a bishop.

Ordination of Schismatics

[From the same Instruction] [1]

(4) Those ordained by schismatic bishops, who have been otherwise **1087** duly ordained, the due form having been observed, receive, indeed, ordina-tion, but not jurisdiction.

Absolution of One in absentia [2]

[From the Decree of the Holy Office, June 20, 1602]

His Holiness . . . condemned and forbade as false, rash, and scandalous **1088** the proposition, namely, "that it is lawful through letters or through a messenger to confess sins sacramentally to an absent confessor, and to receive absolution from that same absent confessor," and orders in turn that that proposition thereafter not be taught in public or private gather-ings, assemblies, and congresses; and that it never in any case be defended as probable, be given the stamp of approval, or be reduced in any way to practice.

According to an opinion of the Holy Office, published repeatedly (espe- **1089** cially on June 7, 1603, and January 24, 1522) under Clement VIII and Paul V, this decree also in a divided sense, i.e., on confession and on absolution separately, is sound; to the decree of the Holy Office a reply was made on July 14, 1605: "The most holy has decreed that the men-tioned interpretation of P. Suarez on the above mentioned decree [namely, on the divided sense] is not adequate," and, according to a decree of the Congregation of the Fathers Theologians on June 7, 1603, it cannot be supported "from that case, when upon only signs of repentance being given and reported to a priest who is present, absolution is given one on the very point of death after confession of sins was made to an absent priest, since it contains an entirely conflicting difficulty." This decree, "by the aforesaid Supreme Pontiffs" is said to have been approved in a decree published on January 24, 1622, by a cardinal, one of the Inquisitors, together with some theologians, and is published a second time: according

---

infants in Italy and adjacent islands, since this was expressly forbidden [see n. 1459] them by Clement VIII in the year 1595.

[1] BR(T) 10, 212 b.

[2] DuPl III, II 171; Viva I 577 a.

to a decree of January 24, 1622, "from the case of that sick person, to whom on the very point of death upon petitioning for confession and after signs of repentance were given, and reported to a priest who is coming, absolution is given, although (the circumstances) contain conflicting reason, no controversy can arise over the spoken decree of Clement VIII." [1]

LEO XI 1605

PAUL V 1605-1621

The Aids or Efficacy of Grace [2]

[From the formula for ending disputes sent to the superior generals of the Order of Preachers and of the Society of Jesus, Sept. 5, 1607]

1090   In the matter of aids [de auxiliis] the right is granted by the Supreme Pontiff not only to the disputants but also to the consultors of returning to their countries and their homes; and it is added that this will be so that His Holiness may promulgate at an opportune time the declaration and conclusion which were awaited. But it was most seriously forbidden by the same Most Holy Lordship that in treating this question anyone either qualify the position opposite his own or note it with any censure. Even more he desires that they in turn abstain from harsh words indicating bitterness of mind. [3]

GREGORY XV 1621-1623   URBAN VIII 1623-1644

---

[1] For this and other documents on this subject, see R. de Scorraille, Francois Suarez II, Parisiis, 1912, 110-114.

[2] Theod. Eleutherius (Meyer) S.J., *Historia controversiarum de divinae gratiae auxiliis,* Antwerp., 1705, 724 a; cf. Jas. Hyac. Serry, O. Pr., *Historia Congregationum de auxiliis divinae gratiae, Antwerp.,* 1709, 587 f.; G. Schneemann, S.J., *Controversiarum de div. gratiae liberique arbitrii Concordia initia et progressus,* Friburgi, 1881, 292 f. When a sharp controversy had arisen between Dominicans and the Jesuit fathers on the aids of grace, whether indeed grace is efficacious from within (from the efficacy of connection with consent) and consists of physical predetermination, as the most reverend Preachers said, or whether the infallibility of divine predestination to grace depends on an intermediate knowledge, Clement VIII established a Congregation on aids to put an end to the strife, which for nine whole years, 1598-1607, sweated over a solution of the case. Finally, when Paul V was in power, after endless disputations were held by the most celebrated theologians of both parties, an end was imposed upon the strife by the Highest Supreme Pontiff.

[3] Furthermore Paul V (decree of the Holy Office, Dec., 1611) prohibited the publication of books on the subject of aids, even under the pretext of commenting on St. Thomas, or in any other way, without first having been proposed to the Holy Inquisitor. Urban VIII reinforced this (through the decrees of the Holy Inquisitor on the days of May 22, 1625 and August 1, 1642) by adding the penalties of deprivation of the faculty

INNOCENT X 1644–1655

Error of the Dual Head of the Church (or the Primacy of R. P.) [1]

[From the decree of the Sacred Office, Jan. 24, 1647]

The most holy . . . has decreed and declared *heretical* this proposition **1091** so presented that it established an exact equality between St. PETER and St. Paul, without subordination and subjection of St. Paul to St. Peter in supreme power, and in the rule of the universal Church: "St. PETER and St. Paul are the two princes of the Church who form one head, or: there are two Catholic heads and supreme leaders of the Catholic Church, joined in highest unity between themselves"; or, "the head of the Catholic Church consists of two who are most divinely united into one"; or, "there are two supreme pastors and guardians of the Church, who form one head only."

---

of teaching and of preaching, of reserving the active and passive voice and excommunication (of an interdict respectively) to the Supreme Pontiff, and to be incurred *ipso facto*. Yet these prohibitions afterwards passed into disuse. Certain of the adversaries of the Molinists falsely contended that the Bull which condemned their doctrine was made by Paul V, and was not only promulgated but that the autograph was preserved in the archive [cf. n. 1097]. The Supreme Pontiff imposed strict silence regarding the conclusion of the Congregation, and gave over to the General of each order a formula by which each would announce the will of the Pope to his man. Not long after Benedict XIV wrote as follows (in the year 1748) to the Supreme Inquisitor of Spain: "You know that there are manifold opinions in the schools on the famous questions about predestination and grace, and on the manner of reconciling human liberty with the omnipotence of God. The Thomists are proclaimed destroyers of human liberty and as followers, not to say of Jansenism but even of Calvinism; but, since they meet the charges with eminent satisfaction, and since their opinion has never been condemned by the Holy See, the Thomists carry on with impunity in this matter, and it is not fitting for any ecclesiastical superior in the present state of affairs to remove them from their opinion. The Augustinians are reported as the followers of du Bay and Jansenism. They represent themselves as supporters of human liberty, and with all their strength banish opposition and, since their opinion has not been condemned by the Holy See, there is no one who does not see that there can be no effort on the part of anyone to cause them to relinquish their opinion. The followers of Molina and Suarez are condemned by their adversaries just as if they were Semipelagians; the Roman Pontiffs thus far have not passed judgment on this system of Molina, and so they continue in its defense and can continue. . . ."—For the decree of Innocent X against Jansenists and what was afterwards published by the Supreme Pontiffs on this matter, see n. 1097.

[1] DuPl. III, II 248.

Errors (5) of Cornelius Jansen [1]

[Excerpts from "Augustinus" and condemned in the Constitutions
"Cum occasione," May 31, 1658]

1092   1. Some of God's precepts are impossible to the just, who wish and strive to keep them, according to the present powers which they have; the grace, by which they are made possible, is also wanting.
Declared and condemned as rash, impious, blasphemous, condemned by anathema, and heretical.

1093   2. In the state of fallen nature one never resists interior grace.
Declared and condemned as heretical.

1094   3. In order to merit or demerit in the state of fallen nature, freedom from necessity is not required in man, but freedom from external compulsion is sufficient.
Declared and condemned as heretical.

1095   4. The Semipelagians admitted the necessity of a prevenient interior grace for each act, even for the beginning of faith; and in this they were heretics, because they wished this grace to be such that the human will could either resist or obey.
Declared and condemned as false and heretical.

1096   5. It is Semipelagian to say that Christ died or shed His blood for all men without exception.
Declared and condemned as false, rash, scandalous, and understood in this sense, that Christ died for the salvation of the predestined, impious, blasphemous, contumelious, dishonoring to divine piety, and heretical.

The Aids or Efficacy of Grace [2]

[From the decree against the Jansenists, April 23, 1654]

1097   But, since at Rome as well as elsewhere there are being circulated certain assertions, acts, manuscripts, and, perchance, printed documents of

---

[1] DuPl III, II 261 ff.; Viva 1 512 b ff.; CICRcht II 138 f.; BR(T) 15, 720 a f.; MBR 5, 486 b; 6, 47 a f. *Bulletin de Littér. Ecclés.* (Toulouse, 1942) 231 f. These propositions of Jansenism were again condemned by Alexander VII with the Constitution, "Ad sanctam B. Patri Sedem" on Oct. 16, 1656; then by Constitution, "Regiminis apostolici" on Feb. 15, 1664, in which he published the formulary [see n. 1099]; finally, by Clement XI with the Constitution, "Vineam Domini Sabaoth" on July 16, 1905 [see n. 1350].

[2] Th. Eleutherus (Meyer) *Hist. controv. de div. gratiae auxiliis,* 707 a; in Serry, *Hist. Congreg. de auxil.,* XXXIV. When the Jansenists appealed against the Molinists to certain acts of the Congregation on aids, and brought forward in place of the true Bull of Paul V the judgments of one or another of the Consultors, to which the solemnity of promulgation alone was lacking, Innocent X in a solemn decree, in which he condemned various books, written in defense of Jansenism, passed this judgment on the pretended Bull of Paul V and the other acts.

the Congregations held in the presence of most happily reigning Clement VIII and Paul V on the question of "Aids of Divine Grace," both under the name of Francis Payne, once Dean of the Roman Rota, and under the name of Fr. Thomas of Lemos, O.P., and of other prelates and theologians, who, as it is asserted, were present at the aforementioned Congregations, besides a certain autograph or exemplar of the Constitution of the same Paul V on the definition of the aforesaid question *On Aids,* and of the condemnation of the opinion or opinions of Louis Molina, S.J., His Holiness by the present decree declares and decrees that no trust at all is to be placed in the above-mentioned assertions, acts, on behalf of the opinion of the Brothers, O.S.D., as well as of Louis Molina and of the other religious, S.J., and in the autograph or exemplar of the above mentioned Constitution of Paul V; and that nothing can or ought to be alleged by either side or by anyone whatsoever; but that on this aforesaid question the decrees of Paul V and Urban VIII, their predecessors, are to be observed.[1]

---

[1] When, indeed, the faculty of Louvain implored Innocent VII that by authority of the Holy See they might be allowed and be free to continue handing down the doctrine of their elders which is contained in the book of censorship of the Universities of Louvain and Douae, together with the apology of Louvain, and that it be declared by the same that the doctrine of grace efficacious by itself, and of predestination before foreseen merits has been condemned and weakened by no Apostolic decrees thus far, the Highest Pontiff (in a brief on the 7th day of Feb., 1694) in the reported words of the "Indiculus," "Profundiores vero etc." [see n. 142] attributed to St. Celestine I, replied: "We do not think it opportune at present to demand a more elaborate discussion of divine helps than that which was instituted by our predecessors, Clement VIII and Paul V." When finally the Jansenists, who, in so far as they could, had not ceased to foment disagreements, and called themselves "Augustinian Thomists," and pretended to battle against the Jesuits alone, lamented that through the Bull "Unigenitus" the doctrine of Sts. Augustine and Thomas had been condemned by the machinations of the Jesuits, Clement VI, who had published that Constitution, refuted those calumnies in the year 1718 by another (Constitution) which begins, "Pastoralis officii" sec. 3. Furthermore, Benedict XIII, who by the Constitution "Pretiosus" (May 26, 1727) confirmed the privileges of the Order of Preachers, prohibited, sec. 30, anyone from condemning in any way whatsoever the doctrine of St. Thomas and his school, and from ridiculing it as condemned in the Bull "Unigenitus." Finally, Clement XII (October 2, 1733) confirmed the decrees of Clement XI and Benedict XIII, and added this: "Yet, having discovered the mind of our predecessors, we do not wish either by our own or their praises conferred on the Thomistic school, which we approve and confirm by our repeated judgment, that there be any disparagement of the other Catholic schools which think differently from the same in explaining the efficacy of divine grace, and whose merits also are clear to the Holy See." He renewed the decrees of Paul V and of others and forbade (all) "from daring to brand any mark or theological censure on the same schools which have different opinions, and to assail their opinions by insults and invectives, until this Holy See shall decide that some definition and pronouncement must be made on the same controversies."

ALEXANDER VII 1655-1667

The Meaning of the Words of Cornelius Jansen [1]

[From the Constitution "Ad sacram beati PETRI Sedem,"
Oct. 16, 1656]

1098   (6) We declare and define that these five propositions have been taken
from the book of the aforementioned Cornelius Jansen, Bishop of Ypres,
entitled AUGUSTINUS, and in the sense understood by that same
Cornelius condemned.

Formulary of Submission Proposed for the Jansenists [2]

[From the Constitution, "Regiminis apostolicis," Feb. 15, 1665]

1099   "I, N., submit to the apostolic Constitution of INNOCENT X, dated
May 31, 1653, and to the Constitution of ALEXANDER VII, dated Oct.
16, 1656, Supreme Pontiffs, and I reject and condemn with a sincere heart,
just as the Apostolic See has condemned them by the said Constitutions,
the five propositions taken from the book of Cornelius Jansen, entitled
Augustinus, and in the sense understood by that same author, and so
I swear: So help me God, and this holy gospel of God." [3]

The Immaculate Conception of the B.V.M.[4]

[From the Bull "Sollicitudo omnium eccl.," Dec. 8, 1661]

1100   (1) The devotion to the most blessed Virgin Mary is indeed of long
standing among the faithful of Christ who believe that her soul, from
the first instant of its creation and infusion into her body, was preserved
immune by a special grace and privilege of God from the stain of original

---

[1] DuPl III, II 281 b (445 b); Viva I 513 b f.; BR(T) 16, 247 a; NBR 6, 47 b.—When,
after the propositions of Jansenism had been condemned by the Supreme Pontiffs, the
Jansenists returned to that sophistry, so as to say that these were indeed to be condemned, and that the meaning was not Jansen's, Alexander VII made these declarations.

[2] DuPl III, II 315 b (446 b); Viva I 514 b; BR(T) 17, 336 b; MBR 6, 212 a.

[3] When some Belgian priests had made certain additions to the formulary, Innocent XII in a brief (Feb. 6, 1694), after confirming the Constitution of Innocent X
and Alexander VII, forbade that this be done, and ordered that the formulary be
taken by all in the obvious sense; but in a second brief (Nov. 24, 1696) declared
that he by no means detracted from the Constitution of Alexander VII by this decree.
Finally, Clement XI in the Constitution, "Vineam Dominis," which we offer below
[see note 1350], closed every way to the subterfuges of the Jansenists as concerns dogmatic fact, and renewed the Constitutions of Innocent X and of Alexander VII.

[4] BR(T) 16, 739 b; MBR 6, 152.

sin, in view of the merits of her Son, Jesus Christ, the Redeemer of our human race, and who, in this sense, esteem and solemnly celebrate the festivity of her conception; the number of these has increased (after the Constitutions of SIXTUS IV renewed by the Council of Trent, note 734 f., 792.) . . . so that . . . now almost all Catholics embrace it. . . .

(4) We renew the Constitutions and decrees published by Roman Pontiffs in favor of the opinion that asserts that the soul of the blessed Virgin Mary at its creation, and at its infusion into her body, was blessed by the grace of the Holy Spirit and was preserved from original sin.

Various Errors on Moral Matters [1]

[Condemned in decrees of Sept. 24, 1665, and of March 18, 1666]

A. On the 24th Day of September, 1665

1. A man is not bound at any time at all in his life to utter an act of 1101 faith, hope, and charity by the force of the divine precepts pertaining to these virtues.

2. A man belonging to the orders of Knights when challenged to a 1102 duel can accept this, lest he incur the mark of cowardice among others.

3. That opinion which asserts that the Bull "Coenae" prohibits ab- 1103 solution of heresy and other crimes only when they are public and that this does not diminish the power of Trent, in which there is a discussion of secret crimes, in the year 1629, July 18th, in the Consistory of the Sacred Congregation of the Most Eminent Cardinals, was seen and sustained.

4. Regular prelates can in the court of conscience absolve any seculars 1104 at all of hidden heresy and of excommunication incurred by it.

5. Although it is evidently established by you that Peter is a heretic, 1105 you are not bound to denounce [him], if you cannot prove it.

6. A confessor who in sacramental confession gives the penitent a 1106 paper to be read afterwards, in which he incites to lust, is not consid- ered to have solicited in the confessional, and therefore is not to be de- nounced.

7. A way to avoid the obligation of denouncing solicitation exists if the 1107 one solicited confesses with the soliciter; the latter can absolve that one without the burden of denouncing.

8. A priest can lawfully accept a twofold stipend for the same Mass by 1108 applying to the petitioner even the most special part of the proceeds

---

[1] DuPl III, II 321 a ff.; Viva I at the beginning; MBR 6, App. 1 ff. Certain moral propositions condemned by Alexander VII and by Innocent XI [see note 1151 ff.], have been taken from the Louvain condemnation of May 4, 1657, and of April 26, 1653.

appropriated to the celebrant himself, and this after the decree of Urban VIII.[1]

1109   9. After the decree of Urban,[2] a priest, to whom Masses are given to be celebrated, can give satisfaction through another, by paying a smaller stipend to him and retaining the other part of the stipend for himself.

1110   10. It is not contrary to justice to accept a stipend for several sacrifices and to offer one sacrifice. Nor, is it contrary to fidelity if I promise, with a promise confirmed also by an oath, to him who gives a stipend, what I offer for no one else.

1111   11. We are not bound to express in a subsequent confession sins omitted in confession or forgotten because of the imminent danger of death or for some other reason.

1112   12. Mendicants can absolve from cases reserved for bishops, when the faculty of the bishop was not obtained for this.

1113   13. He satisfies the precept of an annual confession, who confesses to a regular, presented to a bishop, but unjustly reproved by him.

1114   14. He who makes no confession voluntarily, satisfies the precept of the Church.

1115   15. A penitent by his own authority can substitute another for himself, to fulfill the penance in his place.

1116   16. Those who have provided a benefice can select as confessor for themselves a simple priest not approved by the ordinary.

1117   17. It is permitted a religious or a cleric to kill a calumniator who threatens to spread grave crimes about him or his order, when no other means of defense is at hand; as it seems not to be, if a calumniator be ready to spread the aforesaid about the religious himself or his order publicly or among people of importance, unless he be killed.

1118   18. It is permitted to kill a false accuser, false witnesses, and even a judge, from whom an unjust sentence threatens with certainty, if the innocent can avoid harm in no other way.

1119   19. A husband does not sin by killing on his own authority a wife caught in adultery.

1120   20. The restitution imposed by Pius V [3] upon those who have received benefits but not reciting [the Divine Office in fulfillment of their obligation] is not due in conscience before the declaratory sentence of the judge, because it is a penalty.

1121   21. He who has a collective chaplaincy, or any other ecclesiastical benefit, if he is busy with the study of letters, satisfies his obligation, if he recites the office through another.

---

[1] In the Constitution of Innocent XII "Nuper," Dec. 23, 1697.
[2] In the Constitution of Innocent XII "Nuper," Dec. 23, 1697.
[3] Constit. *"Ex proximo,"* Sept. 20, 1571.

22. It is not contrary to justice not to confer ecclesiastical benefits 1122 gratuitously, because the contributor who contributes those ecclesiastical benefits with money intervening does not exact that money for the contribution of the benefit, but for a temporal profit, which he was not bound to contribute to you.

23. He who breaks a fast of the Church to which he is bound, does 1123 not sin mortally, unless he does this out of contempt and disobedience, e.g., because he does not wish to subject himself to a precept.

24. Voluptuousness, sodomy, and bestiality are sins of the same ulti- 1124 mate species, and so it is enough to say in confession that one has procured a pollution.

25. He who has had intercourse with an unmarried woman satisfies 1125 the precept of confession by saying: "I committed a grievous sin against chastity with an unmarried woman," without mentioning the intercourse.

26. When litigants have equally probable opinions in their defense, 1126 the judge can accept money to bring a sentence in favor of one over the other.

27. If a book is published by a younger or modern person, its opinion 1127 should be considered as probable, since it is not established that it has been rejected by the Holy See as improbable.

28. A nation does not sin, even if without any cause it does not accept 1128 a law promulgated by the ruler.

B. On the 18th day of March, 1666

29. On a day of fasting, he who eats a moderate amount frequently, 1129 even if in the end he has eaten a considerable quantity, does not break the fast.

30. All officials who labor physically in the state are excused from the 1130 obligation of fasting, and need not make certain whether the labor is compatible with fasting.

31. All those are entirely excused from fasting, who make a journey 1131 by riding, under whatever circumstances they make the journey, even if it is not necessary and even if they make a journey of a single day.

32. It is not evident that the custom of not eating eggs and cheese in 1132 Lent is binding.

33. Restitution of income because of the omission of stipends can be 1133 supplied through any alms that a beneficiary has previously made from the income of his service.

34. By reciting the paschal office on the day of Palms one satisfies the 1134 precept.

35. By a single office anyone can satisfy a twofold precept, for the 1135 present day and tomorrow.

1136   36. Regulars can in the forum of conscience use their privileges which were expressly revoked by the Council of Trent.

1137   37. Indulgences conceded to regulars and revoked by Paul V are today revalidated.

1138   38. The mandate of the Council of Trent, made for the priest who of necessity performs the Sacrifice while in mortal sin, to confess as soon as possible [see note 880], is a recommendation, not a precept.

1139   39. The expression "quam primum" is understood to be when the priest will confess in his own time.

1140   40. It is a probable opinion which states that a kiss is only venial when performed for the sake of the carnal and sensible [1] delight which arises from the kiss, if danger of further consent and pollution is excluded.

1141   41. One living in concubinage is not bound to dismiss the concubine, if she is very useful for the pleasure of him so living (in the vernacular, "*regalo*") provided that if she [another reading: he] were missing, he would carry on life with very great difficulty, and other food would affect him living in concubinage with great loathing, and another maid servant would be found with very great difficulty.

1142   42. It is permitted one who borrows money to exact something beyond the principal, if he obligates himself not to seek the principal until a certain time.

1143   43. An annual legacy left for the soul does not bind for more than ten years.

1144   44. So far as the forum of conscience is concerned, when the guilty has been corrected and the contumacy ceases, the censures cease.

1145   45. Books prohibited "until they are expurgated" can be retained until they are corrected by the application of diligence.

All these are condemned and prohibited, at least as scandalous.

Perfect and Imperfect Contrition [2]

[From the decree of the Sacred Office, May 5, 1667]

1146   *Concerning the controversy:* Whether that attrition, which is inspired by the fear of hell, excluding the will to sin, with the hope of pardon, to obtain grace in the sacrament of penance requires in addition some act of love of God, to some asserting this, and to others denying it, and in turn censuring the opposite opinion: . . . His Holiness . . . orders . . . that if they later write about the matter of the aforementioned attrition, or publish books or writings or teach or preach or in any manner whatever instruct penitents or students and others, let them not dare change either opinion with a note of any theological censure or

---

[1] *Viva reads* "sensualis," *but DuPl and MBR as it is here,* "sensibilis."
[2] DuPl III, II 824b f.

contumely, whether it be that of denying the necessity of any love of God in the aforementioned attrition inspired by the fear of hell, which seems to be the more common opinion among scholastics today, or whether that of asserting the necessity of this love, until something has been defined by the Holy See concerning this matter.

CLEMENT IX 1667–1669   CLEMENT X 1670–1676

INNOCENT XI 1676–1689

Frequent and Daily Communion [1]

[From the Decree C. S. Conc., Feb. 12, 1679]

Although the daily and frequent use of the most holy Eucharist has **1147** always been approved by the holy Fathers of the Church, yet never have they appointed certain days either for receiving it more often or certain days of the weeks and months for abstaining from it, which the Council of Trent did not prescribe; but, as if it considered the frailty of human nature, although making no command, it merely indicated what it would prefer when it said: "The Holy Council would indeed wish that at every Mass the faithful present would communicate by the sacramental reception of the Eucharist" [see n. 944]. And this not without cause, for there are very many secret recesses of conscience, various diversions because of the occupations of the spirit, likewise many graces and gifts of God granted to children, and since we cannot scrutinize these with human eyes, nothing can be established concerning the worthiness or integrity of anyone, and consequently nothing concerning the more frequent or daily partaking of the bread of life.

And thus, as far as concerns tradesmen themselves, frequent approach to the receiving of the holy sustenance is to be left to the judgment of the confessors who explore the secrets of the heart, who from the purity of consciences and from the fruit of frequency and from the progress in piety in the case of laity, tradesmen, and married men, will be obliged to provide for them whatever they see will be of benefit to their salvation.

In the case of married persons, however, let them seriously consider this, since the blessed Apostle does not wish them to "defraud one another, except perhaps by consent for a time, that they may give them-

---

[1] Collect. S.C. de Prop. Fide (1907) n. 219; DuPl III, II 346 b f.; Ferraris, *Prompta Bibliotheca*, s.v. "Eucharistis" I 41 (III 244 b ff.).—This decree conforms entirely with the response *S.C. Conc.* already given in the year 1587 (Jan. 24) to the Bishop of Brescia [*Dict. de Théol. cath.* s.v. *Communion eucharist. (fréquente)*, T. 3, col. 534 f.; *Analecta Iuris Pontifici*, ser. 7, col. 789 f.].

selves to prayer" [cf. I Cor. 7:5], let them advise these seriously that they should give themselves more to continence, because of reverence for the most holy Eucharist, and that they should come together for communion in the heavenly banquet with a purer mind.

1148   In this, then, will the diligence of pastors be especially alert, not that some may not be deterred from frequent or daily partaking of holy communion by a single formula of precept, or that days for partaking be established generally, but rather let it be decided what should be permitted to each, or should be decided for themselves by themselves, or by the priests or confessors; and let this be prohibited entirely: that no one be repelled from the sacred banquet, whether he approach it frequently or daily, and yet let it attend that everyone taste of the sweetness of the body of the Lord more rarely or more frequently according to his measure of devotion and preparation.

1149   Similarly nuns who desire holy communion daily will have to be advised to receive communion on the days established by the rule of their order; if some, however, are distinguished by purity of mind and are so enkindled by fervor of spirit that they seem worthy of more frequent or daily reception of the most holy Sacrament, let this be permitted them by the superiors.

It will be of benefit, too, besides the diligence of priests and confessors, to make use also of the services of preachers and to have an agreement with them, that, when the faithful have become used [1] to frequenting the most holy Sacrament (which they should do), they preach a sermon on the great preparation for undertaking that, and show in general that those who by devout zeal are stirred to a more frequent or daily partaking of the health bringing Food, whether lay tradesmen, or married people, or any others, ought to understand their own weakness, so that because of the dignity of the Sacrament and the fear of the divine judgment they may learn to revere the celestial table on which is Christ; and if at any time they should feel themselves not prepared, to abstain from it and to gird themselves for a greater preparation.

But let bishops, in whose dioceses such devotion towards the most Blessed Sacrament flourishes, give thanks to God for this, and they should nurture it by applying to it the proper measure of prudence and judgment, and on their part they will especially prevail upon themselves that no labor or diligence must be spared to do away with every suspicion of irreverence and scandal in the reception of the true and immaculate lamb, and to increase virtues and gifts in those who partake of it; and this will happen abundantly, if those, who are bound by such devoted zeal, by surpassing divine grace, and who desire to be refreshed more frequently

---

[1] It seems that the reading should be "accenderit," "have enkindled."

by the most holy bread, become accustomed to expend their strength and to prove themselves with reverence and love. . . .

Furthermore, let bishops and priests or confessors refute those who 1150 hold that daily communion is of divine right, . . . Let them not permit that a confession of venial sins be made to a simple priest without the approbation of a bishop or ordinary.

Various Errors on Moral Subjects (II) [1]

[Condemned in a decree of the Holy Office, March 4, 1679]

1. It is not illicit in conferring sacraments to follow a probable opinion 1151 regarding the value of the sacrament, the safer opinion being abandoned, unless the law forbids it, convention or the danger of incurring grave harm. Therefore, one should not make use of probable opinions only in conferring baptism, sacerdotal or episcopal orders.

2. I think that probably a judge can pass judgment according to opin- 1152 ion, even the less probable.

3. In general, when we do something confidently according to prob- 1153 ability whether intrinsic or extrinsic, however slight, provided there is no departure from the bounds of probability, we always act prudently.[2]

4. An infidel who does not believe will be excused of infidelity, since 1154 he is guided by a less probable opinion.

5. Even though one sins mortally, we dare not condemn him who 1155 uttered an act of love of God only once in his life.

6. It is probable that the precept of love for God is of itself not of 1156 grave obligation even once every five years.

7. Then only is it obligatory when we are bound to be justified, and 1157 we have no other way by which we can be justified.

8. Eating and drinking even to satiety for pleasure only, are not sinful, 1158 provided this does not stand in the way of health, since any natural appetite can licitly enjoy its own actions.

9. The act of marriage exercised for pleasure only is entirely free of all 1159 fault and venial defect.

10. We are not bound to love our neighbor by an internal and formal 1160 act.

11. We can satisfy the precept of loving neighbor by external acts only. 1161

12. Scarcely will you find among seculars, even among kings, a super- 1162 fluity for [his] state of life. And so, scarcely anyone is bound to give alms from what is superfluous to [his] state of life.

13. If you act with due moderation, you can without mortal sin be 1163

---

[1] DuPl III, II 388 a ff.; Viva I, 175 ff.

[2] The moral system according to these opinions, which is called "Laxismus," is condemned.

sad about the moral life of someone and rejoice about his natural death, seek it with ineffectual desire and long for it, not indeed from dissatisfaction with the person but because of some temporal emolument.

1164   14. It is licit with an absolute desire to wish for the death of a father, not indeed as an evil to the father, but as a good to him who desires it, for a rich inheritance will surely come his way.

1165   15. It is licit for a son to rejoice over the parricide of his parent perpetrated by himself in drunkenness, because of the great riches that came from it by inheritance.

1166   16. Faith is not considered to fall under a special precept and by itself.

1167   17. It is enough to utter an act of faith once during life.

1168   18. If anyone is questioned by a public power, I advise him to confess his faith to a noble person as to God and (to be) proud of his faith; I do not condemn silence as sinful of itself.

1169   19. The will cannot effect that assent to faith in itself be stronger than the weight of reasons impelling toward assent.

1170   20. Hence, anyone can prudently repudiate the supernatural assent which he had.

1171   21. Assent to faith is supernatural and useful to salvation with only the probable knowledge of revelation, even with the fear by which one fears lest God has not spoken.

1172   22. Only faith in one God seems necessary by a necessity of means, not, however, the explicit (faith) in a Rewarder.

1173   23. Faith widely so called according to the testimony of creature or by a similar reason suffices for justification.

1174   24. To call upon God as a witness to a slight lie is not a great irreverence, because of which God wishes or can condemn man.

1175   25. With cause it is licit to swear without the intention of swearing, whether the matter be light or serious.

1176   26. If anyone swears, either alone or in the presence of others, whether questioned or of his own will, whether for sake of recreation or for some other purpose, that he did not do something, which in fact he did, understanding within himself something else which he did not do, or another way than that by which he did it, or some other added truth, in fact does not lie and is no perjurer.

1177   27. A just reason for using these ambiguous words exists, as often as it is necessary or useful to guard the well-being of the body, honor, property, or for any other act of virtue, so that the concealing of the truth is then regarded as expedient and zealous.

1178   28. He who has been promoted to a magistracy or a public office by means of a recommendation or a gift can utter with mental reservation the oath which is customarily exacted of similar persons by order of the king, without regard for the intent of the one exacting it, because he is not bound to confess a concealed crime.

29. A grave, pressing fear is a just cause for pretending the administration of sacraments. 1179

30. It is right for an honorable man to kill an attacker who tries to inflict calumny upon him, if this ignominy cannot be avoided otherwise; the same also must be said if anyone slaps him with his hand or strikes with a club and runs away after the slap of the hand or the blow of the club. 1180

31. I can properly kill a thief to save a single gold piece. 1181

32. It is not only permitted to defend, with a fatal defense, these things we possess actually, but also those things to which we have a partial right, and which we hope to possess. 1182

33. It is permitted an heir as well as a legatee to defend himself against one who unjustly prevents either an inheritance being assumed, or legacies being paid, just as it is permitted him who has a right to a chair or a benefice against one who unjustly impedes his possession of them. 1183

34. It is permitted to bring about an abortion before the animation of the foetus, lest the girl found pregnant be killed or defamed. 1184

35. It seems probable that every foetus (as long as it is in the womb) lacks a rational soul and begins to have the same at the time that it is born; and consequently it will have to be said that no homicide is committed in any abortion. 1185

36. It is permitted to steal not only in extreme, but in grave necessity. 1186

37. Male and female domestic servants can secretly steal from their masters to gain compensation for their work which they judge of greater worth than the salary which they receive. 1187

38. No one is bound under the pain of mortal sin to restore what has been taken away by small thefts, however great the sum total may be. 1188

39. Whoever moves or induces another to bring a serious loss upon a third party is not bound to a restitution of that loss incurred. 1189

40. A usurious contract is permitted even with respect to the same person, and with a contract to sell back previously entered upon with the intention of gain. 1190

41. Since ready cash is more valuable than that to be paid, and since there is no one who does not consider ready cash of greater worth than future cash, a creditor can demand something beyond the principal from the borrower, and for this reason be excused from usury. 1191

42. There is no usury when something is exacted beyond the principal as due because of a kindness and by way of gratitude, but only if it is exacted as due according to justice. 1192

43. What is it but venial sin if one detract authority by a false charge to prevent great harm to himself? 1193

1194   44. It is probable that he does not sin mortally who imposes a false charge on someone, that he may defend his own justice and honor. And if this is not probable, there is scarcely any probable opinion in theology.

1195   45. To give the temporal for the spiritual is not simony, when the temporal is not given for a price, but only as a motive for conferring and effecting the spiritual, or even because the temporal is only a gratuitous compensation for the spiritual, or vice versa.

1196   46. And this also is admissable, even if the temporal is the principal motive for giving the spiritual; furthermore, even if it be the end of the spiritual thing itself, so that it is considered of greater value than the spiritual thing.

1197   47. When the Council of Trent says that they sin mortally by sharing the sins of others who do not promote to the churches those whom they themselves judge to be more worthy and more useful for the Church, the Council either first seems to mean to signify by "more worthy" nothing else than the worthiness of being selected, using the comparative rather than the positive; or secondly, in a less proper expression takes "more worthy" to exclude the unworthy, but not the worthy, or finally, and thirdly, it is speaking of what occurs during an assembly.

1198   48. Thus it seems clear that fornication by its nature involves no malice, and that it is evil only because it is forbidden, so that the contrary seems entirely in disagreement with reason.

1199   49. Voluptuousness is not prohibited by the law of nature. Therefore, if God had not forbidden it, it would be good, and sometimes obligatory under pain of mortal sin.

1200   50. Intercourse with a married woman, with the consent of her husband, is not adultery, and so it is enough to say in confession that one had committed fornication.

1201   51. A male servant who knowingly by offering his shoulders assists his master to ascend through windows to ravage a virgin, and many times serves the same by carrying a ladder, by opening a door, or by cooperating in something similar, does not commit a mortal sin, if he does this through fear of considerable damage, for example, lest he be treated wickedly by his master, lest he be looked upon with savage eyes, or, lest he be expelled from the house.

1202   52. The precept of keeping feast days is not obligatory under pain of mortal sin, aside from scandal, if contempt be absent.

1203   53. He satisfies the precept of the Church of hearing the Holy Sacrifice, who hears two of its parts, even four simultaneously by different celebrants.

1204   54. He who cannot recite Matins and Lauds, but can the remaining hours, is held to nothing, since the great part brings the lesser to it.

55. He satisfies the precept of annual communion by the sacrilegious 1205 eating of the Lord.

56. Frequent confession and communion, even in those who live like 1206 pagans, is a mark of predestination.

57. It is probable that natural but honest imperfect sorrow for sins 1207 suffices.

58. We are not bound to confess to a confessor who asks us about the 1208 habit of some sin.

59. It is permitted to absolve sacramentally those who confess only 1209 half, by reason of a great crowd of penitents, such as for example can happen on a day of great festivity or indulgence.

60. The penitent who has the habit of sinning against the law of God, 1210 of nature, or of the Church, even if there appears no hope of amendment, is not to be denied absolution or to be put off, provided he professes orally that he is sorry and proposes amendment.

61. He can sometimes be absolved, who remains in a proximate occa- 1211 sion of sinning, which he can and does not wish to omit, but rather directly and professedly seeks or enters into.

62. The proximate occasion for sinning is not to be shunned when 1212 some useful and honorable cause for not shunning it occurs.

63. It is permitted to seek directly the proximate occasion for sinning 1213 for a spiritual or temporal good of our own or of a neighbor.

64. A person is fit for absolution, however much he labors under an 1214 ignorance of the mysteries of the faith, and even if through negligence, even culpable, he does not know the mystery of the most blessed Trinity, and of the incarnation of our Lord Jesus Christ.

65. It is enough to have believed the mysteries once. 1215

All condemned and prohibited, as they are here expressed, at least as scandalous and in practice pernicious.

The Holy Pontiff concludes the decree with these words:

Finally, in order that doctors, whether scholastics or any others what- 1216 soever, may refrain from injurious contentions in the future, and that there be deliberations for peace and charity, the same Holy Pontiff commands them in virtue of holy obedience, to be on their guard in printing books and manuscripts, as well as theses, disputations, and sermons against any censure and note, and likewise violent railings against such propositions which are still being carried on among Catholics here and there, until the matter has been considered, and a judgment is rendered [1] by the Holy See upon these same propositions.

---

[1] Benedict XIV sanctioned the same in the Bull, "Sollicita et provide," July 9th, 1753 [BB(M) 10, 251 ff.].

Errors on "donated omnipotence" [1]

[Condemned in the decree of the Holy Office, Nov. 23, 1679]

1217   1. God gives us His omnipotence, that we may use it, just as someone gives another a villa or a book.

1218   2. God submits His omnipotence to us.

They are prohibited as at least rash *and* novel.

Moral Systems [2]

[Decree of the Holy Office, June 26, 1680]

1219   In a report of the contents of the letters of Father Gonzales Thirsus directed to His Holiness through Father Laurea of the Society of Jesus, their most blessed Eminences said that the Secretary of State had written to the Apostolic Nuncio of the Spaniards, asking that he inform the said Father Thirsus what His Holiness commanded, after the letter was kindly received and read not without praise; that he himself freely and boldly preach, teach, and defend with his pen the more probable opinion, and not vigorously attack the opinion of those who assert that in the conflict of the less probable opinion with the more probable so recognized and judged, it is lawful to follow the less probable opinion; and to inform him that whatever he shall do and write in favor of the more probable will be pleasing to His Holiness. Let it be enjoined on the Father General of the Society concerning this order of His Holiness, that he not only permit the Fathers of the Society of Jesus to write in defense of the opinion of the more probable and to oppose the opinion of those who assert that in the controversy of the less probable opinion with the more probable so understood and judged, it is allowed to follow the less probable; but, moreover, let him also write to all the universities of the Society that it is the mind of His Holiness that anyone who will may freely write as he pleases in behalf of the more probable opinion and may attack the contrary opinion above mentioned; and let him order them to submit themselves in all things to the orders of His Holiness.[3]

---

[1] DuPl III, II 352 b: Viva I 564 a.

[2] *Études religieuses* 91 (1902 II), 847 f., where the authentic text appears.—Franc. ter Haar, C.SS.R., contends in his book, *"Ven. Innocentii PP XI de probabilismo decreti historia"* (Tornaci 1904, Casterman) that this decree, disciplinary rather than doctrinal, is prejudicial to "probabilismus"; and others likewise. And on the other hand Aug. Lehmkuhl, S.J., in the work "Probabilismus vindicatus" (Friburgi, 1906, Herder) 78–111 answers that it is not prejudicial to "probabilismus"; and others similarly.

[3] There is added in the copy of the Holy Office: "On the eighth day of July, 1680. When the above-mentioned order of His Holiness was reported to the Father General

Error Concerning the Seal of Confession [1]

[Condemned in the decree of the Holy Office, Nov. 18, 1862]

Concerning the proposition: "It is lawful to use knowledge obtained   1220
in confession, provided it is done without any direct or indirect revelation,
and without burden upon the penitent, unless some much greater evil
follows from its nonuse, in comparison with which the first would be
rightly held of little account," an explanation or limitation then being
added, that it is to be understood concerning the use of the knowledge
obtained from confession with burden to the penitent, any revelation
whatsoever being excluded, and in the case in which a much greater
burden to the same penitent would follow from its nonuse,

it is decided: "that the stated proposition, as far as it admits the use
of said knowledge with the burden upon the penitent, must be altogether
prohibited, even with the aforesaid explanation or limitation."

Errors of Michael of Molinos [2]

[Condemned in the decree of the Sacred Office, August 28, and
in the Constitutions "Coelestis Pastor," Nov. 20, 1687]

1. It is necessary that man reduce his own powers to nothingness, and   1221
this is the interior way.

2. To wish to operate actively is to offend God, who wishes to be   1222
Himself the sole agent; and therefore it is necessary to abandon oneself
wholly in God and thereafter to continue in existence as an inanimate
body.

3. Vows about doing something are impediments to perfection.   1223

4. Natural activity is the enemy of grace, and impedes the operations   1224
of God and true perfection, because God wishes to operate in us without us.

5. By doing nothing the soul annihilates itself and returns to its be-   1225
ginning and to its origin, which is the essence of God, in which it remains transformed and divinized, and God then remains in Himself,
because then the two things are no more united, but are one alone, and

---

of the Society of Jesus through the assessor, he replied that he would obey in every
respect most promptly, although it had never been forbidden by himself or his
predecessors to write in behalf of the more probable opinion and to teach it."

[1] DuPl III, II 354; Viva I 565 b.

[2] DuPl III, II 357 ff.; coll. Viva I 557 a ff.; BR(T) 19, 775 b ff.; MBR 10, 212 b ff.
—Michael de Molinos, born on June 29th, 1628, at Muniessa in Spain, in his works
and letters spread the errors of quietism, so-called, finally was imprisoned, and in
1696, fortified by the sacraments of the Church, died.

in this manner God lives and reigns in us, and the soul annihilates itself in operative being.

1226   6. The interior way is that in which neither light, nor love, nor resignation is recognized, and it is not necessary to understand God, and in this way one makes progress correctly.

1227   7. A soul ought to consider neither the reward, nor punishment, nor paradise, nor hell, nor death, nor eternity.

1228   8. He ought not to wish to know whether he is progressing with the will of God, or whether or not with the same resigned will he stands still; nor is it necessary that he wish to know his own state or his own nothingness; but he ought to remain as an inanimate body.

1229   9. The soul ought not to remember either itself, or God, or anything whatsoever, and in the interior life all reflection is harmful, even reflection upon its human actions and upon its own defects.

1230   10. If one scandalizes others by one's own defects, it is not necessary to reflect, as long as the will to scandalize is not present, and not to be able to reflect upon one's own defects, is a grace of God.

1231   11. It is not necessary to reflect upon doubts whether one is proceeding rightly or not.

1232   12. He who gives his own free will to God should care about nothing, neither about hell, nor about heaven; neither ought he to have a desire for his own perfection, nor for virtues, nor his own sanctity, nor his own salvation, the hope of which he ought to remove.

1233   13. After our free will has been resigned to God, reflection and care about everything of our own must be left to that same God, and we ought to leave it to Him, so that He may work His divine will in us without us.

1234   14. It is not seemly that he who is resigned to the divine will, ask anything of God; because asking is an imperfection, since the act is of one's own will and election, and this is wishing that the divine will be conformed to ours, and not that ours be conformed to the divine; and this from the Gospel: "Seek you shall find" [John 16:24], was not said by Christ for interior souls who do not wish to have free will; nay indeed, souls of this kind reach this state, that they cannot seek anything from God.

1235   15. Just as they ought not ask anything from God, so should they not give thanks to Him for anything, because either is an act of their own will.

1236   16. It is not proper to seek indulgences for punishment due to one's own sins, because it is better to satisfy divine justice than to seek divine mercy, since the latter proceeds from pure love of God, and the former from an interested love of ourselves, and that is not a thing pleasing to God and meritorious, because it is a desire to shun the cross.

1237   17. When free will has been surrendered to God, and the care and thought of our soul left to the same God, no consideration of temptations need any longer be of concern; neither should any but a negative resistence be made to them, with the application of no energy, and if nature is aroused, one must let it be aroused, because it is nature.

18. He who in his prayer uses images, figures, pretension, and his own conceptions, does not adore God "in spirit and in truth" [John 4:23].   1238

19. He who loves God in the way which reason points out or the intellect comprehends, does not love the true God.   1239

20. To assert that in prayer it is necessary to help oneself by discourse and by reflections, when God does not speak to the soul, is ignorance. God never speaks; His way of speaking is operation, and He always operates in the soul, when this soul does not impede Him by its discourses, reflections, and operations.   1240

21. In prayer it is necessary to remain in obscure and universal faith, with quiet and forgetfulness of any particular and distinct thought of the attributes of God and the Trinity, and thus to remain in the presence of God for adoring and loving Him and serving Him, but without producing acts, because God has no pleasure in these.   1241

22. This knowledge through faith is not an act produced by a creature, but it is a knowledge given by God to the creature, which the creature neither recognizes that he has, and neither later knows that he had it; and the same is said of love.   1242

23. The mystics with Saint Bernard in the *Scala Claustralium* [1] (*The Ladder of the Recluses*) distinguished four steps: reading, meditation, prayer, and infused contemplation. He who always remains in the first, never passes over to the second. He who always persists in the second, never arrives at the third, which is our acquired contemplation, in which one must persist throughout all life, provided that God does not draw the soul (without the soul expecting it) to infused contemplation; and if this ceases, the soul should turn back to the third step and remain in that, without returning again to the second or first.   1243

24. Whatever thoughts occur in prayer, even impure, or against God, the saints, faith, and the sacraments, if they are not voluntarily nourished, nor voluntarily expelled, but tolerated with indifference and resignation, do not impede the prayer of faith, indeed make it more perfect, because the soul then remains more resigned to the divine will.   1244

25. Even if one becomes sleepy and falls asleep, nevertheless there is prayer and actual contemplation, because prayer and resignation, resignation and prayer are the same, and while resignation endures, prayer also endures.   1245

26. The three ways: the purgative, illuminative, and unitive, are the   1246

---

[1] Elsewhere: The mystics with St. Bernard or the author of Scala Claustralis under the name of the same St. Bernard.

greatest absurdity ever spoken about in mystical (theology), since there is only one way, namely, the interior way.

1247   27. He who desires and embraces sensible devotion, does not desire nor seek God, but himself; and anyone who walks by the interior way, in holy places as well as on feast days, acts badly, when he desires it and tries to possess it.

1248   28. Weariness for spiritual matters is good, if indeed by it one's own love is purified.

1249   29. As long as the interior soul disdains discourses about God, and disdains the virtues, and remains cold, feeling no fervor in himself, it is a good sign.

1250   30. Everything sensible which we experience in the spiritual life, is abominable, base, and unclean.

1251   31. No meditative person exercises true interior virtues; these should not be recognized by the senses. It is necessary to abandon the virtues.

1252   32. Neither before nor after communion is any other preparation or act of thanksgiving required for these interior souls than continuance in a customary passive resignation, because in a more perfect way it supplies all acts of virtues, which can be practised and are practised in the ordinary way. And, if on this occasion of communion there arise emotions of humility, of petition, or of thanksgiving, they are to be repressed, as often as it is not discerned that they are from a special impulse of God; otherwise they are impulses of nature not yet dead.

1253   33. That soul acts badly which proceeds by this interior way, if it wishes on feast days by any particular effort to excite some sensible devotion in itself, since for an interior soul all days are equal, all festal. And the same is said of holy places, because to souls of this kind all places are alike.

1254   34. To give thanks to God by words and by speech is not for interior souls which ought to remain in silence, placing no obstacle before God, because He operates in them; and the more they resign themselves to God, they discover that they cannot recite the Lord's prayer, i.e., the Our Father.

1255   35. It is not fitting for souls of this interior life to perform works even virtuous ones, by their own choice and activity; otherwise they would not be dead. Neither should they elicit acts of love for the Blessed Virgin, saints, or the humanity of Christ, because since they are sensible objects, so, too, is their love toward them.

1256   36. No creature, neither the Blessed Virgin, nor the saints ought to abide in our heart, because God alone wishes to occupy and possess it.

1257   37. On occasion of temptations, even violent ones, the soul ought not to elicit explicit acts of opposite virtues, but should persevere in the above mentioned love and resignation.

38. The voluntary cross of mortifications is a heavy weight and fruit- 1258
less, and therefore to be dismissed.

39. The more holy works and penances, which the saints performed, 1259
are not enough to remove from the soul even a single tie.

40. The Blessed Virgin never performed any exterior work, and never- 1260
theless was holier than all the saints. Therefore, one can arrive at sanctity
without exterior work.

41. God permits and wishes to humiliate us and to conduct us to a true 1261
transformation, because in some perfect souls, even though not inspired,
the demon inflicts violence on their bodies, and makes them commit
carnal acts, even in wakefulness and without the bewilderment of the
mind, by physically moving their hands and other members against their
wills. And the same is said as far as concerns other actions sinful in
themselves, in which case they are not sins, but in them (*Viva: quia his,*
because with these) the consent is not present.

42. A case may be given, that things of this kind contrary to the will 1262
result in carnal acts at the same time on the part of two persons, for
example man and woman, and on the part of both an act follows.

43. God in past ages has created saints through the ministry of tyrants; 1263
now in truth He produces saints through the ministry of demons, who,
by causing the aforesaid things contrary to the will, brings it about that
they despise themselves the more and annihilate and resign themselves
to God.

44. Job blasphemed, and yet he did not sin with his lips because it 1264
was the result of the violence of the devil.

45. Saint Paul suffered such violences of the devil in his body; thus 1265
he has written: "For the good that I will I do not do; but the evil which
I will not, that I do" [Rom. 7:19].

46. Things of this kind contrary to the will are the more proportionate 1266
medium for annihilating the soul, and for leading [*Viva: et eam*] it to
true transformation and union, nor is there any other way; and this is
the easier and safer way.

47. When things of this kind contrary to the will occur, it is proper 1267
to allow Satan to operate, by applying no effort and making no real
attempt, but man should persist in his own nothingness; and even if
pollutions follow and obscene acts by one's own hands, and even worse,
there is no need to disquiet oneself [*Viva: inquietari*], but scruples must
be banished, as well as doubts and fears, because the mind becomes more
enlightened, more confirmed, and more candid, and holy liberty is acquired. And above all there is no need to confess these matters, and one
acts in a most saintly way by not confessing, because the devil is overcome by this agreement, and the treasure of peace is acquired.

48. Satan, who produces violences of this kind contrary to the will, 1268

afterwards persuades that they are grave sins, so that the mind disturbs itself, lest it progress further in the interior way; hence for weakening his powers it is better not to confess them, because they are not sins, not even venial.

1269   49. Job from the violence of the devil polluted himself with his own hands at the same time as "he offered pure prayer to God" (thus interpreting the passage from chapter 16, Job) [cf. Job. 16:18].

1270   50. David, Jeremias, and many of the holy Prophets suffered violence of this kind, of these impure external operations contrary to the will.

1271   51. In Sacred Scripture there are many examples of violence to the will unto external sinful acts, as that of Samson, who by violence killed himself with the Philistines [Judg. 16:29 f.], entered a marriage with a foreigner [Judg. 14:1 ff.], and committed fornication with the harlot Dalila [Judg. 16:4 ff.], which in other times were prohibited and would have been sins; that of Judith, who had lied to Holofernes, [Judg. 11: 4 ff.]; that of Elisaeus, who cursed children [IV Kings 2:24]; that of Elias, who burned the leaders with the troops of King Achab [cf. IV Kings 1:10 ff.]. But whether violence was immediately executed by God, or by the minister of the demons, as it happens in some souls, is left in doubt.

1272   52. When such things contrary to the will, even impure, happen without confusion of the mind, then the soul can be united to God, and *de facto* is always the more united.

1273   53. To recognize in practice, whether an operation has been violence in some persons, the rule which I have for this is not the protestations of those souls which protest that they have not consented to the said violences or cannot swear that they have consented, and cannot see that they are the souls who make progress in the interior life, but I would adopt a rule from a certain light which is superior to actual human and theological cognition, that makes me recognize for certain, with internal certitude, that such operation is violence; and I am certain that this light proceeds from God, because it comes to me joined with certitude that it comes forth from God, and it leaves in me no shadow of doubt to the contrary, in that way by which it sometimes happens that God in revealing something reassures the soul at the same time that it is He who reveals it, and the soul cannot doubt to the contrary.

1274   54. Persons who lead ordinary spiritual lives, in the hour of death will find themselves deluded and confused with all the passions to be purged in the other world.

1275   55. Through this interior life one reaches the point, although with much suffering, of purging and extinguishing all passions, so that he feels nothing more, nothing, nothing; nor is any disquietude felt, just as if the body were dead, nor does the soul permit itself to be moved any more.

56. Two laws and two desires (the one of the soul, the other of self-love) endure as long as self-love endures; wherefore, when this is purged and dead, as happens through the interior way, those two laws and two desires are no longer present; nor, is any lapse incurred further, nor, is anything felt more, not even venial sin. **1276**

57. Through acquired contemplation one comes to the state of not committing any more sins, neither mortal nor venial. **1277**

58. One arrives at such a state by no longer reflecting on his own actions, because defects arise from reflection. **1278**

59. The interior way is separated from confession, from those who confess, and from cases of conscience, from theology and from philosophy. **1279**

60. For advanced souls, who begin to die from reflections, and who even arrive at the point that they are dead, God sometimes makes confession impossible, and He Himself supplies it with such great preserving grace as they receive in the sacrament; and therefore for such souls it is not good in such a case to approach the sacrament of penance, because it is impossible for them. **1280**

61. When the soul arrives at mystical death, it cannot wish for anything more than what God desires, because it does no longer have a will, since God has taken it away from it. **1281**

62. By the interior way it arrives at a continuous, immobile state in an imperturbable peace. **1282**

63. By the internal way one even arrives at the death of the senses; moreover, it is a sign that one remains in a state of nothingness, that is, of mystical death, if the exterior senses no longer represent sensible things (from which they are) as if they did not exist, because they do not succeed in making the intellect apply itself to them. **1283**

64. A theologian is less disposed than an ignorant man for the contemplative state; in the first place, because he does not have such pure faith; secondly, because he is not so humble; thirdly, because he does not care so much for his own salvation; fourthly, because he has a head full of phantasms, images, opinions, and speculations, and cannot enter into that true light. **1284**

65. One must obey directors in the exterior life, and the latitude of the vow of obedience of religious extends only to the external. In the interior life the matter is different, because only God and the director enter. **1285**

66. A certain new doctrine in the Church of God is worthy of ridicule, that the soul should be governed as far as its interior is concerned by a bishop; but if the bishop is not capable, the soul should go to him with his director. I speak a new doctrine; because neither Sacred Scripture, nor **1286**

councils, nor bulls, nor saints, nor authors have ever transmitted it, nor can transmit it, because the Church does not judge about hidden matters, and the soul has its faculty of choosing whatsoever shall seem good to it [*Viva: anima ius habet eligendi quaecumque sibi bene visum*].

1287 67. To say that the interior must be manifested to the exterior tribunal of directors, and that it is a sin not to do so, is a manifest deception, because the Church does not pass judgment on hidden matters, and they prejudge their own souls by these deceptions and hypocrisies.

1288 68. In the world there is neither faculty nor jurisdiction for commanding that the letters of a director, as far as the interior direction of a soul is concerned, should be made manifest; therefore, it is necessary to assert that it is an insult of Satan, etc.

Condemned as heretical, suspect, erroneous, scandalous, blasphemous, offensive to pious ears, rash, of relaxed Christian discipline, subversive, and seditious respectively.

ALEXANDER VIII 1689–1691

Errors Concerning the Goodness of an Act and Concerning Philosophic Sin [1]

[Condemned in the Decr. S. Off., Aug. 24, 1690]

1289 1. Objective goodness consists in the agreement of an object with rational nature; but formal goodness consists in the conformity of an act with the rule of morals. For this it is sufficient that the moral act tend toward its ultimate end interpretatively. Man is not obliged to love this end, neither in the beginning nor in the course of his moral life.

Declared and condemned as heretical.

1290 2. Philosophic or moral sin is a human act not in conformity with rational nature and right reason; but theological and mortal sin is a free transgression of the divine law. A philosophic sin, however grave, in a man who either is ignorant of God or does not think about God during the act, is a grave sin, but is not an offense against God, neither a mortal sin dissolving the friendship of God, nor one worthy of eternal punishment.

Declared and condemned as scandalous, rash, an offense to pious ears, and erroneous.[2]

---

[1] DuPl III, II 365 a f.; coll. Viva I 363.
[2] Cf. H. Beylard, *Le péché philosophique* [*Nouv. Rev. théol.* 62, (1935), 591 ff., 673 ff.].

Errors of the Jansenists [1]

[Condemned in a Decr. of the Holy Office, Dec. 7, 1690]

1. In the state of fallen nature, for mortal [*Viva: formale*] sin and for demerit that liberty is sufficient by which the mortal sin or demerit was voluntary and free in its cause, namely, in original sin and in the will of Adam sinning.   1291

2. Although there is such a thing as invincible ignorance of the law of nature, this, in the state of fallen nature, does not excuse from formal sin anyone acting out of ignorance.   1292

3. It is not permitted to follow a (probable) opinion or among the probables the most probable.[2]   1293

4. Christ gave Himself for us as an oblation to God, not for the elect only, but for all the faithful only.   1294

5. Pagans, Jews, heretics, and others of this kind do not receive in any way any influence from Jesus Christ, and so you will rightly infer from this that in them there is a bare and weak will without any sufficient grace.   1295

6. Grace sufficient for our state is not so much useful as pernicious, so that we can justly pray: From sufficient grace deliver us, O Lord.   1296

7. Every human act is a deliberate choice of God or of the world; if of God, it is love of the Father; if of the world, it is concupiscense of the flesh, that is, it is evil.   1297

8. Of necessity, an infidel sins in every act.   1298

9. In truth he sins who hates sin merely because of its vileness and its inconsistency with nature, without any reference to the offense to God.   1299

10. The intention with which anyone detests evil and follows after good, merely that he may obtain heavenly glory, is not right nor pleasing to God.   1300

11. Everything which is not in accordance with supernatural Christian faith, which works through charity, is a sin.   1301

12. When in great sinners all love is lacking, faith also is lacking; and even if they seem to believe, their faith is not divine but human.   1302

13. Whoever serves God even in view of an eternal reward, if he lacks charity, is not free from fault, as often as he acts even in view of his eternal reward.   1303

14. Fear of hell is not supernatural.   1304

15. Attrition, which is conceived through a fear of hell and punish-   1305

---

[1] DuPl III, II 371 b ff.; coll. Viva I 364 ff.
[2] By this opinion is condemned absolute "tutiorismus."

ments, with a love of benevolence for God in Himself, is not a good and supernatural motive.

1306   16. Neither the policy nor institution of the Church has introduced the order of placing satisfaction before absolution, but the law and prescription of Christ, since the nature of the thing in a way demands that very order.

1307   17. By that practice of absolving first the order of penance is inverted.

1308   18. The modern custom as regards the administration of the sacrament of penance, even if the authority of many men sustains it and long duration confirms it, is nevertheless not considered by the Church as a usage but as an abuse.

1309   19. Man ought to do penance during his whole life for original sin.

1310   20. Confessions made to religious are generally either sacrilegious or invalid.

1311   21. The parish priest can suspect mendicants who live on common alms, of imposing too light and unsuitable a penance or satisfaction because of the advantage or gain of some temporal aid.

1312   22. They are to be judged sacrilegious who claim the right to receive Communion before they have done worthy penance for their sins.

1313   23. Similarly, they must be prevented from Holy Communion, who have not yet a pure love of God, without any admixture.

1314   24. The oblation in the Temple, which was made by the Blessed Virgin Mary on the day of her purification by means of two turtle doves, one for a holocaust and the other for sins, sufficiently testifies that she was in need of purification, and that her Son (who was being offered) was also stained with the stain of His mother, according to the words of the law.

1315   25. It is unlawful to place in a Christian temple an image of God the Father [*Viva: sedentis,* sitting].

1316   26. Praise which is offered to Mary, as Mary, is vain.

1317   27. Sometimes baptism is valid when conferred under this form: "In the name of the Father, etc. . . . ," omitting these words: "I baptize thee."

1318   28. Baptism is valid when conferred by a minister who observes all the external rite and form of baptizing, but within his heart resolves, I do not intend what the Church does.

1319   29. Futile and many times refuted is the assertion about the authority of the Roman Pontiff being superior to that of an ecumenical Council and about his infallibility in deciding questions of faith.

1320   30. When anyone finds a doctrine clearly established in Augustine, he can absolutely hold and teach it, disregarding any bull of the pope.

1321   31. The Bull of Urban VIII, "In Eminenti," is false.[1]

---

[1] In this Bull of Urban VIII (published in the year 1641) the Constitutions of Pius V and Gregory XIII are confirmed, in which the 79 propositions of Baius are condemned; in the same Bull the book of Cornelius Jansen, which has the title

Condemned and prohibited as rash, scandalous, evil-sounding, injurious, close to heresy, smacking of heresy, erroneous, schismatic, and heretical respectively.

Articles (Erroneous) of the Gallican Clergy (about the Power of the Roman Pontiff) [1]

[Declared void in Constit., "Inter multiplices," Aug. 4, 1690]

1. To blessed Peter and his successors the vicars of Christ, and to the Church herself power over spiritual things and over those pertaining to eternal salvation has been given by God, but not power over civil and temporal affairs, since the Lord said: "My Kingdom is not of this world" [John 18:36], and again: "Render therefore to Caesar the things that are Caesar's, and to God the things that are God's" [Luke 20:25], and hence the statement of the Apostle: "Let every soul be subject to higher powers: for there is no power but from God: and those that are, are ordained of God. Therefore he that resisteth the power, resisteth the ordinance of God" [Rom. 13:1 f.]. Therefore, by the command of God, kings and princes cannot be subject to ecclesiastical power in temporal affairs, nor can they be deposed by the authority of the keys of the Church, either directly or indirectly; nor can their subjects be released from loyalty and obedience and be freed from fulfilling their oath of allegiance; and this opinion, which is necessary for public tranquillity, and which is no less useful to the Church than to the Empire, must by every means be retained as being in harmony with the Word of God, the tradition of the Fathers, and the examples of the saints.[2]

1322

Augustinus, is again prohibited. This Bull the Baians and the Jansenists said was surreptitious, on the ground that it was published by a Pontiff ignorant of the truth, although on the other hand the Pontiff says in it: After mature and diligent reading of the same book, which has the title *Augustinus,* it has been found that in the same book many proscribed propositions of Baius are contained. (Cf. Viva on this proposition. Tournely, *De gratia* q .3; *Historia Iansenismi,* Epoch. I, sec. "The book of Jansenism is announced to Urban VIII and is prohibited by him").

[1] CL I 831 f. and BR(T) 20, 69 a; MBR 10, 217 b; RskRP II 222.—Disapproved, as Pius VI Constit., "Auctorem fidei" [see n. 1599] reports, by Innocent XI by a letter in the form of a Brief, April 11, 1682, and by Alexander III in Constitution, "Inter multiplices" (August 4, 1690). Finally, when resumed by the synod of Pistorium, Pius VI by the Bull "Auctorem fidei" (Aug. 28, 1794) publicly condemned them. These four articles of the declaration, of which the three last concern a dogmatic matter, many of the authors, in a given letter to Innocent XII in the year 1693, retracted.—But these articles of the Gallic clergy do not belong to the year 1682, but with changed form, the six articles of the Sorbonne belong to the year 1663 (Gérin, *Recherches historiques sur l'assemblée du clergé de France de 1682,* ed. 2 [Paris, 1870], p. 17).

[2] How the law for deposing princes, etc., is to be understood, cf. v. gr. *Archiv. für kathol. Kirchenrecht* XXVI (1871), p. lxxx.

1323   2. So there is in the Apostolic See and in the successors of Peter, the vicars of Christ, such full power over spiritual things that the decree concerning the authority of the General Councils which are contained [1] in the fourth and fifth sessions of the sacred ecumenical Council of Constance are valid, and at the same time always remain unchanged, since these decrees have been approved by the Apostolic See and confirmed by the use of the Roman Pontiffs themselves, and by the whole Church and have been observed by the Gallican Church in continuous religious worship; and they are not to be approved by the Gallican Church who destroy the force of these decrees, as if they were of doubtful authority or have been less approved, or who distort the words of the Council in accordance only with the time of the schism.

1324   3. Hence the use of the apostolic power must be moderated by the canons which have been established by the Spirit of God and consecrated by the reverence of the whole world; likewise, the rules, customs, and institutes accepted by the kingdom and the Gallican Church are valid, and the limitations of the Fathers remain unshaken; and this pertains to the fullness of the Apostolic See, namely, that these statutes and customs, confirmed by the consent of both so great a See and of the Churches, retain their proper stability.

1325   4. In questions of faith also, the duties of the Supreme Pontiff are principal ones, and his decrees pertain to all and individual churches, and yet this judgment is not unalterable unless the consent of the Church has been added to it.

Concerning these statements Alexander VIII decreed as follows:

1326   "Each and everything that was considered and decreed in the above mentioned assemblies of the Gallican clergy held in the year 1682, both in regard to the extension of the right of *regalia* and the declaration concerning the ecclesiastical power and the four propositions contained in that declaration, with all and individual mandates, judgments, and confirmations, declarations, epistles, edicts, and decrees edited and published by whatsoever persons, ecclesiastical or lay, in whatever way qualified, and no matter what authority and power they enjoy, even the power which requires individual mention,—all these acts, we declare, by the tenor of these letters, to have been from the very beginning, to be now, and always to be, by right itself, null and void, invalid, useless, entirely and wholly lacking in strength and effectiveness, and that no one is bound to their observance or to the observance of any one of them, even if they have been reinforced by an oath."

---

[1] See n. 657 c. note.

INNOCENT XII 1691–1700

Errors Concerning the Most Pure Love of God [1]

[Condemned in the brief "Cum alias," March 12, 1699]

1. There is an habitual state of the love of God, which is pure charity 1327
and without any admixture of the motive of one's personal interest.
Neither fear of punishment nor desire of reward any longer has a share
in it. God is no longer loved for the sake of merit, nor because of one's
own perfection, nor because of the happiness to be found in loving Him.

2. In the state of the contemplative or unitive life, every interested 1328
motive of fear and hope is lost.

3. That which is essential in the direction of a soul is to do nothing 1329
else than to follow grace, step by step with infinite patience, precaution,
and subtlety. One should restrain himself within these limits so that God
may be permitted to act, and he should never aspire to pure love, except
when God by an interior unction begins to open the heart to this word,
which is so hard for souls heretofore attached to self, and can therefore
scandalize them or cause them confusion.

4. In the state of holy indifference, a soul no longer has voluntary and 1330
deliberate desires for its own interest, with the exception of those occasions on which it does not faithfully cooperate with the whole of its
grace.

5. In the same state of holy indifference we wish nothing for ourselves, 1331
all for God. We do not wish that we be perfect and happy for self
interest, but we wish all perfection and happiness only in so far as it
pleases God to bring it about that we wish for these states by the im-
pression of His grace.

6. In this state of holy indifference we no longer seek salvation as our 1332
own salvation, as our eternal liberation, as a reward of our merits, nor as
the greatest of all our interests, but we wish it with our whole will as
the glory and good pleasure of God, as the thing which He wishes, and
which He wishes us to wish for His sake.

7. Dereliction is nothing else than the abnegation or renunciation of 1333
oneself, which Jesus Christ requires of us in the Gospel, after we have
left all external things. This denial of ourselves is only with regard to our
own interest. . . . The extreme trials in which this abnegation or dere-

---

[1] DuPl III, II 402 ff.; Viva I 562 b ff.; BR(T) 20, 870 b ff.; MBR 10, 21 9 a ff.—
They are contained in the book, *Explicatiòns des maximes des Saints sur la vie in-
térieure*, by Messere Françoise de Salignac Fénelon, Archevêque Duc de Cambray, etc.
(Paris, 1697). Variant readings have been corrected according to the original Gallic
text which DuPl, l.c., supplies.

liction of self must be exercised are the temptations by means of which a jealous God seeks to purify love, by holding out to it no refuge, nor any hope for its welfare, even eternal.

1334   8. All sacrifices, which are wont to be made by souls who are as disinterested as possible about their eternal happiness, are conditional. . . . But this sacrifice cannot be absolute in the ordinary state. Only in the case of extreme trials does this sacrifice become in some manner absolute.

1335   9. In extreme trials a soul can be invincibly persuaded by a reflex persuasion (and this is not the deep foundation of conscience) that it has been justly rejected by God.

1336   10. Then a soul separated from itself expires with Christ on the Cross, saying: "My God, my God, why hast Thou forsaken me?" [Matt. 27:46]. In this involuntary expression of despair there is completed the absolute sacrifice of one's own interest in so far as eternity is concerned.

1337   11. In this state a soul loses all hope of its own interest; but never does it lose in its higher part, that is in its direct and inner acts, a perfect hope, which is a disinterested longing for the promises.

1338   12. Then a director can permit this soul to acquiesce simply in the loss of its own interest, and in the just condemnation which it believes has been enjoined on it by God.

1339   13. The inferior part of Christ on the Cross did not communicate his involuntary disturbances to his superior part.

1340   14. In the extreme trials for the purification of love there takes place a certain separation of the upper part of the soul from the lower. . . . In that separation the acts of the lower part flow from a completely blind and involuntary disturbance, for, whatever is voluntary and intellectual is of the higher part.

1341   15. Meditation consists of discursive acts which are easily distinguished from one another. . . . The putting together of the discursive and reflex acts is the proper exercise of an interested love.

1342   16. There is a state of contemplation so sublime and so perfect that it becomes habitual; so that, as often as a soul actually prays, its prayer is contemplative, not discursive. Then it no longer needs to return to meditation and to its methodical acts.

1343   17. Contemplative souls are deprived of a distinct, sensible, and reflex vision of Jesus Christ at two different times: first, in the newborn fervor of their contemplation; secondly, when the soul loses the vision of Jesus Christ in extreme trials.

1344   18. In the passive state all the distinct virtues are exercised without any thought that they are virtues. At every moment no other thought is in the mind than to do that which God wishes, and a zealous love likewise brings it about that no one any longer desires virtue for himself nor is he ever so endowed with virtue as when he is no longer attached to virtue.

19. In this sense it can be said that a soul in a passive and disinterested 1345
state no longer wishes even love itself, in so far as it is its perfection and
its happiness, but only in so far as it is that which God wishes of us.

20. In confession transformed souls must detest their sins and con- 1346
demn themselves, and desire the remission of their sins not as a personal
purification and liberation, but as the thing which God wills and which
He wills us to will because of His glory.

21. Holy mystics have excluded from the state of transformed souls the 1347
practices of virtues.

22. Although this doctrine (about pure love) was designated a pure 1348
and simple evangelical perfection in universal tradition, the ancient pastors did not propose it indiscriminately to the multitude of the just,
unless the practice of their interested love was proportionate to their grace.

23. Pure love itself alone constitutes the whole interior life; and thence 1349
arises the only principle and the only motive of all acts which are deliberate and meritorious.

Condemned and rejected as, either in the obvious sense of these words,
or in the extended meaning of the thoughts, rash, scandalous, ill-sounding,
offensive to pious ears, pernicious, and likewise erroneous in practice.

CLEMENT XI 1700–1721

Concerning Truths which Necessarily Must be
Explicitly Believed [1]

[Response of the Sacred Office to the Bishop of
Quebec, Jan. 25, 1703]

Whether a minister is bound, before baptism is conferred on an adult, 1349a
to explain to him all the mysteries of our faith, especially if he is at the
point of death, because this might disturb his mind. Or, whether it is
sufficient, if the one at the point of death will promise that when he
recovers from the illness, he will take care to be instructed, so that he
may put into practice what has been commanded him.

Resp. A promise is not sufficient, but a missionary is bound to explain
to an adult, even a dying one who is not entirely incapacitated, the
mysteries of faith which are necessary by a necessity of means, as are
especially the mysteries of the Trinity and the Incarnation.

[Response of the Sacred Office, May 10, 1703]

Whether it is possible for a crude and uneducated adult, as it might be 1349b
with a barbarian, to be baptized, if there were given to him only an

---

[1] ASS 30, (1897/98) 700 with note; Collect. S.C. de Prop. Fide I, n. 254, 1 and
256, 2.

understanding of God and some of His attributes, especially His justice in rewarding and in punishing, according to this remark of the Apostle: "He that cometh to God must believe that he is and that he is a rewarder" [Heb. 11:6], from which it is inferred that a barbarian adult, in a certain case of urgent necessity, can be baptized although he does not believe explicitly in Jesus Christ.

Resp. A missionary should not baptize one who does not believe explicitly in the Lord Jesus Christ, but is bound to instruct him about all those matters which are necessary, by a necessity of means, in accordance with the capacity of the one to be baptized.

An Obsequious Silence in Regard to Dogmatic Facts [1]

[From the Constitution, "Vineam Domini Sabaoth," July 16, 1705]

1350 (Sec. 6 or 25) In order that, for the future, every occasion of error may be prevented, and that all sons of the Catholic Church may learn to listen to the Church herself, not in silence only (for, *"even the wicked are silent in darkness"* [I Kings 2:9]), but with an interior obedience, which is the true obedience of an orthodox man, let it be known that by this constitution of ours, to be valid forever, the obedience which is due to the aforesaid apostolic constitutions is not satisfied by any obsequious silence; but the sense of that book of Jansen which has been condemned in the five propositions (see n. 1092 ff.) mentioned above, and whose meaning the words of those propositions express clearly, must be rejected and condemned as heretical by all the faithful of Christ, not only by word of mouth but also in heart; and one may not lawfully subscribe to the above formula with any other mind, heart, or belief, so that all who hold or preach or teach or assert by word or writing anything contrary to what all these propositions mean, and to what each single one means, we declare, decree, state, and ordain, with this same apostolic authority, that all, as transgressors of the aforementioned apostolic constitutions, come under each and every individual censure and penalty of those constitutions.

---

[1] DuPl III, II 448; Viva I 516 a; BR(T) 21, 235 b; MBR 8, 36 a.

Errors of Paschasius Quesnel [1]

[Condemned in the dogmatic Constitution, "Unigenitus," [2]
Sept. 8, 1713]

(Sec. 3) 1. What else remains for the soul that has lost God and His 1351
grace except sin and the consequences of sin, a proud poverty and a sloth-
ful indigence, that is, a general impotence for labor, for prayer, and for
every good work?

2. The grace of Jesus Christ, which is the efficacious principle of every 1352
kind of good, is necessary for every good work; without it, not only is
nothing done, but nothing can be done.

3. In vain, O Lord, do You command, if You do not give what you 1353
command.

4. Thus, O Lord, all things are possible to him for whom You make 1354
all things possible by effecting those same things in him.

5. When God does not soften a heart by the interior unction of His 1355
grace, exterior exhortations and graces are of no service except to harden
it the more.

6. The difference between the Judaic dispensation and the Christian 1356
is this, that in the former God demanded flight from sin and a fulfillment of the Law by the sinner, leaving him in his own weakness; but in
the latter, God gives the sinner what He commands, by purifying him
with His grace.

7. What advantage was there for a man in the old covenant, in which 1357
God left him to his own weakness, by imposing on him His law? But
what happiness is it not to be admitted to a convenant in which God
gives us what He asks of us?

8. But we do not belong to the new covenant, except in so far as we 1358

---

[1] DuPl III, II 462 ff.; coll. Viva II 1 ff.; CIC Rcht II 140 ff.; BR(T) 21, 569 b ff.;
MBR 8, 119 a ff. Variant, doubtful, and corrected readings are according to the first
Gallic text which DuPl, l.c., presents—Paschasius Quesnel was born on July 14,
1634. After completing his studies in the Sorbonne in 1657, he entered the Congregation of the Oratory; but because of his zeal for the heresy of Jansenism, he was
forced to leave the Congregation. His book, "Reflections morales," was condemned,
to which the Constitution, "Unigenitus," is related. Shortly before his death on
Dec. 2, 1719, he made a profession of faith publicly [Hrt, Sec. rec. II² 822 ff.].

[2] This dogmatic constitution was confirmed by the same Clement XI in the Bull,
"Pastoralis Officii" (Aug. 28, 1718) against the Appellantes, in which he declares
that certain Catholics "who did not accept the Bull "Unigenitus" were clearly outside the bosom of the Roman Church; by Innocent XIII in a decree published on
Jan. 8, 1722; by Benedict XIII and the Roman Synod in 1725; by Benedict XIV
in the encyclical, "Ex omnibus Christiani orbis regionibus" on Oct. 16, 1756; it was
accepted by the Gallic clergy in assemblies in 1723, 1726, 1730, by the councils
of Avignon, 1725 and Ebred, 1727, and by the whole Catholic world.

are participators in that new grace which works in us that which God commands us.

1359   9. The grace of Christ is a supreme grace, without which we can never confess Christ, and with which we never deny Him.

1360   10. Grace is the working of the omnipotent hand of God, which nothing can hinder or retard.

1361   11. Grace is nothing else than the omnipotent Will of God, ordering and doing what He orders.

1362   12. When God wishes to save a soul, at whatever time and at whatever place, the undoubted effect follows the Will of God.

1363   13. When God wishes to save a soul and touches it with the interior hand of His grace, no human will resists Him.

1364   14. Howsoever remote from salvation an obstinate sinner is, when Jesus presents Himself to be seen by him in the salutary light of His grace, the sinner is forced to surrender himself, to have recourse to Him, and to humble himself, and to adore his Savior.

1365   15. When God accompanies His commandment and His eternal exhortation by the unction of His Spirit and by the interior force of His grace, He works that obedience in the heart that He is seeking.

1366   16. There are no attractions which do not yield to the attractions of grace, because nothing resists the Almighty.

1367   17. Grace is that voice of the Father which teaches men interiorly and makes them come to Jesus Christ; whoever does not come to Him, after he has heard the exterior voice of the Son, is in no wise taught by the Father.

1368   18. The seed of the word, which the hand of God nourishes, always brings forth its fruit.

1369   19. The grace of God is nothing else than His omnipotent Will; this is the idea which God Himself gives us in all His Scriptures.

1370   20. The true idea of grace is that God wishes Himself to be obeyed by us and He is obeyed; He commands, and all things are done; He speaks as the Lord, and all things are obedient to Him.

1371   21. The grace of Jesus Christ is a strong, powerful, supreme, invincible grace, that is, the operation of the omnipotent Will, the consequence and imitation of the operation of God causing the incarnation and the resurrection of His Son.

1372   22. The harmony of the all powerful operation of God in the heart of man with the free consent of man's will is demonstrated, therefore, to us in the Incarnation, as in the fount and archetype of all other operations of mercy and grace, all of which are as gratuitous and as dependent on God as the original operation itself.

1373   23. God Himself has taught us the idea of the omnipotent working of His grace, signifying it by that operation which produces creatures from nothing and which restores life to the dead.

24. The right idea which the centurion had about the omnipotence of God and of Jesus Christ in healing bodies by a single act of His will, [Matt. 8:8] is an image of the idea we should have about the omnipotence of His grace in healing souls from cupidity.   1374

25. God illumines the soul, and heals it, as well as the body, by His will only; He gives orders and He is obeyed.   1375

26. No graces are granted except through faith.   1376

27. Faith is the first grace and the source of all others.   1377

28. The first grace which God grants to the sinner is the remission of sin.   1378

29. Outside of the Church, no grace is granted.   1379

30. All whom God wishes to save through Christ, are infallibly saved.   1380

31. The desires of Christ always have their effect; He brings peace to the depth of hearts when He desires it for them.   1381

32. Jesus Christ surrendered Himself to death to free forever from the hand of the exterminating angel, by His blood, the first born, that is, the elect.   1382

33. Ah, how much one ought to renounce earthly goods and himself for this, that he may have the confidence of appropriating, so to speak, Christ Jesus to himself, His love, death, and mysteries, as St. Paul does, when he says: "He who loved me, and delivered Himself for me" [Gal. 2:20].   1383

34. The grace of Adam produced nothing except human merit.   1384

35. The grace of Adam is a consequence of creation and was due to his whole and sound nature.   1385

36. The essential difference between the grace of Adam and of his state of innocence and Christian grace, is that each one would have received the first in his own person, but the second is not received except in the person of the risen Jesus Christ to whom we are united.   1386

37. The grace of Adam by sanctifying him in himself was proportionate to him; Christian grace, by sanctifying us in Jesus Christ, is omnipotent, and worthy of the Son of God.   1387

38. Without the grace of the Liberator, the sinner is not free except to do evil.   1388

39. The will, which grace does not anticipate, has no light except for straying, no eagerness except to put itself in danger, no strength except to wound itself, and is capable of all evil and incapable of all good.   1389

40. Without grace we can love nothing except to our own condemnation.   1390

41. All knowledge of God, even natural knowledge, even in the pagan   1391

philosophers, cannot come except from God; and without grace knowledge produces nothing but presumption, vanity, and opposition to God
Himself, instead of the affections of adoration, gratitude, and love.

1392   42. The grace of Christ alone renders a man fit for the sacrifice of
faith; without this there is nothing but impurity, nothing but unworthiness.

1393   43. The first effect of baptismal grace is to make us die to sin so that
our spirit, heart, and senses have no more life for sin than a dead man
has for the things of the world.

1394   44. There are but two loves, from which all our volitions and actions
arise: love of God, which does all things because of God and which God
rewards; and the love with which we love ourselves and the world,
which does not refer to God what ought to be referred to Him, and
therefore becomes evil.

1395   45. When love of God no longer reigns in the heart of sinners, it needs
must be that carnal desire reign in it and corrupt all of its actions.

1396   46. Cupidity or charity makes the use of the senses good or evil.

1397   47. Obedience to the law ought to flow from the source, and this source
is charity. When the love of God is the interior principle of obedience
and the glory of God is its end, then that is pure which appears externally; otherwise, it is but hypocrisy and false justice.

1398   48. What else can we be except darkness, except aberration, and except sin, without the light of faith, without Christ, and without charity?

1399   49. As there is no sin without love of ourselves, so there is no good
work without love of God.

1400   50. In vain we cry out to God: *My Father,* if it is not the spirit of
charity which cries out.

1401   51. Faith justifies when it operates, but it does not operate except
through charity.

1402   52. All other means of salvation are contained in faith as in their own
germ and seed; but this faith does not exist apart from love and confidence.

1403   53. Only charity in the Christian way makes (Christian actions)
through a relation to God and to Jesus Christ.

1404   54. It is charity alone that speaks to God; it alone that God hears.

1405   55. God crowns nothing except charity; he who runs through any other
incentive or any other motive, runs in vain.

1406   56. God rewards nothing but charity; for charity alone honors God.

1407   57. All fails a sinner, when hope fails him; and there is no hope in
God, when there is no love of God.

1408   58. Neither God nor religion exists where there is no charity.

1409   59. The prayer of the impious is a new sin; and what God grants to
them is a new judgment against them.

60. If fear of punishment alone animates penance, the more intense this 1410 is, the more it leads to despair.

61. Fear restrains nothing but the hand, but the heart is addicted to 1411 the sin as long as it is not guided by a love of justice.

62. He who does not refrain from evil except through fear of punish- 1412 ment, commits that evil in his heart, and is already guilty before God.

63. A baptized person is still under the law as a Jew, if he does not 1413 fulfill the law, or if he fulfills it from fear alone.

64. Good is never done under the condemnation of the law, because 1414 one sins either by doing evil or by avoiding it only through fear.

65. Moses, the prophets, priests, and doctors of the Law died without 1415 having given any son to God, since they produced only slaves through fear.

66. He who wishes to approach to God, should not come to Him with 1416 brutal passions, nor be led to Him by natural instinct, or through fear as animals, but through faith and love, as sons.

67. Servile fear does not represent God to itself except as a stern, 1417 imperious, unjust, unyielding master.

68. The goodness of God has shortened the road to salvation, by 1418 enclosing all in faith and in prayers.

69. Faith, practice of it, increase, and reward of faith, all are a gift of 1419 the pure liberality of God.

70. Never does God afflict the innocent; and afflictions always serve 1420 either to punish the sin or to purify the sinner.

71. For the preservation of himself man can dispense himself from that 1421 law which God established for his use.

72. A mark of the Christian Church is that it is catholic, embracing all 1422 the angels of heaven, all the elect and the just on earth, and of all times.

73. What is the Church except an assembly of the sons of God abiding 1423 in His bosom, adopted in Christ, subsisting in His person, redeemed by His blood, living in His spirit, acting through His grace, and awaiting the grace of the future life?

74. The Church or the whole Christ has the Incarnate Word as head, 1424 but all the saints as members.

75. The Church is one single man composed of many members, of 1425 which Christ is the head, the life, the subsistence and the person; it is one single Christ composed of many saints, of whom He is the sanctifier.

76. There is nothing more spacious than the Church of God; because 1426 all the elect and the just of all ages comprise it.

77. He who does not lead a life worthy of a son of God and a mem- 1427 ber of Christ, ceases interiorly to have God as a Father and Christ as a head.

78. One is separated from the chosen people, whose figure was the 1428

Jewish people, and whose head is Jesus Christ, both by not living according to the Gospel and by not believing in the Gospel.

1429   79. It is useful and necessary at all times, in all places, and for every
kind of person, to study and to know the spirit, the piety, and the
mysteries of Sacred Scripture.

1430   80. The reading of Sacred Scripture is for all.

1431   81. The sacred obscurity of the Word of God is no reason for the
laity to dispense themselves from reading it.

1432   82. The Lord's Day ought to be sanctified by Christians with readings
of pious works and above all of the Holy Scriptures. It is harmful for a
Christian to wish to withdraw from this reading.

1433   83. It is an illusion to persuade oneself that knowledge of the mysteries of religion should not be communicated to women by the reading
of Sacred Scriptures. Not from the simplicity of women, but from the
proud knowledge of men has arisen the abuse of the Scriptures, and have
heresies been born.

1434   84. To snatch away from the hands of Christians the New Testament,
or to hold it closed against them by taking away from them the means of
understanding it, is to close for them the mouth of Christ.

1435   85. To forbid Christians to read Sacred Scripture, especially the Gospels, is to forbid the use of light to the sons of light, and to cause them to
suffer a kind of excommunication.

1436   86. To snatch from the simple people this consolation of joining their
voice to the voice of the whole Church is a custom contrary to the
apostolic practice and to the intention of God.

1437   87. A method full of wisdom, light, and charity is to give souls time
for bearing with humility, and for experiencing their state of sin, for
seeking the spirit of penance and contrition, and for beginning at least
to satisfy the justice of God, before they are reconciled.

1438   88. We are ignorant of what sin is and of what true penance is, when
we wish to be restored at once to the possession of the goods of which sin
has despoiled us, and when we refuse to endure the confusion of that
separation.

1439   89. The fourteenth step in the conversion of a sinner is that, after he
has already been reconciled, he has the right of assisting at the Sacrifice of
the Church.

1440   90. The Church has the authority to excommunicate, so that it may
exercise it through the first pastors with the consent, at least presumed,
of the whole body.

1441   91. The fear of an unjust excommunication should never hinder us
from fulfilling our duty; never are we separated from the Church, even
when by the wickedness of men we seem to be expelled from it, as long

as we are attached to God, to Jesus Christ, and to the Church herself by charity.

92. To suffer in peace an excommunication and an unjust anathema **1442** rather than betray truth, is to imitate St. Paul; far be it from rebelling against authority or of destroying unity.

93. Jesus sometimes heals the wounds which the precipitous haste of **1443** the first pastors inflicted without His command. Jesus restored what they, with inconsidered zeal, cut off.

94. Nothing engenders a worse opinion of the Church among her **1444** enemies than to see exercised there an absolute rule over the faith of the faithful, and to see divisions fostered because of matters which do not violate faith or morals.

95. Truths have descended to this, that they are, as it were, a foreign **1445** tongue to most Christians, and the manner of preaching them is, as it were, an unknown idiom, so remote is the manner of preaching from the simplicity of the apostles, and so much above the common grasp of the faithful; nor is there sufficient advertence to the fact that this defect is one of the greatest visible signs of the weakening of the Church and of the wrath of God on His sons.

96. God permits that all powers be opposed to the preachers of truth, **1446** so that its victory cannot be attributed to anyone except to divine grace.

97. Too often it happens that those members, who are united to the **1447** Church more holily and more strictly, are looked down upon, and treated as if they were unworthy of being in the Church, or as if they were separated from Her; but, "the just man liveth by faith" [Rom. 1:17], and not by the opinion of men.

98. The state of persecution and of punishment which anyone endures **1448** as a disgraceful and impious heretic, is generally the final trial and is especially meritorious, inasmuch as it makes a man more conformable to Jesus Christ.

99. Stubbornness, investigation, and obstinacy in being unwilling either **1449** to examine something or to acknowledge that one has been deceived, daily changes into an odor, as it were, of death, for many people, that which God has placed in His Church to be an odor of life within it, for instance, good books, instructions, holy examples, etc.

100. Deplorable is the time in which God is believed to be honored by **1450** persecution of the truth and its disciples! This time has come. . . . To be considered and treated by the ministers of religion as impious and unworthy of all commerce with God, as a putrid member capable of corrupting everything in the society of saints, is to pious men a more terrible death than the death of the body. In vain does anyone flatter himself on the purity of his intentions and on a certain zeal for religion,

when he persecutes honest men with fire and sword, if he is blinded by his own passion or carried away by that of another on account of which he does not want to examine anything. We frequently believe that we are sacrificing an impious man to God, when we are sacrificing a servant of God to the devil.

1451 101. Nothing is more opposed to the spirit of God and to the doctrine of Jesus Christ than to swear common oaths in Church, because this is to multiply occasions of perjury, to lay snares for the weak and inexperienced, and to cause the name and truth of God to serve sometimes the plan of the wicked.

Declared and condemned as false, captious, evil-sounding, offensive to pious ears, scandalous, pernicious, rash, injurious to the Church and her practice, insulting not only to the Church but also the secular powers, seditious, impious, blasphemous, suspected of heresy, and smacking of heresy itself, and, besides, favoring heretics and heresies, and also schisms, erroneous, close to heresy, many times condemned, and finally heretical, clearly renewing many heresies respectively and most especially those which are contained in the infamous propositions of Jansen, and indeed accepted in that sense in which these have been condemned.

INNOCENT XIII 1721–1724   BENEDICT XIII 1724–1730
CLEMENT XII 1730–1740

BENEDICT XIV 1740–1758

Clandestine Marriages in Belgium (and Holland) [1]

[From the Declaration, "Matrimonia, quae in locis," Nov. 4, 1741]

1452 Marriages which are wont to be entered into in places subject to the dominion of the Federated Orders in Belgium, whether between heretics on both sides, or between an heretical man on one side and a Catholic woman on the other, or, viceversa, without having observed the form prescribed by the Sacred Council of Trent, whether such marriages are valid or not has been for a long time greatly disputed in the minds of men, and there are divided and diverse opinions; a situation which has furnished a rather fruitful source of anxiety and the seed of danger for many years, especially since bishops, parish priests, and missionaries of these regions have no certainty in regard to the matter and do not dare to decree and to declare anything without consulting the Holy See. . . .

---

[1] BR(M) I, 178 ff. [old ed. I n. 34]; MBR 16, 52 a ff.; RskMm II 49 ff.; MThCc 25, 679 ff.—This is the very celebrated "Declaratio Benedictina," whose decisions later were extended to other regions. Cf. A. Lehmkuhl, *Theol. moralis* [12] II n. 905 ff., and ASS 6 (1870) 456; 23 (1890/91) 234 ff.; AE 5 (1897) 263 ff.; 6 (1898) 427 ff.

(1) Our Most Holy Father, having taken time to ponder the matter, **1453** recently enjoined that this declaration and instruction be set down, which should be employed hereafter as a definite rule and norm by all Belgian bishops, priests, and missionaries of these regions, and vicars apostolic, in matters of this kind.

(2) Namely, first, in regard to marriages celebrated between heretics **1454** in places subject to the authority of the Federated Orders, which did not observe the form prescribed by Trent, although His Holiness knows that at other times, in certain particular cases and in circumstances attendant and explained at the time, the Sacred Congregation of the Council has said that they are invalid; nevertheless, His Holiness, being equally certain that nothing has been generally or universally defined by the Apostolic See regarding marriages of this kind, and, on the other hand, that, in order to furnish advice to all the faithful residing in those places and to avert more grave disorders, he ought to declare what must be generally held regarding such marriages, after giving mature consideration to the matter, and sedulously balancing all the weighty reasons pro and con, has declared and decreed that marriages which have been contracted up to now, and which will be contracted hereafter in the said federated provinces of Belgium between heretics, even if the form prescribed by Trent shall not have been observed in their celebration, provided no other canonical impediment interferes, are to be considered as valid; and furthermore, if it should happen that each spouse be received into the bosom of the Catholic Church, they are held bound by the same conjugal tie as before, even if their mutual consent is not renewed before the Catholic priest; but, if only one of the spouses, either man or woman, should be converted, neither can, as long as the other is living, enter into another marriage.

(3) Now as regards those marriages which likewise in the same **1455** federated provinces of Belgium are contracted by Catholics with heretics without the form established by Trent, whether a Catholic man takes an heretical woman in marriage, or a Catholic woman marries an heretical man; grieving very much that there are among Catholics those who, becoming shamefully deranged by a mad love, do not wholeheartedly abhor and think that they should refrain from these detestable marriages which Holy Mother Church has continually condemned and interdicted, and praising greatly the zeal of those bishops, who, by proposing severe penalties, endeavor to restrain Catholics from uniting themselves to heretics in this sacrilegious bond, His Holiness encourages, exhorts, and advises seriously and gravely all bishops, vicars apostolic, parish priests, missionaries, and every other faithful minister of God and of the Church who reside in those regions, to deter, in so far as they can, Catholics of both sexes from entering into marriages of this kind to the destruction of

their own souls, and to make it their business to avert in every good way and efficaciously to hinder these same marriages. But if by chance some marriage of this sort, without observing the Tridentine form, has already been contracted there, or may be contracted in the future (which God forbid!), His Holiness declares that such a marriage, provided that no other canonical impediment exists, must be considered valid, and that neither of the spouses, as long as the other one lives, can in any way enter into a new marriage under the pretext that the prescribed form was not observed; that the Catholic spouse, whether man or woman, should especially bear this in mind, that in proportion to the very grave fault he has committed he should do penance and ask pardon from God, and should try, in proportion to his strength, to draw the other spouse, who is straying from the true faith, back to the bosom of the Catholic Church, and to win her or his soul, which indeed would be a very excellent means of obtaining pardon for the crime committed, knowing besides, as has just been said, that he will be perpetually bound by the bond of that marriage.

1456 (4) In addition, the Holy See declares that whatever up to now has been sanctioned and pronounced about marriages, either between heretics or between Catholics and heretics, in those regions subject to the rule of the Federated Orders in Belgium, is likewise sanctioned and pronounced for similar marriages contracted outside the limits of the dominion of these same Federated Orders by those who have been assigned to the legions, or military forces which are customarily sent by these same Federated Orders to guard and to defend the frontier parts commonly called *di Barriera;* so that, indeed, marriages entered into there without the Tridentine form between heretics on both sides, or between Catholics and heretics, retain their validity, provided the spouse in each case belongs to these same military forces or legions; and His Holiness wishes this declaration to include also the city of Mosa Traiectensis, which is possessed by the Commonwealth of the Federated Orders, not, however, by right of dominion, but only under the name of a pledge, as they say.

1457 (5) Finally, in regard to marriages which are contracted either in the regions of Catholic princes by those who have a domicile in the federated provinces, or in the federated provinces by those who have a domicile in the regions of Catholic princes, His Holiness has thought that nothing new should be decreed and declared, wishing that whenever a dispute arises concerning them, they be decided according to the canonical principles of the common law, and by the resolution approved in similar cases at other times and published by the Sacred Congregation of the Council, and so he has declared and decreed and commanded that it be observed by all for the future.

The Minister of Confirmation [1]

[From the Constitution, "Etsi Pastoralis," for
Italian-Greeks, May 26, 1742]

(3) Let Latin bishops unconditionally confirm infants or others bap- **1458**
tized in their dioceses and signed on the forehead with chrism by Greek
priests, since neither by our predecessors nor by us has the faculty been
granted, nor is it granted to Greek priests in Italy and the adjacent
islands to confer the sacrament of confirmation on baptized infants. . . .[2]

Profession of Faith which Is Prescribed for Orientals (Maronites) [3]

[From the Constitution, "Nuper ad nos," March 16, 1743]

5. . . . I, N., with firm faith, etc. I believe in one, etc., [as in the **1459**
Nicene-Constantinople Creed, see n. 86, 994].

I revere also and accept the universal Synods as follows, namely; The **1460**
first Nicean [see n. 54], and I profess what has been defined in it
against Arius of execrable memory, that the Lord Jesus Christ is the Son
of God, the only-begotten Son of the Father, who is born of the substance of the Father, not made, that He is consubstantial with the Father,
that those impious statements have been rightly condemned in the same
Synod, such as: "That at some time He did not exist," or, "that He was
made of those things which are not, or of some other substance or essence," or, "that the Son of God is mutable or changeable."

The first Constantinople, second in order [see n. 85 f.], and I profess **1461**
that which was defined in it against Macedonius of execrable memory
that the Holy Spirit is not a servant but Lord, not a creature but God,
and possessing the one divinity with the Father and the Son.

The first Ephesian [see n. 111 a f.], third in order, and I profess that **1462**
which was defined against Nestorius of execrable memory, that divinity
and humanity by an ineffable and incomprehensible union in the one

---

[1] BB(M) 1, 352 [ed. old I, n. 57]; MBR 16, 96 b.

[2] The same Benedict XIV in his work, "De Synodo diocesana" (1. VII, c. 8, n. 7:
ed. Mchl. II 70), says: "But whatever there is about this difficult and very complex
controversy, it is clear to all that confirmation conferred by a simple Latin priest
through the sole delegation of the bishop would now be invalid, because the Apostolic
See reserves this right to itself alone." According to a decree of the Holy Office, July
5, 1853 [*Collect. S.C. de Prop. Fide I* (1907), n. 1095], the power of confirming
is taken away from Greek presbyters, whether uniate or schismatic, in Bulgaria, in
Albania, in Cyprus, among the Maronites of Mount Lebanus, in Italy and the adjacent islands, but not in Walachia, Moldavia, and Asia.

[3] BB(M) 2, 82 ff. [old ed. I n. 78]; NBR 16, 148 ff.

person of the Son of God have constituted for us one Jesus Christ, and that for this reason the most Blessed Virgin is truly the Mother of God.

1463   Chalcedon [see n. 148], fourth in order, and I profess that which was defined against Eutyches and Dioscorus, both of execrable memory, that the one and same Son of God, our Lord Jesus Christ, was perfect in divinity and perfect in humanity, true God and true man consisting of rational soul and body, consubstantial with the Father in regard to His divinity, and consubstantial with us in regard to His humanity, in all things similar to us, without sin; that before time He was born of the Father according to divinity, but that in these latter days the same One, for us and for our salvation, was born of the Virgin Mary, Mother of God, according to humanity, and that the one same Christ, Son, Lord, Only-begotten must be recognized in the two natures without confusion, immutably, indivisibly, inseparably, never removing the difference of the natures because of their union, and preserving the peculiar character of each nature joined in one Person and substance; that this same Lord is not separated and divided into two persons, but is one and the same Son and Only-begotten God, the Word, the Lord Jesus Christ: likewise that the divinity of our same Lord Jesus Christ, according to which He is consubstantial with the Father and the Holy Spirit, is impassible and immortal; moreover, the same Lord was crucified and died only in the flesh, as was also defined in the said Synod and in the letter of St. Leo, the Roman Pontiff [cf. n. 143 f.], by whose mouth, the Fathers in the same Synod declared that Blessed Peter the Apostle spoke, and by this definition there is condemned also that impious heresy of those who, when the Trisagion transmitted by the angels was being sung in the aforementioned Synod of Chalcedon: "Holy God, strong God, immortal God, have mercy on us," added these words: "Who was crucified for us," and thereby asserted that the divine nature of the three Persons was passible and mortal.

1464   Second Council of Constantinople [see n. 212 ff.], fifth in order, in which the definition of the aforementioned Synod of Chalcedon was renewed.

1465   Third Council of Constantinople [see n. 289 ff.], sixth in order, and I profess what was defined in it against the Monothelites, that in our one same Lord, Jesus Christ, there are two natural wills and two natural operations without division, change, separation, or confusion, and that His human will is not contrary to, but subject to His divine and omnipotent will.

1466   Second Nicean Council [see n. 302 ff.], seventh in order, and I profess what was defined in it against the Iconoclasts, that images of Christ and of the Virgin Mother of God, as well as of other saints, should be kept and retained, and that due honor and veneration should be given to them.

The fourth of Constantinople [see n. 336 ff.], eighth in order, and I 1467 profess that in it Photius was rightly condemned, and that Saint Ignatius, the Patriarch, was rightly reinstated (restored).

I venerate also and accept all the other universal Synods which have been 1468 lawfully held and confirmed by the authority of the Roman Pontiff, and especially the Synod of Florence; [there follows what is gathered and excerpted as far as the meaning goes from the decree on the union of the Greeks (namely, n. 691–693), and from the decree for the Armenians (see n. 712 f.), of the Council of Florence]. . . .

Likewise, I revere and accept the Council of Trent [see n. 782 ff.], and 1469 I profess what was defined and declared in it, and especially that there is offered to God in the Mass a true, proper, and propitiatory sacrifice, for the living and the dead, and that in the Most Holy Sacrament of the Eucharist, in accordance with the faith that had always been in the Church of God, there is contained truly, really, and substantially the body and blood together with the soul and divinity of our Lord Jesus Christ, and hence the whole Christ, and that there is made a change of the whole substance of the bread into the body, and of the whole substance of the wine into the blood, which change the Catholic Church most fittingly calls transubstantiation, and that under each species and in each single part of each species, when a division is made, the whole Christ is contained.

Likewise, I profess that there are seven sacraments of the New Law 1470 instituted by Christ, our Lord, for the salvation of the human race, although not all of them are necessary for each individual: namely, baptism, confirmation, Eucharist, penance, extreme unction, orders, and matrimony; and (I profess) that these confer grace, and that of these, baptism, confirmation, and orders cannot be repeated without sacrilege. Likewise (I profess) that baptism is necessary for salvation, and hence, if there is imminent danger of death, it should be conferred at once and without delay, and that it is valid if conferred with the right matter and form and intention by anyone, and at any time. Likewise (I profess) that the bond of the sacrament of matrimony is indissoluble, and that, although a separation of bed and board may be possible between the spouses because of adultery, heresy, and some other causes, nevertheless it is not lawful for them to contract another marriage.

Likewise, (I profess) that the apostolic and ecclesiastical traditions 1471 must be accepted and revered; also, that power of granting indulgences has been left to the Church of Christ, and that their use is very salutary for Christian people.

1472   Likewise, I accept and profess what was defined in the aforesaid Synod of Trent about original sin, about justification, about the list and interpretation of the sacred books of both the New Testament and the Old [cf. n. 787 ff., 783 ff.].

1473   Likewise, all other things I accept and profess, which the Holy Roman Church accepts and professes, and I likewise condemn, reject, and anathematize, at the same time all contrary things, both schisms and heresies, which have been condemned, rejected, and anathematized by the same Church. In addition, I promise and swear true obedience to the Roman Pontiff, the successor of Blessed Peter, the prince of the Apostles and the vicar of Jesus Christ. And that this faith of the Catholic Church, without which no one can be saved, etc. . . . [as in the Tridentine profession of faith, see n. 1000].

About not Demanding the Name of an Accomplice [1]

[From the Brief, "Suprema omnium Ecclesiarum sollicitudo," July 7, 1745]

1474   (1) For it came to our attention not so long ago that some confessors of those parts, allowing themselves to be seduced by a false idea of zeal, but straying far from the zeal "according to knowledge" [cf. Rom. 10: 2], have begun to bring in and to introduce a certain evil and pernicious practice in hearing the confessions of the faithful of Christ, and in administering the very saving sacrament of penance: namely, that if by chance they should happen upon penitents who have an associate in their sin, they demand at times from these penitents the name of such an accomplice or companion, and they attempt to induce them to reveal this to them not only by persuasion, but what is more detestable, they directly force and compel them to reveal it, under a threat of denying them sacramental absolution; nay more, they demand that not only the name of the accomplice be made known but also the place of residence, and this intolerable imprudence they do not hesitate to disguise by the specious pretext of procuring the correction of the accomplice and of accomplishing other good effects, nor to defend it by falsifying the opinions of learned men, when, in truth, by following false and erroneous opinions of this sort, or by making a bad application of true and sound principles, they bring destruction not only to their own souls but also to those of their penitents, and, besides, they render themselves guilty before God, the eternal judge, of many serious evils which they ought

---

[1] BB(M) 3, 178 f. [old ed. I n. 134]; NBR 16, 305 a f.—This decree was confirmed and urged by repetition by the same Pontiff in the Constitution "Ubi primum," July 2, 1746 [BB(M) 4, 117 ff.]. Cf. Constit. *Ad eradicandum* September 28, 1746 [BB(M) 4, 303 ff.].

to have foreseen would easily follow from their action. . . . (3) Moreover, in order that we may not seem to be lacking in our apostolic ministry to any degree in so great a danger to souls, and so that we may not permit our mind on this matter to be obscure or ambiguous to you, we wish you to know that the practice mentioned above must be entirely repudiated, and this same practice is reproved and condemned by Us through our present letters in the form of a brief, as scandalous and dangerous, and as harmful to the reputation of one's neighbor as it is to the sacrament itself, and tending to the violation of the most sacred sacramental seal and alienating the faithful from so advantageous and necessary a use of this same sacrament of penance.

Usury [1]

[From the Encyclical "Vix pervenit" to the bishops of Italy,
Nov. 1, 1745]

(Sec. 3), 1. That species of sin which is called usury, and which has its **1475** proper seat and place in a contract of lending, consists in this: that someone, from the loan itself, which of its very nature demands that only as much be returned as was received, wishes more to be returned to him than was received, and therefore contends that some profit beyond the principal, by reason of the lending, is due to him. Therefore, all profit of this sort, which surpasses the principal, is unlawful and is usurious.

2. Nor may any defense be summoned to justify that guilt, either from **1476** this fact, that the gain is not excessive and over much, but moderate, is not great but meager; or from this, that he from whom that profit is asked, because of the loan itself, is not a poor man but rich, who is not going to leave the sum given to him as a loan idle but is going to spend it advantageously to increase his fortune either by buying new estates or by transacting profitable business. Indeed, that person is convicted of acting contrary to the law of lending, which necessarily is concerned with the equality of what is given and returned, who, although that same equality has already once been rendered, does not fear to demand something more from someone, by reason of the lending itself, for which satisfaction has already been made on equal terms; and hence, if he should receive it, he will be obligated to restitution by reason of his obligation in justice, which they call commutative justice, and whose purpose it is both to preserve inviolably in human contracts the equality proper to each one, and to repair it exactly when it is not observed.

3. But by this it is not at all denied that sometimes there can perhaps **1477**

---

[1] BB(M) 3, 269 ff. [ed. vet. I n. 143]; MBR 16, 328 a ff.; cf. M Th Cc 16, 1075 ff. (Decr. S. Poenit., 11, Feb. 1832).

occur certain other titles, as they say, together with the contract of lending, and these not at all innate or intrinsic in general to the nature of a loan, from which titles there arises a just and entirely legitimate cause of rightly demanding something more above the principal than is due from the loan. Likewise, it is not denied that many times one's own money can be rightly invested and expended in other contracts of a different nature from the nature of lending, either to secure an annual income for oneself, or also to practice legitimate commerce and business, and thus procure an honest profit.

1478　　4. But, just as in so many different kinds of contracts of this nature, it is well known that if the equality of each one is not observed, whatever is received more than is just, pertains, if not to usury (for the reason that there is no loan either open or secret), certainly does pertain to some other real injustice carrying likewise the burden of retribution; so, also, if all things are rightly transacted and carried out according to the scale of justice, there is no doubt that in these same contracts there occurs a multifold lawful manner and method of maintaining and carrying on human commerce and profitable business itself for the common good. For, far be it from Christian minds that they should think that, by making use of usury or similar harmful injustices, there could flourish a profitable commerce; since, on the contrary, we should learn from the divine proverb that "justice exalteth a nation, but sin maketh nations miserable" [Prov. 14:34].

1479　　5. But this must be diligently borne in mind, that one would falsely and certainly rashly persuade himself that there is always found and is everywhere present, either some legitimate titles together with a loan, or, even excluding a loan, other just contracts, by the aid of which titles or contracts, it is permitted, as often as money, grain, or something of that kind is lent to another, just so often to receive a moderate increase beyond the whole and sound principal. And so, if anyone thinks in this manner, he will without any doubt be in opposition not only to the divine Scriptures and to the judgment of the Catholic Church about usury, but even to human common sense itself, and to natural reason. For, this at least cannot escape anyone, that in many cases a man is bound to succor another with a pure and simple act of lending, especially when Christ the Lord teaches: "From him that would borrow of thee, turn not away" [Matt. 5:42]; and that, similarly, in many circumstances, besides the loan itself, there can be place for no other just and true contract. Whoever, therefore, is willing to consult his conscience, ought first to inquire whether, with a loan there is truly any other just title, or, apart from a loan there is a just contract, by reason of which the profit which he seeks may be returned immune and free of all guilt.

The Baptism of Jewish Children [1]

[From the epistle "Postremo mense" to the Viceregent
in the City, Feb. 28, 1747]

3. . . . The first point to be considered is whether Hebrew children **1480**
can be lawfully baptized, if the parents are unwilling and reluctant. Secondly, if we say that this is unlawful, then we must consider whether any
case might occur, in which this could not only be done, but would be even
lawful and clearly fitting. Thirdly, we must consider whether the baptism
bestowed on Hebrew children at a time when it is now lawful, should
be considered valid or invalid. Fourthly, we must consider what must be
done when Hebrew children are brought to be baptized, or when it is
discovered that they have been admitted to sacred baptism; finally, how
it can be proved that these same children have already been purified by
the saving waters.

If there is any discussion of the first chapter of the first part, whether **1481**
Hebrew children can be baptized if the parents object, we openly assert
that this has already been defined in three places by St. Thomas, namely,
in Quodl. 2, a. 7; in II-II^{ae}, q. 10, a. 12, where, recalling for examination
the question proposed in the Quodlibeta: "Whether the children of Jews
and of other unbelievers should be baptized against the will of the
parents," he answered thus: "I reply that it must be said that the custom
of the Church has great authority, which should always be followed in all
things, etc. Moreover, the usage of the Church never held that the
children of Jews should be baptized against their parents' wishes. . . ,"
and in addition he says this in III^a, q. 68, a. 10: "I reply that it must be
said that children, sons of unbelievers. . . , if they do not yet have the
use of free will, are, according to the natural law, under the care of their
parents, as long as they cannot provide for themselves. . . , and, therefore, it would be against natural justice, if such children were baptized
without the parents' consent; just as if someone having the use of reason
should be baptized against his will. It would even be dangerous. . . ."

Scotus in 4 Sent. dist. 4, q. 9, n. 2, and in questions related to n. 2, **1482**
thought that a prince could laudably command that small children of
Hebrews and unbelievers be baptized, even against the will of the parents,
provided one could prudently see to it that these same children were not
killed by the parents. . . . Nevertheless, the opinion of St. Thomas prevailed in courts . . . and is more widespread among theologians and
those skilled in canon law [2]. . . .

---

[1] BB(M) 5, 8 ff. [ed. vet. II. n. 28]; MBR 17, 110 ff.

[2] The Pontiff, below in n. 32, decided that the legitimate age up to which Jewish
children may not be baptized against the will of their parents be determined regularly
at the completion of the seventh year.

1483   7. Therefore, this having been established, that it is unlawful to baptize Hebrew children against the will of their parents, now, following the order proposed in the beginning, we must take up the second part: namely, whether any occasion could ever occur in which that would be lawful and fitting. . . .

1484   8. . . . Since this may happen, that a child of Hebrew parentage be found by some Christian to be close to death, he will certainly perform a deed which I think is praiseworthy and pleasing to God, if he furnishes the child with eternal salvation by the purifying water. . . .

1485   9. If, likewise, it should happen that any Hebrew child had been cast out and abandoned by its parents, it is the common opinion of all and has also been confirmed by many decisions, that the child ought to be baptized, even if the parents protest against this and demand the child back. . . .

1486   After we have explained the most obvious cases in which this rule of ours prohibits the baptizing of Hebrew children against the wishes of their parents, we add some other declarations pertaining to this rule, the first of which is this: If parents are lacking, but the infants have been entrusted to the guardianship of a Hebrew, they can in no way be lawfully baptized without the assent of the guardian, since all the authority of the parents has passed to the guardians. . . . 15. The second is this, if the father should enlist in the Christian militia and order his infant son to be baptized, he should be baptized, even though the Hebrew mother protests, since the child must be considered to be, not under the power of the mother, but under that of the father.[1] . . . 16. The third is this, that although the mother does not have her children under her own right, nevertheless, if she belongs to the Christian faith and offers her child for baptism, although the Hebrew father protests, nevertheless, the child should be cleansed by the water of baptism. . . . 17. The fourth is that, if it is a certainty that the will of parents is necessary for the baptism of children, since under the name of parent a paternal grandfather also is included . . . , then it necessarily follows that, if the paternal grandfather has embraced the Catholic faith and brings his grandchild to the font of saving water, although the Hebrew mother objects, when the father is dead, nevertheless, the child should be baptized without hesitation.[2] . . .

1487   18. It is not an imaginary case that sometimes a Hebrew father says that he wants to embrace the Catholic religion and presents himself and his infant sons to be baptized, but afterwards regrets his intention and

---

[1] Gregory IX c. 1, on the exposing of infants and invalids, also decided this.

[2] Benedict XIV in another letter, "Probe te meminisse," Dec. 15, 1751 [BB(M) 9, 88 ff.], declared the same held when the father was dead with regard to a paternal Christian grandmother, even though the Hebrew mother and guardians objected.

refuses to have his son baptized. This happened at Mantua. . . . The case was brought for examination in the Congregation of the Holy Office, and the Pope on the 24th day of September in the year 1699 decreed that action should be taken as follows: "His Holiness, having listened to the wishes of the Cardinals, decreed that two infant sons, one three years old, the other five, be baptized. The other children, namely a son of eight years and a daughter twelve, should be placed in the house of catechumens, if there is one at Mantua, but if not, at the home of a pious and honorable person for the purpose of finding out their will and of instructing them. . . ."

19. Also some unbelievers are accustomed to bring their children to **1488** Christians to be washed with the saving waters, not however that they may merit the satisfactions of Christ, nor that the guilt of original sin may be washed from their soul, but they do this, motivated by some base superstition, namely because they think that by the benefit of baptism, these same children may be freed from malignant spirits, from infection, or some illness. . . .

21. . . . Some unbelievers, when they have represented this idea to **1489** themselves, that by the grace of baptism their children will be freed from illnesses and the persecution of the demons, are brought to such a pass of madness that they have also threatened Catholic priests with death. . . . But, in opposition to this belief, the Congregation of the Holy Office in the presence of the Pope on the 5th day of September, 1625, contested: "The Sacred Congregation of the general Inquisition held in the presence of His Holiness, having read the letters of the Bishop Antibarensis, in which he made supplication for a solution of the doubt written below: Whether, when priests are compelled by Turks to baptize their children, not that they may make them Christians, but for their bodily health, so that they may be freed from infection, epilepsy, the danger of bewitchment, and wolves, whether in such a case they could pretend to baptize them, making use of the matter of baptism without the prescribed form? He replied in the negative, because baptism is the door of the sacraments and a profession of faith, and that in no way can it be simulated. . . ."

29. And so our discourse comes now to those who are presented for **1490** baptism neither by their parents nor by others who have any right over them, but by someone who has no authority. In addition, there is a question about those whose cases are not comprehended under the disposition which permits baptism to be conferred, even if the consent of their elders is withheld. In this case, indeed, they ought not to be baptized, but be sent back to those in whose power and trust they are lawfully placed. But, if they have been already admitted to the sacrament, either they must be detained or recovered from their Hebrew parents and handed over to the faithful of Christ, so that they may be piously and

religiously trained by them; for this is the effect of baptism, which, though it be unlawful, nevertheless is true and valid.

Errors Concerning Duelling [1]

[Condemned in the Constitution, "Detestabilem," Nov. 10, 1752]

1491   1. A military man who would be considered fearful, timid, abject, and unfit for military offices unless he offers or accepts a duel, and hence would be deprived of an office by which he supports himself and his family, or who would be perpetually deprived of the hope of promotion otherwise due him and merited by him, is free from guilt and penalty, whether he offers a duel or accepts one.

1492   2. Those who accept a duel, or even provoke a duel for the sake of protecting their honor, or of avoiding the disrepute of men, can be excused when they know for certain that the combat will not take place, inasmuch as it will be prevented by others.

1493   3. A leader or military officer who accepts a duel through grave fear of losing his reputation or his office, does not incur the ecclesiastical penalties brought by the Church against duelists.

1494   4. It is permitted in the natural state of man to accept and to offer a duel to preserve one's fortunes with honor, when their loss cannot be prevented by any other means.

1495   5. This permission, claimed for the natural state, can also be applied to the state of the commonwealth which is badly regulated, that is to say, in which justice is openly denied, either because of the negligence or the wickedness of the magistracy.

Condemned and prohibited as false, scandalous, and pernicious.

CLEMENT XIII 1758–1769   CLEMENT XIV 1769–1774

PIUS VI 1775-1799

Mixed Marriages in Belgium [2]

[From the Rescript of Pius VI to Card. de Franckenberg,
Archbishop of Mechlin, and to the Bishops of Belgium,
July 13, 1782]

1496   . . . And therefore we must not depart from the uniform opinion of our predecessors and from ecclesiastical discipline, which do not approve marriages between parties who are both heretics, or between a Catholic

---

[1] BB(M) 10, 77 [ed. vet. IV n. 6]; MBR 19, 19 b.
[2] Rsk Mm II 61 ff.; MT h Cc 25, 692 f.

on the one hand and a heretic on the other, and this much less in a case where there is need of a dispensation of some sort. . . .

Passing now to that point about the requested assistance of parish 1497 priests in mixed marriages, we say that if the above named admonition to recall the Catholic party from the unlawful marriage has been fulfilled, and nevertheless he persists in his will to contract it, and it is foreseen that the marriage will inevitably follow, then the Catholic priest can lend his material presence, nevertheless in such wise that he is bound to observe the following precautions: First, that he does not assist at such a marriage in a sacred place, nor clothed in any vestment betokening a sacred function, nor will he recite over the contracting parties any prayers of the Church, and in no way shall he bless them. Secondly, that he will exact and receive from the contracting heretic a declaration in writing, in which with an oath in the presence of two witnesses, who also ought to sign their names, he obligates himself to permit his partner the free use of the Catholic religion, and to educate in it all the children who shall be born without any distinction of sex. . . . Thirdly, that the contracting Catholic make a declaration signed by himself and two witnesses, in which he promises with an oath not only never to apostatize from his Catholic religion, but to educate in it all his future offspring, and to procure effectively the conversion of the other contracting non-Catholic.

Fourthly, that which concerns the proclamations commanded by the 1498 imperial decree, which the bishops hold to be civil rather than sacred acts, we answer: Since they have been preordained for the future celebration of marriage and consequently contain a positive cooperation with it, a thing which certainly exceeds the limits of simple tolerance, we cannot consent that these be made. . . .

It remains now to speak about one more point, concerning which, al- 1499 though we have not been expressly interrogated, nevertheless we do not think it should be passed over in silence, insomuch as, in practice, it could too frequently happen; namely, this: Whether the contracting Catholic, afterwards wishing to share in the sacraments, ought to be admitted to them? To this we say that as long as he shall demonstrate that he is sorry for his sinful union, this can be granted to him, provided he shall sincerely declare before confession that he will procure the conversion of his heretical spouse, that he renews his promise of educating his children in the orthodox religion, and that he will repair the scandal he has given to the other faithful. If these conditions obtain, we are not opposed to the Catholic party receiving the sacraments.[1]

---

[1] Many synods and various Pontiffs have published decrees on (mixed) marriages, e.g., the Synod of Laodicea (between 343 and 381), c. 10, 31; that of Alvira (between 300 and 306), c. 16; that of Carthage III (397), c. 12; that of Agde, c. 67; that of Auvergne (535), c. 4; that of Toulouse (694); that of Chalcedon (451), can. 14;

Concerning the Power of the Roman Pontiff
(Against Febronianism) [1]

[From the Brief, "Super soliditate," Nov. 28, 1786]

1500 And since truly, as Augustine teaches,[2] God has placed the doctrine of truth in the chair of unity, that unfortunate writer on the contrary leaves nothing undone with which to harass and attack in every way this See of Peter, in which See the Fathers have taught with unanimous agreement that that chair was established, in which alone unity might be preserved by all; from which the rights of the venerable communion emanate to all the others; and to which it is necessary that every church and all the faithful everywhere come [cf. Vatican Council, n. 1824]. He has not hesitated to call fanatic the crowd which he saw breaking forth into these words at the sight of the Pontiff: "He is the man who has received from God the keys of the kingdom of heaven with the power of binding and loosing, to whom no other bishop can be made equal, from whom these very bishops receive their authority as he himself received his supreme power from God; moreover, he is the vicar of Christ, the visible head of the Church, the supreme judge of the faithful."

that of Worms (1575); that of Antwerp (1576); that of York (1576); that of Luxeuil (1580); that of Bordeaux (1583); that of Tours (1583); that of Narbonne and Constance (1609); that of Ermeland and Augusta (1610); that of Hertogenbosch (1612); that of Luttich (1618); that of Bordeaux (1624); that of Antwerp (1643); that of Gratianopolis (1690); that of Cologne (1651); that of Paderborn (1658); that of Kulm and of Pressburg (1745); that of Sitten (1651); that of Saint-Omer (1640); that of Ermeland (1726). Furthermore, the Pontiffs: Boniface V (c. 617), Stephen IV (c. 770), Nicholas I (*Resp. ad Consult. Bulgar* n. 22), Boniface VIII (*Decret.* VI 5, 24), Urban VIII (1624), Clement X (ep. d. Aug. 20, 1628), Clement XI (1706), Benedict XIV [cf. n. 1455], Clement XIII (1763), Pius VIII (1830), Gregory XVI (1832 etc.), Pius IX [cf. n. 1640, 1765 ff.], Leo XIII [cf. n. 1853 ff., 1865], Pius X [cf. n. 1991, 2066 ff.]; Codex I. C. can. 1060–1064 c. notis.

[1] BRCC 7, 672 b f.; Rsk RP III 319 f.—Although the book of Febronius or Ioh, Nic. ab. Hontheim: *De statu Ecclesiae et legitima potestate Romani Pontificis,* 1763, had been placed upon the Index of forbidden books, and at the command of the Supreme Pontiff had been especially prohibited by the Bishops of Germany, of Mainz, of Treves, of Cologne, of Bamberg, of Herbipolis, of Constance, of Auguste, of Frising, and of Prague, nevertheless its perverse principles began to be spread and proceed widely throughout Germany. But among those who after Febronius insurrected against the lawful power of the Roman Pontiff, the most unfortunate canonist Eybel was pre-eminent, who, when Pius VI set out on a journey into Germany to move the spirit of Joseph II, published a book: *Was est der Papst?* When it was published in repeated editions and after being translated into other tongues, Pius VI in the Brief, "Super soliditate," condemned it as containing propositions, respectively false, scandalous, bold, injurious, leading to schism, schismatic, erroneous, leading to heresy, heretical, and some condemned by the Church.

[2] Ep. 105, 16 [ML 33, 403]; cf. St. Optatus Milev., *De schismate donatist.* 2, 2 f. [ML 11, 946 f.].

Could, therefore (a thing horrible to say), that voice of Christ have been fanatical, which promised [Matt. 16:19] Peter the keys of the kingdom of heaven with the power of binding and loosing; which keys Optatus Milevitanus, following Tertullian, did not hesitate to confess that Peter alone received to be communicated to the others? Or, are so many solemn decrees of the Popes and Councils repeated so many times to be called fanatic, by which those have been condemned who denied that in blessed Peter, the prince of the Apostles, his successor, the Roman Pontiff, was established by God as the visible head of the Church and the vicar of Jesus Christ, that to him has been transmitted full power of ruling the Church, and that true obedience is due him from all who are considered Christians; and that such is the power of the primacy, which he holds by divine right, that he is superior to other bishops not only by his rank of honor but by the plenitude of his supreme power? All the more must be deplored that blind and rash temerity of the man who was eager to renew in his unfortunate book errors which have been condemned by so many decrees, who has said and insinuated indiscriminately by many ambigui-ties, that every bishop, no less than the pope, was called by God to govern the Church, and was endowed with no less power; that Christ gave the same power Himself to all the apostles; and that whatever some people believe is obtained and granted only by the pope, that very thing, whether it depends on consecration or ecclesiastical jurisdiction, can be obtained just as well from any bishop; that Christ wished His Church to be governed in the manner of a republic; and that, indeed, for that govern-ment there is need of a head for the good of unity, but one who does not dare to interfere in the affairs of others (bishops) who rule at the same time; nevertheless, he has the privilege of exhorting those who are negligent to the fulfillment of their duties; that the power of the primacy is contained in this one prerogative, of making up for the negligence of others, of looking after the preservation of unity by encouragement and example; that the popes have no power in another diocese except in an extraordinary case; that the pope is the head because he holds his power and strength from the Church; that the Pontiffs have made it lawful for themselves to violate the rights of bishops, to reserve to themselves abso-lutions, dispensations, decisions, appeals, bestowal of benefices, in a word all other duties which he enumerates one by one and derides as unjust reservations and injurious to bishops.

The Power of the One Church in the Marriage of Baptized Persons [1]

[From the Epistle, "Deessemus nobis," to the Bishop of Motula, Sept. 16, 1788]

1500a   It is not unknown to us that there are some, who, attributing too much to the authority of the secular princes, and captiously interpreting the words of this canon [see n. 982], have undertaken to defend this: That, since the Tridentine Fathers did not make use of this form of speaking, "to ecclesiastical judges *alone*," or, "*all* matrimonial cases,"—they (the Tridentine Fathers) have left to lay judges the power of at least investigating matrimonial cases which are of pure fact. But we know that even this sophism and this false kind of quibbling are devoid of all foundation. For the words of the canon are so general that they embrace and comprise all cases. Moreover, the spirit or purpose of the law extends so widely that it leaves no place for exception or limitation. For if these cases pertain to the tribunal of the Church alone for no other reason than because the marriage contract is truly and properly one of the seven sacraments of the evangelical law, then, just as this notion of the sacrament is common to all matrimonial cases, so all these cases ought to pertain to the ecclesiastical judges alone.

Errors of the Synod of Pistoia [2]

[Condemned in the Constitution, "Auctorem fidei," Aug. 28, 1794]

[A. Errors about the Church [3]]

Obscuring of Truths in the Church
[From the Decree de Grat., sec. 1]

1501   1. The proposition, which asserts "that in these later times there has been spread a general obscuring of the more important truths pertaining to religion, which are the basis of faith and of the moral teachings of Jesus Christ,"—heretical.

---

[1] A. de Roskovány, *Matrimonium in Ecclesia catholica,* I (1870), 421 f.

[2] Pistoia in Toscana (Italy). BRC 9, 398 b ff.; GI C Rcht II 148 ff.; Rsk RP III 528 ff.; Msi XXXVIII 1261–1282 (cf. also 987–1261).

[3] These collected titles [in so far as they are included individually] are not contained in the Bull itself.

The Power Attributed to the Community of the Church,
in Order That by This the Power May Be Communicated
to the Pastors
[Episcopal Convocation]

2. The proposition which states "that power has been given by God to 1502
the Church, that it might be communicated to the pastors who are its
ministers for the salvation of souls"; if thus understood that the power
of ecclesiastical ministry and of rule is derived from the COMMUNITY
of the faithful to the pastors,—heretical.

The Name Ministerial Head Attributed to the Roman Pontiff
[Decree de fide (on faith), sec. 8]

3. In addition, the proposition which states "that the Roman Pontiff 1503
is the ministerial head," if it is so explained that the Roman Pontiff does
not receive from Christ in the person of blessed Peter, but from the
Church, the power of ministry, which as successor of Peter, true vicar
of Christ and head of the whole Church he possesses in the universal
Church,—heretical.[1]

The Power of the Church for the Establishing and the Sanctioning
of Exterior Discipline
[Decree de fide, secs. 13, 14]

4. The proposition affirming, "that it would be a misuse of the author- 1504
ity of the Church, when she transfers that authority beyond the limits of
doctrine and of morals, and extends it to exterior matters, and demands
by force that which depends on persuasion and love";· and then also,
"that it pertains to it much less, to demand by force exterior obedience
to its decrees"; in so far as by those undefined words, "extends to exterior matters," the proposition censures as an abuse of the authority of
the Church the use of its power received from God, which the apostles
themselves used in establishing and sanctioning exterior discipline—
heretical.

5. In that part in which the proposition insinuates that the Church 1505

---

[1] These propositions 2 and 3, accepted by Febronius, indicate the systems proposed
by Edmund Richereus in his book *De ecclesiastica et politica potestate,* especially approved by the Jansenists. This book was condemned in 1612 by a synod of the province
of Sens under Card. Perronio, and in the same year by a synod of the province of
Bagnères. Paul V, in a brief to the bishops of the province of Sens, approved this condemnation. Furthermore (May 10, 1613), under the same Paul V the book was condemned by a Holy Inquisition and (Dec. 2, 1622) under Gregory XV the book was
again prohibited by the Holy Congregation of the Index, and again (March 4, 1709)
it was prohibited under Clement XI.

"does not have authority to demand obedience to its decrees otherwise than by means which depend on persuasion; in so far as it intends that the Church has not conferred on it by God the power, not only of directing by counsel and persuasion, but also of ordering by laws, and of constraining and forcing the inconstant and stubborn by exterior judgment and salutary punishments" [from Benedict XIV in the Brief, "Ad assiduas," of the year 1755, to the Primate, Archbishops, and Bishops of the Kingdom of Poland],—leading toward a system condemned elsewhere as heretical.

Rights Attributed to Bishops Beyond What is Lawful
[Decree de ord., sec. 25]

1506   6. The doctrine of the synod by which it professes that "it is convinced that a bishop has received from Christ all necessary rights for the good government of his diocese," just as if for the good government of each diocese higher ordinances dealing either with faith and morals, or with general discipline, are not necessary, the right of which belongs to the supreme Pontiffs and the General Councils for the universal Church,—schismatic, at least erroneous.

1507   7. Likewise, in this, that it encourages a bishop "to pursue zealously a more perfect constitution of ecclesiastical discipline," and this "against all contrary customs, exemptions, reservations which are opposed to the good order of the diocese, for the greater glory of God and for the greater edification of the faithful"; in that it supposes that a bishop has the right by his own judgment and will to decree and decide contrary to customs, exemptions, reservations, whether they prevail in the universal Church or even in each province, without the consent or the intervention of a higher hierarchic power, by which these customs, etc., have been introduced or approved and have the force of law,—leading to schism and subversion of hierarchic rule, erroneous.

1508   8. Likewise, in that it says it is convinced that "the rights of a bishop received from Jesus Christ for the government of the Church cannot be altered nor hindered, and, when it has happened that the exercise of these rights has been interrupted for any reason whatsoever, a bishop can always and should return to his original rights, as often as the greater good of his church demands it"; in the fact that it intimates that the exercise of episcopal rights can be hindered and coerced by no higher power, whenever a bishop shall judge that it does not further the greater good of his church,—leading to schism, and to subversion of hierarchic government, erroneous.

The Right Incorrectly Attributed to Priests of Inferior Rank in Decrees of Faith and Discipline
[*Episcopal Convocation*]

9. The doctrine which states, that "the reformation of abuses in regard 1509 to ecclesiastical discipline ought equally to depend upon and be established by the bishop and the parish priests in diocesan synods, and that without the freedom of decision, obedience would not be due to the suggestions and orders of the bishops," [1]—false, rash, harmful to episcopal authority, subversive of hierarchic government, favoring the heresy of Aerius, which was renewed by Calvin [cf. Benedict XIV *De Syn. dioc.* (concerning diocesan synods), 13, 1].

[*From the Episcopal Convocation. From the Epistle to the Vic. For. From the Oration to the Synod, sec. 8. From session 3.*]

10. Likewise, the doctrine by which parish priests and other priests 1510 gathered in a synod are declared judges of faith together with the bishop, and at the same time it is intimated that they are qualified for judgment in matters of faith by their own right and have indeed received it by ordination,—false, rash, subversive of hierarchic order, detracting from the strength of dogmatic definitions or judgments of the Church, at least erroneous.

[*Oration to the Synod, sec. 8*]

11. The opinion enunciating that by the long-standing practice of our 1511 ancestors, handed down even from apostolic times, preserved through the better ages of the Church, it has been accepted that "decrees, or definitions, or opinions even of the greater sees should not be accepted, unless they had been recognized and approved by the diocesan synod,"— false, rash, derogatory, in proportion to its generality, to the obedience due to the apostolic constitutions, and also to the opinions emanating from the legitimate, superior, hierarchic power, fostering schism and heresy.

Calumnies Against Some Decisions in the Matter of Faith Which Have Come Down from Several Centuries
[*Faith, sec. 12*]

12. The assertions of the synod, accepted as a whole concerning deci- 1512 sions in the matter of faith which have come down from several centuries, which it represents as decrees originating from one particular church

---

[1] Almost the same proposition was taught in the system of Richerius (see 1503 n.).

or from a few pastors, unsupported by sufficient authority, formulated for the corruption of the purity of faith and for causing disturbance, introduced by violence, from which wounds, still too recent, have been inflicted,—false, deceitful, rash, scandalous, injurious to the Roman Pontiffs and the Church, derogatory to the obedience due to the Apostolic Constitutions, schismatic, dangerous, at least erroneous.

The So-called Peace of Clement IX
[Oration to the Synod, sec. 2 in the note]

1513   13. The proposition reported among the acts of the synod, which intimates that Clement IX restored peace to the Church by the approval of the distinction of right and deed in the subscription to the formulary written by Alexander VII (see n. 1099),—false, rash, injurious to Clement IX.

1514   14. In so far as it approves that distinction by extolling its supporters with praise and by berating their opponents,—rash, pernicious, injurious to the Supreme Pontiffs, fostering schism and heresy.

The Composition of the Body of the Church
[Appendix n. 28]

1515   15. The doctrine which proposes that the Church "must be considered as one mystical body composed of Christ, the head, and the faithful, who are its members through an ineffable union, by which in a marvelous way we become with Him one sole priest, one sole victim, one sole perfect adorer of God the Father, in spirit and in truth," understood in this sense, that no one belongs to the body of the Church except the faithful, who are perfect adorers in spirit and in truth,—heretical.

[B. Errors about Justification, Grace, the Virtues]

The State of Innocence
[Grace, secs. 4, 7: the sacraments in general, sec. 1;
penance, sec. 4]

1516   16. The doctrine of the synod about the state of happy innocence, such as it represents it in Adam before his sin, comprising not only integrity but also interior justice with an inclination toward God through love of charity, and primeval sanctity restored in some way after the fall; in so far as, understood comprehensively, it intimates that that state was a consequence of creation, due to man from the natural exigency and condition of human nature, not a gratuitous gift of God, false, elsewhere condemned in Baius [see n. 1001 ff.], and in Quesnel [see n. 1384 ff.], erroneous, favorable to the Pelagian heresy.

Immortality Viewed as a Natural Condition of Man
[*Baptism, sec. 2*]

17. The proposition stated in these words: "Taught by the Apostle, **1517** we regard death no longer as a natural condition of man, but truly as a just penalty for original guilt," since, under the deceitful mention of the name of the Apostle, it insinuates that death, which in the present state has been inflicted as a just punishment for sin by the just withdrawal of immortality, was not a natural condition of man, as if immortality had not been a gratuitous gift, but a natural condition,—deceitful, rash, injurious to the Apostle, elsewhere condemned [see n. 1078].

The Condition of Man in the State of Nature
[*On Grace, sec. 10*]

18. The doctrine of the synod stating that "after the fall of Adam, **1518** God announced the promise of a future Redeemer and wished to console the human race through hope of salvation, which Jesus was to bring"; nevertheless, "that God willed that the human race should pass through various states before the plenitude of time should come"; and first, that in the state of nature "man, left to his own lights, would learn to distrust his own blind reason and would move himself from his own aberrations to desire the aid of a superior light"; the doctrine, as it stands, is deceitful, and if understood concerning the desire of the aid of a superior light in relation to the salvation promised through Christ, that man is supposed to have been able to move himself to conceive this desire by his own proper lights remaining after the fall,—suspected, favorable to the Semi-pelagian heresy.

The Condition of Man under the Law
[Ibid.]

19. Likewise, the doctrine which adds that under the Law man "be- **1519** came a prevaricator, since he was powerless to observe it, not indeed by the fault of the Law, which was most sacred, but by the guilt of man, who, under the Law, without grace, became more and more a prevaricator"; and it further adds, "that the Law, if it did not heal the heart of man, brought it about that he would recognize his evil, and, being convinced of his weakness, would desire the grace of a mediator"; in this part it generally intimates that man became a prevaricator through the nonobservance of the Law which he was powerless to observe, as if "He who is just could command something impossible, or He who is pious would be likely to condemn man for that which he could not avoid" (from St. Caesarius *Serm.* 73, in append., St. Augustine, *Serm.* 273,

edit. Maurin; from St. August., *De nat, et grat.*, c. 43; *De grat. et lib. arb.*, c. 16; *Enarr. in psalm.* 56, n. 1),—false scandalous, impious, condemned in Baius (see n. 1504).

1520   20. In that part in which it is to be understood that man, while under the Law and without grace, could conceive a desire for the grace of a Mediator related to the salvation promised through Christ, as if "grace itself does not effect that He be invoked by us" (from Conc. Araus. II, can. 3 [v.n. 176]),—the proposition as it stands, deceitful, suspect, favorable to the Semipelagian heresy.

Illuminating and Exciting Grace
[*Grace, sec. 11*]

1521   21. The proposition which asserts "that the light of grace, when it is alone, effects nothing but to make us aware of the unhappiness of our state and the gravity of our evil; that grace, in such a case, produces the same effect as the Law produced: therefore, it is necessary that God create in our heart a sacred love and infuse a sacred delight contrary to the love dominating in us; that this sacred love, this sacred delight is properly the grace of Jesus Christ, the inspiration of charity by which, when it is perceived, we act by a sacred love; that this is that root from which grow good works; that this is the grace of the New Testament, which frees us from the servitude of sin, makes us sons of God"; since it intimates that that alone is properly the grace of Jesus Christ, which creates in the heart a sacred love, and which impels us to act, or also, by which man, freed from the slavery of sin, is constituted a son of God; and that that grace is not also properly the grace of Jesus Christ, by which the heart of man is touched through an illumination of the Holy Spirit (TRID. sess. 6, c. 5 [see n. 797]), and that no true interior grace of Christ is given, which is resisted,—false, deceitful, leading to the error condemned in the second proposition of Jansen as heretical, and renewing it [see n. 1093].

Faith as the First Grace
[*Faith, sec. 1*]

1522   22. The proposition which declares that faith, "from which begins the series of graces, and through which, as the first voice, we are called to salvation and to the Church": is the very excellent virtue itself of faith by which men are called and are the faithful; just as if that grace were not prior, which "as it precedes the will, so it precedes faith also" (from St. August., *De dono persev.*, c. 16, n. 41),—suspected of heresy, and savoring of it, elsewhere condemned in Quesnel [see n. 1377], erroneous.

The Twofold Love
[*Grace, sec. 8*]

23. The doctrine of the synod about the twofold love of dominating 1523
cupidity and of dominating charity, stating that man without grace
is under the power of sin, and that in that state through the general
influence of the dominating cupidity he taints and corrupts all his actions;
since it insinuates that in man, while he is under the servitude or in the
state of sin, destitute of that grace by which he is freed from the servitude
of sin and is constituted a son of God, cupidity is so dominant that by
its general influence all his actions are vitiated in themselves and corrupted; or that all his works which are done before justification, for
whatsoever reason they may be done, are sins; as if in all his acts the
sinner is a slave to the dominating cupidity,—false, dangerous, leading
into the error condemned by the Tridentine Council as heretical, again
condemned in Baius, art. 40 [see n. 817, 1040].

Sec. 12

24. But in this part, indeed, no intermediate affections are placed be- 1524
tween the dominating cupidity and the dominating charity, planted by
nature itself and worthy of praise because of their own nature, which,
together with love of the beatitude and a natural inclination to good
"have remained as the last outline and traces of the image of God" (from
St. August., *De spirit. et litt.,* c. 28); just as if "between the divine love
which draws us to the kingdom, and illicit human love which is condemned, there should not be given a licit human love which is not
censured" (from St. August., *Serm.* 349 *de car.,* edit. Maurin),—false,
elsewhere condemned [see n. 1038, 1297].

Servile Fear
[*On Penance, sec. 3*]

25. The doctrine which in general asserts that the fear of punishment 1525
"cannot be called evil if it, at least, prevails to restrain the hand"; as if
the fear itself of hell, which faith teaches must be imposed on sin, is not
in itself good and useful as a supernatural gift, and a motion inspired by
God preparing for the love of justice,—false, rash, dangerous, injurious to
the divine gifts, elsewhere condemned [see n. 746], contrary to the
doctrine of the Council of Trent [see n. 798, 898], and to the common
opinion of the Fathers, namely "that there is need," according to the
customary order of preparation for justice, "that fear should first enter,
through which charity will come; fear is a medicine, charity is health"
(from S. August., *In* [*I*] *epist. Io.,* c. 4, *tract.* 9; *in Io. evang., tract,* 41,

n. 10; *Enarr. in psalm.* 127, n. 7; *Serm.* 157 *de verbis Apost,* n. 13; *Serm.* 161 *de verbis Apost.,* n. 8; *Serm.* 349 *de caritate,* n. 7).

The Punishment of Those Who Die with Original Sin Only
[*Baptism, sec. 3*]

1526   26. The doctrine which rejects as a Pelagian fable, that place of the lower regions (which the faithful generally designate by the name of the limbo of children) in which the souls of those departing with the sole guilt of original sin are punished with the punishment of the condemned, exclusive of the punishment of fire, just as if, by this very fact, that these who remove the punishment of fire introduced that middle place and state free of guilt and of punishment between the kingdom of God and eternal damnation, such as that about which the Pelagians idly talk,—false, rash, injurious to Catholic schools.

[C. Errors] about the Sacraments, and First about the Sacramental Form with a Condition Attached
[*Baptism, sec. 12*]

1527   27. The deliberation of the synod which, under pretext of clinging to ancient canons in the case of doubtful baptism, declares its intention of omitting mention of the conditional form,—rash, contrary to practice, to the law, to the authority of the Church.

The Partaking of the Victim in the Sacrifice of the Mass
[*The Eucharist, sec. 6*]

1528   28. The proposition of the synod in which, after it states that "a partaking of the victim is an essential part in the sacrifice," it adds, "nevertheless, it does not condemn as illicit those Masses in which those present do not communicate sacramentally, for the reason that they do partake of the victim, although less perfectly, by receiving it spiritually," since it insinuates that there is something lacking to the essence of the sacrifice in that sacrifice which is performed either with no one present, or with those present who partake of the victim neither sacramentally nor spiritually, and as if those Masses should be condemned as illicit, in which, with the priest alone communicating, no one is present who communicates either sacramentally or spiritually,—false, erroneous, suspected of heresy and savoring of it.

The Efficacy of the Rite of Consecration
[*The Eucharist, sec. 2*]

1529   29. The doctrine of the synod, in that part in which, undertaking to explain the doctrine of faith in the rite of consecration, and disregarding the scholastic questions about the manner in which Christ is in the Eucharist, from which questions it exhorts priests performing the duty of teaching to refrain, it states the doctrine in these two propositions only: 1) after the consecration Christ is truly, really, substantially under the species; 2) then the whole substance of the bread and wine ceases, appearances only remaining; it (the doctrine) absolutely omits to make any mention of transubstantiation, or conversion of the whole substance of the bread into the body, and of the whole substance of the wine into the blood, which the Council of Trent defined as an article of faith [see n. 877, 884], and which is contained in the solemn profession of faith [see n. 997]; since by an indiscreet and suspicious omission of this sort knowledge is taken away both of an article pertaining to faith, and also of the word consecrated by the Church to protect the profession of it, as if it were a discussion of a merely scholastic question,—dangerous, derogatory to the exposition of Catholic truth about the dogma of transubstantiation, favorable to heretics.

The Application of the Fruit of the Sacrifice
[The Eucharist, sec. 8]

30. The doctrine of the synod, by which, while it professes "to believe **1530** that the oblation of the sacrifice extends itself to all, in such a way, however, that in the liturgy there can be made a special commemoration of certain individuals, both living and dead, by praying God specially for them," then it immediately adds: "Not, however, that we should believe that it is in the will of the priest to apply the fruit of the sacrifice to whom He wishes, rather we condemn this error as greatly offending the rights of God, who alone distributes the fruit of the sacrifice to whom He wishes and according to the measure which pleases Him"; and consequently, from this it derides "as false the opinion foisted on the people that they who give alms to the priest on the condition that he celebrate a Mass will receive from it special fruit"; thus understood, that besides the special commemoration and prayer a special offering itself, or application of the Sacrifice which is made by the priest does not benefit, other things being equal, those for whom it is applied more than any others, as if no special fruit would come from a special application, which the Church recommends and commands should be made for definite persons or classes of persons, especially by pastors for their flock, and which, as if coming down from a divine precept, has been clearly expressed by the sacred synod of Trent (sess. 23, c. 1 *de reform;* BENED. XIV, Constit. "Cum semper oblatas," sec. 2),—false, rash, dangerous, injurious to the Church, leading into the error elsewhere condemned in Wycliffe [see n. 599].

The Suitable Order to Be Observed in Worship
[*The Eucharist, sec. 5*]

1531   31. The proposition of the synod enunciating that it is fitting, in accordance with the order of divine services and ancient custom, that there be only one altar in each temple, and therefore, that it is pleased to restore that custom,—rash, injurious to the very ancient pious custom flourishing and approved for these many centuries in the Church, especially in the Latin Church.

[*Ibid.*]

1532   32. Likewise, the prescription forbidding cases of sacred relics or flowers being placed on the altar,—rash, injurious to the pious and approved custom of the Church.

[*Ibid.*, sec. 6]

1533   33. The proposition of the synod by which it shows itself eager to remove the cause through which, in part, there has been induced a forgetfulness of the principles relating to the order of the liturgy, "by recalling it (the liturgy) to a greater simplicity of rites, by expressing it in the vernacular language, by uttering it in a loud voice"; as if the present order of the liturgy, received and approved by the Church, had emanated in some part from the forgetfulness of the principles by which it should be regulated,—rash, offensive to pious ears, insulting to the Church, favorable to the charges of heretics against it.

The Order of Penance
[*Penance, sec. 7*]

1534   34. The declaration of the synod by which, after it previously stated that the order of canonical penance had been so established by the Church, in accord with the example of the apostles that it was common to all, and not merely for the punishment of guilt, but especially for the disposition to grace, it adds that "it (the synod) recognizes in that marvelous and venerable order the whole dignity of so necessary a sacrament, free from the subtleties which have been added to it in the course of time"; as if, through the order in which without the complete course of canonical penance this sacrament has been wont to be administered, the dignity of the sacrament had been lessened,—rash, scandalous, inducing to a contempt of the dignity of the sacrament as it has been accustomed to be administered throughout the whole Church, injurious to the Church itself.

[*Penance, sec. 10, n. 4*]

35. The proposition conceived in these words: "If charity in the begin- 1535
ning is always weak, it behooves the priest, in obtaining an increase of
this charity in the ordinary way, to make those acts of humiliation and
penance which have been recommended in every age by the Church
precede; to reduce those acts to a few prayers or to some fasting after
absolution has already been conferred, seems to be a material desire of
keeping for this sacrament the mere name of penance, rather than an
illuminating and suitable means to increase that fervor of charity which
ought to precede absolution; indeed we are far from blaming the practice of imposing penances to be fulfilled after absolution; if all our good
works have our defects always joined to them, how much more ought
we to fear lest we admit very many imperfections into the very difficult
and very important work of our reconciliation"; since it implies that the
penances which are imposed, to be fulfilled after absolution, are to be
considered as a supplement for the defects admitted in the work of our
reconciliation, rather than as truly sacramental penances and satisfactions for the sins confessed, as if, in order that the true reason for the
sacrament, not the mere name, be preserved, it would be necessary that
in the ordinary way the acts of humiliation and penance, which are imposed as a means of sacramental satisfaction, should precede absolution,—
false, rash, injurious to the common practice of the Church, leading to
the error contained in the heretical note in Peter of Osma [see n. 728;
cf. n. 1306 f.].

The Previous Disposition Necessary for Admitting Penitents to Reconciliation

[*Grace, sec. 15*]

36. The doctrine of the synod, in which, after it stated that "when 1536
there are unmistakable signs of the love of God dominating in the heart
of a man, he can deservedly be considered worthy of being admitted to
participation in the blood of Jesus Christ, which takes place in the sacraments," it further adds, "that false conversions, which take place through
attrition (incomplete sorrow for sins), are not usually efficacious nor
durable," consequently, "the shepherd of souls must insist on unmistakable signs of the dominating charity before he admits his penitents to
the sacraments"; which signs, as it (the decree) then teaches (sec. 17),
"a pastor can deduce from a firm cessation of sin and from fervor in
good works"; and this "fervor of charity," moreover, it prescribes (*De
poenit.* sec. 10) as the disposition which "should precede absolution"; so
understood that not only imperfect contrition, which is sometimes called
by the name of attrition, even that which is joined with the love with

which a man begins to love God as the fountain of all justice [cf. n. 798], and not only contrition formed by charity, but also the fervor of a dominating charity, and that, indeed, proved by a long continued practice through fervor in good works, is generally and absolutely required in order that a man may be admitted to the sacraments, and penitents especially be admitted to the benefit of the absolution,—false, rash, disturbing to the peace of souls, contrary to the safe and approved practice of the Church, detracting from the efficacy of the sacrament and injurious to it.

The Authority for Absolving
[Penance, sec. 10, n. 6]

1537   37. The teaching of the synod, which declares concerning the authority for absolving received through ordination that "after the institution of dioceses and parishes, it is fitting that each one exercise this judgment over those persons subject to him either by reason of territory or some personal right," because "otherwise confusion and disturbance would be introduced"; since it declares that, in order to prevent confusion, after dioceses and parishes have been instituted, it is merely fitting that the power of absolving be exercised upon subjects; so understood, as if for the valid use of this power there is no need of ordinary or delegated jurisdiction, without which the Tridentine Synod declares that absolution conferred by a priest is of no value,—false, rash, dangerous, contrary and injurious to the Tridentine Synod [see no. 903], erroneous.

[Ibid., sec. 11]

1538   38. Likewise, that teaching in which, after the synod professed that "it could not but admire that very venerable discipline of antiquity, which (as it says) did not admit to penance so easily, and perhaps never, that one who, after a first sin and a first reconciliation, had relapsed into guilt," it adds, that "through fear of perpetual exclusion from communion and from peace, even in the hour of death, a great restraint will be put on those who consider too little the evil of sin and fear it less," contrary to canon 13 of the first Council of Nicea [see n. 57], to the decretal of Innocent I to Exuperius Tolos [see n. 95], and then also to the decretal of Celestine I to the Bishops of Vienne, and of the Province of Narbon [see n. 111], redolent of the viciousness at which the Holy Pontiff is horrified in that decretal.

The Confession of Venial Sins
[Penance, sec. 12]

1539   39. The declaration of the synod about the confession of venial sins, which it does not wish, it says, to be so frequently resorted to, lest confessions of this sort be rendered too contemptible,—rash, dangerous, contrary to the practice of the saints and the pious which was approved [see n. 899] by the sacred Council of Trent.

Indulgences
[*Penance, sec. 16*]

40. The proposition asserting "that an indulgence, according to its 1540 precise notion, is nothing else than the remission of that part of the penance which had been established by the canons for the sinner"; as if an indulgence, in addition to the mere remission of the canonical penance, does not also have value for the remission of the temporal punishment due to the divine justice for actual sins,—false, rash, injurious to the merits of Christ, already condemned in article 19 of Luther [see n. 759].

[*Ibid.*]

41. Likewise, in this which is added, i.e., that "the scholastics, puffed 1541 up by their subtleties, introduced the poorly understood treasury of the merits of Christ and of the saints, and, for the clear notion of absolution from canonical penance, they substituted a confused and false notion of the application of merits"; as if the treasures of the Church, whence the pope grants indulgences, are not the merits of Christ and of the saints,— false, rash, injurious to the merits of Christ and of the saints, previously condemned in art. 17 of Luther [see n. 757; cf. n. 550 ff.].

[*Ibid.*]

42. Likewise, in this which it adds, that "it is still more lamentable 1542 that that fabulous application is meant to be transferred to the dead,"— false, rash, offensive to pious ears, injurious to the Roman Pontiffs and to the practice and sense of the universal Church, leading to the error fixed [cf. n. 729] in the heretical note in Peter of Osma, again condemned in article 22 of Luther [see n. 762].

[*Ibid.*]

43. In this, finally, that it most shamelessly inveighs against lists of 1543 indulgences, privileged altars, etc.,—rash, offensive to the ears of the pious, scandalous, abusive to the Supreme Pontiffs, and to the practice common in the whole Church.

The Reservation of Cases
[*Penance, sec. 19*]

44. The proposition of the synod asserting that the "reservation of 1544 cases at the present time is nothing else than an improvident bond for

priests of lower rank, and a statement devoid of sense for penitents who are accustomed to pay no heed to this reservation,"—false, rash, evil-sounding, dangerous, contrary to the Council of Trent [see n. 903], injurious to the hierarchic power.

[Ibid.]

1545   45. Likewise, concerning the hope which it expressed that "when the Ritual and the order of penance had been reformed, there would be no place any longer for reservations of this sort"; in so far as, considering the careful generality of the words, it intimates that, by a reformation of the Ritual and of the order of penance made by a bishop or a synod, cases can be abolished which the Tridentine Synod (sess. 14, c. 7 [n. 903]) declares the Supreme Pontiffs could reserve to their own special judgment, because of the supreme power given to them in the universal Church,—the proposition is false, rash, derogatory, and injurious to the Council of Trent and to the authority of the Supreme Pontiffs.

Censures
[Penance, secs. 20 and 22]

1546   46. The proposition asserting that "the effect of excommunication is merely exterior, because by its nature it merely excludes from exterior communion with the Church"; as if excommunication were not a spiritual punishment, binding in heaven, obligating souls (from St. August., *Epistle* 250 to Bishop Auxilius; *Tract* 50 *in Io.,* 12),—false, dangerous, condemned in art. 23 of Luther [see n. 763], at least erroneous.

[Secs. 21 and 23]

1547   47. Likewise, the proposition which teaches that it is necessary, according to the natural and divine laws, for either excommunication or for suspension, that a personal examination should precede, and that, therefore, sentences called "ipso facto" have no other force than that of a serious threat without any actual effect,—false, rash, pernicious, injurious to the power of the Church, erroneous.

[Sec. 22]

1548   48. Likewise, the proposition which says that "useless and vain is the formula introduced some centuries ago of general absolution from excommunications into which the faithful might have fallen,"—false, rash, injurious to the practice of the Church.

[Sec. 24]

49. Likewise, the proposition which condemns as null and invalid 1549 "suspensions imposed from an informed conscience,"—false, pernicious, injurious to Trent.

[*Ibid.*]

50. Likewise, in that decree which insinuates that a bishop alone does 1550 not have the right to make use of the power which, nevertheless, Trent confers on him (sess. 14, c. 1 *de reform.*) of legitimately inflicting suspensions "from an informed conscience,"—harmful to the jurisdiction of the prelates of the Church.

Orders
[*Orders, sec. 4*]

51. The doctrine of the synod which says that in promoting to orders 1551 this method, from the custom and rule of the ancient discipline, was accustomed to be observed, "that if any cleric was distinguished for holiness of life and was considered worthy to ascend to sacred orders, it was the custom to promote him to the diaconate, or to the priesthood, even if he had not received minor orders; and that at that time such an ordination was not called 'per saltum,' as afterwards it was so called,"—

[Sec. 5]

52. Likewise, the doctrine which intimates that there was no other 1552 title for ordinations than appointment to some special ministry, such as was prescribed in the Council of Chalcedon; adding (Sec. 6) that, as long as the Church conformed itself to these principles in the selection of sacred ministers, the ecclesiastical order flourished; but that those happy days have passed, and new principles have been introduced later, by which the discipline in the choice of ministers for the sanctuary was corrupted;—

[Sec. 7]

53. Likewise, that among these very principles of corruption it men- 1553 tions the fact that there has been a departure from the old rule by which, as it says (Sec. 5) the Church, treading in the footsteps of the Apostle, had prescribed that no one should be admitted to the priesthood unless he had preserved his baptismal innocence, since it implies that discipline has been corrupted by decrees and rules:

1) Whether by these ordinations "per saltum" have been forbidden;

2) or by these, for the need and advantage of churches, ordinations without special title of office are approved, as the ordination for the title of patrimony, specifically approved by Trent, that obedience having been assured by which those so ordained are obliged to serve the necessities of the Churches in fulfilling those duties, for which, considering the time and the place, they were ordained by the bishop, just as it was accustomed to be done from apostolic times in the primitive Church;

3) or, by these a distinction was made by canon law of crimes which render the delinquents irregular; as if, by this distinction, the Church departed from the spirit of the Apostle by not excluding in general and without distinction from the ecclesiastical ministry all, whosoever they be, who have not preserved their baptismal innocence,—the doctrine is false in its several individual parts, rash, disturbing to the order introduced for the need and advantage of the churches, injurious to the discipline approved by the canons and especially by the decrees of the Council of Trent.

[Sec. 13]

1554   54. Likewise, the doctrine which notes as a shameful abuse ever to offer alms for the celebration of Masses, and for administering the sacraments, as well as to accept any offering so-called "of the stole," and, in general, any stipend and honorarium which may be offered on the occasion of prayers or of some parochial function; as if the ministers of the Church should be charged with a shameful abuse because they use the right promulgated by the Apostle of accepting temporal aids from those to whom they furnish spiritual ministrations [Gal. 6: 6],—false, rash, harmful to ecclesiastical and pastoral right, injurious to the Church and its ministers.

[Sec. 14]

1555   55. Likewise, the doctrine by which it professes to desire very much that some way be found of removing the lesser clergy (under which name it designates the clerics of minor orders) from cathedrals and colleges by providing otherwise, namely through approved lay people of mature age, a suitable assigned stipend for the ministry of serving at Masses and for other offices such as that of acolyte, etc., as formerly, it says, was usually done when duties of that sort had not been reduced to mere form for the receiving of major orders; inasmuch as it censures the rule by which care is taken that "the functions of minor orders are to be performed or exercised only by those who have been established in them according to rank" (Conc. prov. IV of Milan), and this also according to the intention of the Tridentine Council (sess. 23, c. 17) "that the duties of sacred orders, from the diaconate to the porter, laudably received in the Church from apostolic times and neglected for a while in many places, should be renewed according to the sacred canons, and should not be considered useless as they are by heretics,"—a rash suggestion, offensive to pious ears, disturbing to the ecclesiastical ministry, lessening of the decency which should be observed as far as possible in celebrating the mysteries, injurious to the duties and functions of minor orders, as well as to the discipline approved by the canons and especially by the Tridentine Synod, favorable to the charges and calumnies of heretics against it.

[Sec. 18]

56. The doctrine which states that it seems fitting that, in the case of **1556** canonical impediments which arise from crimes expressed in the law, no dispensation should ever be granted or allowed,—harmful to the canonical equity and moderation which has been approved by the sacred council of Trent, derogatory to the authority and laws of the Church.

[*Ibid.,* sec. 22]

57. The prescription of the synod which generally and indiscrim- **1557** inately rejects as an abuse any dispensation that more than one residential benefice be bestowed on one and the same person: likewise, in this which it adds that the synod is certain that, according to the spirit of the Church, no one could enjoy more than one benefice, even if it is a simple one,—for its generality, derogatory to the moderation of the Council of Trent (sess. 7, c. 5, and sess. 24, c. 17).

Betrothals and Matrimony
[*Memorial Booklet about Betrothals, etc. sec. 8*]

58. The proposition which states that betrothals properly so-called con- **1558** tain a mere civil act which disposes for the celebrating of marriage, and that these same betrothals are altogether subject to the prescription of the civil laws; as if the act disposing for the sacrament is not, under this aspect, subject to the law of the Church,—false, harmful to the right of the Church in respect to the effects flowing even from betrothals by reason of the canonical sanctions, derogatory to the discipline established by the Church.

[*Matrimony, secs. 7, 11, 12*]

59. The doctrine of the synod asserting that "to the supreme civil **1559** power alone originally belongs the right to apply to the contract of

marriage impediments of that sort which render it null and are called nullifying": which "original right," besides, is said to be "essentially connected with the right of dispensing": adding that "with the secret consent or connivance of the principals, the Church could justly establish impediments which nullify the very contract of marriage"; as if the Church could not and cannot always in Christian marriages, establish by its own rights impediments which not only hinder marriage, but also render it null as regards the bond, and also dispense from those impediments by which Christians are held bound even in the countries of infidels,—destructive of canons 3, 4, 9, 12 of the 24th session of the Council of Trent, heretical [see n. 973 ff.].

[Cit. Memorial Booklet about Betrothals, sec. 10]

1560 60. Likewise, the proposal of the synod to the civil power, that "it remove from the number of impediments, whose origin is found in the Collection of Justinian, spiritual relationship and also that one which is called of public honor"; then, that "it should tighten the impediment of affinity and relationship from any licit or illicit connection of birth to the fourth degree, according to the civil computation through the lateral and oblique lines, in such a way, nevertheless, that there be left no hope of obtaining a dispensation"; in so far as it attributes to the civil power the right either of abolishing or of tightening impediments which have been established and approved by the authority of the Church; likewise, where it proposes that the Church can be despoiled by the civil power of the right of dispensing from impediments established or approved by the Church,—subversive of the liberty and power of the Church, contrary to Trent, issuing from the heretical principle condemned above [see n. 973 ff.].

[D. Errors] Concerning Duties, Practices, Rules Pertaining to Religious Worship

And First, the Adoration of the Humanity of Christ.
[Faith, sec. 3]

1561 61. The proposition which asserts that "to adore directly the humanity of Christ, even any part of Him, would always be divine honor given to a creature"; in so far as, by this word "directly" it intends to reprove the worship of adoration which the faithful show to the humanity of Christ, just as if such adoration, by which the humanity and the very living flesh of Christ is adored, not indeed on account of itself as mere flesh, but because it is united to the divinity, would be divine honor imparted to a creature, and not rather the one and the same adoration with which the Incarnate Word is adored in His own proper flesh (from the 2nd Council of Constantinople, 5th Ecumenical Council, canon 9 [see n. 221; cf. n. 120]),—false, deceitful, detracting from and injurious to the pious and due worship given and extended by the faithful to the humanity of Christ.

[*Prayer, sec. 17*]

62. The doctrine which rejects devotion to the most Sacred Heart of **1562** Jesus among the devotions which it notes as new, erroneous, or at least, dangerous; if the understanding of this devotion is of such a sort as has been approved by the Apostolic See,—false, rash, dangerous, offensive to pious ears, injurious to the Apostolic See.

[*Prayer sec. 10, and the appendix n. 32*]

63. Likewise, in this that it blames the worshipers of the Heart of **1563** Jesus also for this name, because they do not note that the most sacred flesh of Christ, or any part of Him, or even the whole humanity, cannot be adored with the worship of latria when there is a separation or cutting off from the divinity; as if the faithful when they adore the Heart of Jesus, separate it or cut it off from the divinity; when they worship the Heart of Jesus it is, namely, the heart of the person of the Word, to whom it has been inseparably united in that manner in which the bloodless body of Christ during the three days of death, without separation or cutting off from divinity, was worthy of adoration in the tomb,—deceitful, injurious to the faithful worshipers of the Heart of Jesus.

The Order Prescribed in the Undertaking of Pious Exercises
[*Prayer, sec. 14, Appendix n. 34*]

64. The doctrine which notes as universally superstitious "any efficacy **1564** which is placed in a fixed number of prayers and of pious salutations"; as if one should consider as superstitious the efficacy which is derived not from the number viewed in itself, but from the prescript of the Church appointing a certain number of prayers or of external acts for obtaining indulgences, for fulfilling penances and, in general, for the performance of sacred and religious worship in the correct order and due form,— false, rash, scandalous, dangerous, injurious to the piety of the faithful, derogatory to the authority of the Church, erroneous.

[*Penance, sec. 10*]

65. The proposition stating that "the unregulated clamor of the new **1565** institutions which have been called exercises or missions . . . , perhaps

never, or at least very rarely, succeed in effecting an absolute conversion; and those exterior acts of encouragement which have appeared were nothing else than the transient brilliance of a natural emotion,"—rash, evil-sounding, dangerous, injurious to the customs piously and salutarily practiced throughout the Church and founded on the Word of God.

The Manner of Uniting the Voice of the People with the Voice of the Church in Public Prayers
[Prayer, sec. 24]

1566   66. The proposition asserting that "it would be against apostolic practice and the plans of God, unless easier ways were prepared for the people to unite their voice with that of the whole Church"; if understood to signify introducing of the use of popular language into the liturgical prayers,—false, rash, disturbing to the order prescribed for the celebration of the mysteries, easily productive of many evils.

The Reading of Sacred Scripture
[From the note at the end of the decree on grace]

1567   67. The doctrine asserting that "only a true impotence excuses" from the reading of the Sacred Scriptures, adding, moreover, that there is produced the obscurity which arises from a neglect of this precept in regard to the primary truths of religion,—false, rash, disturbing to the peace of souls, condemned elsewhere in Quesnel [sec. 1429 ff.].

The Reading of Proscribed Books Publicly in Church
[Prayer, 29]

1568   68. The praise with which the synod very highly commends the commentaries of Quesnel on the New Testament, and some works of other writers who favor the errors of Quesnel, although they have been proscribed; and which proposes to parish priests that they should read these same works, as if they were full of the solid principles of religion, each one in his own parish to his people after other functions,—false, rash, scandalous, seditious, injurious to the Church, fostering schism and heresy.

Sacred Images
[Prayer, sec. 17]

1569   69. The prescription which in general and without discrimination includes the images of the incomprehensible Trinity among the images to be removed from the Church, on the ground that they furnish an occasion of error to the untutored,—because of its generality, it is rash, and contrary to the pious custom common throughout the Church, as if no images of the Most Holy Trinity exist which are commonly approved and safely permitted (from the Brief "Sollicitudini nostrae" of Benedict XIV in the year 1745).

70. Likewise, the doctrine and prescription condemning in general 1570 every special cult which the faithful are accustomed to attach specifically to some image, and to have recourse to, rather than to another,—rash, dangerous, injurious to the pious custom prevalent throughout the Church and also to that order of Providence, by which "God, who apportions as He wishes to each one his own proper characteristics, did not want them to be common in every commemoration of the saints (from St. Augustine, Epistle 78 to the clergy, elders, and people of the church at Hippo).

71. Likewise, the teaching which forbids that images, especially of the 1571 Blessed Virgin, be distinguished by any title other than the denominations which are related to the mysteries, about which express mention is made in Holy Scripture; as if other pious titles could not be given to images which the Church indeed approves and commends in its public prayers,—rash, offensive to the ears of the pious, and especially injurious to the due veneration of the Blessed Virgin.

72. Likewise, the one which would extirpate as an abuse the custom 1572 by which certain images are kept veiled,—rash, contrary to the custom prevalent in the Church and employed to foster the piety of the faithful.

Feasts
[Libell. memor. for the reformation of feasts, sec. 3]

73. The proposition stating that the institution of new feasts derived 1573 its origin from neglect in the observance of the older feasts, and from false notions of the nature and end of these solemnities,—false, rash, scandalous, injurious to the Church, favorable to the charges of heretics against the feast days celebrated by the Church.

[Ibid., sec. 8]

74. The deliberation of the synod about transferring to Sunday feasts 1574 distributed through the year, and rightly so, because it is convinced that the bishop has power over ecclesiastical discipline in relation to purely spiritual matters, and therefore of abrogating the precept of hearing Mass on those days, on which according to the early law of the Church, even then that precept flourished; and then, also, in this statement which it (the synod) added about transferring to Advent by episcopal authority the fasts which should be kept throughout the year according to the precept of the Church; insomuch as it asserts that it is lawful for a bishop in his own right to transfer the days prescribed by the Church for cele-

brating feasts or fasts, or to abrogate the imposed precept of hearing Mass,—a false proposition, harmful to the law of the general Councils and of the Supreme Pontiffs, scandalous, favorable to schism.

Oaths
[Libell. memor. for the reformation of oaths, sec. 4]

1575   75. The teaching which says that in the happy days of the early Church oaths seemed so foreign to the model of the divine Preceptor and to the golden simplicity of the Gospel that "to take an oath without extreme and unavoidable need had been reputed to be an irreligious act, unworthy of a Christian person," further, that "the uninterrupted line of the Fathers shows that oaths by common consent have been considered as forbidden"; and from this doctrine proceeds to condemn the oaths which the ecclesiastical curia, having followed, as it says, the norm of feudal jurisprudence, adopted for investitures and sacred ordinations of bishops; and it decreed, therefore, that the law should be invoked by the secular power to abolish the oaths which are demanded in ecclesiastical curias when entering upon duties and offices and, in general, for any curial function,—false, injurious to the Church, harmful to ecclesiastical law, subversive of discipline imposed and approved by the Canons.

Ecclesiastical Conferences
[Ecclesiastical Conferences, sec. 1]

1576   76. The charge which the synod brings against the scholastic method as that "which opened the way for inventing new systems discordant with one another with respect to truths of a greater value and which led finally to probabilism and laxism"; in so far as it charges against the scholastic method the faults of individuals who could misuse and have misused it,— false, rash, against very holy and learned men who, to the great good of the Catholic religion, have developed the scholastic method, injurious, favorable to the criticism of heretics who are hostile to it.

[Ibid.]

1577   77. Likewise in this which adds that "a change in the form of ecclesiastical government, by which it was brought about that ministers of the Church became forgetful of their rights, which at the same time are their obligations, has finally led to such a state of affairs as to cause the primitive notions of ecclesiastical ministry and pastoral solicitude to be forgotten"; as if, by a change of government consonant to the discipline established and approved in the Church, there ever could be forgotten and lost the primitive notion of ecclesiastical ministry or pastoral solicitude,—a false proposition, rash, erroneous.

[*Sec. 14*]

78. The prescription of the synod about the order of transacting busi- 1578
ness in the conferences, in which, after it prefaced "in every article that
which pertains to faith and to the essence of religion must be distinguished from that which is proper to discipline," it adds, "in this itself
(discipline) there is to be distinguished what is necessary or useful to
retain the faithful in spirit, from that which is useless or too burdensome for the liberty of the sons of the new Covenant to endure, but more
so, from that which is dangerous or harmful, namely, leading to superstition and materialism"; in so far as by the generality of the words
it includes and submits to a prescribed examination even the discipline
established and approved by the Church, as if the Church which is ruled
by the Spirit of God could have established discipline which is not only
useless and burdensome for Christian liberty to endure, but which is
even dangerous and harmful and leading to superstition and materialism,—false, rash, scandalous, dangerous, offensive to pious ears, injurious
to the Church and to the Spirit of God by whom it is guided, at least
erroneous.

Complaints Against Some Opinions Which are Still Discussed in "Catholic Schools"
[*Oration to the Synod, sec. 1*]

79. The assertion which attacks with slanderous charges the opinions 1579
discussed in Catholic schools about which the Apostolic See has thought
that nothing yet needs to be defined or pronounced,—false, rash, injurious
to Catholic schools, detracting from the obedience to the Apostolic Constitutions.

[*E. Errors Concerning the Reformation of Regulars*]

The "three rules" set down as fundamental by the Synod "for the reformation of regulars"
[*Libell. memor. for the reformation of regulars, sec. 9*]

80. Rule I which states universally and without distinction that "the 1580
regular or monastic state by its very nature cannot be harmonized with
the care of souls and with the duties of parochial life, and therefore, cannot share in the ecclesiastical hierarchy without adversely opposing the
principles of monastic life itself"—false, dangerous to the most holy
Fathers and heads of the Church, who harmonized the practices of the
regular life with the duties of the clerical order,—injurious, contrary to
the old, pious, approved custom of the Church and to the sanctions of

the Supreme Pontiff; as if "monks, whom the gravity of their manners and of their life and whom the holy institution of Faith approves," could not be duly "entrusted with the duties of the clergy," not only without harm to religion, but even with great advantage to the Church. (From the decretal epistle of St. Siricius to Himerius of Tarraco c. 13 [see n. 90].) [1]

1581   81. Likewise, in that which adds that St. Thomas and St. Bonaventure were so occupied in protecting Orders of Mendicants against the best of men that in their defenses less heat and greater accuracy were to be desired,—scandalous, injurious to the very holy Doctors, favorable to the impious slanders of condemned authors.

1582   82. Rule II, that "the multiplicity and diversity of orders naturally produce confusion and disturbance," likewise, in that which sec. 4 sets forth, "that the founders" of regulars who, after the monastic institutions came into being, "by adding orders to orders, reforms to reforms have accomplished nothing else than to increase more and more the primary cause of evil"; if understood about the orders and institutes approved by the Holy See, as if the distinct variety of pious works to which the distinct orders are devoted should, by its nature, beget disturbance and confusion, —false, calumnious, injurious not only to the holy founders and their faithful disciples, but also to the Supreme Pontiffs themselves.

1583   83. Rule III, in which, after it stated that "a small body living within a civil society without being truly a part of the same and which forms a small monarchy in the state, is always a dangerous thing," it then charges with this accusation private monasteries which are associated by the bond of a common rule under one special head, as if they were so many special monarchies harmful and dangerous to the civic commonwealth,—false, rash, injurious to the regular institutes approved by the Holy See for the advancement of religion, favorable to the slanders and calumnies of heretics against the same institutes.

*Concerning the "system" or list of ordinances drawn from rules
laid down and contained in the eight following articles "for
the reformation of regulars"*

[Sec. 10]

1584   84. Art. I. "Concerning the one order to be retained in the Church, and concerning the selection of the rule of St. Benedict in preference to others, not only because of its excellence but also on account of the well-known merits of his order; however, with this condition that in those items which happen to be less suitable to the conditions of the

---

[1] Add URBAN II, in the synod of Nemausen., 1096, can. 2 and 3.

times, the way of life instituted at Port-Royal[1] is to furnish light for discovering what it is fitting to add, what to take away;

Art. II. "Those who have joined this order should not be a part of 1585 the ecclesiastical hierarchy; nor should they be promoted to Holy Orders, except one or two at the most, to be initiated as superiors, or as chaplains of the monastery, the rest remaining in the simple order of the laity;

Art. III. "One monastery only should be allowed in any one city, and 1586 this should be located outside the walls of the city in the more retired and remote places;

Art. IV. "Among the occupations of the monastic life, a proper pro- 1587 portion should be inviolably reserved for manual labor, with suitable time, nevertheless, left for devotion to the psalmody, or also, if someone wishes, for the study of letters; the psalmody should be moderate, because too much of it produces haste, weariness, and distraction; the more psalmody, orisons, and prayers are increased beyond a just proportion of the whole time, so much are the fervor and holiness of the regulars diminished;

Art. V. "No distinction among the monks should be allowed, whether 1588 they are devoted to choir or to services; such inequality has stirred up very grave quarrels and discords at every opportunity, and has driven out the spirit of charity from communities of regulars;

Art. VI. "The vow of perpetual stability should never be allowed; the 1589 older monks did not know it, who, nevertheless, were a consolation of the Church and an ornament to Christianity; the vows of chastity, poverty, and obedience should not be admitted as the common and stable rule. If anyone shall wish to make these vows, all or anyone, he will ask advice and permission from the bishop who, nevertheless, will never permit them to be perpetual, nor to exceed the limits of a year; the opportunity merely will be given of renewing them under the same conditions;

Art. VII. "The bishop will conduct every investigation into their 1590 lives, studies, and advancement in piety; it will be his duty to admit and to dismiss the monks, always, however, after taking counsel with their fellow monks;

Art. VIII. "Regulars of orders which still survive, although they are 1591 priests, may also be received into this monastery, provided they desire to be free in silence and solitude for their own sanctification only; in which case, there might be provision for the dispensation stated in the general rule, n. II, in such a way, however, that they do not follow a rule of life different from the others, and that not more than one, or at most two Masses be celebrated each day, and that it should be satisfactory to the other priests to celebrate in common together with the community;

---

[1] Port-Royal in France, near Paris.

Likewise "for the reformation of nuns"
[*Sec. 11*]

1592   "Perpetual vows should not be permitted before the age of 40 or 45;
nuns should be devoted to solid exercises, especially to labor, turned
aside from carnal spirituality by which many are distracted; consideration must also be given as to whether, so far as they are concerned, it
would be more satisfactory to leave the monastery in the city;—

The system is subversive to the discipline now flourishing and already
approved and accepted in ancient times, dangerous, opposed and injurious to the Apostolic Constitutions and to the sanctions of many
Councils, even general ones, and especially of the Council of Trent;
favorable to the vicious calumnies of heretics against monastic vows and
the regular institutes devoted to the more stable profession of the
evangelical counsels.

[*F. Errors*] *About Convoking a National Council*
[*Libell. memor. for convoking a national council, sec. 1*]

1593   85. The proposition stating that any knowledge whatsoever of ecclesiastical history is sufficient to allow anyone to assert that the convocation of a national council is one of the canonical ways by which
controversies in regard to religion may be ended in the Church of the
respective nations; if understood to mean that controversies in regard to
faith or morals which have arisen in a Church can be ended by an
irrefutable decision made in a national council; as if freedom from
error in questions of faith and morals belonged to a national council,—
schismatic, heretical.

1594   Therefore, we command all the faithful of Christ of either sex not to
presume to believe, to teach, or to preach anything about the said
propositions and doctrines contrary to what is declared in this Constitution of ours; that whoever shall have taught, defended or published them,
or anyone of them, all together or separately, except perhaps to oppose
them, will be subject *ipso facto* and without any other declaration to
ecclesiastical censures, and to the other penalties stated by law against
those perpetrating similar offenses.

1595   But, by this expressed condemnation of the aforesaid propositions and
doctrines, we by no means intend to approve other things contained in
the same book, particularly since in it very many propositions and
doctrines have been detected, related either to those which have been
condemned above, or to those which show an attitude not only of rash
contempt for the commonly approved doctrine and discipline, but of
special hostility toward the Roman Pontiffs and the Apostolic See. In-

deed, we think two must be noted especially, concerning the most august mystery of the Most Holy Trinity, sec. 2 of the decree about faith, which have issued from the synod, if not with evil intent, surely rather imprudently, which could easily drive into error especially the untutored and the incautious.

The first, after it is rightly prefaced that God in His being remains 1596 one and most simple, while immediately adding that God is distinct in three persons, has erroneously departed from the common formula approved in institutions of Christian Doctrine, in which God is said to be one indeed "in three distinct persons," not "distinct in three persons"; and by the change in this formula, this risk of error crept into the meaning of the words, so that the divine essence is thought to be distinct in persons, which (essence) the Catholic faith confesses to be one in distinct persons in such a way that at the same time it confesses that it is absolutely undivided in itself.

The second, which concerns the three divine Persons themselves, that 1597 they, according to their peculiar personal and incommunicable properties, are to be described and named in a more exact manner of speaking, Father, *Word,* and Holy Spirit; as if less proper and exact would be the name "Son," consecrated by so many passages of Scripture, by the very voice of the Father coming from the heavens and from the cloud, and by the formula of baptism prescribed by Christ, and by that famous confession in which Peter was pronounced "blessed" by Christ Himself; and as if that statement should not rather be retained which the Angelic Doctor,[1] having learned from Augustine, in his turn taught that "in the name of the Word the same peculiar property is meant as in the name of the Son," Augustine[2] truly saying: "For the same reason he is called the Word as the Son."

Nor should the extraordinary and deceitful boldness of the Synod be 1598 passed over in silence, which dared to adorn not only with most ample praises the declaration (n. 1322 ff.) of the Gallican Council of the year 1682, which had long ago been condemned by the Apostolic See, but in order to win greater authority for it, dared to include it insidiously in the decree written "about faith," openly to adopt articles contained in it, and to seal it with a public and solemn profession of those articles which had been handed down here and there through this decree. Therefore, surely, not only a far graver reason for expostulating with them is afforded us by the Synod than was offered to our predecessors by the assemblies, but also no light injury is inflicted on the Gallican Church itself, because the synod thought its authority worth invoking in support of the errors with which that decree was contaminated.

---

[1] St. Thomas, *Summa Theol.* Ia, q. 34, a. 2, ad 3.
[2] St. Augustine, *De Trinitate* 1, 7 c. 2 [ML 42 (Aug. VIII), 936].

1599   Therefore, as soon as the acts of the Gallican convention appeared, Our predecessor, Venerable Innocent XI, by letters in the form of a Brief on the 11th day of April, in the year 1682, and afterwards, more expressly, Alexander VIII in the Constitution, "inter multiplices" on the 4th day of August, in the year 1690 (see n. 1322 ff.), by reason of their apostolic duty "condemned, rescinded, and declared them null and void"; pastoral solicitude demands much more strongly of Us that we "reject and condemn as rash and scandalous" the recent adoption of these acts tainted with so many faults, made by the synod, and, after the publication of the decrees of Our predecessors, "as especially injurious" to this Apostolic See, and we, accordingly, reject and condemn it by this present Constitution of Ours, and we wish it to be held as rejected and condemned.

PIUS VII 1800-1823

The Indissolubility of Marriage [1]

[From the Brief to Charles of Dalberg, Archbishop of Mainz, November 8, 1803]

1600   "To the doubts proposed to him the Supreme Pontiff, among other remarks, responds": The decision of lay tribunals and of Catholic assemblies by which the nullity of marriages is chiefly declared, and the dissolution of their bond attempted, can have no strength and absolutely no force in the sight of the Church. . . .

1601   Those pastors who would approve these nuptials by their presence and confirm them with their blessing would commit a very grave fault and would betray their sacred ministry. For they should not be called nuptials, but rather adulterous unions. . . .

Versions of Sacred Scripture [2]

[From the epistle "Magno et acerbo" to the Archbishop of Mohileff, September 3, 1816]

1602   We were overcome with great and bitter sorrow when We learned that a pernicious plan, by no means the first, had been undertaken, whereby the most sacred books of the Bible are being spread everywhere in every vernacular tongue, with new interpretations which are contrary to the wholesome rules of the Church, and are skillfully turned into a distorted sense. For, from one of the versions of this sort already

---

[1] RskMm II 86 ff.

[2] ASS 9 (ed. 1, 1876, ed. 2, 1885) 582 ff.

presented to Us we notice that such a danger exists against the sanctity of purer doctrine, so that the faithful might easily drink a deadly poison from those fountains from which they should drain "waters of saving wisdom" [Ecclus. 15:3]. . . .

For you should have kept before your eyes the warnings which Our **1603** predecessors have constantly given, namely, that, if the sacred books are permitted everywhere without discrimination in the vulgar tongue, more damage will arise from this than advantage. Furthermore, the Roman Church, accepting only the Vulgate edition according to the well-known prescription (see n. 785 f.) of the Council of Trent, disapproves the versions in other tongues and permits only those which are edited with the explanations carefully chosen from writings of the Fathers and Catholic Doctors, so that so great a treasure may not be exposed to the corruptions of novelties, and so that the Church, spread throughout the world, may be "of one tongue and of the same speech" [Gen. 11:1].

Since in vernacular speech we notice very frequent interchanges, **1604** varieties, and changes, surely by an unrestrained license of Biblical versions that changelessness which is proper to the divine testimony would be utterly destroyed, and faith itself would waver, when, especially, from the meaning of one syllable sometimes an understanding about the truth of a dogma is formed. For this purpose, then, the heretics have been accustomed to make their low and base machinations, in order that by the publication of their vernacular Bibles, (of whose strange variety and discrepancy they, nevertheless, accuse one another and wrangle) they may, each one, treacherously insert their own errors wrapped in the more holy apparatus of divine speech. "For heresies are not born," St. Augustine used to say, "except when the true Scriptures are not well understood and when what is not well understood in them is rashly and boldly asserted." [1] But, if we grieve that men renowned for piety and wisdom have, by no means rarely, failed in interpreting the Scriptures, what should we not fear if the Scriptures, translated into every vulgar tongue whatsoever, are freely handed on to be read by an inexperienced people who, for the most part, judge not with any skill but with a kind of rashness? . . .

Therefore, in that famous letter of his to the faithful of the Church **1605** at Meta, Our predecessor, Innocent III,[2] quite wisely prescribes as follows: "In truth the secret mysteries of faith are not to be exposed to all everywhere, since they cannot be understood by all everywhere, but only by those who can grasp them with the intellect of faith. Therefore, to the more simple the Apostle says: "I gave you milk to drink as unto little ones in Christ, not meat" [I Cor. 3:2]. For solid food is for the

---

[1] St. Augustine, *In Io.,* tr. 18, c. 1 [ML 35 (Aug. III b), 1536].
[2] Reg. II, Ep. 141 "Cum ex iniuncto," 1199 [ML 214, 696 CD].

elders, as he said: "We speak wisdom . . . among the perfect" [I Cor. 2:6]; "for I judged not myself to know anything among you, but Jesus Christ and Him Crucified" [I Cor. 2:2]. For so great is the depth of Divine Scripture that not only the simple and the unlettered, but even the learned and prudent are not fully able to explore the understanding of it. Therefore, Scripture says that many "searching have failed in their search" [Ps. 63:7].

1606   "So it was rightly stated of old in the divine law, that even the beast which touched the mountain should be stoned" [Heb. 12:20; Exod. 19:12], lest, indeed, any simple and ignorant person should presume to reach the sublimity of Sacred Scripture, or to preach it to others. For it is written: *Seek not the things that are too high for thee* [Ecclus. 3:22]. Therefore, the Apostle warns "not to be more wise than it behooveth to be wise, but to be wise unto sobriety" [Rom. 12:3]. But, noteworthy are the Constitutions, not only of Innocent III, just mentioned, but also of Pius IV,[1] Clement VIII,[2] and Benedict XIV[3] in which the precaution was laid down that, if Scripture should be easily open to all, it would perhaps become cheapened and be exposed to contempt, or, if poorly understood by the mediocre, would lead to error. But, what the mind of the Church is in regard to the reading and interpretation of Scripture, your fraternity may know very clearly from the excellent Constitution of another of Our predecessors, CLEMENT XI, "Unigenitus," in which those doctrines were thoroughly condemned in which it was asserted that it is useful and necessary to every age, to every place, to every type of person to know the mysteries of Sacred Scripture, the reading of which was to be open to all, and that it was harmful to withdraw Christian people from it, nay more, that the mouth of Christ was closed for the faithful when the New Testament was snatched from their hands [Propositions of Quesnel 79-85; n. 1429-1435].

LEO XII 1823-1829

The Versions of Sacred Scripture[4]

[From the Encyclical "Ubi primum," May 5, 1824]

1607   . . . The wickedness of our enemies is progressing to such a degree that, besides the flood of pernicious books hostile in themselves to

---

[1] The Letter, "Dominici gregis," March 24, 1564 [MBR (L) 2, 116 f.; Hrd X 205 A], in which are approved "Ten Rules about Prohibited Books" [Hrd X 207 ff. (Third and Fourth Rules about the Versions of Sacred Scripture)].

[2] The Letter, "Sacrosanctum catholicae fidei," where the rules of the Index of PIUS IV are confirmed (Oct. 17, 1595) [MBR (L) 3, 56 f.].

[3] The Constitution, "Sollicita ac provida," July 9, 1753 [MBR (L) 19, 59 ff.].

[4] BRC 16, 47 b f.; ASS 9 (ed. 1, 1876, ed. 2, 1885) 591 f.

religion, they are endeavoring to turn to the harm of religion even the Sacred Literature given to us by divine Providence for the progress of religion itself. It is not unknown to you, Venerable Brethren, that a certain "Society," commonly called "Biblical," is boldly spreading through the whole world, which, spurning the traditions of the Holy Fathers and against the well-known decree [see n. 786] of the Council of Trent, is aiming with all its strength and means toward this: to translate—or rather mistranslate—the Sacred Books into the vulgar tongue of every nation. . . .

And to avert this plague, Our predecessors have published many **1608** Constitutions [e.g., PIUS VII; see n. 1602 ff.]. . . . We, also, in accord with our Apostolic duty, encourage you, Venerable Brothers, to be zealous in every way to remove your flock away from these poisonous pastures. "Reprove, entreat, be instant in season, out of season, in all patience and doctrine" [II Tim. 4:2], so that your faithful people, clinging exactly to the regulations of our Congregation of the Index, may be persuaded that, "if the Sacred Books are permitted everywhere without discrimination in the vulgar tongue, more harm will arise therefrom than advantage, because of the boldness of men." Experience demonstrates the truth of this and, besides other Fathers, St. Augustine has declared in these words: "For not . . ." [see n. 1604].

PIUS VIII 1829–1830

Usury [1]

[Response of Pius VIII to the Bishop of Rheims,[2]
given in audience, August 18, 1830]

The Bishop of Rheims in France explains that. . . , the confessors of **1609** his diocese do not hold the same opinion concerning the profit received from money given as a loan to business men, in order that they may be enriched thereby. There is bitter dispute over the meaning of the Encyclical Letter, "Vix pervenit" [see n. 1475 ff.]. On both sides arguments are produced to defend the opinion each one has embraced, either favorable to such profit or against it. Thence come quarrels, dissensions, denial of the sacraments to many business men engaging in that method of making money, and countless damage to souls.

To meet this harm to souls, some confessors think they can hold a middle course between both opinions. If anyone consults them about gain of this sort, they try to dissuade him from it. If the penitent perseveres in his plan of giving money as a loan to business men, and

---

[1] CL VI 681 f.; MThCc 16, 1066 f.
[2] Rheims in France.

objects that an opinion favorable to such a loan has many patrons, and, moreover, has not been condemned by the Holy See, although more than once consulted about it, then these confessors demand that the penitent promise to conform in filial obedience to the judgment of the Holy Pontiff whatever it may be, if he should intervene; and having obtained this promise, they do not deny them absolution, although they believe an opinion contrary to such a loan is more probable. If a penitent does not confess the gain from money given as a loan, and appears to be in good faith, these confessors, even if they know from other sources that gain of this sort has been taken by him and is even now being taken, they absolve him, making no interrogation about the matter, because they fear that the penitent, being advised to make restitution or to refrain from such profit, will refuse.

1610   *Therefore the said Bishop of Rheims inquires:*

I. Whether he can approve the method of acting on the part of these latter confessors.

II. Whether he could encourage other more rigid confessors who come to consult him to follow the plan of action of those others until the Holy See brings out an express opinion on this question.

Pius VIII responded:

To I: They are not to be disturbed. To II: Provided for in the first.

GREGORY XVI 1831–1846

Usury [1]

[Declarations about a response of PIUS VIII [2]]

1611   *A. To the doubts of the Bishop of Viviers:* [3]

1. "Whether the aforesaid judgment of the Most Holy Pontiff must be understood as its words sound, and aside from the title of the law of the prince, about which the Most Eminent Cardinals speak in these responses, so that it is just a matter of a loan made to business men.

2. "Or whether the title from the law of the prince, about which the Eminent Cardinals speak, must be so understood that it is enough that the law of the prince declares that it is licit for anyone to agree about a gain made from a loan only, as happens in the civil code of the Franks, without saying that it (law of the prince) grants the right to receive such gain."

---

[1] CL VI 689ᶜᵈ; MThCc 16, 1073, 1083.
[2] See this response in MThCc 16, 1070, Decr. VIII.
[3] Viviers in France.

The Congregation of the Holy Office responded August 31, 1831:
This has been taken care of in the decree of Wednesday, August 18,
1830, and let the decrees be given.

        B. To the doubt of the Bishop of Nicea: 1612

"Whether penitents, who have taken a moderate gain from a loan only,
under title of the law, in doubtful or bad faith, can be sacramentally
absolved without the imposition of the burden of restitution, provided
they are sincerely sorry for the sin committed because of doubtful or bad
faith, and are ready in filial obedience to observe the commands of the
Holy See."

The Congregation of the Holy Office responded Jan. 17, 1838:
Yes, provided they are ready to observe the commands of the Holy
See. . . .[1]

Indifferentism (against Félicité de Lamennais) [2]

[From the Encyclical "Mirari vos arbitramur," Aug. 15, 1832]

Now we examine another prolific cause of evils by which, we lament, 1613
the Church is at present afflicted, namely indifferentism, or that base
opinion which has become prevalent everywhere through the deceit of
wicked men, that eternal salvation of the soul can be acquired by any
profession of faith whatsoever, if morals are conformed to the standard
of the just and the honest. . . . And so from this most rotten source of
indifferentism flows that absurd and erroneous opinion, or rather insanity,
that liberty of conscience must be claimed and defended for anyone.

    Indeed, to this most unhealthy error that full and immoderate liberty 1614
of opinions which is spreading widely to the destruction of the sacred
and civil welfare opens the way, with some men repeatedly asserting
with supreme boldness that some advantage flows therefrom to religion
itself. But "what death of the soul is worse than freedom for error?"
Augustine used to say [ep. 166 [3]]. For, since all restraint has been re-

---

[1] In the same sense were responses from the Sacred Penitentiary, Sept. 16, 1830,
Aug. 14, 1831, Nov. 11, 1831, Feb. 11, 1832, Nov. 23, 1832, and from the Sacred
Office in a resolution Aug. 31, 1831, approved by GREGORY XVI; cf. CL VI 677 ff.;
MThCc 16, 1067 ff.

[2] BRC 19, 129 a ff.; ASS 4 (1868) 34 ff.; RskRP IV 100 ff.—Félicité de Lamennais,
born June 19, 1782, in Saint Malo in Lower Brittany, together with Montalembert and
Lacordaire founded in 1830 the journal "L'Avenir" to defend the rights of the Church,
which he was compelled to suspend when it was infected with errors. At first he was
submissive to the condemnation, but afterwards he bitterly attacked the Church. He
died at Paris without giving any sign of retraction on Feb. 27, 1854.

[3] Elsewhere, 105; 2, 10 (ML 33, 400).

moved by which men are kept on the paths of truth, since their nature inclined to evil is now plunging headlong, we say that the "bottom of the pit" has truly been opened, from which John [Apoc. 9:3] saw "smoke arising by which the sun was darkened with locusts" coming out of it to devastate the earth. . . .

1615 Nor can we foresee more joyful omens for religion and the state from the wishes of those who desire that the Church be separated from the State, and that the mutual concord of the government with the sacred ministry be broken. For it is certain that that concord is greatly feared by lovers of this most shameless liberty, which has always been fortunate and salutary for the ecclesiastical and the civil welfare.

1616 Having embraced with paternal affection those especially who have applied their mind particularly to the sacred disciplines and to philosophic questions, encourage and support them so that they may not, by relying on the powers of their own talents alone, imprudently go astray from the path of truth into the way of the impious. Let them remember "that God is the guide of wisdom and the director of the wise" [cf. Wisd. 7:15], and that it is not possible to learn to know God without God, who by means of the Word teaches men to know God.[1] It is characteristic of the proud, or rather of the foolish man to test the mysteries of faith "which surpasseth all understanding" [Phil. 4:7] by human standards, and to entrust them to the reasoning of our mind, which by reason of the condition of our human nature is weak and infirm.

The False Doctrines of Félicité de Lamennais [2]

[From the Encyclical, "Singulari nos affecerant gaudio"
to the Bishops of France, June 25, 1834]

1617 But it is a very mournful thing, by which the ravings of human reason go to ruin when someone is eager for revolution and, against the advice of the Apostle, strives "to be more wise than it behooveth to be wise" [cf. Rom. 12:3], and trusting too much in himself, affirms that

---

[1] Cf. S. Irenaeus, *Against Heresies* 1.4, c.6 (MG 7, 986 C ff.).

[2] BRC 19, 380 b; RskRP IV 127.—When the Supreme Pontiff, by Encyclical Letters dated Aug. 15, 1832, condemned the doctrine of Félicité Robert de Lamennais and of the said journal, "L'Avenir," because, in order to protect the freedom of the Church, it was preaching rebellion and full separation of the Church from the State, and was bringing forward some inharmonious things about the powers of reason, Lamennais, indeed, for a time seemed to yield, but a little afterwards he published an infamous book with the title, "Paroles d'un croyant." The Pontiff, therefore, in this Encyclical condemns the book, and he complains bitterly that by repeated changes contrary to the doctrine of the former Encyclical he had impugned the obedience due to the principle, and taught indifferentism and all manner of liberty of conscience. Then he added those things about faith and reason which are gathered above.

truth must be sought outside of the Catholic Church in which truth itself is found far from even the slightest defilement of error, and which therefore, is called and is "the pillar and ground of the truth" [I Tim. 3:15]. But you well understand, Venerable Brothers, that We are here speaking in open disapproval of that false system of philosophy, not so long ago introduced, by which, because of an extended and unbridled desire of novelty, truth is not sought where it truly resides, and, with a disregard for the holy and apostolic traditions, other vain, futile, uncertain doctrines, not approved by the Church are accepted as true, on which very vain men mistakenly think that truth itself is supported and sustained.

Condemnation of the Works of George Hermes [1]

[From the Brief "Dum acerbissimas," Sept. 26, 1835]

To increase the anxieties by which we are overwhelmed day and **1618** night because of this (namely, persecutions of the Church), the following calamitous and highly lamentable circumstance is added: Among those who strive in behalf of religion by published works some dare to intrude themselves insincerely, who likewise wish to seem and who show that they are fighting on behalf of the same religion, in order that, though retaining the appearance of religion yet despising the truth, they can the more easily seduce and pervert the incautious "by philosophy" or by their false philosophic treatises "and vain deceit" [Col. 2:8], and hence deceive the people and extend helping hands more confidently to the enemies who openly rage against it (religion). Therefore, when the impious and insidious labors of any one of these writers have become known to us, we have not delayed by means of our encyclicals and other Apostolic letters to denounce their cunning and depraved plans, and to condemn their errors, and, at the same time, to expose the deadly deceits by which they very cunningly endeavor to overthrow completely the divine constitution of the Church and ecclesiastical discipline, nay, even the whole public order itself. Indeed, it has been proved by a very sad

---

[1] RSkRP IV 150 ff.; A Col 227 ff.—George Hermes, born April 22, 1775, in the village of Dreierwalde on the Rhine in Westphalia, was professor of theology at Münster in 1807, at Bonn in 1820, where on May 26, 1831, he died.—In this Brief are condemned Part 1 (philosophical) and Part 2 (theological) of the "Introduction in Theologiam Christiano-Catholicam" [*Philosophic Introduction to Christian-Catholic Theology*, Münster, 1819, and *Positive Introduction to Christian-Catholic Theology, ibid.* 1829]; Part I of "Dogmatics" (*Christian-Catholic Dogmatics*, Münster, 1834), is condemned in the decree of the Sacred Congregation of the Index, Sept. 26, 1835 (*Analecta Iuris Pont.* II 1442 f.). The Supreme Pontiff, Jan. 7, 1836, ordered that Parts 2 and 3, also of the "Dogmatics" (Münster 1835) be declared to be comprehended by the aforesaid decree. PIUS XI on July 25, 1847, confirmed both decrees.

fact that at length, laying aside the veil of pretense, they have already raised on high the banner of hostility against whatever power has been established by God.

1619 But this alone is not the most grievous cause for mourning. For in addition to those who, to the scandal of all Catholics, have given themselves over to the enemy, to add to our bitter sorrow we see some entering even into the study of theology who, through a desire and passion for novelty "ever learning and never attaining to the knowledge of the truth" [II Tim. 3:7], are teachers of error, because they have not been disciples of truth. In fact, they infect sacred studies with strange and unapproved doctrines, and they do not hesitate to profane even the office of teacher, if they hold a position in the schools and academies; they are known to falsify the most sacred deposit of faith itself, while boasting that they are protecting it. Among the teachers of this sort of error, because of his constant and almost universal reputation throughout Germany, George Hermes is numbered as one who boldly left the royal path, which universal tradition and the most Holy Fathers have marked out in explaining and vindicating the truths of faith; nay, even haughtily despising and condemning it, he is now building a darksome way to error of all kinds on positive doubt as a basis for all theological inquiry, and on the principle which states that reason is the chief norm and only medium whereby man can acquire knowledge of supernatural truths. . . .

1620 Therefore, we ordered that these books be handed over to the theologians most skilled in the German language to be diligently scrutinized in every part. . . . At length . . . [the most Eminent Cardinal Inquisitors], weighing each and everything with great care, as the gravity of the matter demanded, judged that the author "was growing vain in his thoughts" [Rom. 1:21], and had woven into the said works many absurd ideas foreign to the teaching of the Catholic Church; but especially concerning the nature of faith and the rule of things to be believed, about Sacred Scripture, tradition, revelation, and the teaching office of the Church; about motives of credibility, about proofs by which the existence of God is wont to be established and confirmed; about the essence of God Himself, His holiness, justice, liberty, and His purpose in works which the theologians call external; and also about the necessity of grace, the distribution of it and of gifts, recompense of awards, and the infliction of penalties, about the state of our first parents, original sin, and the powers of fallen man; these same books, inasmuch as they contain doctrines and propositions respectively false, rash, captious, inducive to skepticism and indifferentism, erroneous, scandalous, injurious to Catholic schools, destructive of divine faith, suggesting heresy and other things condemned by the Church (the Most Eminent Cardinals) decree must be prohibited and condemned.

And so we condemn and reject the aforesaid books wherever and in 1621 whatever idiom, in every edition or version so far published or to be published in the future, which God forbid, under tenor of these present letters, and we further command that they be placed on the Index of forbidden books.

Faith and Reason (against Louis Eugene Bautain) [1]

[Theses written by Bautain under order of his bishop, Sept. 8, 1840]

1. Reason can prove with certitude the existence of God and the 1622 infinity of His perfections. Faith, a heavenly gift, is posterior to revelation; hence it cannot be brought forward against an atheist to prove the existence of God [cf. n. 1650].

2. The divinity of the Mosaic revelation is proved with certitude by 1623 the oral and written tradition of the synagogue and of Christianity.

3. Proof drawn from the miracles of Jesus Christ, sensible and striking 1624 for eyewitnesses, has in no way lost its force and splendor as regards subsequent generations. We find this proof with all certitude in the authenticity of the New Testament, in the oral and written tradition of all Christians. By this double tradition we should demonstrate it (namely, revelation) to those who either reject it or, who, not having admitted it, are searching for it.

4. We do not have the right to expect from an unbeliever that he 1625 admit the resurrection of our divine Savior before we shall have proposed definite proofs to him; and these proofs are deduced by reason from the same tradition.

5. In regard to these various questions, reason precedes faith and should 1626 lead us to it [cf. n. 1651].

6. Although reason was rendered weak and obscure by original sin, 1627 yet there remained in it sufficient clarity and power to lead us with

---

[1] Cf. Ass. 3 (1867) 224.—Louis Eugene Marie Bautain, born Feb. 17, 1796, at Paris, for a long time professor at Agentoratus (now Strassburg), when he had brought forth (published) certain doctrines about reason and faith different from the common opinions, was warned by his bishop (de Trévern), who also published a pastoral instruction about this matter. Gregory XVI in a Brief dated Dec. 20, 1834, praised the zeal of the bishop, and expressed the hope that the priest would retract his opinions. Bautain, a man highly deserving in other respects, laudably subjected himself, and on Nov. 18, 1835, wrote six orthodox propositions. Nevertheless, when the danger threatened that all his works would be condemned, he set out for Rome and submitted his principal work, "La Philosophie du christianisme," to ecclesiastical judgment and on Sept. 8, 1840, he rewrote the propositions mentioned above, but slightly changed, which, translated word for word (together with the original text) we present. (Cf. De Regny, *L'Abbé Bautain*, Paris, 1884, 248).—He died on the 15th of October, 1867.

certitude to a knowledge of the existence of God, to the revelation made to the Jews by Moses, and to Christians by our adorable Man-God.[1]

The Matter of Extreme Unction [2]

[From the decree of the Sacred Office under Paul V, Jan. 13, 1611, and Gregory XVI, Sept. 14, 1842]

1628   1. *Proposition:* "that without doubt the sacrament of extreme unction can be validly administered with oil not consecrated by episcopal blessing."

The Sacred Office on Jan. 13, 1611, declared: it is destructive and very close to error.

1629   2. *Similarly, to the doubt:* whether in a case of necessity as regards the validity of the sacrament of extreme unction, a parish priest could use oil blessed by himself.

The Sacred Office, Sept. 14, 1842, replied: negatively, according to the form of the decree of Thursday in the presence of His Holiness, Jan. 13, 1611, which resolution Gregory XVI approved on the same day.

---

[1] The original text (written in the French language) in *Der Katholik* 79 (1841), LVI ff.—The theses already written by Bautain Nov. 18, 1835, at the order of his bishop are these: 1. Reasoning can prove with certainty the existence of God.—Faith, a gift from heaven, is posterior to revelation; therefore, it cannot suitably be brought forward against an atheist as a proof of the existence of God.—2. The Mosaic revelation is proved with certainty by the oral and written tradition of the synagogue and of Christianity.—3. The proof of Christian revelation, drawn from the miracles of Jesus Christ, sensitive and striking for eyewitnesses, has not at all lost its strength and its brilliance for subsequent generations. We find this proof in the oral and written tradition of all Christians. It is by this double tradition that we should demonstrate it to those who reject it or who, without yet admitting it, desire it.—4. We have no right to expect an unbeliever to admit the resurrection of our divine Savior before we have given him certain proofs of it; and these proofs are deduced from the same tradition by reasoning.—5. The use of reason precedes faith and leads man to it by revelation and grace.—6. Reason can prove with certainty the authenticity of the revelation made to the Jews by Moses and to the Christians by Jesus Christ (*Der Katholik,* 59 [1836] XXV).—Bautain, April 26, 1844 (when he had in mind to found a religious community) was ordered by the Sacred Congregation of Bishops and Regulars to promise in writing: 1. Never to teach that with the sole light of right reason, leaving divine revelation out of account, one cannot give a true demonstration of the existence of God.—2. . . . that with reason alone one cannot demonstrate the spirituality and immortality of the soul or any other purely natural, rational or moral truth.—3. . . . that with reason alone one cannot have knowledge of principles or of metaphysics, as well as of the truths which depend on them, as a knowledge quite distinct from the supernatural theology which is founded on divine revelation.—4. . . . that reason cannot acquire a true and full certainty of the motives of credibility, that is to say, of those motives that render divine revelation clearly believable, such as are especially the miracles and the prophecies, particularly the resurrection of Jesus Christ" [see n. 1650 f.], (*Dict. de Théol. Cathol.,* II, 482).

[2] A Col 1860, 232.

Versions of Sacred Scripture [1]

[From the Encyclical, "Inter praecipuas," May 6, 1844]

. . . Indeed, you are aware that from the first ages called Christian, **1630** it has been the peculiar artifice of heretics that, repudiating the traditional Word of God, and rejecting the authority of the Catholic Church, they either falsify the Scriptures at hand, or alter the explanation of the meaning. In short, you are not ignorant of how much diligence and wisdom is needed to translate faithfully into another tongue the words of the Lord; so that, surely, nothing could happen more easily than that in the versions of these Scriptures, multiplied by the Biblical societies, very grave errors creep in from the imprudence or deceit of so many translators; further, the very multitude and variety of those versions conceal these errors for a long time to the destruction of many. However, it is of little or no interest at all to these societies whether the men likely to read these Bibles translated into the vulgar tongue, fall into some errors rather than others, provided they grow accustomed little by little to claiming free judgment for themselves with regard to the sense of the Scriptures, and also to despising the divine tradition of the Fathers which has been guarded by the teaching of the Catholic Church, and to repudiating the teaching office itself of the Church.

Toward this end those same Biblical associates do not cease to slander **1631** the Church and this Holy See of PETER, as if it were attempting for these many centuries to keep the faithful people from a knowledge of the Sacred Scriptures; although, on the other hand, there are extant many very illuminating documents of remarkable learning which the Supreme Pontiffs and other Catholic bishops under their leadership, have used in these more recent times, that Catholic peoples might be educated more exactly according to the written and traditional word of God.

Among those rules, which have been written by the Fathers chosen **1632** by the Council of Trent and approved by Pius IV [2] . . . and set in the front part of the Index of prohibited books, in the general sanction of the statutes one reads that Bibles published in a vulgar tongue were not permitted to anyone, except to those to whom the reading of them was judged to be beneficial for the increase of their faith and piety. To this same rule, limited immediately by a new caution because of the persistent deceits of heretics, this declaration was at length appended by the authority of Benedict XIV, that permission is granted for reading vernacular versions which have been approved by the Apostolic See, or have been edited with annotations drawn from the Holy Fathers of the Church or

[1] ASS 9 (1876) 621 ff.
[2] See n. 1606, note 2.

from learned Catholic men. . . . All the aforesaid Biblical societies, condemned a short time ago by our predecessors, we again condemn with Apostolic authority.

1633   Hence, let it be known to everyone that all those will be guilty of a very grave fault in the eyes of God and of the Church who persume to enroll in any one of these societies, or to adapt their work to them or to favor them in any way whatsoever.

PIUS IX 1846–1878

Faith and Reason [1]

[From the Encyclical, "Qui pluribus," Nov. 9, 1846]

1634   For you know, Venerable Brethren, that these hostile enemies of the Christian name, unhappily seized by a certain blind force of mad impiety, proceed with this rashness of thought that "opening their mouth unto blasphemies against God" [cf. Apoc. 13:6] with a boldness utterly unknown, are not ashamed to teach openly and publicly that the most holy mysteries of our religion are the fictions and inventions of men; that the teaching of the Catholic Church is opposed [see n. 1740] to the good and to the advantage of society, and they do not fear even to abjure Christ Himself and God. And, to delude the people more easily and to deceive especially the incautious and the inexperienced, and to drag them with themselves into error, they pretend that the ways to prosperity are known to them alone; and do not hesitate to arrogate to themselves the name of philosophers, just as if philosophy, which is occupied wholly in investigating the truth of nature, ought to reject those truths which the supreme and most clement God Himself, author of all nature, deigned to manifest to men with singular kindness and mercy, in order that men might obtain true happiness and salvation.

1635   Hence, by a preposterous and deceitful kind of argumentation, they never cease to invoke the power and excellence of human reason, to proclaim it against the most sacred faith of Christ, and, what is more, they boldly prate that it (faith) is repugnant to human reason [see n. 1706]. Certainly, nothing more insane, nothing more impious, nothing more repugnant to reason itself can be imagined or thought of than this. For, even if faith is above reason, nevertheless, no true dissension or disagreement can ever be found between them, since both have their origin from one and the same font of immutable, eternal truth, the excellent and great God, and they mutually help one another so much that right reason demonstrates the truth of faith, protects it, defends it;

---

[1] Aexq 5 ff.; AP I 6 ff.; ACol 232 ff.

but faith frees reason from all errors and, by a knowledge of divine things, wonderfully elucidates it, confirms, and perfects it [cf. n. 1799].

And with no less deceit certainly, Venerable Brothers, those enemies **1636** of divine revelation, exalting human progress with the highest praise, with a rash and sacrilegious daring would wish to introduce it into the Catholic religion, just as if religion itself were not the work of God but of men, or were some philosophical discovery which can be perfected by human means [cf. n. 1705]. Against such unhappily raving men applies very conveniently, indeed, what Tertullian deservedly made a matter of reproach to the philosophers of his own time: "Who have produced a stoic and platonic and dialectic Christianity." [1] And since, indeed, our most holy religion has not been invented by human reason but has been mercifully disclosed to men by God, thus everyone easily understands that religion itself acquires all its force from the authority of the same God speaking, and cannot ever be drawn from or be perfected by human reason.

Indeed, human reason, lest it be deceived and err in a matter of so **1637** great importance, ought to search diligently for the fact of divine revelation so that it can know with certainty that God has spoken, and so render to Him, as the Apostle so wisely teaches, "a rational service" [Rom. 12:1]. For who does not know, or cannot know that all faith is to be given to God who speaks, and that nothing is more suitable to reason itself than to acquiesce and firmly adhere to those truths which it has been established were revealed by God, who can neither deceive nor be deceived?

But, how many, how wonderful, how splendid are the proofs at hand **1638** by which human reason ought to be entirely and most clearly convinced that the religion of Christ is divine, and that "every principle of our dogmas has received its root from above, from the Lord of the heavens," [2] and that, therefore, nothing is more certain than our faith, nothing more secure, that there is nothing more holy and nothing which is supported on firmer principles. For, in truth, this faith is the teacher of life, the index of salvation, the expeller of all faults, and the fecund parent and nurse of virtues, confirmed by the birth, life, death, resurrection, wisdom, miracles, prophecies of its author and consummator, Christ Jesus; everywhere resplendent with the light of a supernatural teaching and enriched with the treasures of heavenly riches, especially clear and significant by the predictions of so many prophets, by the splendor of so many miracles, by the constancy of so many martyrs, by the glory of so many saints, revealing the salutary laws of Christ and acquiring greater strength every day from these most cruel persecutions, (this faith) has pervaded

---

[1] Tertullian, *De praescript. haer.*, c. 7 [ML 2, 20 B].

[2] S. Chrysost., *Interpretation on Isaias the prophet,* c. 1 (MG 56, 14).

the whole earth by land and sea, from the rising to the setting of the sun, under the one standard of the Cross, and also, having overcome the deceits of idolaters and torn away the mist of errors and triumphed over enemies of every kind, it has illuminated with the light of divine knowledge all peoples, races, nations, howsoever barbarous in culture and different in disposition, customs, laws, and institutions; and has subjected them to the most sweet yoke of Christ Himself, "announcing peace" to all, "announcing good" [Isa. 52:7]. All of this certainly shines everywhere with so great a glory of divine wisdom and power that the mind and intelligence of each one clearly understands that the Christian Faith is the work of God.

1639 And so, human reason, knowing clearly and openly from these most splendid and equally strong proofs that God is the author of the same faith, can proceed no further; but, having completely cast aside and removed every difficulty and doubt, it should render all obedience to this faith, since it holds as certain that whatever faith itself proposes to man to be believed or to be done, has been transmitted by God.[1]

Civil Marriage[2]

[From the Allocution, "Acerbissimum vobiscum," Sept. 27, 1852]

1640 We say nothing about that other decree in which, after completely despising the mystery, dignity, and sanctity of the sacrament of matrimony; after utterly ignoring and distorting its institution and nature; and after completely spurning the power of the Church over the same sacrament, it was proposed, according to the already condemned errors of heretics, and against the teaching of the Catholic Church, that marriage should be considered as a civil contract only, and that divorce,

---

[1] When the Hermesians dared to interpret these words of the Pontiff as if he were confirming and protecting the doctrine of Hermes, PIUS IX wrote letters, dated July 25, 1847, to John, Archbishop of Cologne, later His Reverend Eminence Cardinal de Geissel, in which he confirmed the Brief of GREGORY XVI, Sept. 26, 1835, and the added decree of the Sacred Congregation of the Index, and he rejected and condemned the works of Hermes.

[2] Aexq 117; AP I 392 f.; cf. ASS 1 (1865), 508 ff.—The commonwealth of New Granada had already in the year 1845 passed a law injurious to the rights of the Church, which merited the attention of GREGORY XVI. But the rulers of that region were so far from withdrawing their steps from the road they had undertaken (*or,* from the journey they had begun) that they harassed the religious orders by new decrees, appropriated ecclesiastical goods for secular uses, persecuted the bishops who were resisting with invincible faith, and finally violated the sanctity of the sacrament by introducing civil marriage. Therefore the Supreme Pontiff decided that he should cry out publicly against such iniquitous laws. Newspapers reported that the Supreme Pontiff exposed the same doctrine about civil marriage, in a letter dated Sept. 19, 1852, to the King of Sardinia, in whose realm this innovation was introduced.

strictly speaking, should be sanctioned in various cases (see n. 1767); and that all matrimonial cases should be deferred to lay tribunals and be judged by them (see n. 1774); because no Catholic is ignorant or cannot know that matrimony is truly and properly one of the seven sacraments of the evangelical law, instituted by Christ the Lord, and that for that reason, there can be no marriage between the faithful without there being at one and the same time a sacrament, and that, therefore, any other union of man and woman among Christians, except the sacramental union, even if contracted under the power of any civil law, is nothing else than a disgraceful and death-bringing concubinage very frequently condemned by the Church, and, hence, that the sacrament can never be separated from the conjugal agreement (see n. 1773), and that it pertains absolutely to the power of the Church to discern those things which can pertain in any way to the same matrimony.

Definition of the Immaculate Conception of the B.V.M.[1]

[From the Bull, "Ineffabilis Deus," Dec. 8, 1854]

. . . To the honor of the Holy and Undivided Trinity, to the glory 1641 and adornment of the Virgin Mother of God, to the exaltation of the Catholic Faith and the increase of the Christian religion, by the authority of our Lord Jesus Christ, of the blessed Apostles, Peter and Paul, and by Our own, We declare, pronounce, and define that the doctrine, which holds that the most Blessed Virgin Mary at the first instant of her conception, by a singular grace and privilege of Almighty God, in virtue of the merits of Christ Jesus, the Savior of the human race, was preserved immaculate from all stain of original sin, has been revealed by God, and on this account must be firmly and constantly believed by all the faithful. Wherefore, if any should presume to think in their hearts otherwise than as it has been defined by Us, which God avert, let them know and understand that they are condemned by their own judgment; that they have suffered shipwreck in regard to faith, and have revolted from the unity of the Church; and what is more, that by their own act they subject themselves to the penalties established by law, if, what they

---

[1] CL VI 842 c f.; AP I 616; ACol 238; *Analecta Iuris Pontificii* I, 1218.—PIUS IX promulgated the definition of the Immaculate Conception of the Blessed Virgin Mary, with the whole Catholic world asking for it and approving. Afterwards, at the time of the Vatican Council, 204 bishops and theologians urged a dogmatic definition concerning the Assumption of the Blessed Virgin Mary for this reason: that, unless the "very firm belief of the Church regarding the Assumption of the Blessed Virgin is to be called a very tenuous belief—which it is impious to think of—, it should be most firmly held, that it (the Assumption) has its origin from the divine-apostolic tradition, i.e., revelation" [CL VII 868 ff.].

think in their heart, they should dare to signify by word or writing or any other external means.

Rationalism and Indifferentism [1]

[From the Allocution, "Singulari quadem," Dec. 9, 1854]

1642 There are, besides, Venerable Brothers, certain men pre-eminent in learning, who confess that religion is by far the most excellent gift given by God to men, who, nevertheless, hold human reason at so high a value, exalt it so much, that they very foolishly think that it is to be held equal to religion itself. Hence, according to the rash opinion of these men, theological studies should be treated in the same manner as philosophical studies [see n. 1708], although, nevertheless, the former are based on the dogmas of faith, than which nothing is more fixed and certain, while the latter are explained and illustrated by human reason, than which nothing is more uncertain, inasmuch as they vary according to the variety of natural endowments and are subject to numberless errors and delusions. Therefore, the authority of the Church being rejected, a very broad field lies open to every difficult and abstract question, and human reason, trusting too freely in its own weak strength, has fallen headlong into most shameful errors, which there is neither time nor inclination to mention here; for, they are well known to you and have been examined by you, and they have brought harm, and that very great, to both religious and civil affairs. Therefore, it is necessary to show to those men who exalt more than is just the strength of human reason that it (their attitude) is definitely contrary to those true words of the Doctor of the Gentiles: "If any man think himself to be something, whereas he is nothing, he deceiveth himself" [Gal. 6:3]. And so it is necessary to show them how great is their arrogance in examining the mysteries which God in His great goodness has deigned to reveal to us, and in pretending to understand and to comprehend them by the weakness and narrowness of the human mind, since those mysteries far exceed the power of our intellect which, in the words of the same Apostle, should be made captive unto the obedience of faith [cf. II Cor. 10:5].

1643 And so, such followers, or rather worshipers of human reason, who set up reason as a teacher of certitude, and who promise themselves that all things will be fortunate under its leadership, have certainly forgotten how grave and terrible a wound was inflicted on human nature from the fault of our first parent; for darkness has spread over the mind, and the will has been inclined to evil. For this reason, the famous philosophers of ancient times, although they wrote many things very clearly, have

---

[1] CL VI 844 d ff.; Aexq 122 ff.; AP I 623 ff.; Rsk RP IV 370 ff.

nevertheless contaminated their teachings with most grave errors; hence that constant struggle which we experience in ourselves, of which the Apostle says: "I see a law in my members fighting against the law of my mind" [Rom. 7:23].

Now, since it is agreed that by the original sin propagated in all the **1644** posterity of Adam, the light of reason has been decreased; and since the human race has most miserably fallen from its pristine state of justice and innocence, who could think that reason is sufficient to attain to truth? Who, lest he fall and be ruined in the midst of such great dangers and in such great weakness of his powers, would deny that he needs the aid of a divine religion, and of heavenly grace for salvation? These aids, indeed, God most graciously bestows on those who ask for them by humble prayer, since it is written: "God resisteth the proud and giveth grace to the humble" [Jas. 4:6]. Therefore, turning toward the Father, Christ our Lord affirmed that the deepest secrets of truth have not been disclosed "to the wise and prudent of this world," who take pride in their own talents and learning, and refuse to render obedience to faith, but rather (have been revealed) to humble and simple men who rely and rest on the oracle of divine faith [cf. Matt. 11:25; Luke 10:21].

You should inculcate this salutary lesson in the souls of those who **1645** exaggerate the strength of human reason to such an extent that they venture by its help to scrutinize and explain even mysteries, although nothing is more inept, nothing more foolish. Strive to withdraw them from such perversity of mind by explaining indisputably that nothing more excellent has been given by the providence of God to man than the authority of divine faith; that this is for us, as it were, a torch in the darkness, a guide which we follow to life; that this is absolutely necessary for salvation; for, "without faith . . . it is impossible to please God" [Heb. 11:6] and *"he that believeth not, shall be condemned"* [Mark 16:16].

Not without sorrow we have learned that another error, no less de- **1646** structive, has taken possession of some parts of the Catholic world, and has taken up its abode in the souls of many Catholics who think that one should have good hope of the eternal salvation of all those who have never lived in the true Church of Christ [see n. 1717]. Therefore, they are wont to ask very often what will be the lot and condition after death of those who have not submitted in any way to the Catholic faith, and, by bringing forward most vain reasons, they make a response favorable to their false opinion. Far be it from Us, Venerable Brethren, to presume on the limits of the divine mercy which is infinite; far from Us, to wish to scrutinize the hidden counsel and "judgments of God" which are "a great deep" [Ps. 35:7] and cannot be penetrated by human thought. But, as is Our Apostolic duty, we wish your episcopal solicitude and vigilance to be aroused, so that you will strive as much as you can to drive from the mind of men that impious and equally fatal opinion, namely, that the way of eternal salvation can be found in any religion whatsoever. May you demonstrate with that skill and learning in which you excel, to the people entrusted to your care that the dogmas of the Catholic faith are in no wise opposed to divine mercy and justice.

1647   For, it must be held by faith that outside the Apostolic Roman Church, no one can be saved; that this is the only ark of salvation; that he who shall not have entered therein will perish in the flood; but, on the other hand, it is necessary to hold for certain that they who labor in ignorance of the true religion, if this ignorance is invincible, are not stained by any guilt in this matter in the eyes of God. Now, in truth, who would arrogate so much to himself as to mark the limits of such an ignorance, because of the nature and variety of peoples, regions, innate dispositions, and of so many other things? For, in truth, when released from these corporeal chains "we shall see God as He is" [I John 3:2], we shall understand perfectly by how close and beautiful a bond divine mercy and justice are united; but, as long as we are on earth, weighed down by this mortal mass which blunts the soul, let us hold most firmly that, in accordance with Catholic teaching, there is "one God, one faith, one baptism" [Eph. 4:5]; it is unlawful to proceed further in inquiry.

1648   But, just as the way of charity demands, let us pour forth continual prayers that all nations everywhere may be converted to Christ; and let us be devoted to the common salvation of men in proportion to our strength, "for the hand of the Lord is not shortened" [Isa. 9:1] and the gifts of heavenly grace will not be wanting those who sincerely wish and ask to be refreshed by this light. Truths of this sort should be deeply fixed in the minds of the faithful, lest they be corrupted by false doctrines, whose object is to foster an indifference toward religion, which we see spreading widely and growing strong for the destruction of souls.

False Traditionalism (against Augustine Bonnetty) [1]

[From the Decree of the S.C. of the Index, 11, (15) June, 1855]

1649   1. "Although faith is above reason, nevertheless no true dissension, no disagreement can ever be found between them, since both arise from the one same immutable source of truth, the most excellent and great God, and thus bring mutual help to each other" [2] [cf. n. 1635 and 1799].

---

[1] ASS 3 (1867) 224.—Augustine Bonnetty, born April 9, 1798, in the town of Entrevaux, France, besides various other philosophical writings, founded the journal: "Annales de philosophie chrétienne." He subscribed to the theses proposed to him by the Sacred Council of the Index; he died March 29, 1879.

[2] From the Encyclical of Pius IX, "Qui pluribus," Nov. 9, 1846 [cf. n. 1634 ff.].

2. Reason can prove with certitude the existence of God, the spiritual- 1650
ity of the soul, the freedom of man. Faith is posterior to revelation, and
hence it cannot be conveniently alleged to prove the existence of God to
an atheist, or to prove the spirituality and the freedom of the rational
soul against a follower of naturalism and fatalism [cf. n. 1622, 1625].

3. The use of reason precedes faith and leads men to it by the help 1651
of revelation and of grace [cf. n. 1626].

4. The method which St. Thomas and St. Bonaventure and other 1652
scholastics after them used does not lead to rationalism, nor has it been
the reason why philosophy in today's schools is falling into naturalism
and pantheism. Therefore, it is not lawful to charge as a reproach against
these doctors and teachers that they made use of this method, especially
since the Church approves, or at least keeps silent.[1]

The Misuse of Magnetism [2]

[From the Encyclical of the Holy Office, Aug. 4, 1856]

. . . Already some responses on this subject have been given by the 1653
Holy See to particular cases, in which those experiments are condemned
as illicit which are arranged for a purpose not natural, not honest, and
not attained by proper means; therefore, in similar cases it was decreed
on Wednesday, April 21, 1841: "The use of magnetism, as it is explained, is not permitted." Similarly, the Sacred Congregation decreed
that certain books stubbornly disseminating errors of this kind should
be condemned. But because, aside from particular cases, the use of
magnetism in general had to be considered, by way of a rule therefore
it was so stated on Wednesday, July 28, 1847: "When all error, sooth-
saying, explicit or implicit invocation of the demon is removed, the use
of magnetism, i.e., the mere act of employing physical media otherwise
licit, is not morally forbidden, provided it does not tend to an illicit end
or to one that is in any manner evil. However, the application of principles and purely physical means to things and effects truly supernatural,
in order to explain them physically, is nothing but deception altogether
illicit and heretical."

Although by this general decree the lawfulness and unlawfulness in the 1654
use or misuse of magnetism were satisfactorily explained, nevertheless
the wickedness of men grew to such an extent that neglecting the legitimate study of the science, pursuing rather the curious, with great loss
to souls and detriment to civil society itself, they boast that they have
discovered the principle of foretelling and divining. Thus, girls with the

---

[1] These propositions are contradictory to the propositions asserted here and there by
Bonnetty.

[2] ASS I (1865) 177 f.; CL VI 103 a; cf. *The Compilation of the Sacred Congregation
for the Propagation of the Faith,* I (1907), n. 1128.

tricks of sleepwalking and of clear-gazing, as they call it, carried away by delusions and gestures not always modest, proclaim that they see the invisible, and they pretend with rash boldness to hold talks even about religion, to evoke the souls of the dead, to receive answers, to reveal the unknown and the distant, and to practice other superstitious things of that sort, intending to acquire great gain for themselves and for their masters through their divining. Therefore, in all these, whatever art or illusion they employ, since physical media are used for unnatural effects, there is deception altogether illicit and heretical, and a scandal against honesty of morals.[1]

The False Doctrine of Anton Guenther [2]

[From the Brief, "Eximiam tuam" to Cardinal de Geissel,
Archbishop of Cologne, June 15, 1857]

1655   Not without sorrow are We especially aware that in these books that erroneous and most dangerous system of rationalism, often condemned by this Apostolic See, is particularly dominant; and likewise we know that in the same books these items among many others are found, which are not a little at variance with the Catholic Faith and with the true explanation of the unity of the divine substance in three distinct, eternal Persons. Likewise, we have found that neither better nor more accurate are the statements made about the mystery of the Incarnate Word, and about the unity of the divine Person of the Word in two natures, divine and human. We know that in the same books there is harm to the Catholic opinion and teaching concerning man, who is so composed of body and soul that the soul, and that rational, may of itself be the true and immediate form of the body.[3] And we are not unaware that in the

---

[1] Cf. the Response of the Sacred Office, July 26, 1899, about the experiments of hypnotism [Compilation of the Sacred Congregation for the Propagation of the Faith, II (1907) n. 2061].

[2] ASS 8 (1874) 446 f.; Aexq 166 f.; AP II 587 f.; RskRP IV 383 f.; ACol 241; *Analecta Iuris Pontificii,* II, 1445 f.—Anton Guenther, born Nov. 17, 1783, in the town of Lindenau, Bohemia, was ordained a priest in 1820; he lived at Vienna from 1824 until his death Feb. 24, 1863, and wrote while there various philosophical and theological works. His works were stopped by a decree of the Sacred Congregation of the Index, promulgated on Jan. 8, 1857, and approved by the Supreme Pontiff on Feb. 17, 1857, to which decree the author submitted in a praiseworthy manner. But when certain followers of Guenther, because his opinions were not enumerated individually in that general decree, took occasion from it to think that he was permitted to persist in them, the Supreme Pontiff in a letter sent to the Cardinal Archbishop of Cologne noted individually the errors of Guenther in these words.

[3] PIUS IX in the letter, "Dolore haud mediocri," to the Bishop of Wratislava (Breslau) on the 30th of April, 1860, declares: "The opinion which places in man one principle of life namely, the rational soul, from which the body also receives movement,

same books those teachings are stated and defended which are plainly opposed to the Catholic doctrine about the supreme liberty of God, who is free from any necessity whatsoever in creating things.

And also that extremely wicked and condemned doctrine which in Guenther's books rashly attributes the rights of a master both to human reason and philosophy, whereas they should be wholly handmaids, not masters in religious matters; and therefore all those things are disturbed which should remain most stable, not only concerning the distinction between science and faith, but also concerning the eternal immutability of faith, which is always one and the same, while philosophy and human studies are not always consistent, and are not immune to a multiple variety of errors. **1656**

In addition, the Holy Fathers are not held in that reverence which the canons of the Councils prescribe, and which these splendid lights of the Catholic Church so altogether deserve, nor does he refrain from the slurring remarks against Catholic Schools, which Our predecessor of cherished memory, PIUS VI, solemnly condemned [see n. 1576]. **1657**

Nor shall we pass over in silence that in Guenther's books "the sound form of speaking" is completely outraged, as if it were lawful to forget the words of the Apostle Paul [II Tim. 1:13], or those which Augustine most earnestly advised: "It is right for us to speak according to a fixed rule, lest liberty with words give birth to an impious opinion, even about the things which are signified by them"[1] [see n. 1714 a]. **1658**

Errors of the Ontologists[2]

[From the decree of the Sacred Office, Sept. 18, 1861,
"they cannot be safely taught"]

1. Immediate knowledge of God, habitual at least, is essential to the human intellect, so much so that without it the intellect can know nothing, since indeed it is itself intellectual light. **1659**

2. That being which is in all things and without which we understand nothing, is the divine being. **1660**

3. Universals considered on the part of the thing are not really distinguished from God. **1661**

---

and all life, and sense, is the most common in the Church of God, and to many highly approved doctors it seems to be so intimately joined with the dogma of the Church that this is the sole legitimate, true interpretation of it, and hence not without error in faith could it be denied." [Aexq 178; RskRP IV 399; A Franz, I B. Baltzer 40]. Therefore, the Cologne Council says: "There can be no doubt that, according to the mind of the Councils, all the operations of our life are accomplished by the rational soul itself created by God" . . . [CL V 293 b; ACol 32; cf. n. 1911 f.].

[1] St. Augustine, *De Civitate Dei* 1, 10, c. 23 [ML 41 (Aug. VII) 300].

[2] ASS 3 (1867) 204 f.

1662   4. Congenital knowledge of God as being simply involves in an eminent way all other cognition, so that by it we hold as known implicitly all being, under whatever aspect it is knowable.

1663   5. All other ideas do not exist except as modifications of the idea by which God is understood as Being simply.

1664   6. Created things exist in God as a part in the whole, not indeed in the formal whole, but in the infinite whole, the most simple, which puts its parts, as it were, without any division and diminution of itself outside itself.

1665   7. Creation can be thus explained: God, by that special act by which He knows Himself, and wills Himself as distinct from a determined creature, man, for example, produces a creature.

The False Freedom of Science (against James Frohschammer) [1]

[From the epistle, "Gravissimas inter," to the Archbishop of Munich-Freising, Dec. 11, 1862]

1666   Amidst the terrible anguish by which we are pressed on all sides in the great restlessness and iniquity of these times, we are sorely grieved to learn that in various regions of Germany are found some men, even Catholics, who, betraying sacred theology as well as philosophy, do not hesitate to introduce a certain freedom of teaching and writing hitherto unheard of in the Church, and to profess openly and publicly new and altogether reprehensible opinions, and to disseminate them among the people.

1667   Hence, We were affected with no light grief, Venerable Brother, when the sad message reached Us that the priest, James Frohschammer, teacher of philosophy in the Academy at Munich, was displaying, beyond all the rest, freedom of teaching and writing in this manner, and was defending these most dangerous errors in his works that have been published. Therefore, with no delay We commanded Our Congregation appointed for censuring books to weigh with great diligence and care the particular volumes which are circulating under the name of the same priest, Frohschammer, and to report all findings to Us. These volumes written in German have the title: *Introductio in Philophiam, De Libertate scientiae, Athenaeum,* the first of which was published in the year 1858, the second in the year 1861, but the third at the turn of this year 1862, by the Munich press. And so the said Congregation . . . judged that the

---

[1] ASS 8 (1874) 429 ff.; Aexq 219 ff.; AP III 548 ff.; RskRP IV 458 ff.—Jacob Frohschammer, born, Jan. 6, 1821, in the village of Illkofen, Bavaria, taught in the University of Munich from the year 1854; he died June 14, 1893.

author in many matters does not think correctly, and that his doctrine is far from Catholic truth.

And this, especially in a twofold direction; the first, indeed, because 1668 the author attributes such powers to human reason which are not at all appropriate to reason itself; and the second, because he grants to the same reason such liberty of judging all things, and of always venturing anything, that the rights of the Church itself, its office and authority are completely taken away.

For the author teaches especially that philosophy, if a right notion of 1669 it is held, cannot only perceive and understand those Christian dogmas which natural reason has in common with faith (as, for instance, a common object of perception), but also those which particularly and properly affect Christian religion and faith, namely, the supernatural end of man, and all that is related to it; and also, that the most holy mystery of the Incarnation of the Lord belongs to the province of human reasoning and philosophy; and that reason, when this object is presented to it, can by its own proper principles, arrive at those (dogmas) with understanding. But, although the author makes some distinction between these (natural) dogmas and those (Christian), and assigns these latter with less right to reason, nevertheless, he clearly and openly teaches that these (Christian) dogmas also are contained among those which constitute the true and proper matter of science or philosophy. Therefore, according to the teaching of the same author, it can and should be definitely concluded that, even in the deepest mysteries of divine wisdom and goodness, nay, even of Its free will, granted that the object of revelation be posited, reason can of itself, no longer on the principle of divine authority, but on its own natural principles and strength, reach understanding or certitude. How "false" and "erroneous" this teaching of the author is, there is no one, even though lightly imbued with the rudiments of Christian doctrine, who does not see immediately and clearly understand.

For, if these worshipers of philosophy were protecting the true and 1670 sole principles and rights of reason and philosophic study, they should certainly be honored with merited praise. Indeed, true and sound philosophy has its own most noble position, since it is the characteristic of such philosophy to search diligently into truth, and to cultivate and illustrate rightly and carefully human reason, darkened as it is by the guilt of the first man, but by no means extinct; and to perceive, to understand well, to advance the object of its cognition and many truths; and to demonstrate, vindicate, and defend, by arguments sought from its own principles, many of those truths, such as the existence, nature, attributes of God which faith also proposes for our belief; and, in this way, to build a road to those dogmas more correctly held by faith, and even to those more profound dogmas which can be perceived by faith alone at first, so that they may in some way be understood by reason. The exacting and most beautiful science of true philosophy ought, indeed, to do such things and to be occupied with them. If the learned men in the academies of Germany would make efforts to excel in this, in proportion to that peculiar well-known inclination of that nation to cultivate the more serious and exacting studies, their zeal would be approved and commended by Us, because they would be turning to the utility and progress of sacred things that which they have learned for their own uses.

1671   But, in truth, We can never tolerate that in so grave a matter as this surely is, that all things be rashly confused, and that reason should seize upon and disturb those things which pertain also to faith, since the limits beyond which reason in its own right has never advanced nor can advance, are fixed and well-known to all. To dogmas of this sort pertain particularly and openly all those which treat of the supernatural elevation of man and his supernatural intercourse with God, and which are known to have been revealed for this purpose. And surely, since these dogmas are above nature, they cannot, therefore, be reached by natural reason and natural principles. For, indeed, reason by its own natural principles can never be made fit to handle scientifically dogmas of this sort. But, if those men dare to assert this rashly, let them know that they are withdrawing, not merely from the opinion of a few learned persons, but from the common and never changing doctrine of the Church.

1672   For, from the divine Scriptures and from the tradition of the Holy Fathers, it is agreed indeed that the existence of God and many other truths were known [cf. Rom. 1] by the natural light of reason, even by those who had not yet received the faith, but that God alone manifested those more hidden dogmas when He wished to make known "the mystery, which had been hidden from ages and generations" [Col. 1:26]. And in such a way indeed that, "at sundry times and in diverse manners He had formerly spoken to the fathers by the prophets, last of all . . . He might speak to us by His Son, . . . by whom He also made the world" [Heb. 1:1 f.]. For "no man hath seen God at any time: the only-begotten Son, who is in the bosom of the Father, he hath declared Him" [John 1:18]. Therefore, the Apostle who testifies that the gentiles knew God by those things which were made, discoursing about "grace and truth" which "came by Jesus Christ" [John 1:17], says, "We speak of the wisdom of God in a mystery, a wisdom which is hidden . . . which none of the princes of this world know . . . But to us God hath revealed them by His Spirit: for the Spirit searcheth all things, yea the deep things of God. For, what man knoweth the things of man but the spirit of a man that is in him? So the things also that are of God, no man knoweth but the Spirit of God" [I Cor. 2:7 f].

Adhering to these and other almost innumerable divine texts, the **1673** Holy Fathers, in transmitting the teaching of the Church, have constantly taken care to distinguish the knowledge of divine things which is common to all by the power of natural intelligence, from the knowledge of those things which is received on faith through the Holy Spirit; and they have continuously taught that through this (faith) those mysteries are revealed to us in Christ which transcend not only human philosophy but even the angelic natural intelligence, and which, although they are known through divine revelation and have been accepted by faith, nevertheless, remain still covered by the sacred veil of faith itself, and wrapped in an obscuring mist as long as we are absent from the Lord [1] in this mortal life. From all this, it is clear that the proposition of Frohschammer is wholly foreign to the teaching of the Catholic Church, since he does not hesitate to assert that all the dogmas of the Christian religion without discrimination are the object of natural science or philosophy, and that human reason, cultivated so much throughout history, provided these dogmas have been proposed to reason itself as an object, can from its own natural powers and principle, arrive at the true understanding concerning all, even the more hidden dogmas [see n. 1709].

But now, in the said writings of this author another opinion prevails **1674** which is plainly opposed to the teaching and understanding of the Catholic Church. For, he attributes that freedom to philosophy which must be called not the freedom of science but an utterly reprobate and intolerable license of philosophy. For, having made a certain distinction between a philosopher and philosophy, he attributes to a "philosopher" the right and duty of submitting himself to the authority which he himself has approved as true, but he denies both (right and duty) to philosophy, so that taking no account of revealed doctrine he asserts that it (philosophy) ought never and can never submit itself to authority. And this might be tolerable and perhaps admissible, if it were said only about the right which philosophy has to use its own principles or methods, and its own conclusions, as also the other sciences, and if its liberty consisted in employing this right in such a way that it would admit nothing into itself which had not been acquired by it under its own conditions, or was foreign to it. But, such true freedom of philos-

---

[1] St. John Chrysostom, Homily 7 (9) on I Cor. (MG 61, 53); St. Ambrose, De fide, to Grat. I, 10 (ML 16, 542 D); St. LEO, Sermon on the Nativity of the Lord 9 (sermo 29: ML 54, 226 B); St. Cyril of Alexandria, Against Nestorius 1, 3 in the beginning [MG 76, 111 A]; Commentary on John 1, 9 [MG 73, 124 C]; St. John Damascene, Exposition of the Orthodox Faith, 1, 2 [MG 94, 794 B]; St. Jerome, Commentary on Gal. 3, 2 [ML 26, 348 C].

ophy must understand and observe its own limitations. For, it will never be permitted either to a philosopher, or to philosophy, to say anything contrary to those things which divine revelation and the Church teaches, or to call any of them into doubt because (he or it) does not understand them, or to refuse the judgment which the authority of the Church decides to bring forward concerning some conclusion of philosophy which was hitherto free.

1675   It also happens that the same author so bitterly, so rashly fights for the liberty, or rather the unbridled license of philosophy that he does not at all fear to assert that the Church not only ought never to pay any attention to *philosophy,* but should even tolerate the errors of philosophy itself, and leave it to correct itself [see n. 1711]; from which it happens that *philosophers* necessarily share in this liberty of *philosophy,* and so even they are freed from all law. Who does not see how forcefully an opinion and teaching of this sort of Frohschammer's should be *rejected, reproved,* and altogether *condemned?* For the Church, from her divine institution, has the duty both to hold most diligently to the deposit of faith, whole and inviolate, and to watch continually with great earnestness over the salvation of souls, and with the greatest care to remove and eliminate all those things which can be opposed to faith or can in any way endanger the salvation of souls.

1676   Therefore, the Church, by the power entrusted to it by its divine Founder, has not only the right, but particularly the duty of not tolerating but of proscribing and condemning all errors, if the integrity of faith and the salvation of souls so demand; and on every philosopher who wishes to be a son of the Church, and also on philosophy, it lays this duty—never to say anything against those things which the Church teaches, and to retract those about which the Church has warned them. Moreover, We proclaim and declare that a doctrine which teaches the contrary is entirely *erroneous* and especially *harmful to faith itself, to the Church and its authority.*

Indifferentism [1]

[From the Encyclical, "Quanto conficiamur moerore," to the bishops of Italy, Aug. 10, 1863]

1677   And here, beloved Sons and Venerable Brothers, We should mention again and censure a very grave error in which some Catholics are unhappily engaged, who believe that men living in error, and separated from the true faith and from Catholic unity, can attain eternal life [see n. 1717]. Indeed, this is certainly quite contrary to Catholic teach-

---

[1] Aexq 229 f.; AP III 613 f.

ing. It is known to Us and to you that they who labor in invincible ignorance of our most holy religion and who, zealously keeping the natural law and its precepts engraved in the hearts of all by God, and being ready to obey God, live an honest and upright life, can, by the operating power of divine light and grace, attain eternal life, since God who clearly beholds, searches, and knows the minds, souls, thoughts, and habits of all men, because of His great goodness and mercy, will by no means suffer anyone to be punished with eternal torment who has not the guilt of deliberate sin. But, the Catholic dogma that no one can be saved outside the Catholic Church is well-known; and also that those who are obstinate toward the authority and definitions of the same Church, and who persistently separate themselves from the unity of the Church, and from the Roman Pontiff, the successor of PETER, to whom "the guardianship of the vine has been entrusted by the Savior," [1] cannot obtain eternal salvation.

But, God forbid that the sons of the Catholic Church ever in any way **1678** be hostile to those who are not joined with us in the same bonds of faith and love; but rather they should always be zealous to seek them out and aid them, whether poor, or sick, or afflicted with any other burdens, with all the offices of Christian charity; and they should especially endeavor to snatch them from the darkness of error in which they unhappily lie, and lead them back to Catholic truth and to the most loving Mother the Church, who never ceases to stretch out her maternal hands lovingly to them, and to call them back to her bosom so that, established and firm in faith, hope, and charity, and "being fruitful in every good work" [Col. 1:10], they may attain eternal salvation.

The Conventions of the Theologians
of Germany [2]

[From the letter, "Tuas libenter," to the Archbishop of
Munich-Freising, Dec. 21, 1863]

. . . Indeed we were aware, Venerable Brother, that some Catholics **1679** who devote their time to cultivating the higher studies, trusting too much in the powers of human ability, have not been frightened by the dangers of errors, lest, in asserting the false and insincere liberty of science, they be snatched away beyond the limits beyond which the obedience due to the teaching power of the Church, divinely appointed to preserve the integrity of all revealed truth, does not permit them to proceed. Therefore, it happens that Catholics of this sort are unhappily deceived, and

---

[1] Council of CHALCEDON in relation to Leo I [cf. n. 149].
[2] ASS 8 (1874) 438 ff.; Aexq 244 f.; AP III 638 ff.; RskRP·IV 487 ff.

often agree with those who decry and protest against the decrees of this Apostolic See and of Our Congregations, that they (decrees) hinder the free progress of science [see n. 1712]; and they expose themselves to the danger of breaking those sacred ties of obedience by which, according to the will of God, they are bound to this same Apostolic See which has been appointed by God as the teacher and defender of truth.

1680   Nor, are We ignorant that in Germany also there prevailed a false opinion against the old school, and against the teaching of those supreme doctors [see n. 1713], whom the universal Church venerates because of their admirable wisdom and sanctity of life. By this false opinion the authority of the Church itself is called into danger, especially since the Church, not only through so many continuous centuries has permitted that theological science be cultivated according to the method and the principles of these same Doctors, sanctioned by the common consent of all Catholic schools, but it (the Church) also very often extolled their theological doctrine with the highest praises, and strongly recommended it as a very strong buttress of faith and a formidable armory against its enemies. . . .

1681   Indeed, since all the men of this assembly, as you write, have asserted that the progress of science and its happy result in avoiding and refuting the errors of our most wretched age depend entirely on a close adherence to revealed truths which the Catholic Church teaches, they themselves have recognized and professed that truth, which true Catholics devoted to cultivating and setting forth knowledge, have always held and handed down. And so, relying on this truth, these wise and truly Catholic men could cultivate these sciences in safety, explain them, and make them useful and certain. And this could not be achieved if the light of human reason, circumscribed by limits in investigating those truths also which it can attain by its own powers and faculties, did not venerate above all, as is just, the infallible and uncreated light of the divine intellect which shines forth wonderfully everywhere in Christian revelation. For, although those natural disciplines rely on their own proper principles, apprehended by reason, nevertheless, Catholic students of these disciplines should have divine revelation before their eyes as a guiding star, by whose light they may guard against the quicksands of errors, when they discover that in their investigations and interpretations they can be led by them (natural principles)—as often happens—to profess those things which are more or less opposed to the infallible truth of things which have been revealed by God.

1682   Hence, We do not doubt that the men of this assembly, knowing and professing the truth mentioned above, have wished at one and the same time clearly to reject and repudiate that recent and preposterous method of philosophizing which, even if it admits divine revelation as an historical fact, nevertheless, submits the ineffable truths made known by divine revelation to the investigations of human reason; just as if those truths had been subject to reason, or, as if reason, by its own powers and principles, could attain understanding and knowledge of all the supernal truths and mysteries of our holy faith, which are so far above human reason that it can never be made fit to understand or demonstrate them by its own powers, and on its own natural principles [see n. 1709]. Indeed, We honor with due praise the men of this same convention because, rejecting, as We think, the false distinction between philosopher and philosophy, about which We have spoken in our other letter to you [see n. 1674], they have realized and professed that all Catholics in their learned interpretations should in conscience obey the dogmatic decrees of the infallible Catholic Church.

While, in truth, We laud these men with due praise because they pro- **1683** fessed the truth which necessarily arises from their obligation to the Catholic faith, We wish to persuade Ourselves that they did not wish to confine the obligation, by which Catholic teachers and writers are absolutely bound, only to those decrees which are set forth by the infallible judgment of the Church as dogmas of faith to be believed by all [see n. 1722]. And We persuade Ourselves, also, that they did not wish to declare that that perfect adhesion to revealed truths, which they recognized as absolutely necessary to attain true progress in the sciences and to refute errors, could be obtained if faith and obedience were given only to the dogmas expressly defined by the Church. For, even if it were a matter concerning that subjection which is to be manifested by an act of divine faith, nevertheless, it would not have to be limited to those matters which have been defined by express decrees of the ecumenical Councils, or of the Roman Pontiffs and of this See, but would have to be extended also to those matters which are handed down as divinely revealed by the ordinary teaching power of the whole Church spread throughout the world, and therefore, by universal and common consent are held by Catholic theologians to belong to faith.

But, since it is a matter of that subjection by which in conscience all **1684** those Catholics are bound who work in the speculative sciences, in order that they may bring new advantages to the Church by their writings, on that account, then, the men of that same convention should recognize that it is not sufficient for learned Catholics to accept and revere the aforesaid dogmas of the Church, but that it is also necessary to subject themselves to the decisions pertaining to doctrine which are issued by the Pontifical Congregations, and also to those forms of doctrine which are held by the common and constant consent of Catholics as theological truths and conclusions, so certain that opinions opposed to these same forms of doctrine, although they cannot be called heretical, nevertheless deserve some theological censure.

The Unity of the Church [1]

[From the letter of the Sacred Office to the bishops
of England, Sept. 16, 1864]

1685   It has been made known to the Apostolic See that some Catholic laymen and ecclesiastics have enrolled in a society to "procure" as they say, *the unity of Christianity,* established at London in the year 1857, and that already many journalistic articles have been published, which are signed by the names of Catholics approving this society, or which are shown to be the work of churchmen commending this same society.

But certainly, I need not say what the nature of this society is, and whither it is tending; this is easily understood from the articles of the newspaper entitled THE UNION REVIEW, and from that very page on which members are invited and listed. Indeed, formed and directed by Protestants, it is animated by that spirit which expressly avows for example, that the three Christian communions, Roman Catholic, Greek-schismatic, and Anglican, however separated and divided from one another, nevertheless with equal right claim for themselves the name Catholic. Admission, therefore, into that society is open to all, wheresoever they may live, Catholics, Greek-schismatics, and Anglicans, under this condition, however, that no one is permitted to raise a question about the various forms of doctrine in which they disagree, and that it is right for each individual to follow with tranquil soul what is acceptable to his own religious creed. Indeed, the society itself indicates to all its members the prayers to be recited, and to the priests the sacrifices to be celebrated according to its own intention: namely, that the said three Christian communions, inasmuch as they, as it is alleged, together now constitute the Catholic Church, may at some time or other unite to form one body. . . .

1686   The foundation on which this society rests is of such a nature that it makes the divine establishment of the Church of no consequence. For, it is wholly in this: that it supposes the true Church of Jesus Christ to be composed partly of the Roman Church scattered and propagated throughout the whole world, partly, indeed, of the schism of Photius, and of the Anglican heresy, to which, as well as to the Roman Church, "there is one Lord, one faith, and one baptism" [cf. Eph. 4:5]. Surely nothing should be preferable to a Catholic man than that schisms and dissensions

---

[1] ASS 2 (ed. 2; 1870) 657 ff.; Compilation of the Sacred Congregation for the Propagation of the Faith I (1907) n. 1262.

among Christians be torn out by the roots and that all Christians be "careful to keep the unity of the Spirit in the bond of peace" [Eph. 4:3]. . . . But, that the faithful of Christ and the clergy should pray for Christian unity under the leadership of heretics, and, what is worse, according to an intention, polluted and infected as much as possible with heresy, can in no way be tolerated. The true Church of Jesus Christ was established by divine authority, and is known by a fourfold mark, which we assert in the Creed must be believed; and each one of these marks so clings to the others that it cannot be separated from them; hence it happens that that Church which truly is, and is called Catholic should at the same time shine with the prerogatives of unity, sanctity, and apostolic succession. Therefore, the Catholic Church alone is conspicuous and perfect in the unity of the whole world and of all nations, particularly in that unity whose beginning, root, and unfailing origin are that supreme authority and "higher principality" [1] of blessed PETER, the prince of the Apostles, and of his successors in the Roman Chair. No other Church is Catholic except the one which, founded on the one PETER, grows into one "body compacted and fitly joined together" [Eph. 4:16] in the unity of faith and charity. . . .

Therefore, the faithful should especially shun this London society, 1687 because those sympathizing with it favor indifferentism and engender scandal.

Naturalism, Communism, Socialism [2]

[From the Encyclical, "Quanta cura," Dec. 8, 1864]

Moreover, although We have not failed to proscribe and frequently 1688 condemn the most important errors of this sort, nevertheless, the cause of the Catholic Church and the salvation of souls divinely entrusted to Us, and the good of human society itself, demand that We again arouse your pastoral solicitude to overcome other base opinions which spring from these same errors as from fountains. These false and perverted errors are to be the more detested because they have this goal in mind: to impede and remove that salutary force which the Catholic Church, according to the institution and command of her divine founder, must exercise freely "unto the consummation of the world" [Matt. 28:20], no less toward individual men, than toward nations, peoples, and their highest leaders; and to remove that mutual alliance of councils between the sacerdotal ministry and the government, and that "happy concord

---

[1] St. Irenaeus, *Against heresies* 3, 3 [MG 7, 849 A].

[2] ASS 3 (1867) 161 ff.; AP III 689 ff. See the letter of His Eminence, Cardinal Antonelli, n. 1700 note.

which has always existed, and is so salutary to sacred and civil affairs." [1]

1689   For, surely you know, Venerable Brothers, that at this time not a few are found who, applying the impious and absurd principles of *naturalism,* as they call it, to civil society, dare to teach that "the best plan for public society, and civil progress absolutely requires that human society be established and governed with no regard to religion, as if it did not exist, or at least, without making distinction between the true and the false religions." And also, contrary to the teaching of Sacred Scripture, of the Church, and of the most holy Fathers, they do not hesitate to assert that "the best condition of society is the one in which there is no acknowledgment by the government of the duty of restraining, by established penalties, offenders of the Catholic religion, except insofar as the public peace demands."

1690   And, from this wholly false idea of social organization they do not fear to foster that erroneous opinion, especially fatal to the Catholic Church and to the salvation of souls, called [2] by Our predecessor of recent memory, GREGORY XVI, *insanity;* namely, that "liberty of conscience and of worship is the proper right of every man, and should be proclaimed and asserted by law in every correctly established society; that the right to all manner of liberty rests in the citizens, not to be restrained by either ecclesiastical or civil authority; and that by this right they can manifest openly and publicly and declare their own concepts, whatever they be, by voice, by print, or in any other way." While, in truth, they rashly affirm this, they do not understand and note that they are preaching a "liberty of perdition," [3] and that "if human opinions always have freedom for discussion, there could never be wanting those who will dare to resist truth, and to trust in the eloquence of human (*al.* mundane) wisdom, when faith and Christian wisdom know from the very teaching of our Lord Jesus Christ how much it should avoid such harmful vanity." [4]

1691   And since, when religion has been removed from civil society, and when the teaching and authority of divine revelation have been repudiated; or the true notion of justice and human right is obscured by darkness and lost; and when in place of true justice and legitimate right, material force is substituted, then it is clear why some, completely neglecting and putting aside the certain principles of sound reason, dare to exclaim: "The will of the people, manifested as they say by public opinion, or in some other way, constitutes the supreme law, freed from all divine and human right; and, that deeds consummated in the political

---

[1] Cf. GREGORY XVI, Encyclical, "Mirari," Aug. 15, 1832 [n. 1613 ff.].

[2] Encyclical of GREGORY XVI, "Mirari," Aug. 15, 1832 (n. 1613).

[3] St. Augustine, Letter 105 (166), c. 2, n. 9 (ML 33, 399).

[4] Epistle of ST. LEO 164 (133), c. 2; ed. Ball (ML 54, 1149 B).

order, by the very fact that they have been consummated, have the force of right." But who does not see and plainly understand that a society of men who are released from the bonds of religion and of true justice can have no other aim, surely, than the goal of amassing and heaping up wealth, and that it (society) can follow no other law in its actions except an uncontrolled cupidity of soul, a slave to its own pleasures and advantages?

Therefore, men of this sort pursue with bitter hatred religious orders, 1692 no matter how supremely deserving because of their Christian, civil, and literary work; and they cry out that these same orders have no legitimate reason for existing, and in this way approve the falsehoods of heretics. For, as Our predecessor of recent memory, PIUS VI, very wisely taught, "abolition of the regulars wounds the status of the public profession of the evangelical counsels; it injures the way of life approved in the Church as suitable to the apostolic teaching; it harms the most distinguished founders whom we venerate on our altars, who established these orders only when inspired by God." [1]

And they also make the impious pronouncement that from the citizens 1693 and the Church must be taken away the power "by which they can ask for alms openly in the cause of Christian charity," and also that the law should be repealed "by which on some fixed days, because of the worship of God, servile works are prohibited," pretending most deceitfully that the said power and law obstruct the principles of the best public economy. And, not content with removing religion from public society, they wish even to banish religion itself from private families.

For, teaching and professing that most deadly error of *communism* 1694 and *socialism,* they assert that "domestic society or the family borrows the whole reason for its existence from the civil law alone; and, hence, all rights of parents over their children, especially the right of caring for their instruction and education, emanate from and depend wholly on the civil law."

In these impious opinions and machinations these most deceitful men 1695 have this particular intention: that the saving doctrine and power of the Catholic Church be entirely eliminated from the instruction and training of youth, and that the tender and impressionable minds of youths may be unfortunately infected and ruined by every pernicious error and vice. For, all who have tried to disturb not only the ecclesiastical but also the public welfare, and to overturn the just order of society, and to destroy all rights, divine and human, have always formed all their evil plans, studies, and work to deceive and deprave especially unsuspecting youth, as we have intimated above, and have placed all their hopes in the cor-

---

[1] Letter to Cardinal de la Rochefoucault, March 10, 1791.

ruption of youth. Therefore, they never cease to harass in every unspeakable way both clergy (secular and regular), from whom, as the genuine documents of history splendidly testify, have flowed so many great advantages for Christian, civil, and literary society; and they never cease to declare that the clergy "as an enemy to the true and useful progress of science and government, must be removed from all responsibility and duty of instructing and training youth."

1696 But, in truth, others, renewing the evil and so-many-times-condemned fabrications of the innovators, dare with signal impudence to subject the supreme authority of the Church and of this Apostolic See, given to it by Christ the Lord, to the judgment of the civil authority, and to deny all rights of the same Church and See with regard to those things which pertain to the exterior order.

1697 For, they are not at all ashamed to affirm that "the laws of the Church do not bind in conscience, except when promulgated by the civil power; that the acts and decrees of the Roman Pontiffs relating to religion and the Church, need the sanction and approval, or at least the assent, of the civil power; that the Apostolic Constitutions,[1] in which secret societies are condemned, whether an oath of secrecy is demanded in them or not, and their followers and sympathizers are punished with anathema, have no force in those regions of the world where societies of this sort are allowed by the civil government; that the excommunication uttered by the Council of Trent and the Roman Pontiffs against those who invade and usurp the rights and possessions of the Church rests upon a confusion between the spiritual order and the civil and political order for the attaining of a mundane good only; that the Church should decree nothing which could bind the consciences of the faithful in relation to the use of temporal goods; that to the Church does not belong the right to coerce by temporal punishments violators of its laws; that it is conformable to the principles of sacred theology, and to the principles of public law for the civil government to claim and defend the ownership of the goods which are possessed by churches, by religious orders, and by other pious places."

1698 Nor do they blush to profess openly and publicly the axiom and principle of heretics from which so many perverse opinions and errors arise. For they repeatedly say that "the ecclesiastical power is not by divine right distinct from and independent of the civil power, and that the distinction and independence of the same could not be preserved without the essential rights of the civil power being invaded and usurped by the Church." And, we cannot pass over in silence the boldness of those

---

[1] CLEMENT XII, "In eminenti," April 28, 1738; BENEDICT XIV, "Providas Romanorum," May 18, 1751 [BB(M) 8, 416 ff.]; PIUS VII, "Ecclesiam," Sept. 13, 1821 [BRC 15, 446 b]; LEO XII, "Quo graviora," March 13, 1825 [BRC 16, 345 a ff.].

who "not enduring sound doctrine" [II Tim. 4:3], contend that "without sin and with no loss of Catholic profession, one can withhold assent and obedience to those judgments and decrees of the Apostolic See, whose object is declared to relate to the general good of the Church and its rights and discipline, provided it does not touch dogmas of faith or morals." There is no one who does not see and understand clearly and openly how opposed this is to the Catholic dogma of the plenary power divinely bestowed on the Roman Pontiff by Christ the Lord Himself of feeding, ruling, and governing the universal Church.

In such great perversity of evil opinions, therefore, We, truly mindful 1699 of Our Apostolic duty, and especially solicitous about our most holy religion, about sound doctrine and the salvation of souls divinely entrusted to Us, and about the good of human society itself, have decided to lift Our Apostolic voice again. And so all and each evil opinion and doctrine individually mentioned in this letter, by Our Apostolic authority *We reject, proscribe, and condemn;* and We wish and command that they be considered as absolutely rejected, proscribed, and condemned by all the sons of the Catholic Church.

"Syllabus," or Collection of Modern Errors [1]

[Excerpted from various Allocutions, Encyclicals, Epistles
of PIUS IX, together with (the above quoted) Bull,
"Quanta cura," edited Dec. 8, 1864]

A. Index of the Acts of Pius IX, from which the Syllabus is excerpted

1. The Encyclical Letter, "Qui pluribus," Nov. 9, 1846 (to this are 1700 referred the propositions of the Syllabus 4-7, 16, 40, 63).

---

[1] *Letter of His Eminence Cardinal I. Antonelli . . . with which the Syllabus compiled by order of His Holiness is sent to the bishops.*

Your Most Illustrious and Reverend Lordship:
Our most holy Lord, PIUS IX, Pontifex Maximus, being especially solicitous concerning the salvation of souls and sound doctrine, even from the very beginning of his Pontificate has never ceased by his Encyclical Letters and Allocutions held in Consistories, and by publishing other Apostolic Letters and Allocutions to proscribe and condemn the most conspicuous errors and false doctrines of this especially unhappy age. But, since it could perhaps happen that all these Pontifical acts have not reached each ordinary, therefore, the Supreme Pontiff wished that a Syllabus of the same errors be made to be sent to all the bishops of the whole Catholic world, by which the same bishops could have before their eyes all the errors and dangerous doctrines which have been condemned and proscribed by Him. To me he gave the command to see to it that this printed Syllabus be forwarded to you, your most Illustrious and Reverend Lordship, on this occasion and at the time when the same Supreme Pontiff because of his supreme anxiety about the safety and welfare of the Catholic Church and of the whole flock of the Lord divinely entrusted to him, decided that another Encyclical letter should be written to all Catholic bishops. Therefore, fulfilling the order of the same Pontiff with

2. The Allocution, "Quisque vestrum," Oct. 4, 1847 (Prop. 63).
3. The Allocution, "Ubi primum," Dec. 17, 1847 (Prop. 16).
4. The Allocution, "Quibus quantisque," Apr. 20, 1849 (Prop. 40, 64, 76).
5. The Encyclical Letter, "Nostis et Nobiscum," Dec. 8, 1849 (Prop. 18, 63).
6. The Allocution, "Si semper antea," May 20, 1850 (Prop. 76).
7. The Allocution, "In consistoriali," Nov. 1, 1850 (Prop. 43, 45).
8. The Condemnation, "Multiplices inter," June 10, 1851 (Prop. 15, 21, 23, 30, 51, 54, 68).
9. The Condemnation, "Ad apostolicae," Aug. 22, 1851 (Prop. 24, 25, 34–36, 38, 41, 42, 65–67, 69–75).
10. The Allocution, "Quibus luctuosissimis," Sept. 5, 1851 (Prop. 45).
11. Letter to the KING of Sardinia, Sept. 9, 1852 (Prop. 73).
12. The Allocution, "Acerbissimum," Sept. 27, 1852 (Prop. 31, 51, 53, 55, 67, 73, 74, 78).
13. The Allocution, "Singulari quadam," Dec. 9, 1854 (Prop. 8, 17, 19).
14. The Allocution, "Probe memineritis," Jan. 22, 1855 (Prop. 53).
15. The Allocution, "Cum saepe," July 26, 1855 (Prop. 53).
16. The Allocution, "Nemo vestrum," July 26, 1855 (Prop. 77).
17. The Encyclical Letter, "Singulari quidem," Mar. 17, 1856 (Prop. 4, 16).
18. The Allocution, "Nunquam fore," Dec. 15, 1856 (Prop. 26, 28, 29, 31, 46, 50, 52, 79).
19. The Letter, "Eximiam tuam," to the Archbishop of Cologne, June 15, 1857 (Prop. 14 NB).
20. The Apostolic Letter, "Cum catholica Ecclesia," Mar. 26, 1860 (Prop. 63, 76 NB).
21. The Letter, "Dolore haud mediocri," to the Bishop of Wratislava (Breslau), Apr. 30, 1860 (Prop. 14 NB).
22. The Allocution, "Novos et ante," Sept. 28, 1860 (Prop. 19, 62, 76, NB).
23. The Allocution, "Multis gravibusque," Dec. 17, 1860 (Prop. 37, 43, 73).
24. The Allocution, "Iamdudum cernimus," Mar. 18, 1861 (Prop. 37, 61, 76, NB, 80).
25. The Allocution, "Meminit unusquisque," Sept. 30, 1861 (Prop. 20).
26. The Allocution, "Maxima quidem," June 9, 1862 (Prop. 1–7, 15, 19, 27, 39, 44, 49, 56–60, 76, NB).

---

all speed and, as is proper, with all obedience, I hasten to send to you, Your Most Illustrious and Reverend Lordship, the same Syllabus together with this letter. . . . [Clausula] Dec. 8, 1864.—ASS 3 (1867) 167 f.

27. The Letter, "Gravissimas inter," to the Archbishop of Munich-Freising, Dec. 11, 1862 (Prop. 9–11).
28. The Encyclical Letter, "Quanto conficiamur moerore," Aug. 10, 1863 (Prop. 17, 58).
29. The Encyclical Letter, "Incredibili," Sept. 17, 1863 (Prop. 26).
30. The Letter, "Tuas libenter," to the Archbishop of Munich-Freising, Dec. 21, 1863 (Prop. 9, 10, 12–14, 22, 33).
31. The Letter, "Cum non sine," to the Archbishop of Friburg, July 14, 1864 (Prop. 47, 48).
32. The Letter, "Singularis Nobisque," to the Bishop of Montreal (?), Sept. 29, 1864 (Prop. 32).

B. Syllabus [1]

Comprising the particular errors of our age, which are noted in consistorial Allocutions, in Encyclical and other Apostolic Letters of His Holiness, our Lord Pope Pius IX [2]

Sec. 1. Pantheism, Naturalism, and Absolute Rationalism

1. No supreme, all wise, and all provident divine Godhead exists, distinct from this world of things, and God is the same as the nature of things and, therefore, liable to changes; and God comes into being in man and in the universe, and all things are God and they have the same substance of God; and God is one and the same as the world, and therefore, also, spirit is one and the same with matter, necessity with liberty, the true with the false, the good with the evil, and the just with the unjust (26).[3]   1701

2. All action of God upon men and the world must be denied (26).   1702

3. Human reason, with absolutely no regard to God, is the only judge of the true and the false, the good and the evil; it is a law unto itself and is, by its own natural powers, sufficient to provide for the good of individuals and of peoples (26).   1703

4. All truths of religion flow from the natural power of human reason; hence, reason is the chief norm by which man can and should come to a knowledge of all truths of whatever kind (1, 17, 26).   1704

---

[1] ASS 3 (1867) 168 ff.; Aexq IX ff.; AP III 701 ff.

[2] In order that the true meaning of this Syllabus may be understood, one must refer to the context of the documents from which the individual propositions have been excerpted [cf. the letter of Cardinal Antonelli quoted above (page 482, note); ASS 3, 167: L. Choupin, "Valeur des décisions doctrinales et disciplinaires du Saint-Siège, 3 ed. 1929, 187 ff.].

[3] These numbers refer to the INDEX "of the Acts of PIUS IX, from which the Syllabus has been excerpted" [see above n. 1700].

1705   5. Divine revelation is imperfect, and therefore subject to continuous and indefinite progress, which corresponds to the progress of human reason (1 [cf. n. 1636] 26).

1706   6. The faith of Christ is opposed to human reason; and divine revelation is not only of no benefit to, but even harms the perfection of man (1 [see n. 1635] 26).

1707   7. The prophecies and miracles described and related in Sacred Scripture are the inventions of poets; and the mysteries of the Christian faith are the culmination of philosophical investigations; and in the books of both Testaments are contained mythical inventions; and Jesus Christ Himself is a mythical fiction (1, 26).

Sec. II. Modified Rationalism

1708   8. Since human reason is equal to religion itself, therefore, theological studies must be conducted just as the philosophical (13 [see n. 1642]).

1709   9. All the dogmas of the Christian religion without distinction are the object of natural science or philosophy; and human reason, cultivated so much throughout history, can by its natural powers and principles arrive at the true knowledge of all, even the more hidden dogmas, provided these dogmas have been proposed to reason itself as its object (27, 30 [see n. 1682]).

1710   10. Since a philosopher is one thing and philosophy another, the former has the right and the duty to submit himself to the authority which he himself has proved to be true; but philosophy cannot and should not submit itself to any authority (27 [see n. 1673] 30 [see n. 1674]).

1711   11. The Church should not only never pay attention to philosophy, but should also tolerate the errors of philosophy, and leave it to correct itself (27 [see n. 1675]).

1712   12. The decrees of the Apostolic See and of the Roman Congregations hinder the free progress of science (30 [see n. 1679]).

1713   13. The method and principles according to which the ancient scholastic doctors treated theology are by no means suited to the necessities of our times and to the progress of the sciences (30 [see n. 1680]).

1714   14. Philosophy is to be treated without any regard to supernatural revelation (30).

N.B. To the system of rationalism are closely connected in great part the errors of Anthony Guenther which are condemned in the Epistle to the Card. Archbishop of Cologne, *"Eximiam tuam,"* Jun. 15, 1857 (19) [see n. 1655], and in the Epistle to the Bishop of Breslau, *"Dolore haud mediocri,"* Apr. 30, 1860 (21).

Sec. III. Indifferentism, Latitudinarianism

15. Everyman is free to embrace and profess that religion which he, 1715
led by the light of reason, thinks to be the true religion (8, 26).

16. In the worship of any religion whatever, men can find the way to 1716
eternal salvation, and can attain eternal salvation (1, 3, 17).

17. We must have at least good hope concerning the eternal salvation 1717
of all those who in no wise are in the true Church of Christ (13 [see
n. 1646] 28 [see n. 1677]).

18. Protestantism is nothing else than a different form of the same 1718
true Christian religion, in which it is possible to serve God as well as
in the Catholic Church (5).

Sec. IV. Socialism, Communism, Secret Societies, Biblical Societies, Clerico-liberal Societies

Evils of this sort have been reproved often and in very severe words 1718a
in the Encyclical Letter, "Qui Pluribus," Nov. 9, 1846 (1); in the Allocution, "Quibus quantisque," Apr. 20, 1849 (4); in the Encyclical Epistle,
"Nostis et Nobiscum," Dec. 8, 1849 (5); in the Allocution, "Singulari
quadam," Dec. 9, 1854 (13); in the Encyclical Epistle, "Quanto conficiamur moerore," Aug. 10, 1863 (28).

Sec. V. Errors Concerning the Church and Its Rights

19. The Church is not a true and perfect society absolutely free, nor 1719
does it operate by its own fixed and proper rights conferred on it by
its divine founder; but it belongs to the civil power to define which
are the rights of the Church, and the limits within which it may exercise
these rights (13, 23, 26).

20. The ecclesiastical power should not exercise its authority without 1720
the permission and assent of the civil government (25).

21. The Church does not have the power of defining dogmatically that 1721
the religion of the Catholic Church is the only true religion (8).

22. The obligation by which Catholic teachers and writers are abso- 1722
lutely bound is restricted to those matters only which are proposed by
the infallible judgment of the Church, to be believed by all as dogmas of
faith (30 [see n. 1683]).

23. The Roman Pontiffs and the Ecumenical Councils have trespassed 1723
the limits of their powers, have usurped the rights of princes, and have
even erred in defining matters of faith and morals (8).

24. The Church does not have the power of using force, nor does it 1724
have any temporal power, direct or indirect (9).

25. Besides the power inherent in the episcopate, there is another 1725
temporal power attributed, either expressly or tacitly granted by the civil

government, to be revoked, therefore, at will by the civil government (9).

1726   26. The Church does not have a natural and legitimate right to acquire and to possess (18, 29).

1727   27. The sacred ministers of the Church and the Roman Pontiff should be entirely excluded from all administration and dominion over temporal things (26).

1728   28. Without the permission of the government, it is not lawful for bishops to issue even Apostolic Letters (18).

1729   29. Favors granted by the Roman Pontiff should be considered void, unless they have been requested through the government (18).

1730   30. The immunity of the Church and of ecclesiastical persons had its origin in civil law (8).

1731   31. The ecclesiastical court for the temporal cases of clerics, whether civil or criminal, should be absolutely abolished, even if the Apostolic See was not consulted, and protests (12, 18).

1732   32. Without any violation of natural right and equity, the personal immunity by which clerics are exempted from the obligation of under-going and practising military service, can be abolished; in truth, civil progress demands this abrogation, especially in a society organized on the form of a more liberal government (32).

1733   33. It does not belong exclusively to the ecclesiastical power of juris-diction, by proper and natural right, to direct the teaching of theological matters (30).

1734   34. The doctrine of those who compare the Roman Pontiff to a free prince acting in the universal Church is a doctrine which prevailed in the Middle Ages (9).

1735   35. There is nothing to forbid that by the vote of a General Council or by the action of all peoples the Supreme Pontificate be transferred from the Roman Bishop and THE CITY to another bishopric and another city (9).

1736   36. The definition of a national council allows no further discussion, and the civil administration can force the matter to those boundaries (9).

1737   37. National churches can be established which are exempt and com-pletely separated from the authority of the Roman Pontiff (23, 24).

1738   38. The excessive decisions of the Roman Pontiffs contributed too much to the division of the Church into East and West (9).

Sec. VI. Errors Concerning Civil Society, Viewed Both in Themselves and in Their Relations to the Church

1739   39. The state of the commonwealth, inasmuch as it is the origin and source of all rights, exercises a certain right bound by no limits (26).

1740   40. The doctrine of the Catholic Church is opposed to the good and to the advantages of human society (1 [see n. 1634], 4).

41. To the civil power, even if exercised by an infidel ruler, belongs 1741
the indirect negative power over sacred things; and hence to the same
belongs not only the right which is called *exsequatur* but also the right,
as they call it, *of appeal as from an abuse* (9).

42. In a conflict between the laws of both powers, the civil law pre- 1742
vails (9).

43. The lay power has the authority of rescinding, of declaring and 1743
making void the solemn agreements (commonly, concordats) made with
the Apostolic See concerning the use of rights pertaining to ecclesiastical
immunity, without its consent and even against its protests (7, 23).

44. The civil authority can interfere in matters which pertain to reli- 1744
gion, morals, and spiritual government. Hence, it can judge about the
instructions which the pastors of the Church, in accordance with their
duty, issue as a guide to consciences; nay even, it can make decrees concerning the administration of the divine sacraments and the dispositions
necessary to receive them (7, 26).

45. The entire government of the public schools in which the youth 1745
of any Christian state is instructed, episcopal seminaries being excepted
for some reason, can and should be assigned to the civil authority; and
assigned in such a way, indeed, that for no other authority is the right
recognized to interfere in the discipline of the schools, in the system of
studies, in the conferring of degrees, in the choice or approval of teachers
(7, 10).

46. Nay, even in the seminaries themselves for the clergy, the plan 1746
of studies to be followed is subject to the civil authority (18).

47. The best state of civil society demands that the peoples' schools 1747
which are open to all children of any class of people, and the public
institutions in general which are destined for the teaching of literature
and the more exact studies, and for caring for the education of youth,
should be exempted from all authority, control, and power of the Church;
and be subjected to the full authority of the civil and political power,
exactly according to the pleasure of the rulers and the standard of current
public opinion (31).

48. Catholic men can approve that method of instructing youth which 1748
has been divorced from Catholic Faith and the power of the Church,
and which regards only, or at least primarily, the natural sciences and
the purposes of social life on earth alone (31).

49. Civil authority can hinder bishops and the faithful people from 1749
freely and reciprocally communicating with the Roman Pontiff (26).

50. The lay authority has of itself the right of presenting bishops, and 1750
can compel them to enter upon the administration of their dioceses before
they receive from the Holy See their canonical appointment and Apostolic Letters (18).

1751   51. Moreover, secular government has the right of deposing bishops from the exercise of their pastoral ministry, and is not bound to obey the Roman Pontiff in those matters which regard the institution of episcopates and bishops (8, 12).

1752   52. The government can by its own right change the age prescribed by the Church for the religious profession of women as well as of men, and can prescribe for all religious orders that they should not admit anyone to the pronouncement of solemn vows without its permission (18).

1753   53. The laws which pertain to the protection of the status of religious orders and to their rights and duties should be abrogated; indeed, the civil government can furnish aid to all those who wish to abandon the institute of the religious life which they once accepted, and to break their solemn vows; and likewise, it can suppress these same religious orders, as well as collegiate churches and simple benefices, even those of the right of patronage, and can lay claim to, and subject their property and revenues to the administration and will of the civil power (12, 14, 15).

1754   54. Kings and princes are not only exempt from the jurisdiction of the Church, but they also are superior to the Church in deciding questions of jurisdiction (8).

1755   55. The Church is to be separated from the state, and the state from the Church (12).

Sec. VII. Errors Concerning Natural and Christian Ethics

1756   56. The laws of morals by no means need divine sanction, and there is not the least need that human laws conform to the natural law, or receive the power of binding from God (26).

1757   57. The science of philosophy and of morals, likewise the civil laws, can and should ignore divine and ecclesiastical authority (26).

1758   58. Other powers should not be recognized except those which have their basis in the material (physical side of man), and all moral discipline and honesty should be employed to accumulate and increase wealth in any way whatsoever, and to satisfy man's pleasures (26, 28).

1759   59. Right consists in a physical fact; all the duties of men are an empty name, and all human deeds have the force of right (26).

1760   60. Authority is nothing more than numbers and the sum of material strengths (26).

1761   61. The chance injustice of an act brings no detriment to the sanctity of the right (24).

1762   62. The principle of "nonintervention" must be proclaimed and observed (22).

1763   63. It is lawful to withhold obedience to legitimate rulers, indeed even to rebel (1, 2, 5, 20).

64. The violation of any most sacred oath, and even any criminal and 1764
disgraceful action repugnant to eternal law, not only must by no means
be reproved, but is even altogether lawful and worthy of the highest
praise, when it is done for love of country (4).

Sec. VIII. *Errors Concerning Christian Marriage*

65. In no way can it be asserted that Christ raised matrimony to the 1765
dignity of a sacrament (9).

66. The sacrament of matrimony is nothing but an appendage to 1766
the contract and separable from it, and the sacrament itself consists
merely in the nuptial blessing (9).

67. By natural law the bond of matrimony is not indissoluble, and in 1767
various cases divorce, properly so-called, can be sanctioned by civil
authority (9, 12 [see n. 1640]).

68. The Church does not have the power to establish impediments 1768
nullifying marriage; but that power belongs to civil authority by which
the existing impediments should be removed (8).

69. The Church in later centuries began to introduce diriment im- 1769
pediments, not by its own right, but by making use of a right which
it had borrowed from the civil power (9).

70. The canons of the Council of Trent which impose the censure of 1770
anathema on those who have the boldness to deny to the Church the
power of introducing diriment impediments [see n. 973 f.], are either
not dogmatic, or are to be understood in accordance with this borrowed
power (9).

71. The formula of the Council of Trent [see n. 990] does not oblige 1771
under penalty of nullity where the civil law prescribes another formula,
and wishes to validate a marriage by the intervention of this new
formula (9).

72. Boniface VIII was the first to declare that the vow of chastity 1772
taken in ordination renders marriages invalid (9).

73. A true marriage can exist between Christians by virtue of a purely 1773
civil contract; and it is false to assert that the contract of marriage between Christians is always a sacrament; or, that there is no contract if
the sacrament is excluded (9, 11, 12 [see n. 1640] 23).

74. Matrimonial cases and betrothals by their very nature belong to 1774
the civil court (9, 12 [see n. 1640]).

N.B. Two other errors can contribute to this subject: about abolishing the 1774a
celibacy of the clergy, and concerning the state of matrimony to be preferred
to the state of virginity. The first is thoroughly discussed in the Encyclical
Epistle, "Qui pluribus," Nov. 9, 1846 (1); the second in the Apostolic Letter
"Multiplices inter," June 10, 1851 (8).

Sec. IX. Errors Concerning the Civil Power of the Roman Pontiff

1775 75. The sons of the Christian and Catholic Church dispute about the compatibility of the temporal power with the spiritual (9).

1776 76. The abolition of the civil power which the Apostolic See possesses, would be extremely conducive to the liberty and prosperity of the Church (4, 6).

1776a N.B. Besides these errors explicitly noted, many others are implicitly condemned, by setting forth and declaring the doctrine which all Catholics should hold firmly regarding the civil power of the Roman Pontiff. Doctrine of this sort is lucidly set forth in the Allocution, "Quibus quantisque," April 20, 1849 (4); in the Allocution, "Si semper antea," May 20, 1850 (6); in the Apostolic Letter, "Cum catholica ecclesia," March 26, 1860 (20); in the Allocution, "Novos et ante," September 28, 1860 (22); in the Allocution, "Iamdudum cernimus," March 18, 1861 (24); in the Allocution, "Maxima quidem," June 9, 1862 (26).

Sec. X. Errors Which Are Related to Modern Liberalism

1777 77. In this age of ours it is no longer expedient that the Catholic religion should be the only religion of the state, to the exclusion of all other cults whatsoever (16).

1778 78. Hence in certain regions of Catholic name, it has been laudably sanctioned by law that men immigrating there be allowed to have public exercises of any form of worship of their own (12).

1779 79. For it is false that the civil liberty of every cult, and likewise, the full power granted to all of manifesting openly and publicly any kind of opinions and ideas, more easily leads to the corruption of the morals and minds of the people, and to the spread of the evil of indifferentism (18).

1780 80. The Roman Pontiff can and should reconcile and adapt himself to progress, liberalism, and the modern civilization (24).

THE VATICAN COUNCIL 1869–1870

Ecumenical XX (on Faith and the Church)

Session iii (April 24, 1870)

Dogmatic Constitution concerning the Catholic Faith [1]

1781 But now, with the bishops of the whole world sitting and judging with Us, gathered together in this Ecumenical Council by Our authority in the Holy Spirit, We, having relied on the Word of God, written and trans-

---

[1] CL VII 248 b ff.; ASS 5 (1869) 462 ff. Cf. EB n. 61 ff.

mitted as We have received it, sacredly guarded and accurately explained by the Catholic Church, from this chair of PETER, in the sight of all, have determined to profess and to declare the salutary doctrine of Christ, after contrary errors have been proscribed and condemned by the power transmitted to Us by God.

Chap. 1. God, Creator of All Things

[*The one, living, and true God and His distinction from all things.*] [1] **1782**
The holy, Catholic, Apostolic, Roman Church believes and confesses that there is one, true, living God, Creator and Lord of heaven and earth, omnipotent, eternal, immense, incomprehensible, infinite in intellect and will, and in every perfection; who, although He is one, singular, altogether simple and unchangeable spiritual substance, must be proclaimed distinct in reality and essence from the world; most blessed in Himself and of Himself, and ineffably most high above all things which are or can be conceived outside Himself [can. 1–4].

[*The act of creation in itself, and in opposition to modern errors, and* **1783** *the effect of creation*]. This sole true God by His goodness and "omnipotent power," not to increase His own beatitude, and not to add to, but to manifest His perfection by the blessings which He bestows on creatures, with most free volition, "immediately from the beginning of time fashioned each creature out of nothing, spiritual and corporeal, namely angelic and mundane; and then the human creation, common as it were, composed of both spirit and body" [Lateran Council IV, see n. 428; can. 2 and 5].

[*The result of creation*]. But God protects and governs by His provi- **1784** dence all things which He created, "reaching from end to end mightily and ordering all things sweetly" [cf. Wisd. 8:1]. For "all things are naked and open to His eyes" [Heb. 4:13], even those which by the free action of creatures are in the future.

Chap. 2. Revelation

[*The fact of positive supernatural revelation*]. The same Holy Mother **1785** Church holds and teaches that God, the beginning and end of all things, can be known with certitude by the natural light of human reason from created things; "for the invisible things of him, from the creation of the world, are clearly seen, being understood by the things that are made" [Rom. 1:20]; nevertheless, it has pleased His wisdom and goodness to reveal Himself and the eternal decrees of His will to the human race in another and supernatural way, as the Apostle says: "God, who at sundry

---

[1] The order of things is indicated here according to the exposition proposed to the Fathers by the speakers of the deputations in the Council itself; CL VII 101 ff.

times and in divers manners, spoke in times past to the fathers by the prophets, last of all, in these days hath spoken to us by His Son" [Heb. 1:1 f; can. 1].

1786 [*The necessity of revelation*]. Indeed, it must be attributed to this divine revelation that those things, which in divine things are impenetrable to human reason by itself, can, even in this present condition of the human race, be known readily by all with firm certitude and with no admixture of error.[1] Nevertheless, it is not for this reason that revelation is said to be absolutely necessary, but because God in His infinite goodness has ordained man for a supernatural end, to participation, namely, in the divine goods which altogether surpass the understanding of the human mind, since "eye hath not seen, nor ear heard, neither hath it entered into the heart of man, what things God hath prepared for them that love Him" [I Cor. 2:9; can. 2 and 3].

1787 [*The source of revelation*]. Furthermore, this supernatural revelation, according to the faith of the universal Church, as declared by the holy synod of Trent, is contained "in the written books and in the unwritten traditions which have been received by the apostles from the mouth of Christ Himself; or, through the inspiration of the Holy Spirit have been handed down by the apostles themselves, and have thus come to us" [Council of Trent, see n. 783]. And, indeed, these books of the Old and New Testament, whole with all their parts, just as they were enumerated in the decree of the same Council, are contained in the older Vulgate Latin edition, and are to be accepted as sacred and canonical. But the Church holds these books as sacred and canonical, not because, having been put together by human industry alone, they were then approved by its authority; nor because they contain revelation without error; but because, having been written by the inspiration of the Holy Spirit, they have God as their author and, as such, they have been handed down to the Church itself (can. 4).

1788 [*The interpretation of Sacred Scripture*]. But, since the rules which the holy Synod of Trent salutarily decreed concerning the interpretation of Divine Scripture in order to restrain impetuous minds, are wrongly explained by certain men, We, renewing the same decree, declare this to be its intention: that, in matters of faith and morals pertaining to the instruction of Christian Doctrine, that must be considered as the true sense of Sacred Scripture which Holy Mother Church has held and holds, whose office it is to judge concerning the true understanding and interpretation of the Sacred Scriptures; and, for that reason, no one is permitted to interpret Sacred Scripture itself contrary to this sense, or even contrary to the unanimous agreement of the Fathers.

---

[1] Cf. St. Thomas, *Summa theol.*, I, q. 1, a. 1.

Chap. 3. Faith

[*The definition of faith*]. Since man is wholly dependent on God as **1789** his Creator and Lord, and since created reason is completely subject to uncreated truth, we are bound by faith to give full obedience of intellect and will to God who reveals [can. 1]. But the Catholic Church professes that this faith, which "is the beginning of human salvation" [cf. n. 801], is a supernatural virtue by which we, with the aid and inspiration of the grace of God, believe that the things revealed by Him are true, not because the intrinsic truth of the revealed things has been perceived by the natural light of reason, but because of the authority of God Himself who reveals them, who can neither deceive nor be deceived [can. 2]. For, "faith is," as the Apostle testifies, "the substance of things to be hoped for, the evidence of things that appear not" [Heb. 11:1].

[*That faith is consonant with reason*]. However, in order that the **1790** "obedience" of our faith should be "consonant with reason" [cf. Rom. 12:1], God has willed that to the internal aids of the Holy Spirit there should be joined external proofs of His revelation, namely: divine facts, especially miracles and prophecies which, because they clearly show forth the omnipotence and infinite knowledge of God, are most certain signs of a divine revelation, and are suited to the intelligence of all [can. 3 and 4]. Wherefore, not only Moses and the prophets, but especially Christ the Lord Himself, produced many genuine miracles and prophecies; and we read concerning the apostles: "But they going forth preached everywhere: the Lord working withal and confirming the word with signs that followed" [Mark 16:20]. And again it is written: "And we have the more firm prophetical word: whereunto you do well to attend, as to a light that shineth in a dark place" [II Pet. 1:19].

[*That faith in itself is a gift of God*]. Moreover, although the assent of **1791** faith is by no means a blind movement of the intellect, nevertheless, no one can "assent to the preaching of the Gospel," as he must to attain salvation, "without the illumination and inspiration of the Holy Spirit, who gives to all a sweetness in consenting to and believing in truth" (Council of Orange, see n. 178 ff.). Wherefore, "faith" itself in itself, even if it "worketh not by charity" [cf. Gal. 5:6], is a gift of God, and its act is a work pertaining to salvation, by which man offers a free obedience to God Himself by agreeing to, and cooperating with His grace, which he could resist [cf. n. 797 f: can. 5].

[*The object of faith*]. Further, by divine and Catholic faith, all those **1792** things must be believed which are contained in the written word of God and in tradition, and those which are proposed by the Church, either in a solemn pronouncement or in her ordinary and universal teaching power, to be believed as divinely revealed.

1793 [*The necessity of embracing faith and retaining it*]. But, since "without faith it is impossible to please God" [Heb. 11:6] and to attain to the fellowship of His sons, hence, no one is justified without it; nor will anyone attain eternal life except "he shall persevere unto the end on it" [Matt. 10:22; 24:13]. Moreover, in order that we may satisfactorily perform the duty of embracing the true faith and of continuously persevering in it, God, through His only-begotten Son, has instituted the Church, and provided it with clear signs of His institution, so that it can be recognized by all as the guardian and teacher of the revealed word.

1794 [*The divine external aid for the fulfillment of the duty of Faith*]. For, to the Catholic Church alone belong all those many and marvelous things which have been divinely arranged for the evident credibility of the Christian faith. But, even the Church itself by itself, because of its marvelous propagation, its exceptional holiness, and inexhaustible fruitfulness in all good works; because of its catholic unity and invincible stability, is a very great and perpetual motive of credibility, and an incontestable witness of its own divine mission.

[*The divine internal aid to the same*]. By this it happens that the Church as "a standard set up unto the nations" [Isa. 11:12], both invites to itself those who have not yet believed, and makes its sons more certain that the faith, which they profess, rests on a very firm foundation. Indeed, an efficacious aid to this testimony has come from supernatural virtue. For, the most benign God both excites the erring by His grace and aids them so that they can "come to a knowledge of the truth" [I Tim. 2:4], and also confirms in His grace those whom "He has called out of darkness into his marvelous light" [I Pet. 2:9], so that they may persevere in this same light, not deserting if He be not deserted [see n. 804]. Wherefore, not at all equal is the condition of those, who, through the heavenly gift of faith, have adhered to the Catholic truth, and of those, who, led by human opinions, follow a false religion; for, those who have accepted the faith under the teaching power of the Church can never have a just cause of changing or doubting that faith [can. 6]. Since this is so, "giving thanks to God the Father, who hath made us worthy to be partakers of the lot of the saints in light" [Col. 1:12], let us not neglect such salvation, but "looking on Jesus, the author and finisher of faith" [Heb. 12:2], "let us hold fast the confession of our hope without wavering" [Heb. 10:23].

Chap. 4. Faith and reason

1795 [*The twofold order of knowledge*]. By enduring agreement the Catholic Church has held and holds that there is a twofold order of knowledge, distinct not only in principle but also in object: (1) in principle, indeed, because we know in one way by natural reason, in another by divine faith; (2) in object, however, because, in addition to things to which natural reason can attain, mysteries hidden in God are proposed to us for belief which, had they not been divinely revealed, could not become known [can. 1]. Wherefore, the Apostle, who testifies that God was known to the Gentiles "by the things that are made" [Rom. 1:20], nevertheless, when discoursing about grace and truth which "was made through Jesus Christ" [cf. John 1:17] proclaims: "We speak the wisdom of God in a mystery, a wisdom which is hidden, which God ordained before the world, unto our glory, which none of the princes of this world know. . . . But to us God hath revealed them by His Spirit. For the Spirit searcheth all things, yea the deep things of God" [I Cor. 2:7, 8, 10]. And the Only-begotten Himself "confesses to the Father, because He hath hid these things from the wise and prudent, and hath revealed them to little ones" [cf. Matt. 11:25].

[*The role of reason in teaching supernatural truth*]. And, indeed, **1796** reason illustrated by faith, when it zealously, piously, and soberly seeks, attains with the help of God some understanding of the mysteries, and that a most profitable one, not only from the analogy of those things which it knows naturally, but also from the connection of the mysteries among themselves and with the last end of man; nevertheless, it is never capable of perceiving those mysteries in the way it does the truths which constitute its own proper object. For, divine mysteries by their nature exceed the created intellect so much that, even when handed down by revelation and accepted by faith, they nevertheless remain covered by the veil of faith itself, and wrapped in a certain mist, as it were, as long as in this mortal life, "we are absent from the Lord: for we walk by faith and not by sight" [II Cor. 5:6 f.].

[*The impossibility of opposition between faith and reason*]. But, al- **1797** though faith is above reason, nevertheless, between faith and reason no true dissension can ever exist, since the same God, who reveals mysteries and infuses faith, has bestowed on the human soul the light of reason; moreover, God cannot deny Himself, nor ever contradict truth with truth. But, a vain appearance of such a contradiction arises chiefly from this, that either the dogmas of faith have not been understood and interpreted according to the mind of the Church, or deceitful opinions are considered as the determinations of reason. Therefore, "every assertion contrary to the truth illuminated by faith, we define to be altogether false" [Lateran Council V, see n. 738].

Further, the Church which, together with the apostolic duty of teach- **1798** ing, has received the command to guard the deposit of faith, has also, from divine Providence, the right and duty of proscribing "knowledge falsely so called" [I Tim. 6:20], "lest anyone be cheated by philosophy and vain deceit" [cf. Col. 2:8; can. 2]. Wherefore, all faithful Christians not only are forbidden to defend opinions of this sort, which are known to be contrary to the teaching of faith, especially if they have been condemned by the Church, as the legitimate conclusions of science, but they shall be altogether bound to hold them rather as errors, which present a false appearance of truth.

1799   [*The mutual assistance of faith and reason, and the just freedom of science*]. And, not only can faith and reason never be at variance with one another, but they also bring mutual help to each other, since right reasoning demonstrates the basis of faith and, illumined by its light, perfects the knowledge of divine things, while faith frees and protects reason from errors and provides it with manifold knowledge. Wherefore, the Church is so far from objecting to the culture of the human arts and sciences, that it aids and promotes this cultivation in many ways. For, it is not ignorant of, nor does it despise the advantages flowing therefrom into human life; nay, it confesses that, just as they have come forth from "God, the Lord of knowledge" [I Kings 2:3], so, if rightly handled, they lead to God by the aid of His grace. And it (the Church) does not forbid disciplines of this kind, each in its own sphere, to use its own principles and its own method; but, although recognizing this freedom, it continually warns them not to fall into errors by opposition to divine doctrine, nor, having transgressed their own proper limits, to be busy with and to disturb those matters which belong to faith.

1800   [*The true progress of knowledge, both natural and revealed*]. For, the doctrine of faith which God revealed has not been handed down as a philosophic invention to the human mind to be perfected, but has been entrusted as a divine deposit to the Spouse of Christ, to be faithfully guarded and infallibly interpreted. Hence, also, that understanding of its sacred dogmas must be perpetually retained, which Holy Mother Church has once declared; and there must never be recession from that meaning under the specious name of a deeper understanding [can. 3]. "Therefore . . . let the understanding, the knowledge, and wisdom of individuals as of all, of one man as of the whole Church, grow and progress strongly with the passage of the ages and the centuries; but let it be solely in its own genus, namely in the same dogma, with the same sense and the same understanding." [1]

Canons (of the Catholic Faith) [2]

1. God the Creator of all things

1801   1. [*Against all errors about the existence of God the Creator*]. If any-one shall have denied the one true God, Creator and Lord of visible and invisible things: let him be anathema [cf. n. 1782].

---

[1] Instruction of Vincent of Lerin, n. 28 [ML 50, 668 (c. 23)].
[2] CL VII 255 a f.; ASS 5 (1869) 469 ff.

2. [*Against materialism*]. If anyone shall not be ashamed to affirm 1802
that nothing exists except matter: let him be anathema [cf. n. 1783].

3. [*Against pantheism*]. If anyone shall say that one and the same 1803
thing is the substance or essence of God and of all things: let him be
anathema [cf. n. 1782].

4. [*Against special forms of pantheism*]. If anyone shall say that finite 1804
things, both corporeal and spiritual, or at least the spiritual, have emanated from the divine substance,

or, that the divine essence by a manifestation or evolution of itself
becomes all things,

or, finally, that God is universal or indefinite being, because by determining Himself, He created all things distinct in genera, in species,
and in individuals: let him be anathema.

5. [*Against pantheists and materialists*]. If anyone does not confess that 1805
the world and all things which are contained in it, both spiritual and
material, as regards their whole substance, have been produced by God
from nothing [cf. n. 1783],

[*Against the Guentherians*], or, shall have said that God created not
by a volition free of all necessity, but as necessarily as He necessarily loves
Himself [cf. n. 1783],

[*Against the Guentherians and the Hermesians*], or, shall have denied
that the world was created to the glory of God: let him be anathema.

2. Revelation

1. [*Against those denying natural theology*]. If anyone shall have said 1806
that the one true God, our Creator and our Lord, cannot be known with
certitude by those things which have been made, by the natural light of
human reason: let him be anathema [cf. 1785].

2. [*Against the deists*]. If anyone shall have said that it is not possible 1807
nor expedient that through divine relation man be taught about God and
the worship to be given to Him: let him be anathema [cf. n. 1786].

3. [*Against the Progressionists*]. If anyone shall have said that man 1808
cannot be drawn by divine power to a knowledge and perfection which
is above the natural, but that he of himself can and ought to reach the
possession of all truth and good by a continual progress: let him be
anathema.

4. If anyone shall not accept the entire books of Sacred Scripture with 1809
all their divisions, just as the sacred Synod of Trent has enumerated
them [see n. 783 f.], as canonical and sacred, or denies that they have
been inspired by God: let him be anathema.

3. Faith

1810   1. [*Against the autonomy of reason*]. If anyone shall have said that human reason is so independent that faith cannot be enjoined upon it by God: let him be anathema [cf. n. 1789].

1811   2. [*Some things must be held as true, which reason itself does not draw from itself*]. If anyone shall have said, that divine faith is not distinguished from a natural knowledge of God and moral things, and that therefore it is not necessary to divine faith that revealed truth be believed because of the authority of God Who reveals it: let him be anathema [cf. n. 1789].

1812   3. [*In faith itself the rights of reason must be preserved*]. If anyone shall have said that divine revelation cannot be made credible by external signs, and for this reason men ought to be moved to faith by the internal experience alone of each one, or by private inspiration: let him be anathema [cf. n. 1790].

1813   4. [*The demonstrability of revelation*]. If anyone shall have said that miracles are not possible, and hence that all accounts of them, even those contained in Sacred Scripture, are to be banished among the fables and myths; or, that miracles can never be known with certitude, and that the divine origin of the Christian religion cannot be correctly proved by them: let him be anathema [cf. n. 1790].

1814   5. [*The liberty of faith and the necessity of grace: against Hermes* (see n. 1618 ff.)]. If anyone shall have said that the assent of the Christian faith is not free, but is necessarily produced by proofs from human reasoning; or, that the grace of God is necessary only for that living faith "which worketh by charity" [Gal. 5:6]: let him be anathema [cf. n. 1791].

1815   6. [*Against the positive doubt of Hermes* (see n. 1619)]. If anyone shall have said that the condition of the faithful and of those who have not yet come to the true faith is equal, so that Catholics can have a just cause of doubting the faith which they have accepted under the teaching power of the Church, by withholding assent until they have completed the scientific demonstration of the credibility and truth of their faith: let him be anathema [cf. n. 1794].

4. Faith and reason
[*Against the pseudo-philosophers and the pseudo-theologians, concerning whom see n. 1679 ff.*]

1816   1. If anyone shall have said that no true mysteries properly so-called are contained in divine revelation, but that all the dogmas of faith can be understood and proved from natural principles, through reason properly cultivated: let him be anathema [cf. n. 1795 f.].

2. If anyone shall have said that the human sciences should be treated 1817
with such liberty that their assertions, although opposed to revealed
doctrine, can be retained as true, and cannot be proscribed by the Church:
let him be anathema [cf. n. 1797–1799].

3. If anyone shall have said that it is possible that to the dogmas 1818
declared by the Church a meaning must sometimes be attributed according to the progress of science, different from that which the Church has
understood and understands: let him be anathema [cf. n. 1800].

And so, fulfilling the obligation of Our supreme pastoral office, by 1819
the incarnation of Jesus Christ We beseech all the faithful of Christ, but
especially those who have charge of, or who perform the duty of teaching; and in fact, by the authority of Our same God and Savior, We
command that they bring their zeal and labor to arrest and banish
these errors from Holy Church, and to extend the light of a most pure
faith.

But, since it is not sufficient to shun heretical iniquity unless these 1820
errors also are shunned which come more or less close to it, we remind
all of the duty of observing also the constitutions and decrees by which
base opinions of this sort, which are not enumerated explicitly here, have
been proscribed and prohibited by this Holy See.

Session iv (July 18, 1870) [1]

Dogmatic Constitution I on the Church of Christ

[*The institution and foundation of the Church*]. "The eternal Pastor 1821
and Bishop of our souls" [I Pet. 2:25], in order to render the saving
work of redemption perennial, willed to build a holy Church, in which,
as in the house of the living God, all the faithful might be contained by
the bond of one faith and charity. Therefore, before His glory was made
manifest, "He asked the Father, not only for the Apostles but also for
those who would believe through their word in Him, that all might be
one, just as the Son Himself and the Father are one" [John 17:20 f.].
Thus, then, as He sent the apostles, whom He had selected from the
world for Himself, as He himself had been sent by the Father [John
20:21], so in His Church He wished the pastors and the doctors to be
"even to the consummation of the world" [Matt. 28:20]. But, that the
episcopacy itself might be one and undivided, and that the entire multitude of the faithful through priests closely connected with one another
might be preserved in the unity of faith and communion, placing the
blessed Peter over the other apostles He established in him the perpetual
principle and visible foundation of both unities, upon whose strength
the eternal temple might be erected, and the sublimity of the Church to

---

[1] CL VII 482 a f.; ASS 6 (1870) 40 ff.

be raised to heaven might rise in the firmness of this faith.[1] And, since the gates of hell, to overthrow the Church, if this were possible, arise from all sides with ever greater hatred against its divinely established foundation, We judge it to be necessary for the protection, safety, and increase of the Catholic flock, with the approbation of the Council, to set forth the doctrine on the institution, perpetuity, and nature of the Sacred Apostolic Primacy, in which the strength and solidarity of the whole Church consist, to be believed and held by all the faithful, according to the ancient and continual faith of the universal Church, and to proscribe and condemn the contrary errors, so pernicious to the Lord's flock.

Chap. 1. The Institution of Apostolic Primacy in Blessed Peter

1822   [*Against heretics and schismatics*]. So we teach and declare that according to the testimonies of the Gospel the primacy of jurisdiction over the entire Church of God was promised and was conferred immediately and directly upon the blessed Apostle Peter by Christ the Lord. For the one Simon, to whom He had before said: "Thou shalt be called Cephas" [John 1:42], after he had given forth his confession with those words: "Thou art Christ, Son of the living God" [Matt. 16:16], the Lord spoke with these solemn words: "Blessed art thou, Simon Bar Jona; because flesh and blood hath not revealed it to thee, but my Father who is in heaven. And I say to thee: That thou art Peter, and upon this rock I will build my church, and the gates of hell shall not prevail against it: and I shall give to thee the keys of the kingdom of heaven. And whatsoever thou shalt bind upon earth, it shall be bound also in heaven: and whatsoever thou shalt loose upon earth, it shall be loosed also in heaven" [Matt. 16:17 ff.]. [*Against Richerius etc. (see n. 1503)*]. And upon Simon Peter alone Jesus after His resurrection conferred the jurisdiction of the highest pastor and rector over his entire fold, saying: "Feed my lambs," "Feed my sheep" [John 21:15 ff.]. To this teaching of Sacred Scriptures, so manifest as it has been always understood by the Catholic Church, are opposed openly the vicious opinions of those who perversely deny that the form of government in His Church was established by Christ the Lord; that to Peter alone, before the other apostles, whether individually or all together, was confided the true and proper primacy of jurisdiction by Christ; or, of those who affirm that the same primacy was not immediately and directly bestowed upon the blessed Peter himself, but upon the Church, and through this Church upon him as the minister of the Church herself.

1823   [Canon]. If anyone then says that the blessed Apostle Peter was not established by the Lord Christ as the chief of all the apostles, and the visible head of the whole militant Church, or, that the same received

---

[1] Cf. St. Leo the Great, *serm. 4 de natali ipsius* c. 2 [ML 54, 150 C].

great honor but did not receive from the same our Lord Jesus Christ directly and immediately the primacy in true and proper jurisdiction: let him be anathema.

Chap. 2. The Perpetuity of the Primacy of Blessed Peter among the Roman Pontiffs

Moreover, what the Chief of pastors and the Great Pastor of sheep, the Lord Jesus, established in the blessed Apostle Peter for the perpetual salvation and perennial good of the Church, this by the same Author must endure always in the Church which was founded upon a rock and will endure firm until the end of the ages. Surely "no one has doubt, rather all ages have known that the holy and most blessed Peter, chief and head of the apostles and pillar of faith and foundation of the Catholic Church, received the keys of the kingdom from our Lord Jesus Christ, the Savior and Redeemer of the human race; and he up to this time and always lives and presides and exercises judgment in his successors, the bishops of the holy See of Rome, which was founded by him and consecrated by his blood, [cf. Council of Ephesus, see n. 112]. Therefore, whoever succeeds Peter in this chair, he according to the institution of Christ himself, holds the primacy of Peter over the whole Church. "Therefore the disposition of truth remains, and blessed Peter persevering in the accepted fortitude of the rock does not abandon the guidance of the Church which he has received." [1] For this reason "it has always been necessary because of mightier pre-eminence for every church to come to the Church of Rome, that is those who are the faithful everywhere," [2] so that in this See, from which the laws of "venerable communion" [3] emanate over all, they as members associated in one head, coalesce into one bodily structure. 1824

[Canon]. If anyone then says that it is not from the institution of Christ the Lord Himself, or by divine right that the blessed Peter has perpetual successors in the primacy over the universal Church, **or** that the Roman Pontiff is not the successor of blessed Peter in the same primacy, let him be anathema. 1825

Chap. 3. The Power and Manner of the Primacy of the Roman Pontiff

[*Assertion of primacy*]. Therefore, relying on the clear testimonies of Sacred Scripture, and adhering to the eloquent and manifest decisions not only of Our predecessors, the Roman Pontiffs, but also of the general Councils, We renew the definition of the Ecumenical Council of Flor- 1826

---

[1] St. Leo, the Great, *sermo 3 de natali ipsius* c. 3 [ML 54, 146 B].
[2] St. Irenaeus, *Adv. haereses* I. 3, c. 3 [MG 7, 849 A].
[3] St. Ambrose, Ep. 11, n. 4 [ML 16, 946 A].

ence, by which all the faithful of Christ most believe "that the Apostolic See and the Roman Pontiff hold primacy over the whole world, and that the Pontiff of Rome himself is the successor of the blessed Peter, the chief of the apostles, and is the true vicar of Christ and head of the whole Church and faith, and teacher of all Christians; and that to him was handed down in blessed Peter, by our Lord Jesus Christ, full power to feed, rule, and guide the universal Church, just as is also contained in the records of the ecumenical Councils and in the sacred canons" [see n. 694].

1827   [*Consequences denied by innovators*]. Furthermore We teach and de-clare that the Roman Church, by the disposition of the Lord, holds the sovereignty of ordinary power over all others, and that this power of jurisdiction on the part of the Roman Pontiff, which is truly episcopal, is immediate; and with respect to this the pastors and the faithful of whatever rite and dignity, both as separate individuals and all together, are bound by the duty of hierarchical subordination and true obedience, not only in things which pertain to faith and morals, but also in those which pertain to the discipline and government of the Church [which is] spread over the whole world, so that the Church of Christ, protected not only by the Roman Pontiff, but by the unity of communion as well as of the profession of the same faith is one flock under the one highest shepherd. This is the doctrine of Catholic truth from which no one can deviate and keep his faith and salvation.

1828   [*The jurisdiction of the Roman Pontiff and of the bishops*]. This power of the Supreme Pontiff is so far from interfering with that power of ordinary and immediate episcopal jurisdiction by which the bishops, who, "placed by the Holy Spirit" [cf. Acts 20:28], have succeeded to the places of the apostles, as true shepherds individually feed and rule the individual flocks assigned to them, that the same (power) is asserted, confirmed, and vindicated by the supreme and universal shepherd, according to the statement of Gregory the Great: "My honor is the universal honor of the Church. My honor is the solid vigor of my brothers. Then am I truly honored, when the honor due to each and everyone is not denied." [1]

1829   [*Free communication with all the faithful*]. Furthermore, it follows that from that supreme power of the Roman Pontiff of ruling the uni-versal Church, the same has the right in the exercise of this duty of his office of communicating freely with the pastors and flocks of the whole Church, so that the same can be taught and guided by him in the way of salvation. Therefore, We condemn and disapprove the opinions of those who say that this communication of the supreme head with pastors and flocks can lawfully be checked, or who make this so sub-

---

[1] St. Gregory's letter to Eulogius, Bishop of Alexandria, l. 8, c. 30 [ML 77, 933 C].

missive to secular power that they contend that whatever is established by the Apostolic See or its authority for the government of the Church has no force or value unless confirmed by an order of the secular power [*Placitum regium,* see n. 1847].

[*Recourse to the Roman Pontiff as the supreme judge*]. And since the 1830 Roman Pontiff is at the head of the universal Church by the divine right of apostolic primacy, We teach and declare also that he is the supreme judge of the faithful [cf. n. 1500], and that in all cases pertaining to ecclesiastical examination recourse can be had to his judgment [cf. n. 466]; moreover, that the judgment of the Apostolic See, whose authority is not surpassed, is to be disclaimed by no one, nor is anyone permitted to pass judgment on its judgment [cf. n. 330 ff.]. Therefore, they stray from the straight path of truth who affirm that it is permitted to appeal from the judgments of the Roman Pontiffs to an ecumenical Council, as to an authority higher than the Roman Pontiff.

[*Canon*]. If anyone thus speaks, that the Roman Pontiff has only the 1831 office of inspection or direction, but not the full and supreme power of jurisdiction over the universal Church, not only in things which pertain to faith and morals, but also in those which pertain to the discipline and government of the Church spread over the whole world; or, that he possesses only the more important parts, but not the whole plenitude of this supreme power; or that this power of his is not ordinary and immediate, or over the churches altogether and individually, and over the pastors and the faithful altogether and individually: let him be anathema.

Chap. 4. The Infallible "Magisterium" of the Roman Pontiff

[*Arguments from public documents*]. Moreover, that by the very 1832 apostolic primacy which the Roman Pontiff as the successor of Peter, the chief of the Apostles, holds over the universal Church, the supreme power of the *magisterium* is also comprehended, this Holy See has always held, the whole experience of the Church approves, and the ecumenical Councils themselves, especially those in which the East convened with the West in a union of faith and charity, have declared. For the fathers 1833 of the fourth council of Constantinople, adhering to the ways of the former ones, published this solemn profession: "Our first salvation is to guard the rule of right faith [. . .]. And since the sentiment of our Lord Jesus Christ cannot be passed over when He says: 'Thou art Peter; and upon this rock I will build my church' [Matt. 16:18], these words which were spoken are proven true by actual results, since in the Apostolic See the Catholic religion has always been preserved untainted, and holy doctrine celebrated. Desiring, then, least of all to be separated from the faith and teaching of this [Apostolic See], We hope that We may deserve to be in the one communion which the Apostolic See proclaims, in which the solidarity of the Christian religion is whole and true"[1]

1834 [cf. n. 171 f.]. Moreover, with the approval of the second council of Lyons, the Greeks have professed, "that the Holy Roman Church holds the highest and the full primacy and pre-eminence over the universal Catholic Church, which it truthfully and humbly professes it has received with plenitude of power from the Lord Himself in blessed Peter, the chief or head of the Apostles, of whom the Roman Pontiff is the successor; and, just as it is bound above others to defend the truth of

1835 faith, so, too, if any questions arise about faith, they should be defined by its judgment" [cf. n. 466]. Finally, the Council of Florence has defined: "That the Roman Pontiff is the true vicar of Christ and head of the whole Church and the father and teacher of all Christians; and to it in the blessed Peter has been handed down by the Lord Jesus Christ the full power of feeding, ruling, and guiding the universal Church" [see n. 694].

1836 [*Argument from the assent of the Church*]. To satisfy this pastoral duty, our predecessors always gave tireless attention that the saving doctrine of Christ be spread among all the peoples of the earth, and with equal care they watched that, wherever it was received, it was preserved sound and pure. Therefore, the bishops of the whole world, now individually, now gathered in Synods, following a long custom of the churches and the formula of the ancient rule, referred to this Holy See those dangers particularly which emerged in the affairs of faith, that there especially the damages to faith might be repaired where faith cannot experience a failure.[2] The Roman Pontiffs, moreover, according as the condition of the times and affairs advised, sometimes by calling ecumenical Councils or by examining the opinion of the Church spread throughout the world; sometimes by particular synods, sometimes by employing other helps which divine Providence supplied, have defined that those matters must be held which with God's help they have recognized as in agreement with Sacred Scripture and apostolic tradition. For, the Holy Spirit was not promised to the successors of Peter that by His revelation they might disclose new doctrine, but that by His help they might guard sacredly the revelation transmitted through the apostles and the deposit of faith, and might faithfully set it forth. Indeed, all the venerable fathers have embraced their apostolic doctrine, and the holy orthodox Doctors have venerated and followed it, knowing full well that the See of St. Peter always remains unimpaired by any error, according to the divine promise of our Lord the Savior made to the chief of His disciples: "I have prayed for thee, that thy faith fail not: and thou, being once converted, confirm thy brethren" [Luke 22:32].

[1] Hrd V 778 f.
[2] Cf. St. Bernard, *Letter* (190) *to Innocent II* [ML 182, 1053 D].

So, this gift of truth and a never failing faith was divinely conferred 1837
upon Peter and his successors in this chair, that they might administer
their high duty for the salvation of all; that the entire flock of Christ,
turned away by them from the poisonous food of error, might be
nourished on the sustenance of heavenly doctrine, that with the occasion
of schism removed the whole Church might be saved as one, and relying
on her foundation might stay firm against the gates of hell.

[*Definition of infallibility*]. But since in this very age, in which the 1838
salutary efficacy of the apostolic duty is especially required, not a few
are found who disparage its authority, We deem it most necessary to
assert solemnly the prerogative which the Only-begotten Son of God
deigned to enjoin with the highest pastoral office.

And so We, adhering faithfully to the tradition received from the begin- 1839
ning of the Christian faith, to the glory of God, our Savior, the elevation
of the Catholic religion and the salvation of Christian peoples, with the
approbation of the sacred Council, teach and explain that the dogma has
been divinely revealed: that the Roman Pontiff, when he speaks *ex
cathedra,* that is, when carrying out the duty of the pastor and teacher
of all Christians in accord with his supreme apostolic authority he explains a doctrine of faith or morals to be held by the universal Church,
through the divine assistance promised him in blessed Peter, operates
with that infallibility with which the divine Redeemer wished that His
church be instructed in defining doctrine on faith and morals; and so
such definitions of the Roman Pontiff ~~from himself~~, but not from the
consensus of the Church, are unalterable. *EX SESE OF THEMSELVES.*

[Canon]. But if anyone presumes to contradict this definition of Ours, 1840
which may God forbid: let him be anathema.

Twofold Power on Earth [1]

[From the Encyclical, "Etsi multa luctuosa," Nov. 2, 1873]

Faith (however) teaches and human reason demonstrates that a two- 1841
fold order of things exists, and that at the same time two powers are to
be distinguished on earth, one naturally which looks out for the tranquillity of human society and secular affairs, but the other, whose origin
is above nature, which presides over the city of God, namely, the Church
of Christ, divinely established for the peace and the eternal salvation of
souls. Moreover, these duties of the twofold power have been very wisely
ordained, that "the things that are God's may be rendered to God," and,
on account of God, "to Caesar the things that are Caesar's" [Matt. 22:21],
who "is great on this account, because he is less than heaven; for he himself

---

[1] ASS 7 (1872) 471 f.

belongs to Him to whom belong heaven and every creature." [1] And from him, surely by divine mandate, the Church has never turned aside, which always and everywhere strives to nurture obedience in the souls of her faithful; and they should inviolably keep, (this obedience) to the supreme princes and their laws insofar as they are secular; and, with the Apostle it has taught that princes "are not a terror to the good work, but to the evil," ordering the faithful "to be subject not only for wrath," because the prince "beareth not the sword as an avenger to execute wrath upon him that doth evil, but also for conscience' sake," because in his office "he is God's minister" [Rom. 13:3 ff.]. Moreover, it itself has restricted this fear of princes to evil works, plainly excluding the same from the observance of the divine law, mindful of that which blessed Peter taught the faithful: "But let none of you suffer as a murderer, or a thief, or a railer, or a coveter of other men's things. But if as a Christian, let him not be ashamed, but let him glorify God in that name" [I Pet. 4:15 f.].

The Liberty of the Church [2]

[From the Encyclical, "Quod nunquam," to the bishops of
Prussia, February 5, 1875]

1842 We intend to fulfill parts of Our duty through this letter, announcing to all to whom this matter pertains, and to the whole Catholic world, that those laws are invalid, namely, which are utterly opposed to the constitution of the divine Church. For, the Lord of holy things did not place the powerful of this world over the bishops in these matters which pertain to the holy ministry, but blessed Peter to whom he commended not only His lambs but also His sheep to be fed [cf. John 21:16, 17]; and so by no worldly power, however elevated, can they be deprived of their episcopal office "whom the Holy Ghost hath placed as bishops to rule the Church of God" [cf. Acts 20:28]. Moreover, let those who are hostile to you know that in refusing to pay to Caesar what belongs to God, you are not going to bring any injury to royal authority, nor to detract anything from it; for it is written: "We ought to obey God, rather than men" [Acts 5:29]; and at the same time let them know that everyone of you is prepared to give tribute and obedience to Caesar, not for wrath, but for conscience [cf. Rom. 13:5 f.] in those matters which are under civil authority and power.

---

[1] Tertullian, *Apology*, c. 30 [ML 1, 442 A].
[2] ASS 8 (1874) 253 ff.

Explanation of Transubstantiation [1]

[From the Decree of the Holy Office, July 7, 1875]

Reply to the question: "Whether the explanation of transubstantiation in the sacrament of the most holy Eucharist can be tolerated, which is comprehended by the following propositions:

1. Just as the formal reason for hypostasis is "to be through itself," or, "to subsist through itself," so the formal reason for substance is "to be in itself" and "actually not to be sustained in another as the first subject"; for, rightly are those two to be distinguished: "to be through itself" (which is the formal reason for hypostasis), and "to be in itself" (which is the formal reason for substance). **1843**

2. Therefore, just as human nature in Christ is not hypostasis, because it does not subsist through itself but is assumed from a superior divine hypostasis, so finite substance, for example, the substance of bread, ceases to be substance by this alone and without any change of itself, because it is sustained supernaturally in another, so that it is not already in itself, but in another as in a first subject. **1844**

3. Thus, transubstantiation, or the conversion of the entire substance of bread into the substance of the body of Christ our Lord, can be explained in this way, that the body of Christ, while it becomes substantially present in the Eucharist, sustains the nature of bread, which by this very fact and without any change in itself ceases to be substance, because it is not now in itself, but in another sustaining; and, indeed, the nature of bread remains, but in it the formal reason for substance ceases; and so there are not two substances, but one only, that, of course, of the body of Christ. **1845**

4. Therefore, in the Eucharist the matter and form of the elements of bread remain; but now, existing supernaturally in another, they do not have the nature of substance, but they have the nature of supernatural accident, not as if in the manner of natural accidents they affected the body of Christ, but on this account, insofar as they are sustained by the body of Christ in the manner in which it has been said." **1846**

The reply is that "the doctrine of transubstantiation, as it is set forth here, cannot be tolerated."

Royal Assent [2]

[From the Allocution, "Luctuosis exagitati," March 12, 1877]

. . . Very recently We have been forced to declare that the following can be tolerated: that the acts of the canonical institution of certain **1847**

---

[1] ASS 11 (1878) 606 f.
[2] ASS 10 (1877/78) 54.

bishops be shown to a secular power, so that, as far as We could, We might avert certain baneful consequences, in which there was no longer question of the possession of temporal goods, but of the consciences of the faithful, their peace, the care and salvation of souls, which is the supreme law for us, and which were called into open risk. But in this which We have done in order to avoid most serious dangers, We wish it to be known publicly and again that We entirely disapprove and abominate that unjust law which is called "royal assent," declaring openly that by it the divine authority of the Church is harmed and its liberty violated. . . . [see n. 1829].

LEO XIII 1878–1903

The Reception of Converted Heretics [1]

[From the Decree of the Holy Office, Nov. 20, 1878]

1848 *To the question:* "Whether baptism should be conferred conditionally on heretics who are converted to the Catholic religion, from whatever locality they come, and to whatever sect they pertain?"

The reply is: "In the negative. But in the conversion of heretics, from whatever place or from whatever sect they come, inquiry should be made regarding the validity of the baptism in the heresy which was adopted. Then after the examination has been established in individual cases, if it is found either that none was conferred, or it was conferred without effect, they shall have to be baptized absolutely. But if according to circumstances and by reason of the localities, after the investigation has been completed, nothing is discovered in favor either of validity or invalidity, or, probable doubt still exists regarding the validity of the baptism, then let them be baptized conditionally, in secret. Finally, if it shall be established that it was valid, they will have to be received only for the profession of faith."

Socialism [2]

[From the Encyclical, "Quod Apostolici muneris," Dec. 28, 1878]

1849 From the records of the Gospels the equality of men consists in this, that all have received the same nature, and are called to the same highest dignity of the sons of God; and at the same time that, since the same end is established for all, each is to be judged individually according to the same law, to obtain punishments or rewards according to merit.

[1] ASS 11 (1878) 605 f.
[2] ASS 11 (1878) 372 ff.; AL I 49 ff.

An inequality of right and power, however, emanates from the very author of nature, "from whom all paternity in heaven and earth is named" [Eph. 3:15]. But the souls of princes and subjects, according to Catholic doctrine and precepts, are so bound by mutual duties and rights that both the passion for ruling is tempered and the way of obedience is made easy, steadfast, and most noble. . . .

If, however, it should ever happen that public power is exercised by **1850** princes rashly and beyond measure, the doctrine of the Catholic Church does not permit rising up against them on one's own terms, lest quiet and order be more and more disturbed, or lest society receive greater harm therefrom. Whenever matters have come to such a pass that no other hope of a solution is evident, it teaches that a remedy is to be hastened through the merits of Christian patience, and by urgent prayers to God. But if the decisions of legislators and princes should sanction or order something that is contrary to divine and natural law, the dignity and duty of the Christian name and the opinion of the apostles urge that "we ought to obey God, rather than men" [Acts 5:29].

But also, Catholic wisdom most skillfully provides for public and **1851** domestic tranquillity, supported by the precepts of divine law, through what it holds and teaches concerning the right of ownership and the distribution of goods which have been obtained for the necessities and uses of life. For when Socialists proclaim the right of property to be a human invention repugnant to the natural equality of man, and, seeking to establish community of goods, think that poverty is by no means to be endured with equanimity; and that the possessions and rights of the rich can be violated with impunity, the Church, much more properly and practically, recognizes inequality among men, who are naturally different in strength of body and of mind; also in the possession of goods, and it orders that right of property and of ownership, which proceeds from nature itself, be for everyone intact and inviolate; for it knows that theft and raping have been forbidden by God, the author and vindicator of every right, in such a way that one may not even look attentively upon (*al.: covet*) the property of another, and "that thieves and robbers, no less than adulterers and idolators are excluded from the kingdom of heaven" [cf. I Cor. 6:9 f.].

And yet she does not on this account neglect the care of the poor, **1852** or, as a devoted mother, fail to take thought for their necessities; but rather, embracing them with maternal affection, and realizing well that they represent the person of Christ Himself, who considers as done to Himself whatever benefit is conferred by anyone on the least of the poor, holds them in great honor; she relieves them by every resource possible; she has erected everywhere in the world homes and hospices to receive them, and to nourish and to care for them, and she takes these institutions under her loving care. By most urgent precept she commands the rich to distribute their superfluous possessions among the poor, and terrifies them by the divine judgment, whereby, unless they go to the aid of the needy poor, they are to be tormented by everlasting punishments. Finally, she especially refreshes and consoles the souls of the poor either by presenting the example of Christ who, "although he was rich, became poor for our sakes" [cf. II Cor. 8:9], or by recalling the words, by which He addressed the poor as "blessed" [cf. Matt. 5:3], and bade them hope for the rewards of eternal blessedness.

Christian Marriage [1]

[From the Encyclical, "Arcanum divinae sapientiae," February 10, 1880]

1853　To the apostles as masters are to be referred the accepted matters which our holy Fathers, the Councils, and the Universal Church have always taught [see n. 970], namely, that Christ our Lord raised matrimony to the dignity of a sacrament, and at the same time brought it about that the spouses strengthened and fortified by heavenly grace which His merits procured, obtain sanctity in the marriage; and that in it, marvelously conformed to the model of the mystical marriage of Himself with the Church, He perfected a love which is befitting to nature [Conc. Trid. sess. 24, c. 1 *de reform. matr.;* cf. n. 969], and He cemented the union of man and woman, indivisible by its own nature, more strongly by the bond of divine love. . . .

1854　And the distinction put forward especially by royal legists must not disturb anyone, in which they separate the nuptial contract from the sacrament, with, of course, this purpose, that, while reserving the conditions of the sacrament to the Church, they may hand over the contract to the power and will of the chiefs of the State. For such a distinction or, more truly, a severance, cannot be approved, since it has been proved that in Christian marriage the contract is inseparable from the sacrament; and so it cannot be a true and legitimate contract without being a sacrament, for this very reason. For, Christ our Lord honored marriage with the dignity of a sacrament; but marriage is the contract itself, provided it is lawfully made. In addition, marriage is a sacrament for this reason, because it is a holy sign, both giving grace and conveying an image of the mystical nuptials of Christ with the Church. Moreover, the form and figure of these nuptials are expressed by the very bond of the supreme union in which man and woman are bound together, and which is nothing other than marriage itself. And thus it is evident that every just union between Christians is in itself and by itself a sacrament;

---

[1] ASS 12 (1879/80) 388 ff.; AL I 120 ff.

and that nothing is more inconsistent with truth than the belief that the sacrament is a kind of added ornament, or an external property which can be disengaged and separated from the contract according to man's pleasure.

The Political Principality [1]

[From the Encyclical, "Diuturnum illud," June 29, 1881]

Although man incited by a kind of arrogance and contumacy often **1855** strives to cast off the reins of government, yet he has never been able to succeed in obeying anyone. In every association and community of men, necessity demands that some be in charge. . . . But it is of interest to note at this point that those who are to be in charge of the state can in certain cases be elected by the will and judgment of the multitude, and Catholic doctrine makes no opposition nor resistance. By this election by which the prince is designated, the rights of principality are not conferred, nor is the power committed, but it is determined by whom it is to be carried on. There is no question here of the kinds of states; for there is no reason why the principality of one person or of several should be approved by the Church, provided it be just and intent upon the common good. Therefore, as long as justice is preserved, peoples are not prohibited from establishing that kind of state for themselves which more aptly befits either their genius or the institutions and customs of their ancestors.

But the Church teaches that what pertains to political power comes **1856** from God. . . . It is a great error not to see what is manifest, that, although men are not solitaries, it is not by congenital free will that they are impelled to a natural community life; and moreover the pact which they proclaim is patently feigned and fictitious, and cannot bestow as much force, dignity, and strength to the political power as the protection of the state and the common welfare of the citizens require. But the principality is to possess these universal glories and aids, only if it is understood that they come from God, the august and most holy source.

That is the one reason for men not obeying, if something is demanded **1857** of them which is openly at odds with natural and divine law; for it is equally wrong to order and to do anything in which the law of nature or the will of God is violated. If, then, it ever happens to anyone to be forced to choose one or the other, namely, to ignore the orders either of God or of princes, obedience must be rendered to Jesus Christ who orders, "the things that are Caesar's, to Caesar; the things that are

---

[1] ASS 14 (1881/82) 4 ff.; AL 211 ff.

God's to God" [cf. Matt. 22:21], and according to the example of the apostles the reply should be made courageously: "We ought to obey God, rather than man" [Acts 5:29]. . . . To be unwilling to refer the right of ordering to God, the author, is nothing else than to wish the most beautiful splendor of political power destroyed, and its nerves cut. . . .

In fact, sudden tumults and most daring rebellions, especially in Germany, have followed that so-called Reformation, whose supporters and leaders have utterly opposed sacred and civil power with new doctrines. . . . From that heresy a falsely called philosophy took its origin in an earlier time, and a right, which they call "new," and a popular power, and an ignorant license which many people consider only liberty. From these we have come to the ultimate plagues, namely, to *communism,* to *socialism,* to *nihilism,* most loathsome monsters and almost destroyers of man's civil society.

1858   Surely the Church of Christ cannot be mistrusted by the princes nor hated by the people. Indeed, she advises the princes to follow justice and in nothing to err from duty; and at the same time she strengthens and aids their authority in many ways. Whatever takes place in the field of civil affairs, she recognizes and declares to be in their power and supreme control; in those matters whose judgment, although for different reasons, pertains to sacred and civil power, she wishes that there exist concord between both, by benefit of which lamentable contentions are avoided for both.

Secret Societies [1]

[From the Encyclical, "Humanum genus," April 20, 1884]

1859   Let no one think that for any reason whatsoever he is permitted to join the Masonic sect, if his profession of Catholicism and his salvation is worth as much to him as it ought to be. Let no pretended probity deceive one; for it can seem to some that the Freemasons demand nothing which is openly contrary to the sanctity of religion and morals, but since the entire reasoning and aim of the sect itself rest in viciousness and shame, it is not proper to permit association with them, or to assist them in any way.

[From the Instruction of the Holy Office, May 10, 1884]

1860   (3) Lest there be any place for error when decision will have to be made as to what the opinions of these pernicious sects are, which are under such prohibition, it is especially certain that Freemasonry and other sects of this kind which plot against the Church and lawful powers,

---

[1] ASS 16 (1883/84) 430 and 17 (1884/85) 44; AL II 71 f.

whether they do this secretly or openly, whether or not they exact from their followers an oath to preserve secrecy, are condemned by automatic excommunication.

(4) Besides these there are also other sects which are prohibited and 1861 must be avoided under pain of grave sin, among which are to be reckoned especially all those which bind their followers under oath to a secret to be divulged to no one, and exact absolute obedience to be offered to secret leaders. It is to be noted, furthermore, that there are some societies which, although it cannot be determined with certainty whether or not they belong to these which we have mentioned, are nevertheless doubtful and full of danger not only because of the doctrines which they profess, but also because of the philosophy of action which those follow under whose leadership they have developed and are governed.

Assistance of a Physician or of a Confessor at a Duel [1]

[From the Response of the Holy Office to the Bishop
of Poitiers, May 31, 1884]

To the question:

I. Can a physician when invited by duelists assist at a duel with the 1862 intention of bringing an end to the fight more quickly, or simply to bind and cure wounds, without incurring the excommunication reserved simply to the Highest Pontiff?

II. Can he at least, without being present at the duel, stay at a neighboring house or in a place nearby, ready to offer his service, if the duelists have need of it.

III. What about a confessor under the same conditions?

The answers are:

To I, he cannot, and excommunication is incurred.

To II and III, that, insofar as it takes place as described, he cannot, and likewise excommunication is incurred.

Cremation of Corpses [2]

[From the Decree of the Holy Office, May 19 and Dec. 15, 1886]

To the question: 1863

I. Whether it is permitted to join societies whose purpose is to promote the practice of burning the corpses of men?

II. Whether it is permitted to command that one's own or the corpses of others be burned?

---

[1] ASS 17 (1884) 601.
[2] ASS 19 (1886), 46 and 25 (1892/93) 63; cf. AE 3 (1895) 98 b f.

The answer on the 19th day of May, 1886 is:

To I. In the negative, and if it is a matter concerned with societies affiliated with the Masonic sect, the penalties passed against this sect are incurred.

To II. In the negative.[1]

Then, on the 15th day of December, 1886:

1864　Insofar as it is a question of those whose bodies are subjected to cremation not by their own will but by that of another, the rites and prayers of the Church can be employed not only at home but also in the church, not, however, at the place of cremation, scandal being avoided. Indeed, scandal can also be avoided if it be known that cremation was not elected by the deceased's own will. But when it is a question of those who elect cremation by their own will, and have persevered in this will definitely and notoriously even until death, with due attention to the decree of Wednesday, May 19, 1886 [given above], action must be taken in such cases according to the norms of the Roman Ritual, Tit. *Quibus non licet dare ecclesiasticam sepulturam* (To whom it is not permitted to give burial in the church). But in particular cases where doubt or difficulty arises, the ordinary will have to be consulted.

Civil Divorce [2]

[From the Decree of the Holy Office, May 27, 1886]

1865　The following questions were raised by some Bishops of France to the inquisition *S.R. et U.:* "In the letter S.R. et U. I. of June 25th, 1885, to all the ordinaries in the territory of France on the law of civil divorce it is decreed thus: "Considering very serious matters, in addition to times and places, it can be tolerated that those who hold magistracies, and lawyers who conduct matrimonial cases in France, without being bound to cede to the office," and it added conditions, of which the second is this: "Provided they are so prepared in mind not only regarding the dignity and nullity of marriage, but also regarding the separation of bodies, about which cases they are obliged to judge, as never to offer an opinion or to defend one to be offered, or to provoke or to incite to that opinion which is at odds with divine and ecclesiastical law."

It is asked:

I. Whether the interpretation is right which is widespread throughout France and even put in print, according to which the judge satisfies the

---

[1] Leo XIII, confirming this decree to the Ordinaries, "ordered that they opportunely have the faithful of Christ instructed on the detestable abuse of cremating human bodies, and that with all their might they deter the flock entrusted to them from this (practice)."

[2] ASS 22 (1889/90) 635 f.

above mentioned condition, who, although a certain marriage is valid in the sight of the Church, ignores that true and unbroken marriage, and applying civil law pronounces that there is ground for divorce, provided he intends in his mind to break only the civil effects and only the civil contract, and provided the terms of the opinion offered consider these alone? In other words, whether an opinion so offered can be said not to be at odds with the divine and ecclesiastical law?

II. After the judge has pronounced that there is ground for divorce, whether the syndic (in French: *le maire*), intent also upon only the civil effects and the civil contract, as is explained above, can pronounce a divorce, although the marriage is valid in the eyes of the Church.

III. After the divorce has been pronounced, whether the same syndic can again join a spouse who strives to enter into other nuptials in a civil ceremony, although the previous marriage is valid in the eyes of the Church and the other party is living?

The answer is:

In the negative to the first, the second,[1] and the third.

The Christian Constitution of States [2]

[From the Encyclical "Immortale Dei," November 1, 1885]

And so God has partitioned the care of the human race between two **1866** powers, namely, ecclesiastical and civil, the one, to be sure, placed over divine, the other over human affairs. Each is highest in its own order; each has certain limits within which it is contained, which are defined by the nature of each and the immediate purpose; and therefore an orbit, as it were, is circumscribed, within which the action of each takes place by its own right.[3] . . . Whatever, then, in human things is in every way sacred, whatever pertains to the salvation of souls or the worship of God, whether it is such by its own nature or again is understood as such because of the purpose to which it is referred, this is entirely

---

[1] But the response of the Holy Penitentiary, given on the 24th day of September, 1887, is worthy of note, according to which it is permitted also for France in a particular case that, after the civil judges have pronounced that there is ground for divorce, the syndic, who would otherwise be ejected from office, pronounced the civil divorce, provided 1) that he profess publicly the Catholic doctrine on matrimony and on matrimonial cases which pertain to ecclesiastical judges only, and provided, 2) in the opinion itself, and as a magistrate speaking in public he declare that he can consider only the civil effects and only the civil contract, that otherwise the bond of matrimony remains entirely firm in the sight of God and conscience" (*Revue de sciences eccles.,* Ambien. 60, 476).

[2] ASS 18 (1885), 166 ff.; AL II 152 ff.

[3] Similarly, the same Pontiff in the Encyclical, "Sapientiae christianae," on the chief duties of Christian citizens, January 10, 1890, says: "The Church and the state, each has its own power; neither obeys the other" [ASS 22 (1889/90), 397].

in the power and judgment of the Church; but other matters, which the civil and political order embraces, are rightly subject to civil authority, since Jesus Christ has ordered: "The things that are Caesar's, render to Caesar; the things that are God's to God" [cf. Matt. 22:21]. But occasions sometimes arise, when another method of concord is also efficacious for peace and liberty, namely, if rulers of public affairs and the Roman Pontiff agree on the same decision in some special matter. On these occasions the Church gives outstanding proof of her motherly devotion, when, as is her wont she shows all possible affability and indulgence. . . .

1867   To wish also that the Church be subject to the civil power in the exercise of her duties is surely a great injustice (to her), and great rashness. By this deed order is disturbed, because the things that are of nature are put over those that are above nature; the frequency of the blessings with which the Church would fill everyday life, if she were not hampered by anything, is destroyed or certainly greatly diminished; and besides a way is prepared for enmities and contentions; and, what great destruction they bring to both powers, the issue of events has demonstrated beyond measure. Such doctrines, which are not approved by human reason and are of great importance for civil discipline, the Roman Pontiffs, Our predecessors, since they understood well what the Apostolic office demanded of them, did by no means allow to pass uncondemned. Thus, Gregory XVI by the encyclical letter beginning, "Mirari vos," on the fifteenth day of August, 1832 [see note 1613 ff.], with great seriousness of purpose struck at those teachings which even then were being preached, that in divine worship no preference should be shown; that individuals are free to form their judgments about religion as they prefer; that one's conscience alone is his guide; and furthermore that it is lawful for everyone to publish what he thinks, and likewise to stir up revolution within the state. On questions of the separation of Church and state the same Pontiff writes thus: "We could not predict happier results both for religion and for the civil government from the wishes of those who desire that the Church be separated from the state, and that the mutual concord between the civil and ecclesiastical authorities be broken off. For, it is manifest that devotees of unhampered freedom fear that concord which has always been beneficial and salutary for both sacred and civil interests."—In a not dissimilar manner Pius IX, as opportunity presented itself, noted many of the false opinions which began to prevail, and afterwards ordered the same to be gathered together so that in, as it were, so great a sea of error, Catholics might have something to follow without mishap.[1]

1868   Moreover, from these precepts of the Pontiffs the following must be

---

[1] Here are cited *ad calcem* from the syllabus propositions 19, 39, 55, 79 [see n. 1719, 1739, 1755, 1779].

thoroughly understood; that the origin of public power should be sought from God Himself, not from the multitude; that free license for sedition is at odds with reason; that it is unlawful for private individuals, unlawful for states to disregard the duties of religion or to be affected in the same way by the different kinds (of religion); that the unrestricted power of thinking and publicly expressing one's opinions is not among the rights of citizens, and is by no means to be placed among matters worthy of favor and support. Similarly, it should be understood that the **1869** Church is a society no less than the state itself, perfect in its kind and in its right; and those who hold the highest power should not act so as to force the Church to serve and to be under them, or so as not to permit her to be free to transact her own affairs, or so as to take from her any of the other rights which have been conferred upon her by Jesus Christ. However, in matters of mixed jurisdiction, it is wholly in accord with **1870** nature, and likewise in accord with the plans of God, that there be no separation of one power from the other, but plainly that there be concord, and this in a manner befitting the closely allied purposes which have given rise to both societies.

This, then, is what is taught by the Church on the establishment and **1871** government of states.—However, by these statements and decrees, if one desire to judge rightly, no one of the various forms of the state is condemned in itself, inasmuch as they contain nothing which is offensive to Catholic doctrine, and they can, if they are wisely and justly applied, preserve the state in its best condition. Neither by any means is this con- **1872** demned in itself, that the people participate more or less in the state; this very thing at certain times and under certain laws can not only be of use to the citizens, but can even be of obligation. Furthermore, neither **1873** does there appear any just cause for anyone charging the Church with being lenient and more than rightly restricted by affability, or with being hostile to that liberty which is proper and lawful. Indeed, if the Church **1874** judges that certain forms of divine worship should not be on the same footing as the true religion, yet she does not therefore condemn governors of states, who, to obtain some great blessing or to prevent an evil, patiently tolerate custom and usage so that individually they each have **1875** a place in the state. And this also the Church especially guards against, that anyone against his will be forced to embrace the Catholic faith, for, as St. Augustine wisely advises: "Man cannot believe except of his free will."[1]

In a like manner the Church cannot approve that liberty which begets **1876** an aversion for the most sacred laws of God and casts aside the obedience due lawful authority. For this is more truly license than liberty. And

---

[1] St. Augustine, *In Io* tr. 26 c. 2 [ML 35 (Aug. III b) 1607].

very rightly is it called "the liberty of ruin" [1] by Augustine, and "a cloak of malice" by the Apostle Peter [I Pet. 2:16]; rather, since it is beyond reason, it is true slavery, for "whosoever committeth sin, is the servant of sin" [John 8:34]. On the other hand, that liberty is genuine and to be sought after, which, from the point of view of the individual, does not permit man to be a slave of errors and passions, most abominable masters, if it guides its citizens in public office wisely, ministers generously to the opportunity for increasing means of well-being, and pro-

1877 tects the state from foreign influence.—This liberty, honorable and worthy of man, the Church approves most of all, and never ceases to strive and struggle for its preservation sound and strong among the nations.—In fact, whatever is of the greatest value in the state for the common welfare; whatever has been usefully established to curb the license of rulers who do not consult the people's good; whatever prevents highest authority from improperly invading municipal and family affairs; whatever is of value for preserving the dignity, the person of man, and the quality of rights among individual citizens, of all such things the records of past ages testify that Catholic Church has always been either the discoverer, or the promoter, or the protector. Therefore, always consistent with herself, if on the one hand she rejects immoderate liberty, which for individuals and states falls into license or slavery, on the other hand she willingly and gladly embraces the better things which the day brings forth, if they truly contain prosperity for this life, which is, as it were,

1878 a kind of course to that other life which is to remain forever. Therefore, when people say that the Church is envious of the more recent political systems, and indiscriminately repudiates whatever the genius of these times has produced, it is an empty and groundless calumny. Indeed, she does repudiate wild opinions; she does disapprove nefarious zeal for seditions, and expressly that habit of mind in which the beginnings of a voluntary departure from God are seen; but since all that is true must come from God, she recognizes whatever has to do with the attaining of truth as a kind of trace of the divine intelligence. And, since there is nothing of truth in the natural order which abrogates faith in teachings divinely transmitted, but many things which confirm it; and since every discovery of truth can lend force to the knowledge and praise of God, accordingly whatever contributes to the extension of the boundaries of knowledge will always do so to the pleasure and joy of the Church; and just as is her custom in the case of other branches of knowledge, so will she also favor and promote those which are concerned with the investigation of nature.

1879   In these studies the Church is not in opposition if the mind discovers

---

[1] Ep. 105 *ad Donatistas* 2, 9 [ML 33, 399].

something new; she does not object to further investigations being made for the refinements and comforts of life; rather, as an enemy of indolence and sloth she wishes especially that the talents of man bear rich fruits by exercise and cultivation; she furnishes incentives to all kinds of arts and works; and by directing through her influence all zeal for such things towards virtue and salvation, she struggles to prevent man from being turned away from God and heavenly blessings by his intelligence and industry. . . .

And so in such a difficult course of events, if Catholics give heed to **1880** us, as they ought, they will easily see what are the duties of each one in matters of opinion as well as of action. And, indeed, in forming opinion, it is necessary to comprehend and hold with a firm judgment whatever the Roman Pontiffs have handed down, and shall hand down, and to profess each publicly as often as occasion demands. And specifically regarding the so-called *liberties* so sought after in recent times, it is necessary for everyone to stand by the judgment of the Apostolic See, and to have the same opinion as that held by it. One should not be deceived by the honorable appearance of these *liberties;* one should consider from what sources they are derived, and by what efforts they are everywhere sustained and promoted. It is well known from experience what results such liberties have achieved in the state; for everywhere they have borne fruits which good and wise man rightly deplore. If such a state really exists anywhere or is imagined in our thoughts, which shamelessly and tyrannically persecutes the name of Christian, and that modern kind of state be compared with it, of which we are speaking, the latter may well seem the more tolerable. Yet the principles upon which it relies are certainly of such a kind, as we have said before, that in themselves they should be approved by no one.

However, action may be concerned with private and domestic affairs or **1881** public affairs.—Certainly in private matters the first duty is to conform life and conduct most diligently to the precepts of the Gospel, and not to refuse to do so when Christian virtue exacts something more than ordinarily difficult to bear and endure. Furthermore, all should love the Church as their common mother; keep her laws obediently; promote her honor, and preserve her rights; and they should try to have her cherished and loved with equal devotion by those over whom they have any authority.

It is also in the public interest to give attention wisely to the affairs of **1882** municipal administration, and in this to strive especially to effect that consideration be given publicly to the formation of youth in religion and in good conduct, in that manner which is right for Christians. On these things especially does the safety of the individual states depend.

Likewise, it is, in general, beneficial and proper for Catholics to extend **1883** their attention further, beyond this, as it were, rather restricted field, and to take in the national government itself. We say "in general," because these precepts of Ours apply to all nations. But it can happen in some places that it is by no means expedient for weighty and just reasons to take part in national politics and to become active in political affairs. But, in general, as we have said, to be willing to take no part in public affairs would be as much at fault as to have no interest and to do nothing for the common good, and even more, because Catholics by the admonition of the very doctrine which they profess are impelled to carry on their affairs with integrity and trust. On the other hand, if they remain indifferent, those whose opinions carry very little hope for the safety of the state will easily seize the reins of government. And this also would be fraught with injury to the Christian religion, because those who were evilly disposed toward the Church would have the greatest power, and those well disposed the least.

1884 Therefore, it is very clear that the reason for Catholics entering public affairs is just, for they do not enter them nor ought they to do so for this reason, so as to approve that which at the moment is not honorable in the methods of public affairs, but to transfer these methods insofar as it can be done, to the genuine and true public good, having in mind the purpose of introducing into all the veins of the state, as a most healthful sap and blood, the wisdom and virtue of the Christian religion. . . .

1885 Lest the union of souls be broken by rash charges, let all understand the following: That the integrity of the Catholic faith can by no means exist along with opinions which border on *naturalism* and *rationalism,* the sum total of which is to tear Christian institutions from their foundations and to establish man's leadership in society, relegating God to second place.—Likewise, that it is not lawful to follow one form of duty in private life, and another in public; for example, so that the authority of the Church is observed in private life, and cast aside in public. For this would be to combine the honorable and the shameful, and to place man in conflict with himself, when on the other hand he should always be in accord with himself, and never in anything or in any manner of life abandon Christian virtue.

1886 But if there is question merely of methods in politics, about the best kind of state, about ordering government in one way or another, surely, in these matters there can be an honorable difference of opinion. Therefore, a dissenting opinion in the matters which we have mentioned on the part of those men whose piety is otherwise known, and whose minds are ready to accept obediently the decrees of the Apostolic See, cannot in justice be considered a sin on their part; and a much greater injury takes place, if they are faced with the charge of having violated or mistrusted the Catholic Faith, which we are sorry to say has taken place more than once.

Let all who are accustomed to express their opinions in writing, and **1887** especially writers for newspapers, bear this precept in mind. In this struggle over most important matters, there can be no place for internal controversies or for party rivalries; and all should strive to preserve religion and the state, which is the common purpose of all. If, therefore, there have been any dissensions before, they should be obliterated by a kind voluntary oblivion; if hitherto there have been rash and injurious actions, those who are in any way to blame for this should make amends with mutual charity, and a kind of special submission should be made on the part of all to the Apostolic See.

In this way Catholics will obtain two very excellent results: one, that of **1888** establishing themselves as helpers of the Church in preserving and propagating Christian wisdom; the other, that of bestowing upon civil society the greatest blessing, the preservation of which is imperiled by evil doctrines, and passions.

Craniotomy and Abortion [1]

[From the Response of the Holy Office to the Archbishop
of Lyons, May 31st, 1899 (May 28th, 1884)]

To the question: Whether it can be safely taught in Catholic schools **1889** that the surgical operation which is called craniotomy is licit, when, of course, if it does not take place, the mother and child will perish; while on the other hand if it does take place, the mother is to be saved, while the child perishes?"

The reply is: "It cannot be safely taught."

[From the reply of the Holy Office to the Archbishop of
Cambrésis, August 19, 1889]

The reply is similar with the following addition: ". . . and every sur- **1890** gical operation that directly kills the fetus or the pregnant mother."

[From the reply of the Holy Office to the Archbishop of
Cambrésis, July 24, 25, 1895] [2]

When the doctor, Titius, was called to a pregnant woman who was **1890a** seriously sick, he gradually realized that the cause of the deadly sickness was nothing else than pregnancy, that is, the presence of the fetus in the

---

[1] ASS 17 (1884) 556 and 22 (1889/90) 749; cf. ASS 7 (1872) 285 ff., 460 ff., 516 ff., and AE 2 (1894) 84, 125, 179, 220, 321 ff.

[2] ASS 28 (1895/96) 383 f.

womb. Therefore, to save the mother from certain and imminent death one way presented itself to him, that of procuring an abortion, or ejection of the fetus. In the customary manner he adopted this way, but the means and operations applied did not tend to the killing of the fetus in the mother's womb, but only to its being brought forth to light alive, if it could possibly be done, although it would die soon, inasmuch as it was not mature.

Yet, despite what the Holy See wrote on August 19th, 1889, in answer to the Archbishop of Cambrésis, that it could not be taught safely that any operation causing the death of the fetus directly, even if this were necessary to save the mother, was licit, the doubting Titius clung to the licitness of surgical operations by which he not rarely procured the abortion, and thus saved pregnant women who were seriously sick.

Therefore, to put his conscience at rest Titius suppliantly asks: Whether he can safely repeat the above mentioned operations under the reoccurring circumstances.

The reply is:

In the negative, according to other decrees, namely, of the 28th day of May, 1884, and of 19th day of August, 1889.

But on the following Thursday, on the 25th day of July . . . our most holy Lord approved a resolution of the Most Eminent Fathers, as reported to him.

[From the reply of the Holy Office to the Bishop of
Sinaboa, May 4, 6, 1898] [1]

1890b   I. Will the acceleration of the birth be licit, when because of the woman's structure the delivery of the fetus would be impossible at its own natural time?

II. And, if the structure of the woman is such that not even a premature birth is considered possible, will it be permitted to cause an abortion, or to perform a Caesarean operation in its time?

III. Is a laparotomy licit, when it is a matter of an extrauterine pregnancy, or of ectopic conceptions?

The reply is:

To I. That the acceleration of the birth *per se* is not illicit, provided it is performed for good reasons at that time, and according to the method by which under ordinary conditions consideration is given to the lives of the mother and the fetus.

To II. With respect to the first part, *in the negative,* according to the decree (issued) on Wednesday, the 24th of July, 1895, on the illicitness of abortion.—As to what pertains to the second part, nothing prevents

---

[1] ASS 30 (1897/98) 703 f.

the woman, who is concerned, from submitting to a Caesarean operation in due time.

To III. That when necessity presses, a laparotomy is licit for extracting ectopic conceptions from the womb of the mother, provided, insofar as it can be done, care is taken seriously and fittingly of the life of the fetus and that of the mother.

On the following Friday, the sixth day of the same month and year, His Supreme Holiness approved the responses of the Most Eminent and Reverend Fathers.

[From the reply of the Holy Office to the Dean of the faculty of theology of the University of Marienburg, the 5th of March, 1902] [1]

To the question: "Whether it is at any time permitted to extract from 1890c the womb of the mother ectopic fetuses still immature, when the sixth month after conception has not passed?"

The reply is:

"In the negative, according to the decree of Wednesday, the 4th of May, 1898, by the force of which care must be taken seriously and fittingly, insofar as it can be done, for the life of the fetus and that of the mother; moreover, with respect to time, according to the same decree, the orator is reminded that no acceleration of the birth is licit, unless it be performed at the time and according to the methods by which in the ordinary course of events the life of the mother and that of the fetus are considered."

Errors of Antonius de Rosmini-Serbati [2]

[Condemned in a Decree of the Holy Office, 14th of Dec., 1887]

1. In the order of created things there is immediately manifested to 1891 the human intellect something of the divine in its very self, namely, such as pertains to divine nature.

2. When we speak of the divine in nature, we do not use that word 1892 *divine* to signify a nondivine effect of a divine cause; nor, is it our mind to speak of a certain thing as *divine* because it is such through participation.

3. In the nature of the universe then, that is in the intelligences that 1893

---

[1] ASS 35 (1902/03) 162.

[2] ASS 20 (1887), 398 ff.; cf. 21 (1888) 709 f.—Antonius, Count de Rosmini-Serbati, born on the 25th of March, 1797, in the town of Roveredo, founder of the clerical congregation, "Instituto della Carità," when some of his writings had been prohibited by the Holy See, praiseworthily submitted. On the first of July, 1855, he died most piously. The propositions here related were excerpted from his works after his death and were condemned by the Holy See.

are in it, there is something to which the term of divine not in a figurative but in a real sense is fitting.—The actuality is not distinct from the rest of divine actuality.

1894   4. Indeterminate being, which without doubt is known to all intelligences, is that divine thing which is manifest to man in nature.

1895   5. Being, which man observes, must be something of the necessary and eternal being, the creating cause, the determining and final cause of all contingent beings; and this is God.

1896   6. In the being which prescinds from creatures and from God, which is indeterminate being, and in God, not indeterminate but absolute being, the essence is the same.

1897   7. The indeterminate being of intuition, initial being, is something of the Word, which the mind of the Father distinguishes, not really, but according to reason from the Word.

1898   8. Finite beings, of which the world is composed, result from two elements, that is, from the real finite terminus and from the initial being, which contributes the form of being to the same terminus.

1899   9. Being, the object of intuition, is the initial act of all beings. Initial being is the beginning both of the knowable and the subsisting; it is likewise the beginning of God, according as He is conceived by us, and of creatures.

1900   10. Virtual and limitless being is the first and most simple of all entities, so that any other entity is composite, and among its components is always and necessarily virtual being.—It is the essential part of absolutely all entities, according as they are divided by reason.

1901   11. The quiddity (that which a thing is) of a finite being does not consist of that which it has of the positive, but of its limits. The quiddity of an infinite being consists of its entity, and is positive; but the quiddity of a finite being consists of the limits of its entity, and is negative.

1902   12. There is no finite reality, but God causes it to exist by adding limitation to infinite reality.—Initial being becomes the essence of every real being.—Being which actuates finite natures, and is joined with them, is cut off by God.

1903   13. The difference between absolute being and relative being is not that which intervenes between substance and substance, but something much greater; for one is being absolutely, the other nonbeing absolutely, and this other is being relatively. But when relative being is posited, being absolutely is not multiplied; hence, absolute and relative (being) absolutely are not one substance, but one being; and in this sense no diversity is being, rather oneness is held as being.

1904   14. By divine abstraction initial being is produced, the first element of finite beings; but by divine imagination the finite real (being) or all realities are produced, of which the world consists.

15. The third operation of absolute being creating the world is divine **1905** synthesis, that is the union of two elements, which are *initial being,* the common beginning of all finite beings, and finite *reality*, or rather different finite realities, the different ends of the same initial being. By this union finite beings are created.

16. Initial being through divine synthesis referred by intelligence, not **1906** as an intelligible but merely as essence, to the real finite ends, causes the finite beings to exist subjectively and really.

17. This alone God effects by creating, that He posits the entire act **1907** wholly as the being of creatures; this act then is properly not made but posited.

18. The love, by which God loves Himself even in creatures, and **1908** which is the reason why He determines Himself to create, constitutes a moral necessity, which in the most perfect being always induces the effect; for such necessity in many imperfect beings only leaves the whole freedom bilateral.

19. The Word is that unseen material, from which, as it is said in **1909** Wisdom 11:18, all things of the universe were created.

20. It is not inconsistent that the human soul, in order that it may be **1910** multiplied by human generation, may thus be conceived, proceed from the imperfect, namely from the sensitive grade, to the perfect, namely to the intellectual grade.

21. When being is capable of being intued by the sensitive principle, **1911** by this influence alone, by this union with itself, only sensing this first, but now, at the same time understanding, it is brought to a more noble state, it changes its nature, and becomes understanding, subsisting, and immortal.

22. It is not impossible to think that it can become a divine power, **1912** so that the intellectual soul is separated from the animate body, and it itself (being) still remains soulful; surely there would remain in it, as the basis of the purely soulful, the soulful principle, which before was in it as an appendage.

23. The soul of the deceased exists in a natural state, as if it did not **1913** exist; since it cannot exercise any reflection upon itself, or have any consciousness of itself, its condition can be said to be like the state of the perpetual shades and eternal sleep.

24. The substantial form of the body is rather the effect of the soul **1914** and the interior terminus of the operation itself; therefore, the substantial form of the body is not the soul itself.—The union of the soul and the body properly consists in immanent perception, by which the subject viewing the idea, affirms the sensible, after it has viewed its essence in this (idea).

25. When the mystery of the Most Blessed Trinity has been revealed, **1915**

its existence can be demonstrated by merely speculative arguments, negative indeed, and indirect; yet such that through them the truth is brought
to philosophic studies, and the proposition becomes scientific like the
rest; for if it were denied, the theosophic doctrine of *pure reason* would
not only remain incomplete, but would also be annihilated, teeming with
absurdities on every side.

1916   26. If the three highest forms of *being,* namely, subjectivity, objectivity, sanctity; or, reality, ideality, and morality, are transferred to absolute being, they cannot be conceived otherwise than as subsisting and
living persons.—The Word, insofar as it is the loved object, and insofar
as it is the Word, that is the object subsisting in itself, known by itself,
is the person of the Holy Spirit.

1917   27. In the humanity of Christ the human will was so taken up by the
Holy Spirit in order to cling to objective Being, that is to the Word,
that it (the will) gave over the rule of man wholly to Him, and assumed the Word personally, thus uniting with itself human nature.
Hence, the human will ceased to be personal in man, and, although
person is in other men, it remained nature in Christ.

1918   28. In Christian doctrine, the Word, the sign and configuration of
God, is impressed on the souls of those who receive the baptism of
Christ with faith.—The Word, that is the sign, impressed on the soul in
Christian doctrine, is real Being (infinite) manifest by itself, which we
thereupon recognize to be the second person of the Most Blessed Trinity.

1919   29. We think that the following conjecture is by no means at variance
with Catholic doctrine, which alone is truth: In the Eucharistic sacrament the substance of bread and wine becomes the true flesh and true
blood of Christ, when Christ makes it the terminus of His sentient
principle, and vivifies it with His life; almost in that way by which
bread and wine truly are transubstantiated into our flesh and blood, because they become the terminus of our sentient principle.

1920   30. When transubstantiation has been accomplished, it can be understood that to the glorious body of Christ some part is added, incorporated
in it, undivided, and equally glorious.

1921   31. In the sacrament of the Eucharist *by the power of words* the body
and blood of Christ are present only in that measure which corresponds
(*a quel tanto*) to the substance of the bread and wine, which are transubstantiated; the rest of the body of Christ is there *through concomitance.*

1922   32. Since he who does not eat the flesh of the Son of man and drink
of His blood, does not have life in him [cf. John 6:54], and nevertheless
those who die with the baptism of water, of blood, or of desire, certainly attain eternal life, it must be said that these who have not eaten

of the body and blood of Christ, are administered this heavenly food in the future life, at the very moment of death.—Hence, also to the saints of the Old Testament Christ was able by descending into hell to communicate Himself under the appearances of bread and wine, in order to make them ready for the vision of God.

33. Since the demons possessed the fruit, they thought that they would enter into man, if he should eat of it; for, when the food was turned into the animated body of man, they themselves were able freely to enter the animality, i.e., into the subjective life of this being, and so to dispose of it as they had proposed. 1923

34. To preserve the Blessed Virgin Mary from the taint of origin, it was enough for the slightest seed in man to remain uncorrupted, neglected perchance by the demon himself, from which uncorrupted seed transfused from generation to generation the Virgin Mary might arise in her time. 1924

35. The more the order of justification in man is considered, the more appropriate appears the Scriptural way of saying that God covers and does not reckon certain sins.—According to the Psalmist [cf. Ps. 31:1] there is a difference between *iniquities* which are *forgiven,* and *sins* which *are covered;* the former, as it seems, are actual and willing faults; but the latter are willing sins on the part of those who pertain to the people of God, to whom on this account they bring no harm. 1925

36. The supernatural order is established by the manifestation of being in the fullness of its real form; the effect of this communication or manifestation is a deiform sense, which begun in this life establishes the light of faith and of grace; completed in the other life establishes the light of glory. 1926

37. The first light rendering the soul intelligent is ideal being; the other first light is also being, not merely ideal, but subsisting and living; that concealing its personality shows only its objectivity; but he who sees the other (which is the Word), even through a reflection or in enigma, sees God. 1927

38. God is the object of the beatific vision, insofar as He is the author of works outwardly. 1928

39. The traces of wisdom and goodness which shine out in creatures are necessary for possessors (of God); for they are collected in the eternal exemplar as that part of Him which can be seen by them (creatures), and they furnish material for the praises which the Blessed sing forever to God. 1929

40. Since God cannot, not even by the light of glory, communicate Himself wholly to finite beings, He was not able to reveal and communicate His essence to possessors (of God), except in that way which 1930

is accommodated to finite intelligences; that is, God manifests Himself to them, insofar as He has relations with them, as their creator, provider, redeemer, sanctifier.

1930a *The judgment:* The Holy Office "has decided that these propositions, in the author's own sense, are to be disproved and proscribed, according as it does disprove, condemn, and proscribe by this general decree. . . . His Holiness has approved, confirmed, and ordered that the decree of the Most Eminent Fathers be observed by all."

Bounds of Liberty, and Human Action [1]

[From the Encyclical, "Libertas, praestantissimum," 20th of June, 1888]

1931 [Finally] many do not approve the separation of Church and state but yet think that the Church ought to yield to the times, and adapt and accommodate herself to what the prudence of the day in administering governments demands. The opinion of these is good, if this is understood of some equitable plan which can be consistent with truth and justice, namely, such that the Church, exploring the hope of some great good, would show herself indulgent and bestow upon the times that which she can, while preserving the sanctity of her office.—But this is not so in matters and doctrines which a change of morals and a fallacious judgment have unlawfully introduced . . .

1932 And so from what has been said it follows that it is by no means lawful to demand, to defend, and to grant indiscriminate freedom of thought, writing, teaching, and likewise of belief, as if so many rights which nature has given to man. For if nature had truly given these, it would be right to reject God's power, and human liberty could be restrained by no law.—Similarly it follows that these kinds of freedom can indeed be tolerated, if there are just reasons, yet with definite moderation, lest they degenerate into caprice and indulgence.

1933 Whenever domination presses or impends such as to hold the state in subjection by an unjust force, or to force the Church to lack due freedom, it is right to seek some tempering of the government in which it is permitted to act with freedom; for in this case that immoderate and vicious freedom is not demanded, but some relief is sought for the good of all, and this only is a concern, that, where license for evil deeds is granted, there opportunity for doing right be not impeded.

1934 And furthermore it is not of itself contrary to one's duty to prefer a form of government regulated by the popular class, provided Catholic doctrine as to the origin and administration of public power be maintained. Of the various kinds of government, the Church indeed rejects

---

[1] ASS 20 (1887), 612 f.; AL III 118 ff.

none, provided they are suited of themselves to care for the welfare of citizens; but she wishes, what nature clearly demands likewise, that each be constituted without injury to anyone, and especially with the preservation of the rights of the Church.

To engage in the affairs of public administration is honorable, unless **1935** somewhere because of a special condition of circumstances and the times it be deemed best otherwise; the Church by all means approves of every one contributing his services to the common interest, and, insofar as everyone can, guarding, preserving, and advancing the state.

Nor does the Church condemn this: to seek to free one's people from **1936** serving a foreign or despotic power, provided it can be done while preserving justice. Finally she does not censure those who wish to have their government live according to its own laws; and their fellow citizens enjoy all possible means for increasing prosperity. The Church has always been a supporter of civic liberties without intemperance, and to this the Italian states especially attest; witness the prosperity, wealth, and glory of their name obtained by municipal law, at a time when the salutary power of the Church had spread to all parts of the state without any opposition.

Love for Church and Fatherland [1]

[From the Encyclical, "Sapientiae christianae," January 10, 1890]

It cannot be doubted that in daily life the duties of Catholics are more **1936a** numerous and more serious than those of such as are either little aware of the Catholic faith or entirely inexperienced in it. . . . The man who has embraced the Christian faith as he ought, by that very fact is subject to the Church as if born of her, and becomes a participant in her worldwide and most holy society, which it is the proper duty of the Roman Pontiff to rule with supreme power, under the invisible head, Jesus Christ.—Now indeed, if we are bidden by the law of nature especially to love and protect the land in which we were brought forth and raised into this light, so that the good citizen does not hesitate even to encounter death for the fatherland, it is a far greater duty for Christians ever to be affected in similar wise toward the Church. For the Church is the holy land of the living God, born of God himself, and established by the same Author, who indeed is on a pilgrimage in the land; calling men, and training and leading them to eternal happiness in heaven. Therefore, the fatherland must be loved, from which we receive the enjoyment of mortal life; but we must love the Church more to whom we owe the love of the soul which will last forever, because it is right to hold the

---

[1] ASS 22 (1889/90) 385 ff.; AL X (At Rome, 1891), 13 ff.

blessings of the spirit above the blessings of the body, and the duties
toward God are much more sacred than those toward man.

1936b   But, if we wish to judge rightly, the supernatural love of the Church
and the natural love of the fatherland are twin loves coming from the
same eternal principle, since God himself is the author and the cause of
both; therefore, it follows that one duty cannot be in conflict with the
other. . . . Nevertheless, the order of these duties, either because of the
troubles of the times or the more perverse will of men, is sometimes
destroyed. Instances, to be sure, occur when the state seems to demand
one thing from men as citizens, and religion another from men as
Christians; and this, clearly, for no other reason than that the rulers of
the state either hold the sacred power of the Church as of no account, or
wish it to be subject to them. . . . If the laws of the state are openly at
variance with divine right, if they impose any injury upon the Church,
or oppose those duties which are of religion, or violate the authority of
Jesus Christ in the Supreme Pontiff, then indeed to resist is a duty, to
obey a crime; and this is bound with injury to the state itself, since
whatever is an offense in religion is a sin against the state.

The Apostolate of the Laity [1]

[From the same Encyclical]

1936c   And there is no reason for anyone to object that Jesus Christ, the
guardian and champion of the Church, by no means needs the help of
men. For, not because of any lack of strength, but because of the magnitude of His goodness does He wish that some effort be contributed by us
toward obtaining and acquiring the fruits of the salvation which He
Himself has procured.

The most important features of this duty are: to profess Catholic
doctrine openly and firmly, and to propagate it as much as each one
can. . . . Surely the duty of preaching, that is of teaching, belongs by
divine right to the masters whom "the Holy Ghost hath placed as
bishops to rule the Church of God" [cf. Acts 20:28], and especially to
the Roman Pontiff, vicar of Jesus Christ, placed with supreme power
over the whole Church, the master of all that is to be believed and to be
practiced. Nevertheless, let no one think that private persons are prohibited from taking any active part in teaching, especially those to whom
God has granted the ability of mind with a zeal for meritorious service.
These, as often as circumstances demand, can well take upon themselves
the role not indeed of teacher, but they can impart to others what they
themselves have received, resounding like an echo with the voice of their
masters. Indeed, this work of the private person has seemed to the

---

[1] ASS 22 (1889/90), 391 f.; AL X (At Rome, 1891) 20 ff.

Fathers of the Vatican Council to be so opportune and fruitful that they have decided furthermore to invite it: "Let all the faithful of Christ contribute their efforts" [See n. 1819].—Moreover, let everyone remember that he can and ought to sow the Catholic faith by the authority of his example, and to preach it by continual profession.—In the duties, then, that bind us to God and to the Church, this especially should be numbered, that the industry of everyone should be exercised, insofar as possible, in propagating Christian truth and in repelling errors.

The Material of the Eucharist (Wine) [1]

[From the Response of the Holy Office, May 8th, 1887; and July 30, 1890]

Two remedies are proposed by the Bishop of Carcassum to guard 1937
against the danger of the spoiling of wine:

1. Let a small quantity of *eau de vie* be added to the natural wine.

2. Let the wine be boiled to the extent of sixty-five degrees.

To the question whether these remedies are lawful in the case of wine for the sacrifice of the Mass, and which is to be preferred,

The answer is:

The wine is to be preferred as is set forth in the second place.

The Bishop of Marseilles explains and asks: 1938

In many parts of France, especially in those located toward the south, the white wine which does service at the bloodless sacrifice of the Mass is so weak and impotent that it cannot be kept for long, unless a quantity of the spirit of wine (spirits of alcohol) is mixed with the same.

1. Is a mixture of this kind lawful?

2. And if so, what quantity of such extraneous matter may be added to the wine?

3. In case of an affirmative answer, is it required to extract the spirit of wine from pure wine or from the fruit of the vine?

The answer is:

Provided that the spirit (alcohol) has been extracted from the fruit of the vine, and the quantity of alcohol added to that which the wine in question naturally contains does not exceed a proportion of twelve percent, and the mixture is made when the wine is very new, there is no objection to this wine being used in the sacrifice of the Mass.[2]

---

[1] ASS 23 (1890/91) 699 f.

[2] A similar response was given for Brazil, August 5, 1896. (ASS 29 [1896/97], 317; AE 4 [1896], 385 a), and in a reply to the Bishop of Tarragona the quantity of alcohol was extended even to 17 or 18 percent, when the wine already naturally has 12 percent or more (ASS *ibid.,* 318; AE *ibid.,* 484 a).

The Right of Private Property, Just Reward for Labor, and the Right of Entering Private Unions [1]

[From the Encyclical, "Rerum novarum," May 15, 1891]

1938a   The right to possess private property as one's own is granted man by nature. . . . Nor is there any reason why the providence of the state should be introduced; for man is older than the state, and therefore he should have had by nature, before any state had come into existence, the right to care for life and body. . . . For those things which are required to preserve life, and especially to make life complete, the earth, to be sure, pours forth in great abundance; but it could not pour it from itself without its cultivation and care by man. Now, when a man applies the activity of his mind and the strength of his body to procuring the goods of nature, by this very act he attaches to himself that part of corporeal nature which he has cultivated, on which he leaves impressed a kind of form as it were, of his personality; so that it should by all means be right for him to possess this part as his own; and by no means should anyone be permitted to violate this right of his.—So obvious is the force of these arguments that it seems amazing that certain ones who would restore obsolete opinions should disagree with them; these, to be sure, concede to the private person the use of the soil and the various fruits of estates, but they deny openly that it is right that either the soil on which he has built, or the estate which he has cultivated be owned by him. . . .

Indeed, rights of this kind which belong to men individually are understood to be much stronger, if they are looked upon as appropriate to and connected with his duties in domestic and social life. . . . This right of property, then, which we have demonstrated to have been assigned to an individual person by nature, through which he is the head of the family, ought to be transferred to man; rather, that right is so much the stronger, as the human person embraces more responsibilities in domestic and social society. The most holy law of nature is that the father of a family provide with training and livelihood all whom he has begotten; and, likewise, it is deduced from nature herself that he seek to acquire and prepare for his children, who bear and continue in a way the father's personality, that by which they can honorably protect themselves from a wretched fate in this uncertain course of life. But this he cannot effect in any way other than by the possession of lucrative property to transmit by inheritance to his children. . . . To wish, therefore, that the civil government at its own option penetrate even to the intimate affairs of the home is a great and pernicious error. . . . The power of the father is such that it can neither be destroyed nor absorbed by the

---

[1] ASS 23 (1890/91), 641 ff.; AL XI (At Rome, 1891), 100 ff.

state. . . . Therefore, when the alleviation of the masses is sought, let this be enduring, that it must be held as fundamental that private property is to be inviolable.

The just possession of money is distinguished from the just use of money. To possess goods privately, as we have seen above, is a natural right of man; and to exercise this right, especially in the society of life, is not only lawful but clearly necessary. . . . But, if indeed this is asked, of what nature must the use of goods be, the Church answers without hesitation: As far as this is concerned, man ought not to hold his exterior possessions as his own, but as common, so that one may easily share them in the need of others. Therefore, the Apostle says: "Charge the rich of this world . . . to give easily, to communicate" [I Tim. 6:17 f.].[1] No one, certainly, is ordered to give assistance to others from that which pertains to his own use and that of the members of his family; nor also to give over to others what he himself needs to preserve what befits his person, and what is proper. . . . But when sufficient care has been given to necessity and decorum, it is a duty to assist the indigent from what remains: "That which remaineth, give alms," [Luke 11:41]. These are not duties of justice, except in extreme cases, but of Christian charity, which of course it is not right to seek by legal action. But the law and judgment of Christ are above the laws and judgments of men, and He in many ways urges the practice of almsgiving . . . and He will judge a kindness conferred upon or denied to the poor as conferred upon or denied to Himself [cf. Matt. 25:34 f.]. **1938b**

Labor by nature has, as it were, placed two marks upon man, namely, that it is personal, because the driving force inheres in the person and is entirely his own by whom it is exercised, and comes into being for his advantage; then, that it is necessary, for this reason, because the fruit of labor is needed by man to guard life; moreover, the nature of things bids (us) to guard life, and especially must we obey nature. Now, if labor is considered only from this viewpoint, that it is personal, there is no doubt but that it is sound for the worker to prescribe a smaller rate of pay; for just as he offers his services of his free will, so, too, of his free will he can be content with a slight pay for his services, or even no pay at all. But the case is to be judged much differently, if with the reason of personality is joined the reason of necessity, separable from the former, to be sure, in theory, not in fact. Actually to continue in life is the common duty of every individual, for whom to lack this persistence is a crime. Therefore, the right to discover that by which life is sustained is born of necessity, and the means to obtain this is supplied to all the poor only by the pay for his labor which is in demand. So, granted that the workman and employer freely agree on the contract, as well as specifically on the **1938c**

---

[1] St. Thomas, *Summa theol.* IIa IIae, q.66, a.2.

rate of pay, yet there is always underlying this something from natural justice, and this greater and more ancient than the will of those who make the contract, namely, that the pay must by no means be inadequate to support the worker, who indeed is frugal and of good character. But if the worker, forced by necessity, or moved by fear of a worse evil, accepts the harder condition, which, even if he does not wish it, must be accepted because it is imposed by the employer or the contractor, this certainly is to submit to force, against which justice cries out. . . . If the worker obtains sufficient pay, so as by it to be able to sustain himself, wife, and children comfortably, he will without difficulty apply himself to thrift, if he is wise, and he will bring it about, as nature herself seems to urge, that, after expenses are deducted, some be left over whereby he may attain a moderate estate. For we have seen that the case which is being discussed cannot be solved by effective reasoning except by this assumption and principle: that the right to private property must be held sacred. . . Nevertheless, these benefits cannot be attained except by the enormity of contributions and taxes. For, since the right to possess private property is granted not by the laws of man but by nature, the authority of the state cannot abolish it, but only temper its practice, and order it to the common good. Therefore, it would act unjustly and inhumanely, if it should detract from private property more than is just, under the name of taxes. . . .

1938d   It is comforting to observe that societies of this kind are being formed generally, either composed entirely of workers, or from both classes; moreover, it is to be desired that they grow in number and in effective influence. . . . For, it is permitted man by the right of nature to enter private societies; moreover, the state is established for the protection of natural right, not for its destruction; and so, if it forbids the formation of associations of citizens, it clearly acts at odds with itself, since it itself, as well as private associations, come into existence from a single principle, that men are by nature social.—Occasions sometimes arise when it is just for laws to forbid such societies, namely, if they deliberately aim at something which is clearly at variance with probity, justice, and the welfare of the state.[1]

---

[1] Cf. the letter of the S.C. Council to the Bishop of Lille, on a certain conflict between workers and contractors which arose in the region on June 5th, 1929 (ASS 21 [1929] 494 ff.).

The Duel [1]

From the Letter, "Pastoralis Officii," to the Bishops of
Germany and Austria, Sept. 12, 1891]

The two divine laws, that which is promulgated by the light of natural **1939** reason, and that by letters written under divine inspiration, strictly forbid the killing or wounding of anyone outside a public cause, unless forced by necessity to defend his own safety. But those who provoke to a private struggle, or accept a challenge do this; they lend their minds and their strength to this, although bound by no necessity, to take the life, or at least to inflict a wound on an adversary. Furthermore, the two divine laws forbid anyone rashly casting aside his own life, subjecting it to grave and manifest danger, when no reason of duty, or of magnanimous charity urges it; but this blind rashness, contemner of life, is clearly in the nature of a duel. Therefore, it can be obscure and doubtful to no one that upon those who engage in individual combat privately, fall both crimes, that of another's destruction, and of voluntarily endangering his own life. Finally, there is scarcely any affliction which is more at variance with the good order of civil life, than the license permitted a citizen to be his own individual defender of the law by private force, and the avenger of honor which he thinks has been violated.

Nor do those who accept combat when it is offered have fear as a **1940** just excuse, because they dread to be held cowards in public if they decline battle. For, if the duties of men were to be measured by the false opinions of the public, there would be no natural and true distinction according to an eternal norm of right and justice between honest actions and shameful deeds. Even the pagan philosophers knew and taught that the false judgments of the public are to be spurned by a strong and stable man. Rather is the fear just and sacred, which turns a man away from unjust slaughter, and makes him sollicitous of his own safety and that of his brothers. Surely, he who spurns the valid judgments of the public, who prefers to undergo the scourges of contumely than to abandon duty in any matter, this man, surely, is of a far greater and higher mind than he who when annoyed by an injury rushes to arms. Yes, indeed, if there is a desire for right judgment, he is the one in whom stout fortitude shines, that fortitude, I say, which is truly called a virtue and whose companion is glory, not counterfeited and not false. For virtue consists in a good in accord with reason, and all glory is foolish except that which depends on the judgment of God who approves.

---

[1] AL (ed. Rom.) xi 283 ff.; ASS 24 (1891/92) 204 b.

The Blessed Virgin Mary, Mediatrix of Graces [1]

[The Encyclical, "Octobri mense," on the Rosary, Sept. 22, 1891]

1940a   The eternal Son of God, when He wished to assume the nature of man for the redemption and glory of man, and for this reason was about to enter upon a kind of mystic marriage with the entire human race, did not do this before He received the wholly free consent of His designated mother, who, in a way, played the part of the human race itself, according to that famous and truthful opinion of Aquinas: "Through the Annunciation the Virgin's consent was looked for in place of all human nature." [2] Therefore, no less truly and properly may it be affirmed that nothing at all of the very great treasure of every grace, which the Lord confers, since "grace and truth came by Jesus Christ" [John 1:17], nothing is imparted to us except through Mary, God so willing; so, just as no one can approach the highest Father except through the Son, so no one can approach Christ except through His Mother.

[From the Encyclical, "Fidentem," on the Rosary, Sept. 20, 1896] [3]

For, surely, no one person can be conceived who has ever made, or at any time will make an equal contribution as Mary to the reconciliation of men with God. Surely, she it was who brought the Savior to man as he was rushing into eternal destruction, at that very time when, with wonderful assent, she received "in place of all human nature" [4] the message of the peace making sacrament brought to earth by the Angel; she it is "of whom was born Jesus" [Matt. 1:16], namely, His true Mother, and for this reason she is worthy and quite acceptable as the *mediatrix to the Mediator.*

The Study of Holy Scripture [5]

[From the Encyclical, "Providentissimus Deus," Nov., 1893]

1941   Since there is need of a definite method of carrying on interpretation profitably, let the prudent teacher avoid either of two mistakes, that of those who give a cursory glance to each book, and that of those who delay too long over a certain part of one. . . . [The teacher] in this [work] will take as his text the Vulgate version, which the Council of Trent decreed [see n. 785] should be considered *as authentic in public*

---

[1] ASS 24 (1891), 196 f.; AL V 10.
[2] *Summa theol.,* IIIa, q.30, a.1.
[3] ASS 29 (1896), 206; AL VI 214.
[4] S. Thomas Aq., *Summa theol.,* IIIa, q.30, a.1.
[5] ASS 26 (1893/94), 278 ff.; AE 2 (1894), 3 ff.; AL V 210 ff.; EB 90 ff.

lectures, disputations, sermons, and expositions, and which the daily custom of the Church commends. Yet account will have to be taken of the remaining versions which Christian antiquity has commended and used, especially of the very ancient manuscripts. For although, as far as the heart of the matter is concerned, the meaning of the Hebrew and the Greek is well elucidated in the expressions of the Vulgate, yet if anything is set forth therein with ambiguity, or if without accuracy "an examination of the preceding language" will be profitable, as Augustine advises.[1]

1942 . . . The Synod of the Vatican adopted the teaching of the Fathers, when, as it renewed the decree of Trent on the interpretation of the divine Word, it declared this to be its mind, that *in matters of faith and morals, which pertain to the building up of Christian doctrine, that is to be held as the true sense of Holy Scripture which Mother Church has held and holds, whose prerogative it is to judge of the true sense and interpretation of Scripture; and, therefore, it is permitted to no one to interpret the Holy Scripture against this sense, or even against the unanimous agreement of the Fathers* [see n. 786, 1788]. By this very wise law the Church by no means retards or blocks the investigations of Biblical science, but rather keeps it free of error, and aids it very much in true progress. For, to every private teacher a large field is open in which along safe paths, by his industry in interpretation, he may labor efficaciously and profitably for the Church. Indeed, in those passages of divine Scripture which still lack certain and definite exposition, it can be so effected by the kindly counsel of a provident God, that by a prepared study the judgment of the Church may be expedited; but in passages which have been explained the private teacher can be of equal help, if he sets these forth very clearly among the masses of the people, and more skillfully among the learned, or defends them more eminently against adversaries. . . .

1943 In the other passages the analogy of faith must be followed, and Catholic doctrine, as received on the authority of the Church, must be employed as the highest norm. . . . Wherefore, it is clear that that interpretation must be rejected as senseless and false, which either makes inspired authors in some manner quarrel among themselves, or opposes the teaching of the Church. . . .

1944 Now, the authority of the Fathers, by whom after the apostles, the growing Church was disseminated, watered, built, protected, and nurtured,[2] is the highest authority, as often as they all in one and the same way interpret a Biblical text, as pertaining to the doctrine of faith and morals.

1945 The authority of the other Catholic interpreters is, indeed, less; yet,

---

[1] St. Augustine, *De doctrina christ.* I. 3, c. 3 and 4 [ML 34, 68].
[2] St. Augustine, *Contra Iulian. Pelag.* I. 2, c. 10, n. 37 [ML 44, 700].

since Biblical studies have had a certain continuous progress in the Church, their own honor must likewise be allotted to their commentaries, and much can be sought opportunely from these to refute contrary opinion and to solve the more difficult problems. But, it is entirely unfitting that anyone should ignore and look down upon the works which our own have left in abundance, and prefer the books of the heterodox; and to the immediate danger to sound doctrine and not rarely to the damage of faith seek from these, explanations of passages to which Catholics have long and very successfully directed their geniuses and labors.

1946   . . . The first [aid to interpretation] is in the study of the ancient Oriental languages, and in the science which is called criticism.[1] Therefore, it is necessary for teachers of Sacred Scripture and proper for theologians to have learned those languages in which the canonical books were originally written by the sacred writers. . . . These, moreover, for the same reason should be more learned and skilled in the field of the true science of criticism; for to the detriment of religion there has falsely been introduced an artifice, dignified by the name of higher criticism, by which from internal evidence alone, as they say, the origin, integrity, and authority of any book emerge as settled. On the other hand it is very clear that in historical questions, such as the origin and preservation of books, the evidences of history are of more value than the rest, and should be gathered and investigated very carefully; moreover, that the methods

---

[1] Leo XIII in the Apostolic Letter, "Vigilantiae," Oct. 30, 1902; "de studiis s. Scripturae provehendis," among other things wrote the following: "Our own [faithful], with Our strong approval, cultivate the field of scientific criticism, for it is very useful in thoroughly perceiving the mind of the sacred writers. They also sharpen this same skill by applying to a passage the resources of the heterodox with no opposition on Our part. But, let them look out lest from this practice they imbibe intemperance of judgment; for the artifice of so-called higher criticism often deteriorates into this, whose dangerous temerity We ourselves have denounced more than once" (ASS 35 [1902/03] 236).

Pius X in a letter given Jan. 11, 1906, to the Bishop of La Rochelle, Le Camus, spoke as follows:

"This especially must be granted you in the way of praise, that you hold to that way of explaining the Sacred Scripture, which under the leadership of the Church must be completely held for allegiance to truth and for the glory of Catholic doctrine. For, as in fact the temerity is to be condemned of those who attribute more to novelty than to the *magisterium* of the Church, and do not hesitate to employ an immoderately free kind of criticism, so is the method of those not to be approved who dare to depart in nothing from the customary exegesis of Scripture, even when with the preservation of faith a good growth of studies demands this. You proceed in the right way between these [extremes], and by your example you show that nothing is to be feared by the Sacred Books from the true progress of the science of criticism, but rather that favorable light can be sought from this; so, surely, if a prudent and honest judgment should be applied to it [*L'Unità cattolica*, Firenza, February 4, 1906; AE 14 (1906), 99. Versio Lat. ex: *Civiltà catt.*, a. 57 (1906) II 484 f.].

of internal criticism are not of such value that they can be applied to a case except for a kind of confirmation. . . . . This same method of higher criticism, which is extolled, will finally result in everyone following his own enthusiasm and prejudiced opinion when interpreting.

Knowledge of the natural sciences will be of great help to the teacher **1947** of Sacred Scripture, by which he can more easily discover and refute fallacious arguments of this kind drawn up against the Sacred Books.— Indeed there should be no real disagreement between the theologian and the physicist, provided that each confines himself within his own territory, watching out for this, according to St. Augustine's [1] warning, "not to make rash assertions, and to declare the unknown as known." But, if they should disagree, a summary rule as to how a theologian should conduct himself is offered by the same author.[2] "Whatever," he says, "they can demonstrate by genuine proofs regarding the nature of things, let us show that it is not contrary to our Scriptures; but whatever they set forth in their volumes contrary to our Scriptures, that is to Catholic faith, let us show by some means, or let us believe without any hesitation to be most false." As to the equity of this rule let us consider, first, that the sacred writers or more truly "the Spirit of God, who spoke through them, did not wish to teach men these things (namely, the innermost constitution of the visible universe) as being of no profit to salvation"; [3] that, therefore, they do not carry an explanation of nature scientifically, but rather sometimes describe and treat the facts themselves, either in a figurative manner, or in the common language of their times, as today in many matters of daily life is true among most learned men themselves. Moreover, when these things which fall under the senses, are set forth first and properly, the sacred writer (and the Angelic Doctor also advised it) "describes what is obvious to the senses," [4] or what God Himself, when addressing men, signified in a human way, according to their capacity.

Because the defense of Holy Scripture must be carried on vigorously, **1948** all the opinions which the individual Fathers or the recent interpreters have set forth in explaining it need not be maintained equally. For they, in interpreting passages where physical matters are concerned have made judgments according to the opinions of the age, and thus not always according to truth, so that they have made statements which today are not approved. Therefore, we must carefully discern what they hand down which really pertains to faith or is intimately connected with it, and what they hand down with unanimous consent; for "in those matters which

---

[1] Cf. St. Augustine, *De Gen. ad litt. imperf.*, lib. c. 9, n. 30 [ML 34, 233].
[2] Idem, *De Gen. ad litt.* l. 1, c. 21, n. 41 [ML 34, 462].
[3] Idem, *ibid.* l. 2, c. 9, n. 20 [ML 34, 270].
[4] St. Thomas, *Summa Theol.* Ia IIae, q. 80, a. 1, ad 3.

are not under the obligation of faith, the saints were free to have different opinions, just as we are," [1] according to the opinion of St. Thomas. In another passage he most prudently holds: "It seems to me to be safer that such opinions as the philosophers have expressed in common and are not repugnant to our faith should not be asserted as dogmas of the faith, even if they are introduced some times under the names of philosophers, nor should they thus be denied as contrary to faith, lest an opportunity be afforded to the philosophers of this world to belittle the teachings of the faith." [2]

Of course, although the interpreter should show that what scientists have affirmed by certain arguments to be now certain in no way opposes [3] the Scriptures rightly explained, let it not escape his notice that it sometimes has happened that what they have given out as certain has later been brought into uncertainty and repudiated. But, if writers on physics transgressing the boundaries of their science, invade the province of the philosophers with perverse opinions, let the theological interpreter hand these opinions over to the philosophers for refutation.

1949   Then these very principles will with profit be transferred to related sciences, especially to history. For, it must regretfully be stated that there are many who examine and publish the monuments of antiquity, the customs and institutions of peoples, and evidences of similar things, but more often with this purpose, that they may detect lapses of error in the sacred books, as the result of which their authority may even be shaken and totter. And some do this with a very hostile mind, and with no truly just judgment; for they have such confidence in the pagan works and the documents of the ancient past as to believe not even a suspicion of error is present in them; but to the books of Holy Scripture, for only a presumed appearance of error, without proper discussion, they deny even a little faith.

1950   It can happen, indeed, that transcribers in copying manuscripts do so incorrectly. This is to be considered carefully and is not to be admitted readily, except in those passages where it has been properly demonstrated; it can also happen that the true sense of some passage remains ambiguous; the best rules of interpretation will contribute much toward the solution of this problem; but it would be entirely wrong either to confine inspiration only to some parts of Sacred Scripture, or to concede that the sacred author himself has erred. For the method of those is not to be tolerated, who extricated themselves from these difficulties by readily granting that divine inspiration pertains to matters of faith and morals, and nothing more.

---

[1] In *Sent.* 2, dist. 2, q. 1, a. 3.

[2] *Opusc.* 10; reply on 42 articles (preface).

[3] E. B., *om* esse.

The books, all and entire, which the Church accepts as sacred and 1951
canonical, with all their parts, have been written at the dictation of the
Holy Spirit; so far is it from the possibility of any error being present to
divine inspiration, that it itself of itself not only excludes all error, but
excludes it and rejects it as necessarily as it is necessary that God, the
highest Truth, be the author of no error whatsoever.

This is the ancient and uniform faith of the Church, defined also by 1952
solemn opinion at the Councils of Florence [see n. 706] and of Trent
[see n. 783 ff.], finally confirmed and more expressly declared at the
Vatican Council, by which it was absolutely declared: "The books of the
Old and New Testament . . . have God as their author" [see n. 1787].
Therefore, it matters not at all that the Holy Spirit took men as instruments for the writing, as if anything false might have slipped, not
indeed from the first Author, but from the inspired writers. For, by
supernatural power He so roused and moved them to write, He stood
so near them, that they rightly grasped in mind all those things, and
those only, which He Himself ordered, and willed faithfully to write
them down, and expressed them properly with infallible truth; otherwise, He Himself would not be the author of all Sacred Scripture. . . .
And so utterly convinced were all the Fathers and Doctors that the holy
works, which were published by the hagiographers, are free of every
error, that they were very eager, no less skillfully than reverently, to
arrange and reconcile those not infrequent passages which seemed to
offer something contrary and at variance (they are almost the very
passages which are now thrown up to us under the name of the new
science); and they professed unanimously that these books, both in whole
and in part, were equally of divine inspiration, and that God Himself,
speaking through the sacred authors, could have set down nothing at all
at variance with the truth.

Let what the same Augustine wrote to Jerome sum this up: ". . . If I
shall meet anything in these works which seems contrary to truth, I shall
not hesitate to believe anything other than that the text is false, or that
the translator did not understand what was said, or that I did not in the
least understand." [1]

. . . For many objections from every kind of teaching have for long 1953
been persistently hurled against Scripture, which now, quite dead, have
fallen into disuse; likewise, at times not a few interpretations have been
placed on certain passages of Scripture (not properly pertinent to the
rule of faith and morals) in which a more careful investigation has seen
the meaning more accurately. For, surely, time destroys the falsities of
opinions, but "truth remaineth and groweth stronger forever and ever." [2]

---

[1] St. August., Ep. 82, 1, n. 3 [ML 33 (Aug. II), 277] and oftener elsewhere.
[2] 3 Esd. 4, 38.

The Unity of the Church [1]

[From the Encyclical, "Satis cognitum," June 29, 1896]

1954   Surely, it is so well established among all according to clear and manifold testimony that the true Church of Jesus Christ is one, that no Christian dare contradict it. But in judging and establishing the nature of this unity various errors have led off the true way. Indeed, not only the rise of the Church, but its entire establishment pertain to that class of things effected by free choice. Therefore, the entire judgment must be called back to that which was actually done, and we must not of course examine how the Church can be one, but how He who founded it wished it to be one.

1955   Now, if we look at what was done, Jesus Christ did not arrange and organize such a Church as would embrace several communities similar in kind, but distinct, and not bound together by those bonds that make the Church indivisible and unique after that manner clearly in which we profess in the symbol of faith, *"I believe in one Church."* . . . Now, Jesus Christ when He was speaking of such a mystical edifice, spoke only of one Church which He called His own: "I will build my Church" [Matt. 16:18]. Whatever other church is under consideration than this one, since it was not founded by Jesus Christ, cannot be the true Church of Christ. . . . And so the Church is bound to spread among all men the salvation accomplished by Jesus Christ, and all the blessings that proceed therefrom, and to propagate them through the ages. Therefore, according to the will of its Author the Church must be alone in all lands in the perpetuity of time. . . . The Church of Christ, therefore, is one and perpetual; whoever go apart (from it) wander away from the will and prescription of Christ the Lord and, leaving the way of salvation, digress to destruction.

1956   But He who founded the only Church, likewise founded it as one; namely, in such a way that whoever are to be in it, would be held bound together by the closest bonds, so much so that they form one people, one kingdom, one body: "One body and one spirit, as you are called in one hope of your calling" [Eph. 4:4]. . . . Agreement and union of minds are the necessary foundation of so great and so absolute a concord among men, from which a concurrence of wills and a similarity of action naturally arise. . . . Therefore, to unite the minds of men, and to effect and preserve the union of their minds, granted the existence of Holy Writ, there was great need of a certain other principle. . . .

1957   Therefore, Jesus Christ instituted in the Church a living, authentic, and likewise permanent *magisterium,* which He strengthened by His

---

[1] ASS 28 (1895/96), 711 ff.; AE 4 (1896), 247 a ff.; AL VI 160 ff.

own power, taught by the Spirit of Truth, and confirmed by miracles. The precepts of its doctrines He willed and most seriously commanded to be accepted equally with His own. . . . This, then, is without any doubt the office of the Church, to watch over Christian doctrine and to propagate it soundly and without corruption. . . .

But, just as heavenly doctrine was never left to the judgment and mind **1958** of individuals, but in the beginning was handed down by Jesus, then committed separately to that *magisterium* which has been mentioned, so, also, was the faculty of performing and administering the divine mysteries, together with the power of ruling and governing divinely, granted not to individuals [generally] of the Christian people but to certain of the elect. . . .

Therefore, Jesus Christ called upon all mortals, as many as were, and **1959** as many as were to be, to follow Him as their leader, and likewise their Savior, not only separately one by one, but also associated and united alike in fact and in mind; one in faith, end, and the means proper to that end, and subject to one and the same power. . . . Therefore, the Church is a society divine in origin, supernatural in its end, and in the means which bring us closest to that end; but inasmuch as it unites with men, it is a human community.

When the divine Founder decreed that the Church be one in faith, and **1960** in government, and in communion, He chose Peter and his successors in whom should be the principle and as it were the center of unity. . . . But, order of bishops, as Christ commanded, is to be regarded as joined with Peter, if it be subject to Peter and obey him; otherwise it necessarily descends into a confused and disorderly crowd. For the proper preservation of faith and the unity of mutual participation, it is not enough to hold higher offices for the sake of honor, nor to have general supervision, but there is absolute need of true authority and a supreme authority which the entire community should obey. . . . Hence those special expressions of the ancients regarding St. Peter, which brilliantly proclaim him as placed in the highest degree of dignity and authority. They everywhere called him *prince of the assembly of disciples, prince of the holy apostles, leader of that choir, mouthpiece of all the apostles, head of that family, superintendent of the whole world, first among the apostles, pillar of the Church.* . . .

But it is far from the truth and openly opposed to the divine constitu- **1961** tion, to hold that it is right for individual bishops to be subordinate to the jurisdiction of the Roman Pontiffs, but not for all taken together. . . . Now this power, about which we speak, over the college of bishops, which Holy Writ clearly discloses, the Church has at no time ceased to acknowledge and attest. . . . For these reasons in the decree of the Vatican Council [see n. 1826 ff.], regarding the power and authority of the primacy of the Roman Pontiff, no new opinion is introduced, but the old and uniform faith of all ages is asserted. Nor, indeed, does the fact that the same (bishops) are subordinate to a twofold power cause any confusion in administration. In the first place, we are prohibited from suspecting any such thing by God's wisdom, by whose counsel that very form of government was established. Secondly, we should note that the order of things and their mutual relations are confused, if there are two magistrates of the same rank among the people, neither of them responsible to the other. But the power of the Roman Pontiff is supreme, universal, and definitely peculiar to itself; but that of the bishops is circumscribed by definite limits, and definitely peculiar to themselves. . . .

1962 But Roman Pontiffs, mindful of their office, wish most of all that whatever is divinely instituted in the Church be preserved; therefore, as they watch with all proper care and vigilance their own power, so they have always seen to it that their authority be preserved for the bishops. Rather, whatever honor is paid the bishops, whatever obedience, all this they attribute as paid themselves.

Anglican Orders [1]

[From the Letter, "Apostolicae curae," Sept. 13, 1896]

1963 In the rite of conferring and administering any sacrament one rightly distinguishes between the ceremonial part and the essential part, which is customarily called *the matter and form*. And all know that the sacraments of the New Law, as sensible and efficient signs of invisible grace, ought both to signify the grace which they effect, and effect the grace which they signify [see n. 695, 849]. Although this signification should be found in the whole essential rite, namely, in matter and form, yet it pertains especially to form, since the matter is the part not determined by itself, but determined by form. And this appears more clearly in the sacrament of orders, for the conferring of which the matter, insofar as it presents itself for consideration in this case, is the imposition of hands. This, of course, by itself signifies nothing, and is employed for certain **1964** orders, and for confirmation. Now, the words which until recent times were everywhere held by the Anglicans as the proper form of priestly ordination, namely, "Receive the Holy Spirit," certainly do not in the least signify definitely the order of priesthood, or its grace and power, which is especially the power "of consecrating and of offering the true body and blood of the Lord," in that sacrifice which is no "nude commemoration of the sacrifice offered on the Cross" [see n. 950]. Such a

---

[1] ASS 29 (1896/97), 198 ff.; AE 4 (1898), 380 a ff.; AL VI 204 ff.

form was indeed afterwards lengthened by these words, "for the office and work of a priest"; but this rather convinces one that the Anglicans themselves saw that this first form was defective, and not appropriate to the matter. But the same addition, if perchance indeed it could have placed legitimate significance on the form, was introduced too late, since a century had elapsed after the adoption of the Edwardine Ordinal; since, moreover, with the extinction of the hierarchy, there was now no power for ordaining.

The same is true in regard to episcopal consecration. For to the **1965** formula "Receive the Holy Ghost" were not only added later the words "for the office and work of a bishop," but also, as regards these very words, as we shall soon see, a different sense is to be understood than in the Catholic rite. Nor is it any advantage in the matter to bring up the prayer of the preface, "Almighty God," since this likewise has been stripped of the words which bespeak the *summum sacerdotium.* It is, of course, not relevant to examine here whether the episcopate is a comple- ment of the priesthood, or an order distinct from it; or whether when conferred, as they say, *per saltum,* that is, on a man who is not a priest, it has its effect or not. But the episcopate without doubt, from institution of Christ, most truly pertains to the sacrament of orders, and is a priest- hood of a pre-eminent grade, that which in the words of the Fathers and in the custom of our ritual is, of course, called "summum sacerdotium," "sacri ministerii summa." Therefore, it happens that since the sacrament of orders and the true *sacerdotium* of Christ have been utterly thrust out of the Anglican rite, and so in the consecration of a bishop of this same rite the *sacerdotium* is by no means conferred; likewise, by no means can the episcopacy be truly and validly conferred; and this is all the more true because among the first duties of the episcopacy is this, namely, of ordaining ministers for the Holy Eucharist and the sacrifice. . . .

So with this inherent *defect of form* is joined the *defect of intention,* **1966** which it must have with equal necessity that it be a sacrament. . . . And so, assenting entirely to the decrees of all the departed Pontiffs in this case, and confirming them most fully and, as it were, renewing them by Our authority, of Our own inspiration and certain knowledge We pronounce and declare that ordinations enacted according to the Anglican rite have hitherto been and are invalid and entirely void. . . .

The Faith and Intention Required for Baptism [1]

[Response of the Holy Office, March 30th, 1898]

Whether a missionary can confer baptism on an adult Mohammedan **1966a** at the point of death, who in his errors is supposed to be in good faith:

---

[1] ASS 30 (1897/98), 700; *Collect. S.c. de Prop. Fide* II, n. 1993, 3.

1. If he still has his full faculties, only by exhorting him to sorrow and confidence, not by speaking about our mysteries, for fear that he will not believe them.

2. Whatever of his faculties he has, by saying nothing to him, since on the one hand, he is not supposed to be wanting in contrition, and on the other, it is supposed to be imprudent to speak with him about our mysteries.

3. If now he has lost his faculties, by saying nothing further to him.

Reply to 1 and 2: in the negative, i.e., it is not permitted to administer baptism absolutely or conditionally to such Mohammedans; and these decrees of the Holy Office were given to the Bishop of Quebec on the 25th of January, and the 10th of May, 1703 [see n. 1349 a f.].

To 3: regarding Mohammedans who are dying and already deprived of their senses, we must rely as in the decree of the Holy Office, Sept. 18, 1850, to the Bishop of Pertois, that is: "If they have formerly given indications that they wish to be baptized, or in their present state either by a nod or any other manner have shown the same disposition, they can be baptized conditionally; but where the missionary after examining all collateral circumstances so judges it wise," . . . His Holiness has approved.

Americanism [1]

[From the Letter, "Testem benevolentiae," to Cardinal
Gibbons, January 22, 1899]

1967   The basis of the new opinions which we have mentioned is established as essentially this: In order that those who dissent may more easily be brought over to Catholic wisdom, the Church should come closer to the civilization of this advanced age, and relaxing its old severity show indulgence to those opinions and theories of the people which have recently been introduced. Moreover, many think that this should be understood not only with regard to the standard of living, but even with regard to the doctrines in which the *deposit of faith* is contained. For, they contend that it is opportune to win over those who are in disagreement, if certain topics of doctrine are passed over as of lesser importance, or are so softened that they do not retain the same sense as the Church has always held.—Now there is no need of a long discussion to show with what a reprehensible purpose this has been thought out, if only the character and origin of the teaching which the Church hands down are considered. On this subject the Vatican Synod says: "For there is to be no receding. . . ." [see n. 1800].

---

[1] ASS 31 (1898/99), 471 ff.; AE 7 (1899) 55 b ff.

Now the history of all past ages is witness that this Apostolic See, to **1968**
which not only the office of teaching, but also the supreme government
of the whole Church were assigned, has indeed continually adhered "to
the same doctrine, in the same sense, and in the same mind" [Conc.
Vatic., see n. 1800]; that it has always been accustomed to modify the
rule of life so as never to overlook the manners and customs of the various
peoples which it embraces, while keeping the divine law unimpaired. If
the safety of souls demands this, who will doubt that it will do so now?—
This, however, is not to be determined by the decision of private individuals who are quite deceived by the appearance of right; but it should be **1969**
the judgment of the Church. . . . But in the case about which we are
speaking, Our Beloved Son, more danger is involved, and that advice is
more inimical to Catholic doctrine and discipline, according to which the
followers of new ideas think that a certain liberty should be introduced
into the Church so that, in a way checking the force of its power and
vigilance, the faithful may indulge somewhat more freely each one his
own mind and actual capacity.

The entire external teaching office is rejected by those who wish to **1970**
strive for the acquisition of Christian perfection, as superfluous, nay even
as useless; they say that the Holy Spirit now pours forth into the souls
of the faithful more and richer gifts than in times past, and, with no
intermediary, by a kind of hidden instinct teaches and moves them. . . .

Yet, to one who examines the matter very thoroughly, when any ex- **1971**
ternal guide is removed, it is not apparent in the thinking of the innovators to what end that more abundant influx of the Holy Spirit should
tend, which they extol so much.—Surely, it is especially in the cultivation
of virtues that there is absolute need of the assistance of the Holy Spirit;
but those who are eager to pursue new things extol the natural virtues
beyond measure, as if they correspond better with the way of life and
needs of the present day, and as if it were advantageous to be endowed
with these, since they make a man better prepared and more strenuous
for action.—It is indeed difficult to believe that those who are imbued
with Christian knowledge can hold the natural above the supernatural
virtues, and attribute to them greater efficacy and fruitfulness. . . .

With this opinion about the natural virtues another is closely con- **1972**
nected, according to which all Christian virtues are divided into two
kinds, as it were, *passive* as they say, and *active;* and they add that the
former were better suited for times past, that the latter are more in
keeping with the present. . . . Moreover, he who would wish that the
Christian virtues be accommodated some to one time and some to another, has not retained the words of the Apostle: "Whom he foreknew,
he also predestined to be made conformable to the image of His Son"
[Rom. 8: 29]. The master and exemplar of all sanctity is Christ, to whose

rule all, as many as wish to be admitted to the seats of the blessed, must conform. Surely, Christ by no means changes as the ages go on, but is "yesterday, and today; and the same forever" [Heb. 13:8]. Therefore, to the men of all ages does the following apply: "Learn of me, because I am meek, and humble of heart" [Matt. 11:29]; and at all times Christ shows himself to us "becoming obedient unto death" [Phil. 2:8]; and in every age the judgment of the Apostle holds: "And they that are Christ's have crucified their flesh with the vices and concupiscences" [Gal. 5:24].

1973   From this contempt, as it were, of the evangelical virtues, which are wrongly called passive, it easily followed that their minds were gradually imbued with a contempt even for the religious life. And that this is common among the advocates of the new opinions we conclude from certain opinions of theirs about the vows which religious orders pronounce. For, they say that these vows are at very great variance with the spirit of our age, and that they are suited to weak rather than to strong minds; and that they are quite without value for Christian perfection and the good of human society, but rather obstruct and interfere with both.—But it is clearly evident how false these statements are from the practice and teaching of the Church, by which the religious way of life has always been especially approved. . . . Moreover, as for what they add, that the religious way of life is of no or of little help to the Church, besides being odious to religious orders, will surely be believed by no one who has studied the annals of the Church. . . .

1974   Finally, not to delay too long, the way and the plan which Catholics have thus far employed to bring back those who disagree with them are proclaimed to be abandoned and to be replaced by another for the future. —But if of the different ways of preaching the word of God that seems to be preferred sometimes by which those who dissent from us are addressed not in temples, but in any private and honorable place, not in disputation but in a friendly conference, the matter lacks any cause for adverse criticism, provided, however, that those are assigned to this duty by the authority of the bishops, who have beforehand given proof to the bishops of their knowledge and integrity. . . .

1975   Therefore, from what We have said thus far it is clear, Our Beloved Son, that those opinions cannot be approved by us, the sum total of which some indicate by the name of Americanism. . . . For it raises a suspicion that there are those among you who envision and desire a Church in America other than that which is in all the rest of the world.

1976   One in unity of doctrine as in unity of government and this Catholic, such is the Church; and since God has established that its center and foundation be in the Chair of Peter, it is rightly called Roman; for "where Peter is, there is the Church." [1] Therefore, whoever wishes to be called by the name of Catholic, ought truly to heed the words of Jerome to Pope Damasus: "I who follow no one as first except Christ, associate myself in communion with your Beatitude, that is, with the Chair of Peter; upon that Rock, I know the Church is built [Matt. 16:18]; . . . whoever gathereth not with thee scattereth" [2] [Matt. 12:30].

The Matter of Baptism [3]

[From a Decree of the Holy Office, August 21, 1901]

The Archbishop of Utrecht [4] relates:

"Many medical doctors in hospitals and elsewhere in cases of necessity 1977 are accustomed to baptize infants in their mother's wombs with water mixed with *hydrargyrus bichloratus corrosivus* (in French: *chloride de mercure*). This water is compounded approximately of a solution of one part of this *chloretus hydrargicus* in a thousand parts of water, and with this solution of water the potion is poisonous. Now the reason why they use this mixture is that the womb of the mother may not be infected with disease."

Therefore the questions:

I. Is a baptism administered with such water certainly or dubiously valid?

II. Is it permitted to avoid all danger of disease to administer the sacrament of baptism with such water?

III. Is it permitted also to use this water when pure water can be applied without any danger of disease?

The answers are (with the approbation of Leo XIII):

To I. This will be answered in II.

To II. It is permitted when real danger of disease is present.

To III. No.

The Use of the Most Blessed Eucharist [5]

[From the Encyclical, "Mirae caritatis," May 28, 1902]

Away then with that widespread and most pernicious error on the 1978 part of those who express the opinion that the reception of the Eucharist is for the most part assigned to those who, free of cares and narrow in

---

[1] St. Ambrose, *In Ps. 40*, n. 30 [ML 14, 1082 A].

[2] St. Jerome, *Ep.* 15, *ad Damasum* [ML 22, 355 f.].

[3] ASS 34 (1901/02), 319 f.; AE 10 (1902), 9.

[4] In Holland.

[5] ASS 34 (1901/02), 644 f.; AE 10 (1902), 191 a.

mind, decide to rest at ease in some kind of a more religious life. For this sacrament (and there is none certainly more excellent or more conducive to salvation than this) pertains to absolutely all, of whatever office or pre-eminence they are, as many as wish (and no one ought not to wish this) to foster within themselves that life of divine grace, whose final end is the attainment of the blessed life with God.

PIUS X 1903–1914

The Blessed Virgin Mary, Mediatrix of Graces [1]

[From the Encyclical, "Ad diem," February 2, 1904]

1978a   As the result of this participation between Mary and Christ in the sorrows and the will, she deserved most worthily to be made the restorer of the lost world," [2] and so the dispenser of all the gifts which Jesus procured for us by His death and blood. . . . Since she excels all in sanctity, and by her union with Christ and by her adoption by Christ for the work of man's salvation, she merited for us *de congruo,* as they say, what Christ merited *de condigno,* and is the first minister of the graces to be bestowed.

"Implicit Citations" in Holy Scripture [3]

[From the Response of the Biblical Commission, February 13, 1905]

The question:

1979   Whether to solve difficulties that occur in some texts of Holy Scripture, which seem to present historical facts, it is permitted the Catholic exegete to state that it is a matter in these texts of the tacit or implicit citation of a document written by an author who was not inspired, all the asser-

---

[1] ASS 36 (1903/04), 453 f.

[2] The monk, Eadmar, *The Excellence of the Virgin Mary,* c. 9 [ML 159, 573]. Cf. what Benedict XV, *Litt. Apost.,* "Inter sodalicia," March 22, 1918 (AAS 10 [1918] 182) holds: "So did she suffer with her suffering and dying son, and almost die; so did she abdicate her maternal rights over her Son for the salvation of men, and to placate God's justice, insofar as was fitting for her, so did she sacrifice her Son, that it can properly be said that she with Christ redeemed the human race"; and also, what Pius XI has, *Litt. Apost.,* "Explorata res," February 2, 1923 (AAS 15 [1923] 104): "The Virgin participated with Jesus Christ in the very painful act of redemption." In the decree of the S.C. of the Holy Office (section on Indulgences), "Sunt quos amor," June 26, 1913 (AAS 5 [1913] 364), he praises the custom of adding to the name of Jesus the name of "His Mother, our coredemptor, the blessed Mary"; cf. also the prayer enriched by the Holy Office with an indulgence, in which the Blessed Virgin Mary is called "coredemptress of the human race" (Jan. 22, 1914; AAS 6 [1914] 108).

[3] ASS 37 (1904/05), 666; AE 13 (1905) 172 b; EB n. 153.

tions of which the inspired author does not at all intend to approve or to make his own, and which therefore cannot be held to be immune from errors?

The answer (with the approbation of Pius X):

In the negative, except in the case where, preserving the sense and judgment of the Church, it is proved by strong arguments: 1) that the sacred writer really is citing the words or documents of another, and 2) that he does not approve the same nor make them his own, so that it is rightly decided that he is not speaking in his own name.

The Historical Nature of Sacred Scripture [1]

[From the reply of the Biblical Commission, June 23, 1905]

The question:

Whether the opinion can be admitted as a principle of sound exegesis, 1980 which holds that the books of Sacred Scripture which are held to be historical, either in whole or in part sometimes do not narrate history properly so called and truly objective, but present an appearance of history only, to signify something different from the properly literal and historical significance of the words?

The answer (with the approbation of Pius X):

In the negative, except in the case, however, not readily or rashly to be admitted, where without opposing the sense of the Church and preserving its judgment, it is proved with strong arguments that the sacred writer did not wish to put down true history, and history properly so-called, but to set forth, under the appearance and form of history a parable, an allegory, or some meaning removed from the properly literal or historical significance of the words.

The Daily Partaking of the Most Holy Eucharist [2]

[From the Decree of the Congregation of the Holy Council, approved by Pius X, December 20th, 1905]

The desire (indeed) of Jesus Christ and of the Church, that all the 1981 faithful of Christ approach the sacred banquet daily, is especially important in this, that the faithful of Christ being joined with God through the sacrament may receive strength from it to restrain wantonness, to wash away the little faults that occur daily, and to guard against more grievous sins to which human frailty is subject; but not principally that consideration be given to the honor and veneration of God, nor that this

---

[1] ASS 38 (1905/06), 24 f.; AE 13 (1905), 353 b; EB n. 154.
[2] ASS 38 (1905/06), 401 ff.; AE 14 (1906), 61 b f.

be for those who partake of it a reward or recompense for their virtues. Therefore, the Sacred Council of Trent calls the Eucharist, "an antidote, by which we are freed from daily faults and are preserved from mortal sins" [see n. 875].

1982   Because of the plague of Jansenism, which raged on all sides, disputes began to arise regarding the dispositions with which frequent and daily communion should be approached, and some more than others demanded greater and more difficult dispositions as necessary. Such discussions brought it about that very few were held worthy to partake daily of the most blessed Eucharist, and to draw the fuller effects from so saving a sacrament, the rest being content to be renewed either once a year or every month, or at most once a week. Such a point of severity was reached that entire groups were excluded from frequenting the heavenly table, for example, merchants, or those *who had been joined in matrimony.*

1983   In these matters the Holy See was not remiss in its proper duty [see n. 1147 ff. and 1313]. . . . Nevertheless, the poison of Jansenism, which had infected even the souls of the good, under the appearance of honor and veneration due to the Eucharist, has by no means entirely disappeared. The question about the dispositions for frequenting communion rightly and lawfully has survived the declarations of the Holy See, as a result of which it has happened that some theologians even of good name rarely, and after laying down many conditions, have decided that daily communion can be permitted the faithful.

1984   . . . But His Holiness, since it is especially dear to him that the Christian people be invited to the sacred banquet very frequently and even daily, and so gain possession of its most ample fruits, has committed the aforesaid question to this sacred Order to be examined and defined.

[Hence the Congregation of the Holy Council on the 16th day of December, 1905] made the following decisions and declarations:

1985   1. Let frequent and daily communion . . . be available to all Christians of every order or condition, so that no one, who is in the state of grace and approaches the sacred table with a right and pious mind, may be prevented from this.

1986   2. Moreover, right mind is in this, that he who approaches the sacred table, indulges not through habit, or vanity, or human reasonings, but wishes to satisfy the pleasure of God, to be joined with Him more closely in charity and to oppose his infirmities and defects with that divine remedy.

1987   3. Although it is especially expedient that those who practice frequent and daily communion be free from venial sins, at least those completely deliberate, and of their effect, it is enough, nevertheless, that they be free from mortal sins, with the resolution that they will never sin in the future. . . .

4. . . Care must be taken that careful preparation for Holy Com- **1988** munion precede, and that actions befitting the graces follow thereafter according to the strength, condition, and duties of each one.

5. . . Let the counsel of the confessor intercede. Yet let confessors **1989** beware lest they turn anyone away from frequent or daily communion, who is found in the state of grace and approaches (it) with a right mind. . . .

9. . . Finally, after the promulgation of this decree, let all ecclesi- **1990** astical writers abstain from any contentious disputation about dispositions for frequent and daily communion.

The Tridentine Law of Clandestinity [1]

[From the Decree of Pius X, "Provida sapientique," Jan. 18, 1906]

I. In the entire German Empire today let the chapter, *Tametsi,* of **1991** the Council of Trent [see n. 990 ff.], although in many places it has not yet been definitely promulgated and introduced by manifest publication or by lawful observance, nevertheless henceforth from the feast day of Easter (i.e., from the 15th day of April) of this year 1906, bind all Catholics, even those up to now immune from observing the Tridentine form, so that they cannot celebrate a valid marriage between one another except in the presence of the parish priest and two or three witnesses [cf. n. 2066 ff.].

II. Mixed marriages, which are contracted by Catholics with heretics **1992** or schismatics, are and remain firmly prohibited, unless, when a just and weighty canonical reason is added, and lawful cautions have been given on both sides, honestly and formally, a dispensation has been duly obtained from the impediment of the mixed religion by the Catholic party. These marriages, to be sure, although a dispensation has been procured, are by all means to be celebrated in the sight of the Church, in the presence of a priest and two or three witnesses, so much so that they sin gravely who contract them in the presence of a non-Catholic minister, or in the presence of only a civil magistrate, or in any clandestine manner. Moreover, if any Catholics in celebrating these marriages seek and accept the service of a non-Catholic minister, they commit another sin and are subject to canonical censures.

Nevertheless, mixed marriages in certain provinces and localities of the **1993** German Empire, even in those which according to the decisions of the Roman Congregations have thus far been subject to the definitely in-

---

[1] ASS 39 (1906/07), 81 ff.; AE 14 (1906), 149 b f.

validating force of the chapter *Tametsi,* already contracted without preserving the Tridentine form or (and, may God forbid this) to be contracted in the future, provided no other canonical impediment stands in the way, and no decision of nullity because of the impediment of clandestinity has been lawfully passed before the feast day of Easter of this year, and the mutual consent of the spouses has persevered up to the said day, these mixed marriages we wish to be upheld as entirely valid, and We declare, define, and decree this expressly.

1994 III. Moreover, that a safe norm may be at hand for ecclesiastical judges, We declare, decide, and decree this same (pronouncement), and under the same conditions and restrictions, with regard to non-Catholic marriages, whether of heretics or of schismatics, thus far contracted between themselves in the same regions without preserving the Tridentine formula, or hereafter to be contracted; so that, if one or both of the non-Catholic spouses should be converted to the Catholic faith, or controversy should occur in an ecclesiastical court regarding the validity of the marriage of two non-Catholics, which is bound up with the question of the validity of the marriage contracted or to be contracted by some Catholic, these same marriages, all other things being equal, are similarly to be held as entirely valid.

The Separation of Church and State [1]

[From the Encyclical, "Vehementer nos," to the clergy
and people of France, February 11, 1906]

1995 We, in accord with the supreme authority which We hold from God, disprove and condemn the established law which separates the French state from the Church, for those reasons which We have set forth: because it inflicts the greatest injury upon God whom it solemnly rejects, declaring in the beginning that the state is devoid of any religious worship; because it violates the natural law, international law, and public trust in treaties; because it is contrary to the divine constitution of the Church and to her essential rights and liberty; because it overturns justice, by suppressing the right of ownership lawfully acquired by manifold titles and by the Concordat itself; because it gravely offends the dignity of the Apostolic See and Our own person, the ranks of bishops, the clergy, and the Catholics of France. Consequently, We protest most vehemently against the proposal of the law, its passage, and promulgation; and We attest that there is nothing at all of importance in it to

---

[1] ASS 39 (1906/07), 12 f.; AE 14 (1906), 56 a.

weaken the laws of the Church, which cannot be changed by the force and rashness of men.[1]

The Shortest Form of Extreme Unction [2]

[From the Decree of the Holy Office, April 25, 1906]

It has been decreed that in the case of true necessity this form suffices: 1996 "By this holy unction may the Lord forgive you whatever you have sinned. Amen."

The Mosaic Authenticity of the Pentateuch [3]

[From the Response of the Commission on Biblical Studies, June 27, 1906]

Question I. Whether the arguments accumulated by critics to impugn 1997 the Mosaic authenticity of the Sacred Books, which are designated by the name of Pentateuch, are of such weight that, in spite of the very many indications of both Testaments taken together, the continuous conviction of the Jewish people, also the unbroken tradition of the Church in addition to the internal evidences drawn from the text itself, they justify affirming that these books were not written by Moses, but were composed for the most part from sources later than the time of Moses? *Reply:* No.

Question II. Whether the Mosaic authenticity of the Pentateuch neces- 1998 sarily demands such a redaction of the whole work that it must be held absolutely that Moses wrote all and each book with his own hand, or dictated them to copyists; or, whether also the hypothesis can be permitted of those who think that the work was conceived by him under the influence of divine inspiration, and was committed to another or several to be put into writing, but in such manner that they rendered his thought faithfully, wrote nothing contrary to his wish, omitted nothing; and, finally, when the work was composed in this way, approved by Moses as its chief and inspired author, it was published under his name. *Reply:* No, for the first part; yes, for the second.

Question III. Whether without prejudice to the Mosaic authenticity of 1999 the Pentateuch it can be granted that Moses for the composition of the work made use of sources, namely written documents or oral tradition,

---

[1] Pius X took up the condemnation of this unjust law with very similar words in the allocution," *Gravissimum apostolici muneris,"* February 21, 1906 (ASS 39 [1906/07], 30 ff.).

[2] ASS 39 (1906/07), 273; AE 14 (1900), 278 a.

[3] ASS 39 (1906/07), 377 f.; AE 14 (1906), 305; EB n. 174 ff.

from which, according to the peculiar goal set before him, and under the influence of divine inspiration, he made some borrowings, and these, arranged word for word according to sense or amplified, he inserted into the work itself? *Reply:* Yes.

2000   *Question IV.* Whether, safeguarding substantially the Mosaic authenticity and the integrity of the Pentateuch, it can be admitted that in such a long course of ages it underwent some modifications, for example: additions made after the death of Moses, or by an inspired author, or glosses and explanations inserted in the texts, certain words and forms of the antiquated language translated into more modern language; finally false readings to be ascribed to the errors of copyists, which should be examined and passed upon according to the norms of textual criticism. *Reply:* Yes, the judgment of the Church being maintained.

The Errors of Modernists, on the Church, Revelation, Christ, the Sacraments [1]

[From the Decree of the Holy Office, "Lamentabili," July 3, 1907]

2001   1. The ecclesiastical law which prescribes that books dealing with the Divine Scriptures be submitted to a previous censorship does not extend to critical scholars, or to scholars of the scientific exegesis of the Old and New Testaments.

2002   2. The Church's interpretation of the Sacred Books is not indeed to be spurned, but it is subject to the more accurate judgment and the correction of exegetes.

2003   3. From the ecclesiastical judgments and censures passed against free and more learned exegesis, it can be gathered that the faith proposed by the Church contradicts history, and that Catholic teachings cannot in fact be reconciled with the truer origins of the Christian religion.

2004   4. The *magisterium* of the Church, even by dogmatic definitions, cannot determine the genuine sense of the Sacred Scriptures.

2005   5. Since in the deposit of faith only revealed truths are contained, in no respect does it pertain to the Church to pass judgment on the assertions of human disciplines.

2006   6. In defining truths the learning Church and the teaching Church so collaborate that there is nothing left for the teaching Church but to sanction the common opinions of the learning Church.

2007   7. When the Church proscribes errors, she cannot exact any internal assent of the faithful, by which the judgments published by her are embraced.

---

[1] ASS 40 (1907), 470 ff.; AE 15 (1907), 276 b f.; EB n. 183 ff.—Cf. Heiner, *Der neue Syllabus Pius' X* (Mainz, 1907).

8. They are to be considered free of all blame who consider of no 2008 account the reprobations published by the Sacred Congregation of the Index, or by other Sacred Roman Congregations.

9. They display excessive simplicity or ignorance, who believe that 2009 God is truly the author of the Sacred Scripture.

10. The inspiration of the books of the Old Testament consists in this; 2010 that the Israelite writers have handed down religious doctrines under a peculiar aspect which is little known, or not known at all to the Gentiles.

11. Divine inspiration does not so extend to all Sacred Scripture that 2011 it fortifies each and every part of it against all error.

12. The exegete, if he wishes to apply himself advantageously to Bib- 2012 lical studies, should divest himself especially of any preconceived opinion about the supernatural origin of Sacred Scripture, and should interpret it just as he would other merely human documents.

13. The Evangelists themselves and the Christians of the second and 2013 third generation have artificially distributed the parables of the Gospels, and thus have given a reason for the small fruit of the preaching of Christ among the Jews.

14. In many narratives the Evangelists related not so much what is 2014 true, as what they thought to be more profitable for the reader, although false.

15. The Gospels up to the time of the defining and establishment of 2015 the canon have been augmented continually by additions and corrections; hence, there has remained in them only a slight and uncertain trace of the doctrine of Christ.

16. The narrations of John are not properly history, but the mystical 2016 contemplation of the Gospel; the discourses contained in his Gospel are theological meditations on the mystery of salvation, devoid of historical truth.

17. The Fourth Gospel exaggerated miracles, not only that the extraor- 2017 dinary might stand out more, but also that they might become more suitable for signifying the work and glory of the Word Incarnate.

18. John, indeed, claims for himself the character of a witness concern- 2018 ing Christ; but in reality he is nothing but a distinguished witness of the Christian life, or of the life of the Christian Church at the end of the first century.

19. Heterodox exegetes have more faithfully expressed the true sense 2019 of Scripture than Catholic exegetes.

20. Revelation could have been nothing other than the consciousness 2020 acquired by man of his relation to God.

21. Revelation, constituting the object of Catholic faith, was not com- 2021 pleted with the apostles.

22. The dogmas which the Church professes as revealed are not truths 2022

fallen from heaven, but they are a kind of interpretation of religious facts, which the human mind by a laborious effort prepared for itself.

2023   23. Opposition can and actually does exist between facts which are narrated in Sacred Scripture, and the dogmas of the Church based on these, so that a critic can reject as false, facts which the Church believes to be most certain.

2024   24. An exegete is not to be reproved who constructs premises from which it follows that dogmas are historically false or dubious, provided he does not directly deny the dogmas themselves.

2025   25. The assent of faith ultimately depends on an accumulation of probabilities.

2026   26. The dogmas of faith are to be held only according to a practical sense, that is, as preceptive norms for action, but not as norms for believing.

2027   27. The divinity of Jesus Christ is not proved from the Gospels; but is a dogma which the Christian conscience has deduced from the notion of the Messias.

2028   28. When Jesus was exercising His ministry, He did not speak with this purpose, to teach that He was the Messias, nor did His miracles have as their purpose to demonstrate this.

2029   29. It may be conceded that the Christ whom history presents, is far inferior to the Christ who is the object of faith.

2030   30. In all the evangelical texts the name, *Son of God,* is equivalent to the name of *Messias;* but it does not at all signify that Christ is the true and natural Son of God.

2031   31. The doctrine about Christ, which Paul, John, and the Councils of Nicea, Ephesus, and Chalcedon hand down, is not that which Jesus taught, but which the Christian conscience conceived about Jesus.

2032   32. The natural sense of the evangelical texts cannot be reconciled with that which our theologians teach about the consciousness and the infallible knowledge of Jesus Christ.

2033   33. It is evident to everyone, who is not influenced by preconceived opinions, that either Jesus professed an error concerning the immediate coming of the Messias, or the greater part of the doctrine contained in the Synoptic Gospels is void of authenticity.

2034   34. The critic cannot ascribe to Christ knowledge circumscribed by no limit, except on the supposition which can by no means be conceived historically, and which is repugnant to the moral sense, namely, that Christ as man had the knowledge of God, and nevertheless was unwilling to share the knowledge of so many things with His disciples and posterity.

2035   35. Christ did not always have the consciousness of His Messianic dignity.

36. The resurrection of the Savior is not properly a fact of the his- 2036
torical order, but a fact of the purely supernatural order, neither demonstrated nor demonstrable, and which the Christian conscience gradually
derived from other sources.

37. Faith in the resurrection of Christ was from the beginning not so 2037
much of the fact of the resurrection itself, as of the immortal life of
Christ with God.

38. The doctrine of the expiatory death of Christ is not evangelical but 2038
only Pauline.

39. The opinions about the origin of the sacraments with which the 2039
Fathers of Trent were imbued, and which certainly had an influence on
their dogmatic canons, are far different from those which now rightly
obtain among historical investigators of Christianity.

40. The sacraments had their origin in this, that the apostles and their 2040
successors, swayed and moved by circumstances and events, interpreted
some idea and intention of Christ.

41. The sacraments have this one end, to call to man's mind the ever 2041
beneficent presence of the Creator.

42. The Christian community has introduced the necessity of baptism, 2042
adopting it as a necessary rite, and adding to it the obligation of professing Christianity.

43. The practice of conferring baptism on infants was a disciplinary 2043
evolution, which was one reason for resolving the sacrament into two,
baptism and penance.

44. There is no proof that the rite of the sacrament of confirmation 2044
was practiced by the apostles; but the formal distinction between the
two sacraments, namely, baptism and confirmation, by no means goes
back to the history of primitive Christianity.

45. Not all that Paul says about the institution of the Eucharist [I Cor. 2045
11:23–25] is to be taken historically.

46. There was no conception in the primitive Church of the Christian 2046
sinner reconciled by the authority of the Church, but the Church only
very gradually became accustomed to such a conception. Indeed, even
after penance was recognized as an institution of the Church, it was not
called by the name, sacrament, for the reason that it would have been
held as a shameful sacrament.

47. The words of the Lord: "Receive ye the Holy Ghost; whose sins 2047
ye shall forgive they are forgiven them, and whose sins ye shall retain
they are retained" [John 20:22, 23], do not refer at all to the sacrament
of penance, whatever the Fathers of Trent were pleased to say.

48. James in his Epistle [Jas. 5:14 f.] does not intend to promulgate 2048
some sacrament of Christ, but to commend a certain pious custom, and
if in this custom by chance he perceives some means of grace, he does

not accept this with that strictness with which the theologians have accepted it, who have established the notion and the number of the sacraments.

2049   49. As the Christian Supper gradually assumed the nature of a liturgical action, those who were accustomed to preside at the Supper acquired the sacerdotal character.

2050   50. The elders who fulfilled the function of watching over gatherings of Christians were instituted by the apostles as presbyters or bishops to provide for the necessary arrangement of the increasing communities, not properly for perpetuating the apostolic mission and power.

2051   51. Matrimony could not have emerged as a sacrament of the New Law in the Church, since in order that matrimony might be held to be a sacrament, it was necessary that a full theological development of the doctrine on grace and the sacraments take place first.

2052   52. It was foreign to the mind of Christ to establish a Church as a society upon earth to endure for a long course of centuries; rather, in the mind of Christ the Kingdom of Heaven together with the end of the world was to come presently.

2053   53. The organic constitution of the Church is not immutable; but Christian society, just as human society, is subject to perpetual evolution.

2054   54. The dogmas, the sacraments, the hierarchy, as far as pertains both to the notion and to the reality, are nothing but interpretations and the evolution of the Christian intelligence, which have increased and perfected the little germ latent in the Gospel.

2055   55. Simon Peter never even suspected that the primacy of the Church was entrusted to him by Christ.

2056   56. The Roman Church became the head of all the churches not by the ordinances of divine Providence, but purely by political factors.

2057   57. The Church shows herself to be hostile to the advances of the natural and theological sciences.

2058   58. Truth is no more immutable than man himself, inasmuch as it is evolved with him, in him, and through him.

2059   59. Christ did not teach a defined body of doctrine applicable to all times and to all men, but rather began a religious movement adapted, or to be adapted to different times and places.

2060   60. Christian doctrine in its beginnings was Judaic, but through successive evolutions it became first Pauline, then Johannine, and finally Hellenic and universal.

2061   61. It can be said without paradox that no chapter of Scripture, from the first of Genesis to the last of the Apocalypse, contains doctrine entirely identical with that which the Church hands down on the same subject, and so no chapter of Scripture has the same sense for the critic as for the theologian.

62. The principal articles of the Apostles' Creed did not have the same meaning for the Christians of the earliest times as they have for the Christians of our time. 2062

63. The Church shows herself unequal to the task of preserving the ethics of the Gospel, because she clings obstinately to immutable doctrines which cannot be reconciled with present day advances. 2063

64. The progress of the sciences demands that the concepts of Christian doctrine about God, creation, revelation, the Person of the Incarnate Word, the redemption, be recast. 2064

65. Present day Catholicism cannot be reconciled with true science, unless it be transformed into a kind of nondogmatic Christianity, that is, into a broad and liberal Protestantism. 2065

Censure of the Holy Pontiff: "His Holiness has approved and confirmed the decree of the Most Eminent Fathers, and has ordered that all and every proposition enumerated above be held as condemned and proscribed" [See also n. 2114]. 2065a

Betrothal and Marriage [1]

[From the Decree *Ne temere* of the Holy Council, August 2, 1907]

Betrothal.—I. Those betrothals alone are held valid and carry canonical effects, which have been contracted in writing signed by the parties, and either by the pastor or ordinary of the place, or at least by two witnesses. 2066

Marriage. III. The above marriages are valid, which are contracted in the presence of the pastor or ordinary of the place, or a priest delegated by either of the two, and at least two witnesses. . . . 2067

VII. If the danger of death is imminent, when the pastor or ordinary of the place, or a priest delegated by either of the two cannot be had, out of consideration for the conscience (of the betrothed) and (if occasion warrants) for legitimizing offspring, marriage can be validly and licitly contracted in the presence of any priest and two witnesses. 2068

VIII. If it happens that in some region the pastor or ordinary of the place or priest delegated by them, in the presence of whom marriage can be celebrated, cannot be had, and this condition of things has lasted now for a month, the marriage can be validly and licitly entered upon after a formal consent has been given by the betrothed in the presence of two witnesses. 2069

XI. Sec. 1. All who have been baptized in the Catholic Church and have been converted to her from heresy or schism, even if one or the other has afterwards apostasized, as often as they enter upon mutual betrothal or marriage, are bound by the laws above established. 2070

---

[1] ASS 40 (1907), 527 ff.; AE 15 (1907), 320 ff.

Sec. 2. They also hold for the same Catholics mentioned above, if they contract betrothal or marriage with non-Catholics, whether baptized or not baptized, even after having obtained dispensation from the impediment of mixed marriage, or of difference of worship, unless it has otherwise been established by the Holy See for some particular place or region.

Sec. 3. Non-Catholics, whether baptized or not baptized, if they make contracts between themselves, are nowhere bound to keep the Catholic form of betrothal or of marriage.

Let the present decree lawfully published and promulgated be kept by its transmission to the ordinaries of places; and let what has been disposed in it begin to have the force of law everywhere, from the solemn day of the Pasch of the Resurrection D.N.I.C. [April 19] of next year, 1908.

The False Doctrines of the Modernists [1]

[From the Encyclical, "Pascendi dominici gregis," Sept. 8, 1907]

2071   Since it is a very clever artifice on the part of the modernists (for they are rightly so-called in general) not to set forth their doctrines arranged in orderly fashion and collected together, but as if scattered, and separated from one another, so that they seem very vague and, as it were, rambling, although on the contrary they are strong and constant, it is well, Venerable Brothers, first to present these same doctrines here in one view, and to show the nexus by which they coalesce with one another, that we may then examine the causes of the errors and may prescribe the remedies to remove the calamity. . . . But, that we may proceed in orderly fashion in a rather abstruse subject, this must be noted first of all, that every modernist plays several roles, and, as it were, mingles in himself, (I) the philosopher of course, (II) the believer, (III) the theologian, (IV) the historian, (V) the critic, (VI) the apologist, (VII) the reformer. All these roles he must distinguish one by one, who wishes to understand their system rightly, and to discern the antecedents and the consequences of their doctrines.

2072   [I] Now, to begin with the philosopher, the modernists place the foundation of their religious philosophy in that doctrine which is commonly called *agnosticism*. Perforce, then, human reason is entirely restricted to *phenomena,* namely, things that appear, and that appearance by which they appear; it has neither the right nor the power to transgress the limits of the same. Therefore, it cannot raise itself to God nor recognize His existence, even through things that are seen. Hence, it is inferred that God can by no means be directly an object of science; yet,

---

[1] ASS 40 (1907), 593 ff.; AE 15 (1907), 361 ff.; EB n. 250 ff. [*inde* a n. 2073].

as far as pertains to history, that He is not to be considered an historical subject.—Moreover, granting all this, everyone will easily see what becomes of *Natural Theology,* of the *motives of credibility,* of *external revelation.* These, of course, the modernists completely spurn, and relegate to intellectualism, an absurd system, they say, and long since dead. Nor does the fact that the Church has very openly condemned such portentous errors restrain them, for the Vatican Synod so decreed: "If anyone, etc.," [see n. 1806 f., 1812].

But in what way do the Modernists pass from agnosticism, which **2073** consists only in nescience, to scientific and historic *atheism,* which on the other hand is entirely posited in denial; so, by what law of reasoning is the step taken from that state of ignorance as to whether or not God intervened in the history of the human race, to the explanation of the same history, leaving God out altogether, as if He had not really intervened, he who can well knows. Yet, this is fixed and established in their minds, that science as well as history should be atheistic, in whose limits there can be place only for phenomena, God and whatever is divine being utterly thrust aside.—As a result of this most absurd teaching we shall soon see clearly what is to be held regarding the most sacred person of Christ, the mysteries of His life and death, and likewise about His resurrection and ascension into heaven.

Yet this agnosticism is to be considered only as the negative part of **2074** the system of the modernists; the positive consists, as they say, in *vital immanence.* Naturally, they thus proceed from one to the other of these parts.—Religion, whether this be natural or supernatural, must, just as any fact, admit of some explanation. But the explanation, with natural theology destroyed and the approach to revelation barred by the rejection of the arguments of credibility, with even any external revelation utterly removed, is sought in vain outside man. It is, then, to be sought within man himself; and, since religion is a form of life, it is to be found entirely within the life of man. From this is asserted the principle of religious immanence. Moreover, of every vital phenomenon, to which it has just been said religion belongs, the first actuation, as it were, is to be sought in a certain need or impulsion; but, if we speak more specifically of life, the beginnings are to be posited in a kind of motion of the heart, which is called a *sense.* Therefore, since God is the object of religion, it must be concluded absolutely that faith, which is the beginning and the foundation of any religion, must be located in some innermost sense, which has its beginning in a need for the divine. Moreover, this need for the divine, since it is felt only in certain special surroundings, cannot of itself pertain to the realm of consciousness, but it remains hidden at first beneath consciousness, or, as they say with a word borrowed from modern philosophy, in the *subconsciousness,* where, too, its root remains hidden and undetected.—Someone perhaps will ask in what way does this need of the divine, which man himself perceives within himself, finally evolve into religion? To this the modernists reply: "Science and history are included within a twofold boundary: one external, that is the visible world; the other internal, which is consciousness. When they have reached one or the other, they are unable to proceed further, for beyond these boundaries is the *unknowable.* In the presence of this unknowable, whether this be outside man and beyond the perceptible world of nature, or lies concealed within the *subconsciousness,* the need of the divine in a soul prone to religion, according to the tenets of *fideism,* with no judgment of the mind anticipating, excites a certain peculiar *sense;* but this sense has the divine *reality* itself, not only as its object but also as its intrinsic cause implicated within itself, and somehow unites man with God." This sense, moreover, is what the modernists call by the name of faith, and is for them the beginning of religion.

2075　　But this is not the end of their philosophizing, or more correctly of their raving. For in such a sense the modernists find not only faith, but together with faith and in faith itself, as they understand it, they affirm that there is place for revelation. For will anyone ask whether anything more is needed for revelation? Shall we not call that religious sense that appears in the conscience "revelation," or at least the beginning of revelation; why not God himself, although rather confusedly, manifesting Himself to souls in the same religious sense? But they add: Since God is alike both object and cause of faith, that revelation is equally of God and from God, that is, it has God as the Revealer as well as the Revealed. From this, moreover, Venerable Brothers, comes that absurd affirmation of the modernists, according to which any religion according to its various aspects is to be called natural and also supernatural. From this, consciousness and revelation have interchangeable meanings. From this is the law according to which *religious consciousness* is handed down as a universal rule, to be equated completely with revelation, to which all must submit, even the supreme power in the Church, whether this teaches or legislates on sacred matters or discipline.

2076　　Yet in all this process, from which according to the modernists, faith and revelation come forth, one thing is especially to be noted, indeed of no small moment because of the historico-critical sequences which they pry from it. For the *unknowable,* of which they speak, does not present itself to faith as something simple or alone, but on the contrary adhering closely to some phenomenon, which, although it pertains to the fields of science and history, yet in some way passes beyond them, whether this phenomenon be a fact of nature containing some secret within itself, or be any man whose character, actions, and words do not seem possible of being reconciled with the ordinary laws of history. Then faith, attracted by the unknowable which is united with the phenomenon, embraces the whole phenomenon itself and in a manner permeates it with its own life. Now from this two things follow: first, a kind of *transfiguration* of the phenomenon by elation, that is, above its true conditions, by which its matter becomes more suitable to clothe itself with the form of the divine, which faith is to introduce; second, some sort of *disfiguration,* (we may call it such) of the same phenomenon, arising from the fact that faith attributes to it, when divested of all adjuncts of place and time, what in fact it does not possess; and this takes place especially when phenomena of times past are concerned, and the more fully as they are the older. From this twofold source the modernists again derive two canons, which, when added to another already borrowed from agnosticism, constitute the foundations of historical criticism. The subject will be illustrated by an example, and let us take that example from the person of Christ. In the person of Christ, they say, science and history encounter nothing except the human. Therefore, by virtue of the first canon deduced from agnosticism whatever is redolent of the divine must be deleted from His history. Furthermore, by virtue of the second canon the historical person of Christ was *transfigured* by faith; therefore, whatever raises it above historical conditions must be removed from it. Finally, by virtue of the third canon the same person of Christ is disfigured by faith; therefore, words and deeds must be removed from it, whatever, in a word, does not in the least correspond with His character, state, and education, and with the place and time in which He lived. A wonderful method of reasoning indeed! But this is the criticism of the modernists.

　　Therefore, *the religious sense,* which through *vital* immanence comes **2077** forth from the hiding places of the subconsciousness, is the germ of all religion, and the explanation likewise of everything which has been or is to be in any religion. Such a *sense,* crude in the beginning and almost unformed, gradually and under the influence of that mysterious principle, whence it had its origin, matured with the progress of human life, of which, as we have said, it is a kind of form. So, we have the origin of any religion, even if supernatural; they are, of course, mere developments of the *religious sense.* And let no one think that the Catholic religion is excepted; rather, it is entirely like the rest; for it was born in the consciousness of Christ, a man of the choicest nature, whose like no one has ever been or will be, by the process of *vital immanence.* . . . [adduced by can. 3 of the Vatican Council on revelation; see n. 1808].

　　Yet up to this point, Venerable Brethren, we have discovered no place **2078** given to the intellect. But it, too, according to the doctrine of the modernists, has its part in the act of faith. It is well to notice next in what way. In that *sense,* they say, which we have mentioned rather often, since it is *sense,* not knowledge, God presents himself to man, but so confusedly and disorderly that He is distinguished with difficulty, or not at all, by the subject believer. It is necessary, therefore, that this sense be illuminated by some light, so that God may completely stand out and be separated from it. Now, this pertains to the intellect, whose function it is to ponder and to institute analysis, by which man first brings to light the vital phenomena arising within him, and then makes them known by words. Hence the common expression of the modernists, that the religious man must *think* his faith.—The mind then, encountering this sense, reflects upon it and works on it, as a painter who brightens up the faded outline of a picture to bring it out more clearly, for essentially thus does one of the teachers of the modernists explain the matter. Moreover, in such a work the mind operates in a twofold way: first, by a natural and spontaneous act it presents the matter in a simple and popular judgment; but then after reflection and deeper consideration, or, as they say, by *elaborating the thought,* it speaks forth its thoughts in *secondary* judgments, derived, to be sure, from the simple first, but more precise and distinct. These *secondary* judgments, if they are finally sanctioned by the supreme *magisterium* of the Church, will constitute *dogma.*

2079   Thus, then, in the doctrine of the modernists we have come to an outstanding chapter, namely, the origin of dogma and the inner nature of dogma. For they place the origin of dogma in those primitive simple formulae, which in a certain respect are necessary for faith; for revelation, to actually be such, requires a clear knowledge of God in consciousness. Yet the dogma itself, they seem to affirm, is properly contained in the *secondary* formulae.—Furthermore, to ascertain its nature we must inquire above all what revelation intervenes between the *religious formulae* and the religious *sense* of the soul. But this he will easily understand, who holds that such formulae have no other purpose than to supply the means by which he (the believer) may give himself an account of his faith. Therefore, they are midway between the believer and his faith; but as far as faith is concerned, they are inadequate signs of its object, usually called *symbolae;* in their relationship to the believer, they are mere instruments. —So by no means can it be maintained that they absolutely contain the truth; for, insofar as they are symbols, they are images of the truth, and so are to be accommodated to the religious sense, according as this refers to man; and as *instruments* they are the vehicles of truth, and so they are in turn to be adapted to man, insofar as there is reference to the religious sense. But the object of *the religious sense,* inasmuch as it is contained in the *absolute,* has infinite aspects of which now one, now another can appear. Likewise, the man who believes can make use of varying conditions. Accordingly, also, the formulae which we call dogma should be subject to the same vicissitudes, and so be liable to change. Thus, then, the way is open to the *intrinsic* evolution of dogma.—Surely an infinite piling up of sophisms, which ruin and destroy all religion.

Yet that dogma not only can but ought to be evolved and changed, even **2080** the modernists themselves in fragmentary fashion affirm, and this clearly follows from their principles. For among the chief points of doctrine they hold this, which they deduce from the principle of *vital immanence,* that religious formulae, to be really religious and not only intellectual speculations, should be alive, and should live the life of the religious sense. This is not to be understood thus, as if these formulae, especially if merely imaginative, were invented for the religious sense; for their origin is of no concern, nor is their number or quality, but as follows: that the religious sense, applying some modification, if necessary, should join them to itself *vitally.* Of course, in other words, it is necessary that the *primitive* formula be accepted by the heart and sanctioned by it; likewise that the labor by which the secondary formulae are brought forth be under the guidance of the heart. Hence it happens that these formulae, to be vital, should be and should remain adapted alike to the faith and to the believer. Therefore, if for any cause such an adaptation should cease, they lose the original notions and need to be changed.—Furthermore, since this power and the fortune of the dogmatic formulae are so unstable, it is no wonder that they are such an object of ridicule and contempt to modernists, who say nothing to the contrary and extol nothing but the religious sense and religious life. And so they most boldly attack the Church as moving on a path of error, because she does not in the least distinguish the religious and moral force from the superficial significance of the formulae, and by clinging with vain labor and most tenaciously to formulae devoid of meaning, permits religion itself to collapse.— Surely, "blind and leaders of the blind" [Matt. 15:14] are they who, puffed up by the proud name of science, reach such a point in their raving that they pervert the eternal concept of truth, and the true sense of religion by introducing a new system, "in which from an exaggerated and unbridled desire for novelty, truth is not sought where it certainly exists, and neglecting the holy and apostolic traditions, other doctrines empty, futile, uncertain, and unapproved by the Church are adopted, on which men in their extreme vanity think that truth itself is based and maintained." [1] So much, Venerable Brothers, for the modernist as a philosopher.

[II] Now if, on advancing to the believer, one wishes to know how **2081** he is distinguished from the philosopher among the modernists, this must be observed that, although the philosopher admits the reality of the divine as the object of faith, yet this reality is not found by him any-

---

[1] The Encyclical of Gregory XVI, "Singulari Nos," June 25, 1834 [n. 1617].

where except in the heart of the believer, since it is the object of sense and of affirmation, and so does not exceed the confines of phenomena; furthermore, whether that reality exists in itself outside that sense and affirmation, the philosopher passes over and neglects. On the other hand for the modernist believer it is established and certain that the reality of the divine definitely exists in itself, and certainly does not depend on the believer. But if you ask on what then the assertion of the believer rests, they will reply: In the personal *experience* of every man.—In this affirmation, while they break with the rationalists, to be sure, yet they fall in with the opinion of Protestants and pseudomystics [cf. n. 1273]. For they explain the subject as follows: that in the religious sense a kind of intuition of the heart is to be recognized, by which man directly attains the *reality* of God, and draws from it such conviction of the existence of God and of the action of God both within and without man, that it surpasses by far all conviction that can be sought from science. They establish, then, a true experience and one superior to any rational experience. If anyone, such as the rationalists, deny this, they say that this arises from the fact that he is unwilling to establish himself in the moral state which is required to produce the experience. Furthermore, 2082 this experience, when anyone has attained it, properly and truly makes a believer.—How far we are here from Catholic teachings. We have already seen [cf. n. 2072] such fabrications condemned by the Vatican Council. When these errors have once been admitted, together with others already mentioned, we shall express below how open the way is to atheism. It will be well to note at once that from this doctrine of experience joined with another of symbolism, any religion, not even excepting paganism, must be held as true. For why should not experiences of this kind not occur in any religion? In fact, more than one asserts that they have occurred. By what right will modernists deny the truth of an experience which an Islamite affirms, and claim true experiences for Catholics alone? In fact, modernists do not deny this; on the contrary some rather obscurely, others very openly contend that all religions are true. But it is manifest that they cannot think otherwise. For on what basis, then, should falsity have been attributed to any religion according to their precepts? Surely it would be either because of the falsity of the religious sense or because a false formula was set forth by the intellect. Now the religious sense is always one and the same, although sometimes it is more imperfect; but that the intellectual formula be true, it is enough that it respond to the religious sense and to the human believer, whatever may be the character of the perspicacity of the latter. In the conflict of different religions the modernists might be able to contend for one thing at most, that the Catholic religion, inasmuch as it is the more vivid, has more truth; and likewise that it is more worthy of the name of Christian, inasmuch as it corresponds more fully with the origins of Christianity.

There is something else besides in this part of their doctrine, which **2083** is absolutely inimical to Catholic truth. For the precept regarding experience is applied also to *tradition,* which the Church has hitherto asserted, and utterly destroys it. For the modernists understand tradition thus: that it is a kind of communication with others of an *original experience,* through preaching by means of the intellectual formula. To this formula, therefore, besides, as they say, *representative* force, they ascribe a kind of *suggestive* power, not only to excite in him who believes the religious sense, which perchance is becoming sluggish, and to restore the experience once acquired, but also to give birth in them who do not yet believe, to a religious sense for the first time, and to produce the experience. Thus, moreover, religious experience is spread widely among the people; and not only among those who are now in existence, but also among posterity, both by books and by oral transmission from one to another.—But this communication of experience sometimes takes root and flourishes; sometimes it grows old suddenly, and dies. Moreover, to flourish is to the modernists an argument for truth; for they hold truth and life to be the same. Therefore, we may infer again: that all religions, as many as exist, are true; for otherwise they would not be alive.

Now with our discussion brought to this point, Venerable Brethren, **2084** we have enough and more to consider accurately what relationship the modernists establish between faith and science; furthermore, history, also, is classed by them under this name of science.—And in the first place, indeed, it is to be held that the object-matter of the one is entirely extraneous to the object-matter of the other and separated from it. For faith looks only to that which science professes to be unknowable to itself. Hence to each is a different duty: science is concerned with phenomena where there is no place for faith; faith, on the other hand, is concerned with the divine, of which science is totally ignorant. Thus, finally, it is settled that there can never be dissension between faith and science; for if each holds its own place, they will never be able to meet each other, and so contradict each other. If any persons by chance object to this, on the ground that certain things occur in visible nature which pertain also to faith, as, for example, the human life of Christ, the modernists will deny it. For, although these things are classified with phenomena, yet, insofar as they are imbued with the life of faith, and in the manner already mentioned have been transfigured and disfigured by faith [cf. n. 2076], they have been snatched away from the sensible world and transferred into material for the divine. Therefore, to him who asks further whether Christ performed true miracles and really divined the future; whether He truly rose from the dead and ascended into heaven, agnostic science will give a denial, faith an affirmation; yet as a result of this there will be no conflict between the two. For one, addressing philosophers as a philosopher, namely, contemplating Christ only according to historical reality, will deny; the other, speaking as a believer with believers, viewing the life of Christ as it is lived again by the faith and in the faith, will affirm.

2085   A great mistake, however, is made as a result of this by anyone who thinks that he can believe that faith and science are subject to each other in no way at all. For, as regards science he does indeed think rightly and truly; but it is otherwise with faith, which must be said to be subject to science not only on one, but on three grounds. For, first, we must observe that in any religious fact, after the *divine reality* has been taken away, and whatever experience he who believes has of it, all other things, especially religious formulae, do not pass beyond the confines of phenomena, and so fall under science. By all means let it be permitted the believer, if he wills, to go out of the world, yet as long as he remains in it, whether he likes it or not, he will never escape the laws, the observations, the judgments of science and history.—Furthermore, although it is said that God is the object of faith alone, this is to be granted with regard to the *divine reality,* but not with regard to the *idea* of God. For this is subject to science, which, while it philosophizes in the logical order, as they say, attains also what is absolute and ideal. Therefore, philosophy or science has the right to learn about the idea of God, and to direct it in its evolution, and, if anything extraneous enters it, to correct it. Hence the axiom of the modernists: Religious evolution should be reconciled with the moral and the intellectual, that is, as one teaches whom they follow as a master, it should be subject to them.—Finally it happens that God does not suffer duality within Himself, and so the believer is urged on by an innermost force so to harmonize faith with science that it never disagrees with the general idea which science sets forth about the entire universe. Thus, then, is it effected that science is entirely freed from faith, that faith on the other hand, however much it is proclaimed to be extraneous to science, is subject to it.—All this, Venerable Brethren, is contrary to what Pius IX, Our predecessor, handed down teaching: "It is the duty of philosophy, in those matters which pertain to religion, not to dominate but to serve, not to prescribe what is to be believed, but to embrace what is to be believed with reasonable obedience, and not to examine the depths of the mysteries of God, but to revere them piously and humbly.[1] The modernists completely invert the matter; so what Our predecessor, Gregory IX, similarly wrote about certain theologians of his age can be applied to these: "Some among

---

[1] Brief to the Archbishop of Cologne, June 15, 1857 [see n. 1655].

you, distended like bladders by the spirit of vanity, strive by novelty to cross the boundaries fixed by the Fathers; twisting the meaning of the sacred text . . . to the philosophical teaching of the rationalists, to make a show of science, not for any benefit to their hearers. . . . These men, lead astray by various strange doctrines, reduce the head to the tail, and force the queen to serve the handmaid." [1]

This, surely, will be quite clear to one who observes how the modernists **2086** act quite in conformity with what they teach. For much seems to have been written and spoken by them in contrary fashion so that one might easily think them doubtful and uncertain. But this takes place deliberately and advisedly, namely, in accord with the opinion which they hold on the mutual exclusion of faith and science. Thus in their books we find certain things which a Catholic entirely approves, yet on turning the page certain things which one could think were dictated by a rationalist. So, when writing history they make no mention of the divinity of Christ, but when preaching in the churches they profess it most strongly. Likewise, when discussing history they have no place for the Councils and the Fathers, but when teaching catechism, they refer to the former and the latter with respect. Thus, too, they separate theological and pastoral exegesis from the scientific and the historical. Similarly, on the principle that science in no wise depends on faith, when they are treating of philosophy, history, and criticism, with no special horror about following in the tracks of Luther [cf. n. 769], they display in every way a contempt for Catholic precepts, the Holy Fathers, the Ecumenical Synods, and the ecclesiastical *magisterium;* and if they are criticized for this, they complain that they are being deprived of their freedom. Finally, professing that faith must be made subject to science, they rebuke the Church generally and openly, because she refuses most resolutely to subject and accommodate her teachings to the opinions of philosophy; but they, repudiating the old theology for this purpose, endeavor to bring in the new, which follows the ravings of the philosophers.

[III] Here now, Venerable Brethren, we approach the study of the **2087** modernists in the theological arena, a rough task indeed, but to be disposed of briefly. It is a question, indeed, of conciliating faith with science, and this in no other way than by subjecting one to the other. In this field the modernist theologian makes use of the same principles that we saw employed by the philosopher, and he adapts them to the believer; we mean the principles of *immanence* and *symbolism.* Thus, moreover, he accomplishes the task most easily. It is held as certain by the philosopher that *the principle of faith is immanent;* it is added by the believer that *this principle is God;* and he himself (the theologian) concludes: *God,* then, *is immanent in man.* From this comes *theological immanence.*

---

[1] Letter to the theological masters of Paris, July 7, 1223 [cf. n. 442 f.].

Again, to the philosopher it is certain that *the representations of the object of faith are only symbolical;* to the believer, likewise, it is certain that *the object of faith is God in Himself;* so the theologian gathers that *the representations of the divine reality are symbolical.* From this comes *theological symbolism.*—Surely the greatest errors, and how pernicious each is will be clear from an examination of the consequences.—For to speak at once about *symbolism,* since such symbols are symbols with regard to their object, but with regard to the believer are instruments, the believer must first of all be on his guard, they say, lest he cling too much to the formula, as formula, but he must make use of it only that he may fasten upon the absolute truth, which the formula at the same time uncovers and covers, and struggles to express without ever attaining it. Besides, they add, such formulae are to be applied by the believer insofar as they help him; for they are given as a help, not as a hindrance, with full esteem indeed, which out of social respect is due the formulae which the public *magisterium* has judged suitable for expressing the common consciousness, as long, of course, as the same *magisterium* shall not declare otherwise. But regarding *immanence* what the modernists mean really, is difficult to show, for they do not all have the same opinion. There are some who hold on this subject, that God working in man is more intimately present in him than man is even in himself; which, if rightly understood, bears no reproach. Others on this matter lay down that the action of God is one with the action of nature, as the action of the first cause is one with that of the second cause, which really destroys the supernatural order. Finally, others so explain it in a way that causes a suspicion of a pantheistic meaning; yet this fittingly coincides with the rest of their doctrines.

2088   Now to this axiom of immanence is added another which we can call divine permanence; these two differ from each other in about the same way as private experience does from experience transmitted by tradition. An example will illustrate the point, and let us take it from the Church and the sacraments. The Church, they say, and the sacraments are by no means to be believed as having been instituted by Christ Himself. Agnosticism stipulates this, which recognizes nothing but the human in Christ, whose religious conscience, like that of the rest of men, was formed gradually; the law of immanence stipulates this, which rejects external applications, to use their terms; likewise the law of evolution stipulates this, which demands time and a certain series of circumstances joined with it, that the germs may be evolved; finally, history stipulates this, which shows that such in fact has been the course of the thing. Yet it is to be held that the Church and the sacraments have been *mediately* established by the Christ. But how? All Christian consciences, they affirm, were in a way virtually included in the conscience of Christ, as the plant in the seed. Moreover, since the germs live the life of the seed, all Christians are to be said to live the life of Christ. But the life of Christ according to faith is divine; thus, also, is the life of Christians. If, then, this life in the course of the ages gave origin to the Church and the sacraments, quite rightly will such an origin be said to be from Christ, and be divine. Thus they effect completely that the Sacred Scriptures also are divine, and that dogmas are divine.—With this, then, the theology of the modernists is essentially completed. Surely a brief provision, but very abundant for him who professes that science must always be obeyed, whatever it orders. Everyone will easily see for himself the application of these principles to the other matters which we shall mention.

Up to this point we have touched upon the origin of faith and its **2089** nature. But since faith has many outgrowths, chiefly the Church, dogma, worship, and devotions, the Books which we call "sacred," we should inquire what the modernists teach about these also. To take dogma as a beginning, it has already been shown above what its origin and nature are [n. 2079 f.]. It arises from a kind of impulse or necessity, by virtue of which he who believes elaborates his own thoughts so that his own conscience and that of others may be the more clarified. This labor consists entirely in investigating and in refining the primitive formula of the mind, not indeed in itself, according to the logical explanation, but according to circumstances, or *vitally,* as they say, in a manner less easily understood. Hence it happens that around that formula certain secondary formulae, as We have already indicated, gradually come into being [cf. n. 2078]; these afterwards brought together into one body, or into one edifice of faith, as responding to the common consciousness, are called dogma. From this the dissertations of the theologians are to be well distinguished, which, although they do not live the life of dogma, are not at all useless, not only for harmonizing religion with science and for removing disagreements between them, but also for illumining and protecting religion from without, even perchance as a means for preparing material for some new future dogma.—It would by no means have been necessary to discuss worship at length, did not the sacraments also come under this term, on which the errors of the modernists are most serious. They say that worship arises from a twofold impulse or necessity; for, as we have seen, all things in their system are said to come into existence by innermost impulses or necessities. The first need is to attribute something sensible to religion; the second is to express it, which surely cannot be done without a sensible form, or consecrating acts which we call sacraments. But for the modernists sacraments are mere symbols or signs, although not lacking efficacy. To point out this efficacy, they make use of the example of certain words which are popularly said to have caught on, since they have conceived the power of propagating certain ideas which are vigorous and especially shake the mind. Just as these words are ordered in relation to ideas, so are the sacraments to the religious sense, nothing more. Surely they would speak more clearly if they affirm that the sacraments were instituted solely to nourish faith. But this the Synod of Trent has condemned: "If any one says that these sacraments were instituted solely to nourish the faith, let him be anathema" [n. 848].

2090   We have already touched somewhat on the nature and origin of the Sacred Books. According to the principles of the modernists one could well describe them as a collection of *experiences,* not such as come in general to everyone, but extraordinary and distinguished, which have been had in every religion.—Precisely thus do the modernists teach about our books of both the Old and the New Testament. Yet, in accord with their own opinions they note very shrewdly that, although experience belongs to the present, yet one can assume it equally of the past and of the future, inasmuch as naturally he who believes either, lives the past by recollection in the manner of the present, or the future by anticipation. Moreover, this explains how the historical and apocalyptic books can be classified among the Sacred Books. Thus, then, in these Books God certainly speaks through the believer, but as the theology of the modernists puts it, only by *immanence* and *vital permanence.*—We shall ask, what then about inspiration? This, they reply, is by no means distinguished from that impulse, unless perhaps in vehemence, by which the believer is stimulated to reveal his faith by word or writing. What we have in poetic inspiration is similar; wherefore a certain one said: "God is in us, when he stirs we are inflamed." [1] In this way God should be called the beginning of the inspiration of the Sacred Books.—Furthermore, regarding this inspiration, the modernists add that there is nothing at all in the Sacred Books that lacks such inspiration. When they affirm this one would be inclined to believe them more orthodox than some in more recent times who restrict inspiration somewhat as, for example, when they introduce so-called *tacit citations.* But this is mere words and pretense on their part. For, if we judge the Bible according to the precepts of agnosticism, namely, as a human work written by men for men, although the theologian is granted the right of calling it divine by immanence, just how can inspiration be forced into it? Now, the modernist assuredly asserts a general inspiration of the Sacred Books, but admits no inspiration in the Catholic sense.

2091   What the school of modernists imagines about the Church offers a richer field for discussion.—They lay down in the beginning that the Church arose from a twofold necessity: one in any believer, especially

---

[1] Ovid, *Fasti* 6, 5.

in him who has found an original and special experience, to communicate his faith to others; the other, after faith has communicated among many, in collectivity to coalesce into a society and to watch over, increase, and propagate the common good. What, then, is the Church? It is the fruit of the *collective conscience,* or of the association of individual consciences which, by virtue of *vital permanence,* depends on some first believer, that is, for Catholics, on Christ. Moreover, any society needs a directing authority, whose duty it is to direct all associates toward the common end, to foster prudently the elements of cohesion, which in a religious society are fulfilled by doctrine and worship. Hence, the triple authority in the Catholic Church: *disciplinary, dogmatic, liturgical.*—Now the nature of the authority is to be gathered from its origin; from its nature, indeed, its rights and duties are to be sought. In past ages a common error was that authority came to the Church from without, namely, immediately from God; therefore it was rightly held to be autocratic. But this conception has now grown obsolete. Just as the Church is said to have emanated from the collectivity of consciences, so in like manner authority emanates vitally from the Church itself. Authority, then, just as the Church, originates from religious conscience, and so is subject to the same; and if it spurns this subordination, it veers towards tyranny. Moreover, we are now living at a time when the sense of liberty has grown to its highest point. In the civil state public conscience has introduced popular government. But conscience in man, just as life, is only one. Unless, then, ecclesiastical authority wishes to excite and foment an intestine war in the conscience of men, it has an obligation to use democratic forms (of procedure), the more for this reason, because unless it does so, destruction threatens. For, surely, he is mad who thinks that with the sense of liberty as it now flourishes any recession can ever take place. If it were restricted and checked by force, it would break forth the stronger, with the destruction alike of the Church and religion. All this do the modernists think, who as a result are quite occupied with devising ways to reconcile the authority of the Church with the liberty of believers.

But the Church has not only within the walls of its own household **2092** those with whom she should exist on friendly terms, but she has them outside. For the Church does not occupy the world all by herself; other societies occupy it equally, with which communications and contacts necessarily take place. These rights, then, which are the duties of the Church in relation to civil societies, must be determined, and must not be determined otherwise than according to the nature of the Church herself, as the modernists have indeed described to us.—In this, moreover, they clearly use the same rules as were introduced above for science and faith. There discussion centered on *objects,* here on *ends.* So, just as by reason of the object we see faith and science extraneous to each other, so the state and Church are extraneous to each other because of the ends which they pursue; the former pursuing a temporal, the latter a spiritual end. Of course it was once permitted to subordinate the temporal to the spiritual; it was permitted to interject discussion on *mixed* questions, in which the Church was held as mistress and queen, since the Church, of course, was declared to have been instituted by God without intermediary, inasmuch as He is the author of the supernatural order. But all this is repudiated by philosophers and historians. The state, then, must be disassociated from the Church, just as even the Catholic from the citizen. Therefore, any Catholic, since he is also a citizen, has the right and the duty, disregarding the authority of the Church, pushing aside her wishes, counsels, and precepts, yes, spurning her rebukes, of pursuing what he thinks is conducive to the good of the state. To prescribe a way of action for a citizen on any pretext is an abuse of ecclesiastical power, to be rejected by every means.—Of course, Venerable Brothers, the source from which all this flows is indeed the very source which Pius VI, Our predecessor, solemnly condemned [cf. n. 1502 f.] in the Apostolic Constitution, *Auctorem fidei*.

2093　　But it is not enough for the school of modernists that the state should be separated from the Church. For, just as faith, as far as phenomenal elements are concerned, as they say, should be subordinated to science, so in temporal affairs should the Church be subject to the state. This, indeed, they do not by chance say openly, but by reason of their thinking are forced to admit. For laying down the principle that the state alone has power in temporal matters, if it happens that the believer, not content with internal acts of religion, proceeds to external acts, as for example, the administration or reception of the sacraments, these will necessarily fall under the dominion of the state. What, then, about the authority of the Church? Since this is not explained except through external acts, it will be entirely responsible to the state. Obviously forced by this conclusion, many of the liberal Protestants entirely reject all external sacred worship, rather, even any external religious association, and strive to introduce individual religion, as they say. But if the modernists do not yet proceed openly to this point, they ask meanwhile that the Church of her own accord tend in the direction in which they themselves impel her, and that she adapt herself to the forms of the state. Now these are their ideas on *disciplinary* authority.—On the other hand, by far more evil and pernicious are their opinions on *doctrinal* and *dogmatic* power. On the *magisterium* of the Church they comment, for example, as follows: A religious society can never truly coalesce into one unless the conscience of the associates be one, and the formula which they use one. But this twofold unity demands a kind of common mind whose duty it is to find and determine the formula which corresponds best with the common conscience; and this mind must have sufficient authority to impose on the community the formula which it has determined upon. Moreover, in this union and fusion, as it were, both of the mind which draws up the formula, and of the power which prescribes it, the modernists place the notion of the *magisterium* of the Church. Since, then, the *magisterium* finally arises at some time from the individual consciences, and has as a mandate the public duty to the benefit of the same consciences, it necessarily follows that the *magisterium* depends on these, and so must bend to popular forms. Therefore, to prohibit the consciences of individuals from expressing publicly and openly the impulses which they feel; to obstruct the way of criticism whereby it impels dogma in the path of necessary evolutions, is not the use but the abuse of the power permitted for the public weal. Similarly, in the very use of power, measure and moderation are to be applied. To censure and proscribe any book without the knowledge of the author, without permitting any explanation, without discussion, is surely very close to tyranny.—Thus, here also a middle course must be found to preserve the rights at once of authority and liberty. Meanwhile the Catholic must so conduct himself as to proclaim publicly his strict respect for authority, yet not to fail to obey his own mind.—In general they prescribe as follows for the Church: that, since the end of ecclesiastical power pertains only to the spiritual, all external trappings must be abolished, by which it is adorned most magnificently for the eyes of the onlookers. In this the following is completely overlooked, that religion, although it pertains to souls, is not confined to souls exclusively, and that the honor paid to authority redounds to Christ as its founder.

Moreover, to complete this whole subject of faith and its various 2094 branches, it remains for us, Venerable Brethren, to consider finally the precepts of the modernists on the development of both.—Here is a general principle: In a religion which is living nothing is without change, and so there must be change. From here they make a step to what is essentially the chief point in their doctrines, namely, *evolution*. Dogma, then, Church, worship, the Books that we revere as sacred, even faith itself, unless we wish all these to be powerless, must be bound by the laws of evolution. This cannot appear surprising to you, if you bear in mind what the modernists have taught on each of these subjects. So, granted the law of evolution, we have the way of evolution described by the modernists themselves. And first, as regards faith. The primitive form of faith, they say, was crude and common to all men, since it had its origin in human nature and human life. Vital evolution contributed progress; to be sure, not by the novelty of forms added to it from the outside, but by the daily increasing pervasion of the religious sense into the conscience. Moreover, this progress was made in two ways: first, in a negative way, by eliminating anything extraneous, as for example, that might come from family or nation; second, in a positive way, by the intellectual and moral refinement of man, whereby the notion of the divine becomes fuller and clearer, and the religious sense more accurate. The same causes for the progress of faith are to be brought forward as were employed to explain its origins. But to these must be added certain extraordinary men (whom we call prophets, and of whom Christ is the most outstanding), not only because they bore before themselves in their lives and works something mysterious which faith attributed to the divinity, but also because they met with new experiences never had before, corresponding to the religious needs of the time of each.—But the progress of dogma arises chiefly from this, that impediments to faith have to be overcome, enemies have to be conquered, objections have to be refuted. Add to this a perpetual struggle to penetrate more deeply the things that are contained in the mysteries of faith. Thus, to pass over other examples, it happened in the case of Christ: in Him that divine something or other, which faith admitted, was slowly and gradually expanded, so that finally He was held to be God.—The necessity of accommodating itself to the customs and traditions of the people especially contributed to the evolution of worship; likewise, the necessity of employing the power of certain acts, which they have acquired by usage.— Finally, the cause of evolution as regards the Church arose in this, that she needs to be adjusted to contemporary historical conditions, and to the forms of civil government publicly in vogue. This do they think regarding each. But before we proceed we wish that this doctrine of necessities or needs be well noted; for beyond all that we have seen, this is, as it were, the basis and foundation of that famous method which they call historical.

2095   To linger still on the doctrine of evolution, this is to be noted especially, that, although needs or necessities impel to evolution, yet if driven by this alone, easily trangressing the boundaries of tradition and thus separating itself from the primitive vital principle, it would lead to ruin rather than to progress. Thus, following the mind of the modernists more completely, we shall say that evolution comes out of the conflict of two forces, one of which leads to progress, the other holds back to conservation. The conserving force flourishes in the Church and is contained in tradition. Indeed, religious authority makes use of it; and this it does both by right itself, for it is in the nature of authority to guard tradition, and in fact, for authority remote from the changes of life is pressed on not at all, or very little by the incentives that drive to progress. On the contrary the force which attracts to progress and responds to the inner needs, lies hidden, and works in the consciences of individuals, especially of those who attain life, as they say, more closely and intimately.—Behold here, Venerable Brethren, we perceive that most pernicious doctrine raise its head, which introduces into the Church the members of the laity as elements of progress.—By a kind of covenant and pact between these two forces, the conserver and the promoter of progress, namely, between authority and the consciences of individuals, advances and changes take place. For the consciences of individuals, or certain of them, act on the collective conscience; but this last acts upon those who have authority, and forces them to effect agreements and to abide by the pact.—As a result of this, moreover, it is easy to understand why the modernists marvel so, when they realize that they are caught or are punished. What is held up to them as a fault, they themselves hold as a religious duty to be fulfilled. No one knows the needs of consciences better than they themselves, because they come in closer touch with them than does ecclesiastical authority. Therefore, they gather all these needs, as it were, within themselves; and so they are bound by the duty of speaking and writing publicly. Let authority rebuke them, if it wishes; they themselves are supported by the conscience of duty, and they know by intimate experience that they deserve not criticism but praise. Surely it does not escape them that progress is by no means made without struggles, nor struggles without victims; so let they themselves be victims, just as the prophets and Christ. Because they are held in evil repute, they do not look askance at authority on this account; they even concede that it is carrying out its duty. They complain only that they are not heard; for thus the course of souls is impeded; yet the time to put an end to delays will most certainly come, for the laws of evolution can be halted, but they can by no means be broken. Therefore, they continue on their established road; they continue, although refuted and condemned, concealing their incredible audacity with a veil of feigned humility. Indeed, they bow their heads in pretense, yet with their hands and minds they boldly follow through what they have undertaken. Moreover, thus they act quite willingly and wittingly, both because they hold that authority must be stimulated and not overturned, and because it is a necessity for them to remain within the fold of the Church, that they may gradually change the collective conscience. Yet when they say this, they do not remark that they confess that the collective conscience is apart from them, and thus without right they commend themselves as its interpreters. . . . [Then is adduced and explained what is contained in this Enchiridion n. 1636, 1705, 1800].—But after we have observed the philosopher, believer, and theologian among the followers of modernism, it now remains for us to observe the historian, critic, apologist, and reformer in like manner.

[IV] Certain of the modernists who have given themselves over to **2096** composing history, seem especially solicitous lest they be believed to be philosophers; why, they even profess to be entirely without experience of philosophy. This they do with consummate astuteness, lest, for example, anyone think that they are imbued with the prejudiced opinions of philosophy, and for this reason, as they say, are not at all *objective*. Yet the truth is that their history or criticism bespeaks pure philosophy; and whatever conclusions are arrived at by them, are derived by right reasoning from their philosophic principles. This is indeed easily apparent to one who reflects.—The first three canons of such historians and critics, as we have said, are those same principles which we adduced from the philosophers above: namely, *agnosticism,* the theorem of the *transfiguration* of things by faith, and likewise another which it seemed could be called *disfiguration*. Let us now note the consequences that come from them individually.—According to *agnosticism,* history, just as science, is concerned only with phenomena. Therefore, just as God, so any divine intervention in human affairs must be relegated to faith, as belonging to it alone. Thus, if anything occurs consisting of a double element, divine and human, such as are Christ, the Church, the sacraments, and many others of this kind, there will have to be a division and separation, so that what was human may be assigned to history, and what divine to faith. Thus, the distinction common among the modernists between the Christ of history and the Christ of faith, the Church of history and the Church of faith, the sacraments of history and the sacraments of faith, and other similar distinctions in general.—Then this human element itself, which we see the historian assume for himself, must be mentioned, such as appears in documents, raised above historical conditions by faith through *transfiguration*. So, the additions made by faith must in turn be dissociated, and relegated to faith itself, and to the history of faith; so when Christ is being discussed, whatever surpasses the natural condition of man, as is shown by psychology, or has been raised out of the place and the time in which He lived, must be dissociated.—Besides, in accord with the third principle of philosophy those things also which do not pass beyond the field of history, they view through a sieve, as it were, and eliminate all and relegate likewise to faith, which in their judgment, as they say, are not in the logic of facts or suited to the characters. Thus they do not will that Christ said those things which appear to exceed the capacity of the listening multitude. Hence from His *real* history they delete and transfer to faith all his allegories that occur in His discourses. Perhaps we shall ask by what law these matters are dissociated? From the character of the man, from the condition which He enjoyed in the state; from His education, from the complexus of the incidents of any fact, in a word, if we understand well, from a norm which finally at some time recedes into the merely *subjective*. They aim, of course, themselves to take on the character of Christ and, as it were, to make it their own;

whatever, in like circumstances they would have done, all this they transfer to Christ.—Thus then to conclude, *a priori* and according to certain principles of philosophy which they in truth hold but profess to ignore, they affirm that Christ, in what they call *real* history, is not God and never did anything divine; indeed, that He did and said as a man what they themselves attribute to Him the right of doing and saying, taking themselves back to His times.

[V] Moreover, as history receives its conclusions from philosophy, so criticism takes its conclusions from history. For the critic, following the indications furnished by the historian, divides documents in two ways. Whatever is left after the threefold elimination just mentioned he assigns to *real* history; the rest he delegates to the history of faith or *internal* history. For they distinguish sharply between these two histories; the history of faith (and this we wish to be well noted) they oppose to the *real* history, as it is real. Thus, as we have already said, the two Christs: one real, the other, who never was in fact, but pertains to faith; one who lived in a certain place and in a certain age; another, who is found only in the pious commentaries of faith; such, for example, is the Christ whom the Gospel of John presents, which, according to them is nothing more or less than a meditation.   **2097**

But the domination of philosophy over history is not ended with this. After the documents have been distributed in a twofold manner, the philosopher is again on hand with his dogma of *vital immanence;* and he declares that all things in the history of the Church are to be explained by *vital emanation.* But either the cause or the condition of *vital emanation* is to be placed in some need or want; therefore, too, the fact must be conceived after the need, and the one is historically posterior to the other. —Why then the historian? Having scrutinized the documents again, either those that are contained in the Sacred Books or have been introduced from elsewhere, he draws up from them an index of the particular needs which relate not only to dogma but to liturgy, and other matters which have had a place one after the other in the Church. He hands over the index so made to the critic. Now he (the critic) takes in hand the documents which are devoted to the history of faith, and he so arranges them age by age that they correspond one by one with the index submitted, always mindful of the precept that the fact is preceded by the need, and the need by the fact. Surely, it may at times happen that some parts of the Bible, as for example the epistles, are the fact itself created by the need. Yet whatever it is, the law is that the age of any document is not to be determined otherwise than by the age of any need that has arisen in the Church.—Besides, a distinction must be made between the origin of any fact and the development of the same, for what can be born on one day, takes on growth only with the passage of time. For this reason the critic   **2098** must, as we have said, again divide the documents already distributed through the ages, separating the ones which have to do with the origin of the thing, and those which pertain to its development, and he must in turn arrange them by periods.

2099   Then again there is place for the philosopher, who enjoins upon the historian so to exercise his zeal as the precepts and laws of evolution prescribe. Thereupon the historian examines the documents again; examines carefully the circumstances and conditions which the Church has experienced for period after period: her conserving power, the needs both internal and external which have stimulated her to progress, the obstacles which have been in her way, in a word, everything whatsoever which helps to determine how the laws of evolution have been kept. Finally, after this he describes the history of the development in broad outlines, as it were. The critic comes in and adapts the rest of the documents. He applies his hand to writing. The history is finished.—Now we ask, to whom is this history to be ascribed? To the historian or to the critic? Surely to neither; but to the philosopher. The whole business is carried on through *apriorism;* and indeed by an apriorism reeking with heresy. Surely such men are to be pitied, of whom the Apostle would have said: "They become vain in their thoughts . . . professing themselves to be wise they became fools" [Rom. 1:21–22]; but yet they move us to anger, when they accuse the Church of so confusing and changing documents that they may testify to her advantage. Surely they charge the Church with that for which they feel that they themselves are openly condemned by their own conscience.

2100   Furthermore, as a result of this division and arrangement of the documents by ages it naturally follows that the Sacred Books cannot be attributed to those authors to whom in fact they are ascribed. For this reason the modernists generally do not hesitate to assert that those same books, especially the Pentateuch and the first three Gospels, from the brief original account grew gradually by additions, by interpolations, indeed, in the manner of either theological or allegorical interpretations; or even by the interjection of parts solely to join different passages together.—To state it briefly and more clearly, there must certainly be admitted the *vital* evolution of the Sacred Books, born of the evolution of faith and corresponding to the same.—Indeed, they add that the traces of this evolution are so manifest that its history can almost be described. Nay, rather, they do in fact describe it with no hesitation, so that you would believe that they saw the very writers with their own eyes as they applied their hand in every age to amplifying the Sacred Books. Moreover, to support these actions they call to their aid a criticism which they call textual; and they strive to convince us that this or that fact or expression is not in its own place, and they bring forward other such arguments.—You would indeed say that they had prescribed for themselves certain types, as it were, of narrations and discourses, as a result of which they decide with certainty what stands in its own place or in a strange place.—Let him who wishes judge how skilled they can be to make decisions in this way. Moreover, he who gives heed to them as they talk about their studies on the Sacred Books, as a result of which it was granted them to discover so many things improperly stated, would almost believe that no man before them had turned the pages of these same books; and that an almost infinite number of doctors had not examined them from every point of view, a group clearly far superior to them in mind, and erudition, and sanctity of life. These very wise doctors indeed, far from finding fault with the Sacred Scriptures in any part, rather, the more thoroughly they investigated them, the more they gave thanks to divine authority for having deigned so to speak with men. But alas, our doctors with respect to the Sacred Books did not rely upon those aids on which the modernists did; thus they did not have philosophy as a master and guide, nor did they choose themselves as their own authority in making decisions. Now, then, we think that it is clear of what sort the method of the modernists is in the field of history. The philosopher goes ahead; the historian succeeds him; right behind, in order, works criticism, both internal and textual. And since it is characteristic of the first cause to communicate its power to its consequences, it becomes evident that such criticism is not criticism at all; that it is rightly called *agnostic, immanentist,* and *evolutionist;* and that so, he who professes it and *uses* it, professes the errors implicit in the same and opposes Catholic doctrine.—For this reason it can seem most strange that criticism of this kind has such weight today among Catholics. This obviously has a twofold cause: first of all the pact by which the historians and the critics of this kind are so closely joined, the differences of nationality and the dissension of religions being placed in the background; then the endless effrontery by which all with one voice extol whatever each of them prattles, and attribute it to the progress of science; by which in close array they attack him who wishes to examine the new marvel or his own; by which they accuse him who denies it of ignorance, adorn him with praises who embraces and defends it. Thus no small number are deceived who, if they should examine the matter more closely, would be horrified.—From this powerful domineering on the part of those in error, and this heedless compliance on the part of fickle souls, a corruption in the surrounding atmosphere results which penetrates everywhere and diffuses its pestilence.

[VI] But let us pass on to the apologist. He, too, among the modernists **2101** depends in a twofold manner upon the philosopher. First, *indirectly,* taking history as his subject matter, written at the dictation of the philosopher, as we have seen; then directly, having obtained his doctrines and judgments from him. Hence that precept widespread in the school of the modernists that the new apologetics should resolve controversies over religion by historical and psychological investigations. Therefore, the modernist apologist approaches his task by advising the rationalists that they defend religion not by means of the Sacred Books, nor by history as widely employed in the Church which is written in the old way, but by *real* history composed of modern principles and the modern method. And this they assert not as if using an *argumentum ad hominem,* but because in very fact they think that only such history hands down the truth. They are indeed unconcerned about asserting their sincerity in what they write; they are already known among the nationalists; they are already praised for doing service under the same banner; and on this praise, which a real Catholic would reject, they congratulate themselves, and, hold it up against the reprimands of the Church.—But now let us see how one of them proceeds in his apologies. The end which he places before himself for accomplishment, is this: to win a person thus far inexperienced in the faith over to it, that he may attain this *experience* of the Catholic religion, which according to the modernists is the only basis of faith. A twofold way is open to this: one *objective,* the other *subjective.* The first proceeds from agnosticism, and it strives to show that that vital virtue is in religion, especially the Catholic religion, which persuades every psychologist and likewise historian of good mind that in its history something of the *unknown* must be concealed. To this end it is necessary to show that the Catholic religion, as it exists today, is exactly that which Christ founded, or that it is nothing other than the progressive development of that germ which Christ introduced. First, then, it must be determined of what nature the germ is. This, furthermore, they wish to prove by the following formula: The Christ announced the coming of the kingdom of God, which was to be established shortly; and that He Himself would be its Messias, that is, the divinely given founder and ordainer. Then it must be shown in what way this germ, always *immanent* and *permanent* in the Catholic religion, has evolved gradually, and according to history, and has adapted itself to succeeding circumstances, taking to itself from these *vitally* whatever of the doctrinal, cultural, and ecclesiastical forms was useful to it, but meanwhile overcoming such obstacles as met it, scattering its enemies, and surviving all attacks and combats. Yet after it has been shown that all these, namely, obstacles, enemies, attacks, combats, and likewise the vitality and fecundity of Church have been of such nature that, although the laws of evolution appear unimpaired in the history of the Church, yet they are not alike to be fully developed by the same history; the unknown will stand before it, and will present itself of its own accord.—Thus do they argue. In all this reasoning, however, they fail to notice one thing, that that determination of the primitive germ is due solely to the apriorism of the agnostic and evolutionist philosopher, and the germ itself is so gratuitously defined by them as to fit in with their case.

Yet while by reciting arguments the new apologists struggle to proclaim **2102** and bring conviction to the Catholic religion, of their own accord they grant and concede that there is much in it which offends. With a kind of ill-concealed pleasure they even declare repeatedly and openly that they find errors and contradictions also in the field of dogma; yet they add that these not only admit of an excuse, but, which should be an object of wonder, that these have been produced rightly and lawfully. Thus, even according to themselves much in the Sacred Books within the field of science and history is affected by error. But they say that here it is not a question of science or history, but only of religion and morals. There science and history are a kind of covering with which the religious and moral experiences are bound, so that they may be more easily spread among the masses; since, indeed, the masses would not understand this otherwise, a more perfect kind of science and history would not have been a help but a harm to them. But, they add, the Sacred Books, because they are religious by nature, necessarily possess life; now, life also has its own truth and logic, quite different from rational truth and rational logic, rather of an entirely different order, namely, the truth of comparison and proportion not only with reference to the *medium* (so they themselves call it) in which it is lived, but also with reference to the end for which it is lived. Finally, they proceed to such a point that, abandoning all restraint, they assert that whatever is evolved through life, is entirely true and legitimate.—Now We, Venerable Brethren, for whom there is one, unique truth, and who regard the Sacred Books thus, "that written under the inspiration of the Holy Spirit they have God as their author" [see n. 1787], declare that this is the same as giving the lie of utility, or the officious lie to God Himself, and We assert in the words of St. Augustine: "Once some officious lie is admitted against so high an authority, there will remain not a clause in those books which, according as it will appear to anyone difficult to practise or incredible of belief, is not referred according to this same pernicious rule to the plan and purpose of a lying author." [1] Therefore it will happen, as the same Holy Doctor adds: "In these, namely the Scriptures, everyone will believe what he wishes; what he does not wish, he will not believe."—But the modernist apologists move forward rapidly. They also concede that in the Sacred Books such reasonings are frequently discovered which attempt to prove a certain doctrine without rational foundation; such kind are those which rest upon the prophecies. And they defend these as a kind of artifice for preaching, which are made legitimate by life. What more? They admit, rather, they assert that Christ

---

[1] St. Augustine, *Letter 28,* c. 3 [ML 33 (Aug. II), 112, 3].

Himself manifestly erred in indicating the time of the coming of the kingdom of God; and this should not seem strange, they say, for He, too, was bound by the laws of life! Again, what about the dogmas of the Church? These also abound in open contradictions; but in addition to the fact that they are admitted by vital logic, they are not opposed to symbolic truth; for in these it is a question of the infinite, to which belong infinite considerations. Finally, they so prove and defend all this that they do not hesitate to profess that no more noble honor is shown the Infinite than the affirming of contradictions about Him.—But when a contradiction is approved, what will not be approved?

2103   He who does not yet believe can be disposed toward faith not only by *objective* but also by *subjective* arguments. To this end the modernist apologists return to the doctrine of *immanence*. They labor in fact to persuade man that in him, and in the innermost recesses of his nature and life are concealed a desire and need for some religion; not for any religion, but for such a one as is the Catholic religion; for this, they say, is absolutely postulated by the perfect development of life.—Here, moreover, we should again complain vigorously that there are not lacking among Catholics those who, although they reject the doctrine of *immanence* as a doctrine, yet employ it as a method of apology; and they do this so heedlessly that they seem to admit in human nature not only a capacity and a suitability for the supernatural order, as certain Catholic apologists have always demonstrated within proper bounds, but a genuine need in the true sense of the word.—To speak more accurately, this need of the Catholic religion is introduced by modernists who wish to be known as the more moderate. For, those who can be called *integralists* wish that the germ be demonstrated to the man who does not yet believe, as being hidden in him, the very germ which was in the consciousness of Christ and was transmitted to men by Him.—Thus then, Venerable Brethren, we recognize the apologetic method of the modernists, summarily described, as quite in keeping with their doctrine; a method indeed, as also the doctrines, full of errors, not suited for edifying, but for destroying, not for making Catholics, but for dragging Catholics into heresy, yes, even for the complete subversion of every religion.

2104   [VII] Finally, a few words must be said about the modernist as a reformer. What we have said thus far shows abundantly with how great and keen a zeal for innovating these men are carried away. Moreover, this zeal extends to absolutely everything which exists among Catholics. They wish philosophy to be reformed, especially in ecclesiastical seminaries, so that, after relegating scholastic philosophy to the history of philosophy along with the other obsolete systems, youth may be taught modern philosophy which alone is true and in accord with our age.—To reform theology, they wish that that which we call rational have modern philosophy as a basis, but they demand that positive theology be based especially upon the history of dogma.—They also demand that history be written and be taught according to their method and modern prescriptions. Dogmas and the evolution of the same, they declare, must be brought into harmony with science and history.—As regards catechesis, they demand that only those dogmas be noted in catechism, which have been reformed, and are within the capacity of the masses. As for worship they say that external devotions are to be reduced in number, and that steps be taken to prevent their increase, although some who are more favorable toward symbolism show themselves more indulgent on this score.—They cry out that the government of the Church must be reformed in every respect, but especially on the disciplinary and dogmatic side. Thus, both within and without it is to be brought in harmony with the modern conscience, as they say, which tends entirely towards democracy; so to the lower clergy and to laity itself appropriate parts in the government should be assigned, and when authority has been unified too much and too centralized, it is to be dispersed.—The Roman congregations they likewise wish to be modified in the performance of their holy duties, but especially that which is known as the *Holy Office* and is also called the *Index*. Likewise, they contend that the action of ecclesiastical authority must be changed in the political and social fields, so that it may at the same time live apart from civil affairs, yet adapt itself to them in order to imbue them with its spirit.—In the field of morals they adopt the principle of the Americanists, that the active virtues are to be placed before the passive, and should be put ahead of them in practice.—They desire that the clergy be prepared to practise the ancient humility and poverty; moreover, that in thought and deed they conform with the precepts of modernism.—Finally, there are some who, giving heed to the words of their Protestant masters, desire the removal of holy celibacy itself from the priesthood— What, then, do they leave untouched in the Church, that is not to be reformed by them or according to their pronouncements?

In explaining all this doctrine of the modernists, Venerable Brethren, **2105** We shall seem to some, by chance, to have delayed too long. Yet it was quite necessary to do so, both that, as is customary, We might not be charged by them with ignorance of their tenets, and that it might be clear that when it is a question of modernism we are dealing not with scattered teachings in no way connected with one another, but with a single and compact body, as it were, in which, if you admit one thing, the rest necessarily follows. Thus we have made use of what amounts to didactic reasoning, and sometimes we have not rejected the atrocious words which the modernists have employed.

Now as we look back upon the whole system in one glance, as it were, no one will be surprised when we define it as the synthesis of all heresies.

Surely, if anyone had proposed this to himself, to bring together into one the sap and blood of all the errors that have ever existed about the faith, no one would have performed the task more completely than the modernists have done it. Rather they have gone so much beyond this as not only to destroy completely the Catholic religion, but all religion, as We have already intimated. Hence, the applause of the rationalists; for this reason do those among the rationalists who speak more freely and openly congratulate themselves on having found no more efficacious allies than the modernists.

2106   Now let us return for a moment, Venerable Brothers, to that most pernicious doctrine of *agnosticism*. By it evidently, as far as the intellect is concerned, every way to God is barred to man, while a more fitting approach is supposed to be open through a certain sense of the soul and action. Who does not see how wrong this is? For the sense of the soul is the response to the action of the thing which the intellect and the external senses have proposed. Take away the intellect and man will be prone to follow the external senses, in which direction he is already proceeding. Again this is bad; for any phantasies of the religious sense will not destroy common sense; moreover, by common sense we are taught that any disturbance or occupation of the soul is not a help but rather a hindrance to the search for truth, for truth, we say, as it is in itself; for that other *subjective* truth, the fruit of the internal sense and action, if indeed it is adapted to play, contributes nothing at all to man whose chief concern it is to learn whether outside himself there is a God into whose hands he will one day fall.—But the modernists do introduce experience as an aid to so great a task. Yet, what will this add to that sense of the soul? Nothing at all, except to make it more vehement; and as a result of this vehemence to make its conviction of the truth of the object proportionately stronger. Now these two certainly never make the sense of the soul cease to be sense, nor do they change its nature which is always liable to deception, unless it is directed by the intellect; but rather they confirm and assist it, for the more intense the sense, by that greater right it is sense.

2107   Now since we are here dealing with religious sense and the experience contained in it, you know well, Venerable Brethren, how much there is need of prudence in this matter; likewise how much doctrine to guide prudence itself. You know this from your own experience with souls, especially certain ones in whom the sense is pre-eminent; you know it from your habit of reading books which treat of asceticism, which works, although they are of little worth in the estimation of the modernists, yet present a doctrine far more solid and more profound for observing wisdom than that which they arrogate to themselves. Indeed, it seems to Us the part of madness, or at least consummate imprudence, to hold as true without investigation the intimate experiences which the modernists recommend.

But why, to speak cursorily, if there is so much force and value in these experiences, should not the same value be attributed to that experience which many thousands of Catholics assert that they have regarding the erroneous path on which the modernists tread? Is not all this false and fallacious? But the great majority of men firmly hold this, and will hold this: that through sense alone and experience, with no guidance and light of the mind, man can never attain God. And so we again have atheism, and no religion.

The modernists promise themselves nothing better by proclaiming the   **2108** doctrine of symbolism. For if all intellectual elements, as they say, are merely symbols of God, will not the very name of God, or of the divine personality be a symbol. And if this is so, then there will be a possibility of doubt about the divine personality and the way is open to pantheism. Moreover, in the same way the other doctrine of divine immanence leads to pure and unmixed pantheism. For we ask this: Does such immanence distinguish God from man or not? If it does so distinguish, in what then does it differ from Catholic doctrine, or why does it reject the doctrine of external revelation? If it does not so distinguish, we have pantheism. But this immanence of the modernists holds and grants that every phenomenon of conscience proceeds from man as man. Thus good reasoning infers from this that God and man are one and the same; and so we have pantheism.

Indeed, the distinction which they proclaim between science and faith   **2109** admits no other conclusion. For, they place the object of science in the reality of the knowable; the object of faith, on the contrary, in the reality of the unknowable. Now, the unknowable is fully established from this, that between the material object and the intellect there is no proportion, and this defect of proportion can never be removed, not even in the doctrine of the modernists. Therefore, the unknowable will always remain unknowable, to the believer as well as to the philosopher. Therefore, if we will possess any religion, it will be of an unknowable reality. Why this cannot also be the soul of the universe, as certain rationalists admit, we certainly do not see. But let these words suffice now to show fully how the doctrine of the modernists leads by manifold routes to atheism, and to the destruction of all religion. Indeed, the error of the Protestants was the first to take the step down this road; the error of the modernists follows; atheism will be the next step. [After fixing the causes of these errors—curiosity, pride, ignorance of true philosophy—certain rules are laid down for the support and organization of philosophical, theological, and profane studies, and for the cautious selection of teachers, etc.]

The Author and Historical Truth of the Fourth Gospel [1]

[Response of the Biblical Commission, May 29, 1907]

2110   *Question I:* Whether from the constant, universal, and solemn tradition of the Church coming down from the second century, inasmuch as it is taken chiefly a) from the testimonies and allusions of the Holy Fathers, ecclesiastical writers, even heretics, which, since they must derive from the disciples and first successors of the apostles, are necessarily closely connected with the very origin of the work itself; b) from the acceptance always and everywhere of the name of the author of the fourth Gospel in the Canon and in the catalogues of the Sacred Scriptures; c) from the oldest manuscripts, codices, and versions in various languages of the same Books; d) from the public liturgical practice obtaining in the whole world from the beginnings of the Church; prescinding from theological proof, it is demonstrated by such strong historical proof that John the Apostle and no other is to be recognized as the author of the fourth Gospel, that the reasons adduced by critics in opposition by no means weaken this tradition?—*Answer:* In the affirmative.

2111   *Question II:* Whether the internal reasons also, which are taken from the text of the fourth Gospel, considered separately, from the testimony of the author and the manifest relationship of the Gospel itself with the First Epistle of the Apostle John, are to be considered as confirming the tradition which undoubtedly attributes the fourth Gospel to the same Apostle?—And whether the difficulties which are assumed from a comparison of the Gospel with the other three, the diversity of the times, purposes, and audiences, for whom and against whom the author wrote, being kept in view, can be reasonably solved, just as the most Holy Fathers and exegetes have shown in different places?—*Answer:* In the affirmative to both parts.

2112   *Question III:* Whether, not withstanding the practice which flourished constantly in the whole Church from the earliest times, of arguing from the fourth Gospel as from a truly historical document, in consideration, nevertheless, of the peculiar nature of the same Gospel, and of the manifest intention of the author to illustrate and to prove the divinity of Christ from the very deeds and words of the Lord, it can be said that the deeds related in the fourth Gospel are totally or partially so invented that they are allegories or doctrinal symbols; but that the words of the Lord are not properly and truly the words of the Lord himself, but theological compositions of the writer, although placed in the mouth of the Lord?—*Answer:* In the negative.

---

[1] ASS 40 (1907), 383 f.; AE 15 (1907), 259 f.; EB n. 180 ff.

The Authority of the Decisions of the Biblical Commission [1]

[From *Motu proprio*, "Praestantia Scripturae," Nov. 18, 1907]

... After long discussions and most conscientious deliberations, certain **2113** excellent decisions have been published by the Pontifical Biblical Commission, very useful for the true advancement of Biblical studies and for directing the same by a definite norm. Yet we notice that there are not lacking those who have not received and do not receive such decisions with the obedience which is proper, even though they are approved by the Pontiff.

Therefore, we see that it must be declared and ordered as We do now declare and expressly order, that all are bound by the duty of conscience to submit to the decisions of the Biblical Pontifical Commission, both those which have thus far been published and those which will hereafter be proclaimed, just as to the decrees of the Sacred Congregations which pertain to doctrine and have been approved by the Pontiff; and that all who impugn such decisions as these by word or in writing cannot avoid the charge of disobedience, or on this account be free of grave sin; and this besides the scandal by which they offend, and the other matters for which they can be responsible before God, especially because of other pronouncements in these matters made rashly and erroneously.

In addition to this, intending to repress the daily increasing boldness of **2114** spirit of many Modernists, who by sophisms and artifices of every kind endeavor to destroy the force and the efficacy not only of the Decree, "Lamentabili sane exitu," which was published at Our command by the Sacred Roman and Universal Inquisition on the third of July of the current year [see n. 2071 ff.], but also of Our Encyclical Letter, "Pascendi Dominici gregis," given on the eighth of September of this same year [see n. 2071 ff.] by Our Apostolic authority, We repeat and confirm not only that Decree of the Sacred Supreme Congregation, but also that Encyclical Letter of Ours, adding the penalty of excommunication against all who contradict them; and We declare and decree this: if anyone, which may God forbid, proceeds to such a point of boldness that he defends any of the propositions, opinions, and doctrines disproved in either document mentioned above, he is *ipso facto* afflicted by the censure imposed in the chapter *Docentes* of the Constitution of the Apostolic See, first among those excommunications *latae sententiae* which are reserved simply to the Roman Pontiff. This excommunication, however, is to be understood with no change in the punishments, which those who have committed anything against the above mentioned documents may incur, if at any

---

[1] ASS 40 (1907), 724 ff.; AE 15 (1907), 425 f.; EB n. 278 ff.

time their propositions, opinions, or doctrines are heretical; which indeed has happened more than once in the case of the adversaries of both these documents, but especially when they defend the errors of modernism, that is, the refuge of all heresies.

The Nature and Authorship of the Book of Isaias [1]

[Response of the Biblical Commission, June 29th, 1908]

2115   *Question I:* Whether it can be taught that the prophecies which are read in the book of Isaias, and here and there in the Scriptures, are not prophecies in the true sense of the word, but either accounts composed after the event or, if it is necessary that they be acknowledged as being foretold before the event, that the prophet foretold them not from any natural revelation of God who knows the future, but by a kind of happy sagacity and natural acumen of the mind from things that have already happened?—*Reply:* In the negative.

2116   *Question II:* Whether the opinion which prevails that Isaias and the other prophets uttered only prophecies which were to take place in the near future, or after no great space of time, can be reconciled with those prophecies, especially the Messianic and eschatological, which were certainly pronounced by these same prophets a long time in advance, and also with the common opinion of the Holy Fathers who assert with one accord that the prophets foretold those things also which were to be fulfilled after many ages?—*Reply:* In the negative.

2117   *Question III:* Whether it can be admitted that the prophets, not only as reformers of human depravity, and heralds of the divine Word for the benefit of those who heed it, but also as foretellers of future events, must have continually addressed themselves, not to future listeners but to contemporary ones, on an equal footing with themselves, and in a manner to make possible a clear understanding; that as a consequence the second part of book of Isaias (chapter 40, 66), in which the prophet living among them addresses and consoles not the Jews on an equal footing with Isaias, but the lamenting in Babylonian exile, cannot have had Isaias himself, who was already dead, as its author, but should be assigned to some unknown prophet living among the exiles?—*Reply:* In the negative.

2118   *Question IV:* Whether the philological argument taken from the language and style to impugn the identity of the author of the book of Isaias, is to be considered of such importance as to force a serious person, skilled in the art of criticism and in the Hebrew language, to recognize in the same book a plurality of authors?—*Reply:* In the negative.

2119   *Question V:* Whether solid arguments stand out, even taken collectively,

---

[1] ASS 41 (1908), 613 f.; AE 16 (1908), 297; EB n. 287 ff.

to induce the conviction that the Book of Isaias is not to be attributed to Isaias himself alone, but to two, or even to several authors.—*Reply:* In the negative.

The Relationship Between Philosophy and Theology [1]

[From the Encyclical, "Communium rerum," April 21, 1909]

. . . (Therefore) the task of philosophy is chiefly to set forth promi- **2120** nently the "reasonable service" [Rom. 12:1] of our faith, and the duty which follows from that of joining faith to divine authority which proposes the most profound mysteries which, proven by many evidences of truth, "are become exceedingly credible" [Ps. 92:5]. Far different from this is the task of theology, which relies on divine revelation and makes more solid in the faith those who confess that they rejoice in the honor of the Christian name; for no Christian should dispute how what the Catholic Church believes in heart, and confesses in words is not so; but always unhesitatingly holding to the same faith, but loving and living according to it, humbly seek the reason, insofar as he can, how it is so. If he can understand, let him give thanks to God; if he cannot let him not push his horns to the struggle [Cf. I Mach. 7:46], but let him submit his head to veneration.

The Historical Character of the Earlier Chapters of Genesis [2]

[Response of the Biblical Commission, June 30th, 1909]

Question I: Whether the various exegetical systems which have been **2121** proposed to exclude the literal historical sense of the three first chapters of the Book of Genesis, and have been defended by the pretense of science, are sustained by a solid foundation?—*Reply:* In the negative.

Question II: Whether, when the nature and historical form of the Book **2122** of Genesis does not oppose, because of the peculiar connections of the three first chapters with each other and with the following chapters, because of the manifold testimony of the Old and of the New Testaments; because of the almost unanimous opinion of the Holy Fathers, and because of the traditional sense which, transmitted from the Israelite people, the Church always held, it can be taught that the three aforesaid chapters of Genesis do not contain the stories of events which really happened, that is, which correspond with objective reality and historical truth; but are either accounts celebrated in fable drawn from the mythologies and cosmogonies of ancient peoples and adapted by a holy writer to mono-

---

[1] AAS I (1909), 381; AE 17 (1909), 170.
[2] AAS I (1909), 567 ff.; AE 17 (1909), 334; EB n. 332 ff.

theistic doctrine, after expurgating any error of polytheism; or allegories and symbols, devoid of a basis of objective reality, set forth under the guise of history to inculcate religious and philosophical truths; or, finally, legends, historical in part and fictitious in part, composed freely for the instruction and edification of souls?—*Reply:* In the negative to both parts.

2123   *Question III:* Whether in particular the literal and historical sense can be called into question, where it is a matter of facts related in the same chapters, which pertain to the foundations of the Christian religion; for example, among others, the creation of all things wrought by God in the beginning of time; the special creation of man; the formation of the first woman from the first man; the oneness of the human race; the original happiness of our first parents in the state of justice, integrity, and immortality; the command given to man by God to prove his obedience; the transgression of the divine command through the devil's persuasion under the guise of a serpent; the casting of our first parents out of that first state of innocence; and also the promise of a future restorer?—*Reply:* In the negative.

2124   *Question IV:* Whether in interpreting those passages of these chapters, which the Fathers and Doctors have understood differently, but concerning which they have not taught anything certain and definite, it is permitted, while preserving the judgment of the Church and keeping the analogy of faith, to follow and defend that opinion which everyone has wisely approved?—*Reply:* In the affirmative.

2125   *Question V:* Whether all and everything, namely, words and phrases which occur in the aforementioned chapters, are always and necessarily to be accepted in a special sense, so that there may be no deviation from this, even when the expressions themselves manifestly appear to have been taken improperly, or metaphorically or anthropomorphically, and either reason prohibits holding the proper sense, or necessity forces its abandonment?—*Reply:* In the negative.

2126   *Question VI:* Whether, presupposing the literal and historical sense, the allegorical and prophetical interpretation of some passages of the same chapters, with the example of the Holy Fathers and the Church herself showing the way, can be wisely and profitably applied?—*Reply:* In the affirmative.

2127   *Question VII:* Whether, since in writing the first chapter of Genesis it was not the mind of the sacred author to teach in a scientific manner the detailed constitution of visible things and the complete order of creation, but rather to give to his people a popular notion, according as the common speech of the times went, accommodated to the understanding and capacity of men, the propriety of scientific language is to be investigated exactly and always in the interpretation of these?—*Reply:* In the negative.

2128   *Question VIII:* Whether in that designation and distinction of six days, with which the account of the first chapter of Genesis deals, the word (dies) can be assumed either in its proper sense as a natural day, or in the improper sense of a certain space of time; and whether with regard to such a question there can be free disagreement among exegetes?—*Reply:* In the affirmative.

The Authors and the Time of the Composition of the Psalms [1]

[Reply of the Biblical Commission, May 1, 1910]

Question I: Whether the designations *Psalms of David, Hymns of* 2129 *David, Davidian Psalter,* used in the ancient collections and in the Councils themselves to designate the Book of 150 psalms of the Old Testament, just as also the opinion of many Fathers and Doctors who held that absolutely all the psalms of the Psalter are to be ascribed to David alone, have such force that David ought to be held as the only author of the entire Psalter?—*Reply:* In the negative.

Question II: Whether from a comparison of the Hebraic with the 2130 Alexandrian Greek text and with other old versions it can rightly be argued that the titles of the psalms prefixed to the Hebraic text are more ancient than the so-called version of the seventy men; and therefore have derived, if not directly from the authors themselves of the psalms, at least from an old Judaic tradition?—*Reply:* In the affirmative.

Question III: Whether the aforesaid titles of the psalms, witnesses of 2131 the Judaic tradition, since there is not serious argument against their authenticity, can prudently be called into doubt?—*Reply:* In the negative.

Question IV: Whether, if the by no means infrequent testimonies of 2132 Holy Scripture about the natural skill of David, illustrated by the grace of the Holy Spirit in composing the religious hymns, are considered, the institutions established by him on the liturgical singing of the psalms, the attributing of the psalms to him both in the Old Testament and the New, and in the inscriptions themselves which were prefixed to the psalms from antiquity, besides the consensus of opinion of the Jews, Fathers, and Doctors of the Church, it can be prudently denied that David is the chief author of the hymns of the Psalter; or on the other hand affirmed that only a few hymns of the Psalter are to be attributed to him? *Reply:*—In the negative to both parts.

Question V: Whether in appearance the Davidian origin can be denied 2133 to those psalms which are cited in the Old and New Testament distinctly under the name of David, among which to be considered before the rest come: psalm 2, *Quare fremuerunt gentes;* psalm 15, *Conserva me, Domine;* psalm 17, *Diligam te, Domine, fortitudo mea;* psalm 31, *Beati, Quorum*

---

[1] AAS 2 (1910), 354 f.; EB n. 340 ff.

remissae sunt iniquitates; psalm 68, *Salvum me fac, Deus;* psalm 109, *Dixit Dominus Domino meo?—Reply:* In the negative.

2134   *Question VI:* Whether the opinion of those can be admitted who hold that among the psalms of the psalter some, whether of David or of other authors, which for liturgical and musical reasons, the listlessness of the amanuenses, or for other unknown reasons, have been divided into several groups or joined into one; and likewise that there are other psalms, such as *Miserere mei, Deus,* which, that they may be made to fit in better with historic circumstances or the solemnities of the Jewish people, have been lightly revised and modified by the subtraction or addition of one or two verses, although preserving the inspiration of the entire sacred text?— *Reply:* In the affirmative to both parts.

2135   *Question VII:* Whether the opinion can probably be sustained of those among more recent writers who, relying on internal indications only, or on an inaccurate interpretation of the sacred text, tried to show that not a few psalms were composed after the times of Esdras and Nehemias, even in the late period of the Machabees.—*Reply:* In the negative.

2136   *Question VIII:* Whether because of the many testimonies of the Sacred Books of the New Testament, and the unanimous consent of the Fathers, together also with the indications of the writers of the Judaic nation, more psalms should be recognized as prophetic and messianic, which have predicted the coming of the future Liberator, the kingdom, the priesthood, the passion, the death, and resurrection; and therefore their opinion ought to be completely rejected, who pervert the prophetic and messianic nature of the psalms and restrict the same oracles on Christ only to pronouncing the future lot of the elect people?—*Reply:* In the affirmative for both parts.

The Age for Admitting to First Eucharistic Communion [1]

[From the Decree, "Quem singulari," of the Congregation on the Sacraments, August 8, 1910]

2137   I. The age of discretion both for confession and for Holy Communion is that at which the child begins to reason, that is, at about the seventh year, more or less. The obligation of satisfying both precepts of confession and communion begins from that time [see n. 437].

2138   II. For first confession and for first communion a full and perfect knowledge of Christian doctrine is not necessary. But the child will be obliged afterwards to learn gradually the whole catechism in accord with his intelligence.

2139   III. The knowledge of religion which is required in a child, that he may prepare himself fittingly for his first communion, is that by which in accord

---

[1] AAS 2 (1910), 582 f.

with his capacity he perceives the mysteries of faith necessary by a necessity of means, and by which he distinguishes Eucharistic bread from the common and corporeal, in order that he may approach the most blessed Eucharist with that devotion which his age carries.

IV. The obligation of the precept of confession and communion which 2140 rests upon a child, falls especially upon those who should have care of him, that is, upon parents, confessor, teachers, and pastor. But to the father, or to those who take his place, and to the confessor, it pertains, according to the Roman Catechism, to admit the child to first communion.

V. Once or several times a year let the pastors take care to announce 2141 and to hold general communion for children, and to admit to it not only new communicants but also others who by the consent of their parents or confessor, as has been mentioned above, have already partaken for the first time from the holy altar. Let some days for instruction and preparation be set aside in advance.

VI. Those who have charge over children must make every effort to see 2142 that these same children after first communion approach the holy table often, and, if it can be done, daily, just as Jesus Christ and Mother Church desire [see n. 1981 ff.]; and that they do this with that devotion of mind which is appropriate to such an age. Let those who have this responsibility remember besides the very serious obligation by which they are bound, see to it that the children themselves continue to be present at the public instructions in catechism, or otherwise in some manner supply the same with religious instruction.

VII. The custom of never admitting children to confession, or of never 2143 absolving them when they have arrived at the use of reason, is to be disapproved entirely. Therefore, the local ordinaries will see to it, even by applying the remedy of the law, that this custom is entirely abandoned.

VIII. The abuse of not administering Viaticum and extreme unction 2144 to children past the age of reason, and of burying them according to the rite of infants is entirely an abuse. Let the local ordinaries deal severely with those who do not abandon such a custom.

The Oath Against the Errors of Modernism [1]

[From *Motu proprio*, "Sacrorum antistitum," September 1, 1910]

I . . . firmly embrace and accept all and everything that has been 2145 defined, affirmed, and declared by the unerring *magisterium* of the Church, especially those chief doctrines which are directly opposed to the errors of this time. And first, I profess that God, the beginning and end of all things, can be certainly known and thus can also be demon-

---

[1] ASS 2 (1910), 669 ff.

strated by the natural light of reason "by the things that are made" [cf.
Rom. 1:20], that is, by the visible works of creation, as the cause by
the effects. Secondly, I admit and recognize the external arguments of
revelation, that is, divine facts, and especially miracles and prophecies,
as very certain signs of the divine origin of the Christian religion; and
I hold that these same arguments have been especially accommodated
to the intelligence of all ages and men, even of these times. Thirdly,
likewise, with a firm faith I believe that the Church, guardian and mistress of the revealed word, was instituted proximately and directly by
the true and historical Christ Himself, while he sojourned among us, and
that the same was built upon Peter, the chief of the apostolic hierarchy,
and his successors until the end of time. Fourthly, I accept sincerely the
doctrine of faith transmitted from the apostles through the orthodox
fathers, always in the same sense and interpretation, even to us; and so
I reject the heretical invention of the evolution of dogmas, passing from
one meaning to another, different from that which the Church first had;
and likewise I reject all error whereby a philosophic fiction is substituted
for the divine deposit, given over to the Spouse of Christ and to be
guarded faithfully by her, or a creation of the human conscience formed
gradually by the efforts of men and to be perfected by indefinite progress
in the future. Fifthly, I hold most certainly and profess sincerely that
faith is not a blind religious feeling bursting forth from the recesses
of the subconscious, unformed morally under the pressure of the heart
and the impulse of the will, but the true assent of the intellect to the
truth received extrinsically *ex auditu,* whereby we believe that what has
been said, attested, and revealed by the personal God, our Creator and
Lord, to be true on account of the authority of God the highest truth.

2146   I also subject myself with the reverence which is proper, and I adhere
with my whole soul to all the condemnations, declarations, and prescriptions which are contained in the Encyclical letter, "Pascendi" [see n.
2071 ff.] and in the Decree, "Lamentabili" [see n. 2001 f.], especially
on that which is called the history of dogma. In the same manner I
disapprove the error of those who affirm that the faith proposed by the
Church can be in conflict with history, and that Catholic dogmas, in
the sense in which they are now understood, cannot be reconciled with
the more authentic origins of the Catholic religion.—I also condemn and
reject the opinion of those who say that the more erudite Christian puts
on a dual personality, one of the believer, the other of the historian,
as if it were permitted the historian to hold what is in contradiction to
the faith of the believer; or to establish premises from which it follows
that dogmas are either false or doubtful, provided they are not directly
denied.—I disapprove likewise that method of studying and interpreting
Sacred Scripture, which disregards the tradition of the Church, the

analogy of faith, and the norms of the Apostolic See, and adheres to the fictions of the rationalists, and no less freely than boldly adopts textual criticism as the only and supreme rule.—Besides I reject the opinion of those who hold that to present the historical and theological disciplines the teacher or the writer on these subjects must first divest himself of previously conceived opinion either on the supernatural origin of Catholic tradition, or on the aid promised by God for the perpetual preservation of every revealed truth; then that the writings of the individual Fathers are to be interpreted only by the principles of science, setting aside all divine authority, and by that freedom of judgment with which any profane document is customarily investigated. Finally, in short, 2147 I profess to be utterly free of the error according to which the modernists hold that there is nothing divine in the sacred tradition; or, what is far worse, admit this in the pantheistic sense, so that nothing remains but the bare and simple fact to be assimilated with the common facts of history, namely, of men by their industry, skill, and genius continuing through subsequent ages the school inaugurated by Christ and His disciples. So I retain most firmly the faith of the Fathers, and shall retain it until the final breath of life, regarding the certain gift of truth, which is, was, and will be always in the succession of the episcopacy from the apostles,[1] not so that what may seem better and more fitting according to each one's period of culture may be held, but so that the absolute and immutable truth preached [2] by the apostles from the beginning may never be believed otherwise, may never be understood otherwise.

All these things I promise that I shall faithfully, completely, and sincerely keep and inviolably watch, never deviating from them in word and writing either while teaching or in any other pursuit. So I promise, so I swear, so may God, etc.

Certain Errors of the Orientals [3]

[From the letter, "Ex quo," to the Archbishops Apostolic
Delegates in Byzantium, in Greece, in Egypt, in Mesopotamia,
in Persia, in Syria, and in the Oriental Indies,
December 26, 1910]

No less rashly than falsely does one approach this opinion, that the 2147a dogma concerning the procession of the Holy Spirit from the Son by no means is taken from the very words of the Gospel, or is sanctioned by the faith of the ancient Fathers;—most imprudently, likewise, is doubt

---

[1] Iren. 4, c. 26, 2 [MG 7, 1058 c.].
[2] Tertullian, *De praescr.* c. 28 [ML 2, 40].
[3] AAS 3 (1911), 118 f.

raised as to whether the sacred dogmas on purgatory and on the Immaculate Conception of the Blessed Virgin Mary were acknowledged by the holy men of earlier years;— . . . regarding the constitution of the Church . . . first of all an error, long since condemned by Our predecessor, Innocent X, is being renewed [cf. n. 1091], in which it is argued that St. Paul is held as a brother entirely equal to St. Peter;—then, with no less falsity, one is invited to believe that the Catholic Church was not in the earliest days a sovereignty of one person, that is a *monarchy;* or that the primacy of the Catholic Church does not rest on valid arguments.—But . . . the Catholic doctrine on the most Blessed Sacrament of the Eucharist is not left untouched when it is taught inflexibly that the opinion can be accepted which maintains that among the Greeks the words of consecration do not produce an effect unless preceded by that prayer which they call *epiclesis,*[1] although, on the other hand, it is well known that to the Church there belongs no right whatsoever to innovate anything touching on the substance of the sacraments; and no less inharmonious with this is the view that confirmation conferred by any priest at all is to be held valid.

These opinions are noted as "grave errors."

The Author, the Time of Composition, and Historical Truth of the Gospel According to Matthew [2]

[Response of the Biblical Commission, June 19, 1911]

2148 I. Whether after noting the universal and constant agreement of the Church from the earliest times, which is clearly shown by the eloquent testimonies of the Fathers, the inscriptions of the manuscripts of the Gospels, even the most ancient versions of the Sacred Scriptures, and the catalogues handed down by the Holy Fathers, the ecclesiastical writers, the Highest Pontiffs, and the Councils, and finally the liturgical practice of the Eastern and Western Church, it can and should be affirmed with certainty that Matthew, the Apostle of Christ, is in fact the author of the vulgate Gospel under his name?—*Reply:* In the affirmative.

2149 II. Whether the opinion should be considered as sufficiently supported

---

[1] That epiclesis is not required for consecration the following, before Pius X, taught: Benedict XII by the communication, *"Iam dudum,"* in the year 1341, condemning among the errors of the Armenians, error n. 66 (cf. above 532 ff.); Clement VI by the letter, *"Super quibusdam,"* to Consolator, Cathol. Armen. (Bar [Th] ad 1351, n. 11); Benedict XIII, Instr. 31st of May, 1729 sent to the Patriarch Melchit. Antioch. (CL 2, 439); Benedict XIV in the Brief, *"Singularis Romanorum,"* Sept. 1, 1741, confirming the synod provinc. Maronit. (CL 2, 197); Pius VII in the Brief, "Adorabile Eucharistiae," 8th of May, 1822, to the Patriarch Graeco-Melchit. Antioch. (CL 2, 551).

[2] AAS 3 (1911), 294–296; EB n. 401 ff.

by the assent of tradition, which holds that Matthew preceded the other evangelists in his writing, and that he composed the first Gospel in the native language then employed by the Jews of Palestine, to whom that work was directed?—*Reply:* In the affirmative to both parts.

III. Whether the redaction of this original text can be placed beyond the time of the overthrow of Jerusalem, so that the prophecies which are read there about this same overthrow were written after the event; or whether what is customarily alleged to be the testimony of Irenaeus [*Adv. haer.,* lib. 3, cap. 1, n: 2] of uncertain and controversial interpretation, is to be considered of such weight that it forces us to reject the opinion of those who think, more in accord with tradition, that the same redaction was composed even before Paul's arrival in the City? —*Reply:* In the negative to both parts.   2150

IV. Whether that opinion of certain moderns can even with some probability be sustained, according to which Matthew did not properly or strictly compose the Gospel such as has been handed down to us, but only some collection of the words or conversations of Christ, which another anonymous author has made use of as sources, whom they make the redactor of the Gospel itself.—*Reply:* In the negative.   2151

V. Whether from the fact that the Fathers and all ecclesiastical writers, indeed the Church herself from her own incunabula used, as canonical, only the Greek text of the Gospel known under the name of Matthew, not even excepting those who taught expressly that Matthew the Apostle wrote in his native language, it can be proved with certainty that the Greek Gospel is identical as to substance with that Gospel written in his native language by the same Apostle?—*Reply:* In the affirmative.   2152

VI. Whether from the fact that the author of the first Gospel pursues especially the dogmatic and apologetic aim, namely, of demonstrating to the Jews that Jesus is the Messias foretold by the prophets, and descended from the lineage of David, and from the fact that when arranging the deeds and words which he narrates and sets forth anew, he does not always hold to the chronological order, it may be deduced that these matters are not to be accepted as true; or, also, whether it can be affirmed that the accounts of the accomplishments and discourses of Christ, which are read in the Gospel itself, have undergone a kind of alteration and adaptation under the influence of the prophets of the Old Testament, and the status of the more mature Church, and so are by no means in conformity with historical truth?—*Reply:* In the negative to both parts.   2153

VII. Whether in particular the opinions of those persons should be rightly considered as devoid of solid foundation, who call into question the historical authenticity of the two first chapters, in which the genealogy and infancy of Christ are related; as also of certain opinions on dogmatic matters of great moment, as are those which have to do with the primacy   2154 of Peter [Matt. 16:17–19], the form of baptizing, together with the universal mission of preaching handed over to the apostles [Matt. 28:19–20], the apostles' profession of faith in the divinity of Christ [Matt. 14:33], and other such matters which occurred in Matthew announced in a special way?—*Reply:* In the affirmative.

The Author, the Time of Composition, the Historical Truth of the Gospels According to Mark and According to Luke [1]

[Reply of the Biblical Commission, June 26, 1912]

2155 I. Whether the evident judgment of tradition, from the beginnings of the Church in wonderful agreement with and confirmed by manifold arguments, namely, the eloquent testimonies of the Holy Fathers and ecclesiastical writers, the citations and allusions which occur in the writings of the same, the practice of the ancient heretics, the versions of the Books of the New Testament, the most ancient and almost entire body of manuscripts, and also the internal reasons taken from the very text of the Sacred Books, definitely compels the affirmation that Mark, the disciple and expounder of Peter, and Luke the physician, the hearer and companion of Paul, are in fact the authors of the Gospels which are respectively attributed to them?—*Reply:* In the affirmative.

2156 II. Whether the reasons by which some critics strive to demonstrate that the last twelve verses of the Gospel of Mark [Mark 16:9–20] were not written by Mark himself, but were added by another hand, are such as to give the right to affirm that they are not to be accepted as inspired and canonical; or at least demonstrate that the author of the said verses is not Mark?—*Reply:* In the negative to both parts.

2157 III. Whether one may likewise doubt the inspiration and canonicity of the accounts given by Luke of the infancy of Christ [Luke 1–2]; or the apparition of the Angel strengthening Christ, and the sweat of blood [Luke 22:43 f.]; or whether it can at least be shown by solid reasons—as pleased the ancient heretics, and is agreeable also to some more recent critics—that the said accounts do not belong to the genuine Gospel of Luke?—*Reply:* In the negative to both parts.

2158 IV. Whether those most rare and very peculiar documents, in which the Canticle *Magnificat* is directed not to the Blessed Virgin but to Elizabeth, can and should in any way prevail against the harmonious testimony of almost all manuscripts, both of the original Greek text and of the versions, as well as against the interpretation which the context no less than the spirit of the Virgin herself, and the constant tradition of the Church clearly exacts?—*Reply:* In the negative.

---

[1] AAS 4 (1912), 463–465; EB n. 408 ff.

V. Whether, with respect to the chronological order of the Gospels, **2159** it is right to withdraw from that opinion which, strengthened equally by the most ancient and continued testimony of tradition, testifies that Mark was the second in order to write and Luke the third, after Matthew, who was the first of all to write his Gospel in his native tongue; or, whether their opinion, which asserts that the Gospel was composed second and third before the Greek version of the first Gospel, is to be regarded in turn as in opposition to this idea?—*Reply:* In the negative to both parts.

VI. Whether the time of composition of the Gospel of Mark and **2160** Luke may be postponed until the overthrow of the city of Jerusalem; or, because the prophecy of the Lord in Luke about the overthrow of this city seems more definite, it can be sustained that his Gospel at least was composed after the siege had already begun?—*Reply:* In the negative to both parts.

VII. Whether it ought to be affirmed that the Gospel of Luke preceded **2161** the book of the *Acts of the Apostles;* and although this book, with same author Luke [Acts 1:1 f.], was finished before the end of the Apostle's Roman captivity [Acts 28:30 f.], his Gospel was not composed after this time?—*Reply:* In the affirmative.

VIII. Whether, keeping in mind both the testimonies of tradition and **2162** internal evidence, as regards the sources which both evangelists used in composing the Gospels, that opinion can prudently be called into question which holds that Mark wrote according to the preaching of Peter, but Luke according to the preaching of Paul; and which also asserts that other sources worthy of trust were also at hand for these same evangelists, either oral or even already consigned to writing?—*Reply:* In the negative.

IX. Whether the words and deeds which are described accurately and, **2163** as it were, graphically by Mark according to the preaching of Peter, and are most sincerely set forth by Luke, following everything diligently from the beginning through witnesses clearly worthy of trust, inasmuch as they themselves from the beginning were eyewitnesses and ministers of the word [Luke 1:2 f.], rightly vindicate that complete historical faith in themselves which the Church has always given them; or, whether on the contrary the same deeds and actions are to be judged void of historical truth, at least in part, either because the writers were not eyewitnesses, or because in both Gospels defects in order and discrepancies in the succession of the deeds are not rarely caught; or because, since they came and wrote later, they were obliged to represent conceptions necessarily extraneous to the minds of Christ and the apostles, or deeds now more or less distorted by the imagination of the people; or, finally, because they indulged in preconceived dogmatic ideas, each one according to his purpose?—*Reply:* In the affirmative to the first part; in the negative to the second.

The Synoptic Question or the Mutual Relations between the Three Earlier Gospels [1]

[Reply of the Biblical Commission, June 26, 1912]

2164   I. Whether, preserving what must be jealously preserved according to the decisions made above, especially on the authenticity and integrity of the three Gospels of Matthew, Mark, and Luke; on the substantial identity of the Greek Gospel of Matthew with its early original; also on the order of time in which the same were written, to explain their mutual likenesses and differences, midst so many varying and opposite opinions of the authors, it is impossible for exegetes to dispute freely and to appeal to the hypotheses of tradition whether written or oral, or even of the dependence of one upon a preceding or upon several preceding?—*Reply:* In the affirmative.

2165   II. Whether they should be advised to preserve what was established above, who, supported by no testimony of tradition or by historical argument, easily taken in by the hypothesis publicly proclaimed of two sources, which labors to explain the composition of the Greek Gospel of Matthew and of the Gospel of Luke chiefly by their dependence upon the Gospel of Mark and a so-called collection of the Lord's discourses; and whether they are thus able to defend this freely?—*Reply.* In the negative to both parts.

The Author, Time of Composition, Historical Veracity of the Book of the Acts of the Apostles

[Reply of the Biblical Commission, June 12, 1913]

2166   I. Whether in view especially of the tradition of the whole Church going back to the earliest ecclesiastical writers, and noting the internal reasons of the book of Acts, considered in itself or in its relation to the third Gospel, and especially because of the mutual affinity and connection between the two prologues [Luke 1:1–4; Acts 1:1 f.], it must be held as certain that the volume that is entitled *Actus Apostolorum,* or, Πράξεις Ἀποστόλων, has Luke the Evangelist as author?—*Reply:* In the affirmative.

2167   II. Whether for critical reasons taken from the language and style, and from the manner of narrating, and from the oneness of aim and doctrine, it can be demonstrated that the book of the Acts of the Apostles

---

[1] AAS 4 (1912), 465; EB n. 417 f.

should be attributed to one author alone; and therefore that the opinion of more recent writers which holds that Luke is not the only author of the book, but that different persons are to be recognized as authors of the same book is devoid of any foundation?—*Reply:* In the affirmative to both parts.

III. Whether in outward appearance, the prominent chapters in the **2168** Acts where the use of the third person is broken off and the first person plural introduced, weaken the unity and authenticity of composition; or rather historically and philologically considered are to be said to confirm it?—*Reply:* In the negative to the first part; in the affirmative to the second.

IV. Whether because of the fact that the book itself is abruptly con- **2169** cluded after scarcely making mention of the two years of Paul's first Roman captivity, it may be inferred that the author had written a second volume now lost, or had intended to write it; and so the time of composition of the Book of Acts can be deferred long after this captivity; or whether it should rather rightly and worthily be held that Luke toward the end of the first Roman captivity of the Apostle Paul had completed his book?—*Reply:* In the negative to the first part; in the affirmative to the second.

V. Whether, if there is considered together the frequent and easy com- **2170** munication which Luke undoubtedly had with the first and prominent founders of the Palestinian church, and also with Paul, the Apostle of the Gentiles, whose assistant in the preaching of the Gospel and companion in travel he was; also his customary industry and diligence in seeking witnesses, and in observing things with his own eyes; also, and finally, the evident and amazing agreement for the most part of the Book of Acts with the letters of Paul and the more genuine monuments of history, it should be held with certainty that Luke had at hand sources worthy of all trust, and applied them accurately, well, and faithfully, so that he rightly indicates for himself full historical authority?—*Reply:* In the affirmative.

VI. Whether the difficulties which are usually raised from the super- **2171** natural deeds related by Luke, and from the narration of certain discourses which, since they are handed down in summary, are considered fictitious and adapted to circumstances; also from certain passages, apparently at least, in disagreement with history whether profane or biblical; finally also from certain accounts which seem to be at odds with the author of the Acts, or with other sacred authors, are such as can call the historical authority of the Acts into doubt or at least in some manner diminish it?—*Reply:* In the negative.

The Author, Integrity, and Time of Composition of the Pastoral Letters of Paul the Apostle [1]

[Response of the Biblical Commission, June 12, 1913]

2172 I. Whether, keeping in mind the tradition of the Church which continues universally and steadily from the earliest times, just as the ancient ecclesiastical records testify in many ways, it should be held with certainty that the so-called pastoral letters, that is, the two to Timothy and another to Titus, notwithstanding the rashness of certain heretics who have eliminated them as being contrary to their dogma from the number of Pauline epistles, without giving any reason, were composed by the Apostle Paul himself, and have always been reckoned among the genuine and canonical?—*Reply:* In the affirmative.

2173 II. Whether the so-called fragmentary hypothesis introduced by certain more recent critics and variously set forth, who for no otherwise probable reason, rather while quarreling among themselves, contend that the pastoral letters were constructed at a later time from fragments of letters, or from corrupt Pauline letters by unknown authors, and notably increased, can bring some slight prejudice upon the clear and very strong testimony of tradition?—*Reply:* In the negative.

2174 III. Whether the difficulties which are brought up in many places whether from the style and language of the author, or from the errors especially of the Gnostics, who already at that time are described as serpents; or from the state of the ecclesiastical hierarchy, which is supposed to have been already evolved, and other such reasons in opposition in some way, weaken the opinion which holds the authenticity of the pastoral letters as valid and certain?—*Reply:* In the negative.

2175 IV. Whether, since no less from historical reasons as from ecclesiastical tradition, in harmony with the testimonies of the oriental and occidental most holy Fathers; also from the indications themselves which are easily drawn from the abrupt conclusion of the Book of the Acts and from the Pauline letters written at Rome, and especially from the second letter to Timothy, the opinion of a twofold Roman captivity of the Apostle Paul should be held as certain, it can be safely affirmed that the pastoral letters were written in that period of time which intervenes between the liberation from the first captivity and the death of the Apostle?—*Reply:* In the affirmitive.

---

[1] AAS 5 (1913), 292 ff.; EB n. 425 ff.

The Author and Method of Composition of the Epistle to the Hebrews [1]

[Reply of the Biblical Commission, June 24, 1914]

I. Whether so much force is to be attributed to the doubts which in **2176** the first centuries possessed the minds of some in the Occident regarding the divine inspiration and Pauline origin of the Epistle to the Hebrews, because of the special abuse of heretics, that, although aware of the perpetual, unanimous, and continued affirmation of the Oriental Fathers, to which was added after the fourth century the full agreement of the entire Western Church; weighing also the acts of the Highest Pontiffs and of the sacred Councils, especially of Trent, and also the perpetual practice of the universal Church, one may hesitate to classify it with certainty not only among the canonical—which is determined regarding faith—but also among the genuine epistles of the Apostle Paul?—*Reply:* In the negative.

II. Whether the arguments which are usually drawn from the un- **2177** usual absence of the name of Paul, and the omission of the customary introduction and salutation in the Epistle to the Hebrews—or from the purity of the same Greek language, the elegance and perfection of diction and style,—or from the way by which the Old Testament is cited in it and arguments made from it,—or from certain differences which supposedly existed between the doctrine of this and of the other epistles of Paul, somehow are able to weaken the Pauline origin of the same; or whether, on the other hand, the perfect agreement of doctrine and opinions, the likeness of admonitions and exhortations, and also the harmony of the phrases and of the words themselves celebrated also by some non-Catholics, which are observed between it and the other writings of the Apostle of the Gentiles, demonstrate and confirm the same Pauline origin?—*Reply:* In the negative to the first part; in the affirmative to the second.

III. Whether the Apostle Paul is so to be considered the author of **2178** this epistle that it should necessarily be affirmed that he not only conceived and expressed it all by the inspiration of the Holy Spirit, but also endowed it with that form with which it stands out?—*Reply:* In the negative, save for a later judgment of the Church.

---

[1] ASS 6 (1914), 417 f.; EB n. 429 ff.

BENEDICT XV 1914–1922

Parousia, or the Second Advent of Our Lord Jesus Christ in the Epistles of St. Paul the Apostle [1]

[Reply of the Biblical Commission, June 18, 1915]

2179   I. Whether to solve the difficulties which occur in the epistles of St. Paul and of the other apostles, where there is mention of "parousia," as they say, or of the second coming of our Lord Jesus Christ, a Catholic exegete is permitted to assert that the apostles, although under the inspiration of the Holy Spirit, taught no error, nevertheless express their own human feelings in which error or deception can lie concealed?— *Reply:* In the negative.

2180   II. Whether, bearing in mind the genuine notion of the apostolic gift, and the undoubted fidelity of St. Paul with regard to the doctrine of the Master, likewise the Catholic dogma on the inspiration and inerrancy of the Holy Scriptures, according to which all that the sacred writer asserts, declares, and introduces ought to be maintained as asserted, declared, and introduced by the Holy Spirit; weighing also the texts of the epistles of the Apostle considered in themselves, especially in harmony with the method of speaking of the Lord himself, one should affirm that the Apostle Paul in his writings said nothing at all which does not agree perfectly with that ignorance of parousia of the time, which Christ Himself proclaimed to belong to man?—*Reply:* In the affirmative.

2181   III. Whether, noting the Greek expression, "ἡμεῖς οἱ ζῶντες οἱ περιλειπόμενοι," weighing also the explanation of the Fathers, especially of John Chrysostom, who was most versed in the native idiom and in the epistles of Paul, it is permitted to reject the traditional interpretation in the Catholic schools as more remotely desired and devoid of solid foundation (which was retained by the renewers themselves also of the sixteenth century), which explains the words of St. Paul in chapter 4, epist. I to the Thessalonians, vv. 15–7, without in any way involving the affirmation of parousia so proximate that the Apostle numbers himself and his readers among those faithful who are to go to meet Christ as survivers?—*Reply:* In the negative.

---

[1] ASS 7 (1915), 357 f.; EB n. 432 ff.

On Dying and Dead Schismatics [1]
[Reply of the Holy Office to various local ordinaries, May 17, 1916]

I. Whether when material schismatics at the point of death, in good **2181a**
faith seek either absolution or extreme unction, these sacraments can be
conferred on them without their renouncing errors?—*Reply:* In the negative, but that it be required that they reject errors as best they can, and
make a profession of faith.

II. Whether absolution and extreme unction can be conferred on
schismatics at the point of death when unconscious?—*Reply:* Conditionally, in the affirmative, especially if from additional circumstances it can
be conjectured that they at least implicitly reject their errors, yet effectually
removing scandal, at least by manifesting to bystanders that they accept
the Church and have returned at the last moment to unity.

III. As regards ecclesiastical burial the Roman Ritual must stand firm.

Spiritism [2]
[Reply of the Holy Office, April 24, 1917]

Whether it is permitted through a *medium,* as they call him, or with- **2182**
out a *medium,* with or without the application of hypnotism, to be present
at spiritistic conversations or manifestations of any kind, even though
these phenomena present the appearance of honesty or piety, whether by
interrogating souls or spirits, or by listening to responses, or only by
looking on, even with a tacit or expressed protestation that one does not
wish to have anything to do with wicked spirits.—*Reply:* In negative in
all cases.

*From the Codex of Canon Law promulgated on May 19, 1918,
variously, see in Index systematicus.*

Certain Propositions on Knowledge of the Soul of Christ [3]
[Decree of the Holy Office, June 5, 1918]

When the question was proposed by the Sacred Congregation on
Seminary and University Studies, whether the following propositions
can be safely taught:

I. It is not established that there was in the soul of Christ while living **2183**

---

[1] *Kolner Pastoralblatt* 50 (1916), 504 f.; *Linzer Diözesanblatt* 1916, 11: *Theol.-prakt.
Quartalschrift* 69 (Linz, 1916), 693.

[2] AAS 9 (1917), 268.

[3] AAS 10 (1918), 282.

among men the knowledge which the blessed and the comprehensors have [cf. Phil. 3:12, 13].

2184   II. Nor can the opinion be called certain which has established that the soul of Christ was ignorant of nothing, but from the beginning knew all things in the Word, past, present, and future, or all things that God knows by the knowledge of vision.

2185   III. The opinion of certain more recent persons on the limited knowledge of the soul of Christ is to be accepted in Catholic schools no less than the notion of the ancients on universal knowledge.

The Most Eminent and Reverend Cardinals, general Inquisitors in matters of faith and morals, the prayer of the Consultors being held first, decreed that the answer must be: In the negative.

The Inerrancy of Holy Scripture [1]

[From the Encyclical, "Spiritus Paraclitus," September 15, 1920]

2186   By the doctrine of Jerome those statements are well confirmed and illustrated by which Our predecessor, Leo XIII, solemnly declared the ancient and constant faith of the Church in the absolute immunity of Scriptures from any errors: *Tantum abest . . .* [see n. 1951]. And, introducing the definitions of the Councils of Florence and Trent, confirmed in the Vatican Synod, he has the following: "Therefore, nothing at all matters . . . otherwise He Himself were not the Author of all Sacred Scripture" [See n. 1952].

Although these words of Our predecessors leave no place for ambiguity or evasion, We must grieve, Venerable Brothers, that not only were there not lacking some among those outside the Church, but even among the sons of the Catholic Church, moreover—which wounds Our soul more severely—among the clergy itself and the teachers of the sacred disciplines, who relying proudly on their own judgment, either openly reject the *magisterium* of the Church on this subject or secretly oppose it. Indeed, We approve the plan of those who, to extricate themselves and others from the difficulties of the Sacred Codex, in order to eliminate these difficulties, rely on all the aids of scholarship and literary criticism, and investigate new avenues and methods of research; but they will wander pitifully from their purpose, if they disregard the precepts of Our predecessor and *pass beyond* certain limits and *bounds which the Fathers have set* [Prov. 22:28]. Yet by these precepts and limits the opinion of the more recent critics is not restrained, who, after introducing a distinction between the primary or religious element of Scripture, and the secondary or profane, wish, indeed, that inspiration itself pertain to all the ideas,

---

[1] AAS 12 (1920), 393 ff.; EB n. 465 ff.

rather even to the individual words of the Bible, but that its effects and especially immunity from error and absolute truth be contracted and narrowed down to the primary or religious element. For their belief is that that only which concerns religion is intended and is taught by God in the Scriptures; but that the rest, which pertains to the profane disciplines and serves revealed doctrine as a kind of external cloak of divine truth, is only permitted and is left to the feebleness of the writer. It is not surprising, then, if in physical, historical, and other similar affairs a great many things occur in the Bible, which cannot at all be reconciled with the progress of the fine arts of this age. There are those who contend that these fabrications of opinions are not in opposition to the prescriptions of Our predecessor, since he declared that the sacred writer in matters of nature speaks according to external appearance, surely fallacious [see n. 1947]. But how rashly, how falsely this is affirmed, is plainly evident from the very words of the Pontiff.

And no less do they dissent from the doctrine of the Church who **2187** think that the historical parts of Scriptures depend not on the *absolute* truth of facts, but only on what they call *the relative* and harmonious opinion of the multitude; and they do not hesitate to infer this from the very words of Pope Leo, because he said that the principles established regarding the things of nature can be transferred to the historical disciplines [see n. 1949]. And so they contend that the sacred writers, just as in physical matters they spoke according to what was apparent, so they related events unwittingly, inasmuch as these seemed to be established according to the common opinion of the multitude or the false testimonies of others; and that they did not indicate the sources of their knowledge, and did not make the narrations of others their own. Why shall we refute at length a matter plainly injurious to Our predecessor, and false and full of error? For what is the similarity of the things of nature and history, when the physical are concerned with what "appears to the senses," and so should agree with phenomena; while on the other hand the law of history is chiefly this, that what is written must be in agreement with the things accomplished, according as they were accomplished in fact? If the opinion of these men is once accepted, how will that truth of sacred story stand safe, immune from every falsehood, which Our predecessor declares must be retained in the entire text of its literature? But if he affirms that the same principles that have a place in physics can to advantage be transferred to history and related disciplines, he certainly does not establish this on a universal basis, but is only professing that we use the same methods to refute the fallacies of adversaries as we use to protect the historical faith of Sacred Scripture against their attacks. . . .

Nor is Sacred Scripture lacking other detractors; We recognize those **2188** who, if they are restrained within certain limits, so abuse right principles indeed that they cause the foundations of the truth of the Bible to totter, and undermine the Catholic doctrine handed down by the Fathers in common. Among these Fathers Jerome, if he were still alive, would surely hurl the sharpest weapons of his speech, because, neglecting the sense and judgment of the Church, they very smoothly take refuge in citations which they call implicit, or in accounts historical in appearance; or, they contend that certain kinds of literature are found in the sacred books, with which the whole and perfect truth of the divine word cannot be reconciled; or, they have such an opinion on the origin of the Bible that its authority collapses and utterly perishes. Now, what must be thought of those who in expounding the Gospels themselves diminish the human faith due them and overturn divine faith? For what our Lord Jesus Christ said, and what He did they are of the opinion did not come down to us entire and unchanged, although they are witnesses of all those who wrote down religiously what they themselves had seen and heard; but that—especially with reference to the fourth Gospel— part came down from the evangelists who themselves planned and added much, and part was brought together from the account of the faithful of another age.

Now, Venerable Brethren, with the passing of the fifteenth generation after the death of the greatest Doctor We have communicated with you not to delay to bring these words to the clergy and your people, that all, under the patronage and leadership of Jerome, may not only retain and guard the Catholic doctrine of the divine inspiration of the Scriptures, but may also cling most zealously to the principles which are prescribed in the Encyclical Letter, "Providentissimus Deus," and in this Our own. . . .

The Doctrines of Theosophy [1]

[Reply of the Holy Office, July 18, 1919]

2189   Whether the doctrines, which today are called theosophical, can be in harmony with Catholic doctrine; and thus whether it is permitted to join theosophical societies, attend their meetings, and read their books, daily papers, journals, and writings.—*Reply:* In the negative in all cases.

---

[1] AAS 11 (1919), 317.

PIUS XI 1922–1939

The Relation Between Church and State [1]

[From the Encyclical, "Ubi arcano," December 23, 1922]

But if the Church thinks it unlawful to mingle in these worldly affairs, 2190 concerned in the mere controlling of politics, without reason, yet by her own right she strives that civil power invent no cause for obstructing in any way those higher blessings in which man's eternal salvation is contained, or for threatening harm or destruction by unjust laws and orders; or for undermining the divine constitution of the Church; or, finally, of trampling upon the sacred laws of God in the civil community of men.

The Law and Method of Following the Doctrine of St. Thomas Aquinas [2]

[From the Encyclical, "Studiorum Ducem," June 29, 1923]

We desire very much that those especially who hold the *magisteria* 2191 of the higher disciplines in the schools of the clergy note carefully and observe inviolably all the precepts which both Our predecessors, and first of all Leo XIII [3] and Pius X,[4] have decreed and We ourselves have ordered last year.[5] Moreover, let them be convinced that they will then satisfy the demands of their office and will likewise fulfill Our expectation, if, when they begin truly to love the Doctor Aquinas, by a long and intensive study of his works, and by interpreting the Doctor himself, they communicate the warmth of this love to the students under their instruction, and render them capable of exciting a similar zeal in others.

Naturally among lovers of St. Thomas, such as all the sons of the 2192 Church who are concerned with the highest studies should be, We desire that there exist that honorable rivalry with just freedom from which studies make progress, but no detraction which is not favorable to truth and which serves only to break the bonds of charity. Therefore, let whatever is prescribed [6] in the Code of Canon Law be sacred to each one of them, that "the professors may carry on the study of rational [7] philosophy

---

[1] AAS 14 (1922), 698.
[2] AAS 15 (1923), 323 f.
[3] *Litt. Encyclical,* "Aeterni Patris," August 4, 1879 [AAS 12 (1879), 97 ff.].
[4] *Motu proprio,* "Doctoris Angelici," June 29, 1914 [AAS 6 (1914), 336 ff.].
[5] Encyclical, "Officiorum omnium," August 1, 1922 [AAS 14 (1922), 449 ff.].
[6] Can. 1366, Sec. 2.
[7] The 24 theses [AAS 6 (1914), 383 ff.] to be proposed are referred to here as "the

and of theology and the instruction of their students in these disciplines according to the method, doctrines, and principles of the Angelic Doctor, and may hold them sacred," and that all so conduct themselves according to this norm as to be truly able to call him that master. "But let not some exact from others anything more than this which the Church, the mistress and mother of all demands of all; for in those matters about which there is wont to be varied opinions among teachers of higher distinction among our Catholic schools no one is to be prevented from following the opinion which seems to him the more probable."

The Revival of Merits and Gifts [1]

[From the Bull of Jubilee, "Infinita Dei misericordia," May 29, 1924]

2193　Now when the Hebrews in the year of the Sabbath, after recovering their goods which had passed into the ownership of others, were returning *"to their own possession,"* and the servants, now free, were betaking themselves *"to their former family"* [Lev. 25:10], and the debt of the debtors was cancelled, all this more happily happens and is accomplished among us in the year of atonement. For, all who by doing penance carry out the salutary orders of the Apostolic See in the course of the great Jubilee, the same regain anew and receive that abundance of merits and gifts which they had lost by sinning, and they are so set free from the cruel domination of Satan that they regain the freedom "wherewith Christ has made us free" [Gal. 4:31], and, finally, of all the punishment which they would have been obliged to pay for their faults and sins, because of the highly accumulated merits of Jesus Christ, the Blessed Virgin Mary, and the saints, they are fully absolved.

The Kingship of Christ [2]

[From the Encyclical, "Quas primas," December 11, 1925]

2194　Moreover, on what foundation this dignity and power of our Lord rests, Cyril of Alexandria aptly observes: "He obtained his dominion over all creatures, to speak in a word, not by having wrested it by force or brought it in from some other source, but by His own essence and

---

greatest principles and pronouncements," of St. Thomas (S.C. de Sem. et Stud. Univ. AAS 8 [1916], 157), containing "safe norms for directing, without imposing any duty to embrace all" (Benedict XV, *Ench. Cleric.* 1938, n. 929); furthermore, the arguments of St. Thomas for the existence of God are "today also the strongest of all" (Pius XI, AAS 15 [1923], 317).

[1] AAS 16 (1924), 210. On this passage, see *Zeitschr. f. kath. Theol.* 49 (1925), 298 ff. (J. B. Umberg).

[2] AAS 17 (1925), 598 ff.

nature"; [1] naturally, His kingdom depends on that wonderful union which is called hypostatic. Therefore, it follows not only that Christ is to be adored as God by angels and men, but also that angels and men obey and are subject to His power as man, namely, that Christ obtains His power over all creatures solely in the name of the hypostatic union. —But yet what could be more pleasing to us and more pleasant to contemplate than that Christ commands us not only by right of birth but also by an acquired right, that is, of redemption? Would that all forgetful men would recall what price they have cost our Savior, for, "not with corruptible things as with gold or silver were you redeemed but by the precious blood of Christ, as of a lamb unspotted and undefiled" [I Pet. 1:18, 19]. Now we are not our own, since Christ has bought us "with a great price" [I Cor. 5:20]; our very bodies "are members of Christ" [I Cor. 6:15].

Now to explain briefly the force and nature of this kingship, it is **2195** hardly sufficient to say that it consists of a threefold power, and if it lacked this, it is scarcely recognized as a kingship. Testimonies drawn and gathered from Sacred Scriptures indicate more than sufficiently this fact about the universal power of our Redeemer, and according to the Catholic faith it must be believed that Jesus Christ was given to men as a Redeemer, in whom to trust; but at the same time as a legislator, to whom to give obedience (Conc. Trid., sess. VI, can. 21 [see n. 831]). But the Gospels do not insist so much on the fact that He established laws, as they do of Him observing laws; and, indeed, whoever keep these precepts, the same are said in different words in different places by the divine Master both to prove their love for Him, and to remain in His love [John 14:15; 15:10]. Jesus Himself declared to the Jews, who accused Him of violating the quiet of Sabbath by the wonderful healing of the sick man, that the Father had bestowed judicial power on Him: "For neither doth the Father judge any man, but hath given all judgment to the Son" [John 5:22]; by which this also is understood— since the fact cannot be separated from the judgment—that by His own right He confers rewards and punishments upon men while still living. And furthermore that power which is called executive is to be attributed to Christ, since it is necessary that all obey His power, and since no one can escape what has been imposed upon the contumacious in the imposing of punishment.

Nevertheless, that such a kingdom is spiritual in a special way, and pertains to spiritual things, not only do the words which we have quoted above from the Bible show, but Christ the Lord by His manner of action confirms. For, on more than one given occasion, when the Jews, or rather the apostles themselves were of the opinion through error that the Messias would deliver the people into liberty and would restore the

---

[1] *In Ioann.* l. 12, c. 18 [MG 74, 622].

kingdom of Israel, He Himself destroyed and dispelled their vain opinion and hope; when He was about to be proclaimed king by a surrounding multitude, He declined the name and honor by fleeing and hiding; in the presence of the Roman governor He declared that His kingdom was not "of this world" [John 18:36]. Indeed. this kingdom is presented in the Gospels as such, into which men prepare to enter by doing penance; moreover, they cannot enter it except through faith and baptism, which, although an external rite, yet signifies and effects an interior regeneration; it is opposed only to the kingdom of Satan and to the powers of darkness, and demands of its followers not only that, with mind detached from wealth and earthly things, they prefer gentleness of character, and hunger and thirst after justice, but also that they renounce themselves and take up their cross. Moreover, since Christ as Redeemer has acquired the Church by His blood, and as Priest has offered and continues to offer Himself as a victim for our sins, does it not seem right that He assume the nature of both offices and participate in them?

2196 Otherwise he would err basely, who should deprive Christ, the man, of power over all civil affairs, since He has received the most absolute right over created things from the Father, so that all have been placed under His authority. But yet, as long as He led His life on earth, He abstained entirely from exercising such domination; and just as He once belittled the possession and desire of human things, so He then permitted and today permits the possession of them. And regarding this the following is very aptly said: "He does not snatch away mortal things, who gives heavenly kingdoms" [Hymn, "Crudelis Herodes," in the Office of the Epiphany]. And so the kingdom of our Redeemer embraces all men, and in this matter We gladly make the words of Our predecessor of immortal memory Our own: "Clearly His power is not only over Catholic peoples, or over those alone who, cleansed by holy baptism, surely belong to the Church, if right is considered, though error of opinion leads them in devious ways, or dissension separates them from charity, but it embraces even those who are reckoned as destitute of Christian faith, so that in all truth all mankind is under the power of Jesus Christ" [Encyclical, "Annum sacrum," given May 25, 1899]. Nor is there in this matter any difference among individuals and domestic and civic groups, because men united in society are no less under the power of Christ. Surely the same (Christ) is the source of individual and common salvation: "Neither is there salvation in any other; for there is no other name under heaven given to men, whereby we must be saved" [Acts 4:12]; the same Person is the author of prosperity and true happiness for individual citizens and for the state: "For the city is not made happy from one source, and man from another,

since the state is nothing else than a harmonious multitude of men." [1]
Therefore, let the rulers of nations not refuse to offer the public service
of reverence and obedience to the power of Christ through themselves and
through the people, if they truly wish, while preserving their authority to
advance and increase the fortunes of their country.

Laicism [2]

[From the same Encyclical, "Quas primas," December 11, 1925]

Now, if we order that Christ the King be worshiped by all of Catholic 2197
name, by this very fact we intend to provide for the necessity of the times
and to apply a special remedy for the plague which infects human society. [3]

We call the plague of our age so-called laicism, with its errors and
nefarious efforts. . . . For the power of Christ over all nations has begun
to be denied; hence, the right of the Church which exists from the very
right of Christ, to teach the human race, to pass laws and to rule for the
purpose of leading people especially to eternal salvation has been denied.
Then, indeed, little by little the religion of Christ was placed on the same
level with false religions, and was put in the same class most shamefully;
it was then subjected to civil power, and was almost given over to the
authority of rulers and magistrates; some proceeded further, who thought
that a kind of natural religion, and some sort of natural impulse of the
mind should be substituted for divine religion. States have not been lacking which proclaimed that they could live without God, and that their
religion should consist in an impious neglect of God.

The Johannine Comma [4]

[From the Decree of the Holy Office, January 13, 1897,
and the Declaration of the Holy Office, June 2, 1927]

To the question: "Whether it can safely be denied, or at least called into 2198
doubt that the text of St. John in the first epistle, chapter 5, verse 7, is
authentic, which read as follows: 'And there are three that give testimony
in heaven, the Father, the Word, and the Holy Ghost. And these three are
one?' "—the response was given on January 13, 1897: In the negative.

At this response there arose on June 2, 1927, the following declaration,
at first given privately by the same Sacred Congregation and afterwards

---

[1] St. Augustine, *Letter to Macedonius* c. 3, n. 9 [ML 33, 670].
[2] AAS 17 (1925), 604 f.
[3] The institution, that is, of the Feast of Christ the King.
[4] ASS 29 (1896/97), 639 and EB n. 120 f.

repeated many times, which was made a part of public law in EB n. 121 by authority of the Holy Office itself:

"This decree was passed to check the audacity of private teachers who attributed to themselves the right either of rejecting entirely the authenticity of the Johannine comma, or at least of calling it into question by their own final judgment. But it was not meant at all to prevent Catholic writers from investigating the subject more fully and, after weighing the arguments accurately on both sides, with that moderation and temperance which the gravity of the subject requires, from inclining toward an opinion in opposition to its authenticity, provided they professed that they were ready to abide by the judgment of the Church, to which the duty was delegated by Jesus Christ not only of interpreting Holy Scripture but also of guarding it faithfully."

Meetings to Procure the Unity of All Christians [1]

[From the Decree of the Holy Office, July 8, 1927]

2199 Whether it is permitted Catholics to be present at, or to take part in conventions, gatherings, meetings, or societies of non-Catholics which aim to associate together under a single agreement all who in any way lay claim to the name of Christian?

Reply: In the negative, and there must be complete adherence to the decree (*De participatione catholicorum societati,* "ad procurandam christianitatis unitatem") on the participation of Catholics in a society "to procure the unity of Christianity." [2]

The Connection of the Sacred Liturgy with the Church [3]

[From the Apostolic Constitution, "Divini cultus," December 20, 1928]

2200 Since the Church has received from her founder, Christ, the duty of guarding the holiness of divine worship, surely it is part of the same, of course after preserving the substance of the sacrifice and the sacraments, to prescribe the following: ceremonies, rites, formulas, prayers, chant— by which that august and public ministry is best controlled, whose special name is *Liturgy,* as if an exceedingly sacred action. And the liturgy is an undoubtedly sacred thing; for, through it we are brought to God and are joined with Him; we bear witness to our faith, and we are obligated to it

---

[1] AAS 19 (1927), 278.

[2] AAS 11 (1919), 309; letter of the Holy Office, "Apostolicae Sedis," September 16, 1864, to all the Bishops of England, and another letter, "Quod vos," November 8, 1865, to certain Anglican Puseyites, *ibid.,* 310 ff. Cf. also the Encyclical, "Mortalium animos," of Pius XI, January 6, 1928 [AAS 20 (1928), 5 ff.].

[3] AAS 21 (1929), 33 f.

by a most serious duty because of the benefits and helps received, of which we are always in need. Hence a kind of intimate relationship between dogma and sacred liturgy, and likewise between Christian worship and the sanctification of the people. Therefore, Celestine I proposed and expressed a canon of faith in the venerated formulas of the Liturgy: "Let the law of supplication establish the law of believing. For when the leaders of holy peoples administer legislation enjoined upon themselves they plead the cause of the human race before divine Clemency, and they beg and pray while the entire Church sighs with them" [see n. 139].

Masturbation Procured Directly [1]

[From the Decree of the Holy Office, August 2, 1929]

Whether masturbation procured directly is permitted to obtain sperm, 2201 by which a contagious disease *blenorragia* (gonorrhea) may be detected and, insofar as it can be done, cured.
Reply: In the negative.

The Christian Education of Youth [2]

[From the Encyclical, "Divini illius magistri," December 31, 1929]

Since every method of education aims for that formation of man which 2202 he ought to acquire in this mortal life, in order to attain the ultimate goal destined for him by the Creator, it is plainly evident that as no education can be truly so called which is not entirely ordered to that final end, in the present order of things established by the providence of God, namely after He revealed Himself in His Only-begotten, who alone is "the way, the truth, and the life" [John 14:6], no full and perfect education can exist except that which is called Christian. . . .

The task of educating does not belong to individual men but necessarily 2203 to society. Now necessary societies are three in number, distinct from one another, yet harmoniously combined by the will of God, to which man is assigned from birth; of these, two, namely, the family and civil society, are of the natural order; and the third, the Church, to be sure, is of the supernatural order. Family living holds first place, and, since it was established and prepared by God Himself for this purpose, to care for the generation and upbringing of offspring, thus by its nature and by its inherent rights it has priority over civil society. Nevertheless, the family is an imperfect society, because it is not endowed with all those things by which it may attain its very noble purpose perfectly; but civil associa-

---

[1] AAS 21 (1929), 490.
[2] AAS 22 (1930), 49 ff.

tion, since it has in its power all things necessary to achieve its destined end, namely, the common good of this earthly life, is a society absolute in all respects and perfect; for this same reason, therefore, it is pre-eminent over family life, which indeed can fulfill its purpose safely and rightly only in civil society. Finally, the third society, in which man by the waters of baptism enters a life of divine grace, is the Church, surely a supernatural society embracing the whole human race; perfect in herself, since all things are at her disposal for attaining her end, namely the eternal salvation of man, and thus supreme in her own order.

Consequently, education, which is concerned with the whole man, with man individually and as a member of human society, whether established in the order of nature or in the order of divine grace, pertains to these three necessary societies, harmoniously according to the proper end of each, proportionately according to the present order divinely established.

2204 But in the first place, in a more pre-eminent way education pertains to the Church, namely, because of a twofold title in the supernatural order which God conferred upon her alone; and thus by an entirely more powerful and more valid title than any other title of the natural order.

The first reason for such a right rests on the supreme authority of the *magisterium* and on the mission which the divine Founder of the Church bestowed upon her in those words: "All power is given to me in heaven and on earth. Going therefore teach ye . . . even unto the consummation of the world" [Matt. 28:18–20]. Upon this *magisterium* Christ the Lord conferred immunity from error, together with the command to teach His doctrine to all; therefore, the Church "has been established by her divine Founder as the pillar and foundation of truth, to teach all men the divine faith, to guard its deposit given to her whole and inviolate, and to direct and fashion men in their public and private actions unto purity of morals and integrity of life, according to the norm of revealed doctrine." [1]

The second reason for the right arises from that supernatural duty of a mother, by which the Church, most pure spouse of Christ, bestows upon men a life of divine grace, and nurtures and promotes it by her sacraments and precepts. Worthily then does St. Augustine say: "He will not have God as father, who would not be willing to have the Church as mother." [2]

2205 Therefore, the Church promotes letters, the sciences, and the arts, insofar as they are necessary or useful for Christian education and for everyone of her activities for the salvation of souls, founding and supporting her schools and institutions, in which every discipline is taught and an approach is made to all grades of erudition. [3] And it must not be thought

---

[1] Pius IX, Encyclical Epistle, "Quum non sine," July 14, 1864 [AP I, 3, 652].
[2] *De Symbolo ad catech.* 13 [ML 40, 668].
[3] *Cod. Jur. Can.* c. 1375.

that so-called physical education is alien to her maternal *magisterium,* since this also has the capacity to benefit or harm Christian education.

And this action of the Church in every kind of culture of the mind, just as it is of the highest benefit to families and nations, which with Christ removed from their midst are rushing into destruction,—as Hilary rightly says: "What can be so perilous to the world as not to have accepted Christ?" [1]—so it causes no inconvenience to the civil organization in these things; for the Church, as she is a most prudent mother, does not in the least prevent her schools and institutions in every nation educating the laity from conforming with the prescribed laws of the authorities, but is ready in every way to cooperate with the authorities, and if any difficulties by chance should arise, to dissolve them by a mutual understanding.

Besides, it is the right of the Church which she cannot surrender, and the duty which she cannot abandon, to watch over all education, such as is imparted to her children, namely, the faithful in either public or private institutions, not only insofar as pertains to religious doctrine as it is taught there, but also with regard to any other discipline or arrangement of affairs, according as they have some relationship with religion and moral precepts.[2]

The rights of the family and of the state, even the very rights which 2206 belong to individual citizens with reference to just freedom in investigating the things of science and of the methods of science, and of any profane culture of the mind, not only are not at variance with such a special right of the Church, but are even quite in harmony with it. For, to make known at once the cause and origin of such concord, the supernatural order, on which the rights of the Church depend, far from destroying and weakening the natural order, to which the other rights which we have mentioned pertain, rather elevates and perfects it; indeed, of these orders one furnishes help and, as it were, the complement to the other, consistent with the nature and dignity of each one, since both proceed from God, who cannot be inconsistent with Himself: "The works of God are perfect and all His ways are judgment" [Deut. 32:4].

Indeed, this matter will appear clearer if we consider the duty of educating, which pertains to the family and to the state, separately and more closely.

And, first, the duty of the family agrees wonderfully with the duty of 2207 the Church, since both very similarly proceed from God. For God communicates fecundity directly to the family, in the natural order, the principle of life and thus the principle of education to life, at the same time along with authority, which is the principle of order.

On this subject the Angelic Doctor with his customary clarity of

---

[1] *Commentary on Matthew,* chap. 18, n. 3 [ML 9, 1019].

[2] *Cod. Jur. Can.* c. 1381, 1382.

thought and precision in speaking says: "The father according to the flesh in a particular way shares in the method of the principle which is found universally in God. . . The father is the principle of generation and of education, and of all things which pertain to the perfection of human life." [1]

The family, then, holds directly from the Creator the duty and the right to educate its offspring; and since this right cannot be cast aside, because it is connected with a very serious obligation, it has precedence over any right of civil society and of the state, and for this reason no power on earth may infringe upon it. . . .

2208 From this duty of educating, which especially belongs to the Church and the family, not only do the greatest advantages, as we have seen, emanate into all society, but no harm can befall the true and proper rights of the state, insofar as pertains to the education of citizens, according to the order established by God. These rights are assigned to civil society by the Author of nature himself, not by the right of fatherhood, as of the Church and of the family, but on account of the authority which is in Him for promoting the common good on earth, which indeed is its proper end.

2209 From this it follows that education does not pertain to civil society in the same way as it does to the Church or the family, but clearly in another way, which naturally corresponds to its proper end. This end, moreover, that is, the common good of the temporal order, consists in peace and security, which families and individual citizens enjoy by exercising their rights; and at the same time in the greatest possible abundance of spiritual and temporal things for mortal life, which abundance is to be attained by the effort and consent of all. The duty, then, of the civil authority, which is in the state, is twofold, namely, of guarding and advancing but by no means, as it were, of absorbing the family and individual citizens or of substituting itself in their place.

Therefore, as far as education is concerned, it is the right or, to speak more accurately, the office of the state to guard the priority right of the family by its laws, as we have mentioned above; that is, of educating offspring in the Christian manner, and so of acknowledging the supernatural right of the Church in such a Christian education.

It is likewise the duty of the state to guard this right in the child itself, if at any time the care of parents—because of their inertia, or ignorance, or bad behavior—fails either physically or morally; since their right of educating, as we have said above, is not absolute and despotic, but dependent on the natural and divine law, and for this reason subject not only to the authority and judgment of the Church, but also to the vigilance and care of the state for the common good; for the family is not a perfect society, which possesses within itself all things necessary for bringing itself

---

[1] *Summa theol.*, IIa IIae, q. 102, a. 1.

to full and complete perfection. In these cases, otherwise very rare, the state does put itself in the place of the family, but, always in keeping with the natural rights of the child and the supernatural rights of the Church, considers and provides for the needs of the moment by opportune assistance.

In general, it is the right and duty of the state to guard the moral and 2210 religious education of youth according to the norms of right reason and faith, by removing the public impediments that stand in the way of it. But it is especially the duty of the state, as the common good demands, to promote the education and instruction of youth in several ways; first and by itself, by favoring and aiding the work undertaken by the Church and the family, the extent of whose success is demonstrated by history and experience; where this work is lacking or does not suffice, by performing the work itself, even by establishing schools and institutions; for the state more than the other societies abounds in resources, which, having been given it for the common needs of all, it is quite right and proper that it expend these for the benefit of those from whom it received them. Besides, the state can prescribe and then see to it that all citizens learn both civil and political duties; also that they be instructed in science and in the learning of morals and of physical culture, insofar as it is fitting, and the common good in our times actually demands. Nevertheless, it is quite clear that the state is bound by this duty, not only to respect, while promoting public and private education in all these ways, the inherent rights of the Church and family of a Christian education, but also to have regard for justice which attributes to each one his own. Thus, it is not lawful for the state to reduce the entire control of education and instruction to itself so that families are forced physically and morally to send their children to the schools of the state, contrary to the duties of their Christian conscience or to their legitimate preference.

Yet, this does not prevent the state from establishing schools which may be called preparatory for civic duties, especially for military service, for the proper administration of government, or for maintaining peace at home and abroad; all of which, indeed, since they are so necessary for the common good, demand a peculiar skill and a special preparation, provided that the state abstains from offending the rights of the Church and of the family in matters that pertain to them.

It belongs to civil society to supply, not only for youth but also for all 2211 ages and classes, an education which can be called civic, and which on the positive side, as they say, consists in this, that matters are presented publicly to men belonging to such a society which by imbuing their minds with the knowledge and image of things, and by an emotional appeal urge their wills to the honorable and guide them by a kind of moral compulsion; but on the negative side, that it guards against and obstructs the things that oppose it. Now this civic education, so very broad and complex that it includes almost the entire activity of the state for the common good, ought to conform with the laws of justice, and cannot be in conflict with the doctrine of the Church, which is the divinely constituted teacher of these laws.

2212   It should never be forgotten that in the Christian sense the entire man is to be educated, as great as he is, that is, coalescing into one nature, through spirit and body, and instructed in all parts of his soul and body, which either proceed from nature or excel it, such as we finally recognize him from right reason and divine revelation, namely, man whom, when fallen from his original estate, Christ redeemed and restored to this supernatural dignity, to be the adopted son of God, yet without the preternatural privileges by which his body had before been immortal, and his soul just and sound. Hence, it happened that the defilements which flowed into the nature of man from Adam's sin, especially the infirmity of the will and the unbridled desires of the soul, survive in man.

And, surely, "folly is bound up in the heart of a child and the rod of correction shall drive it away" [Prov. 22:15]. Therefore, from childhood the inclination of will, if perverse, must be restrained; but if good, must be promoted, and especially the minds of children should be imbued with the teachings that come from God, and their souls strengthened by the aids of divine grace; and, if these should be lacking, no one could be restrained in his desires nor be guided to complete perfection by the training and instruction of the Church, which Christ has endowed with heavenly doctrine and divine sacraments for the purpose of being the efficacious teacher of all men.

2213   Therefore, every form of teaching children, which, confined to the mere forces of nature, rejects or neglects those matters which contribute with God's help to the right formation of the Christian life, is false and full of error; and every way and method of educating youth, which gives no consideration, or scarcely any, to the transmission of original sin from our first parents to all posterity, and so relies wholly on the mere powers of nature, strays completely from the truth. For the most part those systems of teaching which are openly proclaimed in our day tend to this goal. They have various names, to be sure, whose chief characteristic is to rest the basis of almost all instruction on this, that it is sound for children to instruct themselves, evidently by their own genius and will, spurning the counsel of their elders and teachers, and putting aside every human and even divine law and resource. Yet, if all these are so circumscribed by their own limits that new teachers of this kind desire that youth also take an active part in their own instruction, the more properly as they advance in years and in the knowledge of things, and likewise that all force and severity, of which, however, just correction is by no means a part, this indeed is true, but not at all new, since the Church has taught this, and Christian teachers, in a manner handed down by their ancestors, have retained it, imitating God who wished all created things and especially all men to cooperate actively with Him according to their proper nature, for divine Wisdom "reaches from end to end and orders all things sweetly" [Wisd. 8:1]. . . .

But much more pernicious are those opinions and teachings regarding 2214 the following of nature absolutely as a guide. These enter upon a certain phase of human education which is full of difficulties, namely, that which has to do with moral integrity and chastity. For here and there a great many foolishly and dangerously hold and advance the method of education, which is disgustingly called "sexual," since they foolishly feel that they can, by merely natural means, after discarding every religious and pious aid, warn youth against sensuality and excess, by initiating and instructing all of them, without distinction of sex, even publicly, in hazardous doctrines; and what is worse, by exposing them prematurely to the occasions, in order that their minds having become accustomed, as they say, may grow hardened to the dangers of puberty.

But in this such persons gravely err, because they do not take into account the inborn weakness of human nature, and that *law* planted *within our members,* which, to use the words of the Apostle Paul, "fights against the law of my mind" [Rom. 7:23]; and besides, they rashly deny what we have learned from daily experience, that young people certainly more than others fall more often into disgraceful acts, not so much because of an imperfect knowledge of the intellect as because of a will exposed to enticements and unsupported by divine assistance.

In this extremely delicate matter, all things considered, if some young people should be advised at the proper time by those to whom God has entrusted the duty, joined with opportune graces, of educating children, surely those precautions and skills are to be employed which are well known to Christian teachers.

Surely, equally false and harmful to Christian education is that method 2215 of instructing youth, which is commonly called "coeducation." Both the sexes have been established by God's wisdom for this purpose, that in the family and in society they may complement each other, and may aptly join in any one thing; for this reason there is a distinction of body and of soul by which they differ from each other, which accordingly must be maintained in education and in instruction, or, rather ought to be fostered by proper distinction and separation, in keeping with age and circumstances. Such precepts in accord with the precepts of Christian prudence are to be observed at the proper time and opportunely not only in all schools, especially through the disturbed years of youth, upon which the manner of living for almost all future life entirely depends, but also in gymnastic games and exercises, in which special care must be taken for the Christian modesty of girls, inasmuch as it is especially unbecoming for them to expose themselves, and to exhibit themselves before the eyes of all.

2216 But to obtain perfect education care must be taken that all the conditions which surround children while they are being trained, fittingly correspond with the end proposed.

And surely from the necessity of nature the environment of the child for his proper training must be regarded as his family, established by God for this very purpose. Therefore, finally, we shall rightly consider that institution stable and safest which is received in a family rightly ordered and well disciplined; and the more efficacious and stable as the parents especially and other members of the household present themselves before the children as an example of virtue.

2217 Moreover, for the weaknesses of human nature, rendered weaker by the ancestral sin, God in His goodness has provided the abundant helps of His grace and that plentiful supply of assistance which the Church possesses for purifying souls and for leading them on to sanctity; the Church, we say, that great family of Christ, which is the educational environment most intimately and harmoniously connected with individual families.

2218 Since, however, new generations would have to be instructed in all those arts and sciences by which civil society advances and flourishes; and since the family alone did not suffice for this, accordingly public schools came into being; yet in the beginning—note carefully—through the efforts of the Church and the family working together, and only much later through the efforts of the state. Thus the seats and schools of learning, if we view their origin in the light of history, were by their very nature helps, as it were, and almost a complement to both the Church and the family. So the consequence is that public schools not only cannot be in opposition to the family and the Church, but must ever be in harmony with both, as far as circumstances permit, so that these three, namely, school, family, and Church seem to effect essentially one sanctuary of Christian education, unless we wish the school to stray from its clear purpose and be converted into a disease and the destruction of youth.

2219 From this it necessarily follows that through schools which are called *neutral* or *lay,* the entire foundation of Christian education is destroyed and overturned, inasmuch as religion has been entirely removed from them. But they will be *neutral* schools in no way except in appearance, since they are in fact plainly hostile to religion or will be.

It is a long task and there is indeed no need to repeat what Our predecessors, especially Pius IX and Leo XIII openly declared, in whose reigns especially it happened that the serious disease of such laicism invaded the public schools. We repeat and confirm their declarations [1] and likewise the prescripts of the Sacred Canons, according to which Catholic youths are prohibited from frequenting for any reason either neutral or mixed schools, namely, those which Catholics and non-Catholics attend for instruction; but it will be permitted to attend these, provided in the judgment of a prudent ordinary, in certain conditions of place and time, special precautions be taken.[2] For no school can be tolerated (especially if it is the "only" school and all children are bound to attend it) in which, although the precepts of sacred doctrine are taught separately to Catholics, yet the teachers are not Catholics, and who imbue Catholic and non-Catholic children generally with a knowledge of the arts and letters.

For, because the instruction in religion is given in a certain school 2220 (usually too sparingly), such a school for this reason does not satisfy the rights of the Church and family; nor is it thus made suitable for the attendance of Catholic pupils; for, in order that any school measure up to this, it is quite necessary that all instruction and doctrine, the whole organization of the school, namely, its teachers, plan of studies, books, in fact, whatever pertains to any branch of learning, be so permeated and be so strong in Christian spirit, under the guidance and the eternal vigilance of the Church, that religion itself forms both the basis and the end of the entire scheme of instruction; and this not only in the schools in which the elements of learning are taught but also in those of higher studies. "It is necessary," to use the words of Leo XIII, "not only that youth be taught religion at definite times, but that all the rest of their instruction be pervaded with a religious feeling. If this be lacking, if this sacred condition does not permeate and stimulate the minds of the teachers and those taught, small benefit will be received from any learning, and no little damage will often follow." [3]

Moreover, whatever is done by the faithful of Christ to promote and 2221 protect the Catholic school for their children, is without any doubt a religious work, and thus a most important duty of "Catholic Action"; accordingly, all those sodalities are very pleasing to Our paternal heart and worthy of special praise, which in many places in a special manner and most zealously are engaged in so essential a work.

Therefore, let it be proclaimed on high, well noted, and recognized by all that the faithful of Christ in demanding a Catholic School for their children are nowhere in the world guilty of an act of a political dissension,

---

[1] Pius IX, Ep., "Quum non sine," July 14, 1864; Syllabus, Prop. 48 [see note, 1748]; Leo XIII, Alloc., "Summi Pontificatus," August 20, 1880; Encyclical letter, "Nobilissima," February 8, 1884; Encyclical letter, "Quod multum," August 22, 1886; Epistle, "Officio sanctissimo." December 22, 1887; Encyclical letter, "Caritatis," March 19, 1894; etc. Cf. *Cod. Iur. Can. cum Fontium Annot;* ad can. 1374.

[2] *Cod. Iur. Can.,* c. 1374.

[3] Encyclical letter, "Militantis Ecclesiae," August 1, 1897.

but perform a religious duty which their own conscience peremptorily demands; and, these Catholics do not intend to withdraw their children from the training and spirit of the state, but rather to train them for this very end, in a manner most perfect, and best accommodated to the usefulness of the nation, since a true Catholic, indeed, well instructed in Catholic teaching, is by this very fact the best citizen, a supporter of his country, and obedient with a sincere faith to public authority under any legitimate form of government.

2222 The salutary efficiency of schools, moreover, is to be attributed not so much to good laws as to good teachers, who, being well prepared and each having a good knowledge of the subject to be taught the students, truly adorned with the qualities of mind and spirit, which their most important duty obviously demands, glow with a pure and divine love for the youth committed to them, just as they love Jesus Christ and His Church, —whose most beloved children these are—and by this very fact sincerely have the true good of the family and the fatherland at heart. Therefore, We are greatly consoled and We acknowledge the goodness of God with a grateful heart, when we see that in addition to the men and women of religious communities who devote themselves to the teaching of children and youth, there are so many and such excellent lay teachers of both sexes, and that these—for their greater spiritual advancement joining in associations and spiritual sodalities, which are to be praised and promoted as a noble and strong aid to "Catholic Action"—unmindful of their own advantage, devote themselves strenuously and unceasingly to that which St. Gregory of Nazianzus calls "the art of arts and the science of sciences," [1] namely, the direction and formation of youth. Yet, since those words of the divine Master apply to them also: "The harvest indeed is great, but laborers are few" [Matt. 9:37], such teachers of Christian education— whose training should be of special concern to the pastors of souls, and superiors of religious orders—we exhort the Lord of the harvest with suppliant prayers to provide such teachers in greater numbers.

2223 Furthermore, the education of the child, inasmuch as he is "soft as wax to be molded into vice" [2] in whatever environment he lives, must be directed and watched by removing occasions of evil, and by supplying opportunely occasions for good in times of relaxation of mind, and enjoyment of companions, because "evil communications corrupt good manners" [I Cor. 15:33].

Yet, such watchfulness and vigilance, as we have said should be applied, does not at all demand that young people be removed from association with men with whom they must live their lives, and whom they must consult in regard to the salvation of their souls; but only that they be

---

[1] *Oratio* 2, 16 [MG 35, 426].
[2] Horace, *De arte poetica*, 1, 163.

fortified and strengthened in a Christian manner—especially today—against the enticements and errors of the world, which, according to the words of John, are entirely "concupiscence of the flesh, concupiscence of the eyes, and pride of life" [I John 2:16], so that, as Tertullian wrote of the early Christians: "Let our people keep themselves as Christians who should at all times be sharers in the possession of the world, not of its error." [1]

Christian education aims properly and immediately to make man a true 2224 and perfect Christian by cooperating with divine grace, namely, to mold and fashion Christ Himself in those who have been reborn in baptism, according to the clear statement of the Apostle: "My little children of whom I am in labor again, until Christ be formed in you" [Gal. 4:19]. For, the true Christian must live a supernatural life in Christ: "Christ our life" [Col. 3:4], and manifest the same in all his actions, "that the life of Jesus may be made manifest in our mortal flesh" [II Cor. 4:11].

Since this is so, Christian education embraces the sum total of human actions, because it pertains to the workings of the senses and of the spirit, to the intellect and to morals, to individuals, to domestic and civil society, not indeed, to weaken it, but according to the example and teaching of Jesus Christ, to elevate, regulate, and perfect it.

Thus the true Christian, molded by Christian education, is none other than the supernatural man who thinks, judges, and acts constantly and consistently in accordance with right reason; supernaturally inspired by the examples and teachings of Jesus Christ; that is, a man outstanding in force of character. For whoever follows his own inclination and acts stubbornly, intent on his own desires, is not a man of strong character; but only he who follows the eternal principles of justice, just as even the pagan host himself recognizes when he praises "the just" man together with "the man tenacious of purpose"; [2] but these ideas of justice cannot be fully observed unless there is attributed to God whatever is God's due, as is done by the true Christian.

The true Christian, far from renouncing the activities of this life and from suppressing his natural talents, on the contrary fosters and brings them to perfection by so cooperating with the supernatural life that he embellishes the natural way of living, and supports it by more efficacious aids, which are in accord not only with spiritual and eternal things but also with the necessities of natural life itself.

---

[1] *De idolatria,* 14 [ML 1, 682].

[2] Horace, *Od.,* 1. 3, od. 3, v. 1.

Christian Marriage [1]

[From the Encyclical, "Casti Connubii," Pius XI, Dec. 31, 1930]

2225   First, then, let this remain as an unchangeable and inviolable basis;
marriage was not instituted or restored by man but by God; not by man
but by the very author of nature, God; and by the restorer of the same
nature was it fortified, confirmed, and elevated through laws; and these
laws, therefore, cannot be subject to any decision of man and not even to
any contrary agreement on the part of the spouses themselves. This is a
doctrine of Holy Scripture [Gen. 1:27 f.; 2:22 f.; Matt. 19:3 ff.; Eph.
5:23 ff.]; this is the continued and unanimous tradition of the Church; this
is the solemn definition of the sacred Council of Trent, which declares
and confirms [sess. 24; see n. 969 ff.] that the perpetual and indissoluble
bond of marriage, and the unity and the stability of the same emanate
from God as their author.

But, although marriage by its nature was instituted by God, nevertheless
man's will has its own role, and a most noble one in it; for, every individual marriage, inasmuch as it is a conjugal union between a certain
man and a certain woman, it arises only from the free consent of both
spouses, and indeed this free act of the will, by which both parties hand
over and accept the rights [2] proper to matrimony, is so necessary to constitute a true marriage that it cannot be supplied by any human power.[3]
Yet such freedom has this purpose only, to establish that contracting
parties really wish to enter upon marriage and wish to do so with a certain
person or not; but the nature of marriage is wholly removed from the
freedom of man, so much so that as soon as man has contracted marriage
he is subject to its divine laws and essential properties. For the Angelic
Doctor, discussing good faith in marriage and offspring, says: "These
things are so effected in marriage by the conjugal agreement itself that if
anything contrary were expressed in the consent which makes the marriage,
it would not be a true marriage." [4]

By wedlock, then, souls are joined and made as one, and the souls are
affected earlier and more strongly than bodies; not by any transient
affection of the senses or the spirit, but by a deliberate and firm decision
of the will; and from this joining of souls, with God so decreeing, a sacred
and inviolable bond arises.

This entirely proper and peculiar nature of this contract makes it completely different not only from the connections of animals performed by

---

[1] AAS 22 (1930), 539 ff.
[2] Cf. *Cod. Iur. Can.*, can. 1081, sec. 2.
[3] Cf. *Cod. Iur. Can.*, can. 1081, sec. 1.
[4] *Summa theol.*, Suppl., q. 49, a. 3.

blind instinct of nature alone, in which there is no reason nor free will, but also from those unrestrained unions of men, which are far removed from every true and honorable bond of wills, and destitute of any right to family life.

From this it is now well established that truly legitimate authority has 2226 the power by law and so is compelled by duty to restrain, to prevent, and to punish base marriages, which are opposed to reason and to nature; but since a matter is involved which follows upon human nature itself, that is no less definitely established which Our predecessor, Leo XIII, of happy memory, plainly taught: [1] "In choosing a state of life there is no doubt but that it is within the power and discretion of individuals to prefer either one of two: either to adopt the counsel of Jesus Christ with respect to virginity, or to bind himself with the bonds of matrimony. To take away the natural and primeval right of marriage, or in any way to circumscribe the chief purpose of marriage established in the beginning by the authority of God, "Increase and multiply" [Gen. 1:28], is not within the power of any law of man."

Now as We come to explain what are these blessings, granted by God, 2227 of true matrimony, and how great they are, Venerable Brethren, there come to Us the words of that very famous Doctor of the Church, whom not so long ago We commemorated in Our Encyclical Letter, *Ad Salutem,* published on the fulfillment of the fifteenth century after his death. St. Augustine says: "All these are blessings, because of which marriage is a blessing: offspring, conjugal faith, and the sacrament." [2] How these three headings are rightly said to contain a very splendid summary of the whole doctrine on Christian marriage, the Holy Doctor clearly shows when he says: "By conjugal faith care is taken that there be no intercourse outside the marriage bond with another man or another woman; by offspring, that children be begotten in love, nourished with kindness, and brought up religiously; but by the sacrament, that the marriage be not broken, and that the separated man or woman have intercourse with another not even for the sake of offspring. This is, as it were, the law of marriage, whereby the fruitfulness of nature is adorned and the depravity of incontinence is controlled." [3]

[1] Thus the child holds the first place among the blessing of matri- 2228 mony. Clearly the Creator of the human race Himself, who because of His kindness wished to use men as helpers in propagating life, taught this in Paradise, when He instituted marriage, saying to our first parents, and through them to all spouses: "Increase and multiply and fill the earth"

---

[1] Encyclical letter, "Rerum novarum," May 15, 1891 [AAS 23 (1890/91), 645; AL XI (Rome) 104].

[2] St. Augustine, *De bona conjugali,* 24, 32 [ML 40, 394].

[3] St. Augustine, *Op. cit.,* 24, 32 [ML 40, 394].

[Gen. 1:28]. This thought St. Augustine very beautifully infers from the words of St. Paul the Apostle to Timothy [I Tim. 5:14], when he says: "So the Apostle is witness that marriage is accomplished for the sake of generation. *I wish,* he says, *young girls to marry.* And as if someone said to Him: *Why?* he immediately adds: *To bear children, to be mothers of families"* [I Tim. 5:14].[1]

2229   Indeed, Christian parents should further understand that they are destined not only to propagate and to preserve the human race on earth, nay rather, not to raise any kind of worshipers of the true God, but to produce offspring of the Church of Christ; to procreate "fellow-citizens of the saints and members of God's household" [Eph. 2:19], that the people devoted to the worship of God and our Savior may increase daily. For, even if Christian spouses, although they themselves are sanctified, have not the power to transfuse sanctification into their offspring, surely the natural generation of life has become a way of death, by which original sin passes into the offspring; yet in some manner they share something of that primeval marriage of Paradise, since it is their privilege to offer their own offspring to the Church, so that by this most fruitful mother of the sons of God they may be regenerated through the laver of baptism unto supernatural justice, and become living members of Christ, partakers of immortal life, and, finally, heirs of eternal glory which we all desire with all our heart. . . .

2230   But the blessing of offspring is not completed by the good work of procreation; something else must be added which is contained in the dutiful education of the offspring. Surely, the most wise God would have made insufficient provision for the child that is born, and so for the whole human race, unless He had also assigned the right and duty of educating to the same ones to whom He had given the power and right of generating. For it cannot escape anyone that offspring, not only in matters which pertain to the natural life, and much less in those which pertain to the supernatural life, cannot be sufficient unto itself or provide for itself, but is for many years in need of the assistance of others, of care, and of education. But it is certain that, when nature and God bid, this right and duty of educating offspring belongs especially to those who began the work of nature by generating, and they are also absolutely forbidden to expose this work to ruin by leaving it unfinished and imperfect. Surely, the best possible provision has been made in matrimony for this most necessary education of children, in which, since parents are joined to each other by an insoluble bond, there is always at hand the care and mutual assistance of both. . . .

Nor can this be passed over in silence, that, since the duty committed to parents for the good of offspring is of such great dignity and importance,

---

[1] St. Augustine, *Op. cit.,* 24, 32 [ML 40, 394].

any honorable use of this faculty given by God to procreate new life, at the command of the Creator Himself and the laws of nature, is the right and privilege of matrimony alone, and must be confined within the sacred limits of marriage.

[2] Another blessing of matrimony which we have spoken of as mentioned by Augustine, is the blessing of faith, which is the mutual fidelity of spouses in fulfilling the marriage contract, so that what by this contract, sanctioned by divine law, is due only to one spouse, cannot be denied him nor permitted to anyone else; nor is that to be conceded to the spouse, which can never be conceded, since it is contrary to divine rights and laws and is especially opposed to conjugal faith. 2231

Thus this faith demands in the first place the absolute unity of marriage, which the Creator Himself established in the matrimony of our first parents when He willed that it exist only between one man and one woman. And although afterwards God, the supreme legislator, somewhat relaxed this primeval law for a time, nevertheless there is no doubt that the Evangelical Law entirely restored that original and perfect unity and did away with all dispensations, as the words of Christ and the uniform way either of teaching or acting on the part of the Church plainly show [see note 969]. . . .

Nor did Christ the Lord wish to condemn only polygamy and polyandry, whether successive [1] or simultaneous, as they are called, or any other dishonorable act; but, in order that the sacred bonds of marriage may be absolutely inviolate, He forbade also even the willful thoughts and desires about all these things: "But I say to you that whosoever shall look on a woman to lust after her hath already committed adultery with her in his heart" [Matt. 5:28]. These words of Christ the Lord cannot become void even by the consent of one spouse; for they express the law of God and of nature, which no will of man can ever break or bend.[2]

Even mutual familiar intercourse between spouses, that the blessing of conjugal faith may shine with due splendor, should be so distinguished by the mark of chastity that husband and wife conduct themselves in all things according to the law of God and of nature, and strive always to follow the will of the most wise and most holy Creator, with great reverence for the work of God.

Moreover, this conjugal fidelity, most aptly called by St. Augustine [3] the "faith of chastity," will flourish more readily, and even much more pleasantly, and as ennobling coming from another most excellent source, namely, from conjugal love, which pervades all duties of the married life 2232

---

[1] Successive polygamy is here understood as illicit wherein a wife, while the conjugal bond remains, is rejected, and another like companion is adopted.

[2] Cf. decree of the Holy Office, March 2, 1679, prop. 50 [see n. 1200].

[3] *De bono conjugali*, 24, 32 [ML 40, 394].

and holds a kind of primacy of nobility in Christian marriage. "Besides, matrimonial fidelity demands that husband and wife be joined in a peculiarly holy and pure love, not as adulterers love each other, but as Christ loved the Church; for the Apostle prescribed this rule when he said: "Husbands, love your wives, as Christ also loved the Church" [Eph. 5:25; cf. Col. 3:19]; which Church certainly He embraced with tremendous love, not for His own advantage, but keeping before Him only the good of His Spouse." [1]

We speak, then, of a love that rests not only on a carnal inclination that very quickly disappears, nor on pleasing words only, but that is also set in the innermost affection of the heart; and, "since the proof of love is a manifestation of deeds," [2] that is proven by external deeds. Now these deeds in home life include not only mutual assistance, but also should extend to this, rather should aim especially for this, that husband and wife help each other daily to form and to perfect the interior man more fully, so that through their partnership in life they may advance in the virtues more and more, and may grow especially in true love toward God and their neighbors, on which indeed "dependeth the whole Law and the Prophets" [Matt. 22:40]. Manifestly the most perfect example of all holiness set before men by God is Christ the Lord. All, in whatever condition and whatever honorable way of life they have entered, with God's help should also arrive at the highest degree of Christian perfection, as is proven by the examples of many saints.

This mutual interior formation of husband and wife, this constant zeal for bringing each other to perfection, in a very true sense, as the Roman Catechism teaches, can be said to be the very first reason and purpose of matrimony; if, however, matrimony be not accepted too narrowly as instituted for the proper procreation and education of children, but more broadly as the mutual participation in all life, companionship, and association.

With this same love the remaining rights as well as duties of marriage must be regulated, so that not only the law of justice, but also the norm of love may be that of the Apostle: "Let the husband render the debt to the wife, and the wife also in like manner to the husband" [I Cor. 7:3].

2233   Finally, after the domestic society has been confirmed by the bond of this love, of necessity there must flourish in it that which is called by Augustine *the order of love*. Now this order includes both the primacy of the husband over the wife and the children, and the prompt and not unwilling subjection and obedience of the wife, which the Apostle commends with these words: "Let women be subject to their husbands as to

---

[1] *Catech. Rom.*, II, 8, 24.

[2] St. Gregory the Great, *Homil. 30 in Evange.* (John 14:23–31), n. 1 [ML 76, 1220].

[3] Cf. *Catech. Rom.*, II, 8, 13.

the Lord, because the husband is the head of the wife, as Christ is the head of the Church" [Eph. 5:22 f.].

Yet this obedience does not deny or take away the liberty which by full right belongs to a woman, both in view of her dignity as a human being, and in view of her noble duties of wife, mother, and companion; nor does it demand that she obey every desire of her husband, that is, not in keeping with right reason or with her dignity as a wife; nor, finally, does it mean that a wife is to be placed on the same level with persons who in law are called minors, to whom the free exercise of their rights is not customarily granted because of lack of mature judgment, or because of inexperience in human affairs; but it forbids that exaggerated liberty which has no care for the good of the family; it forbids that in this body of the family the heart be separated from the head, to the great detriment of the whole body and the proximate danger of ruin. For, if the man is the head, the woman is the heart, and just as he holds primacy in ruling, she can and ought to claim primacy in love for herself as her own.

Furthermore, this obedience of the wife to her husband, insofar as pertains to degree and manner, can be different, according to different persons, places, and conditions of the time; rather, if a husband fail in his duty, it is the wife's responsibility to take his place in directing the family. But the very structure of the family and its chief law, as constituted and confirmed by God, can never and nowhere be overturned or tainted.

On this point of maintaining order between husband and wife Our predecessor of happy memory, Leo XIII, wisely taught in his Encyclical Letter on Christian marriage which We have mentioned: "The man is the ruler of the family and the head of the woman; yet, since she is flesh of his flesh, and bone of his bone, let her be subject and obedient to the man, not in the manner of a maidservant but of a companion, so that of course, neither honor nor dignity be lacking in the obedience rendered. But let divine charity be the unfailing guide of duty in him who is at the head, and in her who obeys, since both bear the image, the one, of Christ, the other of the Church. . . ." [1]

[3] Yet the sum total of such great benefits is completed and, as it were, 2234 brought to a head by that blessing of Christian marriage which we have called, in Augustine's words, a sacrament, by which is denoted the indissolubility of the bond and the raising and hallowing by Christ of the contract into an efficacious sign of grace.

In the first place, to be sure, Christ Himself lays stress on the indissoluble firmness of the nuptial bond when he says: "What God hath joined together, let no man put asunder" [Matt. 19:6]; and, "Everyone that putteth away his wife, and marrieth another committeth adultery,

---

[1] Encyclical letter, "Arcanum divinae sapientiae," February 10, 1880 [ASS **12** (1879/80), 389; AL 2 (Romae) 18].

and he that marrieth her that is put away from her husband committeth adultery" [Luke 16:18].

Moreover, St. Augustine places in this indissolubility what he calls "the blessing of the sacrament," in these clear words: "But in the sacrament it is intended that the marriage be not broken, and that the man or the woman dismissed be not joined with another, even for the sake of off-spring."[1]

2235   And this inviolable stability, although not of the same perfect measure in every case, pertains to all true marriages; for that saying of the Lord, "What God hath joined together, let no man put asunder," although, said of the marriage of our first parents, the prototype of every future marriage, must apply to all true marriages. Therefore, although before Christ the sublimity and severity of the primeval law were so tempered that Moses allowed the citizens of the people of God because of the hard-ness of their hearts to grant a bill of divorce for certain causes; yet Christ in accord with His power as Supreme Legislator revoked this permission of greater license, and restored the primeval law in its entirety through those words which are never to be forgotten: "What God hath joined together, let no man put asunder." So, most wisely did Pius VI, Our predecessor of happy memory, writing to the Bishop of Agria,[2] say: "From this it is manifestly clear that matrimony, even in the state of nature, and surely long before it was raised to the dignity of a sacrament properly so called, was so established by God that it carries with it a perpetual and indissoluble bond, which, accordingly, cannot be dissolved by any civil law. And so, although the sacramental element can be separated from matrimony, as is true in a marriage between infidels, still in such a marriage, inasmuch as it is a true marriage, there must remain and surely does remain that perpetual bond which by divine right is so inherent in marriage from its very beginning that it is not subject to any civil power. And so whatever marriage is said to be contracted, either it is so contracted that it is in fact a true marriage, and then will have that perpetual bond inherent by divine law in every true marriage, or it is supposed to be contracted without that perpetual bond, and then is not a marriage, but an illicit union repugnant by its purpose to the divine law, and therefore cannot be entered upon or maintained.[3]

2236   If this stability seems subject to exception, however rare, as in the case of certain natural marriages entered into between unbelievers, or if be-tween the faithful of Christ, those which are valid but not consummated, that exception does not depend on the will of man or of any merely

---

[1] St. Augustine, *De Gen. ad litt.*, IX 7, 12 [ML 34, 397].

[2] Erlau (Eger) in Hungary.

[3] Pius VI, Rescript to the Bishop of Agria, July 11, 1789 [A. de Roskovány, *Matri-monium in Eccl. cath.*, I (1870), 291].

human power, but on divine law, whose only guardian and interpreter is the Church of Christ. Yet, not even such a power can for any cause ever affect a Christian marriage which is valid and consummated. For, since the marriage contract is fully accomplished in such case, so also absolute stability and indissolubility by God's will are apparent, which cannot be relaxed by any human authority.

If we wish to investigate with due reverence the intimate reason for this divine will, we shall easily discover it in the mystical signification of Christian marriage, which is fully and perfectly had in a marriage consummated between the faithful. For with the Apostle, in his Epistle to the Ephesians as witness [Eph. 5:32] (to which we referred in the beginning), the marriage of Christians recalls that most perfect union which exists between Christ and the Church: "This is a great sacrament, but I speak in Christ and in the church," which union, indeed, as long as Christ shall live and the Church through Him, surely can never be dissolved by any separation. . . .

In this blessing of the sacrament, in addition to its indissoluble firm-   **2237** ness, far higher emoluments are also contained, very aptly indicated by the word, "sacrament"; for to Christians this is not a hollow and empty name, since Christ the Lord, "the Institutor and Perfector" [1] of the sacraments, raising the marriage of His faithful to a true and proper sacrament of the New Law, made it in very fact a sign and source of that peculiar interior grace by which it perfects natural love, confirms an indissoluble union, and sanctifies the spouses.[2]

And since Christ established valid conjugal consent between the faithful as a sign of grace, the nature of the sacrament is so intimately bound up with Christian marriage that no true matrimony can exist between baptized persons "unless by that very fact it be a sacrament." [3]

When then the faithful with sincere minds give such consent, they open up a treasure of sacramental grace for themselves, from which they draw supernatural strength for fulfilling their obligations and duties faithfully, nobly, and perseveringly even until death.

This sacrament, in the case of those who, as they say, place no *obex* in its way, not only increases the permanent principle of supernatural life, namely sanctifying grace, but also bestows peculiar gifts, good dispositions of mind, and seeds of grace, by increasing and perfecting the natural powers, so that the spouses are able not only to understand by reason, but to know intimately, to hold firmly, to wish efficaciously, and to carry out, indeed, whatever pertains to the marriage state, both its ends and obligations; finally, it grants them the right to obtain the actual

---

[1] Council of Trent, sess. 24 [See n. 969].

[2] Council of Trent, *ibid.*

[3] *Cod. Iur. Can.*, c. 1012.

assistance of grace as often as they need it for fulfilling the duties of this state.

2238   And yet, since it is a law of divine Providence in the supernatural order that men do not gather the full fruit of the sacraments which they receive after acquiring the use of reason, unless they cooperate with grace, the grace of marriage will remain in great part a useless talent hidden in the field, unless the spouses exercise supernatural strength and cultivate and develop the seeds of grace which they have received. But if they do all they can to make themselves docile to grace, they will be able to bear the burdens of their state and fulfill its duties, and will be strengthened and sanctified and, as it were, consecrated by so great a sacrament. For, as St. Augustine teaches, just as by baptism and holy orders a man is set aside and assisted either to lead his life in a Christian manner, or to fulfill the duties of the priesthood, and is never devoid of sacramental help, almost in the same manner (although not by a sacramental sign) the faithful who have once been joined by the bond of marriage can never be deprived of its sacramental assistance and tie. But rather, as the same Holy Doctor adds, they take that holy bond with them even when they may have become adulterers, although not now to the glory of grace, but to the crime of sin, "as the apostate soul, as if withdrawing from union with Christ, even after faith has been lost, does not lose the sacrament of faith which it received from the laver of regeneration."[1]

But let these same spouses, not restrained but adorned by the golden tie of the sacrament, not impeded but strengthened, struggle with all their might for this end, that their wedlock, not only by the strength and significance of the sacrament, but also by their mentality and character, be and always remain the living image of that most fruitful union of Christ with the Church, which surely is to be revered as the mystery of the most perfect love.

The Abuse of Matrimony[2]

[From the same Encyclical, "Casti Connubii," Dec. 31, 1930]

2239   Let us discuss the offspring, which some have the audacity to call the troublesome burden of marriage, and which they declare should be studiously avoided not by honorable continence (permitted even in matrimony when both spouses consent), but by frustration of the natural act. Indeed, some vindicate themselves for this criminal abuse on the ground that they are tired of children and wish merely to fulfill their

---

[1] St. August., *De nupt. et concup.*, 1, 10 [ML 44, 420]; cf. *De bono coniug.*, 24, 32 [ML 40, 394].
[2] AAS 22 (1930), 559 ff.

desires without the consequent burden; others on the ground that they can neither observe continence, nor because of difficulties of the mother or of family circumstances cannot have offspring.

But surely no reason, not even the gravest, can bring it about that what is intrinsically against nature becomes in accord with nature, and honorable. Since, moreover, the conjugal act by its very nature is destined for the generating of offspring, those who in the exercise of it deliberately deprive it of its natural force and power, act contrary to nature, and do something that is shameful and intrinsically bad.

Therefore, it is no wonder that Sacred Scripture itself testifies that the divine Majesty looks upon this nefarious crime with the greatest hatred, and sometimes has punished it with death, as St. Augustine relates: "It is illicit and disgraceful for one to lie even with his legitimate wife, when conception of offspring is prevented. Onan did this; God killed him therefor." [1]

Since, therefore, certain persons, manifestly departing from Christian **2240** doctrine handed down from the beginning without interruption, have recently decided that another doctrine should be preached on this method of acting, the Catholic Church, to whom God himself has entrusted the teaching and the defense of the integrity and purity of morals, placed in the midst of this ruination of morals, in order that she may preserve the chastity of the marriage contract immune from this base sin, and in token of her divine mission raises high her voice through Our mouth and again proclaims: Any use of the marriage act, in the exercise of which it is designedly deprived of its natural power of procreating life, infringes on the law of God and of nature, and those who have committed any such act are stained with the guilt of serious sin.

Therefore, We admonish the priests who devote time to hearing confessions, and others who have care of souls, in accord with Our highest authority, not to permit the faithful committed to them to err in this most serious law of God, and much more to keep themselves immune from false opinions of this kind, and not to connive in them in any way.

---

[1] St. Augustine, *De coniug. adult.*, 2, 12 [ML 40, 482]; cf. Gen. 38:8–10; S. Poenitent., April 3, June 3, 1916.—The following responses first appeared in the work *Institutiones Alphonsianae,* authored by Cl. Marc, t. II, (1917), n. 2116 f.

In the response of April 3, it is declared: a) that a wife because of a threat of death or grave injury can cooperate in an interrupted copulation with her husband; b) but by no means can she do so, not even for the sake of avoiding death, in a sodomitic copulation.

In the response of June 3, it is declared: a) that a wife is bound to positive resistance, when a man wishes to use an instrument to practice onanism;—b) that in this case passive resistance does not suffice;—c) that a man who uses such instruments is truly likened to an oppressor, against whom the woman should oppose that resistance which a virgin does to an invader. [See the text itself in the cited work; or, in A. Veermeersch, *De castitate* (1919), n. 263, and in other authors.]

If any confessor or pastor of souls, which may God forbid, either himself leads the faithful entrusted to him into these errors, or at least either by approval or by guilty silence confirms them in these errors, let him know that he must render a strict accounting to God, the Supreme Judge, for the betrayal of his trust, and let him consider the words of Christ as spoken to himself: *"They are blind, and the leaders of the blind; and if the blind lead the blind, both fall into the pit"* [Matt. 15:14].[1]

2241   Holy Church knows very well that not rarely one of the spouses is sinned against rather than commits a sin, when for a very grave reason he permits a perversion of the right order, which he himself does not wish; and on this account he is without fault, provided he then remembers the law of charity and does not neglect to prevent and deter the other from sinning. Those spouses are not to be said to act against the order of nature who use their right in a correct and natural way, although for natural reasons of time, or of certain defects new life cannot spring from this. For in matrimony itself, as in the practice of the conjugal right, secondary ends are also considered, such as mutual aid, the cultivation of mutual love, and the quieting of concupiscence, which spouses are by no means forbidden to attempt, provided the intrinsic nature of that act is preserved, and so its due ordering is towards its primary end. . . .

Every care must be taken lest the calamitous conditions of external affairs give occasion for a much more disastrous error. For no difficulties can arise which can nullify the obligation of the mandates of God which forbid acts that are evil from their interior nature; but in all collateral circumstances spouses, strengthened by the grace of God, can always perform their duty faithfully, and preserve their chastity in marriage untainted by this shameful stain; for the truth of the Christian faith stands expressed in the teaching of the Synod of Trent: "Let no one rashly assert that which the Fathers of the Council have placed under anathema, namely, that there are precepts of God impossible for the just to observe. God does not ask the impossible, but by His commands instructs you to

---

[1] Decree of the Holy Office, November 22, 1922.—By this decree [*Nederlandsche Katholicke Stemmen* 23 (1923), 35 ff.] *copula dimidiata* is discussed:

I. "Whether it can be tolerated that confessors of their own accord teach the practice of *copula dimidiata*, and promiscuously persuade all penitents of it, who fear the birth of more children."

II. "Whether a confessor must be criticized, who, after all remedies have been attempted in vain to turn the penitent who abuses matrimony away from this evil, teaches the practice of *copula dimidiata* for the avoidance of moral sins."

III. "Whether a confessor must be criticized, who in circumstances under II persuades a penitent of *copula dimidiata* noted elsewhere, or to the penitent who asks whether this method is licit, replies simply that it is licit without any restriction or explanation."

The reply is: "To question I: In the negative. To II and III: In the affirmative."

do what you are able, to pray for what you are not able, and assists you that you may be able" [see n. 804]. This same doctrine was again solemnly repeated and confirmed in the condemnation of the Jansenist heresy, which dared to utter this blasphemy against the goodness of God: "Some precepts of God are impossible of fulfillment, even for just men who wish and strive to keep the laws according to the powers which they have; grace also is lacking to them which would render this possible" [see n. 1092].

The Killing of the Foetus [1]

[From the same Encyclical, "Casti Connubii," Dec. 31, 1930]

Another very grave crime is also to be noted, by which the life of the offspring hidden in the mother's womb is attempted. Moreover, some wish this to be permitted according to the pleasure of the mother or father; others, however, call it illicit unless very grave reasons attend, which they call by the name of medical, social, eugenic "indication." Since this pertains to the penal laws of the state, according to which the destruction of the offspring begotten but not yet born is prohibited, all of these demand that the "indication," which they defend individually in one way or another, be recognized even by the public laws, and be declared free of all punishment. Nay rather, there are not lacking those who demand that public magistrates lend a helping hand to these death-dealing operations, something which unfortunately we all know is taking place very frequently in some places. 2242

Now as for the medical and therapeutic "indication," to use their words, We have already said, Venerable Brethren, how sorry We are for the mother, whose health and even life are threatened by grave dangers resulting from nature's duty; but what reason can ever be strong enough to excuse in any way the direct murder of the innocent? For this is the case in point here. Whether this is brought upon the mother or the offspring, it is contrary to God's precept and the voice of nature: "Thou shalt not kill!" [Exod. 20:13].[2] The life of each person is an equally sacred thing, and no one can ever have the power, not even public authority to destroy it. Consequently, it is most unjust to invoke the "right of the sword" against the innocent since this is valid against the guilty alone; nor is there any right in this case of a bloody defense against an unjust aggressor (for who will call an innocent child an unjust aggressor?); nor is there present any "right of extreme necessity," as it is called, which can extend even to the direct killing of the innocent. 2243

---

[1] AAS 22 (1930), 562 ff.
[2] Cf. the decree of the Holy Office, May 5, 1898; July 24, 1895; May 31, 1884 [see n. 1889 ff.; AAS 28 (1895/96), 383 f.; 17 (1884), 556].

Therefore, honorable and experienced physicians praiseworthily endeavor to protect and to save the lives of both the mother and the offspring; on the other hand, most unworthy of the noble name of physician and of commendation would they prove themselves, as many as plan for the death of one or the other under the appearance of practising medicine or through motives of false pity. . . .

2244   Now what is put forth in behalf of *social* and *eugenic indication,* with licit and honorable means and within due limits, may and ought to be held as a solution for these matters; but because of the necessities upon which these problems rest, to seek to procure the death of the innocent is improper and contrary to the divine precept promulgated by the words of the Apostle: "Evil is not to be done that good may come of it" [Rom. 3:8].

Finally, those who hold high office among nations and pass laws may not forget that it belongs to public authority by appropriate laws and penalties to defend the lives of the innocent, and the more so as those whose lives are endangered and are attacked are less able to defend themselves, among whom surely infants in their mothers' wombs hold first place. But if public magistrates not only do not protect those little ones, but by their laws and ordinances permit this, and thus give them over to the hands of physicians and others to be killed, let them remember that God is the judge and the avenger of innocent "blood which cries from earth to heaven" [Gen. 4:10].

The Right to Marriage, and Sterilization [1]

[From the same Encyclical, "Casti Connubii," Dec. 31, 1930]

2245   Finally, that pernicious practice should be condemned which is closely related to the natural right of man to enter into matrimony, and also in a real way pertains to the good of the offspring. For there are those who, overly solicitous about the ends of *eugenics,* not only give certain salutary counsels for more certainly procuring the health and vigor of the future offspring—which certainly is not contrary to right reason—but also place *eugenics* before every other end of a higher order; and by public authority wish to prohibit from marriage all those from whom, according to the norms and conjectures of their science, they think that a defective and corrupt offspring will be generated because of hereditary transmission, even if these same persons are naturally fitted for entering upon matrimony. Why, they even wish such persons even against their will to be deprived by law of that natural faculty through the operation of physicians; and this they propose not as a severe penalty for a crime

---

[1] AAS 22 (1930), 664 f.

committed, to be sought by public authority, nor to ward off future crimes of the guilt,[1] but, contrary to every right and claim, by arrogating this power to the civil magistrates, which they never had and can never have legitimately.

Whoever so act completely forget that the family is more sacred than the state, and that men are generated primarily not for earth and for time, but for heaven and eternity. And, surely, it is not right that men, in other respects capable of matrimony, who according to conjecture, though every care and diligence be applied, will generate only defective offspring, be for this reason burdened with a serious sin if they contract marriage, although sometimes they ought to be dissuaded from matrimony.

In fact, public magistrates have no direct power over the bodies of **2246** their subjects; therefore, they can never directly do harm to, or in any way affect the integrity of the body, where no crime has taken place, and no cause for serious punishment is at hand, either for reasons of *eugenics,* or any other purpose. St. Thomas Aquinas taught the same, when, inquiring whether human judges have the power to inflict some evil on man to ward off future evils, concedes this to be correct with reference to certain other evils, but rightly and worthily denies it with regard to injuring the body: "Never ought anyone, according to human judgment, to be punished when without guilt, by a penalty of flogging to death, or of mutilation, or of beating." [2]

Christian doctrine has established this, and by the light of human reason it is quite clear that private individuals have no other power over the members of their bodies, and cannot destroy or mutilate them, or in any other way render them unfitted for natural functions, except when the good of the whole body cannot otherwise be provided for.

The Emancipation of Women [3]

[From the same Encyclical, "Casti Connubii," Dec. 31, 1930]

Whoever, then, obscure the luster of conjugal faith and chastity by **2247** writing and speaking, these same teachers of error easily undermine the trustful and honorable obedience of the woman to the man. Many of them also boldly prattle that it is an unworthy form of servitude on the part of one spouse to the other; that all rights between spouses are equal; and when these are violated by the servitude of one, they proudly proclaim that a kind of *emancipation* has been or ought to be effected. This *emancipation,* moreover, they establish in a threefold way: in the ruling

---

[1] Cf. AAS 22 (1930), 604.

[2] *Summa theol.,* IIa, IIae, q. 108, a. 4, ad 2.

[3] AAS 22 (1930), 567 f.

of domestic society, in the administration of family affairs, and in preventing or destroying of the life of the offspring, and they call these *social, economic,* and *physiological:* physiological, indeed, in that they wish women freed, or to be freed of the duties of wife, whether conjugal or maternal, at her own free will (but we have already said enough to the effect that this is not emancipation but a wretched crime); economic, of course, whereby they wish woman, even unbeknown to or with the opposition of the man, to be able freely to possess, carry on, and administer her own business affairs, to the neglect of children, husband, and the entire family; finally, social, insofar as they remove from the wife domestic cares whether of children or of family, that she may be able while neglecting these, to follow her own bent, and even to devote herself to business and public affairs.

2248　　But this is not a true emancipation of woman, nor is it a freedom which is in accord with reason, nor worthy of her and due to the office of a noble Christian mother and wife; rather it is a corruption of the feminine nature and of maternal dignity, and a perversion of the entire family, whereby the husband is deprived of a wife, the offspring of a mother, and the house and entire family of an ever watchful guardian. Rather, indeed, such false liberty and unnatural equality with man are turned to the destruction of the woman herself; for, if the woman descends from that royal seat to which she was raised within the walls of the home by the Gospel, she will shortly be reduced to ancient servitude (if not in appearance, yet in very fact), and will become, as she was among the pagans, a mere instrument of man.

But that equality of rights which is so greatly exaggerated and extended, ought to be recognized of course among those which are proper to a person and human dignity, and which follow upon the nuptial contract and are natural to marriage; and in these, surely, both spouses enjoy absolutely the same right and are bound by the same obligations; in other matters a kind of inequality and just proportion must exist, which the good of the family and the due unity and stability of domestic society and of order demand.

Nevertheless, wherever the social and economic conditions of the married woman, because of changed ways and practices of human society, need to be changed in some manner, it belongs to public authority to adapt the civil rights of woman to the necessities and needs of this time, with due consideration of what the different natural disposition of the feminine sex, good morality, and the common good of the family demand; provided, also, that the essential order of domestic society remains intact, which is founded on an authority and wisdom higher than human, that is, divine, and cannot be changed by public laws and the pleasure of individuals.

Divorces [1]

[From the same Encyclical, "Casti Connubii," Dec. 31, 1930]

The advocates of neopaganism, having learned nothing from the **2249** present sad state of affairs, continue daily to attack more bitterly the sacred indissolubility of marriage and the laws that support it, and contend that there must be a decision to recognize divorces, that other and more humane laws be substituted for the obsolete laws.

They bring forward many different causes for divorce, some deriving from the wickedness or sin of persons, others based on circumstances (the former they call subjective, the latter objective); finally, whatever makes the individual married life more harsh and unpleasant. . . .

So there is prattle to the effect that laws must be made to conform to these requirements and changed conditions of the times, the opinions of men, and the civil institutions and customs, all of which individually, and especially when brought together, most clearly testify that opportunity for divorce must forthwith be granted for certain causes.

Others, proceeding further with remarkable impudence, believe that inasmuch as matrimony is a purely private contract, it should be left directly to the consent and private opinion of the two who contracted it, as is the case in other private contracts, and so can be dissolved for any reason.

But opposed to all these ravings stands the one most certain law **2250** of God, confirmed most fully by Christ, which can be weakened by no decrees of men or decisions of the people, by no will of legislators: "What God hath joined together, let no man put asunder" [Matt. 19:6]. And if a man, contrary to this law puts asunder, it is immediately illegal; so rightly, as we have seen more than once, Christ Himself has declared: "Everyone that putteth away his wife and marrieth another, committeth adultery, and he that marrieth her that is put away, committeth adultery" [Luke 16:18]. And these words of Christ refer to any marriage whatsoever, even that which is purely natural and legitimate; for indissolubility is proper to every true marriage, and whatever pertains to the loosening of the bond is entirely removed from the good pleasure of the parties concerned and from every secular power.

"Sexual Education" and "Eugenics" [2]

[From the Decree of the Holy Office, March 21, 1931]

I) Can the method be approved, which is called "sexual education," **2251** or even "sexual initiation?"

---

[1] AAS 22 (1930), 572 ff.
[2] AAS 23 (1931), 118 f.

Response: In the negative, and that the method must be preserved entirely as set forth up to the present by the Church and saintly men, and recommended by the Most Holy Father in the Encyclical Letter, "On the Christian Education of Youth," given on the 31st day of December, 1929 [see n. 2214]. Naturally, care must especially be taken that a full and solid religious instruction be given to the youth of both sexes without interruption; in this instruction there must be aroused a regard, desire, and love for the angelic virtue; and especially must it be inculcated upon them to insist on prayer, to be constant in the sacraments of penance and the most Holy Eucharist, to be devoted to the Blessed Virgin, Mother of holy purity, with filial devotion and to commit themselves wholly to her protection; to avoid carefully dangerous reading, obscene plays, association with the wicked, and all occasions of sin.

By no means, then, can we approve what has been written and published in defense of the new method especially in these recent times, even on the part of some Catholic authors.

2252   II) What is to be thought of the so-called theory of "eugenics," whether "positive" or "negative," and of the means indicated by it to bring human progeny to a better state, disregarding the laws either natural or divine or ecclesiastical which concern the rights of the individual to matrimony?

Response: That this theory is to be entirely disapproved, and held as false and condemned, as in the Encyclical Letter on Christian marriage, "Casti connubii," dated on the 31st day of December, 1930 [see n. 2245 f.].

The Authority of the Church in Social and Economic Affairs [1]

[From the Encyclical, "Quadragesimo anno," May 15, 1931]

2253   The principle which Leo XIII clearly established long ago must be layed down, that there rest in us the right and the duty of passing judgment with supreme authority on these social and economic problems.[2] . . . For, although economic affairs and moral discipline make use of their own principles, each in its own sphere, nevertheless, it is false to say that the economic and the moral order are so distinct and alien to each other that the former in no way depends on the latter.

---

[1] AAS 23 (1931), 190.

[2] Cf. Encycl., "Rerum novarum," n. 13 [ASS 23 (1890/91), 647; Al XI (Romae, 1891), 107].

The Ownership or Right of Property [1]

[From the same Encyclical, "Quadragesimo anno," May 15, 1931]

Its individual and social nature. First, then, let it be held as acknowl- **2254**
edged and certain that neither Leo nor those theologians who taught
under the leadership and direction of the Church have ever denied or
called into question the twofold nature of ownership, which is called
individual and social, according as it regards individuals or looks to
the common good; but have always unanimously affirmed that the right
to private ownership has been assigned to men by nature, or by the
Creator himself, both that they may be able individually to provide for
themselves and their families, and that by means of this institution the
goods which the Creator has destined for the entire human family may
truly serve this end, all of which can by no means be attained except by
the maintenance of a definite and fixed order. . . .

Obligations inherent in ownership. In order to place definite limits to **2255**
the controversies which have begun to arise over ownership and the
duties inherent therein, we must first lay down the fundamental principle
which Leo XIII established, namely, that the right of property is distinguished from its use.[2] For that justice which is known as "commutative" directs men to preserve the division of property as sacred, and not
to encroach on the rights of others by exceeding limits of proper ownership; but that owners make only honorable use of their property is not
the concern of this justice, but of other virtues whose duties "it is not
right to seek by passing a law." [3] Therefore, some unjustly declare that
ownership and its honorable use are bounded by the same limits; and,
what is much more at odds with the truth, that because of its abuse or
nonuse the right to property is destroyed and lost. . . .

What the power of the state is. From the very nature of ownership **2256**
which We have called both individual and social it follows that men
must in very fact take into account in this matter not only their own
advantage but also the common good. To define these duties in detail,
when necessity demands it, and the natural law does not prescribe them,
is the duty of those who are in charge of the state. Therefore, what is
permitted those who possess property in consideration of the true necessity of the common good, what is illicit in the use of their possessions,
public authority can decide more accurately, following the dictates of the
natural and the divine law. Indeed, Leo XIII wisely taught that the
description of private possessions has been entrusted by God to man's

---

[1] AAS 23 (1931), 191 ff.
[2] Encycl., "Rerum novarum," n. 19 [ASS 23 (1890/91), 651; AL XI 113].
[3] Cf. Encycl., "Rerum novarum," n. 19 [see n. 1938b].

industry and to the laws of peoples. . . ." [1] Yet it is plain that the state may not perform its duty arbitrarily. For the natural right of possessing private property and of transmitting goods by inheritance should always remain intact and unviolated, "for man is older than the state," [2] and also, "the domestic household is prior both in idea and in fact to the civil community." [3] Thus the most wise Pontiff had already declared it unlawful for the state to exhaust private funds by the heavy burden of taxes and tributes. "Public authority cannot abolish the right to hold private property, since this is not derived from the law of man but of nature, but can only control its use and bring it in harmony with the common good.[4] . . .

2257 *Obligations regarding superfluous income.* Superfluous incomes are not left entirely to man's discretion; that is, wealth that he does not need to sustain life fittingly and becomingly; but on the other hand Sacred Scripture and the holy Fathers of the Church continuously declare in clearest words that the rich are bound most seriously by the precept of practicing charity, beneficence, and liberality.

The investment of rather large incomes so that opportunities for gainful employment may abound, provided that this work is applied to the production of truly useful products, we gather from a study of the principles of the Angelic Doctor,[5] is to be considered a noble deed of magnificent virtue, and especially suited to the needs of the time.

2258 *Titles in acquiring ownerships.* Moreover, not only the tradition of all times but also the doctrine of Our predecessor, Leo, clearly testify that ownership in the first place is acquired by the occupation of a thing that belongs to no one, and by industry, or specification as it is called. For no injury is done anyone, whatever some may say to the contrary, when property is occupied which rests unclaimed and belongs to no one; but the industry which is exercised by man in his own name, and by the aid of which a new kind, or an increase is added to his property, is the only industry that gives a laborer a title to its fruits.

Capital and Labor [6]

[From the same Encyclical, "Quadrágesimo anno," May 15, 1931]

2259 Far different is the nature of the labor which is hired out to others and is exercised on another's capital. This statement is especially in harmony

---

[1] Encycl., "Rerum novarum," n. [ASS 23 (1890/91), 644; AL XI 102].
[2] *Ibid.,* n. 6 [ASS 23 (1890/91), 644; AL XI 102].
[3] *Ibid.,* n. 10 [ASS 23 (1890/91), 646; AL XI 105].
[4] *Ibid.,* n. 35 [ASS 24 (1890/91), 663; AL XI 133].
[5] Cf. *Summa theol.,* IIa, IIae, q. 9, a. 1, 3, 4.
[6] AAS 23 (1931), 194 ff.

with what Leo XIII says is *most true,* "that the riches of the state are produced only by the labor of the working man." [1]

Neither without the other is able to produce anything. Hence it follows that unless one performs labor on his own property, the property of the one should be associated in some way with the labor of the other; for neither effects anything without the other. And this Leo XIII had in mind when he wrote: "There can be no capital without labor, nor labor without capital." [2] Therefore, it is entirely false to ascribe to one or the other alone whatever was obtained from the combined effort of both; and it is entirely unjust that either deny the efficacy of the other, and arrogate to himself whatever has been accomplished. . . .

The directive principle of just distribution. Without doubt, lest by these 2260 false decisions they block the approach to justice and peace, both should have been forewarned by the wise words of Our predecessor: "Although divided among private owners, the earth does not cease to serve the usefulness of all.[3] . . ." Therefore, wealth which is being continuously increased through economic and social progress should be so distributed to individual persons and classes of men, that the common good of all society be preserved intact. By this law of social justice one class is forbidden to exclude the other from a share in the profits. None the less, then, the wealthy class violates this law of social justice, when, as it were, free of all anxieties in their good fortune, it considers that order of things just by which all falls to its lot and nothing to the worker; and the class without property violates this law, when, strongly incensed because of violated justice, and too prone to vindicate wrongly the one right of their own of which it is conscious, demands all for itself, on the ground that it was made by its own hands, and so attacks and strives to abolish ownership and income, or profits which have not been gained by labor, of whatever kind they are, or of whatever nature they are in human society, for no other reason than because they are such. And we must not pass over the fact that in this matter appeal is made by some, ineptly as well as unworthily, to the Apostle when he says: "If any man will not work, neither let him eat" [II Thess. 3:10]; for the Apostle utters the statement against those who abstain from work, even though they can and ought to work; and he advises us that we should make zealous use of time and strength, whether of body or mind, and that others should not be burdened, when we can provide for ourselves. But by no means does the Apostle teach that labor is the only title for receiving a livelihood and profits [cf. II Thess. 3:8-10].

To each, then, is his own part of property to be assigned; and it must

---

[1] Encycl., "Rerum novarum," n. 27 [ASS 23 (1890/91), 657; AL XI 123].

[2] *Ibid.,* n. 15 [ASS 23 1890/91), 649; AL XI 109].

[3] *Ibid.,* n. 7 [ASS 28 (1890/91), 644; AL XI 102].

be brought about that distribution of created goods be made to conform
to the norms of the common good or social justice. . . .

The Just Wage or Salary of Labor [1]

[From the same Encyclical]

Let us consider the question of wages which Leo XIII said "was of
great importance," [2] stating and explaining the doctrine and precepts
where necessary.

2261   *The wage contract not unjust in its essence.* And first, indeed, those
who declare that the contract of letting out and of accepting labor for
hire is unjust in its essence, and that therefore in its place there has to be
substituted a contract of partnership, are in complete error, and gravely
calumniate Our predecessor, whose Encyclical Letter "On Wages" not
only admits such a contract, but treats it at length according to the principles of justice. . . .

2262   [*On what basis a just portion is to be estimated*]. Leo XIII has already
wisely declared in the following words that a fair amount of wages is to
be estimated not on one but on several considerations: "In order that a
fair measure of wages may be established, many conditions must be considered. . . ." [3]

The individual and social nature of labor. It must be observed both
of ownership and of labor, especially of that which is let out to another,
that besides their personal or individual concerns there must be considered also a social aspect; for, unless there be a truly social and organic
body; unless the social and juridical order protect labor; unless the various trades which depend on one another, united in mutual harmony, are
mutually complementary; and unless, which is more important, the intellect, capital, and labor come together as in a unit, man's efforts cannot produce due fruits. Therefore, man's efforts cannot be estimated
justly nor adequately repaid, if its social and individual nature is overlooked.

Three fundamental matters to be considered. Moreover, from this
twofold character, which is the deep-seated nature of human labor,
flow most serious conclusions by which wages should be regulated and
determined.

2263   a) *The support of the workingman and his family.* First, wages must
be paid to the workingman which are sufficient for the support of himself and of his family. [4] It is right, indeed, that the rest of the family

---

[1] AAS 23 (1931), 198 ff.
[2] Encyclical, "Rerum novarum," n. 34 [ASS 23 (1890/91), 661; AL XI 129].
[3] *Ibid.*, n. 17 [ASS 23 (1890/91), 649; AL XI 111].
[4] Cf. Encycl., "*Casti connubii,*" December 31, 1930 [AAS 22 (1930), 587].

according to their ability contribute to the common support of all, as one can see in the families of rural people especially, and also in many families of artisans and minor shopkeepers; but it is wrong to abuse the tender years of children and the weakness of women. Especially in the home or in matters which pertain to the home, let mothers of families perform their work by attending to domestic cares. But the worst abuse, and one to be removed by every effort, is that of mothers being forced to engage in gainful occupation away from home, because of the meagerness of the father's salary, neglecting their own cares and special duties, and especially the training of their children. Every effort, then must be made that the fathers receive a sufficiently ample wage to meet the ordinary domestic needs adequately. But if in the present state of affairs this cannot always be carried out, social justice demands that changes be introduced as soon as possible, whereby every adult workingman may be made secure by such a salary. It will not be amiss here to bestow praise upon all those who in a very wise and useful plan have attempted various plans by which the wage of the laborer is adjusted to the burdens of the family, so that when burdens are increased, the wage is made greater; surely, if this should happen, enough would be done to meet extraordinary needs.

b) *The condition of business.* An account must also be taken of a   **2264** business and its owner; for, unjustly would immoderate salaries be demanded, which the business cannot endure without its ruin and the ruin of the workers consequent on this. And yet if the business makes less profit because of dilatoriness, or laziness or neglect of technical and economic advance, this is not to be considered a just cause for lowering the wages of the worker. However, if no such amount of money returns to a business which is sufficient to pay the workers a just wage, because it is oppressed by unjust burdens or because it is forced to sell its product at a price lower than is just, those who so harass a business are guilty of a serious offense; for they deprive the workers of just wage, who, forced by necessity, are compelled to accept a wage less than is just. . . .

c) *The demands of the common good.* Finally, the wage scale must   **2265** be adjusted to the economic welfare of the people. We have already shown above how conducive it is to the welfare of the people, that workers and officials by setting aside whatever part of their wage is not used for necessary expenses, gradually acquire a modest fortune; but another thing, of scarcely less importance, and especially necessary in our time, must not be passed over, namely, that an opportunity to work be furnished to those who are both able and willing to work. . . . Another thing, then, is contrary to social justice, that, for the sake of personal gain, and with no consideration of the common welfare, the wages of workers be lowered or raised too much; and this same justice demands that by a concerted planning and good will, insofar as it can be done, salaries be so regulated that as many as possible can have employment and receive suitable means for the maintenance of life.

Very properly, also a reasonable proportion between salaries is of importance, with which is closely connected the proper proportion of prices at which those goods are sold which are produced by the various groups such as agriculture, industry, and others. If all these are kept in harmony, the various skills will combine and coalesce as into one body, and like members of one body will bring to each other mutual help and perfection. Then at length will the economic and social order be truly established and attain its ends, if all those benefits are supplied to all and to each, which can be furnished by the wealth and resources of nature, by technical skills, and by the social constitution of economic affairs. Indeed, these benefits should be as numerous as are necessary to satisfy the necessities and the honorable conveniences of life, and to raise men to that happier way of life which, provided it be conducted prudently, not only is no hindrance to virtue, but a great help to it.[1]

The Right Social Order [2]

[From the same Encyclical, "Quadragesimo anno," May 15, 1931]

2266   [*The duty of the state*]. When we now speak of the reformation of institutions, we have in mind chiefly the state, not as if all salvation is to be expected from its activity, because on account of the evil of individualism, which we have mentioned, matters have reached such a state that the highly developed social life, which once flourished compositely in diverse institutions, has been brought low and almost wiped out; and individual men and the state remain almost alone, to the by no means small detriment of the state, which, having lost its form of social regimen and having taken on all the burdens formerly borne by the associations now destroyed, has been almost submerged and overwhelmed by an endless number of functions and duties. . . .

Therefore, the supreme authority of the state should entrust to the smaller groups the expediting of business and problems of minor importance, by which otherwise it would be greatly distracted. Thus it will be brought about that all matters which pertain to the state will be executed more freely, more vigorously, and more efficiently, since it alone is qualified to perform them, directing, guarding, urging, and compelling, according as circumstances prompt and necessity demands. Therefore, let those who are in power be convinced that the more perfectly the

---

[1] Cf. St. Thomas, *De regimine principum* I, 15—Encycl., "Rerum novarum," n. 27 [ASS 23 (1890/91), 656; AL; AL XI 121].
[2] AAS 23 (1931), 202 ss.

principle of the duty of the "subsidiary" is kept, and a graded hierarchial order flourishes among the various associations, the more outstanding will be the social authority and efficiency, and the happier and more prosperous the condition of the state.

The mutual harmony of "orders." Moreover, both the state and every 2267 outstanding citizen should look especially and strive for this, that with the suppression of the conflicts between classes a pleasing harmony may be aroused and fostered between the orders. . . .

Therefore the social political policy must work for a restoration of the "orders" . . . , "orders," namely, in which men are placed not according to the position which one holds in the labor market, but according to the diverse social roles which they exercise individually. For just as it happens through natural impulse that, those who are united by proximity of place establish municipalities, so, also, those who labor at the same trade or profession—whether it be economic or of some other kind—form guilds or certain groups (*collegia seu corpora quaedam*), so that these groups, being truly autonomous, are customarily spoken of, if not as essential to civil society, yet at least as natural to it. . . .

It is scarcely necessary to recall that what Leo XIII taught about the form of political government is equally applicable, with due proportion, to the guilds or groups, namely, that it is sound for men to choose whatever form they prefer, provided that the demands of justice and of the common good be given consideration.[1]

[*Freedom of association*]. Now just as the inhabitants of a municipal- 2268 ity are accustomed to establish associations for very different purposes, with which each one has full power to join or not, so those who practice the same trade will enter equally free associations with one another for purposes in some way connected with the practice of their trade. Since these free associations are explained clearly and lucidly by Our predecessor, we consider it enough to stress this one point: that man has complete freedom not only to form such associations, which are of private right and order, but also to freely choose within these that organization and those laws which are considered especially conducive to that end which has been proposed." [2] The same freedom is to be maintained in instituting associations which extend beyond the limits of a single trade. Moreover, let these free associations which already flourish and enjoy salutary fruits, according to the mind of Christian social teaching make it their aim to prepare the way for those more outstanding guilds or "orders" about which we made mention above, and let them manfully carry this out.

---

[1] Cf. Encyclical Letter, "Immortale Dei," November 1, 1885 [see n. 1871 f.].

[2] Cf. Encyclical Letter, "Rerum novarum," n. 42 [ASS 23 (1890/91), 667; AL (Rome) XI 138 f.].

2269 *The guiding principle of economics to be restored.* Still another matter, closely connected with the former, must be kept in mind. Just as the unity of society cannot rest on mutual opposition of classes, so the right ordering of economic affairs cannot be given over to the free competition of forces . . . Therefore, higher and more noble principles are to be sought, with which to control this power firmly and soundly; namely, social justice and social charity. Therefore, the institutions of the people, and of all social life, must be imbued with this justice, so that it be truly efficient, or establish a juridical and social order, by which, as it were, the entire economy may be fashioned. Social charity, moreover, should be as a soul of this order, and an alert public authority should aim to protect and guard this effectively, a task which it will be able to accomplish with less difficulty, if it will rid itself of those burdens which we have declared before are not proper to it.

Furthermore, the various nations should strive for this by combining their zeal and labors, so that, since in economic affairs they depend for the most part on one another and need one another's help, they may by wise pacts and institutions promote a favorable and happy cooperation in the world of economics.

Socialism [1]

[From the same Encyclical, "Quadragesimo anno," May 15, 1931]

2270 We declare as follows: Whether socialism be considered as a doctrine, or as an historical fact, or as an "action," if it truly remain socialism, even after it has yielded to truth and justice in the matters which we have mentioned, it cannot be reconciled with the dogmas of the Catholic Church, since it conceives a human society completely at variance with Christian truth.

Socialism conceives of a society and the social character of man entirely at variance with Christian truth. According to Christian doctrine man, endowed with a social nature, is placed on this earth, so that by leading a life in society and under an authority ordained by God [cf. Rom. 13:1] he may develop and evolve fully all his faculties to the praise and glory of his Creator; and by faithfully performing the duty of his trade, or of any other vocation, he may acquire for himself both temporal and eternal happiness. Socialism, however, entirely ignorant of this sublime end both of man and of society, and unconcerned about it, affirms that human society was instituted for material advantages alone. . . .

Catholic and socialist have contradictory meanings. But if socialism,

---

[1] AAS 23 (1931), 215 ff.

as all errors, contains some truth in itself (which, indeed, the Sovereign Pontiffs have never denied), nevertheless it is based on a doctrine of human society, peculiar to itself, and at odds with true Christianity. "Religious Socialism," "Christian Socialism" have contradictory meanings: no one can at the same time be a good Catholic and a socialist in the true sense of the word. . . .

The Universal Motherhood of the Blessed Virgin Mary [1]

[From the Encyclical, "Lux veritatis," December 25, 1931]

She (to be sure), by reason of the fact that she bore the Redeemer of 2271 the human race, in a certain manner is the most benign mother of us all, whom Christ the Lord wished to have as brothers [cf. Rom. 8:29]. Our predecessor of happy memory, Leo XIII,[2] so speaks: "Such did God show her to us, whom, by the very fact that He chose her as the Mother of His Only-begotten, He clearly endowed with maternal feelings which express nothing but love and kindness; such did Jesus Christ show her by His own deed, when He wished of His own will to be under and obedient to Mary, as son to mother; such did He declare her from the Cross when He committed her, as the whole human race, to John the disciple, to be cared for and cherished by Him" [John 19:26 f.]; such, finally, did she herself give herself, who embraced with her great spirit that heritage of great labor left by her dying Son, and immediately began to exercise her maternal duties toward all.

The False Interpretation of Two Biblical Texts [3]

[Response of the Biblical Commission, July 1, 1933]

I. Whether it is right for a Catholic person, especially when the 2272 authentic interpretation of the chief apostles has been given [Acts 2:24–33; 13:35–37], so to interpret the words of Psalm 15:10–11: "Thou wilt not leave my soul in hell; nor wilt thou give thy holy one to see corruption. Thou hast made known to me the ways of life," as if the sacred author did not speak of the resurrection of our Lord Jesus Christ? —*Reply:* In the negative.

II. Whether it is permitted to assert that the words of Jesus Christ 2273 which are read in St. Matthew 16:26: "For what doth it profit a man, if he gain the whole world, and suffer the loss of his own soul? Or what exchange shall a man give for his soul?"; and likewise the words which

---

[1] AAS 23 (1931), 514.

[2] Encyclical, *"Octobri mense,"* September 22, 1891 [ASS 24 (1891/92), 196; AL (Rome), 11, 304 f.].

[3] AAS 25 (1933) 344.

are found in St. Luke 9:25: "For what is a man advantaged, if he gain the whole world, and lose himself, and cast away himself," do not in a literal sense have reference to the eternal salvation of the soul, but only to the temporal life of man, notwithstanding the tenor of the words themselves and their context, and also the unanimous Catholic interpretation? —*Reply:* In the negative.

The Need and the Office of the Priesthood [1]

[From the Encyclical, "Ad catholici sacerdotii," December 20, 1935]

2274 The human race has always experienced the need of priests, that is, of men who, by the office lawfully entrusted to them, are mediators between God and humanity; whose entire duty in life embraces those activities which pertain to the eternal Godhead, and who offer prayers, remedies, and sacrifices in the name of society, which is obliged in very fact to cherish religion publicly, to acknowledge God as the Supreme Lord and first beginning, to propose Him as its last end, to offer Him immortal thanks, and to offer Him propitiation. In fact, among all peoples, whose customs are known, provided they are not compelled to act against the most sacred laws of nature, attendants of sacred affairs are found, although very often they serve vain superstitions, and likewise wherever men profess some religion and wherever they erect altars, far from lacking priests, they venerate them with special honors.

Yet, when divine revelation shone forth, the sacerdotal office was distinguished by greater dignity; this dignity, indeed, in a hidden manner Melchisedech, priest and king [cf. Gen. 14:18], foretells, whose example Paul the Apostle refers [cf. Heb. 5:10; 6:20; 7:1–11, 15] to the person and priesthood of Jesus Christ.

But if the attendant of sacred things, according to the famous definition of the same Paul, is a man "taken from amongst men," yet "ordained for men in the things that pertain to God" [Heb. 5:1], his office surely looks not to human and transitory things, however much they seem worthy of regard and praise, but to divine and eternal things. . . .

In the sacred writings of the Old Testament, when the priesthood was established by the norms which Moses, influenced by the instigation and urging of God, had promulgated, special functions, duties, and rites were attributed to it. . . .

The priesthood of the Old Testament derived its majesty and glory from nothing other than the fact that it foretold that priesthood of the New and eternal Testament given by Jesus Christ, namely, that established by the blood of the true God and of the true man.

---

[1] AAS 28 (1936), 8 ff.

The Apostle of the Gentiles treating summarily and briefly of the greatness, dignity, and office of the Christian priesthood expresses his opinion in these words, as it were, in a nutshell: "Let a man so account of us as of the ministers of Christ and the dispensers of the mysteries of God" [I Cor. 4:1].

The Effects of the Order of the Priesthood [1]

[From the Encyclical, "Ad catholici sacerdotii," December 20, 1935]

The minister of Christ is the priest; therefore, he is, as it were, the **2275** instrument of the divine Redeemer, that He may be able to continue through time His marvelous work which by its divine efficacy restored the entire society of men and brought it to a higher refinement. Rather, as we customarily say rightly and properly: "He is another Christ," since he enacts His role according to these words: "As the Father has sent me, I also send you" [John 20:21]; and in the same way and through the voice of the angels his Master sings: "Glory to God in the highest," and exhorts peace "to men of good will" [cf. Luke 2:14]. . . . Such powers, conferred upon the special sacrament of the priesthood, since they become imprinted on his soul with the indelible character by which, like Him whose priesthood he shares, he becomes "a priest forever" [Ps. 109:4], are not fleeting and transitory, but stable and permanent. Even if through human frailty he lapse into errors and disgraces, yet he will never be able to delete from his soul this sacerdotal character. And besides, through the sacrament of orders the priest not only acquires the sacerdotal character, not only high powers, but he is also made greater by a new and special grace, and by special helps, through which indeed— if only he will faithfully comply, by his free and personal cooperation, with the divinely efficient power of these heavenly gifts, surely he will be able worthily and with no dejection of spirit to meet the arduous duties of his ministry. . . .

From holy retreats [of spiritual exercises] of this kind such usefulness can also at times flow forth, that one, who has entered "in sortem Domini" not at the call of Christ Himself but induced by his earthly motives, may be able "to stir up the grace of God" [cf. II Tim. 1:6]; for since he is now bound to Christ and the Church by an everlasting bond, he can accordingly do nothing but adopt the words of St. Bernard: "For the future make good your ways and your ambitions and make holy your ministry; if sanctity of life did not precede, at least let it follow." [2] The grace which is commonly given by God and is given in a special

---

[1] AAS 28 (1936), 10, 15, 50 f.
[2] Ep. 27, *ad Ardut.* [ML 182, 131].

manner to him who accepts the sacrament of orders, will undoubtedly aid him, if he really desires it, no less for emending what in the beginning was planned wrongly by him, than for executing and taking care of the duties of his office.

The Divine Office, the Public Prayer of the Church [1]

[From the Encyclical, "Ad catholici sacerdotii," December 20, 1935]

2276   Finally, the priest in this matter, also, performing the work of Jesus Christ, who "passed the whole night in the prayer of God" [Luke 6:12], and "always lived to make intercession for us" [Heb. 7:25], is by office the intercessor with God for all; it is among his mandates to offer not only the proper and true sacrifice of the altar in the name of the Church to the heavenly Godhead, but also "the sacrifice of praise" [Ps. 49:14] and common prayers; he, indeed, by the psalms, the supplications, and the canticles, which are borrowed in great measure from Sacred Scripture, daily, again and again discharges the duty of adoration due to God, and he performs the necessary office of such an accomplishment for men. . . .

If private supplication is so powerful because of the solemn and great promises given by Jesus Christ [Matt. 7:7–11; Mark 11:24; Luke 11:9–13], then the prayers, which are uttered in the Office in the name of the Church, the beloved spouse of the Redeemer, without doubt enjoy greater force and virtue.

Social Justice [2]

[From the Encyclical, "Divini Redemptoris," March 19, 1937]

2277   [51] For in reality besides the justice which is called commutative, social justice also must be fostered which demands duties from which neither workingmen nor employers can withdraw themselves. Now it is the part of social justice to exact from the individual what is necessary for the common good. But just as in the case of the structure of any living body, there is no regard for the good of the whole, unless each individual member be endowed with all those things which they need to fulfill their roles, so in the case of the constitution and composition of the community, there can be no provision for the good of the whole society, unless the individual members, namely, men endowed with the dignity of personality, are supplied with all they need to exercise their social duties. If, then, provision is made for social justice, the rich fruits

---

[1] AAS 28 (1936), 18 f.
[2] AAS 29 (1937), 921.

of active zeal will grow from economic life, which will mature in an order of tranquillity, and will give proof of the strength and solidarity of the state, just as the strength of the body is discerned from its undisturbed, complete, and fruitful functioning.

[52] Social justice will not be satisfied unless workingmen can furnish for themselves and for their families a livelihood in a secure way, based on an acceptable salary consistent with reality; unless an opportunity is given them of acquiring a modest fortune for themselves, so as to avoid that plague of universal pauperism, which is so widely diffused; unless, finally, opportune plans are made for their benefit, whereby the workers by means of public or private insurances may be able to have some provision for their old age, periods of illness, and unemployment. In this connection it is well to repeat what we said in the Encyclical Letter, "Quadragesimo anno": "Then only will the economic and social order be soundly established, etc." [see n. 2265].

Resistance Against the Abuse of Power [1]

[From the Encyclical, "Firmissimam constantiam," to the Mexican Bishops, March 28, 1937]

Surely it must be granted that for the development of the Christian **2278** life external aids, which are perceptible to the senses, are necessary, and likewise that the Church, as a society of men, has great need of a just freedom of action for the enjoyment and expansion of life, and that the faithful in civil society possess the right to live according to the dictates of reason and conscience.

Consequently, then, when the natural freedoms of the religious and civil order are impugned, Catholic citizens cannot endure and suffer this. Yet the vindication of these rights and freedoms, according to attendant circumstances, can be more or less opportune, more or less strenuous.

But you yourselves, Venerable Brothers, have often taught your faithful that the Church, despite serious trouble to herself, is the supporter of peace and order, and condemns all unjust rebellion and violence against constituted powers. Yet it has also been affirmed among you that, if at any time these powers manifestly impugn justice and truth, so as to overturn the foundations of authority, it is not evident why those citizens should be condemned who unite to protect themselves, and to preserve the nation by employing licit and proper means against those who abuse power to overthrow the state.

But if the solution of this question necessarily depends on individual

[1] AAS 29 (1937), 196 f.

attendant circumstances, nevertheless some principles should be brought to light:

1. Such vindications have the nature of means, or of relative end, not of ultimate and absolute end.

2. These vindications, as means, should be licit actions, not evils in themselves.

3. Since the vindications themselves should be appropriate and proportionate to the end, they are to be applied insofar as they conduce entirely or in part to the proposed end, yet in such a manner that they do not bring greater evils to the community and justice, than the very evils to be reformed.

4. Now the uses of such means and the full exercise of civil and political rights, since they include also problems of a purely temporal and technical order or of violent defense, do not belong directly to the duty of Catholic Action, although to Catholic Action does belong the duty of instructing Catholic men in the right exercise of their proper rights, and in the defense of the same by just means, according to the demand of the common good.

5. The clergy and Catholic Action, since, because of the mission of peace and love entrusted to them, they are bound to unite all men "in the bond of peace" [Eph. 4:3], should contribute very much to the prosperity of the nation, both by encouraging the union of citizens and classes, and by supporting all social initiatives which are not at odds with the doctrine and moral law of Christ.

PIUS XII 1939–

The Natural Law [1]

[From the Encyclical, "Summi Pontificatus," October 20, 1939]

2279   It is well established that the first and profound source of the evils by which the modern state is afflicted, issues from this fact, that the universal standard of morality is denied and rejected, not only in the private life of individuals but also in the state itself, and in the mutual relationships which exist between races and nations; that is, the natural law is being nullified by detraction and neglect.

This natural law rests on God as its foundation, the omnipotent creator and author of all, and likewise the supreme and most perfect legislator, the most wise and just vindicator of human actions. When the eternal Godhead is rashly denied, then the principle of all probity totters and sways, and the voice of nature becomes silent, or gradually is weak-

---

[1] AAS 31 (1939), 423.

ened, which teaches the unlearned as well as those who have not as yet acquired the experience of civilization what is right and what is not right; what is permitted, and what is not permitted, and warns them that some day they must render an account for their good and evil deeds before the Supreme Judge.

The Natural Unity of the Human Race [1]

[From the same Encyclical, "Summi Pontificatus," October 20, 1939]

[Pernicious error] is contained in the forgetfulness of that mutual 2280 relationship between men and of the love which both a common origin and the equality of the rational nature of all men demands, to whatever races they belong. . . . The Bible narrates that from the first marriage of man and woman all other men took their origin; and these, it relates, were divided into various tribes and nations, and were scattered over various parts of the world. . . . [Acts 17:26]: Therefore, by a wonderful insight of mind we can behold and contemplate the human race as a unity, because of its common origin from the Creator, according to these words: "One God and Father of all, who is above all, and through all, and in us all" [Eph. 4:6]; and likewise, one in nature which consists of the materiality of the body and of the immortal and spiritual soul. . . .

International Law [2]

[From the same Encyclical, "Summi Pontificatus," October 20, 1939]

Venerable Brothers, that opinion which attributes almost infinite 2281 power to the state not only is an error fatal to the internal life of nations and to the promotion of greater growth, but also does harm to the mutual relations of peoples, since it infringes upon that unity by which all nations should be contained in their relations with one another, strips international laws of their force and strength, and, paving the way to the violation of other laws, renders it very difficult for them to live together in peace and tranquillity.

For the human race, although by the law of natural order established by God it is disposed into classes of citizens, and likewise into nations and states, yet is bound by mutual bonds in juridical and moral affairs, and coalesces into a single great congregation of peoples destined to pursue the common good of all nations, and is ruled by special norms which both preserve unity and direct them daily to more prosperous circumstances.

---

[1] AAS 31 (1939), 426 f.
[2] AAS 31 (1939), 437 ff.

Surely, there is no one who does not see, if rights are claimed for the state, which is quite absolute and responsible to no one, that this is entirely opposed to naturally ingrained law, and wholly refutes it; and it is clear, likewise, that such rights place at the discretion of rulers of the state the bonds lawfully agreed upon by which nations are joined to one another; and they impede an honest agreement of minds and mutual collaboration for helpful action. If, Venerable Brothers, properly organized and long lasting understandings between states demand this, the bonds of friendship, from which rich fruits arise, demand that peoples recognize the principles and norms of the natural law by which nations are joined to one another, and be obedient to the same. In similar fashion these same principles demand that for every nation its own liberty be preserved, and that those rights be assigned to all by which they may live and may advance day by day on the road of civil progress to more prosperous circumstances; finally, they demand that pacts entered upon, as exacted and sanctioned by international law, remain unimpaired and inviolable.

There is no doubt that then only can nations live peacefully together, then only can they be governed publicly by established bonds, when mutual trust exists between them; when all are convinced that the trust given will be preserved on both sides; finally when all accept these words as certain, "better is wisdom than weapons of war" [cf. Eccles. 9:18]; and, furthermore, when all are prepared to inquire into and discuss a matter more extensively, but not by force and threats to bring about a critical situation, if delays, disputes, difficulties, changes of front stand in the way, all of which indeed can arise not only from bad faith but also from a change of circumstances and from a mutual clash of individual interests.

But then to separate the law of nations from the divine law, so that it depends upon the arbitrary decisions of the rulers of the state as its only foundation, is nothing other than to pull it down from its throne of honor and security, and to hand it over to a zeal which is excessive and concerned with private and public advantage, and which strives for nothing other than to assert its own rights and deny those of others.

2282   Surely, it must be affirmed that in the course of time, because of serious changes in attendant circumstances—which, while the pact was being made, were not foreseen, or perhaps could not even have been foreseen— either entire agreements or certain parts of these sometimes become unjust to either of the stipulating parties, or could seem so, or at least turn out exceedingly severe, or, finally, become such that they cannot be carried out to advantage. If this should happen refuge must necessarily, of course, be taken in a sincere and honest discussion, with a view to making opportune changes in the pact, or to composing an entirely new one. But, on the other hand, to hold proper pacts as fluid and fleeting things, and to attribute to oneself the tacit power, as often as one's own advantage seems to demand this, of infringing on the same of one's own free will, that is, without consulting, and overlooking the other party in the pact, certainly deprives states of due and mutual trust; and so the order of nature is completely destroyed, and peoples and nations are separated from one another as by precipitous and deep chasms.

Sterilization [1]

[Decree of the Holy Office, February 24, 1940]

To the question proposed to the Supreme Sacred Congregation of the 2283 Holy Office; "Whether direct sterilization, either perpetual or temporary, is permitted on a man or a woman," the Most Eminent and Reverend Fathers, Doctors, and Cardinals, appointed to guard matters of faith and morals, on Thursday, the 21st day of February, 1940, have decided that the following answer must be given:

"In the negative, and indeed that it is prohibited by the law of nature, and that, insofar as it pertains to eugenic sterilization, it has already been disapproved by the decree of this Congregation, on the 21st day of March, 1931.

The Corporal Origin of Man [2]

[From an address of Pius XII November 30, 1941,
at the beginning of the year of the Pontifical
Academy of Sciences]

God has placed man in the highest place in the scale of living creatures; 2285 endowed, as he is, with a spiritual soul, the chief and the highest of all the animal kingdom. Manifold investigations in the fields of paleontology, biology, and morphology regarding other questions concerning the origin of man have thus far produced nothing clear and certain in a positive way. Therefore, we can only leave for the future the reply to the question, whether some day, science illumined and guided by revelation will offer certain and definite solutions to so serious a question.

Members of the Church [3]

[From the Encyclical, "Mystici Corporis," June 29, 1943]

Actually only those are to be numbered among the members of the 2286 Church who have received the laver of regeneration and profess the true

---

[1] AAS 32 (1940), 73.

[2] AAS 33 (1941), 506.

[3] AAS 35 (1943), 202 f.

faith, and have not, to their misfortune, separated themselves from the structure of the Body, or for very serious sins have not been excluded by lawful authority. "For in one spirit," says the Apostle, "were we all baptized into one Body, whether Jews or Gentiles, whether bond or free" [I Cor. 12:13]. So, just as in the true community of the faithful of Christ there is only one Body, one Spirit, one Lord, and one Baptism, so there can be only one faith [cf. Eph. 4:5]; and so he who refuses to hear the Church, as the Lord bids "let him be as the heathen and publican" [cf. Matt. 18:17]. Therefore, those who are divided from one another in faith or in government cannot live in the unity of such a body, and in its one divine spirit.

The Jurisdiction of Bishops [1]

[From the same Encyclical, "Mystici Corporis," June 29, 1943]

2287   Therefore, the bishops of the sacred rites are to be considered as the more illustrious members of the Universal Church not only because they are bound with the divine Head of the whole Body by a very special bond, and so are rightly called "principal parts of the members of the Lord," [2] but, as far as each one's own diocese is concerned, because as true shepherds they individually feed and rule in the name of Christ the flocks entrusted to them [Conc. Vat., *Const. de Eccl.,* cap. 3; see n. 1828]; yet while they do this, they are not entirely independent, but are placed under the due authority of the Roman Pontiff, although they enjoy the ordinary power of jurisdiction obtained directly from the same Highest Pontiff. So they should be revered by the people as divinely appointed successors of the apostles [cf. *Cod. Iur. Can.,* can. 329, 1]; and more than to the rulers of the world, even the highest, are those words befitting to our bishops, inasmuch as they have been anointed with the chrism of the Holy Spirit: "Touch ye not my anointed" [I Par. 16, 22; Ps. 104:15].

The Holy Spirit as the Soul of the Church [3]

[From the same Encyclical, "Mystici Corporis," June 29, 1943]

2288   If we closely examine this divine principle of life and virtue given by Christ, insofar as He established it as the source of every gift and created grace, we easily understand that this is nothing else than the Paraclete, the Spirit, who proceeds from the Father and the Son, and who in a special manner is called "the Spirit of Christ," or "the Spirit of the Son" [Rom.

---

[1] AAS 35 (1943), 211 f.
[2] Greg. the Great, *Moral.,* XIV, 35, 43; ML 75, 1062.
[3] AAS 35 (1943), 218 ff.

8:9; II Cor. 3:17; Gal. 4:6]. For by this Breath of grace and truth did the Son of God anoint His soul in the uncontaminated womb of the Virgin; this Spirit holds it a delight to dwell in the beloved soul of the Redeemer as in His most beloved temple; this Spirit, Christ by shedding His own blood merited for us on the Cross; this Spirit, finally, when He breathed upon the apostles, He bestowed on the Church for the remission of sins [cf. John 20:22]; and, while Christ alone received this Spirit according to no measure [cf. John 3:34], yet to the members of the mystical body He is imparted only according to the measure of the giving of Christ, out of Christ's own fullness [cf. Eph. 1:8; 4:7]. And after Christ was glorified on the Cross, His Spirit is communicated to the Church in the richest effusion, that she and her individual members may more and more daily become like our Savior. It is the Spirit of Christ that has made us God's adopted sons [cf. Rom. 8:14–17; Gal. 4:6–7], that someday "we all beholding the glory of God with open face may be transformed into the the same image from glory to glory" [II Cor. 3:18].

Moreover, to this Spirit of Christ as to no visible principle is this also to be attributed, that all parts of the Body are joined to one another as they are with their exalted head; for He is entire in the Head, entire in the Body, entire in the individual members, and with these He is present, and these He assists in various ways, according to their various duties and offices, according to the greater or less degree of spiritual health which they enjoy. He is the one who by His heavenly grace is to be held as the principle of every vital and in fact every salutary act in all the parts of any body. He is the one who, although He Himself is present of Himself in all members, and is divinely active in the same, yet in the inferior members also operates through the ministry of the higher members; finally, He is the one who, while He always day by day produces the growth of the Church by imparting grace, yet refuses to dwell through sanctifying grace in members wholly cut off from the Body. Indeed, the presence and activity of the Spirit of Jesus Christ are succinctly and vigorously expressed by Our most wise predecessor, Leo XIII, of immortal memory in the Encyclical, "Divinum illud," in these words: "Let it suffice to state this, that, as Christ is the Head of the Church, the Holy Spirit is her soul." [1]

Knowledge of the Soul of Christ [2]

[From the same Encyclical, "Mystici Corporis," June 29, 1943]

But such a most loving knowledge as the divine Redeemer from the **2289** first moment of His Incarnation bestowed upon us, surpasses any zealous

---

[1] ASS 29 (1896), 650.
[2] ASS 35 (1943), 230.

power of the human mind; since through that beatific vision, which He began to enjoy when He had hardly been conceived in the womb of the Mother of God, He has the members of His mystical body always and constantly present to Him, and He embraces all with His redeeming love.

The Indwelling of the Holy Spirit in Souls [1]

[From the same Encyclical, "Mystici Corporis," June 29, 1943]

2290   Surely we are not ignorant of the many veils that stand in the way of our understanding and explaining this profound doctrine, which is concerned with our union with the divine Redeemer, and with the indwelling of the Holy Spirit in a special way in souls; veils by which this profound doctrine is enveloped as by a kind of cloud, because of the weakness of the minds of those who make inquiry. And we know also that from correct and persistent investigation of this subject, and from the conflict of various opinions and the clash of ideas, provided love of truth and due obedience to the Church direct such investigations, precious light abounds and comes forth, by which also in the sacred science akin to this actual progress is attained. Therefore, we do not censure those who enter upon diverse ways and methods of reasoning to understand, and according to their power to clarify the mystery of this marvelous union of ours with Christ. But let this be a general and unshaken truth, if they do not wish to wander from sound doctrine and the correct teaching of the Church: namely, that every kind of mystic union, by which the faithful in Christ in any way pass beyond the order of created things and wrongly enter among the divine, so that even a single attribute of the eternal Godhead can be predicated of these as their own, is to be entirely rejected. And, besides, let them hold this with a firm mind as most certain, that all activities in these matters are to be held as common to the Most Holy Trinity, insofar as they depend upon God as the supreme efficient cause.

Let them note also that there necessarily is here a question of a hidden mystery, which in this earthly exile, being covered by a veil, can never be looked into or be described by human tongue. Indeed, the divine Persons are said to indwell inasmuch as being present in an inscrutable manner in animate creatures endowed with intellect they are attained by them through knowledge and love,[2] yet in a manner intimate and unique that transcends all nature. Indeed, to contemplate this so as at least to approach it slightly, that way and method are not to be overlooked which the Vatican Synod [sess. 3, *Const. de fid. cath.*, cap. 4; see n. 1795] strongly recommended in matters of this kind; this method,

---

[1] AAS 35 (1943), 231 f.

[2] Cf. St. Thomas, *Summa theol.*, Ia, q. 43, a. 3.

indeed, struggling to obtain light by which the hidden things of God may be recognized at least slightly, proceeds thus, comparing these mysteries with one another and with the final end to which they are directed. Opportunely then does Our very wise predecessor, Leo XIII of happy memory, when he spoke of this union of ours with Christ and of the divine Paraclete dwelling within us, turn His eyes to that beatific vision by which at sometime in heaven this same mystic union will obtain its consummation and perfection. He says: "This wonderful union, which is called by the name 'indwelling,' differs only by our created state from that by which God gives joy and embraces the inhabitants of heaven." [1] In this heavenly vision it will be proper in an utterly ineffable manner to contemplate the Father, Son, and divine Spirit with the eyes of the mind increased by the higher light, and to assist throughout eternity at the processions of the divine Persons, and to rejoice with a happiness very like that with which the most holy and undivided Trinity is happy.

The Relationship between the B.V.M. and the Church [2]

[From the same Encyclical, "Mystici Corporis," June 29, 1943]

It was she [the Virgin Mother of God] who, free from sin either   2291
personal or original, always most closely united with her Son, offered Him on Golgotha to the Eternal Father, together with the holocaust of her mother's rights and mother's love, as a new Eve, for all the sons of Adam stained by his pitiful fall, so that she, who in the flesh was the mother of our Head, by the new title also of grief and glory, in the spirit was made the mother of all His members. She it was who by very powerful prayers accomplished that the Spirit of the divine Redeemer, already given on the Cross, should be bestowed with wonderful gifts on the day of Pentecost upon the recently risen Church. Finally, she herself by enduring her tremendous griefs with a strong and confident spirit, more than all the faithful of Christ, the true Queen of the Martyrs, "filled up those things that are wanting of the sufferings of Christ . . . for His Body, which is the Church" [Col. 1:24]; and she has attended the mystical body of Christ, born [3] of the torn heart of our Savior, with the same mother's care and deep love with which she cherished and nurtured the Infant Jesus nursing in the crib.

So may she, the most holy Mother [4] of all the members of Christ, to whose Immaculate Heart We have confidently consecrated all men, and

---

[1] Cf. "Divinum illud"; ASS 29 (1896), 653.

[2] AAS 35 (1943), 247 f.

[3] Cf. *Off. Ssmi. Cordis, in hymno ad Vesp.*

[4] Cf. Pius X, "Ad diem illum": ASS 36 (1903/04), 453.

who now is resplendent in heaven in the glory of body and soul, and reigns together with her Son, earnestly request and strive to obtain from Him that copious streams of grace flow from the exalted Head upon all the members of the mystical body without interruption.

The Authenticity of the Vulgate [1]

[From the Encyclical, "Divino afflante Spiritu," September 30, 1943]

2292   But that the Synod of Trent wished the Vulgate to be the Latin version "which all should use as authentic," applies, as all know, to the Latin Church only, and to the public use of Scripture, and does not diminish the authority and force of the early texts. For at that time no consideration was being given to early texts, but to the Latin versions which were being circulated at that time, among which the Council decreed that that version was rightly to be preferred which was approved by the long use of so many centuries within the Church. So this eminent authority of the Vulgate, or, as it is expressed, *authenticity,* was established by the Council not especially for critical reasons, but rather because of its authorized use in the Church continued through the course of so many centuries; and by this use it is demonstrated that this text, as the Church has understood and understands, in matters of faith and morals is entirely free of error, so that, on the testimony and confirmation of the Church herself, in discussions, quotations, and meetings it can be cited safely and without danger of error; and accordingly such authenticity is expressed primarily not by the term *critical* but rather *juridical.* Therefore, this authority of the Vulgate in matters of doctrine does not at all prevent—rather it almost demands today—this same doctrine being called upon for help, whereby the correct meaning of Sacred Scripture may daily be made clearer and be better explained. And not even this is prohibited by the decree of the Council of Trent, namely, that for the use and benefit of the faithful in Christ and for the easier understanding of divine works translations be made into common languages; and these, too, from the early texts, as we know has already been praiseworthily done with the approval of the authority of the Church in many regions.

The Literal and Mystical Sense of Holy Scripture [2]

[From the same Encyclical, "Divino afflante Spiritu," September 30, 1943]

2293   Well equipped with a knowledge of ancient languages and with the help of critical scholarship, let the Catholic exegete approach that task

---

[1] AAS 35 (1943), 309 f.
[2] AAS 35 (1943), 310 f.

which of all those imposed upon him is the highest, namely, to discover and set forth the true meaning of the Sacred Scriptures. In this work let interpreters keep in mind that their greatest care should be to discern and define what the so-called *literal* sense of the language of the Bible is. Let them bring out this *literal* meaning of the words with all diligence through a knowledge of languages, employing the aid of the context and of comparison with similar passages; indeed, all these are customarily used for assistance in the interpretation of profane writers also, so that the mind of the author may become quite clear. Moreover, let the exegetes of Sacred Scriptures, mindful of the fact that they are dealing with the divinely inspired word, no less diligently take into account the explanations and declarations of the *magisterium* of the Church, and likewise the explanation given by the Holy Fathers, and also the "analogy of faith," as Leo XIII in the Encyclical letter, *Providentissimus Deus,* very wisely notes.[1] Indeed, let them see to this with special zeal, that they explain not only those matters which are of concern to history, archaeology, philology, and other such disciplines as we grieve to say is done in certain commentaries, but, after bringing in such matters opportunely, insofar as they can contribute to exegesis, point out especially what is the theological doctrine on matters of faith and morals in the individual books and texts, so that this explanation of theirs may not only help teachers of theology to set forth and confirm the dogmas of faith, but also be of assistance to priests in clarifying Christian doctrine to the people, and finally serve all the faithful to lead holy lives worthy of a Christian.

When they have given such an interpretation, especially, as we have said, theological interpretation, let them effectively silence those who assert that with difficulty do they find anything by way of Biblical commentary to raise the mind to God, nourish the soul, and promote the interior life, and declare that recourse must be had to a certain spiritual and so-called mystical interpretation. How far from rightly they profess this the experience of many shows, who frequently considering and meditating upon the word of God, perfect their souls, and are moved by a strong love toward God; and this is clearly proved by the everlasting institution of the Church and the admonitions of the most eminent Doctors. Surely, all spiritual meaning is not excluded from Sacred Scripture. For what was said and done in the Old Testament, was most wisely so ordered and disposed by God that past events in a spiritual manner presignified what would take place in the new covenant of grace. So the exegete, just as he should find and expound the so-called *literal* significance of the words, which the sacred writer intended and expressed, so also he should the spiritual significance, provided it can be

[1] Leo XIII, *Acta* XIII, pp. 345–346; *Ench. Bibl.* n. 94–96.

rightly established that it was given by God. For God alone could know this spiritual significance and reveal it to us. Indeed, the divine Savior Himself indicates such a sense to us in the Holy Gospels and teaches us; the apostles, also, imitating the example of the Master, in speaking and writing profess this; so does the teaching handed down by the Church; finally, the ancient practice of the liturgy declares, wherever that famous pronouncement can rightly be applied: The law of praying is the law of believing. So, let Catholic exegetes make clear and set forth this spiritual sense, intended and ordained by God Himself, with that diligence which the dignity of the divine Word demands; but let them beware religiously lest they proclaim other transferred meanings of things as the genuine sense of Sacred Scripture.

Kinds of Literature in Holy Scripture [1]

[From the same Encyclical, "Divino afflante Spiritu," September 30, 1943]

2294　　Therefore, let the interpreter with all care and without neglect of the light which the more recent investigations have shed, strive to discern what the real character and condition of life of the sacred writer were; in what age he flourished; what sources he used whether written or oral, and what forms of expression he employed. Thus he will be able to know better who the sacred writer was, and what he wished to indicate by his writing. For it escapes no one that the highest norm of interpretation is that by which what the writer intends to say is perceived and defined, as St. Athanasius advises: "Here, as it is fitting to do in all other passages of divine Scripture, we observe that it must be accurately and faithfully considered on what occasion the Apostle has spoken; what is the person and what is the subject on which he has written, lest anyone ignorant of these things, or understanding something else besides them, wander from the true meaning." [2]

But what the literal sense is in the words and writings of the old oriental authors is very often not as clear as it is among the writers of our age. For what they wish to signify by words is not determined by the laws of grammar or philology alone, nor by the context of the passage alone; the interpreter should by all means return mentally, as it were, to those remote ages of the Orient, in order that rightly assisted by the aid of history, archaeology, ethnology, and of other disciplines, he may discern and perceive what so-called literary genres the writers of that age sought to employ and in fact did employ. For the old Orientals, to express what they had in mind, did not always use the same forms and

---

[1] AAS 35 (1943), 314 f.
[2] *Contra Arianos,* I, 54: MG XXVI, col. 123.

the same modes of speaking as we do today, but rather those which were accepted for use among men of their own times and localities. What these were, the exegete cannot determine, as it were, in advance, but only by an accurate investigation of the ancient literatures of the Orient. Furthermore, such investigation carried on within the last ten years with greater care and diligence than before, has shown more clearly what forms of speaking were employed in those ancient times, whether in describing matters in poetry, or in proposing norms and laws of life, or finally in narrating the facts and events of history. This same investigation has also proven this clearly, that the people of Israel were especially pre-eminent among the rest of the ancient nations of the Orient in writing history properly, both because of the antiquity and the faithful recountal of events; which indeed, is surely the effect of divine inspiration, and the result of the special purpose of biblical history which pertains to religion. Indeed, let no one who has a right understanding of Biblical inspiration, be surprised that among the Sacred Writers, as among the other ancients, certain definite ways of explaining and narrating are found; certain kinds of idioms especially appropriate to Semitic languages, so called *approximations,* and certain hyperbolic methods of speaking, yes, sometimes even paradoxes by which events are more firmly impressed upon the mind. For none of those methods of speaking is foreign to the Sacred Scriptures which among ancient peoples, especially among Orientals, human speech customarily used to express its thought, yet on this condition, that the kind of speaking employed be not at odds with the sanctity and truth of God, just as with his usual perspicacity the Angelic Doctor has noted in the following words: "In Scripture divine matters are made known to us in the manner we customarily employ." [1] For just as the substantial Word of God was made like man in all things "without sin," [2] so also the words of God, expressed in human language, in all things have been made like human speech, without error, which Saint John Chrysostom has already extolled with highest praise as the συνκατάβασις, or, condescension of a provident God; and which he has asserted [3] again and again is the case in the Sacred Scriptures. Therefore, let the Catholic exegete, in order to satisfy the present day needs of Biblical matters, in explaining Sacred Scripture, and in showing and proving it free of all error, prudently use this aid, to inquire how the form of expression and the kind of literature employed by the Sacred writer, contribute to a true and genuine interpretation; and let him be convinced that this part of his office cannot be neglected

---

[1] *Comment. ad Heb.,* cap. I, lect. 4.

[2] Heb. 4:15.

[3] Cf. *In Gen.* I: 4 (MG LIII, col. 34–35); *In Gen.* II: 21 (*ibid.,* col. 121); *In Gen.* III: 8 (*ibid.,* col. 135); *Hom. 15 in Ioan.,* ad I, 18 (MG LIX, col. 27 f.).

without great harm to Catholic exegesis. For not uncommonly—to touch upon one thing only—when some propose by way of rebuke that the Sacred Authors have strayed away from historical truth, or have not reported events accurately, it is found to be a question of nothing other than the customary natural methods of the ancients in speaking and narrating, which in the mutual intercourse among men were regularly employed, and in fact were employed in accord with a permissible and common practice. Therefore, intellectual honesty requires that when these matters are found in divine speech which is expressed for man in human words, they be not charged more with error than when they are uttered in the daily use of life. Therefore, by a knowledge and accurate appraisal of the modes and skills of speaking and writing among the ancients, many problems will be possible of solution, which are raised against the truth and historical trustworthiness of the divine Scripture; and no less fittingly will such study contribute to a fuller and clearer understanding of the mind of the Sacred Writer.

The Purposes of Matrimony [1]

[Decree of the Holy Office, April 1, 1944]

2295 Certain publications concerning the purposes of matrimony, and their interrelationship and order, have come forth within these last years which either assert that the primary purpose of matrimony is not the generation of offspring, or that the secondary purposes are not subordinate to the primary purpose, but are independent of it.

In these works different primary purposes of marriage are designated by other writers, as for example: the complement and personal perfection of the spouses through a complete mutual participation in life and action; mutual love and union of spouses to be nurtured and perfected by the psychic and bodily surrender of one's own person; and many other such things.

In the same writings a sense is sometimes attributed to words in the current documents of the Church (as for example, primary, secondary purpose), which does not agree with these words according to the common usage by theologians.

This revolutionary way of thinking and speaking aims to foster errors and uncertainties, to avoid which the Most Eminent and Very Reverend Fathers of this supreme Sacred Congregation, charged with the guarding of matters of faith and morals, in a plenary session, on Wednesday, the 29th of March, 1944, when the question was proposed to them: "Whether the opinion of certain recent persons can be admitted, who either deny

---

[1] AAS 36 (1944), 103.

that the primary purpose of matrimony is the generation and raising of offspring, or teach that the secondary purposes are not essentially subordinate to the primary purpose, but are equally first and independent," have decreed that the answer must be: In the negative.

Millenarianism (Chiliasm) [1]

[Decree of the Holy Office, July 21, 1944]

In recent times on several occasions this Supreme Sacred Congregation 2296 of the Holy Office has been asked what must be thought of the system of mitigated Millenarianism, which teaches, for example, that Christ the Lord before the final judgment, whether or not preceded by the resurrection of the many just, will come visibly to rule over this world. The answer is: The system of mitigated Millenarianism cannot be taught safely.

The Presence of Christ in the Mysteries of the Church [2]

[From the Encyclical, "Mediator Dei," November 20, 1947]

In every liturgical act there is present together with the Church her 2297 divine Founder; Christ is present in the august Sacrifice of the altar, not only in the person of His minister, but especially in the species of the Eucharist; He is present in the sacraments through His power which He transfuses into them as instruments for effecting sanctity; finally, He is present in the praises and supplications directed to God, according to these words: "For where there are two or three gathered together in my name, there am I in the midst of them" [Matt. 18:20]. . . .

Therefore, the liturgical year, which the piety of the Church fosters and follows, is no cold and indifferent representation of those things which belong to times of the past, or a simple and bare recollection of things of an earlier age. But rather, it is Christ Himself, who perseveres in His Church, and who is pursuing the way of His great mercy; indeed, when He made His way through this mortal life doing good,[3] He entered upon it with this purpose, that His mysteries might penetrate the minds of men and that through them in some way they might live; and these mysteries surely are present and operate continuously not in that uncertain and obscure manner about which certain more recent writers babble, but in the manner that is taught us by the Church; since, according to the opinion of the Doctors of the Church, the ex-

---

[1] AAS 36 (1944), 212.
[2] AAS 39 (1947), 528, 580.
[3] Cf. Acts 10:38.

amples of Christian perfection are pre-eminent, and the sources of divine grace, because of the merits and deprecations of Christ and by their effect endure in us, although they exist individually in their own way according to each one's own character for the sake of our salvation.

The Full Notion of Liturgy [1]

[From the same Encyclical, "Mediator Dei," November 20, 1947]

2298 The sacred Liturgy, then, constitutes the public worship which our Redeemer, the Head of the Church, has shown to the heavenly Father; and which the society of the faithful in Christ attribute to their Founder, and through Him to the eternal Father; and, to sum up briefly, it constitutes the public worship of the mystical body of Jesus Christ, namely, the Head and its members.

Therefore, they wander entirely away from the true and full notion and understanding of the Sacred Liturgy, who consider it only as an external part of divine worship, and presented to the senses; or as a kind of apparatus of ceremonial proprieties; and they no less err who think of it as a mere compendium of laws and precepts, by which the ecclesiastical Hierarchy bids the sacred rites to be arranged and ordered.

The Relationship Between the Ascetic Life and the Piety of the Liturgy [2]

[From the same Encyclical, "Mediator Dei," November 20, 1947]

2299 Therefore in the spiritual life there can be no difference and no conflict between that divine action which infuses grace into souls to perpetuate our redemption, and the kindred and laborious work of man which should not render [3] God's gift in vain; and likewise between the efficacy of the external rite of the sacraments, which arises *ex opere operato* (from an accomplished task), and a well deserving act on the part of those who partake of and accept the sacraments; which act indeed we call *opus operantis* (the work of the worker); and in like manner between public supplications and private prayers; between the right way of acting and the contemplation of supernal things; between the ascetic life and the piety of the Liturgy; and, finally, between the jurisdiction of the ecclesiastical Hierarchy and that legitimate *magisterium* and that power, which are properly called sacerdotal, and which are exercised in the sacred ministry.

---

[1] AAS 39 (1947), 528 f., 532.
[2] AAS 39 (1947), 537.
[3] Cf. II. Cor. 6:1.

For serious cause the Church urges that those who serve the altar as an intrusted duty, or who have entered an institution of the religious life devote [1] themselves at stated times to pious meditation, to diligent self examination and criticism, and other spiritual exercises, since they are appointed in a special way to the liturgical functions of regularly performing the Sacrifice and of offering due praise. Without doubt liturgical prayer, since it is the public supplication of the illustrious Spouse of Jesus Christ, stands out with greater excellence than private prayers. But this greater excellence by no means indicates that these two kinds of prayer are different from and at odds with each other. For, since they are animated by one and the same zeal, they also come together and are united according to these words: "Christ is all and in all" [Col. 3:11], and strive for the same purposes, until Christ be formed in us. [2]

The Participation of the Faithful in the Priesthood of Christ [3]

[From the same Encyclical, "Mediator Dei," November 20, 1947]

It is expedient that all the faithful in Christ understand that it is their   **2300** supreme duty and dignity to participate in the Eucharistic Sacrifice. . . .

Yet, because the faithful in Christ participate in the Eucharistic Sacrifice, they do not on this account enjoy sacerdotal power. It is indeed quite necessary that you keep this clearly before the eyes of your flocks.

For there are those . . . who today revive errors long since condemned, and teach that in the New Testament the name "priesthood" includes all who have been cleansed by the water of baptism; and likewise that that precept by which Jesus Christ at the Last Supper entrusted to the apostles the doing of what He Himself had done, pertained directly to the entire Church of the faithful in Christ; and that hence, and hence only, has arisen the hierarchical priesthood. Therefore, they imagine that the people enjoy true sacerdotal power, but that the priest acts only by virtue of an office delegated by the community. So they believe that the Eucharistic Sacrifice is truly called a "concelebration," and they think that it is more expedient for priests standing together with the people to "concelebrate" than to offer the Sacrifice privately in the absence of the people.

It is superfluous to explain how captious errors of this kind contradict those truths which we have stated above, when treating of the rank

---

[1] Cf. *CIC* can. 125, 126, 565, 571, 595, 1367.

[2] Cf. Gal. 4:19.

[3] AAS 39 (1947), 552 ff.

Translator's note: In the 30th edition the numeration of nos. 2300 to 2333 is corrected. In previous editions no. 2300 had been 3000. Note in indexes of previous editions.

which the priest enjoys in the mystical body of Christ. Yet we think that we must call this to mind namely, that the priest acts in place of the people only for this reason, that he plays the part of our Lord, Jesus Christ, insofar as He is the Head of all the members, and offers himself for them, and that for this reason he approaches the altar as a minister of Christ, inferior to Christ, but superior to the people.[1] The people, on the other hand, inasmuch as they do not in any way play the part of the divine Redeemer, and are not a conciliator between themselves and God, can by no means enjoy the sacerdotal right.

All this, indeed, is established by the certitude of faith; yet, furthermore, the faithful in Christ are also to be said to offer the divine victim, but in a different way.

Now some of Our predecessors and doctors of the Church have declared this very clearly. "Not only," says Innocent III of immortal memory, "do the priests offer the Sacrifice, but all the faithful also; for what is specially fulfilled by the ministry of the priests, this is done collectively by the prayers of the faithful."[2] And it is pleasing to bring to bear on this subject at least one of the many statements of St. Robert Bellarmine: "The Sacrifice," he says, "is offered chiefly in the person of Christ. And so the oblation that follows the Consecration is a kind of attestation that the whole Church consents in the oblation made by Christ, and offers it at the same time with him."[3]

The rite and the prayers of the Eucharistic Sacrifice no less clearly point out and show that the oblation of the victim is performed by the priests together with the people. . . .

It is not surprising that the faithful of Christ are raised to such a dignity. For, by the waters of baptism, by the general title of Christian they are made members of the mystical body of Christ, the priest, and by the "character", as it were, imprinted upon their souls, they are assigned to divine worship; and so they participate in the priesthood of Christ Himself according to their condition. . . .

But there is also a very profound reason why all Christians, especially those who are present at the altar, are said to offer the Sacrifice.

In this very important subject, lest insidious error arise, we should limit the word "offer" by terms of exact meaning. For that unbloody immolation, by which, when the words of consecration are uttered, Christ is made present on the altar in the state of a victim, is performed by the priest alone, because he bears the role of Christ, and not because he plays the role of the faithful in Christ. And so, because the priest places the victim upon the altar, he offers to God the Father, the same

---

[1] Cf. S. Robert Bellarm., *De Missa* 2, c. 4.

[2] *De sacro Altaris mysterio* 3, 6.

[3] *De Missa* 1, c. 24.

Victim by which he offers an oblation for the glory of the Most Holy Trinity and for the good of the whole Church. But the faithful in Christ participate in this oblation in a restricted sense in their own fashion, and in a twofold manner, namely, because they offer the Sacrifice not only through the hands of the priest, but also, in a manner, together with him; indeed, because of this participation the oblation of the people is also referred to the liturgical worship.

Moreover, it is clear that the faithful in Christ offer the Sacrifice through the hands of the priest from this, that the minister at the altar plays the part of Christ, as of the Head, making His offering in the name of all His members, whereby indeed it happens that the whole Church is rightly said to offer the oblation of the Victim through Christ. But that the people together with the priest himself offer the Sacrifice is not established because of this, because the members of the Church, just as the priest himself, perform a visible liturgical rite, which belongs only to the minister divinely assigned to this; but for the reason that they join their prayer of praise, impetration, expiation, and thanksgiving with the prayers or intention of the priest, even of the High Priest Himself; so that in the very same oblation of the Victim, also according to an external rite by the priest, they may be presented to God, the Father. For the external rite must by its very nature manifest internal worship; but the Sacrifice of the New Law signifies that supreme allegiance by means of which the principal Offerer Himself, who is Christ, and together with Him and through Him all of His mystical members attend and venerate God with due honor.

The Material and Form of the Sacrament of Orders [1]

[Apostolic Constitution, "Sacramentum Ordinis," November 30, 1947]

1. The sacrament of orders instituted by Christ the Lord, by which **2301** spiritual power is handed down and grace is conferred to perform ecclesiastical duties properly, the Catholic faith professes to be one and the same for the universal Church. . . . And for these sacraments instituted by Christ the Lord in the course of the ages the Church has not, and could not substitute other sacraments, since, as the Council of Trent teaches, the seven sacraments of the New Law have all been instituted by Jesus Christ, our Lord, and the Church has no power over the "substance of the sacraments," that is, over those things which, with the sources of divine revelation as witnesses, Christ the Lord Himself decreed to be preserved in a sacramental sign. . . .

3. It is established moreover, among all that the sacraments of the

---

[1] AAS 40 (1948), 5–7.

New Law, as sensible and efficient signs of invisible grace, owe and signify the grace which they effect, and effect the grace which they signify. Indeed the effects which should be produced and so signified by the sacred ordination of the diaconate, presbyterate, and episcopate, namely, power and grace, are found to have been sufficiently signified in all the rites of the universal Church of different times and regions by the imposition of hands, and by the words that determine this. Furthermore, there is no one who does know that the Roman Church always considered valid the ordinations conferred in the Greek rite, without the handing over of the instruments, so that at the Council of Florence, in which the union of the Greeks with the Church of Rome was accomplished, it was not imposed on the Greeks that they change the rite of ordination, or that they insert in it the tradition of the instruments; rather, the Church wished that in the City itself (Rome) Greeks be ordained according to their own rite. From all this it is gathered that according to the mind of the Council of Florence the tradition of the instruments is not required for the substance and validity of this sacrament, according to the will of our Lord Jesus Christ Himself. But if, according to the will and prescription of the Church, the same should some day be held necessary for validity also, all would know that the Church is able even to change and to abrogate what she has established.

4. Since these things are so, invoking divine light by Our supreme apostolic authority and certain knowledge We declare, and, according as there is need, decree, and determine that the matter of sacred orders of the diaconate, priesthood, and episcopate, and this alone, is the imposition of the hands; but that the form, and likewise alone, is the words which determine the application of this matter, by which the sacramental effects are signified with but one meaning, namely, the power of orders, and grace of the Holy Spirit, and which as such are accepted and applied by the Church. Hence it follows that in order to do away with all controversy and to preclude the way to anxieties of conscience, by Our Apostolic Authority We do declare, and, if ever it has been otherwise lawfully arranged, decide that the tradition of the instruments at least for the future is not necessary for the validity of the sacred orders of the diaconate, priesthood, and episcopate.

5. But regarding the matter and form in the conferring of every order, by Our same supreme apostolic authority We decree and establish the following: In the ordination of deacons the matter is the one imposition of the bishop's hand, which occurs in the rite of that ordination. But the form consists of the words of the "Preface," of which the following are essential and so required for validity: "Send forth upon him, we beseech, O Lord, the Holy Spirit, by which for the work of faithfully performing your ministry he may be strengthened by the gift of Thy sevenfold

grace." In the ordination of priests the matter is the first imposition of the bishop's hands which is done in silence, but there is no continuation of the same imposition by an extension of the right hand, nor the last to which these words are joined: "Receive the Holy Spirit: whose sins you shall forgive, etc." But the form consists of the words of the "preface," of which the following are essential and so required for validity: "Bestow, we beseech, almighty Father, upon this thy servant the dignity of the priesthood; renew in his vitals the spirit of sanctity, that he may obtain the gift of good merit acceptable to Thee, O God, and may by the example of his conversation introduce rigid judgment of morals." Finally, in the episcopal ordination or consecration the matter is the imposition of the hands by the consecrating bishop. But the form consists of the words of the "Preface," of which the following are essential and thus required for validity: "Fulfill in Thy priest the completion of Thy ministry, and adorned in the ornaments of all glorification sanctify him with the moisture of heavenly unguent." . . .

6. That no occasion for doubt may be offered, we command that in any conferring of orders the imposition of hands be made by physically touching the head of the one to be ordained, although even the moral touch suffices for performing a sacrament validly. . . . The disposition of this Our Constitution does not have retroactive force.

The Time of the Documents of the Pentateuch, and the Literary Genre of the Eleven First Chapters of Genesis [1]

[Letter of the Secretary of the Biblical Commission to Cardinal Suhard, Archbishop of Paris, January 16, 1948]

Our Most Holy Father has decided to commit to the consideration of **2302** the Pontifical Biblical Commission two questions which were recently submitted to His Holiness on the sources of the Pentateuch and the historicity of the eleven first chapters of Genesis. These two questions, together with their doctrines and prayers, were examined most attentively by the Most Reverend Consultors and Most Eminent Cardinals assigned to the aforesaid Commission. At the end of their deliberations His Holiness has deigned to approve the response which follows, in audience on the 16th day of January, 1948, granted to the undersigned.

The Pontifical Biblical Commission with a joyful heart praises the sense of filial confidence which inspired this consultation, and desires to respond to it in a sincere effort to promote Biblical studies, since within the limits of the traditional doctrine of the Church the fullest freedom is granted them. This freedom is affirmed explicitly in the Encyclical,

---

[1] AAS 40 (1948), 45 ff.

Divino afflante Spiritu, of the Supreme Pontiff, who is reigning gloriously, with these words: "The Catholic exegete, impelled by an active and strong love of his science, and sincerely devoted to Holy Mother Church, should by no means be kept from attacking difficult questions as yet unresolved, again and again, not only to refute what is raised in opposition by adversaries, but to strive also to find a solid explanation which is in faithful accord with the doctrine of the Church, namely with what has been taught about Sacred Scripture free of all errors, and also satisfies in due measure certain conclusions of the profane sciences.

But let all the other sons of the Church remember that the attempts of these strenuous workers in the vineyard of the Lord should be judged not only with an honest and just heart, but also with the highest charity; indeed, these men should beware of that zeal, which is by no means prudent, whereby it is thought that whatever is new, for this very reason should be attacked or brought into suspicion" [AAS 35 (1943), 319].

If anyone under the light of this commendation of the Supreme Pontiff should consider and interpret the three replies given officially by the Biblical Commission on the questions already mentioned, i.e., on the 23rd day of June, 1905, regarding the stories in the historical books of Sacred Scripture, which have only the appearance of history [n. 1980] on the 27th day of June, 1906, on the Mosaic authenticity of the Pentateuch [n. 1997–2000], on the 30th day of June 1909, on the historical character of the three first chapters of Genesis [n. 2121–2128], will concede that these responses are by no means opposed to the earlier and truly scientific examination of these questions, which was instituted according to the information obtained within the last forty years. Therefore, the Biblical Commission does not think that, at least for the present, new decrees on these questions should be issued.

As for what pertains to the composition of the Pentateuch, the Biblical Commission in the above mentioned decree of the 27th day of June, 1906, recognized that it could be affirmed that "Moses in the composition of his work had made use of sources, namely, written documents or oral tradition" [n. 1999], and that modifications and additions later than Moses can also be admitted [cf. n. 2000]. There is no one today who doubts the existence of these sources, or who does not admit the successive additions which are due to the social and religious conditions of later times, and which are evident also in the historical narrative. However, among non-Catholic exegetes today very different opinions are offered regarding the nature and number of these documents, and their identification and time. Authors are not lacking in various countries who, from purely critical and historical reasons, without any apologetic zeal, definitely reject the theories set forth up to now, and try to explain certain peculiarities of the composition of the Pentateuch not so much from the diversity of supposed sources as from the special psychology and peculiar method, more thoroughly known today, of thinking and speaking on the part of the ancient Orientals; or also from the literary genre which varies according to subject matter. Therefore, we urge Catholic scholars to examine these questions with open minds in the light of sane criticism, and according to the findings which other sciences interested in the subject have obtained. For such an examination will undoubtedly show how great a part and what a profound influence Moses had as author and legislator.

The question of the literary forms of the eleven first chapters of Genesis is more obscure and more complicated. These literary forms do not correspond exactly with any classical category, and are not to be judged according to Greco-Latin or modern literary forms. Hence the historicity of these chapters can neither be denied nor affirmed simply, without undue application to them of the norms of a literary form under which they cannot be classed. If, then, it is admitted that in these chapters history in the classic and modern sense is not found, it must also be confessed that modern science does not yet offer a positive solution to all the problems of these chapters. . . . If anyone should contend *a priori* that their narratives contain no history in the modern sense of the word, he would easily insinuate that these are in a sense of the word historical, although in fact they relate in simple and figurative words, which correspond to the capacity of men who are less erudite, fundamental truths with reference to the economy of health, and also describe in popular manner the origin of humankind and of an elect people. . . .

Artificial Fertilization [1]

[From the Address of Pius XII on September 29, 1949, before the fourth international convention of Catholic physicians]

1. The practice of artificial fertilization, insofar as it concerns man, **2303** cannot be judged exclusively, or even principally, according to the norms of biology and medicine, neglecting moral and juridical norms.

2. Artificial fertilization outside of marriage is to be condemned purely and simply as immoral.

In fact, natural law and positive divine law demand that procreated new life be the fruit of marriage alone. Only marriage guards the dignity of spouses (especially of the wife, as far as this question is concerned), and their personal good. Only marriage of itself provides for the good and education of the child. Therefore, it follows that there can be no divergence of opinion among Catholics in condemning artificial fertiliza-

---

[1] AAS 41 (1949), 559 f.

tion outside the conjugal union. Offspring conceived in such a manner would be by the very fact illegitimate.

3. Artificial fertilization, which is effected within marriage but by an active element of a third party, is in the same way immoral, and as such is to be condemned absolutely.

Only spouses have a reciprocal right over the body to procreate new life, which right is exclusive and inalienable. The child also demands this. For upon him, who communicates new life to the child, nature itself by the force of this relationship imposes the obligation both of protecting and raising this offspring. Indeed, between the legitimate husband and the child procreated by the active element of the third party (even if the husband should consent) no bond of origin, nor any moral and juridical bond of matrimonial procreation exists.

4. As for the morality of artificial fertilization within marriage, let it suffice for the present for Us to call to mind the principles of the natural law; the mere fact that the end which is intended is actually achieved in this way does not make the use of this means lawful; and the desire of spouses (in itself, moreover, lawful) of having offspring does not yet prove sufficiently that the use of artificial fertilization, by which this desire is fulfilled, is licit.

It is an erroneous opinion which holds that marriage between persons incapable of contracting marriage because of the impediment of impotence can be rendered valid by the use of this means.

On the other hand it goes without saying that the active element is always procured illicitly by acts which are contrary to nature.

Although *a priori* new methods cannot be excluded merely because they are new, nevertheless, as far as artificial fertilization is concerned, not only is there need of the greatest circumspection, but it simply must be avoided. By these words We do not necessarily forbid the use of artificial means, which are destined only either to render the natural act easier or to bring it about that the completed act attain its end in a natural way.

Let it not be forgotten: only the procreation of new life, which takes place according to the will and order of the Creator, obtains to a truly perfect degree the ends intended by it. Such procreation corresponds at once to the corporal and spiritual nature and the dignity of the spouses and to the normal and happy development of the infant.

The Intention to be Possessed in Baptism [1]

[Response of the Holy Office, December 28, 1949]

To this Supreme Sacred Congregation . . . the question has been 2304 proposed:

"Whether, in judging matrimonial cases, baptism conferred in the sects of the Disciples of Christ, the Presbyterians, Congregationalists, Baptists, Methodists, when the necessary matter and form have been used, is to be presumed as invalid because of the lack of the required intention in the minister of doing what the Church does, or what Christ instituted; or whether it is to be presumed as valid unless in a particular case it is proven to the contrary." *The reply:* In the negative to the first part; in the affirmative to the second.

Some False Opinions that Threaten to Undermine the Foundations of Catholic Doctrine [2]

[From the Encyclical, "Humani generis," August 12, 1950]

The discord and departure from truth on the part of the human race 2305 in religious and moral affairs have always been a source and a cause of very painful grief to all good men, and especially to the faithful and sincere sons of the Church, and more than ever today when we perceive the very principles of Christian culture offended on all sides.

Indeed, it is no wonder that such discord and wandering have always flourished outside the fold of Christ. For although human reason, speaking simply, by its natural powers and light can in fact arrive at true and certain knowledge of one personal God who in His providence guards and directs the world, and also of the natural law infused into our souls by the Creator, nevertheless, not a few obstacles prevent man's reason from efficaciously and fruitfully using this natural faculty which it possesses. For matters which pertain to God and have to do with relationships between men and God, are truths which completely transcend the order of sensible things, and, when they are introduced into the action of life and shape it, demand devotion of self and self-abnegation. The human intellect, moreover, in acquiring such truths labors with difficulty not only on account of the impulse of the depraved senses and the imagination, but also of the desires which have their source in original sin. Therefore it happens that men in matters of this kind easily

---

[1] AAS 41 (1949), 650.

[2] AAS 42 (1950), 561–577. We present almost the entire text. See emendations of the text AAS 42 (1950), 960.

persuade themselves that what they do not wish to be true, are false or at least doubtful.

For this reason divine "revelation" must be considered morally necessary, in order that those truths, which in the realm of religion and morals are not of themselves beyond the scope of reason, yet in the present condition of the human race, may be readily grasped by all with strong certitude and with no admixture of error.[1]

Yet on the other hand the human mind can sometimes experience difficulties in forming a certain judgment "of credibility" about the Catholic faith, although so many wonderful external signs have been disposed by God, through which, even by the natural light of reason alone, the divine origin of the Christian religion can be proven with certainty. For man, whether induced by prejudiced opinions or instigated by desires and evil will, can refuse and resist not only the evidence of external signs, which is pre-eminent, but also the supernal inspirations which God brings into our hearts.

Anyone who observes those who are outside the fold of Christ, can easily see the chief ways upon which many learned men have entered. There are those who contend that the so-called system of evolution, not yet irrefutably demonstrated within the scope of the natural sciences, and admitted imprudently and indiscreetly, extends to the origin of all things, and who boldly entertain the monistic and pantheistic theory that the whole world is subject to continuous evolution. Indeed, the supporters of communism gladly employ this theory, to bring out more efficaciously and defend their "dialectic materialism," casting out of mind every notion of God.

2306   Such fictions of evolution, by which whatever is absolute, firm, and immutable, is repudiated, have paved the way for a new erroneous philosophy which, in opposition to "idealism," "immanence," and "pragmatism," has obtained the name of "existentialism," since it is concerned only with the "existence" of individual things, and neglects the immutable essence of things.

There is also a kind of false "historicism," which attends only to events of human life, and razes the foundations of all truth and absolute law, not only insofar as it pertains to the philosophical matters, but to Christian teachings as well.

2307   In such a great confusion of opinions as this it gives Us some solace to note those who not rarely today desire to return from the principles of "realism," in which they had once been instructed, to the well-springs of truth revealed by God, and to acknowledge and profess the word of God as preserved in Holy Scripture. Yet at the same time We must grieve that by no means a few of these, the more firmly they cling to the word

---

[1] Conc. Vatic., D.B., 1876, *Const. De Fide cath.,* cap. 2, *De revelatione.*

of God, that much more diminish human reason; and the more they exalt the authority of God who reveals, the more sharply they spurn the *magisterium* of the Church, instituted by Christ the Lord to guard and interpret the truths revealed by God. This indeed is not only in open contradiction to Sacred Scripture, but is proved false from actual experience. Often the very ones who disagree with the true Church openly complain about their own discord in matters of dogma, so that they unwillingly confess to the necessity of the living *magisterium*.

Indeed, Catholic theologians and philosophers, upon whom falls the serious duty of protecting divine and human truth, and of inculcating these in the minds of men, may not ignore or neglect these opinions which more or less stray from the straight road. Moreover, they should thoroughly examine these opinions, because diseases cannot be cured unless they have been rightly diagnosed; also because sometimes in false fabrications something of truth lies hidden; finally, because such theories provoke the mind to scrutinize and weigh certain truths, philosophical or theological, more carefully. 2308

But, if our philosophers and theologians strive to gather only such fruit from these doctrines, after cautious examination, there would be no reason for the intervention of the *magisterium* of the Church. However, although We have found that Catholic doctors in general are on their guard against those errors, yet it is well established that there are not lacking today, just as in apostolic times, those who, in their extreme zeal for novelty and also in their fear of being held ignorant of those matters which the science of a progressive age has introduced, strive to withdraw themselves from the temperateness of the sacred *magisterium;* and thus they become involved in the danger of gradually and imperceptibly departing from the truth revealed by God, and of leading others into error along with themselves.

Indeed, even another danger is observed, and is more serious, since it is more concealed under the appearance of virtue. There are many who, deploring the discord of the human race and the confusion of minds, and roused by an imprudent zeal for souls, are moved by a kind of impulse, and burn with a vehement desire to break down the barriers by which good and honest men are mutually separated, embracing such an irenicism that, forgetting the questions that separate men, they not only seek to refute destructive atheism by common strength, but even to reconcile opposing ideas in dogmatic matters. And just as once there were those who asked whether the traditional study of apologetics constituted an obstacle rather than an aid to the winning of souls for Christ, so today there are not lacking those who dare proceed to the point of seriously raising the question whether theology and its method, as they flourish in the schools with the approval of ecclesiastical authority, ought not only to be perfected, but even to be entirely reformed, so that the kingdom of Christ may be propagated more efficaciously everywhere in the land, among men of every culture, and of every religious opinion. If these men aimed at nothing else than the better adaptation of ecclesiastical science and its method to present day conditions and demands, by introducing a kind of new plan, there would be little reason to fear; but, burning with an imprudent irenicism, some seem to consider as obstacles to the restoration of fraternal unity those matters which rest upon the very laws and principles given by Christ, and upon the institutions founded by Him, or which are the bulwarks and pillars of the integrity of faith, by the collapse of which all things are united to be sure, but only in ruin. . . .

2309   As far as theology is concerned, some propose to diminish as much as possible the significance of dogmas, and to free dogma itself from the manner of speaking long accepted in the Church, and from the philosophical notions which are common among Catholic teachers; so that in explaining Catholic doctrine there may be a return to the manner of speaking of the Holy Scripture and of the Holy Fathers. They cherish the hope that the time will come when dogma, stripped of the elements which they say are extrinsic to divine revelation, may be profitably compared with the dogmatic opinions of those who are separated from the unity of the Church; and in this way gradually a mutual assimilation will be reached between Catholic dogma and the principles of the dissidents.

2310   In addition, when Catholic doctrine has been reduced to this condition, they think that the way is paved to satisfy present-day needs, by expressing dogma in the terms of contemporary philosophy, whether of "immanence" or of "idealism," or "existentialism," or of any other system. Certain more daring persons contend that this can and ought to be done for this reason, because they maintain that the mysteries of faith can never be expressed by notions that are adequately true, but only by so-called "approximative" notions, always changeable, by which truth is indicated to a certain degree, but is also necessarily deformed. So they think that it is not absurd, but quite necessary that theology in place of the various philosophies which it has used as its instruments in the course of time, substitute new notions for old ones, so that in ways that are different, and even in some degree opposite, yet possessing the same value, as they say, render the same divine truths in a human way. They add also that the history of dogmas consists in presenting the various successive forms with which revealed truth has clothed itself, according to the different doctrines and opinions which have arisen in the course of the ages.

2311   But it is clear from what we have said that such endeavors lead not only to dogmatic "relativism," as it is called, but actually contain it; indeed, the contempt for the doctrine as commonly handed down, and for the phraseology by which the same is expressed, more than sufficiently bear this out. Surely there is no one who does not see that the phraseology of such notions not only as employed in the schools but also by the *magisterium* of the Church herself, can be perfected and polished; and, besides, it is noted that the Church has not always been constant in employing the same words. It is also evident that the Church cannot be bound to any system of philosophy which flourishes for a brief period of time; for, what has been set in order over many centuries by common consent of Catholic teachers, in order to achieve some understanding of dogma, without doubt does not rest on so perishable a foundation. Rather they are based on principles and notions derived from a true knowledge of created things; and surely in deriving this knowledge, truth divinely revealed has through the Church illumined the mind like a star. Therefore, it is no wonder that some such notions were not only employed by ecumenical councils but also so sanctioned that it is not right to depart from them.

Therefore, to neglect, or to reject, or to deprive so many great things   2312
of their value, which in many instances have been conceived, expressed, and perfected after long labor, by men of no ordinary genius and sanctity, under the watchful eye of the holy *magisterium,* and not without the light and guidance of the Holy Spirit for the expression of the truths of faith ever more accurately, so that in their place conjectural notions may be substituted, as well as certain unstable and vague expressions of a new philosophy, which like a flower of the field exists today and will die tomorrow, not only is the highest imprudence, but also makes dogma itself as a reed shaken by the wind. Moreover, the contempt for the words and ideas which the scholastic theologians customarily use, tends to weaken so-called speculative philosophy, which they think is void of true certitude, since it rests on theological reasoning.

Surely it is lamentable that those eager for novelty easily pass from a   2313
contempt for scholastic theology to a neglect, and even a disrespect for the *magisterium* of the Church, which supports that theology by its authority. For, this *magisterium* is considered by them as a hindrance to progress and an obstacle to science; indeed, by certain non-Catholics it is looked upon as an unjust restraint by which some learned theologians are prevented from pursuing their science. And, although this sacred *magisterium,* in matters of faith and morals, should be the proximate and universal norm of faith to any theologian, inasmuch as Christ the Lord entrusted the entire deposit of faith to it, namely, the Sacred Scriptures and divine "tradition," to be guarded, and preserved, and interpreted; yet its office, by which the faithful are bound to flee those errors which more or less tend toward heresy, and so, too, "to keep its constitutions

and decrees, by which such perverse opinions are proscribed and prohibited," [1] is sometimes ignored as if it did not exist. There are some who consistently neglect to consult what has been set forth in the Encyclical Letters of the Roman Pontiffs on the character and constitution of the Church, for the reason that a certain vague notion prevails drawn from the ancient Fathers, especially the Greek. For the popes, as they repeatedly say, do not wish to pass judgment on those matters which are in dispute among theologians, and so there must be a return to the early sources, and the more recent constitutions and decrees of the *magisterium* are to be explained from the writings of the ancients.

Even if perchance these things seem to have been wisely said, yet they are not without error. It is true that, in general, the Pontiffs grant freedom to theologians in those matters which are disputed with varying opinions, but history teaches that many things, which formerly were subject to free discussion, later cannot permit any discussion.

It is not to be thought that what is set down in Encyclical Letters does not demand assent in itself, because in this the popes do not exercise the supreme power of their *magisterium*. For these matters are taught by the ordinary *magisterium,* regarding which the following is pertinent: "He who heareth you, heareth me." [Luke 10:16]; and usually what is set forth and inculcated in the Encyclical Letters, already pertains to Catholic doctrine. But if the Supreme Pontiffs in their acts, after due consideration, express an opinion on a hitherto controversial matter, it is clear to all that this matter, according to the mind and will of the same Pontiffs, cannot any longer be considered a question of free discussion among the theologians.

2314 It is also true that theologians must always have recourse to the sources of divine revelation; for it is their duty to indicate how what is taught by the living *magisterium* is found, either explicitly or implicitly, in Sacred Scripture and in divine "tradition." In addition, both sources of doctrine, divinely revealed, contain so many and such great treasures of truth that they are in fact never exhausted. Therefore, the sacred disciplines always remain vigorous by a study of the sacred sources, while, on the other hand, speculation, which neglects the deeper investigation of sacred deposit, as we know from experience, becomes sterile. But for this reason even positive theology, as it is called, cannot be placed on equal footing with merely historical science. For, together with these sacred sources God has given a living *magisterium* to His Church, to illumine and clarify what is contained in the deposits of faith obscurely and implicitly. Indeed, the divine Redeemer entrusted this deposit not to individual Christians, nor to the theologians to be interpreted authentically,

---

[1] CIC, can. 1324; cf. Conc. Vat., D.B., 1820, *Const. De Fide cath.,* cap. 4; *De fide et ratione,* post canones.

but to the *magisterium* of the Church alone. Moreover, if the Church exercises this duty of hers, as has been done again and again in the course of the ages, whether by ordinary or extraordinary exercise of this function, it is clear that the method whereby clear things are explained from the obscure is wholly false; but rather all should follow the opposite order. Therefore, Our predecessor of immortal memory, Pius IX, teaching that the most noble function of theology is to show how a doctrine defined by the Church is contained in the sources, added these words, not without grave reason: "By that very sense by which it is defined."[1] . . .

But to return to the new opinions which We have touched upon above, 2315 many things are proposed or instilled in the mind (of the faithful) to the detriment of the divine authority of Sacred Scripture. Some boldly pervert the meaning of the definition of the Vatican Council, with respect to God as the author of Sacred Scripture; and they revive the opinion, many times disproved, according to which the immunity of the Sacred Writings from error extends only to those matters which are handed down regarding God and moral and religious subjects. Again, they speak falsely about the human sense of the Sacred Books, under which their divine sense lies hidden, which they declare is alone infallible. In interpreting Sacred Scripture they wish that no account be taken of the analogy of the faith and of "the tradition" of the Church, so that the teaching of the Holy Fathers and of the holy *magisterium* is to be referred, as it were, to the norm of Sacred Scripture as explained by exegetes in a merely human manner, rather than that Sacred Scripture be interpreted according to the mind of the Church, which was established by Christ the Lord as the guardian and interpreter of the whole deposit of truth revealed by God.

And besides, the literal sense of Sacred Scripture and its exposition, 2316 as elaborated by so many great exegetes under the watchful eye of the Church, according to their false opinions, should yield to the new exegesis which they call symbolic and spiritual; by which the Sacred Books of the Old Testament, which today are as a closed source in the Church, may be opened sometime to all. They declare that by this method all difficulties vanish, by which they only are shackled who cling to the literal sense of Scripture.

Surely, everyone will see how foreign all this is to the principles and norms of interpretation rightly established by Our predecessors of happy memory, Leo XIII in the Encyclical Letter "Providentissimus," Benedict XV in the Encyclical Letter, "Spiritus Paraclitus," and also by us in the Encyclical Letter, "Divino Efflante Spiritu."

And it is not strange that such innovations, as far as pertains to almost 2317

---

[1] Pius IX, *Inter gravissimas*, October 26, 1870; *Acta P.I.*, Vol. V, p. 260.

all branches of theology, have already produced poisonous fruit. It is doubtful that human reason, without the aid of divine "revelation" and divine grace, can demonstrate the existence of a personal God by arguments deduced from created things; it is denied that the world had a beginning, and it is disputed that the creation of the world was necessary, since it proceeds from the necessary liberality of divine love; eternal and infallible foreknowledge of the free actions of men is likewise denied to God; all of which, indeed, are opposed to the declarations of the Vatican Council.[1]

2318　　The question is also raised by some whether angels are personal creatures; and whether matter differs essentially from spirit. Others destroy the true "gratuity" of the supernatural order, since they think that God cannot produce beings endowed with intellect without ordering and calling them to the beatific vision. This is not all: the notion of original sin, without consideration of the definitions of the Council of Trent, is perverted, and at the same time the notion of sin in general as an offense against God, and likewise the concept of the satisfaction made by Christ for us. And there are those who contend that the doctrine of transubstantiation, inasmuch as it is founded on an antiquated philosophical presence of Christ in the Most Holy Eucharist, is reduced to a kind of symbolism, so that the consecrated species are no more than efficacious signs of the spiritual presence of Christ, and of His intimate union with the faithful members in the mystical body.

2319　　Some think that they are not bound by the doctrine proposed a few years ago in Our Encyclical Letter, bearing upon the sources of "revelation," which teaches that the mystical body of Christ and the Church are one and the same.[2] Some reduce to any empty formula the necessity of belonging to the true Church in order to attain eternal salvation. Others, finally, do injury to the reasonable nature of the "credibility" of the Christian faith.

2320　　It is well known how much the Church values human reason, in what is concerned with definitely demonstrating the existence of one personal God; and likewise with proving irrefutably from divine signs the foundations of the Christian faith itself; and, in like manner, with expressing rightly the law which the Creator has placed in the souls of men; and finally, with attaining some understanding, and this a most fruitful understanding, of the mysteries.[3] Yet reason will be able to fulfill this function only when it has been trained in the required manner; namely, when it has become imbued with that sound philosophy which has long stood out as a patrimony handed down from the earlier Christian ages,

---

[1] Cf. Conc. Vat., *Const. De Fide cath.*, cap. 1, *De Deo rerum omnium creatore.*

[2] Cf. Enc., *Mystici Corporis Christi*, AAS, vol. XXXV, p. 193 f.

[3] Cf. Conc. Vat., D.B., 1796.

and so possesses the authority of an even higher order, because the *magisterium* of the Church has carefully weighed its principles and chief assertions, which were gradually made clear and defined by men of great genius, by the test of divine "revelation" itself. Indeed, this philosophy, recognized and accepted within the Church, protects the true and sincere value of human understanding, and constant metaphysical principles —namely, of sufficient reason, causality, and finality—and, finally, the acquisition of certain and immutable truth.

To be sure in this philosophy many things are treated with which **2321** matters of faith and morals are neither directly nor indirectly concerned, and which, therefore, the Church entrusts to free discussion of learned men; but in regard to other matters, especially the principles and chief assertions which we mentioned above, the same freedom is not granted. In such essential questions, one may indeed clothe philosophy with a more fitting and richer dress, fortify it with more efficacious words, rid it of certain supports of scholars which are not fitting, and also cautiously enrich it with certain sound elements of progressive human study; but it is never right to subvert it, or to contaminate it with false principles, or to consider it a great but obsolete monument. For truth and its philosophic declaration cannot be changed from day to day, especially when it is a question of principles known to the human mind *per se,* or of those opinions which rest both on the wisdom of the ages, and on the consent and support of divine revelation. Whatever truth the human mind in its honest search will be able to discover, surely cannot be opposed to truth already acquired, since God, the highest Truth, created and directs the human intellect not that it may daily oppose new truths to those rightly acquired, but that by the removal of errors, which perchance have crept in, it can build truth upon truth in the same order and structure by which the very nature of things, from which truth is drawn, is perceived to have been constituted. Therefore, the Christian, whether philosopher or theologian, does not hastily and easily adopt every new thing thought up from day to day, but with the greatest care places it in the scale of justice, and weighs it, lest he lose or corrupt the truth already acquired, indeed with grave danger and harm to faith itself.

If these matters are thoroughly examined, it will be evident why the **2322** Church demands that future priests be instructed in the philosophic disciplines "according to the manner, doctrine, and principles of the Angelic Doctor," [1] since it knows well from the experience of many ages that the method and system of Aquinas, whether in training beginners or investigating hidden truth, stand out with special prominence; moreover, that his doctrine is in harmony, as in a kind of symphony, with divine "revelation," and is most efficacious in laying safe foundations of

---

[1] CIC, can. 1366, 2.

faith, and also in collecting usefully and securely the fruits of sound progress.[1]

2323   For this reason it is to be exceedingly deplored that the philosophy accepted and recognized within the Church is today held in scorn by some; so much so that it is impudently renounced as antiquated in form, and rationalistic, as they say, in its process of thinking. For they insist that this philosophy of ours defends the false opinion that an absolutely true metaphysics can exist, while on the other hand they assert that things, especially the transcendent, cannot be expressed more aptly than by disparate doctrines, which complement each other, although, in a manner they are opposed to each other. So, they concede that the philosophy of our schools, with its clear description and solution of questions, with its accurate demarcation of notions and clear distinctions, can indeed be useful for a training in scholastic theology, well accommodated to the minds of men of the Middle Ages, but does not offer a system of philosophizing which corresponds with our modern culture and its needs. Then they raise the objection that an unchanging philosophy is nothing but a philosophy of immutable essences, while the modern mind must look to the "existence" of individual objects, and to life, which is always in a state of flux. While they despise this philosophy, they extol others, whether ancient or modern, whether of the peoples of the Orient or of the Occident, so that they seem to insinuate that any philosophy or belief with certain additions, if need be, as corrections or supplements, can be reconciled with Catholic dogma. No Catholic can doubt that this is quite false, especially since it involves those fictions which they call "immanence," or "idealism," or "materialism," whether historic or dialectic, or even "existentialism," whether professing atheism, or at least rejecting the value of metaphysical reasoning.

2324   And, finally, they find this fault with the traditional philosophy of our Schools, namely, that in the process of cognition it is concerned only with the intellect, and overlooks the function of the will, and of the affections of the mind. This certainly is not true. For never has Christian philosophy denied the usefulness and the efficacy of the good disposition of the entire mind for fully comprehending and embracing religious and moral truths; on the other hand, it has always taught that the lack of such dispositions can be the cause of the intellect becoming affected by disordered desires and an evil will, and of being so obscured that it does not see rightly. On the other hand the Common Doctor is of the opinion that the intellect can in some way perceive the higher goods that pertain to the moral order, whether natural or supernatural, since it experiences in the mind a kind of passionate "relationship" with these goods, whether

---

[1] AAS, vol. XXXVIII, 1946, p. 387.

natural, or added by the gift of grace; [1] and it is evident how much even such an obscure understanding can be an aid to the investigations of reason. Yet, it is one thing to recognize the force of the will for the disposition of the affections in aiding reason to acquire a more certain and firmer understanding of matters of morals; but these innovators make a different claim, namely, they assign to the faculties of desiring and coveting a kind of intuition, and that man, when he cannot through the process of reason decide with certainty what is to be accepted as true, turns to the will, by which he decides freely and chooses between opposite opinions, thus stupidly confusing the act of cognition and of the will.

It is not strange that because of these new opinions two branches of   2325 philosophy are endangered, which by their nature are closely connected with the doctrine of faith, namely, theodicy and ethics. Indeed, some believe that the function of these disciplines is not to demonstrate anything certain about God or any other transcendental being, but rather to show that what faith teaches about a personal God and His precepts is in perfect harmony with the needs of life, and thus should be embraced by all, so that despair may be avoided and eternal salvation attained. Since all such opinions are openly opposed to the teachings of Our predecessors, Leo XIII and Pius X, they cannot be reconciled with the decrees of the Vatican Council. Surely, it would be superfluous to deplore these wanderings from the truth, if all, even in philosophical matters, would accept with due reverence the *magisterium* of the Church, whose duty it surely is not only to guard and interpret the deposit of truth revealed by God, but also to watch over these philosophical disciplines, lest Catholic dogma suffer any harm from incorrect opinions.

It remains for Us to say something on the questions which, although   2326 they have to do with the disciplines which are customarily called "positive," yet are more or less connected with the truths of Christian faith. Not a few insistently demand that the Catholic religion give as much consideration as possible to these disciplines. Surely, this is praiseworthy when it is a case of actually proven facts, but caution must be exercised when the question concerns "hypotheses," although in some manner based on human knowledge, in which hypotheses doctrine is discussed which is contained in the Sacred Scriptures or in "tradition." When such conjectural opinions are opposed directly or indirectly to the doctrine revealed by God, then their demand can in no way be admitted.

Wherefore, the *magisterium* of the Church does not forbid that the   2327 teaching of "evolution" be treated in accord with the present status of human disciplines and of theology, by investigations and disputations by learned men in both fields; insofar, of course, as the inquiry is concerned

---

[1] Cf. St. Thomas, *Summa theol.,* IIa IIae, q. 1, a. 4, ad 3; q. 45, a. 2, c.

with the origin of the human body arising from already existing and living matter; and in such a way that the reasonings of both theories, namely of those in favor and of those in opposition, are weighed and judged with due seriousness, moderation, and temperance; and provided that all are ready to yield to the judgment of the Church, to which Christ has entrusted the duty of interpreting Sacred Scriptures authentically, and of preserving the dogmas of faith.[1] Yet some with daring boldness transgress this freedom of discussion, acting as if the origin of the human body from previously existing and living matter, were already certain and demonstrated from certain already discovered indications, and deduced by reasoning, and as if there were nothing in the sources of divine revelation which demands the greatest moderation and caution in this thinking.

2328   When there is a question of another conjectural opinion, namely, of polygenism so-called, then the sons of the Church in no way enjoy such freedom. For the faithful in Christ cannot accept this view, which holds that either after Adam there existed men on this earth, who did not receive their origin by natural generation from him, the first parent of all; or that Adam signifies some kind of multitude of first parents; for it is by no means apparent how such an opinion can be reconciled with what the sources of revealed truth and the acts of the *magisterium* of the Church teaches about original sin, which proceeds from a sin truly committed by one Adam, and which is transmitted to all by generation, and exists in each one as his own.[2]

2329   Just as in the biological and anthropological sciences, so also in the historical there are those who boldly transgress the limits and precautions established by the Church. And, We especially deplore a certain entirely too liberal manner of interpreting the historical books of the Old Testament, the supporters of which defend their case by reference without warrant to a letter given not long ago by the Pontifical Council on Biblical Affairs to the Archbishop of Paris.[3] This Letter plainly advises that the eleven first chapters of Genesis, although they do not conform properly with the methods of historical composition which distinguished Greek and Latin writers of past events, or the learned men of our age have used, nevertheless in a certain sense, to be examined and determined more fully by exegetes, are truly a kind of history; and that the same chapters, in simple and figurative speech suited to the mentality of a people of little culture, both recount the principal truths on which the attainment of our eternal salvation depends, and also the popular de-

---

[1] Cf. Address of the Pope to the members of the Academy of Sciences, November 30, 1941: AAS, vol. XXXIII, p. 506.

[2] Cf. Rom. 5:12–19; Conc. Trid., sess. V, can. 1–4.

[3] January 16, 1948: AAS 40, 45–48.

scription of the origin of the human race and of the chosen people. But if the ancient sacred writers draw anything from popular narrations (which indeed can be conceded) it must never be forgotten that they did so assisted by the impulse of divine inspiration, by which in selecting and passing judgment on those documents, they were preserved free from all error.

Moreover, these matters which have been received into Sacred Litera- **2330** ture from popular narrations are by no means to be identified with mythologies or other things of this kind, which proceed from undue imagination rather than from that zeal for truth and simplicity which so shines forth in the Sacred Books of the Old Testament that our sacred writers must evidently be said to excel the ancient profane writers.

The Definition of the Assumption of the Blessed Virgin Mary [1]

[From the Apostolic Constitution, "Munificentissimus Deus,"
Nov. 1, 1950]

All these arguments and considerations of the Holy Fathers and of **2331** the theologians are based on the Holy Scriptures as their ultimate foundation, which indeed place before us as though before our eyes the loving Mother of God as most closely joined with her divine Son, and as ever sharing His lot. Therefore, it seems almost impossible to think of her who conceived Christ, bore Him, nourished Him with her milk, held Him in her arms, and pressed Him to her breast, as separated from Him after this earthly life in her body, even though not in soul. Since our Redeemer is the Son of Mary, surely, as the most perfect observer of divine law, He could not refuse to honor, in addition to His Eternal Father, His most beloved Mother also. And, since He could adorn her with so great a gift as to keep her unharmed by the corruption of the tomb, it must be believed that He actually did this.

But this especially must be remembered, that ever since the second century the Virgin Mary has been presented by the Holy Fathers as the new Eve, very closely connected with the new Adam, although subject to Him in that struggle with the enemy of hell, which, as is presignified in the protevangelium [Gen. 3:15] was to result in a most complete victory over sin and death, which are always joined together in the writings of the Apostle of the Gentiles [Rom. 5:6; I Cor. 15:21–26; 54–57]. Therefore, just as the glorious resurrection of Christ was an essential part, and the final evidence of this victory, so the Blessed Virgin's common struggle with her Son was to be concluded with the "glorification" of her virginal body, as the same Apostle says: "When . . . this

---

[1] AAS 42 (1950), 767–770.

mortal hath put on immortality, then shall come to pass the saying that is written: Death is swallowed up in victory" [I Cor. 15:54].

Therefore, the august Mother of God, joined in a secret manner with Jesus Christ, from all eternity "by one and the same decree" [1] of predestination, immaculate in her conception, a most pure virgin in her divine maternity, noble ally of the divine Redeemer, who has gained full triumph over sin and its consequences, has finally attained as the highest crown of her privileges, that she should be immune from the corruption of the tomb, and that in the same manner as her Son she would overcome death and be taken away soul and body to the supernal glory of heaven, where as Queen she would shine forth at the right hand of the same Son of hers, the immortal King of Ages [I Tim. 1:17].

2332 Since, then, the universal Church, in which the Spirit of Truth flourishes, who infallibly directs it to achieve a knowledge of revealed truths, has through the course of the ages repeatedly manifested its own faith; and since the bishops of the whole world with almost unanimous consent request that the truth of the bodily Assumption of the Blessed Virgin Mary into heaven be defined as a dogma of the divine and Catholic faith—a truth which is founded on the Sacred Scriptures, has been fixed deeply in the minds of the faithful in Christ, has been approved by ecclesiastical worship even from the earliest times, is quite in harmony with the other revealed truths, and has been splendidly explained and declared by the zeal, knowledge, and wisdom of the theologians—We think that the moment appointed in the plan of a provident God has now come to proclaim solemnly such an extraordinary privilege of the Virgin Mary. . . .

2333 Accordingly, after We directed Our prayers in supplication to God again and again, and invoked the light of the Spirit of Truth, for the glory of Almighty God, who lavishes His special benevolence on the Virgin Mary, for the honor of her Son, the immortal King of the Ages and the victor over sin and death, for the increasing glory of the same august Mother, and for the joy and exultation of the whole Church, by the authority of our Lord Jesus Christ, of the Blessed Apostles, Peter and Paul, and by Our own authority We pronounce, declare, and define that the dogma was revealed by God, that the Immaculate Mother of God, the ever Virgin Mary, after completing her course of life upon earth, was assumed to the glory of heaven both in body and soul.

Therefore, if anyone, which may God forbid, should dare either to deny this, or voluntarily call into doubt what has been defined by Us, he should realize that he has cut himself off entirely from the divine and Catholic faith.

[1] Bull, "Ineffabilis Deus," Acta Pii IX, P. 1, vol. I, p. 599.

Appendix

ST. BONIFACE I, 418-422

The Primacy of the Roman Pontiff [1]

[From the Letter, "Manet beatum," to Rufus and the other Bishops throughout Macedonia, etc., March 11, 422]

The watchful care over the universal Church confided to Peter abides **5000** with him by reason of the Lord's statement; for he knows on the testimony of the Gospel [Matt. 16:18] that the Church was founded on him. His office can never be free from cares, since it is certain that all things depend on his deliberation. These considerations turn my mind to the regions of the Orient, which we behold in a way with genuine solicitude. Far be it from the priests of the Lord, that anyone of them fall into the offense of making the decrees of our elders foreign to him, by attempting something in the way of a novel and unlawful usurpation, realizing that he thus makes him a rival, in whom our Christ has placed the highest power of the priesthood, and whoever rises to reproach him cannot be an inhabitant of the heavenly regions. "To you," He said, "I shall give the keys of the kingdom of heaven" [Matt. 16:19] into which no one shall enter without the favor of the door-keeper. He said: "Thou art Peter, and upon this rock I shall build my church" [Matt. 11:29]. Whoever, therefore, desires before God to be judged worthy of the dignity of the priesthood, since one reaches God with the support of Peter, on whom, as we have said above, it is certain that the Church was founded, <should> be "meek

---

[1] C. Silva-Tarouca, S.J., *Epistularum Rom. Pontificum ad vicarios per Illyricum aliosque episcopos. Collectio Thessalonicensis,* 1937, p. 27 ff. [*Textus et documenta Ser. theol.,* 23].

and humble of heart" [Matt. 11:29], lest as a contumacious disciple of him, whose <pride> he has imitated, he undergo the punishment of the teachers. . . .

5001   Since the circumstances demand, examine if you please, the decrees of the canons; you will find, what church ranks second after the church at Rome, or what is third. In these (decrees) there appears a distinct order, so that the pontiffs of the other churches recognize that they nevertheless are under one church . . . and share the same priesthood, and to whom they, preserving charity, should be subject because of ecclesiastical discipline. Indeed this teaching of the canons has persisted from antiquity, and continues even at the present time, through the grace of Christ. No one has ever boldly raised his hands in opposition to the apostolic supremacy, from whose judgment there may be no withdrawal; no one in this has been rebellious, except him who wished judgment to be passed on himself. The above mentioned great churches preserve . . . their authority through the canons: the churches of Alexandria and of Antioch [cf. n. 163, 436], having the knowledge of ecclesiastical law. They preserve, I say, the statutes of our elders . . . in all things rendering and receiving an interchange of that grace which they know that they owe to us in the Lord who is our peace. But since the situation demands it, it must be shown by documents that the greatest churches of the Orient in important affairs, in which there was need of greater inquiry, have always consulted the See of Rome, and, as often as experience demanded, asked for its help. Athanasius of holy memory and Peter, priests of the church of Alexandria, sought the aid of this See.[1] When the Church of Antioch was afflicted during a very long period, with the result that conferences because of this were often held, it is clear that the Apostolic See was consulted, first under Meletius and later under Flavianus. According to its authority, after the many things which were accomplished by our church, no one doubts that Flavianus received the grace of communion, which he would have lacked forever if his writing had not gone forth hence upon this basis.[2] The emperor Theodosius of most kindly memory, thinking that the ordination of Nectarius did not possess stability, since it did not take place in our way, sending from his presence members of his court together with bishops, demanded that it be performed in this case by the Roman See, and that they direct it in the regular way, so as to strengthen the priesthood.[3] A short time ago, that is under my predecessor of happy memory, Innocent, the Pontiffs of the Oriental

---

[1] Cf. the letters of St. Julius I, J f 183, 185 f. 188; and St. Damasus' letter J f. 233, 236.

[2] Cf. St. Damasus' letter Jf. 235.

[3] Cf. Epistle of the Council of Constantinople to St. Damasus, Cst p. 567.

churches, grieving that they were separated from the communion of blessed Peter, through envoys asked for peace, as your charity remembers.[1] And at this time the Apostolic See without difficulty granted all, obeying the Master who says: "And to whom you have pardoned any thing, I also. For what I have pardoned, if I have pardoned anything, for your sakes have I done it in the person of Christ. That we be not overreached by Satan. For we are not ignorant of his devices [II Cor. 2:10 f.], that is, who always rejoices at dissension. Since then, most beloved Brethren, I think that the examples which we have given suffice to prove the truth, although more are retained in your own minds, without harm to our brotherhood we wish to meet your assembly, as you see by this letter which has been directed by Us through Severus, a notary of the Apostolic See, most acceptable to Our heart, chosen from Our circle. Thus in agreement, as befits brothers, let not anyone wishing to endure in our communion bring up again for discussion the name of our brother and fellow priest, Bishop Perigenas,[2] whose sacerdotal office the Apostle Peter has already confirmed at the suggestion of the Holy Spirit, leaving no question about this for the future, and let there be no objection to this, since he was appointed by Us during the space of that time in which the office was vacant. . . .

ST. SIXTUS III, 432–440

The Incarnation [3]

["The formula of union" of the year 433, by which the peace between St. Cyril of Alexandria and the Antiochenes was established, was approved by St. Sixtus III]

But how we know and speak regarding the Virgin Mother of God,   5002 and about the manner of the incarnation of the only-begotten Son of God, necessary not because of increase but for satisfaction, we have taken and possess from above, from the divine Scriptures as well as

---

[1] Cf. Epistle of St. Innocent I, Jf 305–310; Cst p. 843 ff.

[2] St. Boniface I had confirmed Perigenas as Bishop of Corinth, but not all had acquiesced in this appointment.

[3] The Greek text from the epistle of John of Antioch to Sixtus, ACOec. I, 1, 7, p. 159; ML 50, 603 ff.;—the Latin from the epistle of the same John to Cyril, insofar as it exists, ACOec. I, 2 p. 103. The same creed is found in the epistle of Cyril of Alexandria to John of Antioch, MG 77, 176; see R n. 2060 "Although indeed no proper sentence of approbation of the formula of union through the Pontiff of Rome has been preserved, yet all that Xystus writes on the fact of the union between John and Cyril seems to leave no doubt that he approved a formula," says B. Silva-Tarouca, S.J., Institutiones hist. eccl. Pars II, fasc. I (1933) 135. Cf. letter 5 of Sixtus to Cyril, ML 50, 602 ff.

from the tradition of the holy fathers, and we speak briefly, adding
nothing at all to the faith of the holy Fathers, which was set forth at
Nicea. For, as we have already said, this suffices for all understanding
of piety and for all renunciation of heretical perfidy. But we speak not
presuming the unlawful, but by confession of special weakness excluding
those who wish to rise up against what we regard as beyond man.

5003   We confess our Lord Jesus Christ, the only begotten son of God,
perfect God and perfect man, of a rational soul and of a body, born
of the Father before the ages according to the Godhead, but in the last
days the same on account of us and on account of our salvation according to the incarnation from the Virgin Mary, consubstantial with the
Father, the same according to the Godhead, and consubstantial with
us according to the incarnation. For the unity of the two natures was
made; wherefore, we confess one Christ, one son, one Lord. According
to this unmingled unity we confess the holy Virgin Mother of God, because the Word of God was made flesh and was made man, and by the
conception united to Himself a temple assumed from her. Moreover, we
recognize the evangelical and apostolic voices about the Lord as men
speaking with divine inspiration, joining these sometimes as if spoken
of one person, but sometimes separating them as if of two natures, and
these indeed befitting God according to the Godhead of Christ, but
humbly teaching according to the incarnation.

URBAN IV, 1261–1264

The Object and Force of Rememorative Liturgical Action [1]

[From the Bull, "Transiturus de hoc mundo," August 11, 1264]

5004   For other things whose memory we keep, we embrace in spirit and
mind; but we do not for this reason hold their real presence. In this
sacramental commemoration, however, Jesus Christ is present with us,
under another form to be sure, but in His substance.

ALEXANDER VII, 1655–1667

Gravity of Matter in Actions of Impurity [2]

[From the Response of the Holy Office, February 11, 1661]

5005   Whether a confessor is to be denounced for solicitation on account
of scarcity of material?

---

[1] BR (T) III (1858), 705.

[2] F. M. Cappello S.J., *Tract can. mor. de sacramentis* II, P. 1, De Poenit., ed. 2
(1929), n. 668, nota 39.

Reply: Since in actions of impurity scarcity of matter is not present, and if it should be present, is not in the matter at hand, they have decided that it should be denounced, and that a contrary opinion is not probable.

To the decrees of the Holy Office of February 11th, 1661, Benedict XIV referred readers in the Constitution "Sacramentum Poenitentiae," of June 1, 1741 (Docum. V in Cod. Iuris. Can.).

INNOCENT XII, 1691–1700

Matrimony as a Contract and a Sacrament [1]

[Reply of the Holy Office to Mission. Capucc., July 23, 1698]

Whether matrimony between apostates from the faith and those   5006 previously rightly baptized, entered upon after the apostasy, publicly according to the custom of pagans or Mohammedans, is truly matrimony and a sacrament.

Reply: If any agreement of dissolubility be at hand, there is no matrimony and no sacrament, but if none is at hand, there is matrimony and a sacrament.

---

[1] P. Gasparii, *Codicis Iuris Can. fontes* IV, n. 761; *Collectanea S.C. de Prop. Fide* I, n. 243.

INDEXES

Index of Scriptural Passages

*(Numbers on the right side of the columns refer
to the marginal numbers in the text)*

[3]

Systematic Index of

Dogmatic and Moral Matters

(A canon of the Code of canon law *is indicated by the letter* C; *a condemned proposition by the number in italics)*

REVELATION

THE POSSIBILITY AND NECESSITY OF REVELATION

I a Revelation strictly so-called or the speaking of God to man is possible and useful *1706,* 1807 f.; supernatural 1636, 1787, *2020 ff.;* morally (necessary) concerning natural religious truths 1642 ff.; absolutely necessary concerning the supernatural 1786, 1808; can be made believable by external signs 1622 ff., 1627 f., 1638 f., 1651, 1790, 1793, 1812 f.

THE FACT AND OBJECTS (MYSTERIES) OF REVELATION

I b The Most Holy Trinity revealed some things, through Moses, the prophets and their other servants, and finally through Christ 428, 1785; Christ, so that he might teach that He is the Messias, spoke and performed miracles *2028.*

Revelation is not a work of men or some philosophical discovery 1636, 1639, 1705, 1800, *2020 f.,* or a mere evolution of Christian understanding 2054, *2074 ff.,* but a determined body of doctrine applicable to all times and men 2059, *2078 ff.*

Besides truths accessible even to human reason Christian revelation contains mysteries widely so-called, as the eternal decrees of God, 1785; strictly so-called, which are inaccessible to reason 1616 f., 1642 ff., 1655, *1662,* 1668 f., 1682, 1709, 1795, 1816, *1915 f.;* moreover, they even transcend angelic understanding 1673, which with the progress of science cannot be understood or demonstrated 1642 ff., 1668 f., 1671 ff., *1704, 1709,* 1796, 1816, 1818; nevertheless, they do not contradict reason 1634 f., 1649, *1706,* but exceed it 1635, 1671, 1795, and always remain obscure 442, 1796; are not inventions of men contrary to the common good 1634, *1707.*

Revelation is not imperfect 1705, nor as such to be made perfect through progress 1636, 1639, 1656, *1705, 1800*; nor is it to be changed in any way into another meaning 1800, 1818; it is immutable 125, 148, 160 f., 212, 293, 308, 336, 1656, *2060 f.*, 2145; it was complete with the Apostles 783, *2021*.

THE ACCEPTANCE OF REVELATION (FAITH)

I c Divine Revelation requires internal faith 1637, 1681, 1789, 1810; and that divine (i.e. because of the pre-eminent authority of God revealing) 1789, 1811, C1323, sec. 1, which presupposes revelation previously made 1622, 1650, and known by the use of reason *1068*, 1626, 1651, 1670, 1790, 2146 (even in the scholastic method 1652).

Knowledge does not suffice that is only probable *1171*, nor merely subjective (of the Pseudo-mystics) *1273*, nor merely internal experience *2081*, or private inspiration 1812; but there is required a secure knowledge of the fact of revelation *1171*, 1623 ff., 1634 ff., 1639, *1715*, 1790, 1812, 2106 f. (although an infidel lead by a less probable opinion, not believing is not excused from infidelity *1154*). No one invited to embrace the faith is to be forced 1875; but revelation once accepted under the teaching authority of the Church cannot be called into doubt by a suspended assent 1794, 1815; hence a positive doubt is not the basis of theological investigation (Hermes) 1619 ff., 1815; all indifferentism and latitudinarianism is to be rejected 1613 f., 1646 f., 1677, 1689, 1715 ff., 1815, 1874, 1932, 2199.

THE POWERS, DUTIES, LIMITS OF REASON

I d Not all certitude is founded on faith *553 f.*; natural certitude is had not only of the first principle or those things which can be resolved to it *558*, 3020 f., but with a certitude of evidence (admitting of grades *556*) we know material substance 557, the

efficient causality of things *559 ff.*, 3020; the distinction of things from God *562 ff.*, and temporal existence *565;* the existence of one's own intellect and will *566;* that not all appearances are true *567;* that God and creatures are something *568*. The first and unique principle is not "If something is, something is" 570. Future, even contingent, things have a determined truth *719 ff.* Immediate knowledge of God (according to the mind of the Ontologists) is not essential to the human intellect 1659 ff.—Truth itself is immutable *2058, 3010 f.*, 3021 ff. Reason without revelation and even without grace can know some religious truths before the faith is accepted *1022, 1391*, 1616 ff., 1626, 1650, 1652, 1670, 1785, 1795, 1806, 2072, like the existence of God 1622, 1650, 1670, 1672, 1785, 1806, *2072 ff.* (and demonstrate it 1670, 2145, as even His nature and attributes 1670); the infinity of God 1622, the spirituality and immortality of souls 1650, the freedom of man 1650, the fact of creation 1806, miracles 1813, the divinity of Mosaic revelation 1623, 1627, and Christian 1624 f., 1627.

Before the reception of faith reason can and ought to know for certain (besides the fact of revelation) the motives for credibility (besides the preambles of faith) 1171, 1622 ff., 1634 f., 1637 ff., 1651, 1790 ff., 1799, 1812, 2145, 3005, *3019*, 3020, among which the prophecies and miracles of Christ *1707*, 1790, 1813, *2028*, 2145, and the Church itself, of itself, are outstanding 1638, 1794, 1957.

After the reception of the faith reason can attain a kind of understanding of the mysteries 1796, 3020, not, however, perceive all revealed truths or prove them with evident argument 282, 442, 1616, 1626 f., 1642, 1655 f., 1668 f., 1671 ff., 1682, *1704, 1709*, 1796, 1816, *1915*, 2120; thus, v.g., with the natural light it cannot attain its supernatural end and its means 1668 f., 1671 ff., 1791.

Human reason is not immune from all error 1618; wherefore it is not to be relied upon very much 1679; it is not autonomous, but subject to uncreated truth 1789, 1810; it is not the sole norm by which truths (necessary for salvation) are known 1616 f., 1619 ff., 1634 f., 1636, 1639, *1703 f.*, 1786, 1793, 1808; nor is it to be made equal to religion 1642, *1708*.

Man does not have an unmodified freedom of feeling, speaking, writing 1613 f., 1666 ff., 1674, 1679, 1690, *1779*, 1877, but limited 1932.

THE MUTUAL RELATIONSHIP BETWEEN REASON AND REVELATION

I e Revelation and reason cannot contradict one another 738, 1634 f., 1649, 1797 ff., 1878, 1947, 2023 f., 2109, 2146, nor is faith opposed to human reason 1635, 1706.

Reason explains, guards, and defends revealed truths 1635, 1652, 1799.

Revelation, on the other hand, frees reason from errors, enlightens, and strengthens it 195, 1616, 1635, 1642 ff., 1786, 1799, 1807, 3005; fosters the rectitude and purity of natural knowledge 1786; is the infallible director of philosophy 1656, 1681, and its negative norm 1681, *1714;* not only the philosopher but philosophy itself is under the teaching authority of faith 1674 ff., 1682 f., *1710, 1714*, 2073, 2085 f., and ought to be ancillary to theology 442 f., 1656, *1710*, 2087, 2120; hence errors of reason are rightly and beneficially proscribed by the Church 1674 ff., 1711, 1798, 1817, 2093; whose judgment is to be followed even with regard to things not yet expressly defined 1683 f., *1712, 1722*, 1820, *2008*, 2113 f., 3013, C1324.

Theology is to be treated otherwise than natural science 442 f., 1642, 1656, 1666 f., 1670 ff., 1681, *1708*, 1795, 1808, 2104; the method and principles of scholastic theology are not to be rejected 1657, 1680, *1713, 3008;* all

speculation concerning revealed truths should be founded upon the teaching of the Church and the Fathers 320, 323, 325, 1616 f., 1619 ff., 1657, 2086, 2120, 3012 f., and even a reasonable form in words is to be retained and the commonly received terminology is to be preserved 320, 442 f., 1658, 1800, *3009 ff.*

THE SOURCES OF REVELATION

The written source of revelation is *the canonical books of both Testaments* 32, 84, 92, 162, 245, 706 f., 783 f., 1787, 1809, 2001 ff., 2116 ff., C1323 sec. 1, of which the authentic version is had in the Vulgate 785, 1787, 2292.

These complete books with all their parts are to be received as sacred and canonical 784, 1787, and to be faithfully guarded 2198, as from God, who is the author of both Testaments 28, 348, 421, 464, 706 f., 783, 1787, 1952, *2009 ff.*, or from the Holy Ghost speaking 1951; inspired 706 (the nature of inspiration: 1952, *2009 f.*) and as such handed down to the Church 783 f., 1787, 1809, *2010 f.*, *2061*, 2090, 2100, 2102, 2115, 2179 f.; and to be judged and interpreted according to the unanimous consent of the Fathers and the sense of the Church 786, 995, 1788, 1944, according to sound principles 1946 ff., *2012 ff.*, *2061*, 2146, 2186 ff., 2293, 3002, 3016, 3029 f., in particular the books which are considered historical 1979 f., *2013 ff.*, 2186 f., 2294; Pentateuch 1997 ff., and its early chapters 2121 f., 3002; the Book of Isaias 2115 ff.; Book of Psalms 2129 ff.; the Gospels according to Matthew 2148 f., 2164 ff., Mark, and Luke 2155 ff., 2164 ff., John 2110 ff.; Acts of the Apostles 2166 ff.; pastoral epistles of St. Paul 2171 ff.; Epistle to the Hebrews 2176 ff.

True inerrancy belongs to Sacred Scripture 494, 570 f., 783, *1707*, 1787, *2011 ff.*, 2102, 2179 ff., 2186 ff., *3015*.

The reading of Sacred Scripture is not necessary for all *1429, 1567;* nor fitting

THE CHURCH

ESSENCE

II a   The Church is a *society* instituted by Christ God 703, 1618, 1821 ff., 1959, *2052 ff.,* 2088, 2091 ff., 2145, C100, sec. 1; a people one in faith, end, and things conducing to the end; subject to one and the same power, a society divine in origin, by its end and things proximately serving, insofar as it pertains to its end, are human members 1959, constituting one mystical body

under Christ the head 468, 705, *3019;* formed from the side of Christ 480, 2291. The end of the Church is to pour forth salvation procured through Christ and at the same time the benefits emanating therefrom upon all men of all ages 1821, 1955, 2203; and especially to protect the doctrine of Christ by a living and authentic teaching authority and to propagate it complete and uncorrupted 1957, 2145.

It is a society perfect and independent 330 ff., *498,* 1698, *1719 f.,* 1841 f., 1847, 1867, 1869, 2203; an immutable organization *2053;* with the right to possess even temporal things 1697, *1726 f.,* and with temporal power *1725,* and immunity *1730, 1732,* and its proper court *1731;* visible and knowable from the *marks* inherent in it and distinguishing it from the other religious bodies 86, 223, 247, 347, 430 f., 464, 468, 999, 1686, 1793 f., 1821 ff., 1955 f.; it is hierarchical 41 f., 44 f., 150 ff., 272, 361, 424, 426, 434, *498,* 675, 687, 853, 960, 966 f., 2145, C107, C108, C329 sec. 1, C948, and so lay persons have no power to dispose of ecclesiastical goods 361, in fact, not even priests of lesser rank by reason of their ordination *1509;* nor is the power derived into the hierarchies from the community of the faithful *1500, 1502 f., 1822 f.;* it is a monarchy i.e., constituted under one head having supreme power 44, *498, 633, 658 f., 1325,* 1500, *1503,* 1698 f., 1821, 2091, *2147a,* C218 f.; it is one (in faith, rule, and communion 1960) and unique 14, 86, 246 f., 347, 423, 430, 464, 468, 480, 1685 ff., 1954 ff. (not twofold, carnal and spiritual *485*); holy 1, 2, 6, 9, 86, 288, 347, 423, 464, 468, 1686; catholic 1, 6, 9, 14, 54, 86, 288, 347, 423, 464, 468, 1686; apostolic 14, 86, 247, 288, 347, 423, 464, 468, 570a, 1686; which is Roman 460, 570a, 1686, 1794, see IIIa-i; it is perpetual 1793, 1821, 1955, *2052;* it is necessary to all for salvation; "outside the Church there is no salvation," nor remission of sins 2 ff., 14, 39 f., 246 f., 423, 430, 468 f., 570b, 714, 999 f., 1473, 1613 f., 1646 ff., 1677, 1716 ff., 1954 ff., 2199, 3019, C731 sec. 2, C1322 sec. 2; hence:

II b Those ought (at least in desire) to be members of the Church who wish to be saved 388, 468, 629, 1646 f., C1322 sec. 2; members are the baptized (even children 869 f.) not only the predestined or faithful *627, 629, 631 f.,* 647, *1422, 1515,* but the perfect and sinners *473, 838, 1358, 1413, 1422-1438,* even the foreknown *631 f., 646,* princes and kings 1688, 1754, eastern and western *1738;* but the predestined are not necessarily always members of the Church *631 f.*

The Church is not divided into carnal and spiritual *485,* nor divided into three branches, namely, Roman-Catholic, Greek-schismatic, Anglican 1685 f., 2199.

The non-baptized do not belong to the body of the Church 895; falling away from a defined doctrine they fall away from the unity of the Church 1641.

POWER

Power of Teaching (Infallibility)

II c The fact of infallibility. The Church has by divine right the right and the office of guarding revealed doctrine 1675, and of expounding it *1444,* C1322 sec. 1, and in this function it is infallible 160, 767, *1512,* 1617, 1839, 1957 f., 1969, 2147, through the indwelling Holy Spirit 302, by whose assistance it preserves inviolably the deposit of faith 159 f., *1445, 1501,* C1322, nor has it ever erred *1723.*

II d The subject of infallibility: The *Pope* is infallible even without the consent of the Church *1325,* C1323 sec. 2; cf. III f.

Ecumenical Councils together with the Pope confirming them 164, 173, 212, 226 f., 250*, *768 f., 1723,* C222 sec. 2, C227 f., which represent the universal Church 270 ff., 349, 657 ff.,

769 f., 999 f., 1085 f.; they are taught by the Holy Spirit 930, C1322 f.; for which reason they have never erred in matters of faith and morals *1723;* they are constituted by the bishops 340, and others according to the norm of C223; they do not depend upon the presence of princes 331, 340. Particular and national councils are not infallible 1593, *1736,* C*1326;* hence in matters of faith and morals they do not give unalterable judgments *1511, 1593, 1736;* furthermore, diocesan councils do not judge concerning the decrees of higher sees 1511.

The Church dispersed throughout the world is infallible in proposing the doctrines of Christ handed down 1683, 1792, C1323 sec. 1.

Individual Bishops, although they are not infallible in teaching, nevertheless are the true doctors and masters, under the authority of the Roman Pontiff, of the faithful committed to their care *1506,* C1326; not however, *presbyters* —although joined in a synod *1510 f.,* not the *laity* 1936c, 1958, 2006.

The object of infallibility is things pertaining to faith and morals 767, 786, *1449 f.,* 1797 f., 1800, *2005;* and the teaching that the religion of the Catholic Church alone is true *1721,* and what are especially joined with the faith 1948 (not however ordinations for rule 333), the interpretation of the true sense of Sacred Scripture 32, 786, 995, 1788, *2202 ff., 2061;* the condemnation of errors concerning faith and morals 161, 2146, 2211, *2253;* and even dogmatic facts 224 ff., 1098 f., 1350, *1513 f.,* in such a way that dogmas are the norm of believing and acting *2026.* **II e**

The exercise of infallibility: The Church exercises her infallibility either in solemn judgment or in ordinary universal teaching 1683, 1792, C1323 sec. 1, by defining revealed truths *1721,* by watching over the faith of its subjects 1444, C247, and this by right and office 1797 f.; it cannot neglect truth *1449,* nor impugn it *1450,* nor **II f** permit obscurity in the more important truths of faith and morals *489, 1445 f., 1449, 1501, 1552 f., 1567, 1576 f.,* 1821, *1967;* nor again treat of errors once (definitely) condemned 161; nor change the sense of defined dogma *2080;* nor can it establish harmful discipline *1578;* hence acquiescence is to be given to its judgment even in things not yet expressly defined 1683 f., *1712, 1722,* 1820, 2113 f., 3013, C1324; nor does obsequious silence suffice 1350.

In its right and office of teaching all nations the Church is independent of all civil power C1322 sec. 2.

By right it demands a previous censorship of books *2001.*

THE POWER OF RULING (JURISDICTION)

II g The *nature* of jurisdiction: The Church has the jurisdiction given to the Apostles and to their successors *379,* for obtaining the salvation of souls and the purity of faith 1675, complete and total in religious matters *1285 ff., 1502, 1505,* 1841, 1847, 1866, C1553, and at least indirect in temporal matters 469 (two swords) 1697, *1724;* and that divine 469, and perpetual 287, *1577,* 1688, 1696, 2093, even relative as to the external order 1696 f.; wherefore legislative, judicial, and coactive power belong to her 411, *499 f., 1504 f.,* 1697, *1724;* it punishes especially with ecclesiastical censures 357, 499, *591 ff.,* 610, *643 ff.,* 681 ff., *763 f., 1440 ff., 1546 ff.,* C2214 sec. 1 (which does not cease when the guilty one is corrected and the contumacy comes to an end *1144*), not however of itself by bloody execution 401; and this jurisdiction does not depend upon the probity or the predestination of the subject *486, 545, 588, 595, 637, 646, 648, 650, 656,* 661. Even the perfect are bound by the precepts of the Church 473.

II h The *objects* and *functions* of ecclesiastical jurisdiction are especially these: the administration of the sacraments 437,

491 ff., 931, 1744, C731; in particular, matrimonial cases 973 f., 978, 982, 1454, 1500a, *1559 f.,* 1600, 1640, *1768 ff.,* 1865, 1991 ff., 2066 ff., C1016, C1960; preaching the divine word 434, *449 ff.,* 594, 687 f., C1327 f.; the election and ordination of bishops 339, 363, 1750 f., 1842, C109, and clerics 960, 967, C109, C1352; the care of religious and nuns *1752 f.,* C487 ff.; the granting of indulgences 467, 550, *622, 676, 729,* 989, 998, 1471, C911; the institution of feasts *1573,* C1247; the direction of theological study 422, 1666 ff., *1733, 1746,* 1843 ff., C589, C1365; of the reading and interpretation of Sacred Scripture *1567,* 1602 ff., 1630 ff., 1941 ff., 1979 f., 1997 ff., 2001 ff.; of the religious institution (in schools) 1695, *1745 ff.,* C1372 f., C1381; *see* XIp; generally the care of all sacred things and in some way even of temporal and external things 361, *458 f.,* 495, 685 f., *1286 f., 1322, 1504, 1696 f., 1724 ff.,* 1841, 2253, C1495 f., C1499.

RELATIONSHIPS

To the State: The Church in its own af- **II ii** fairs is independent of the civil power 161*, 305, 333, 361, *1575,* 1688, 1697 f., 1719 f., 1728 ff., *1741 ff.,* 1841 f., 1847, 1867, 1869, 2190, C1556, C1597, C2198, C2214, especially in matrimonial cases: cf. IIh; it is not an obstacle to the temporal prosperity of the state 333, 1936; nor hostile "to the more recent discipline of states" 1878 f.; let there be a single religion of the State *1777 ff.*

Its jurisdiction extends even over princes and kings 469, 1322, 1688, *1754,* C1557 sec. 1, C2227; even nations 1688; over public life, the family, education (in Christian schools) *1745 ff.,* 1995, 2197, C1372-1383, *see* XIp; for this reason it can invalidate unjust laws 1842, and call upon the secular arm 401, 468 f., *640, 682, 773,* 1689 ff., C2198; the Church cannot however, involve itself without reason merely in political or earthly business 1841, 2190; and it recognizes the power of a civil ruler, even a sinner *595, 597, 656.* The Church has the right to possess independently of the State *495, 596,* 685; it is rightly endowed by secular rulers *619.* In a conflict of laws the Church is to be obeyed, not the state *1742,* 1841 f., 1850, 1936b.

National churches independent of the Pope are not to be tolerated *1324, 1737.*

The Church is not to be separated from the State 1615, 1688, *1755,* 1867, 1995, 2092 f., but a way of concord is to be entered upon 1866, 1870, 2205.

The Church recognizes the State and its laws 1841, 1855 ff., 1866 ff., 1933 ff. The State cannot govern without concern for religion, and that the Catholic religion 1689; nor can it proclaim freedom of conscience and worship 1690 (saving the necessary tolerance of worships 1874); nor the right of openly manifesting any sort of concept 1690, or substitute the force of fact for the notion of true law 1691, *1759;* nor persecute religious families 1692, or take away the permission to collect alms 1693, or permit servile work on certain days 1693. The State is not the source of all law *1739;* nor does it have an indirect negative power in sacred things (so called, *exequatur, appellatio ab abusu) 1741,* 1866; nor the prevailing right in a conflict *1742,* nor the right to rescind a concordat *1743.*

II k *To Sciences:* The Church has authority over philosophers and philosophy 1682, 1710, even in things not yet expressly defined 1683 f.; for which reason it should not tolerate philosophic errors 1674 ff., *1711 f.;* errors in faith cannot be legitimate scientific conclusions 1797 f., 1947; the Church does not restrain sciences from their proper methods 1681, 1799, nor does it condemn scientific studies 609, 1878 f., *2057.*

To Culture: The Church is of benefit to **II l** human culture 609, 1740, 1799, 1878 f., 1936, 2205 f.; its teachings are not hostile to the good and benefit of human society *1634, 1740;* nor does it impede the free progress of science 1679, *1712 f.* (not even through the scholastic method 1680, *1713);* it ought not be reconciled with liberalism and politics *1780;* it is not an obstacle to true freedom 1873, 1876 f., 1932, 1936; it can in disciplinary matters accommodate itself to the various conditions of the times 1931, 1968, without however omitting or weakening any sections of doctrine 1800, 1967, *2065.*

THE ROMAN PONTIFF

SAINT PETER, PRINCE OF THE APOSTLES

Christ promised and gave to blessed **III a** Peter the primacy of jurisdiction over the universal Church 163, 466, 570c, 1821 ff.; hence Peter is the prince of the Apostles 351, 466, *496,* 570c, *655,* 694, 1823 f., and greater than St. Paul *1091, 2147a;* he is the Vicar of Christ *496,* 673, the foundation of the Church 351, 1821, 1824, 1976, 2145, and head *633,* and visible principle of unity 247, 1821, 1960 f.; "from whom the episcopacy and all authority have emerged" 100. Peter was aware of his own primacy 2055.

Peter has successors 468 f., *570d,* 766, and these are perpetual by divine right 1824 f.; which succession is found in the episcopacy of the City of Rome 570a ff., 1824, C218.

Three seats of St. Peter are shown 163. He himself founded the Roman Church 1824, and together with Paul was given over by Nero to be killed 163.

THE ROMAN PONTIFF SUCCESSOR TO ST. PETER

The Primacy of Jurisdiction

The *Existence* of Primacy: The Roman **III b** Pontiff holds (and always has held) primacy in the universal Church 41, 57a ff., 87, 100, 100*, 109 f., 112, 149, 149*, 161*, 163, 230, 247, 298, 326, 332, 341, 350 f., 357, 436, 466, 468, *484, 570*d, *589,* 674, 694, 740, *765 ff.,* 999 f., *1319 f., 1322 ff.,* 1473, 1500, 1734, *1826 ff.,* 1831 ff., 1960 f., *2055 ff.,* 2147a, 5000 f.; this primacy is supreme and full 466, 694, C218; was not introduced through the Church 332, *1503,* nor by the Emperor (Roman) *635,* but was instituted immediately by Christ *765 f.,* who in the person of Peter made the Roman Bishop the head of the entire Church 570c ff., 694, *765 f.,* 999, 1500, 1824 ff., that alone 468 f., *653, 1091,* not only ministerial *1503,* but so that by divine right he may have supreme power 466, 694, 1500, 1825 f., 1831, C109, C219, and that ordinary and immediate over all and each 1831, and immutable privileges 332, provided he is duly elected *652,* 674, although perchance he be evil *588, 638 f., 646, 650,* or not predestined *637, 646, 648.*

The Roman Pontiff is Peter's successor 57b, 57e, 87, 109, 112, 466, 570d, *639,* 674, 694, 740a, 999, 1473, 1677, 1824 ff., 1832 ff., 5000 f., C218 sec. 1, and the Vicar of Christ *617,* 694, 740a, *765,* 999, 1473, 1500, 1826.

III c The extent of the primacy: The Roman Pontiff has authority over Councils 446, 717, 740, 768, *1319, 1323 f., 1506 ff., 1574, 1598 f.,* C2332; he has jurisdiction over bishops 57a ff., 149, 570h, 1500, *1506 ff.,* 1823, 1961; for which reason he is the ordinary superior of dioceses 1500, C218 sec. 2, and of all churches 466; which however is not injurious to the jurisdiction of bishops but strengthens it 466, 1828, 1962; he has a certain power over princes and nations *1322, 1754,* C1557; and in general everyone baptized is subject to him as far as sacred things are concerned 468 f., 570a, *1734,* 1827, 1831, C87; and whoever refuses to be subject to the Roman Pontiff or refuses to communicate with members of the Church subject to him is a schismatic 570a, C1325 sec. 2.

The functions of primacy: The Roman **III d** Pontiff nourishes, rules and governs the whole Church 109 f., 468 f., 694, 1500, 1698 f., 1826, 1831, 1961, C218; and particularly the Roman *636 f.;* he alone establishes canons *570k;* he himself gives out legitimate decretals *618 f.;* has the full power over spiritual things *1323 f.;* hence he disposes of the treasury of the Church (see XII l), concedes indulgences (see XII l), calls transfers, dissolves councils 740, C222, sec. 2; makes bishops 968, 1750 f., C329, sec. 2; transfers, judges, and punishes them 570h, 570p; dispenses in the laws of the Church *491 ff., 731,* C81; is the supreme judge 57a ff., 330, 352, 469, 570 f., *731, 1440,* 1830, C1569, from whom no appeal is granted 330 f., 333, 341, 353, 469, 570g, 717, 1830, 5001, C1880, who can be judged by no one 330, 333, 353, 570g, 1830 f., C1556; he can establish reserved cases 903, C893, and these for the whole Church *1545,* C895, C2245; sometimes he excommunicates without the presumed consent of the entire Church *1440.*

Consequences: The Roman Pontiff is the **III e** father and teacher of all Christians 694; head of the whole Church 694; is the root of the unity of the Church 1686, 1960, 1976; hence to be subject to him is "necessary for salvation" 469, 570b, 570, 5000, and "where the Pope is there is the Church" 1500, 1686; national churches separated from him are a contradiction 1738; obedience should be shown him in respect to the laws of the Church 999, 1698 f., C2231; he is not subordinate to the Emperor (Roman) *497,* 570i; he acts freely in the universal Church *1734;* for which reason even if the ruler is unwilling he can carry on business with the bishops and all the faithful *1749,* 1829, C2333; to whom his court is always open 446, 1830, C1569; his letters are valid and can be promulgated even without the permission of the civil ruler (or "regal approval") *1728*, 1829, 1847; even without his acknowledgement they are valid 1729. He ought not to adapt himself to modern liberalism 1780. He is rightly called "Most Holy" *649*.

The Infallibility of the Roman Pontiff

III f The Roman Pontiff can establish articles of faith and laws of morals and of good works *767*, and in establishing these (and in determining the sense of the words of any book of a theologian 1098 f.) he is infallible 100, 100*, 109, 110, 129, 139, 142, 160, 171 f., 351, 570q, 1000, *1319*, when he speaks ex cathedra 1838 ff., C1323 sec. 2; hence he is the supreme Teacher of the Church 694, 1832 ff., C218; whose final decision is irretractable 109, 110, 159, 1830, 1880, even before the consent of the Church (teaching) *1325*, 1839, or a universal council 768, 1839, C1332 sec. 2.

The Roman Pontiff has never erred in matters of faith or morals 171 ff., 273, *1723*, 1836 (not even Liberius 93); for this reason he is rightly called the protagonist of the faith 129, whose office is to define and defend the truths of faith 466, 570q, 1836, which is never done to the detriment of science 1679, *1712*. Assent and obedience are due to his decrees, even if they do not pertain to the dogmas of faith and morals 1698.

The Civil Rule of the Roman Pontiff

III g The spiritual kingdom of the Roman Pontiff is compatible with temporal rule *613, 1775;* abrogation of this rule is not to the benefit of the Church *1776;* for this reason he is not to be deprived of all dominion and temporal responsibility *1727*.

Election and Person

III h The Roman Pontiff according to law is elected by the Cardinals *620*, C160;

rightly elected he is the true Pastor of the Church 674, C219, and its head 1500, although perchance he be **not** predestined or evil: see IIIb.

The Roman See

The Roman See is the See of Saint Peter **III i** 57b, 57e, 163, 298, 351, 694, 1824, which (if the Pope is unwilling) cannot be transferred *1735;* for this reason the Church of the City of Rome is the mistress and vindicator of truth 1679, mother and (as such immune from error 740b) mistress of all the faithful 433, 436, 460, *617, 2056,* and of all churches 859, 910, 946, 999 f., to which it is superior 163, *621,* over which it holds a primacy of power 436, and it is their head 57e,—and this not from merely political conditions, but from the ordination of divine providence 1827, *2056*.

ONE GOD

HIS EXISTENCE AND KNOWABILITY

God exists 1 f., 6 f., 9 ff., 13, 15, 17, 19, **IV a** 39, 54, 86, 428, 703, 994, 1782, 1801; which can be known with certainty by the light of reason 1622, 1650, 1670 ff., 1785, 1806, 2072, 2106 f., 2145, and also demonstrated 1670, 2145, even without grace *1391, 3017,* 3020; moreover, God has revealed Himself 429, 1785 ff.; hence His existence also can and ought to be believed 1782; but the immediate vision of God is not natural to the soul *475;* much less is it (vision) essential or congenital to it, or identical with the light of the intellect itself *1659, 1662 f., 1927;* nor is God immediately manifest in things *1891 ff.;* "God is" and "God is not" do not mean the same thing 555.

THE ESSENCE AND ATTRIBUTES OF GOD

God is only one 1 f., 6 f., 9 ff., 13, 15, **IV b** 17, 19, 39, 54, 86, 420 f., 462, 703, 994, 1782, 1801; distinct from the world 433, *507, 523, 1660 f., 1664,*

1701, 1782, 1803 f., *1891 ff.*, 2108, *2189*, 3005; He did not begin at the same time as the world 501; He is high above all 1782.

In God various attributes are distinguished: He is simple 389, 428, 993, 1782, and immutable 254, 346, 428, 463, 703, *1701*, 1782, 1804, uncreated 39, eternal 39, 254, 346, 428, 463, 703, 1782 (and He alone 391), immense 39, 428, 1782, incomprehensible 254, 428, 1782, ineffable 428, 1782, a spiritual substance 1782, happy in and of Himself 1782; there is, however, no real distinction between the nature and the attributes, nor among themselves 294, 389, 993; and on this account ought all distinction in God to be rejected *523 f.*

THE RELATIONS OF GOD TO THINGS OUTSIDE HIMSELF

IV c God is infinitely intelligent 1782, knowing all things 300, 316, 321 f., 1784, even free things in the future 321, 1784, 3017, the past, present, and future by a knowledge of vision *2184*, and willing in an infinitely perfect way 1782, omnipotent 1 ff., 39, *210*, 316, 346, *374*, 428, 461 ff., 703, 1782, with a free will in operating outside Himself *374*, 706, 1655, 1783, 1805; ought not to obey the devil 586, was able to do what He did not 374.

There does not exist a twofold principle of the world, good and evil 19 ff., 29, 54, 86, 237, 343, 421, 461, 469, 706 f., 994, 1783, 1801; God is the source of all truth and power 1649; He is also one and the same in the Old and New Testament 28, 348, 421, 464, 706.

THE TRIUNE GOD

UNITY OF NATURE

V a In God there are three Persons, who nevertheless are one God 1 ff., 13, 15, 17, 19, 22 ff., 39, 42a, 48, 51, 54, 58 ff., 82 f., 201, 213, 231, 254, 275, 278 ff., 294, 296, 343, 346, 389 f., 420 f., 428, 431 f., 461, 691, 703 f., 993, 994, 1595 f., *1915;* they are,

namely, one nature, one essence or co-essential, one substance, or consubstantial 19, 59, 66, 74, 83, 86, 213, 254, 275, 277 ff., 343, 420, 428, 431 f., 461, 703 f., 708, 993 f.; they are co-equal, coeternal, coomnipotent 13, 19, 39, 54, 68, 70, 75, 78 f., 254, 276 ff., 343, *368*, 428, 461 ff., 703 f., 708; equally omnipresent, adorable, omniscient, immense, vivifying 39, 75, 79 f., 254, 703 f.; inseparable in being 48, 281, 461, in acting (creating) 19, 77, 79, 281, 284, 428, 461; one principle of operation outside 77, 254, 281, 284, 421, 428, 703, especially in effecting the Incarnation 284, 429.

THE TRINITY OF PERSONS

The Father is a simple and indivisible **V b** substance 432; is not made, not created, nor born, nor proceeding 3, 19, 39, 275, 345 f., nor by generating does He lose anything of His substance 432; but He has everything of Himself; He is the principle without principle 428, 703 f.; He is omnipotent 1 f., 6, 9, 13, 15, wise and benign *381*, invisible, incapable of suffering, immortal, incomprehensible, immutable 3; with the Son He is the cause (according to the Greeks) or (according to the Latins) the principle of the Holy Spirit 691; He is the creator of heaven and earth 3, 6, of things visible and invisible 9, 13, 54, 86, 994.

The Son is God 2 ff., 13, 16 ff., 39, 49 ff., **V c** 54, 57*, 61, 68 ff., 77 ff., 86, 148, 233, 276, 461 f., 705, 708, 993 f.; consubstantial (ὁμοούσιος) with the Father 13, 54, 86, 276, 462, 708; He is not a kind of extension of the Father 66, nor a portion of Him 276; He is not created 13, 39, 48, 61, 86; but He is a principle from a principle 704, born of the nature or substance of the Father 13, 19 f., 48, 54, 69, 86, 275 f., 281, 344 ff., 432, 462, 703 f., 708, 994, and only the Father 40, 428, 703 f.; and that from eternity 214; neither by will nor necessity 276; He is His natural, not adopted Son 276; He is immutable 14, incapable of suffering 72, 344, sempiternal 276.

The Son is not the matter from which God created *1909*, but through Him all things are made 54, 77, 86; He rules all 422; as the Son He is not pre-destined 285; He alone is incarnate 282, 285, 422, and suffered 42a; He is not better called "Word" than "Son" 1597. [On the Incarnate Word see VIIIa ff.]

V d The Holy Spirit is true God 2 ff., 13 ff., 39, 51, 54, 58 ff., 74, 275 ff., 296, 344, 461, 463, 1084, 1461, neither born, nor created 39, 277, proceeding from the Father and the Son 15, 19, 83, 277, 345 f., 369, 428, 460, 463, 574a, 691, 703, 994, 1084, *2147a*, as from one principle 460, 691, 704; He is immutable 14; He is not made 14, 76; but all things are made through Him 77; He is to be adored as the Father and the Son 80, 86; He is sent by the Father and the Son 277; He is not the Father of Christ 282, nor the soul of the world *370;* He is the inspirer of the Law and the Prophets 86, 344, of both Testaments 13, 345 f., 706 f., 783, 1787; He is the cause of the Incarnation 290, 344, 429; He is the vivifier 86; He dwells in the Church 302; He is sent to the apostles and the faithful and works in them 13; He teaches a universal council 930; He acts in the sacraments 424; He is received with sanctifying grace 799; He is sevenfold 83; He gives seven gifts 83; He is given in a special way in confirmation 697, and ordina-tion 964.

VARIOUS EXPLANATIONS AND MANNER OF SPEAKING

V e These three Persons are among them-selves really distinct 39, 231, 281, *523 f.*, 703 ff.; but each is whole in the others (circumincession) 704; in them there is nothing before or after 39; the Deity is not diminished in each, it is not increased in the Three 279.

There are in God relations numerically distinct 280, 703, and properties 281, 296, 428.

The Persons together with the essence do not constitute a quaternity 431 f.; nor because of the Incarnation is a quaternity made 283.

Reality, idealness, and morality are not persons *1916*.

God is not to be called threefold, but triune 278; not "one God distinct in three Persons," but "in three distinct Persons" 1596, 1655.

A real distinction is not to be established between the nature and the Persons (subsistences) 389, 431; some dis-tinction, however, is to be made *523 f.*

The formulas: "Will generates will," "Wisdom generates wisdom" are to be rightly understood 294, 296.

This revealed truth is a mystery 1655, *1915*, falsely explained by Ant. Guen-ther 1655.

GOD THE CREATOR

CREATION

The triune God 48, 79, 281, 421, created **VI a** the world from nothing 1 ff., 19, 21, 29, 54, 86, 235, 343, 421, 428, 461, 706, 994, 1782 f., 1801, 1805, when He willed *374, 706,* not from eternity 391, *501 ff., 3017*, but from the be-ginning of time 428, 1783, 2123; not of necessity *501, 503,* but freely from His goodness *374, 607, 706, 1655,* 1783, 1805, 1908, 3017; nevertheless God is not the only cause of true effects 559 ff., nor did He create the best world *569,* nor another world, so that Adam was not the first man *717c.*

Creation is falsely explained by the Origenists 203 ff., Priscillianus and the Manicheans *237 ff.*, Ekard 501 ff., the ontologists *1664 f.*, Rosmini *1905 ff.*, the pantheists *1701,* 1803 f., the emanatianists 34, 232, *1665,* 1804.

Creatures

Creatures of two kinds are to be dis- **VI b** tinguished (distinct from God *1701,* 1782, 1803): visible and invisible, bodily and spiritual 9, 13, 19, 54, 86, 343, 421, 428, 461, 706, 994, 1783,

1802, 1804 f., *3018;* created nature, even material, is of itself good 37, 236 f., 242, 421, 425, 706, 713; it is changeable 706; it is not the same as the Word *1909;* nor is it purely nothing *526, 1901 ff.*, nor are all things one *522.*

Heaven, the stars, and water are not animate *208;* nor is flesh-food of itself unclean *244.*

VI c Angels exist and are spiritual 428, 461, 706, 994, 1783, 1802, 1804 f., 3018, they are not propagated 533; the devil himself was created and good 237; likewise also the other demons 428, 574a.

VI d Man is not of the substance of God 1701, but is created 241 f., 1783, 1801, 1806, 2123; he consists of two substances 295, namely of a soul or spirit and a body (not made by the devil 242) or flesh 295, 428, 481, 1783, 1914; he is therefore flesh intellectually animated 255. The end of man is so that leading a life in society and ordered under God he may cultivate fully all his faculties for the praise of His Creator, and by fulfilling faithfully the office of his art or any other vocation he may obtain for himself both temporal and eternal happiness 2270.

Adam was the first man 101, 228a, 2123, from whom the whole human race is derived 2280, 3028; nor before him were there any men in the world 717c. On the origin of the body of Adam: 2123, 2285, 3027.

The human soul is not a part of the divine substance or one reality with the Word 20, 31, 235, 348, *511 ff.;* nor is it uncreated or uncreatable 527; but it is created by God 20, 144*, 170, 527, 3027, from nothing 348; it does not pre-exist 203, 236; it is not generated by parents 170, *533, 1910;* nor does it evolve from sensitive to intellectual *1910 ff.;* it is a substance 295; it is not one in all 738; but one in each 338; infused before birth *1185;* it is not naturally either good or evil 236, 243, 642.

The soul is rational and intellectual 148,

216, 255, 290, 338, 344, 393, 422, 429, 480, 738; but it is not itself the unique object of evident knowledge *557;* it is immortal 2 ff., 16, 40, 86, 738; it is not united with the body accidentally *1911 f.*, *1914*, but *per se* and essentially it is truly the form of the body 480 f., 738, 1655; it is endowed with liberty 129 f., 133 ff., 140, 174, 181, 186, 316 f., 322, 325, 348, *373, 776, 793, 797, 1027 f., 1039, 1065 ff., 1093 ff., 1291, 1360 f., 1912, 1914*, which liberty can be proved not only from Scripture 1041, but also from reason 1650.

[On the separated soul see XIVa and b]

Man by his nature is a social being 1856, **VI e** 2270; wherefore all cannot be equal 1849, 1851; cf. XIi-p.

THE END OF CREATION AND PROVIDENCE

The *end,* which God had in creating, is **VI f** not His own beatitude 1783, but the manifestation of His goodness 1783. The end of the world is the glory of God 134, 1805, 2270, the beginning and end of all things 1785. This end nevertheless is not obtained equally by the evil and the good work of man *504 ff.;* it is obtained not only by complete renunciation 508, cf. XIa ff. XIIId.

By His providence God governs things **VI g** visible and invisible 421, 1784, and He protects them 254, by truly acting upon the world and men *1702;* He does not will evil as He wills good 514; and He only permits sin 816; He could have prevented evil *375;* He ought not to obey the devil *586;* He neither communicates nor subjects His omnipotence to us 1217 f. Man is not under the direction of the stars 35, 239 f., nor is he ruled by fate 607.

GOD ELEVATING

THE SUPERNATURAL ORDER

God elevated rational creatures (angels **VII a** and men) to a state exceeding the needs of nature *1001-1007, 1009, 1021,*

1023 f., *1079*, *1671 ff.*, *3018;* which is not transformation into God *510*, or into the Only Begotten Son of God *511 ff.*, *520 ff.*, nor is it identification with the humanity of Christ *520 ff.*, nor a manifestation of being itself in the fullness of its real form *1926;* but it is an ordering to a supernatural end *1786* (unapproachable to reason without revelation *1669*), which consists in the vision and fruition of God *530*, *693;* to which man ought to tend through supernatural acts *180*, *190*, *198*, *714*, *809*, *842*, *1002*, *1004 f.*, *1011 ff.*, *1023*, *1027;* for this reason a distinction is to be made between works naturally (morally) good and works meritorious of a supernatural end *190*, *1008*, *1034*, *1036 ff.*, *1061 f.*, *1065*, *1289 f.*, *1394*, *1524.*

The natural is perfected by the supernatural order *2206*, *2224*, **2237.**

ORIGINAL MAN

(The State of Integral Nature)

VII b The first man was formed without sin *316*, *793*, in sanctity and justice *788;* he had free will *133*, *186*, *316*, *793*, and supernatural gifts *1008*, *1024*, of integrity *192*, *1026*, *2123*, *2212*, and of immortality *101*, *175*, *788*, *793*, *1006*, *1078*, *1517*, *2123*, *2212.*

The grace (justice) of the first man was not a consequence of creation nor due to nature itself *1008*, *1023 ff.*, *1026*, *1385 ff.*, but God could have created man without this supernatural grace *1021*, *1023 f.*, *1079*, *1516 f.*, even such as he is now born *1055.*

To preserve the original state man needed grace *192*, *1001 ff.;* and his merits were not merely human and natural *1001 ff.*, *1007*, *1009*, *1384.*

ORIGINAL SIN

VII c Man at the suggestion of the devil sinned *428*. Adam lost through (originating) sin sanctity and justice and was wholly changed for the worse in body and soul *174*, *200b*, *788*, *2123*, *2212*, was made a "mass of perdition" *316*, under the power of the devil *788*, *793.*

The fall of Adam hurt not only himself, but from it his whole progeny contracted sin (original) *102*, *109a*, *130*, *144**, *175*, *316*, *348*, *376*, *536*, *574a*, *711*, *789 ff.*, *793*, *1643 ff.;* which nevertheless does not consist in concupiscence, which in an improper sense is called sin *792.*

Original sin is passed on not by imitation but by propagation or generation from the seed of Adam *109a*, *711*, *790 f.*, *795*, *2229;* it is true sin *101*, *174 f.*, *789 ff.*, *3018*, *3028*, and guilt of sin, not only of penalty *376;* it is proper to everyone *790*, *795*, although not personal *532;* it is in children themselves *102*, *410*, *532*, *791;* equally of Christians and infidels *534;* it is voluntary, not by the habitual will of the child *1048*, but by reason of origin *1047*, and it differs from actual sin by reason of consent *410*, and also by reason of penalty, which for original sin alone is the lack of the vision of God *410*, since non-baptized children are condemned indeed (with the penalty of damnation) yet they did not hate God in act *1049*, nor did they suffer the penalty of fire (sense) *493a*, *1526.*

Original sin is taken away in the baptism of regeneration *101* f., *109a*, *160b*, *329*, *348*, *790 ff.*, which must be received at least in desire *388*, *413.*

A man should not do penance throughout his whole life for original sin *1309.*

The Blessed Virgin Mary did not at all contract original sin; see VIIIk.

FALLEN MAN

(The Consequences of Original Sin. The State of Fallen Nature.)

Man through the sin of Adam was **VII d** changed for the worse *188*, *195*, *200b*, *1643* f.; he was made mortal *101*, *109a*, *175*, *793*, and under the power of the devil *711*, *788*, *793*, prevented from entering heaven *711*, subject to eternal death *734.*

His intellect was obscured *195*, *788*, *1616*, *1627*, *1634*, *1643*, *1670.*

Freedom of will as a capacity for good (supernatural) was wholly lost, 105, 130, 133-135, 181, 186, 194, 317, 811, and as concerns the rest (natural things) his free will was not indeed destroyed *160a, 766, 793, 797, 815, 1065, 1298, 1388,* but it was weakened 160a, 181, 186, 199, 793; man can, however, do certain good things even without grace *1008, 1022, 1025, 1027 ff., 1037 f., 1065, 1351 ff., 1372, 1388 ff., 1414,* 1524; even if without a special privilege he cannot avoid all venial sins 107 f., 471, 804, 833, *1275 f., 1282.*

Therefore not all works of infidels or sinners are sins or splendid vices *1025, 1035, 1298, 1388;* nor in all acts do they serve a dominant desire *1040, 1523 f.;* and material sins, which are from force or from invincible ignorance are not formal because of the will of Adam *1291 f.*

There is in fallen man the inclination to sin, from which he cannot completely free himself 792, *1275;* by which, however, he is not prevented from entering heaven *743, 792;* for involuntary motions of concupiscence are not transgressions of the law *1050 f., 1074 ff.*

God could have from the beginning created a man such as is now born *1055.*

GOD THE REDEEMER: CHRIST

(Incarnation; Christology)

TRUE GOD

VIII a Christ is true God 2 ff., 13, 20, 33, 39, 42a, 54, 57*, 86, 111a, 113 f., 116 f., 143 f., 148, 220, 224, 255, 283, 288, 290, 344, 392, 422, 462, 480, 708, 710, 993, 994, *2027 ff.,* 2088, 5003; hence he is rightly called the Word of the Father 118 f., 224; and likewise the Son of the Father 1597, consubstantial with Him 13, 54, 86, 148, 220, 480, 708, 993, 1460, 5003; equal to the Father 118, not separated from Him 66, not His extension or gathering 66;

God of God 13, 54, 86, born, not made 13, 39, 54, 61, only-begotten 13, 54, 86, one of the Trinity 216, 222, 255, 291, 372, 708, through whom all things are made 54, 86, 422; He is unchangeable 27, 54, eternal 54, 66, incapable of suffering 27. The divinity of Christ is proved in the Gospels *2027, 2030, 2096 f.;* cf. Vc.

TRUE MAN

The same Christ is true man 13, 18, 25, **VIII b** 33, 40, 111a, 114, 143 f., 148, 220, 258, 283, 288, 290, 344, 393, 422, 429, 462, 480, 708, 1463; conceived of the Holy Spirit 2, 6, 9, 13, etc., not of man 13, 20; truly born of a mother 2, 6, 9, 13, 257, 285, 422, 708, 993; He has a rational soul 25, 111a, 148, 216, 255, 283, 290, 344, 422, 429, 462, 480, 709 f., 1463, 5003, intellectual 13, 216, 255, 422, 429, 480, not merely sensitive 710, truly human 13, 65, *204,* which however did not previously exist *204;* and He has a body 26, 31, 111a, 148, 290, 480, 708, 1463, 5003, i.e., true human flesh 20, 216, 255 ff., 393, 422, 429, not imaginary 20, 344, 462, 710, nor celestial 710, joined to divinity right from the very beginning 205; and His soul is truly, *per se* and essentially, the form of His body 216, 480. And so Christ is in all things like us without sin 1463.

TWO NATURES

There are therefore in Christ two natures **VIII c** 18, 20, 33, 42a, 111a, 143 f., 148, 168, 213 ff., 283, 288, 344, 422, 429, 462, 710, 1463, 5003, which are indeed substantially different 260; nevertheless they are undivided 148, 259 ff., 1463, 5003, inseparable 148, 283, 288, 290, 314a, 1463, unconfused 11a, 148, 168, 219 f., 259 f., 288, 290, 314a, 1463; for this reason He is said to be "of two natures and in two natures" 259, 462, 708.

Each nature retains its own properties 72, 258, 262, 288, 290, 708, 1462, and faculties of knowing and willing 263, 265 ff., 288, 344, 1465: He has two operations 144, 251 ff., 264 ff., 288 f., 291 f., 344, 710, 1465. The two wills are not contrary to each other 251 f., 288 ff., 1465; the operation θεανδρική, so-called, is to be rightly understood 268.

ONE PERSON
(The Hypostatic Union)

VIII d Christ is only one Person 20, 42a, 143, 215 ff., 261, 269, 283, 312, 314a, 344, 422, 429, 462, 480, 710, 876, 1462 f., 1655, so that God and man in Him are one and the same 13, 111a, 215 ff., 257, 259, 288 ff., 312, 708, whole God-man and whole man-God 168; He is consubstantial with God and with man 148, 220, 257, "a third person in the Trinity" 372, but neither the Father nor the Holy Spirit 422.

The natures are united not only through having the same name, grace, dignity, authority, operation, relation, confusion, affection, and virtue 111a, 115, 121, 216, 708, 710, nor only through denomination or adoration 216, nor through the conversion of one nature into the other 40;

but they are united according to subsistence (ὑπόστασιν), which is called hypostatic union 13, 111a, 115 f., 148, 216 ff., 226, 261, 288, 292, 344, 429, 462, 480, 708, 710, 1463, which was accomplished from the first moment of the Incarnation 111a, 204 f., 234, 250. The hypostatic union (falsely explained by Ant. Guenther 1665, and Rosmini 1917) is ineffable and incomprehensible and a mystery strictly so-called 1462, 1669.

CONSEQUENCES AND MANNERS
OF SPEAKING

VIII e Christ is not to be called only θεοφόρος, or godly 117, 312, or the dwelling place of God 123, 708, nor one composite nature 288, nor simply "two natures" 630.

From unity of person there follows a communication of idioms, or reciprocal predication of properties and operations 16, 116, 121, 124, 201, 222, 224,

248, 372, 480, 1339; hence the "agnoeti" erred 248.

The operations of the human nature are made more dignified by being joined with the divinity 550, 1019.

The humanity of Christ itself is to be adored 120, 221; and indeed directly as united with divinity 224, 1561, with one adoration, not two 120, 221; and also to be loved by the perfect 1255; this cult of latria is fitting especially to the Eucharistic Christ 478, 878, 888, C1255 sec. 1; and to the Most Sacred Heart of Jesus 1563.

The Man Christ is the only Son of God 2, 64, and natural 143, 1460, in no way adopted 299, 309 ff., 314a, 344, 462; a "servant" only allegorically through obedience 310, 313; He is not the Son of the Holy Spirit 282; but truly a Son of man; see VIIIi; He can be called less than the Father and Holy Spirit, greater or less than Himself 285; He cannot be called incapable of being born 26; rather He has two nativities, eternal as God and temporal as man 257, 285, 290, 344, 1463.

VIII f Christ was conceived holy and without sin, born and died 13, 18, 65, 122, 148, 224 f., 251, 258, 286, 290, 711, 1463; rather impeccable even before the resurrection 224; for this reason He did not need purification 1314; He had the seven gifts of the Holy Spirit 83, in particular even fear of God 378; He was not subject to passions nor improved by progress 224; He did not offer sacrifice for Himself 122; He was free in the Passion 215, 253, 255; He performed miracles 215, 1624, 1790, 1813, 2084, by His own power 121, and gave forth prophecies 1790, and His soul knew from the beginning all things in the Word, which God knows by a knowledge of vision 2183 ff., 2289, even the last day 248, 2032 ff.

In Christ three substances can indeed rightly be distinguished: the Word, the soul, the flesh 285, 295; but He is better called a person and two sub-

stances of God and of man 148, 312.
Christ as Word is born only, as man He
is born, made, and predestined 285;
as man he is not omnipresent 307.

GOD THE REDEEMER:
THE WORK OF
CHRIST

(Redemption, Soteriology)

VIII g Since neither through the powers of nature nor the Mosaic law fallen man
could be restored 793, 811, but only
through the merits of Christ 711, 790,
795, 809, 820, *1011,* Christ was made
man for our salvation 9 f., 13, 16, 40,
54, 86, *371,* 429, 708, and died that
He might repair the nature lost
through Adam 194, 794, 800, and free
us from the yoke of the devil *371,* and
from original sin *536,* 790; through
the death of the Cross (which He, not
the Father suffered, 42a, and which
was a true sacrifice 122, 938, 940,
2195), He redeemed us from sin and
reconciled us to the Father 286, 993 f.,
2212, and that out of love for the human race, not from fate *717d;* He
satisfied (by His Passion) for all men
or for the sins of the whole world
122 ff., 160a f., 286, 319, 323, 344,
462, 480, 550, 790, 794 *f.,* 799, 809,
820, *1096, 1294 ff., 1382, 3018,* which
satisfaction is infinite *319, 552, 1019,*
and superabundant 740a. Christ in the
next world will not be crucified for
the demons 209.

Christ is the Redeemer 328, 355, 494,
550, 794, 831, 874, 877, 907, 1100,
2195, the Savior 1, 251, 253, 269, 271,
337, 796, 809, 874, 875, 913, the
Mediator of God and men 143, 251,
253, 333, 711, 790, our Lord 1 (and
frequently elsewhere), and King 13,
333, and He is as man a king with
legislative, judicial, coactive, adminis-
trative jurisdiction over both the members of His spiritual kingdom and over
all men 2194 ff.; over all civil states
2196; He passed laws in fact as a true
legislator 831; hence laicism is to be

condemned 2197. Likewise Christ as
man is a Priest 122, 333, 430, 938,
940, 2136, 2195; He is present in the
mysteries of the Church 2297.

THE MYSTERIES OF THE
LIFE OF CHRIST

Christ about to come is foreshadowed **VIII h**
through all the sacred things, sacrifices,
sacraments, ceremonies of the Old
Testament 695, 711 f.; in fact, promised even before the Law 794, to our
first parents 2123. He is not a mythical
fiction *1707.*

Christ was made flesh and conceived of
the Holy Spirit from the Virgin Mary
2 ff., 13, 40, 63, 86, 148, 255, **422,**
429, 708, 933, 944;

then He was born of the Virgin Mary
2 ff., 122, 143 f., 148, 233, 282 f.,
314a n, 344, 422, 709 ff., as legitimate
717 f.; He was not the son of Saint
Joseph 993;

during His life He ate, drank, slept, and
became tired 422; He was hungry,
thirsted, grieved, He wept 20; He was
poor but not absolutely *494, 577;* He
had a right to property 577 (of using
things, selling them or giving them
away, of acquiring other things from
them 494); willingly He paid tribute to
Caesar 495; He always had a consciousness of His Messianic dignity *2035;*

He suffered 2 ff., 13, 34, 54, 86, 143 f.,
422, 480; and that willingly 255,
717d, as man 72, 344, 709;

He was crucified under Pontius Pilate
2 ff., 20, 86, 222, 255; nor can it be
said that the inferior part of Christ
on the Cross did not communicate to
the superior part its involuntary disturbance *1339;*

He died 3 ff., 16, 20, 42a, 286, 344, 422,
429, 462, 993, 1463, a pious death
(according to the Gospels) *2038;* He
was made sin for us 286, and He
offered sacrifice 938 f., 951; from His
side opened after death true water
flowed, not phlegm 416 f., 480; (concerning the blood that was shed the
Church has defined nothing 718);

He was buried 2 ff., 20, 86, 255, 344, 462;

He descended into hell 3, 6, 40, 429, 462, in His soul (not in power only) *385*, 429; but He did not do away with hell *532*, 574a;

He rose (on the third day) 2 ff., 13, 16, 20, 40, 54, 86, 255, 429, 462, 994, 2036, 2084, as Psalm 15, 10 f., foretold 2272, by His own power 286, with a true resurrection of the flesh 344, 422, 429, 462, 709, by a reassuming of the soul to the body 422, 462, historically demonstrable *2036 f.;* and truly then, but without need, He ate 344, 422;

He ascended into heaven 2 ff., 13, 20, 54, 86, 255, with body and soul 13, 344, 429, 462, 709;

He is seated at the right hand of the Father 2 ff., 13, 16, 86, 255, 344, in the flesh 73, 422, 462, 709, according to a natural manner of existing 874;

He sent the Holy Spirit 344;

He rules unto eternity 9, 13, 16, 86;

He will judge the living and the dead 2 ff., 13, 40, 54, 86, 228a, 287, 334, 422, 427, 429, 462, 994, coming in His body 13, 73, 255, 422, 709.

MARY THE MOTHER OF GOD AND VIRGIN

VIII i Mary is the Mother of Christ and hence truly and properly the mother of God 20, 91, 111a, 113, 144, 201 f., 214, 218, 256 f., 290, 422, 708, 993, 1462, 5002; but she generated only the Son, not the Trinity 284.

VIII k Mary was an inviolate virgin 13, 20, 91, 113, 144, 201 f., 214, 255 f., 282, 290, 344, 429, 462, 708, 735, 993, 1462; and remained perpetually (before birth and in birth and after birth) 91, 256, 282, 314a n, 734, 993; for this reason she did not need purification 1314.

She was conceived immaculate, i.e., without the stain of original sin 256, 734 f., 792, *1073*, 1100, 1641, 2147a, but not because of an uncorrupted seed passed on to her *1924;* nor did she suffer or die because of original sin *1073.*

By a special privilege she was free from all sin, even venial 256, 833; excels all in sanctity 1978a; performed external good works *1260;* intercedes before God for men 734; because of which she is worthy of praise *1316*, and even to be loved by the perfect *1255 f.*

She is the mediatrix of all graces 1940a, 1978a, and in a certain way a coredemptrix with Christ 1978a n.

She was assumed with her body into heaven 1641 note, 2291, 3031 ff.

GOD THE SANCTIFIER: THE FRUITS OF THE REDEMPTION

THE NOTION OF JUSTIFICATION

IX a Justification does not consist in the fact that sins are only covered over or not imputed 742, 792, 804, *1925*, nor in only, although true, remission of sins 483, 799, 821 (which indeed is always conjoined to it 103, 742, 792, *1031 ff., 1043*), nor in obedience to the commandments *1042*, nor in the external favor of God 821, nor in the mere external imputing of the merits of Christ 820 f., nor formally in the justice of Christ Himself 799, 820; but it is such a condition of a man, in which in himself he is made just and a friend of God 799, taken into a state of adoption of the sons of God 794, 796, *1042, 1523,* 2212, and of an heir of eternal life 799, 2229, consort of the divine nature *1021, 1042;* it is a sanctification and internal renewal through sanctifying grace (as a "permanent principle of supernatural life" 2237) 197, *539*, 792, 795 f., 799 f., 809, *1069*, with the infusion of faith, hope, and charity 410, 800.

The various causes of justification are enumerated 799, 807.

THE WAY OF JUSTIFICATION

IX b Although nothing of the things which lead to justification merit it, but all are done through grace 176 ff., 187,

194 f., 790, 797 ff., 811, 813, *1042,* and are founded upon the merits of Christ 103 f., 186, 197 f., 790, 794 f., 800, 809, 820, 993, man (an adult) nevertheless can and ought to dispose himself to justification 797 ff., 814, 817, 819, 823, 897, 915, *1029 f., 1418,* by supernatural acts 797 f., 811 ff., *1042,* by freely assenting and cooperating with grace exciting and helping 797, which he can cast aside 797 f., *1093, 1095;* to the measure of his disposition the subsequent justification corresponds 799.

A disposition is made by acts of faith, hope, charity and penance 798, 813, by observing the commandments 798, 897.

Faith is the beginning of human salvation 801, and the necessary foundation and root of justification 178, 200b, 801, 1789, 1793; but it is not the first grace *1376 f.,* 1522.

But faith alone does not suffice *751 f.,* 798, 800 ff., 819, *822 f.,* 829 f., 839, 847, 851, 902, 914, nor only with prayers *1418,* nor "confident" faith 802, 822 f., 851, 922, nor faith so-called from the testimony of creatures 200, *1173,* nor faith in one God without explicit faith of a rewarder *1172,* 1349b, and of the Trinity and Incarnation 1214, 1349a, 1966a. In the Creed (*see* n. 86) as a unique and first principle all the faithful of Christ should agree 782.

Penance consists not only in an amendment of life *747,* nor only in confident faith 802, 822; but is a hatred and detestation for sin with desire for the sacrament 798, with the purpose of a new life and an observing of the commandments 798, 829 ff.

Contrition is always necessary for justification 894, 897, 902; it can be twofold: one perfect with charity, and the other imperfect or attrition 898, 915.

Attrition without charity is not evil *744, 746,* 798, 818, 898, 915, *1416, 1525;* and it can be supernatural *1304 f., 1525;* and ought to be supernatural for justification *1207, 1299.*

Contrition (perfect with charity) with desire of the sacrament justifies even before its (the sacrament's) reception *1033,* even outside the case of necessity or martyrdom 1070 f.

THE CONSEQUENCES OF JUSTIFICATION (BAPTISMAL)

IX c *See* effects of Baptism XIIc. No one is able with certitude of faith or ought to know that he is justified 802, 833 f. Concupiscence remains in the reborn 792, *1393.* It is not enough to believe and to pray *1418.* Even the innocent are afflicted by God *1420.* Man to preserve himself cannot dispense himself from the observance of divine law given for his utility 1421.

ACTUAL GRACE

The Nature of Grace (Actual)

X a Grace (actual) is a supernatural help of God, by which a man is made fit to act as he should to obtain eternal life 103 ff., 132 ff., 177 ff., 200a f., 797 ff.; it is not only an external help 104; but through grace God "operates in us without us" 193, although all things are not done by grace alone *1352 ff.*

Grace gives us not only the ability to act more easily, but the absolute possibility 105, 812; it heals nature vitiated by original sin and restores the liberty (of the sons of God) 105, 130, 181, 317, 325.

Names and Divisions

X b There is given a grace of illumination (in the intellect) and of inspiration (in the will) 135 ff., 180, 797, *1521,* 1791; arousing grace (calling) and helping 179, 200, 317, 797 ff., 807, 813 f.; antecedent, concomitant, and subsequent 809, beginning and perfecting 806, anticipating 177, 187, 191, 196, 317, 348, 797, 813, *1377, 1522;* operating (moving) 317, 797, 813, 898, *1036;* external and internal *1355;* elevating 130, healing (medicinal) 317; efficacious, sufficient, merely suffi-

see VIIIg *1096*, not only for the pre-destined *1096, 1382*, not for only the faithful 1294; although not all receive the benefit of redemption 319, 322 f., *717b*, 795, *1362, 1380* [Cf. VIIIh.].

God positively predestines all good works 196, 300, 316 ff., 322, 348, 816, and the glory of those to be saved 316, 322, so that nevertheless "in the election of those to be saved the mercy of God precedes good merit" 322, but He has predestined no one to evil *160a*, 200, 300, 316 ff., 321 f., 514, 816, 827; and as no one is saved un-willingly *1362 f.*, 1380, likewise, who-ever is to be lost "is condemned be-cause of the merit of his own iniq-uity" 200, 316, 318, 321; God fore-knew however and predestined the punishments of the impious 300, 316, in such a way however that "in the condemnation of those who are to be lost the evil deserving it precedes the just judgment of God" 322.

X h God "does not abandon the justified, un-less He is first abandoned by them" 804, 806, 1648, 1677, 1794; but rightly gives grace to penitents, nor permits us to be tempted more than we can sustain 980; hence the commandments of God are impossible to no one 200, 804, 828, *1092, 1519;* the grace of conversion is offered to sinners 807; and God does not deny grace even to the foreknown (i.e., non-predestined) 319, 827; they can be Christians and members of the Church *627 ff., 1422;* while on the other hand predestined persons can be outside it *628, 631.* Even those living in this world and possessing personal property can be saved 427, 430.

It is false that frequent confession and communion in one living in a worldly way is a mark of predestination *1206;* or that the prayer of the foreknown person is of no value *606;* or that outside of the Church no grace is given *1295*, 1379, 1646; or that the first grace is faith *1376 f., 1522*, or remission of sins *1378, 1521*, conse-quently as if no grace were given one who is not justified *1043 f.*

Without a special revelation no one can be certain that he himself is either of the number of the predestined 805 f., 825, or after sin that he will turn himself back 805, or that he enjoys perseverance 183, 806, 826, which is "the great gift" 826, 832.

The Catholic doctrine concerning justi-fication is the only true one 809; it is not derogatory to the glory of God or the merits of Christ 843.

THE ECONOMY OF SALVATION

In the state of the Law of Nature suf- **X i** ficient grace was not lacking to men *160a, 1295, 1356 ff.;* nor however could they desire grace with their own powers 1518; some were saved through hope of the coming of Christ and by His blood 160b.

"The Law" or the Old Testament was good and a work of the one God 28, 348, 421, 464, 706; it had not only fear *1413 ff.*, but even grace *1356 f., 1519 f.;* nevertheless the law of itself did not justify 189, 194, 793; men were justified under law by the blood of Christ 160b and in the hope of His coming 160b.

After the promulgation of the New Testa-ment the "Legal Precepts" of the Old Testament became deadly 712; the ob-servance of the commandments how-ever belongs even to the New Testa-ment 804, 828 ff., 837, 863; for Christ was not only a Redeemer but a Legis-lator 831. One fulfilling His Law from fear alone is not under the Law as a Jew *1413*. The New Law will not cease with the coming of another law 717i.

GOD THE SANCTIFIER: THE APPLICATION OF THE FRUIT

THE VIRTUES AND PRECEPTS

The Virtues and Laws Viewed in General

In justification at the same time as **XI a** sanctifying grace there are infused the habits of virtues 410, 483, 800, 821, more probably even in the baptism of children 410, 483; the theological and moral virtues are distinguished 410.

The acts of theological virtues fall under divine precept *1101, 1155 f., 1166 f., 1215, 1289;* active virtues are necessary in the spiritual life *1221 ff.,* and they are fitting even for the perfect *476;* the passive virtues are not to be preferred to the active 1972.

There exists a twofold divine law, natural and positive 1851, 1939.

There exists a natural right and a natural law 1756, 1936a, 1938c d, 1939, 2279, to which human laws are to be conformed 1756f., and the law of nations 2281.

Even human laws should take their binding force from God 1756, 1851.

Right does not consist in a material fact *1759, 1761.*

Custom can obtain the force of law *1132,* but in the Church it receives it from the superior hierarchical power *1507,* C25.

A people accepting a law promulgated by a prince without any cause sins *1128.*

A man for his own preservation cannot *dispense* himself from that law which God established for his benefit *1421.*

The Pope can dispense in the laws of the universal Church *731.*

One does not always act prudently by following a weak probable opinion *1153;* but it is licit to follow the most probable among probable opinions *1293,* and it is licit to attack that opinion which allows one to follow a less probable rather than a more probable opinion 1219.

In the administration of the sacraments it is not licit, having left aside a more probable opinion, to follow a less probable one *1151.* Any opinion should not be considered probable by the fact that it is contained in a book of someone younger or more modern *1127.*

Regulars cannot use in the forum of conscience their privileges expressly revoked by the Council of Trent *1136.*

Faith

(Concerning faith as it is an acceptance of revelation and of the preambles of faith, see: Ic d, as it is the foundation of justification: IXb.)

Faith is a theological virtue 530, super- **XI b** natural 178, 1789, 1795, which is infused in justification 800 f., more probably even in the baptism of children 410, 483; it is not to be attributed to merits 200, but is to be attributed to internal grace 178, 200a f., 442, 1626, 1791, 1814;

Hermes 1620 and the modernists 2074 ff., erred concerning the *nature* of faith.

Faith is not a certain religious sense 2074 ff., but an intellectual assent 420, 798, 1789, 1791, 1814, 2145, the supernatural principle of knowledge 1789, 1795, 1814, but an act produced by a creature, not merely infused by God *1242,* distinct from natural science 1656, 1811; even if it does not perceive truths from intrinsic reasons 442, 1789; it is not, however, for this reason a blind assent 1625, 1637, 1790 f., 1812, or contrary to reason 1797 ff., *1915;* but it is above reason 1649, 1671 ff., 1796 f.; not necessarily is it produced by arguments of reason 1814; and hence it is at the same time an act of the will commanding 420, 1789, by which a man offers free submission to God 1791, 1814, who can even command faith 1810.

It is, then, a certain assent, infallible, unchangeable by reason of its motive, which is not the convergence of probabilities 2025, nor the private experience of anyone *2081,* but it is the authority of God revealing 723, 1637 ff., 1656, 1789 f., 1794, 1800, 1811 f., 1815, 1968, *2025, 2081,* 2145; it is with the help of grace above all firm, by reason of its adherence 428, 460, 468, 706 ff., 1637, 1794, 1815, which the will commands *1169.*

Faith which is called confident is not true and justifying faith 802, 822 f., 851, 922, *1383.*

Although faith is absolutely necessary for salvation (see IXb), yet it is not necessary for every naturally good work *1022, 1025, 1301, 1398;* nor is purely negative infidelity a sin *1068.*

The act of faith falls under a special precept *1166,* and should be elicited several times in life *1101, 1167, 1215;* the hiding of faith can be sinful 1168, C1325 sec. 1.

By divine and Catholic faith those things are to be believed which are revealed by God (in writing or tradition) and proposed by the Church defining or teaching ordinarily 1792. Religious assent is required in doctrines proposed but not yet defined (for example, in the decisions of the Roman Congregations) 1684, 1880, *2007 f.,* 2113; and in dogmatic facts 1350, 1513 f. Necessarily the articles concerning the existence and justice of God, the Trinity, and the Incarnation are to be believed explicitly *1172, 1214,* 1349a b, 1966a.

He especially sins against faith, whether a heretic, i.e., one baptized, who retaining the name Christian pertinaciously doubts or denies any of the truths to be believed by divine and Catholic faith, or an apostate, i.e., one baptized and falling away from the Christian faith totally C1325 sec. 2. Heretics are to be denounced *1105,* and societies harmful to the faith are to be avoided *1859 ff.* Books prohibited "until expurgated" cannot be retained before they are expurgated *1145.*

To burn heretics cannot be said to be against the will of the Spirit *773,* and to fight the Turks is not repugnant to God *774.*

Faith is not lost by any sort of sin 808, 838, *1302,* but only by infidelity 808, *1302;* hence it can exist without charity *1302, 1401 f., 1791,* and without hope 1407; and thus indeed it is dead 800, 838, *1401 ff.,* but a gift of God 1791. In the next life faith will be done away with 530.

Hope

XI c The habit of hope is infused at justification 800 f., more probably even in the baptism of children 410, 483; it can

exist without charity *1407;* and in the next life it will be done away with 530.

The act of hope should be elicited at times during life *1101.*

The act from a motive of hope is good 804, 841, *1300, 1303,* even for the perfect *1232, 1234, 1327 f., 1331 ff., 1337.*

Charity

Charity toward God.

The habit of charity is infused at justifica- **XI d** tion 800 f., more probably already in the baptism of children 410, 483; it is never present without grace 198; charity is to be distinguished from the natural love of God 1034, 1036.

Perfect charity destroys sin *1031 ff., 1070;* it does not exclude fear and hope *1327 f.;* it is not the only motive for a good act 508, *1349, 1394-1408;* it is not necessary for obedience to the law *1016,* nor for attrition 1146, nor the most pure (act) for communion *1313;* when it is not present not all works are sins 1297, *1394 ff., 1523 f.*

God is to be loved more than one's neighbor 525.

Imperfect charity is not dishonorable 744.

The act of charity is produced by a creature; it is not merely infused by God *1242;* it should be elicited not only once in a lifetime *1155,* or only in case of necessity *1157,* but several times in a lifetime *1156,* 1289, and that by divine right *1101.*

Charity toward one's neighbor.

Man is bound to love his neighbor not only through external acts *1161,* but also by an internal and formal act *1160.*

Thus it is not permitted to be sad over the life of another or rejoice in his death, to seek this with an inefficacious longing and desire it because of some temporal advantage *1163,* nor to desire the death of one's father because of an inheritance which will accrue *1164,* nor to rejoice in parricide of **a** parent brought about by himself in drunkenness, because of an inheritance *1165*.

The rich are urged by a most grave precept to give alms to the poor from their superfluity 1852, 1938b, 2257.

It is false to say that scarcely any can be found in the world, who have anything superfluous to their state, and hence are bound to give alms *1162*.

Those giving the mendicant Friars alms are not by that fact excommunicated *600, 614;* it is not licit for the state to take away from citizens and the Church the faculty by which they can openly ask for alms for the sake of Christian charity 1693.

The souls in purgatory are helped by alms 427, 464, 693.

Lest anyone scandalize others by his own defects, care should be taken even when the will to scandalize is not present *1230*.

Mortally sinful cooperation is realized in a servant who by submitting his shoulders helps his master to ascend through windows to ravish a virgin, or by cooperating in something similar, even if he does this through fear of a notable loss, for example lest he be expelled from the house 1201.

The First Precept of the Decalogue

XI e Religion is falsely explained by the modernists 2074 ff. Religion can exist where there is no charity (as a motive) *1408*. God ought to be worshiped even by external and public acts 120, 221, 302, 478, 941, 950, *1254, 1573,* even by those striving for perfection *1254* (for example, by prayer *472*); in particular adoration is due to the humanity of Christ 120, 221, 224, *1255, 1561;* likewise to the Most Holy Eucharist 878, 888, C1255, sec. 1, even by the perfect and contemplatives *478;* and the same is true of the Most Sacred Heart of Jesus *1562 f.*

The true notion of the Liturgy is explained 2298; likewise its necessity for the ascetical life 2299.

The worship (and invocation) of the Saints is laudable 342, 941, 952, 984, 998, C1276, which should be offered even by the perfect *1255 f.;* praise is especially due to the Blessed Virgin Mary *1255 f., 1316,* C1276; John the Baptist sent by God is holy and just and filled with the Holy Spirit in the womb of his mother 421. The Church does not pray for the saints 535.

Likewise the veneration of images is licit 250*, 302 ff., 306, 337, 679, 985 ff., 998, 1466, C1276; also of God the Father and the Trinity *1315, 1569,* and the veneration of relics 303, 342, 440, 679, 985, 998, C1276; in either case however it is only relative 302, 337, 985 f., C1255 sec. 2; the special cult shown to some images is not to be maligned *1570 ff.* Nor does anyone act badly in seeking a devout feeling on solemn days and in sacred places *1253.*

The rite of the Church in the solemn administration of the sacraments should not be contemned, omitted, or changed 665, 856, 931, 996, C773; the same holds true concerning the canon and ceremonies of the Mass 942 f., 953 f., C818; concerning the customary mixing of water with the wine 698, 945, C814; concerning blessings, the chant, and offices 424, 426, *1463, 1587;* concerning baptismal water and exorcisms 665, C757; concerning the prayers added to the absolution 896, C885; concerning the blessing of matrimony 981, C1101; concerning the anointing in conferring orders 965; likewise the multiplication and ornamentation of altars are to be held in respect *1531 f.;* concerning the magnificence of worship and the institution of feasts *1533, 1573 f.;* concerning the application and certain number of prayers *599, 1564;* concerning ecclesiastical burial (the cremation of dead bodies being reprobated) 1863 f.

To take away or to invade ecclesiastical property is a sacrilege 685 f.

Simony is illicit (concerning orders, ecclesiastical gifts, the sacraments, blessings, relics, etc.) 354, 359, 364, 400, 440, *1122*, *1195 f.*, C727; prayers offered for benefactors is not necessarily simoniacal *605;* but it is simony to give food for a spiritual thing *364*, or a price for reception into a monastery 400, or the temporal for the spiritual precisely as the motive for conferring or effecting the spiritual or as a gratuitous compensation for the spiritual—or the reverse—*1195;* or if the temporal is the principal motive for giving the spiritual or its end *1196*. It is also against justice not to confer ecclesiastical benefices gratuitously *1122.*

No custom exempts from simony 364.

To assist at certain spiritualistic demonstrations is illicit 2182; mesmerism is to be employed cautiously 1653 f.; theosophy attacks Catholic doctrine 2189.

XI f Prayer is either private or (in the divine office said by a priest in the name of the Church) public 2276; it is good *509;* not however that of quietism (Molinos) *1221-1288;* it is not the same as resignation *1245;* nor is it an absolute quiet of soul *1241;* it does not exclude reasoning *1240;* it is helped by images *1238;* it is hindered by impious thoughts that are permitted *1244,* likewise by sleep *1245.* One seeking sensible devotion in this does not thereby do wrong *1247,* 1249 f.

Prayer presupposes grace 176; it is necessary 183, 804, 979, even for the perfect *472;* it benefits especially those to whom it is applied *599,* even the souls detained in purgatory 464, 535, 693, 983, 988; it is fitting even for the perfect *1234, 1254,* as is also the act of thanksgiving *1235;* in a sinner it is not a new sin *1409;* the prayer of the foreknown is not useless *606;* the petition of anything is not injurious to God *507, 1234.* In liturgical prayers the use of the vernacular language is not to be introduced 946, *1566.*

The Second Precept of the Decalogue

A vow is a good and supernatural act **XI g** 184, and it does not derogate from the promise made to God in baptism 865; nor is it an impediment to perfection *1223.*

An oath, which is made with truth and judgment and justice, is licit 425, *487, 662, 1451,* even when made to confirm human contracts or civil business *623,* especially at the command of a judge concerning speaking the truth 663, or from some other cause, as for purification of infamy 663,—in ecclesiastical court, in investitures and in the sacred ordinations of bishops *1575.*

Perjury knowingly committed for any cause, even if for the sake of one's life, or even in favor of the faith, is a mortal sin 644, *1174;* perjury is committed even by swearing with a purely mental restriction *1176,* although the hiding of truth is considered expedient and zealous *1177,* or although any otherwise hidden crime might have to be made manifest 1178.

A fictitious oath is not licit for any cause, whether the matter be light or grave *1175.*

The Third Precept of the Decalogue

The precept of observing feasts obliges **XI h** under mortal sin *1202.* New feasts are not instituted from neglect of old feasts and by false notions of the nature and end of feasts 1573. It is not licit to observe Saturday 712.

The state cannot permit servile works on certain days 1693.

One hearing two parts (of Mass) by different celebrants at the same time does not satisfy the precept of the Church concerning hearing Mass *1203.*

The soul does not act badly by arousing itself to sensible devotion by a particular effort on certain solemn days *1253.*

A bishop by his own right cannot transfer feasts of the universal Church *1574.*

The Fourth Precept of the Decalogue

Authority is not the mere sum of num- **XI i**

bers and of material powers *1760,* but a right given by God 1849, 1851, as a principle of order 2207.

Obedience is not always to be offered in externals only *1285,* but can be shown even without charity *1016,* and shown to human laws also even by the perfect *473.*

XI k The family does not receive its reason for existence from civil law 1694, but from the natural law 2203, 2207, especially with regard to the power of parents over children 1694, 1938a, 2207.

The family is an imperfect society 2203, 2209, in which the man is the head, the woman the heart 2233.

Spouses owe one another fidelity 2231, and love in affection and effect 2232, preserving the rights and dignity of the person 2233, 2248.

The economic emancipation of women, physiological, is to be rejected completely; the social (civil) is to be admitted only very cautiously 2247 f.

Parents are to be loved by their children *1164 f.* But the children are free to choose marriage or virginity 2226.

XI l In the Church a man through baptism is constituted a person with all the rights and duties of Christians, unless, so far as the rights are concerned, an impeding obstacle stands in the way of the bond of ecclesiastical communion, or a censure imposed by the Church C87, 1936a; cf. XIIc.

A member of the Church has the right to receive from a cleric spiritual goods C682, especially the helps necessary for salvation C682, such as participation in the sacrifice of the Mass C1248, reception of the sacraments cf. C785, C853, C886, C892, C939, instruction in Christian doctrine C1331 ff.

XI m Obligations: The love of piety toward the Church is greater than toward the fatherland 1881, 1936b.

Subjection to the jurisdiction of the Church, even on the part of kings and princes 469, *1322,* 1688, *1754,* and recognition of the Church and its au-

thority not only in private but also in public life 1885;

observance of the universal law of Christ 200, 411, 829 f., 863, 1881, and of the precepts of the Church 200, 411, 830, 864, 1881 (even on the part of those baptized in infancy 869 f.), according to the expressed authority of Sacred Scripture *641;* reception of instruction in religion 2138, 2142;

reception of the sacraments 2137 ff.; cf. XIIc ff.;

support of the clergy according to the precept of the Lord 427, *598;*

apostolate (lay) 1819, 1881 f., 1884, 1888, 1936c, 1974, especially on the part of editors of magazines 1887.

The law of ecclesiastical fast binds under **XI n** pain of grave sin 1123;

it is broken by frequently eating a little bit, if a notable quantity is reached 1129.

All officials doing physical work in the state are not absolutely excused 1130, or those making an unnecessary journey of one day by horseback 1131.

In the selection of foods custom can create an obligation *1132,* cf. C1251 sec. 1.

A bishop of his own right cannot transfer the day of fast of the universal Church *1574.*

There is to be no fast on the Nativity of our Lord, nor on Sunday 234.

Feast days: see XI h.

The State is a perfect society 1869, 2203, **XI o** with its own laws recognized by the Church 161*, 469, 1841 f., 1851, 1858, 1866; its end is the common good of this earthly life 1841, 2203, 2208 f., in human things (not divine) 1866, so that, nevertheless, it should promote the true religion 1615, 1688 ff., *1757, 1777 ff.,* 2197 (without however forcing anyone who is unwilling to join the Catholic faith 1875), and to repress the unregulated liberty of feeling and the sense of propagandizing publicly 1868, 1876, 1932 (preserving the admission of a moderate freedom for just causes 1932). Likewise it cannot proclaim freedom of worship as the natural law *1777 ff.*, 1874, 1932 (although freedom of worship can be patiently borne in customs and practice, where either the necessity of obtaining a greater good or of preventing an evil demands it 1874).

Licitly, justice being preserved, one can free himself from external dominion 1876, 1936.

The principle of "non-intervention" is reprobated *1762*.

Political rule as such is required by natural law 1855 f., 1866, 1868; its form can be diverse 1855, 1871 f., 1886, 1934, 2221, and once taken up can be changed again 1933.

But sedition and rebellion are illicit *1763*, 1850, 1868, 1878, 2278; for the authority of the government in itself is given immediately by God 1856 f., 1868, 1934 (it does not arise from a contract 1856), and is even in a sinner *595, 597, 656*.

The right order of the state demands that, individualism rejected and the struggle "of the classes" excluded, "orders" be maintained 2267, so that matters of minor moment and concern be relegated to inferior groups 2266, and it involve itself in only a subsidiary way 2266, so that when necessity demands it may define the use of property 1938c, 2256, and always serve and guard social justice 2277.

[The relation between Church and state, see II i].

The obligations of the state and the rights of citizens: The state ought to preserve and guard the natural rights of the family 1877, 1938a, 2277,

and of private persons 1877, 1938a, 2277 (even of fetuses 2244 and of infants 2209), for example with regard to the right of entering matrimony 2245, 2252,

and of "orders" 2266, and of the Church 1719ff., 2208 ff., 2278.

Let it not involve itself without necessity in the intimate affairs of citizens 1877, 1938a, or of cities 1877, or of "orders" 2266 ff., or of families 1877 (it can-

not circumscribe the begetting of children 2226);

let it recognize the rights of citizens to live according to the precepts of reason and of conscience 2278, of private property 2256, of inheritance 2256, of coalition 1938d, 2268, not however of societies secretly conspiring against the rights of the state 1860.

The obligations of citizens and the rights of the state: The state (if it is the fatherland, to be loved 1936a) is also to be guarded by the citizens 1936a by the giving even of one's life 1936a; but for the love of the fatherland it is not lawful to violate oaths or commit crimes *1764*, nor to violate the laws of the Church 1936b, on the other hand it is licit to resist the abuse of power according to the circumstances 1936b, 2278.

Just taxes are to be paid 1938c, 2256. Just laws are to be fulfilled *1763*, 1841, 1876.

Each one should work according to his capacity for the public good of the municipality 1882, and of the state by accepting public office 1883 ff., 1935, editors of magazines by their writing 1887.

Education, is entirely ordered to the **XI p** last end, accordingly it should be Christian 2202, 2212, 2224.

The office of educating belongs to the Church, the family, and the state 2203 ff.

It belongs to the Church as the supreme teacher and supernatural mother 1695, 1745 ff., 2204, 2217, who ought to oversee the whole of education 2205, 2220.

Hence neither clergy is to be kept from gathering youths into institutions or educating 1695, 2222.

The right and office of the family to educate is from God 2207, 2216, 2230, of protecting children 2223, of sending them to truly Catholic schools (not mixed or neutral) 2219 ff., C1374, with Catholic teachers, especially religious 2222.

The state has the office of educating in a subsidiary way 2208, by safeguarding by laws the right of the family and children 2209 f., and by observing the right of the Church 2209 f., by promoting education and scholarship 2210, by commanding and taking care of instruction in civil and national laws 2210 or civic education 2211.

"Sexual" education is reprobated 2214, 2251, likewise education that is merely natural 2213, and coeducation 2215.

The Fifth Precept of the Decalogue

XI q Man is bound to preserve his own life 1938c, C1240.

Hence he should not rashly throw it away 1939.

A public magistrate has no direct power over the members (of the body) of those subject to him 2246, private persons have no other than that which pertains to the natural ends of the bodily members 2246; hence he cannot destroy or mutilate them except if otherwise he cannot provide for the good of the whole body 2246; nor is it permitted the state to deprive citizens of the generative power 2245 f.

To wound or to kill a man for a private reason (*per se*) is not lawful 1939, 2354; but for a public reason it is lawful to kill or wound a man 1939 if it is done as punishment for a crime 425, 2245 f.

The killing of an unjust aggressor is lawful 1939, not however of a calumniator *1117*, *1180*, or a false witness or an unjust judge *1118*, or of an adulterous spouse *1119*, or of one running away after striking a blow *1180*, or on stealing a gold piece *1181*, or impeding the hope of possessing 1182, of an inheritance, or legacy, or office, or an allowance *1183*.

The direct killing of the innocent is (intrinsically) evil 1890, 2243, C2354. Tyrannicide is illicit 690.

Abortion is illicit (even before the animation of the fetus *1184 f.*) 1890a, 2242 ff., C2350 sec. 1; likewise crani-

otomy 1889 f., even of an ectopic fetus 1890b f.

A duel is illicit *1102*, 1491 ff., 1939 f., C2351, and likewise with the assistance of a doctor or a confessor 1862, C2351 sec. 1.

The Sixth Precept of the Decalogue

1. Outside and within matrimony: Temp- **XI r** tations of the flesh are to be resisted (even in the midst of prayer) 1261 ff.

The kiss of a woman is not always a mortal sin 477.

Pollution (prohibited by the law of nature *717g*, *1199*), sodomy, and bestiality are sins of the lowest different species *1124*. Masturbation to care for health is illicit 2201.

Intercourse (illicit) is a grave sin specifically different from an imperfect act *1125*.

A concubine is to be put out, even if it seems difficult *1141*.

Artificial insemination is to be avoided 3303.

2. Outside of matrimony: voluptuousness and a carnal act are sins 477, and this is against the natural law *717g*, 2231, not admitting of lightness of matter *1140*, 5005.

Fornication is a mortal sin 43, 453, and that by the law of nature *1198*.

3. Within marriage: the function of marriage is not by its own nature a sin 241, 537, 2230; moreover it is due the one who seeks it 2231, 2248; but exercised for voluptuousness alone it does not lack venial sin *1159*.

Intercourse with a married woman, even with the consent of the husband is adultery *1200*, 2231, C2357 sec. 2.

Onanism is intrinsically gravely sinful 2239 ff.

Because of adultery the separation of spouses is licit 702, C1129.

The union of blood relatives is prohibited by divine law 362.

The Seventh Precept of the Decalogue

The right of property is natural 1851, **XI s** 1938abc, 2256, necessary for the common good 1851, 2254, and for the good of the family 1851, 1938a, 2254, and for the individual good 1851, 1938a, joined to the most grave precept of charity of giving superfluities to the poor 1852, 1938b, 2257.

A distinction is to be made between dominion and use 1938a, 2255, that (dominion) is not lost by abuse 2255, this (use) can be determined by laws for the necessary good of the community 1938c, 2256.

Property is acquired by inheritance 1938a, 2256, by occupation of a thing belonging to no one 2258, by prescription (presupposing continuing good faith) 439, C1512, by industry 2258, not only by work 2260.

Labor can be allocated justly 1938b, 2261; its just reward according to the individual and social nature of the work should be adequate for the sustenance of the worker and his family 1038c, 2263, and to his official status 2264, and the necessity of the common good 2264.

Dominion is injured *by theft* 1851, for to take a thing belonging to another against the will of the owner is a mortal sin *717h*, 1851, nor is it licit in grave necessity *1186*. Occult compensation is held as illicit, if domestic servants pilfer secretly from their masters, if they judge their work to be greater than the salary which they receive *1187*.

But in extreme need to take another's things is just 1938b.

A contract of sale can be illicit 394, as fictitious and real exchange 1081 f., exchange of money 403, 448, 716, 739, *1142*, 1191 f., 1475 ff., although it can become licit 1609 f., 1611 f. A contract which is called usurious is illicit *1190*.

Agreements entered upon according to the law of nations are to be preserved 2281 f.

It is a matter of social justice "to exact from each all that is necessary for the common good" 2277, and hence it governs the allocation of the fruits

from capital and labor 2260, 2265, and offers the opportunity to work 2265, and to receive a just wage 2263, 2277, that the order may become juridical and social 2269.

The Eighth Precept of the Decalogue

A calumnious lie concerning a man of great authority can be mortal *1193*, and mortal it certainly is to impose a false charge upon another to defend justice and honor *1194*. Purely mental restriction is illicit *1176-1178*.   **XI t**

THE SACRAMENTS
The Sacraments in General

Essence: The sacraments are means of grace 139, 844 ff., C731, sec. 1 or "the symbols of a sacred thing and the visible forms of invisible grace" 876, 1963, 2237.   **XII a**

The sacraments of the Old Law differed from the sacraments of the New Law 845, 857, in that they did not cause grace but symbolized it 695; they foretold the Messias 711, at whose coming they ceased 712.

The sacraments of the New Law "through which all true justice either begins, or begun is increased, or lost is regained" 843a, contain and confer the grace signified: see Effect; they differ among themselves in dignity 846; they are not contemned without sin 424, *484, 669*, nor condemned without heresy 367.

They are instituted by Christ 570m, 844, 996 f., 1470, *2039 ff.*, 2088, 2096, C731 sec. 1, or perfect 969, 2237, not only to nourish faith alone 848, *2041*, nor as mere signs of justice received 849; they are neither more nor fewer than seven 402, 424, 449 ff., 465, 695, 844, 996 f., 1470.

They are accomplished with due matter and form 98, 672, 695, 895, 959, 1489, 1963, C742 sec. 1, "with the intention on the part of the minister of doing what the Church does" 672, 695, 854, 860, *1318*, 3004; the ceremonies accompanying the administration can be changed by the Church as long as the substance is preserved 931, 570m, 2147a, 3001, not however by the minister 856, 1963 f., C733.

Holy oils ought to be blessed by the legitimate minister 1086.

The effect: The sacraments of the New Testament not only nourish faith 848, but confer grace 324, 410, *539*, 695, 741, 847, 849 f., 996, 1470, *2039 f.*, C731 sec. 1, from the work worked (*ex opere operato*) 851, 2089, by the power of the Holy Spirit 424, upon all not placing an obstacle 411, 741, 849, and that always 850, and "whenever anyone uses them" 876, and hence no pious person should doubt concerning the power and efficacy of the sacraments 802.

Three (only 695, 2238) sacraments furthermore imprint a character (which is not the Word *1918*) and cannot be repeated 411, 695, 852, 960, 996 f., 1470, C732, sec. 1.

The significance of "Sacrament and reality . . ." etc. 415.

XII b *The minister:* Not any Christian can validly administer all sacraments 853, 1958; but the proper minister for each sacrament, even if he is by chance a sinner 169, 424, *486, 488, 545, 584,* 855; who although unworthy, "truly consecrates," absolves" etc., 672, 855, 902, 920, indeed even if he is a heretic 860, or a schismatic 169 (a sinful person does not necessarily experience infidelity concerning the sacraments etc. *634*), and he is the cause (ministerial) of justification *1058*. Moreover, the minister ought to be a legitimate one 967.

In the conferring of the sacraments it is not licit for a minister to follow a probable opinion passing over a safer one *1151;* he ought to have the right intention 672, 695, *752, 854, 1318, 1966,* 3004, and not use simulation 418, *1179,* 1489; and not at will omit sacramental rites 570 0, 856, 996, C733; sometimes the sacraments should be conferred conditionally 339, 446, *1527,* 1848, C746.

The subject is a man (adult) who is

willing 411, and disposed although lacking the fervor of a governing charity and long tried in it *1536*. The legitimate subject is neither a heretic nor a schismatic C731, sec. 2, unless perhaps a dying heretic with regard to absolution and extreme unction 2181a.

The necessity: Generally the sacraments are necessary for salvation (although not all for each person 847, 996), either in fact or in desire 388, 413, 847, *1071*, C737, sec. 1.

Baptism

The essence: Baptism is the first sacra- **XII c** ment 86, 287, 402, 430, 465, 696, 857 ff., 994, C737 sec. 1; it is one 9, 140, 347, 464, 482; it succeeded circumcision 410.

The remote matter is natural water (only) 412, 430, 449, 482, 542, 574a, 696, 858, C737 sec. 1, with which in case of necessity there can be mixed bichloride of mercury 1977; saliva is not valid 412, nor beer 447; the proximate matter is the washing 449, threefold 229, or one 250*, C737 sec. 1, or immersion 229, 398, 413, C758.

The form is not the invocation of the angels 82, nor merely the invocation of the Trinity *1317*, but the words "I baptize thee in the name of the Father, and of the Son, and of the Holy Spirit" 82, 97, 229, 249, 297, 334a f., 398, 413, 430, 482, *542*, 696, 860, *1317*, or (among the Greeks): "Let him be baptized. . . ." 696, with a condition added, where there is need 399, 1527, ["in the name of Christ" 47, 94, 97, 229, 335; ["in the name of the Trinity" 82, 97, 334a, 335, 430; ["in the Holy Spirit" 11].

The effects are: an application of the merits of Christ 790, and hence a change into a new creature 895, the remission of sins in general 86, 109a, 130, 250*, 287, 324, 410, 464, 482, 742, 792, 895, *1057,* especially original sin 102, 109a, *160a,* 329, 348, 410 f., 424, 574a, 696, 792, and personal sin 424, 574a, 696, 895, provided man consents 410, the remission of temporal punishment 464, 696, 792, 807, 904, the conferring of grace 130, 483, 792, 799, 933, adoption into the sonship of God 712, regeneration 102, 109a, 140, 324, 695 f., 933, the infusion of virtues 410, 483, 800, union with Christ, whose member the baptized person is made 197, 696, 790, 895, 933, 2229, liberation from the power of the devil 140, 712, 904, the conferring of the gifts of the Holy Spirit 904, the beginning of the spiritual life 696, reception into the Church 324, 570a, 696, 864, 870, *1413*, 1936a, 2203, C87, the opening of heaven 139, 410, 424, 530, 693, 696, 792, the imprinting of a character 411, 695, 852, 960, the obligation of preserving the law of Christ 200, 411, 829 f., 863 f., 869, C87, and the power 200, 804, 828, *1042, 1054, 1092.*

But baptism does not give inamissible grace 862; nor does it take away concupiscence 792, *1393;* nor does it make actual grace superfluous 132; nor does it of itself dissolve legitimate marriage (Pauline Priv.) 407, C1126; does not impede subsequent vows 865; nor does the mere recollection of it destroy sin 806.

The end of baptism is that a man may live his life in a Christian way 806.

XII d *The minister* ought to be someone other than the baptized 413, and in solemn baptism either a priest 696, C738 (even in the presence of a bishop 98) or a deacon 52e, C741; in private baptism a good faithful person 52d, a layman, or even a woman 712, indeed a sinner or heretic 52d, 46 f., 53, 55 f., 88, 94, 97, 249, 297, 334a, 696, 1470, C742, so long as he has the intention 672, 696, 860, *1318,* 1470, 1848, C742 sec. 1, 3004.

The subject: Every man ought of necessity to receive baptism 348, 482, 696, 712, 796, 799, 861, 870, 895, 1470, *2042,* C737 sec. 1, at least in desire (baptism of desire) 388, 413, 796, C737 sec. 1; even children (after the eighth day 574a, or as soon as it can conveniently be done 712) and insane are to be baptized 102, 140, 367, 410 f., 424, 430, 482, 574a, 712, 868, *2043,* C745; in certain cases it is lawful to baptize the children of Jews 1480 ff., 1490, and non-Catholics C750 f.; adults should have the intention 411, 1966a, and prepare themselves by various acts 798, especially by explicit faith in the existence of one God and His remunerative and avenging justice, the Trinity and the Incarnation 1349a b, 1966a; reception is not to be put off until the time of death 868.

The administration: Baptism cannot be repeated 46, 53, 88, 97, 435, 464, 574a, 695, 852, 867, 869, 895, 996 f., C732 sec. 2; some however are to be rebaptized because of invalidity 56, 97, sometimes conditionally 399, 1537, 1848, C737 sec. 2, C746, C752 sec. 3; let exorcisms precede 140; let anointings be used 449; let patrons acting for the person baptized be present 870, C762; confirmation and communion are not required for the validity of baptism *542.*

Confirmation

Essence: Confirmation is a true and **XII e** proper sacrament 52d, 98, 419, 424, 465, *543,* 669, 697, 871, *2044.*

The remote matter is chrism 419, 450, 872, made of oil and balsam 450, 697, 1458; blessed by a bishop 93*, 98, 450, 571, 697, 1086, C781 sec. 1; the proximate matter is the imposition of hands 424, 1963, with the anointing with chrism 419, 450, 697, C780, C781 sec. 2.

The form is "I sign thee. . . ." 697.

The effect is the communication of the Holy Spirit 98, 450, for strength 419, 695, 697; a character is imprinted upon the soul and hence this sacrament cannot be repeated 695, 852, 960, 996, C732 sec. 1.

The minister, ordinary, is the bishop alone 52d f., 93*, 98, 250*, 419, 424, 450, 465, *543,* 572, *608,* 697, 873, 960, 967, 1458, 2147a, C782, sec. 1, and that is not established for evil motives *608;* the extraordinary minister is a priest having the faculty from the Supreme Pontiff *543,* 573 f., 697, C782 sec. 2. Cf. above AAS 38 (1946) 349 ff. (The Power of the Greek priests 1459n).

The subject is anyone baptized 465, 871, C786 (even an infant 98); he is not bound however by a necessity of means of salvation 52e, C787, anyone contemning it sins mortally 669.

The Eucharist

The Real Presence; the Sacrament

XII f *The presence of Christ* in the Eucharist is true, real, identical 355, 414, 424, 430, 465, *544,* 574a, *583,* 666, 698, *717 f.,* 874 ff., 883 ff., 890, 997, 1469, 5004, not only with regard to His divinity *717 f.;* it is accomplished by transubstantiation 355, 416, 424, 430, 465, *544, 581,* 666, 698, 715, 877, 884, 997, 1469, *1529, 1919, 3018,* which is not impanation *1845;* the substances of bread and wine cease *581 f.,* 877, 884; likewise the nature of bread with its elements *1843 ff.,* the appearances (accidents) remaining without a subject 416, *582,* 884; and by force of the words the body and blood of Christ exist under the different appearances, the rest by concomitance 876, 885, *1921,* and that not only in use 715, 876, 886, but as long as the appearances remain *578 ff.,* so that Christ is whole under each appearance 626, 667, 698, 874, 932, 936, 997, 1469, and (when a separation is made) under each part 698, 876, 885, 1469, *1921;* which mode of existing is sacramental, not natural 874; this transubstantiation concerning which the faithful are explicitly to be taught *1529,* was not rightly explained by Rosmini and others *1843 ff., 1919 ff.*

Essence: The Eucharist is a true sacrament 367, 402, 430, 437, 465, 542, 626, 666, 698, instituted by Christ at the last supper 874 f., *2045,* as a symbol of mystical union 873a, 875, 882.

The Matter is wheat bread 692, 698, 715, 876, C815 sec. 1, either without leaven

(among those of the Latin Church) 350, 465, 692, or leavened (among the Greeks) 692, C816, and wine of grapes 414, 416, 430, 698, 945, 956, C815 sec. 2 (which, where there is need, may be allowed to boil to 65° 1937, and to have an alcoholic strength of 12% or 18% 1938); with which a little water ought to be mixed 416, 441, 452, 698, C814, because of the mystical signification 698, 945, 956; the water however is not changed into phlegm 416 f.

The Form is the words of Christ 414, 424, 452, 698, 715, 876, 938, not however the epiclesis 416 f.

The Minister: A priest rightly ordained having the proper intention validly consecrates 424, 430, 574a, 715, C802, not however a deacon 53*, C802, nor anyone else (although holy) 424, 430, 574a; for lawfulness the state of grace is required 418, 880, C807.

Worship: The Eucharist is to be kept (not beyond fifteen days 452) 879, 886, 889, C1265, and honored with a worship of latria 878, 888, C1255, even by the perfect *478.*

Communion

Consuming the Eucharist is distinguished **XII g** in three ways: sacramental, spiritual and both together 881, 890, C863; the sacramental is in this life alone and is had only in the New Testament *1922;* the whole Christ is consumed under each appearance 626, 876, 932, 936, hence communion can be made under either appearance alone 626, 931, 935, while the consuming of the chalice is not of divine precept for those not sacrificing 930, 934 ff.; for this reason communion under one appearance is to be preserved (according to the statute of the Church 626, 931, 935) 626, 668, 756, C852, it is to be distributed to the faithful ordinarily by a priest 881 f., 892, C845 sec. 1, extraordinarily by a deacon C845 sec. 2.

The subject: Children are not obliged to receive communion 933, 937 C854, sec. 1, but those who reach the age of discretion are bound to communicate each year at least at Paschal time 437, 891, *1922*, 2137, C859; but a sacrilegious communion does not satisfy this precept *1205*, C861.

For the lawful reception faith alone does not suffice 755, 893, but there is required (and as far as the soul is concerned suffices *1439*) "a great reverence and sanctity" 880 f., that is the state of grace which is acquired by confession, not only by contrition 880, 893, C856; moreover, one receiving should be fasting 626, C858 (unless he be infirm 626), rightly prepared (by positive acts) 755, 880, *1252;* but penance fulfilled is not necessary nor must the most pure charity be attained *1312 f.;* the Eucharist is to be kept for the sick 452, not however too long 452, and transported with honor 879, 889, C847, even to the young 2144.

In danger of death Viaticum should be received C864.

Frequent or even daily communion is not necessary by divine law 1150, but it is commended to all who approach it with a right mind 881 f., 944, 955, 1147 ff., 1978, 1981 ff., C863; even the young 2137 ff., C863.

The effect is not bodily sustenance *546*, nor especially nor solely remission of sins 882, 887; but union with Christ (without the changing of Christ into the subject 546) and an increase of grace and the virtues 546, 698; the remission of venial sins and penalties 546, 875, 887, 1981; preservation from mortal sins 875, 1981; perseverance in good 882; communion is the spiritual food of the soul 695, 698, and the pledge of future glory 875, 882, 887; which effect does not depend upon confidence alone 755; frequent communion of itself is not a mark of predestination *1206*.

The Sacrifice of the Mass

XII h *Essence:* The Mass is a sacrifice 424, 430, 441, 452, 464, 938 ff., 948 ff., 957, 997, divine 940, singular 937a, but true 937a, 948, 997, *1045*, 1469, and

proper 948, 997, 1469, prefigured by the sacrifices of nature and the Law 938 f., visible 938, 957; instituted by Christ at the Last Supper 938 f., 949, 957, 961, 963, as is established in the Gospel *585;* by which the sacrifice of the Cross is represented and applied 938, 940; from which it then does not detract 940, 951.

The sacrifice does not consist in the communion alone 948, nor is there required the presence of the faithful or the (even spiritual) communion of those assisting 944, 955, 1528; which (even sacramental) is recommended 944, 1981 ff., C863.

The victim of the Mass is Christ Himself 424, 430, 940, 2195, offered in another way than on the Cross 940.

The principal one offering is Christ Himself 424, 430, 940, 2195, 3000, by the ministration of priests 424, 434, 940.—The priest who after mortal sin cannot confess and has to celebrate, having made a perfect act of contrition, after celebrating should confess as soon as possible 880, and that according to precept *1138 f.* The faithful in their own way coöffer 3000.

The Effect: The Mass is a sacrifice of latria 950; hence it is offered to God alone, not to the saints 941, in whose honor nevertheless it can be offered 952; it is in thanksgiving 950; it is in supplication and propitiation 940, 950, 996 f., 1469, 2195.

By this sacrifice sins (even grave) are remitted indirectly 940, temporal punishments, however for contrite penitents even directly 940, 950; it is of benefit not only to the one receiving 950, but especially for him to whom the fruit is applied *1530*, C828; it can be offered for the faithful departed 427, 464, 693, 940, 944, 950, 983, 996, C809. For the celebration and application of one Mass it is not lawful to accept a double stipend by offering a most special fruit *1108*, and one injures justice who accepts stipends for many Masses and offers only one *1110*, and likewise he injures fidelity by promising what he offers for no other *1110*. An annual legacy endures only for ten years *1143*.

The manner of offering: The Church rightly instituted the various ceremonies to be observed in the sacrifice and retains the Latin language 943, 946, 954, 956, *1436*, C818 f.; in particular the Canon of the Mass is to be venerated 414, 942, and retained 953; a little water should be mixed with the wine 416 f., 452, 698, 945, 956, C814; simulated celebration is illicit 418; consecration outside of Mass or under only one appearance never is licit C817. Mass can be said on many altars of the same Church 1531.

Penance

XII i *Essence:* Penance is a true sacrament of the New Testament 146, 402, 424, 465, 699, 807 ff., 894 f., 911 ff., 2046; different from baptism and capable of being repeated 839, 894 f., 897, 911 ("a second plank after shipwreck" 807); instituted by Christ (John 20, 23) 732, 807, 894, 913, in the form of a judgment 895, 899, 902, 919, 2047; to whose dignity the usages introduced by the Church are not contrary *1534*.

The sacramental form is not an anointing 451, but a judicial sentence 807, 895, 902, 919, through the words of the priest: "I absolve thee. . . ." *538*, 699, 807, 895, 896, which ought to be proffered to one present *1088 f.* By its power sins are forgiven *538*, 896, not however by reason of the confidence of a man that he is absolved 802, 823 f.

The matter or quasi-matter is the acts of the penitent 699, 896, 914, contrition, confession, satisfaction, which are also called "parts" 146, 671, 699, 745, 896, 914.

Contrition is a "grief of soul and detestation for sin committed, with a purpose of not sinning again" *514 f.*, 747, 897, so that a man would completely wish not to have sinned *514 f.;* it is a free and voluntary act 898; it is divided

according to motives into natural which (although not sinful *1299*, nevertheless) is not sufficient for justification *1207*, and supernatural which is necessary for absolution 699, *751 f.*, 897 f., *1536*. Contrition is to be manifested to a confessor *754*, and should be the foundation for the hope of improvement *1210*, and especially with regard to the flight of the proximate free occasion *1211 ff*.

One kind is perfect proceeding from charity 898, which without desire for the sacrament is inefficacious 898; with desire for it always justifies 898, *1071;* it does not make confession superfluous 587.

Another kind is imperfect (attrition) proceeding "commonly from a consideration of the shamefulness of sin or from a fear of hell and punishment" 898, 915, *1305*.

Attrition does not necessarily include the love of God 1146, *1305;* it is however a good motion *746*, 898, 915, *1411 f.*, *1417*, a free and voluntary act 897, 915, *1300*, and likewise useful *1410*, disposing to grace 898, 915, nevertheless without the sacrament it does not justify 898, 915, *1305*, *1410*, but with the sacrament suffices for justification 898.

Confession is necessary for salvation by divine right 699, *724 f.*, 899, 916 f., 919, and ought to include the grave sins committed after baptism 146, 430, 437, 699, *724 f.*, 807, 894 f., 911, C901 (not yet directly forgiven by the power of the keys 470, *491*, *493*), which should be manifested integrally 574a, 899, 917, *1111*, *1209*, according to the last species *1124 f.*, *1200*, C901, with a material integrity or at least formal 147, 699, 900 f., *1111;* for this reason sins both merely internal and manifest should be brought in to the accusation *726 f.*, *748*, 899, and even circumstances changing the species 899, 917; sins inculpably omitted are to be indicated in a subsequent confession *1111;* evil customs are not to be denied *1208;* and this formal integrity is of divine law 699, 724 f., 899, 917; nor does a crowd of people excuse from it 1209. Confession of this kind is neither impossible 900, 918, nor a torture of conscience 900.

Venial or grave sins already directly forgiven are not necessarily but laudably confessed 470, 748 f., 899, 917, 1539, C902.

Confession should be external and oral 587, 699; secret facts however known made to the priest alone suffices 145, 727, 901, 916, and can even be by signs 147; or through an interpreter C903.

Salutary and appropriate satisfaction (by the power of the keys 925) should be imposed 146, 671, 699, 899, 904 ff., 925, C887, as a medicine 904, and a punishment 904 f., and it should be fulfilled by the penitent (himself) 437, 807, 1115, C887, not necessarily and by divine law before the absolution 728, 1306-1308, 1437 f., 1534 f., or before communion 1312; it does not consist in a confident faith 922, not in any anointing 451, but in good works 699, by which God is truly worshiped 924, especially in prayer, fasting and alms 699, 807; which have their power from the merits of Christ 904 f., 923, and that sacramental 1535, and from the work of the one working they have merit condignly 1077.

XII k   The effect of this sacrament, unless it is a "false penance" 366, is spiritual healing 695, recovery of lost justice 839, reconciliation with God and remission of sins committed after baptism 424, 430, 464, 671, 699, 840, 894, 896, 911, 1057 f., C870, even if they are not "believed" to be remitted 750 ff.; which can all be forgiven by this sacrament 43, 167, even if after penance they are again committed 540; remission of penalty especially eternal 807, 840, 1057 f.; not however of all the temporal punishment 456, 535, 807, 840, "without our great tears and labors" 895, peace and consolation 896; likewise the perfect revival of

merits killed and grace lost 2193; liberation from censures 1144, C2247 ff.

The necessity of the sacrament is of divine law 724 ff., indeed is of means or of salvation 574a, 670, 839, in itself or in desire 807, 895, even to one of the faithful who is contrite 587, 725.

The minister of penance is not a layman 670, 753, but only a priest 95*, 146, 807, 902, 920, 957, C871, who ought to have jurisdiction 437, 574a, 699, 903, 919, 921, 1113, 1116, 1537, C872 (different for different reserved cases 753, 903, 921, 1103 f., 1112, 1545, which reservation ceases in danger of death 903), even for the absolution of venial sins 1150, C872; he ought not always of necessity to be the pastor of the one confessing 470, 492, 574a, 1310, but it is necessary that he act sincerely 752, 902, 919.

The sacramental seal is to be strictly preserved 145, 438, 1220, C889 f., and the name of an accomplice is by no means to be sought 1474, C888.

Solicitation is held to be avoided, even when the confessor gives the penitent a card (with a written solicitation) to be read afterward 1106, and the obligation of denouncing does not cease, if the one solicited confesses to the one soliciting 1107.

The subject is man baptized and fallen 146, 430, 807, 894 f., 899, 911, 913 ff., C901; who ought to be present 1088 f.; absolution is not to be denied to penitents about to die 57, 88*, 95, 95*, 111, 1538, nor destitute of his senses, if it is certain that he had and manifested the desire 147, 1089, neither even to usurers rightly disposed 1612, nor to the relapsed or recidivists 1538, nor to fornicators or adulterers 43; nor for one disposed is it to be put off 1437 f., C886, but for habitual and occasional sinners who are indisposed it is to be denied or put off 1210 ff.; likewise for those ignorant of the mysteries of the faith, such as the Trinity and the Incarnation 1214 (which it does not suffice to have believed once *1215*).

Confession is to be made at least once a year *437*, *470*, *901*, *918*, C906; it is advisable that it be done in Lent *901*, *918*, not necessarily to one's own pastor *492*, C905, but it can be made to a religious *491*; sacrilegious confession does not satisfy the precept of the Church *1114*, C907.

INDULGENCES

XII l *Essence:* They are not pious frauds of the faithful *758*, but the remission of the temporal punishment (after the sin has been taken away) *740a*, *1060*, C911, to be paid before God *622*, *677*, *740a*, *759*, *1540*, through the application of the treasury of the Church (that is, of the merits or satisfactions of Christ and of the saints *550* ff., *723a*, *740a*, *757*, *1060*, *1471*, *1541*, *2193*, C911, made to the living by way of an absolution, for the dead as a suffrage *740a*, C911, through the Roman Pontiff *551*, *570k*, *676*, *723a*, *729*, *740a*, *989*, *998*, *1471*, C912, especially in a jubilee *467*, *2193*, or through a bishop for his subjects *678*, C349 sec. 2, for reasonable causes *551*, *676*, *740a*; they were in use from ancient times *989*.

Effects are salutary and useful *622*, *723a*, *740a*, *758*, *760 ff.*, *989*, *998*, *1236*, *1471*, C911; they take away the temporal punishment due even to hidden sins *761* f.; they can be applied to the dead *723a*, *740a*, *1542*, C911 f., whom they truly benefit *762*.

The effect depends on the reception of baptism, freedom from excommunication (the state of grace *551*, *676*, *740a*, C925), the fulfilling of the prescribed work *677*, C925. The lists of indulgences are laudably established *1543*; those revoked, however, have no value *1137*.

Extreme Unction

XII m *Essence:* It is a true sacrament instituted by Christ and promulgated by St. James *99*, *315*, *424*, *451*, *465*, *669*, *700*, *907* ff., *926* ff., *2048*; hence it is not a rite instituted by the Fathers *926*, nor the same as the grace of curing *927*.

The matter is the anointing with oil of the infirm blessed by a bishop *99*, *424*, *700*, *908*, *1628*, C937, C945, not by a simple priest *1629*, except with an apostolic faculty C945.

The form is either the longer ordinary form *700*, *908*, or the extraordinary and very short one *1996*, C946 sec. 1.

The effect is the grace of the Holy Spirit *909*, *927*, remission of sins *315*, *909*, *927*, spiritual health *695*, *700*, arousing of the confidence of divine mercy *909*, alleviation of soul *909*, *927*, cleansing of the remains of sin *909*, strength against the temptations of the devil *909*; sometimes even the health of the body *315*, *700*, *909*.

The minister is the priest *99*, *700*, *908*, *910*, *929*, each and alone C938 sec. 1.

The subject is a man gravely ill *451*, *700*, *908*, *910*, C940, as often as he should fall back into danger of his life even after convalescence *910*, C940 sec. 2; of itself it is presupposed that the person is in the state of grace *99*, *315*.

The necessity is not *per se* the means C944, but anyone contemning it sins mortally *669*, *910*, *928*.

The rites customarily employed by the Church are to be observed *910*, *928*.

Orders

The priesthood is in general necessary **XII n** and existed in every law *957*, *2274*, with its functions *2274*, especially in revealed law *957*, *2274*. In the New Law the priest is "another Christ," whose person he acts *2275*, *3000*.

The essence: There are distinguished major and minor orders *150* ff., *454*, *958*, *962*, C949, constituting an ecclesiastical hierarchy *42*, *45*, *89*, *150* ff., *305*, *360*, *960*, *962*, *966*, C109; the episcopacy, the priesthood, and diaconate are of divine institution *42*, *305*, *356*, *958*, *966*, C108 sec. 3; the subdiaconate is a major order *45*, *153*, *305*, *958*, C949.

The minor orders are acolyte, exorcist, lector, ostiarius 45, 154 ff., 426, 547, 958, *1555*, C949, C111 sec. 2; they should precede the sacred orders 958, 962, *1551;* they are not however required for the validity of the sacred orders 454; they are to be put into use *1556*. The tonsure is a sign of the clerical state 958, C108.

There exists a true sacrament of orders 367, 465, 701, 957 f., 959 f., 961, 963 f.; instituted by Christ 949, 957 ff., 963, *2049 f.;* in which a visible and external priesthood is established 957; the diaconate equally as the priesthood is a sacrament 356; and it does not consist in the mere rite of choosing ministers of the Word of God 963.

The form of sacramental orders is the words (prayer) of the one ordaining for the various ones 150 ff., 445, *547,* 701, 959, 964, 1963 ff., 3001.

The matter is the imposition of hands 150 ff., 305, 445, 701n, 910, 950, 3001, to which is added the handing over of the instruments 150 ff., 701, the anointing and the other ceremonies 965.

The end is the governance and increase of the Church 695, the perpetual conservation of the mission and of the power of the apostles *2050*, the ministration of divine worship 2238, C948.

The effect is grace (with which the one ordained should freely cooperate 2275) and communication of the Holy Spirit 701, 902, 959, 964, 3001, the indelible sacramental character 695, 852, 960, 964, 996 f., 2275, C732 sec. 1 (for this reason it cannot be repeated 695, 852, 960, C732), with the power (arising from the character 2275) various in the various orders 960;

in the episcopacy: the succession in the place of the Apostles 960, the power of ordaining 150 ff., 424, 701, 960, 967, of confirming 419, 424, 465, 572, 697. 873, 960, 967, 1458, C951; of blessing the chrism of confirmation 98, 571, 697, 1086, C734 sec. 1, C781 sec. 1, and the oil of the infirm 99, 700, 908, 1628, C734 sec. 1, C945;

in the priesthood: the power of celebrating Mass and of absolving 957, 961, 2049 f., 3000, C802, C871, of conferring anointing 99, 910, C938 sec. 1, of imposing hands upon those to be ordained priests 151, of baptizing (even in the presence of a bishop) not however of confirming 98, 1458, C738, C782 sec. 1, unless he is especially delegated by the Supreme Pontiff 573 f., 697, C782 sec. 2;

in the major orders: those thus constituted cannot again become laymen 960, 964, C211 sec. 1. They ought to preserve celibacy 52b f., 89, 301, 360, 979, *1774a*, C132, and they are obliged to the Divine Office C135; which obligation one holding a benefice does not satisfy by occupying himself in study, if he recites the Office through another 1121, or who on Palm Sunday recites the Paschal Office *1134,* or who performs one Office recited if for today and yesterday *1135,* or who excused from the recitation of Matins and Lauds omits the rest of the hours *1204*. The restitution imposed by Pius V on those holding benefices and not reciting the Office obliges in conscience before the sentence of a judge *1120*, and it cannot be done through alms from the fruits of the benefice made before the omission *1133*.

The ordinary *minister* is the bishop alone 150 ff., 424, *608,* 701, 960, 967, C951; hence the priest cannot confer the diaconate *548*.

Ordinations conferred by heretical or schismatic bishops are illicit to be sure, but valid (55, 57*) 169, 249, 354, 358, 1087, C951; likewise orders simoniacally conferred or received 364, C2372; Anglican orders, however, are invalid because of a defect of form 1963 ff.

The subject is only a baptized man 56 C968 sec. 1 (even if perhaps fallen *1553*), examined 301, and rightly

Anyone contemning the solemnizing of marriage sins mortally 669, 981. Civil matrimony is to be reproved 1640; even cooperation in it 1865.

The Sacramentals

XII p *They are* things or actions which the Church in a kind of imitation of the sacraments uses to obtain effects, especially spiritual ones, through their impetration C1144; they are consecrations, blessings—whether constitutive or invocative C1148 sec. 2, and exorcism 140, C1151.

The minister of the sacramentals is a cleric endowed with the due power 99, C1146; *the subjects* are Catholics, catechumens, and in some ways non-Catholics C1149, C1152. They should be employed in the Mass and in the prescribed administration of the sacraments 856, 931, 943, 945, 954, 956, 965, 982; none are to be spurned 665, 965, nor simoniacally acquired 364.

GOOD WORKS (MERIT) AND EVIL; CHRISTIAN PERFECTION

The nature of works

XIII a The works of a man are not indifferent 804, 828 ff., 834, not even external 386, 516 ff. (God also accomplishes them 517), nor those done by the perfect 472 f., 476, 478, 1260; a good work or an evil one does not equally glorify God 504 f., 514 f.

The works of man are not immediately divided into virtuous and vicious according to the virtuousness or viciousness of the agent 642, 1297, but there are also naturally good works, which yet do not merit beatitude 642, 817, 1002 ff., 1012, 1037, 1301, which (good works) can be done without grace 1025, 1037 f., 1352 f., 1388 ff., 1392, 1395 ff.

The goodness of works is not realized, if the natural appetite enjoys its acts 1158 f.; it does not depend on an accord with reason alone with reference to God 1289.

Not all works done before justification

are sins 817, 898, 915, 1063, 1523; for this reason infidels do not sin in all their works 1022, 1025, 1035, 1040, 1065, 1068, 1298, 1375, 1401 f., 1523; nor do the impious act badly in everything 642, 1035, 1040, 1395, 1523; nor do they always serve vicious concupiscence 1038, 1297 ff., 1394 ff., 1523. It is not a vice to act without charity in view of an eternal reward 1303.

A just man does not sin in every good work 771 f., 775 f., 804, 835, not even venially 772, 804, 835; nor is it a sin to reject evil because of its shamefulness without reference to its being an offense against God 1299; nor evil to look to a reward 804, 841, 1300, 1303.

Fear of penalties is good and useful 744, 798, 898, 915, 1411 ff., and can be supernatural 898, 1304, 1525.

The observance of the commandments is necessary 804, 829 f., 2273, with a fight against the flesh, the world, and the devil 806 (since faith alone does not suffice 800, 804, 829 ff.), and it is not impossible 200, 804, 828, 832, 1054, 1519, 2238, 2241, it obliges even the perfect 472 ff.

Merit

The good works of the just make a man **XIII b** better 380, and, provided they are done freely 1094, they truly merit an increase in grace and glory 191, 517 ff., 803, 809, 834, 836, 842, 1008, 1013-1017, 1044, 1261, 1419.

The just at the same time by good works or penances inflicted by God, if they suffer them patiently, satisfy for temporal punishments 807, 904 ff., 923 f., 1010, 1059, and that condignly 1077 (without, however, all afflictions being punishments for sins 1072); which power is derived from grace by which a man is made a son of God and a member of Christ 134, 140, 191, 287, 309, 708, 809, 812, 842, 904 f., 1011-1018, 1031 ff., 1062, 1070, 1077, with the cooperation of faith 287, 430, 714, 803, 809, 1008, 1062, so that merits and satisfactions are in some way ours

842, *1008, 1010, 1419.* Merits that have been lost, with the recovery of the state of grace, revive perfectly at the same time as the grace 2193.

Sin *(personal)*

XIII c To sin (actual) there is presupposed a knowledge of the law, whence it is not committed with invincible ignorance *775, 1068, 1292,* but nevertheless with vincible *377;* moreover, it ought to be a voluntary act *410, 775, 1046, 1050 f.,* by a personal will *1291;* placed with true freedom, not only from coercion *1094,* but from necessity *1039, 1041, 1066 f., 1291;* nor is the suggestion to sin made by the devil by only placing stones or herbs *383.* A grave sin, by which God is not offended (a philosophical sin) does not exist *1290.* By sin (actual) a guilt of sin (habitual sin) is contracted, which is not only the obligation of the penalty *1056 ff.;* personal sins however are not passed on like original sin *1052 f.*

Even one who is justified (although he be perfect *471 f.*) can sin mortally 805, 833, 862.

Mortal sins are those by which God is always offended *1290, 3018,* and man is made an enemy of God 899, and even a member of the devil 628, to whose power he has handed himself over 894, and a servant of sin 894, by which the grace of justification is lost 808, 837, 862, and eternal damnation is incurred 410, 464, 531, 693; and there are also sins venial in nature 106 ff., 804, 835, *1020,* by which justice is not taken away 804, 899, which are a common evil 107 f., and without a special privilege cannot be avoided completely 833.

All mortal sins can be remitted 43, 167, and taken away by perfect charity with the desire for the sacrament 898, even before baptism *1033,* or by the sacrament of penance (even without charity) 430, *724, 726 f.,* 798, 898, 1146, *1536,* sometimes even by extreme unction 909.

Venial sins can be taken away in many ways 899, C902; in confession they are praiseworthily mentioned 470, *748 f.,* 899, *1539,* C902.

Christian *Perfection*

It is possible to increase the justice received through the grace of Christ *471,* 803; the virtues ought to be increased *1044,* by observance of the commandments *1044.* **XIII d**

The way to perfection is the imitation of Christ, who is the "master and example of all sanctity" 1972, 2224, 2232.

In the threefold way—purgative, illuminative, and unitive (*1246*) no one proceeds through quietism (Molinos) *1221–1288,* but

there is required also the exercise of external works *1260,* positive resistance against temptation *1237, 1257,* and against the suggestions of the demon *1261 f.;* the use of voluntary mortifications is of help *1258 f.,* confession and direction according to theology and philosophy *1279 f., 1286 f., 1329;*

progress is *impeded* by a tedium with spiritual things *1248.*

Extreme trials do not separate the superior part of the soul (with its voluntary acts) from the inferior (with its involuntary disturbances) *1340.*

Perfection does not consist in this, that a man lack either concupiscence, which he suffers involuntarily *1050 f., 1074 ff.,* or every thing of his own and dominion 494, *575 f.,* 2224, or his own act of choice of will 576, or that he does not pursue things, honors, usefulness, internal devotion, sanctity, reward, the kingdom of heaven 508.

One does not reach so far, that a man lacks all venial sin 107 f., 804, 810 (except from a special privilege 833) *1276 f.,* or that he become impeccable *471;* so that he cannot will anything other than what God wills *1281,* so that he cannot make further progress in grace *471,* so that he can be found more perfect than Christ *471,* so that he may attain an immobile state in imperturbable peace *1282,* or death of the senses *1283,* or finally that in this life he might have final happiness *474*, and that he may be transformed into God *1225* (as totally as in the Eucharist the bread into the body of Christ *510*), so that he may be made one, not only like to God *510*, and hence he may have the whole that the Father gave to the Son *511 ff.*, *520 ff.*, and he may do whatever God does and may generate the Son Himself *513;*

so that he is not bound to keep the commandments 804, 830, and obey human power or that of the Church *472,* 1970, to pray and to conquer concupiscence *472, 1275 ff.;* to exercise himself in acts of virtue *476,* 806, *1251, 1347,* or in internal acts only *518,* to show reverence to the Eucharistic Christ *478,* to love God more than his neighbor *525;*

so that he may habitually love God without there being any admixture of his own motive *1327 ff.*, even with regard to eternity *1335 ff.*, with regard to discursive acts (in meditation) *1341 ff.*, with regard to the love of God Himself as a perfection of his own *1345,* and with regard to the remission of sins *1346;*

so that he may know with the certitude of faith that he is in the state of grace 802, or (without special revelation) that he is predestined 805, 825, 833, and that he will persevere 802, 806, 826.

XIII e Religious perfection (in a community) is especially commended by the Church 980, 1973, and it is defended against detractors: against William of St. Amour *458 f.*, against Wiclif *600-604*, *614 f.,* *624 f.,* 680, against the Jansenists *1310 f.*, against the Pistorians *1580-1590*, against naturalists 1692, *1752 f.*

In particular the Order of Preachers and Friars Minor are praised *459.*

Vows made after baptism are not invalid by force of the promise made in baptism 865.

Vows are not impediments to perfection *1223,* 1973.

The scope of the vow of obedience of religious does not always pertain to the exterior *1285.*

The solemn vow of chastity prevents a valid marriage 979, C1073, and dissolves a sanctioned nonconsummated marriage 976, C1119.

GOD THE CONSUMMATOR

THE LAST THINGS FOR INDIVIDUAL MEN

Death is a penalty for sin 101, 175, 793; **XIV a** the Judgment (particular) follows immediately after this 464, 530 f., 693. —Before the time of the redemption the patriarchs etc., did not dwell in Paradise 160a, nor did they go to heaven before the death of Christ 410.

Those who die after baptism without personal sin or otherwise without sin and penalty, immediately (the inclinations to sin being no obstacle *743*) attain heaven 457, 464, 530, 570s, 693, 696, to enter which the state of grace is required 800, 809, 842, *1011.* Heaven or the state of happiness is not a substantial transformation into God *510,* but the elevation of man to supernatural happiness 1808, which cannot be investigated by reason alone 1669, nor had in this life *474 f.*, but in the future 287; and consists in the immediate, intuitive, face to face vision and enjoyment of God 530, 570s, 574a, 693, 1647, *1928 ff.*, in which God is seen not merely as acting toward things outside Himself *1928*, nor merely shining forth from created vestiges *1929*, nor merely as provider, redeemer, sanctifier *1930,* but as He is in Himself 530; faith and hope are done away with 530, but chaste fear is not excluded *382.* The vision takes place through the light of glory *475, 1928 ff.*: it is had without interruption 530, and it is eternal 16, 40, 228a, 347, 429, 464, *1716,* 1793; it is the reward of good works 714, 809, 936, 842; it admits of degrees 693, 842;

but it is greater than works (in the sense of Baius) *1014*.

The souls of those who die in the state of grace, but with venial faults or temporal penalties not yet satisfied are detained in Purgatory 456, 570s, 693, 840, 983, 998, 2147a, concerning the existence of which it is certain from Scripture 456, *777;* which does not consist in only the fears of one about to die *744;* but in satisfactory penalties which the souls suffer 464, 530, 570s, 693, 840, 983, while they are tormented by fire 570s, secure, nevertheless, concerning their salvation, but are outside the state of merit 778, they do not sin by seeking rest or by abhorring the penalties *779;* they are helped by the prayers, satisfactory acts, and alms of the living 427, 456, 464, *535,* 693, 780, 983, 998, by indulgences 723a, 729, *1542,* C911, especially by the sacrifice of the Mass 427, 693, 983, 1469.

Those on the other hand who die in original sin or grave personal sin (or outside the Church 714) immediately descend into Hell 40, 321, 410, 429, 457, 464, 493a, 531, 574a, 693, 714, *1290, 1525,* which was not destroyed through Christ *536, 574a;* where they are punished by different punishments 493a, namely, by loss or by the lack of the vision of God for sin both original and personal 321, 410, 464, 693, and by the sensation or torments (of fire) by which those "who lived evilly" are punished 40, 160b, 228a, 410, 429, 531, 714, 1677.

The punishments of Hell are eternal 16, 40, 160b, *211,* 228a, 410, 429, 457, 570, 714; but little children (in Limbo) who died without baptism do not suffer the punishment of fire 410, *1526;* who, however, do not go into an earthly paradise *534,* but to a place different from the place of the other damned 228a, 531, with their own and blaspheming God from an habitually dominating will 1049.

The soul of a person who dies in a natural state does not completely lack all activity *1913*.

THE END OF THE WORLD

(Chiliasmus)

Chiliasm cannot safely be taught 2296. XIV b
The world ought not to be consumed naturally *717a*.

In the consummation of the world there will be a resurrection of the dead 1 ff., 13, 16, 20, 30, 86, 242, 347, and indeed of all 40, 287, even of the damned 228a 531, with their own bodies 20, 40, 347, 427, 429, 464, 531, which will not be purely spiritual or orbicular 207, 287.

Then there will follow a universal Judgment 54, 86, 531, 994, which will not be carried out by the Father 384, but through Christ 13, 40, 86, 255, 287, 422, 427, 462, 464, who renders to each according to his works 228a, 287, 344, 427, 429, 462, 531, 693; when this is done, then the Church will reign with Him forever 287; —nor will there ever be by any metamorphosis of the demons or of impious men *211*.

Alphabetic Index of Proper Names and Things

Abelard, *368 ff.*, 393 fn.

Abortion, *1184 f.*, 1890a-c

Absolution of the absent, *1088 f.; see* Systematic Index XII i

Abstinence from meat, 37, *1132*

Acacius of Constantinople, 169, 171

Accidents of the Eucharist, *582, 884*

Accomplice, name of (in confession), 1474

Acoemetae, 201 fn.

Acolyte (order of), *see* Syst. Ind. XII n

Action (Catholic), 2221 f., 2278; (civil), 1882 ff., 1933 ff.

Acts of the Apostles, 2161, 2166 ff.; *see* Canon, of sacred books (Syst. Ind. I f)

Acts, carnal, *see* Syst. Ind. XI r, *477;* external, *516 f., 1501;* good or evil, *642;* necessary for penance, *see* Syst. Ind. XII i

Advent (second) of Christ, *see* Syst. Ind. XIV b

Aerian heresy, *1509*

Aethelstan's psalter, 4

Affairs, public (state), 1885 ff., 2190; sacred, *see* Syst. Ind. II 1; of the sacrament (effects), 411, 415

Afflictions, 1072

Africans, and rebaptism, 53; and their bishops on freedom and grace, 134

Agatho, Pope, 254 fn., 288 ff.

Agde, council of (a. 506), 1499 fn.

Agnoëtae, 248

Agnosticism (of modernists), 2072 ff.

Albania (confirmation), 1458 fn.

Albigenses, 367 fn., 401 f., 428 ff.

Alexander II, Pope, 359 fn.

Alexander III, Pope, 358 fn., 365 fn., **393 ff.**

Alexander IV, Pope, 458 f.

Alexander V, Pope, 698

Alexander VII, Pope, 1091 fn., 1098 ff., *1513,* 5005

Alexander VIII, Pope, 128 fn., 1080 fn., *1289 ff.,* 1322 fn., 1599

Alexandrian church, 163, 436, 5001; synod (a. 430), 113 fn.

Almaric, 433

Alms, *see* Syst. Ind. XI d

Altars, several, *1531;* adorned, *1532;* privileged, *1543*

Ambrose, St., 39 fn., 320, 442 fn., 1673 fn., 1824 fn., 1976 fn.

Americanism, 1967 ff.

Amour, William of St., *458 f.*

Amphibologia (ambiguity of language), 1176 ff.

Analogy, of faith, 1796, 1943, 2146

Anastasius I, Pope, 93

Anastasius II, Pope, 39 fn., 169 f.

Angels, *see* Syst. Ind. VI c

Anglican, church, 1685 f.; ordination, 1963 ff.

Anima (soul, human), *see* Syst. Ind. **VI d**

Anniversaries, of martyrs, 92

Anomians, 85

Constitutions of the Apostles, 12

Consummation; *see* Syst. Ind. XIV a f.

Contract, of property, 716; matrimonial; *see* Syst. Ind. XII o

Contrition; *see* Syst. Ind. IX b, XII i

Convention, of theologians of Germany, 1679 ff.; to unite all Christians, 2199

Cooperation, in evil, *1201*

Copulation, carnal; *see* Syst. Ind. XI r; interrupted, 2239 fn.

Cor Jesu, Heart of Jesus, *1562 f.*

Cornelius I, Pope, 44 f.

Corpses; *see* cadavers

Corpus Christi (Body of Christ); *see* Syst. Ind. VIII b and 12f ff.; hominis (of man); *see* ibid., VI d

Correction, of princes, 597

Councils, ecumenical, particular, diocesan, national; *see* Syst. Ind. II d

Councils, particular, more celebrated; *see* under special names

Councils, universal (ecumenical): of Chalcedon, 148 f.; of Constance, 581 f.; of Constantinople I, 80 f.; II, 212 ff.; III, 289 ff.; IV, 336 ff.; of Ephesus, 111a ff.; of Florence, 691 ff.; Lateran I, 359 ff.; II, 364 ff.; III, 400 ff.; IV, 428 ff.; V, 738 f.; of Lyons II, 460 ff.; Nicene I, 54 ff.; II, 302 ff.; of Trent, 782 ff.; Vatican, 1781 ff.; of Vienna, 471 ff.; *see* also individual councils

Council, of Constance (a. 1414 to 1418), 581 ff., *657 ff., 770,* 1323; *see* Chron. Index; (a. 1609), 1499 fn.

Counsels, evangelical, *1584 ff.,* 1973

Craniotomy, 1889 f.

Creation, of the creature; *see* Syst. Ind. VI a ff.

Cremation, of corpses, 1863 f.

Criticism, art of, 1946

Cross, of the Lord, *302, 304*

Culm (Kulm), council of (a. 1745), 1499 fn.

Culpa peccati (fault of sin); *see* Syst. Ind. XII k, XIII c

Culture, 1799; *see* Syst. Ind. II l

Cult; *see* Syst. Ind. XI e; freedom of; *see* Syst. Ind. XI o

Custom, of sinning, 1208, 1210

Cyprian, St., 47, 230, 247, 430

Cyprus, confirmation in, 1458 fn.

Cyril, St., of Alexandria, 111a, 113 ff., 171,
226 f., 269, 290, 292, 1673 fn., 2194

Cyril, St., of Jerusalem, 12

Cyrus, of Alexandria, 271 f.

Damasus, Pope, 58 ff., 83 fn., 84 fn., 1976; "Faith of Damasus," 15 f.

Damnation, to hell; *see* Syst. Ind. Xg h, XIV a

Davidian, psalter, 2129 ff.

Day, Biblical, 2128

Deacon, ordination of, 152, 445, 701

Death, 101, 175, 793; *see* Syst. Ind. XIV a

Decalogue, 899

Decisions, in matters of faith; *see* Syst. Ind. II c, II k, III f

Decretals, 165, *618*

Definition, dogmatic, 1836; *see* Syst. Ind. II c, III f

Defunct; *see* Purgatory (in Syst. Ind. XIV a)

Deity, one, one God; *see* Syst. Ind. IV a ff.; triune, *ibid.,* V a ff.

Democracy, ecclesiastical, 2091

Denunciation, of a heretic, *1105;* of one who solicits, *1106 f.*

Deposition, of clerics, 127, 304, 354, 438

Deposit, of faith, 1800, 1836

Der-Balyzeh, Papyrus of, 1

Desire, involuntary, *1050;* of death of father, *1164*

Desperation, *1336*

Devil, 237, *383,* 427, *1261, 1923*

Devotion, sensible, *1247*

Diaconate, 356; *see* Syst. Ind. XII n

Dictinius, 245

Didymus, 271

Diodorus, 271

Dionysius, St., Pope, 48 ff.

Dionysius, St., Bishop of Alexandria, 8

Dionysius, Bishop of Milan (352-355), 93

Dionysius, Foullechat, 575 ff.

Dioscorus, 171, 341, 1463

Discipline, ecclesiastical, 1578

Dispensation, *731, 1421, 1546*

Disposition, for frequent communion; *see* Syst. Ind. XII g; for justification, *see* ibid., IX b

Divinity, of Christ; *see* Syst. Ind. VIII a; the Church, *ibid.,* II a

Divorce; *see* Syst. Ind. XII o

Intention, in prayer, *599;* in the sacraments; see Syst. Ind. XII a f.

Intercessions, for the dead; see Syst. Ind. XIV a

Interdict, 682

Interpretations, of Holy Scripture, 786; see Syst. Ind. I f, II e and h

Interrogations, to be proposed to Wyclifites and Hussites, 657 ff.

Investiture, 361, 363

Irenaeus, St., 2, 1616 fn., 1824, 2147, 2150

Irregularities, *1553, 1556*

Isaias, 2115 ff.

Italo-Greeks, and confirmation, 1458 fn.

Jacobites, united, 703 ff.

Janduno, John de, 495 ff.

Jansen, Cornelius, 1092 ff., 1098 f., 1451

Jansenists, 1099, 1291 ff.

Jerome, St., 165, 320, 1673 n, 1976, 2186

Jerome de Praga, 659 f.

Jerusalem, Church of, 436

Joachim, abbot, 431

Job, 310, *1264*

John, St., the Apostle, 162; Gospel of, *2016 ff.,* 2110 f.; see *Canon* (in Syst. Ind. I f)

John the Baptist, 421, 857

John, Patriarch of Constantinople, 171 fn.

John Chrysostom, St., 1638, 1673 fn., 2181

John Damascene, St., 1673 fn.

John II, Pope, 201 f.

John IV, Pope, 253

John XV, Pope, 342

John XXII, Pope, *484 ff.;* see Chron. Index

Joseph, St., 993

Josephini, 444

Joy, sinful, *1163 ff.*

Jubilee, 467

Judaeans (Jews), 793 f., 811, 1480 ff.

Judge, *1126, 1152,* 1865

Judgment, particular, 464, 530 f., 693; see Syst. Ind. XIV a; universal; see *ibid.,* XIV b

Julius I, Pope, 57a ff., 698

Julius II, Pope, 717 fn.

Julius III, Pope, 873a ff.

Jurisdiction, of the Church; see Syst. Ind. II g ff.; of the Roman Pontiff, *ibid.,* III b ff.

Jus gentium (international law), 1995, 2281 f.

Jus gladii (law of the sword), 425, 2245 f.

Justification; see Syst. Ind. IX a ff.

Justinian, emperor, 201 f.

Justin, Martyr, St., 1, 8

Justice, as sanctity; see *Syst. Ind.* IX a ff.; as virtue: commutative, 2255; see *ibid.,* XI s; social, *ibid.*

Kiss, *477, 1140*

Knowledge, of the soul of Christ, 248, 2032 ff., 2183 ff.

Labor, worthy of reward and sufficient for caring for family; see Syst. Ind. XI s; of mother of family, 2263

Laics, 42, 687, *753,* 902, 920, 930, 934 ff.; apostolate of (laity), 1678, 1936c

Laicism, 2197, 2219

Lamennais, Felicitas de, 1613 ff.

"Lamentabili," syllabus, 2001 ff., 2114

Langres, council of (a. 859), 320 fn.

Language, vernacular in liturgy, 946, *1436,* 1566; studies of oriental, 1946

Languor (spiritual), *acedia, 1248*

Laodicea, council of (a. 364), 88 fn., 924 fn., 1499n; council of (a. 1618), 1499 fn.

Lateran, council of Martin I (a. 649), 254 ff.; of Paschal II (a. 1102), 357; Lateran council (ecum.) I (a. 1123), 359 ff.; II (a. 1139), 364 ff.; III (a. 1179), 400 f.; IV (a. 1215), 428 ff., 492, 901, 918, 990; see Chron. Index; V (a. 1512–1517), 738 ff.

Latitudinarianism; see Syst. Ind. I c

Latone, John de, *578 ff.*

Latria (the veneration of God); see Syst. Ind. XI e

Laudianus codex, 4

Law, Old and New; see Syst. Ind. X i

Laws; see Syst. Ind. XI a i, XIII a

Laxism, *1153*

Lectorate, 45, 156, 958

Legalia (matters pertaining to the law), of the Old Testament abrogated, 712

Legacies, annual for the dead, *1143*

Leo I, Pope, 143 ff., 165, 172, 231 fn., 246, 289, 292, 401, 1463, 1499 fn., 1673 fn., 1690 fn., 1821 fn., 1824; see Chron. Index

Leo III, Pope, 86 fn., 314a fn.
Leo IX, Pope, 343 ff., 355 fn., 358 fn., 359 fn., 360 fn., 362 fn.
Leo X, Pope, *738 ff.*
Leo XII, Pope, 1607 f., 1697 fn.
Leo XIII, Pope, 1848 ff., 701 fn., 1499 fn., 2186 f., 2196, 2219 f., 2226, 2233, 2253 ff.; *see* Chron. Index
Levite, 42, 89
"Lex supplicandi, lex credendi" (law of supplication, law of believing), 139, 2200
Libanus (Mt.), Maronites of (confirmation), 1458 fn.
Liberalism, *1777 ff.,* 2093
Liberius, Pope, 88, 93
Liberty (freedom), of God; *see* Syst. Ind. VI a; of man, *ibid.,* II i, III e; immoderate of men, *ibid.,* I d, XI a
Life, of Christ; *see* Syst. Ind. VIII h; supernatural man; *see* Syst. Ind. VII a, IX, X
Light, of faith, of grace, of glory, *475,* 1926
Limbo, of little children, 493a, *1526*
Liturgy (rites, cults, ceremonies); *see* Syst. Ind. XI e, XII a f.; connection with the Church, 2200; efficacy, 5004, 2297
Love, 1036 ff., 1239 ff.; love of Church and fatherland, 1936a; *see* Charity in Syst. Ind. IX b, XI d
Liturgy, Mozarabic, 4
Luke, St., 2155 ff., 2164 ff., 2166 ff.; *see* Canon (in Syst. Ind.)
Lucian, martyr, 12
Lucidus, presbyter, 160a f.
Lucius III, Pope, 402
Ludovicus XIV, king, 1322 fn.
Lyons, council of II (a. 1274), 86 fn., 460, 1834
Luther, Martin, *741 ff., 1540 f.*
Luxeuil, council of (a. 1580), 1499 fn.
Luxury; *see* Syst. Ind. XI s

Macarius, Bishop of Jerusalem, 12
Macarius, of Antioch, 710
Macedonius, Macedonians, 58 fn., 62, 85, 228, 271, 705, 1461
Magisterium (teaching function), of the Church, ordinary, 1683, 1782; *see* Syst. Ind. II c ff.

Magnetism, 1653 f.
Magnificat, 2158
Mahometes, 717c
Major orders; *see* Syst. Ind. XII n
Man, created; *see* Syst. Ind. VI d; primitive, *ibid.,* VII b; lapsed, *ibid.,* VII d
Mandates, observance of; *see* Syst. Ind. X h
Manichaeans, 234 ff., 367n, 707, 710
Marcellians, 85
Marcellus of Ancyra, 4
Marcion, 48, 234, 710
Mark, St., founder of the see of Alexandria, 163; gospel of, 2155 to 2165; *see* Canon in Chron. Index
Maronites, confirmation of, 1458 fn.; profession of faith, 1459 ff.
Marsilius of Padua, *495 ff.*
Martin I, St., 254 ff.
Martin V, Pope, *581 ff.,* 716 fn.; *see* Chron. Index
Martin of Bracara, 4
Martyrs, acts of, 165
Mary, Mother of God and Virgin; *see* Syst. Ind. VIII i f.
Masons (free), *1718a,* 1859 ff.
Mass, of perdition, 316, 322; Mass, sacrifice of; *see* Syst. Ind. XII h
Masturbation, 2201; *see mollities*
Matter of the sacrament; *see* Syst. Ind. XII a
Materialism, *1758,* 1802
Mathesis (astrology), 35, 239 f.
Matrimonial cases; *see* Syst. Ind. XII o; mixed (marriages), 301, 1452 ff., 1496 ff., with note to 1499
Matthew, St., 2148 ff., 2164 f.; *see* Canon in Chron. Index
Maximus, St., 4
Mechitritz (Armenus), 533
Mediator; *see* Syst. Ind. VIII g
"Mediator Dei" Encycl., 2297 ff.
Medic (at duel), 1862
Meditation, discursive, *1341 f.*
Melchisedech, 333, 938
Melitius, 57*, 5001
Members, of the Church; *see* Syst. Ind. II b
Mendicants, *458 f., 614, 781, 1311,* 1581.
Mennas, Patriarch of Constantinople, 171 fn.

Oath, vow; *see* Syst. Ind. XI g

Oath, antimodernistic, 2145 ff.

Obex (impediment), of a sacrament, 411, 849

Obedience; *see* Syst. Ind. XI i m o

Obsession, demoniac, *1923*

Occasion, of sin, 366, *1141, 1211 ff.*

Occupation, 2258

Odium (hate), of God, 1049; of sin; *see* Attrition, Contrition (in Syst. Ind. IX b, XII i)

Offices (duties), of a Catholic man, 1870 ff., 1935

Oils, holy; *see* Syst. Ind. XII a c m

Oligarchy, 1855

Olivi, Peter John, 480 ff.

Omnipotence, of God, 1217 f.; *see* Syst. Ind. IV c

"Omnis utriusque sexus," cap. conc. Lat. IV, 437

Onanism, conjugal, 2239 f.

Ontologism (Ontologists), 1659 ff.

Operations, two in Christ; *see* Syst. Ind. VIII c

Ordinal, Edwardian (Anglican), 1964

Ordination, of clerics; *see* Syst. Ind. II h, XII n

"Orders," as colleges (guilds) in the same art (skill), 2267

Orders, religious, *1580 ff.*, 1973; *see* Mendicants

Order (sacrament); *see* Syst. Ind. XII n; public in society, 2266

Ordo, Roman, 7

Origen (Origenists), 93 fn., 203 ff., 223, 271; *see also* 3 ff.

Osius, 57 b ff.

Osma, Peter de, *724 ff., 1535, 1542*

Ostiariatus (order of porter), 45, 157, 958

Paderborn, council of (a. 1658), 499 fn.

Pantheism (Pantheists), 31, 1652, *1701 ff.*, 1782, 1803, 2074 f.

Pope; *see* Syst. Ind. III a ff.

Paradise, terrestrial, *534*

Parents; *see* Syst. Ind. XI k p

Parochus (pastor), 437, *491 ff.*, 990, *1509 f., 2067 ff.*

Parousia (or the second coming of our Lord, Jesus Christ); 2179 ff.; *see* Syst. Ind. XIV b

Paschal II, Pope, 357 f., 361 fn.

"Pascendi," Encyclical on modernists, 2071 ff., 2114

Passagini, 444

Passion, of Christ; *see* Syst. Ind. VIII h

Passive virtues, 1972

Pastoral letters of St. Paul, 2172 ff.

Patareni, 401, 444

Patarinus, Marsilius, *495 f.*

Patriarchs, of the Old Testament, 199; ecclesiastical, 341, 436, 466

Patrinus, 870

Paulianists, 56, 88 fn., 97

Paul, St., Apostle, 163, 1091, *1265* and *passim;* epistles of, 2172 ff., 2176 ff.; *see* Canon

Paul III, Pope, 782 ff.

Paul IV, Pope, 993

Paul V, Pope, 1089, 1090, 1097, 1503 fn., 1628

Paul, of Constantinople, 271 f.

Paul, of Samosata, 233, 271, 710

Pauperes of Lyons, 444

Pay (just), for labor; *see* Syst. Ind. XI s

Peculiarities, communication of, in Christ; *see* Syst. Ind. VIII s

Poverty (of Christ); *see* Syst. Ind. VIII h

Pelagius (Pelagians, Pelagianism), 101 ff., 126 f., 129, 174 f.

Pelagius I, Pope, 228a ff.

Pelagius II, Pope, 246 f.

Penalties, *1072, 1420*

Penance, sacrament of; *see* Syst. Ind. XII i; virtue of, *ibid.,* IX b

Penances, false, 366

Pentateuch, 1997 ff., 2121 ff., 3002, 3029 f.

Perfect (perfection); *see* Syst. Ind. XIII d e

Perjury, 664, *1174 ff.*

Perseverance; *see* Syst. Ind. X h

Person, of Christ; *see* Syst. Ind. VIII d; of the Blessed Trinity, *ibid.,* V b ff.

Pertinacious, 640

Peter, St.; *see* Syst. Ind. III a

Peter, of Alexandria, 171, 5001

Peter, of Antioch, 171

Peter de Bruis, 367 fn.

Peter Chrysologus, St., 4

Peter Deacon, 129 fn.

Peter Lombard, 393 fn., 431 f., 442 fn.

Peter of Osma, *724 ff.*

Phenomena, 2072

Philip IV, king, 468 fn.

CORRIGENDA

(*The Sources of Catholic Dogma*)

Page 31, number 74, read "is true God" for "is not true God."

Page 49, number 111a, from lines 3 through 6 read: "that the Word, in an ineffable and inconceivable manner, having hypostatically united to Himself flesh animated by a rational soul, became Man and was called the Son of Man," also lines 11 through 14, read: "For it was no ordinary man who was first born of the Holy Virgin and upon whom the Word afterwards descended; but being united from the womb itself He is said to have undergone fleshly birth, claiming as His own the birth of His own flesh."

Page 61, number 148, second column, line 15, read "nowhere removed" for "removed."

Page 87, number 218, read "but not as if the word of God" for "but as if the Word of God."

Page 87, number 219, substitute the following for the first three lines: "If anyone speaking on two natures does not confess that our Lord Jesus Christ is acknowledged as in His Divinity as well as in His Manhood, in order that by this he may signify the difference of the natures in which". Also the following for the last six lines but one: "if he accepts such an expression as this with regard to the mystery of Christ, or, acknowledging a number of natures in the same one Lord our Jesus Christ the Word of God made flesh, but does not accept the difference of these [natures] of which He is also composed, which is not destroyed by the union (for one is from both, and through one both), but in this uses number in such a way"

Page 102, number 257. Insert after "Jesus Christ" and before "consubstantial": "consubstantial with God and His Father according to His divine nature and".

Page 117, number 296. Insert in line 5 after Holy Spirit: "just as God is the Father, God is the Son, God is the Holy Spirit"; also read: "which according to substance" for "according to substance which"

Page 194, line 3, read "voiding" for "voicing"

Page 219, number 691, for lines 12 through 16, read: "And since all that the Father has, the Father himself, in begetting, has given to His only begotten Son, with the exception of Fatherhood, the very fact that the Holy Spirit proceeds from the Son, the Son himself has from the Father eternally, by whom He was begotten also eternally"

Page 225, number 703, add after "one eternity" "and all these things are one"

Page 250, number 797, read "does not do nothing at all" for "does nothing at all"

Page 259, number 818, "we flee to the mercy of God" for "we flee the mercy of God"

Page 316, number 1096, read "intended" for "understand", and add "alone" after "predestined"

Page 457, number 1839, read "by virtue of his supreme apostolic authority he defines" for "in accord with his supreme apostolic authority he explains"; also "possesses that infallibility" for "operates with that infallibility"; also "His church be endowed" for "His church be instructed", and "of themselves" for "from himself"

Page 556, number 2164, read "it is permitted for exegetes to dispute freely" for "it is impossible etc."

Page 633, number 2302, last sentence. Read "in no sense of the word historical", for "in a sense of the word historical"

CORRIGENDA

(The Sources of Catholic Dogma)